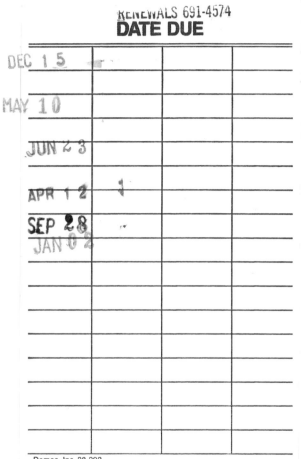

Education and Society in Late Imperial China, 1600–1900

This volume and the conference from which it resulted were sponsored by the Joint Committee on Chinese Studies, of the American Council of Learned Societies and the Social Science Research Council, with funds provided by the National Endowment for the Humanities and the Andrew W. Mellon Foundation. The UCLA Center for Chinese Studies provided organizational and editorial support.

Education and Society in Late Imperial China, 1600–1900

EDITED BY

Benjamin A. Elman and Alexander Woodside

UNIVERSITY OF CALIFORNIA PRESS

Berkeley   Los Angeles   London

The publisher gratefully acknowledges the contribution of the UCLA International Studies and Overseas Programs for preparation of the index to this volume.

University of California Press
Berkeley and Los Angeles, California

University of California Press, Ltd.
London, England

Library of Congress Cataloging-in-Publication Data

Education and society in late imperial China, 1600–1900 / edited by Benjamin A. Elman and Alexander Woodside.
    p.   cm. — (Studies on China; 19)
  Includes bibliographical references and index.
  ISBN 0-520-08234-6
  1. Education — Social aspects — China — History — Congresses. 2. China — Social conditions — 1644–1912 — Congresses. 3. Learning and scholarship — China — Congresses. I. Elman, Benjamin A., 1946–   . II. Woodside, Alexander. III. Series.
LA1131.8.E38   1994
379.19'0951'0903 — dc20   92-42292
                                                CIP

Printed in the United States of America
1 2 3 4 5 6 7 8 9

STUDIES ON CHINA

A series of conference volumes sponsored by the Joint Committee on Chinese Studies of the American Council of Learned Societies and the Social Science Research Council.

1. *The Origins of Chinese Civilization*
edited by David N. Keightley
University of California Press, 1982

2. *Popular Chinese Literature and Performing Arts in the People's Republic of China, 1949–1979*
edited by Bonnie S. McDougall
University of California Press, 1984

3. *Class and Social Stratification in Post-Revolution China*
edited by James L. Watson
Cambridge University Press, 1984

4. *Popular Culture in Late Imperial China*
edited by David Johnson, Andrew J. Nathan, and Evelyn S. Rawski
University of California Press, 1985

5. *Kinship Organization in Late Imperial China, 1000–1940*
edited by Patricia Buckley Ebrey and James L. Watson
University of California Press, 1986

6. *The Vitality of the Lyric Voice: Shih Poetry from the Late Han to the T'ang*
edited by Shuen-fu Lin and Stephen Owen
Princeton University Press, 1986

7. *Policy Implementation in Post-Mao China*
edited by David M. Lampton
University of California Press, 1987

8. *Death Ritual in Late Imperial and Modern China*
edited by James L. Watson and Evelyn S. Rawski
University of California Press, 1988

9. *Neo-Confucian Education: The Formative Stage*
edited by Wm. Theodore de Bary and John W. Chaffee
University of California Press, 1989

10. *Orthodoxy in Late Imperial China*
edited by Kwang-Ching Liu
University of California Press, 1990

11. *Chinese Local Elites and Patterns of Dominance*
edited by Joseph W. Esherick and Mary Backus Rankin
University of California Press, 1990

12. *Marriage and Inequality in Chinese Society*
edited by Rubie S. Watson and Patricia Buckley Ebrey
University of California Press, 1991

13. *Chinese History in Economic Perspective*
edited by Thomas G. Rawski and Lillian M. Li
University of California Press, 1991

14. *Bureaucracy, Politics, and Decision Making in Post-Mao China*
edited by Kenneth G. Lieberthal and David M. Lampton
University of California Press, 1992

15. *Pilgrims and Sacred Sites in China*
edited by Susan Naquin and Chün-fang Yü
University of California Press, 1992

16. *Ordering the World: Approaches to State and Society in Sung Dynasty China*
edited by Robert Hymes and Conrad Schirokauer
University of California Press, 1993

17. *Chinese Families in the Post-Mao Era*
edited by Deborah Davis and Stevan Harrell
University of California Press, 1993

18. *Voices of the Song Lyric in China*
edited by Pauline Yu
University of California Press, 1993

19. *Education and Society in Late Imperial China, 1600–1900*
edited by Benjamin A. Elman and Alexander Woodside
University of California Press, 1994

CONTENTS

LIST OF MAPS AND TABLES / *ix*
PREFACE / *xi*
CONTRIBUTORS / *xiii*
INTRODUCTION / *1*
Alexander Woodside and Benjamin A. Elman

PART 1 • EDUCATION, FAMILY, AND IDENTITY / *17*

1. The Education of Daughters in the Mid-Ch'ing Period / *19*
   Susan Mann

2. Four Schoolmasters: Educational Issues in Li Hai-kuan's
   Lamp at the Crossroads / *50*
   Allan Barr

3. Education for Its Own Sake:
   Notes on Tseng Kuo-fan's *Family Letters* / *76*
   Kwang-Ching Liu

PART 2 • EXAMINATIONS AND CURRICULA / *109*

4. Changes in Confucian Civil Service Examinations
   from the Ming to the Ch'ing Dynasty / *111*
   Benjamin A. Elman

5. Fang Pao and the *Ch'in-ting Ssu-shu-wen* / *150*
   R. Kent Guy

6. Discourse, Examination, and Local Elite:
The Invention of the T'ung-ch'eng
School in Ch'ing China   /   *183*
Kai-wing Chow

PART 3 • TECHNICAL LEARNING AND INTELLECTUAL CHALLENGE IN CH'ING EDUCATIONAL LIFE   /   *221*

7. Learning Mathematical Sciences during
the Early and Mid-Ch'ing   /   *223*
Catherine Jami

8. Tai Chen and Learning in the Confucian Tradition   /   *257*
Cynthia J. Brokaw

9. Legal Education in Ch'ing China   /   *292*
Wejen Chang

10. Manchu Education   /   *340*
Pamela Kyle Crossley

PART 4 • THE THEORY AND PRACTICE OF SCHOOLS AND COMMUNITY EDUCATION   /   *379*

11. Elementary Education in the Lower Yangtze Region in
the Seventeenth and Eighteenth Centuries   /   *381*
Angela Ki Che Leung

12. Education and Empire in Southwest China:
Ch'en Hung-mou in Yunnan, 1733–38
William T. Rowe   /   *417*

13. The Divorce between the Political Center and
Educational Creativity in Late Imperial China   /   *458*
Alexander Woodside

14. Lung-men Academy in Shanghai and the Expansion
of Kiangsu's Educated Elite, 1865–1911   /   *493*
Barry Keenan

AFTERWORD: THE EXPANSION OF
EDUCATION IN CH'ING CHINA   /   *525*
Alexander Woodside and Benjamin A. Elman

INDEX   /   *561*

MAPS AND TABLES

MAPS

Administrative Map of China / *xv*
The Yangtze Delta (Chiang-nan) / *xvi*
11.1 *I-hsueh* Established in the Lower Yangtze Region / *387*
14.1 Kiangsu / *496*

TABLES

3.1 Tseng Kuo-fan's Brothers and Sons / *77*
4.1 Format of Provincial and Metropolitan Civil Service Examinations during the Ming Dynasty / *114*
4.2 Format of Provincial and Metropolitan Civil Service Examinations during the Early Ch'ing Dynasty, 1646–1756 / *118*
4.3 Format of Provincial and Metropolitan Civil Service Examinations during the Early Ch'ing Dynasty Reform of 1663 / *119*
4.4 Format of Provincial and Metropolitan Civil Service Examinations during the Mid-Ch'ing Dynasty, 1757–87 / *120*
4.5 Format of Provincial and Metropolitan Civil Service Examinations during the Late Ch'ing Dynasty, 1787–1901 / *121*
4.6 Format of Provincial and Metropolitan Civil Service Examinations during the Late Ch'ing Dynasty after the 1901 Reform / *122*
11.1 Early Ch'ing Elementary Schools in the Lower Yangtze Region / *386*
12.1 Local Schools Established in Yunnan, 1644–1737 / *426*
12.2 Yunnan *I-hsueh* and Population Density by Prefecture / *431*
12.3 Textbooks Housed at Each Yunnan *I-hsueh* / *441*
14.1 Number of Academies in Southern Kiangsu Province, by Prefecture / *497*
14.2 Headmasters of Lung-men Academy, 1865–1904 / *509*

PREFACE

It is sometimes jokingly said that academic conferences are beset by the contradiction between their function of promoting intellectually unsettling additions to knowledge and their equally important function as a scholarly solidarity ritual. The conference that produced the following chapters became an involuntary and peculiarly painful exercise in the reconciliation of these allegedly contradictory functions. It was held at La Casa de Maria, an ecumenical retreat and conference center in Santa Barbara, California, June 8 through 14, 1989, just four days after the armed repression of the student movement in China.

The nightmare of what was happening in China weighed very heavily on all of the conference's members. Obviously, it created a very different atmosphere for the conference from the one the editors had sought. Our first evening together was devoted to a discussion of the private clinics in Peking that might accept foreign blood donations and to a consideration of which Chinese intellectuals were in the greatest danger. Eventually, we found that our solidarity as a group lay in trying to create an image of affirmative scholarship as a contrast to the images of evil then on our television screens. At no time was it possible to conjure up a spirit of business as usual.

The conference had been planned by various people from about 1985. The original suggestion came from Professor Evelyn Rawski, acting as chairperson of the Joint Committee on Chinese Studies of the American Council of Learned Societies, and the editors wish to express their gratitude to her. The conference was in fact sponsored by that committee, and our thanks are also due to Jason H. Parker, its executive associate. Additional funding for the conference came from the Mellon Foundation and the U.S. National Endowment for the Humanities. While the University of British Columbia and the University of California, Los Angeles, were both involved in the conference's preparation, making it a multinational affair, the UCLA Center for Chinese Studies was the matrix and the command center of the conference. For his help, the editors thank Professor Philip Huang, the center's director. We also owe a strong debt of gratitude to Richard Gunde, the center's assistant director, whose advice and assistance and heroic organizational skills in dealing with the continuing business of the conference were indispensable to us.

The members of the conference included Professor Suzanne W. Barnett of the University of Puget Sound and Professor Harriet Zurndorfer of the Sinologisch Instituut, University of Leiden. We are grateful to them for coming to the conference and for so generously sharing their ongoing research about Ch'ing dynasty education with us. Our discussants included a Sung dynasty scholar, an anthropologist of Africa, and a historian of modern Japan. For helping us to hold up a mirror to ourselves and offering stimulating guidance about our chapters, our thanks are due to Professors Peter Bol, Jack Goody, Tetsuo Najita, Peter Perdue, Frederic Wakeman, Jr., and Ying-shih Yü. The editors also wish to thank Adam Schorr and Regie Stites of UCLA for being such exemplary rapporteurs to the conference.

In addition to writing a somewhat cursory introduction to the volume, the editors have chosen to write a concluding chapter in which we offer our particular views, but not necessarily the views of the other conference members, about the conference's general subject.

Alexander Woodside, Vancouver
Benjamin A. Elman, Los Angeles

CONTRIBUTORS

Allan Barr is associate professor of Chinese at Pomona College. He has published a number of articles on seventeenth-century Chinese literature and is currently undertaking a study of the classical tale in the Ming period.

Cynthia J. Brokaw is associate professor of history at the University of Oregon. Princeton University has published her *Ledgers of Merit and Demerit: Social Change and Moral Order in Late Imperial China* (1991).

Wejen Chang is senior research fellow at the Institute of History and Philology, Academia Sinica, Taiwan, and professor of law at National Taiwan University. Harvard University will publish his recent study of the Ch'ing legal system. He has previously published *Ch'ing-tai fa-chih yen-chiu* (Study of the Ch'ing legal system) in Taiwan (Academia Sinica, 1983, 3 vols.).

Kai-wing Chow is assistant professor of history and Asian studies at the University of Illinois at Urbana-Champaign. Stanford University has published his *Ritual and Ethics: Classical Scholarship and Lineage Institutions in Late Imperial China, 1600–1830* (1994).

Pamela Kyle Crossley is associate professor of history at Dartmouth College. She is the author of *Orphan Warriors: Three Manchu Generations and the End of the Qing World* (Princeton, 1990) and a forthcoming study of Ch'ing imperial ideology.

Benjamin A. Elman is professor of history at the University of California, Los Angeles. He has published *From Philosophy to Philology* (Harvard University, 1984, 1990) and *Classicism, Politics, and Kinship* (University of California, Berkeley, 1990), which received the 1991 Berkeley Prize. Currently he is researching the social and intellectual role of civil examinations in China from 1400 to 1900.

R. Kent Guy is associate professor of history and East Asian studies at the University of Washington. He has published *The Emperor's Four Treasures: Scholars and the State in the Late Ch'ien-lung Era* (Harvard University, 1987). He is currently researching personnel procedures in the Ch'ing dynasty, and the political history of the mid-Ch'ing era.

Catherine Jami is chargé de recherche, Centre National de la Recherche Scientifique, Paris. Her current research is on mathematics in late imperial China and on scientific contacts with Europe. She has published *Les Méthodes Rapides pour la Trigonométrie et le Rapport Précis du Cercle (1774): Tradition chinoise et rapport occidental en mathématiques* (Collège de France, Institut des Hautes Études Chinoises, 1990).

Barry Keenan is professor of history at Denison University, Granville, Ohio. He is the author of *The Dewey Experiment in China: Educational Reform and Political Power in the Early Republic* (Harvard, 1977). His current research interest is in the autonomy of China's educated elite in the Lower Yangtze from 1865 to 1911.

Angela Ki Che Leung is research fellow in the Sun Yat-sen Institute of Social Sciences and Philosophy, Academia Sinica, Taiwan. She received her doctorate in history from the École des Hautes Études en Sciences Sociales, Paris, and is currently completing a book on Ming-Ch'ing philanthropy, in addition to publishing a number of articles in English, French, and Chinese on Ming-Ch'ing sociocultural history.

Kwang-Ching Liu is professor of history at the University of California, Davis. His recent publications include *Orthodoxy in Late Imperial China* (University of California, 1990), which he edited, and a collection of articles entitled *Ching-shih ssu-hsiang yü hsin-hsing ch'i-yeh* (Statecraft and the rise of enterprise) in Taiwan (Lien-ching, 1990). Currently, he is researching Tseng Kuo-fan and the Tseng family of Hsiang-hsiang, Hunan.

Susan Mann teaches history at the University of California, Davis. She is author of *Local Merchants and the Chinese Bureaucracy 1750–1950* (Stanford University, 1987) and is currently researching women's history in China.

William T. Rowe is professor of history at Johns Hopkins University. He has published *An Early Modern Chinese City: Conflict and Community in Nineteenth-Century Hankow* (Stanford University, 1989) and *Hankow: Commerce and Society in a Chinese City 1796–1889* (Stanford University, 1984). Currently, he is researching a biography of Ch'en Hung-mou.

Alexander Woodside is professor of modern Chinese and Southeast Asian history at the University of British Columbia. He is author of *Vietnam and the Chinese Model* (1971, 1988) and *Community and Revolution in Modern Vietnam* (1976) and a coauthor of *In Search of Southeast Asia: A Modern History* (1971, 1987). He is currently completing a study of politics and education in late imperial China.

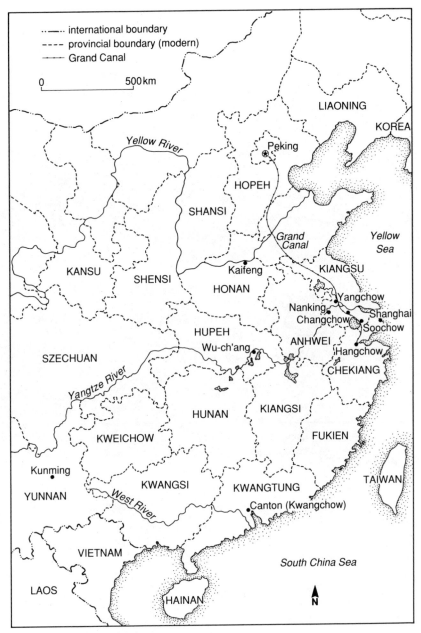

Administrative Map of China

SOURCE: Benjamin A. Elman, *From Philosophy to Philology: Intellectual and Social Aspects of Change in Late Imperial China* (Cambridge, Mass.: Council on East Asian Studies, Harvard University, 1984), reprinted here with the publisher's permission.

NOTE: In this volume, most common place names are given in the Post Office system of romanization. Otherwise, the Wade-Giles system is generally used.

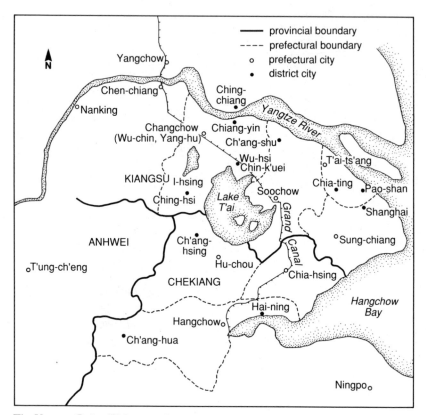

The Yangtze Delta (Chiang-nan)

SOURCE: Benjamin A. Elman, *Classicism, Politics, and Kinship* (Berkeley: University of California Press, 1990).

Introduction

Alexander Woodside and Benjamin A. Elman

Compared with other civilizations, China has placed an inordinately high value on education. During the classical era (600–250 B.C.), influential Chinese thinkers from Confucius (551–479 B.C.) to Mencius (372–298? B.C.), from Mo-tzu (470–391? B.C.) to Hsun-tzu (298–238? B.C.), advanced the unprecedented notion that merit and ability measured by training should take precedence over race or birth in state appointments. Since the early empire (200 B.C.–A.D. 200), clans and families had, whenever possible, mobilized their financial and cultural resources to provide young boys (and in some cases girls) with the tools of classical literacy. For the most part, however, a society based on merit remained an unattained ideal, and for much of the early empire an education remained the privilege of landed aristocrats and to a lesser degree prosperous merchants.

Beginning in the middle empire (A.D. 600–900), the Chinese state dramatically increased its expenditures on education and created in the process the first national examination system for selecting civil officials in the world. Such developments, which challenged the educational monopoly for advancement in official life held by northwestern aristocratic clans, climaxed during the Northern and Southern Sung dynasties (960–1280), when a national school system was erected to mainstream bright young men from local counties throughout the empire into public service. In addition, the rise of Buddhism in medieval China created new local institutions for education in which many commoners —male and female—were now educated in Buddhist schools and monasteries. Thereafter, state and society, except for the occasional Taoist eccentric, were agreed that education, particularly a Confucian moral education, was one of the foundations of public order and civilized life.

These pioneering educational achievements gathered momentum during the Sung dynasties, when various strands of Confucian statecraft and moral

1

philosophy were reinvigorated, particularly the metaphysical strand associated with Ch'eng I (1033–1107) and Chu Hsi (1130–1200) later called *Tao-hsueh* (Studies of the Way) and usually referred to today as "Neo-Confucianism." The latter school became orthodox during the Mongol Yuan dynasty (1280–1368), especially for the civil service curriculum when the selection process was renewed in 1313. Moreover, the Mongol co-option of Neo-Confucian orthodoxy served as an important model for the later Ming (1368–1644) and Manchu Ch'ing dynasty (1644–1911), which both made the Ch'eng-Chu school the cornerstone of Confucian orthodoxy. A recent conference volume on education in Sung China has, for example, highlighted the long-term educational contributions that Neo-Confucian educators such as Chu Hsi have made to Chinese cultural life.[1]

Such contributions are said by the editors of *Neo-Confucian Education* to have laid the groundwork for the contemporary success of the Chinese in a post-Confucian age. For example, it is increasingly common today to hear scholars and journalists say that the traditional Chinese stress on education is a product of a Confucian legacy whose intellectual spirit undergirds the remarkable economic transformation of Taiwan, Hong Kong, and Singapore in the twentieth century. While such claims tend to be more rhetorical than historically accurate, it is nonetheless clear that Sung Neo-Confucian education represented a first step in the later evolution of Chinese state and society and that the Sung-Yuan Ch'eng-Chu orthodoxy was mastered by millions of civil service examination candidates from 1400 until 1900.

But what sorts of Neo-Confucian education emerged after the Sung period? Beyond the elite competition for cultural and examination prestige, what forms of education were available for commoners and women? To date, we have had only impressionistic and anecdotal evidence. Too often preliminary and overstated conclusions about the "debilitating" educational effects of Neo-Confucian orthodoxy or the "rigidly compartmentalized structure" of the imperial civil service examination system (an especially misunderstood and understudied educational agency) have precluded research and discussion of education in China rather than stimulating further inquiry. Our conference volume serves as a forum to reevaluate earlier conferences on Chinese education, which we hope will enable the reader to gain a firmer hold on what aspects of earlier research require revision or reformulation.

Europeans first marveled at the educational achievements of the Chinese in the sixteenth century when Catholic missionaries wrote approvingly of the civil service examinations regularly held under government auspices. Such admiration carried over into the accounts of China prepared by eighteenth-century *philosophes*, who praised the "Mightie Kingdome" for its rational policies and enlightened education. In the nineteenth century, however, such admiration dissipated as Protestant missionaries increasingly noted instead the rampant illiteracy and widespread poverty of the Chinese people living under the leaking umbrella of a corrupt mandarin elite. By the end of the century, Chinese patriots themselves called for an educational revolution that would cast out what they now considered the backward habits of thought ingrained for centuries through the rote memorization required in the despised Confucian civil examinations. Educational revolution must accompany political revolution, they said.

This volume seeks to integrate the history of late imperial China with the history of education there. We hope to reveal thereby the role education played in Chinese society and the significance of education in political and intellectual life. Contributors were asked to address education in late imperial China as a prism of analysis for delineating in precise terms the complex relation between Confucian educational theory and actual processes of education, learning, and socialization. Our efforts to probe beneath the educational ideals enunciated by Neo-Confucian philosophers and get a more precise historical glimpse of how education actually was practiced in China from 1600 until 1900 was guided by our conference goal of highlighting the relationship between society and education in Ch'ing China. To this end, contributors were asked: How was education affected by kinship relations and gender? What was the content and perceived function of elementary education for the society and state at large? How did the civil examinations represent elite educational ideals? How did the doubling of the size of the late empire under Manchu rule influence the extension of education and schooling in a multiethnic political culture? By placing Sung-inspired Neo-Confucian education in its late Ming and Ch'ing dynasty social and political context, the chapters that follow attempt to illuminate why education (although its content and meaning varied widely) was so valued by Chinese regardless of class or gender. The authors try to show how education meant different things to different people and to different constituencies.

But what *was* education? In his famous 1790 essay on the education of youth in America, Noah Webster tried to disarm his readers by remarking that the subject of education had been "exhausted" by the ablest writers, both ancients and moderns. Few of Webster's contemporaries in Ch'ing China would have agreed with him. Their whole lives revolved around the proper definition, and competitive redefinition, of what to them were the three inexhaustible categories of "teaching" (*chiao*), "learning" (*hsueh*), and "culture/literature" (*wen*).

"Teaching" tended generally to mean the production or reproduction of a highly literate elite and the socialization of the far less literate, or even illiterate, common people by means of exhortations and rituals. But even this concept never hardened fatally into a tidy formula, given the permanent condition of dissatisfaction with the educational status quo that characterized Chinese history. "Teaching" could be the functional opposite of "learning," as in Chu Hsi's argument that because schools were failing to instruct and nourish their pupils China's educational failures inhered in the faults of poor "teaching," not in the crimes of bad "learning." On the other hand, the line between the two categories could also be blurred by political turmoil. When the Chia-ch'ing emperor (r. 1796–1820) told his court in 1814 that heterodox popular religions were spreading because of the excessive numbers of unlearned people in his empire, he practically conflated "learning" with indoctrinative teaching from above.[2] In an era of mounting corruption and rebellions, even some ostensibly Mencian philosophers of the Ch'ing period such as Chiao Hsun (1763–1820) were driven to give "teaching" a much larger historical authority than Mencius himself might have recognized. Chiao Hsun denied that the inherent goodness of human nature could activate decent behavior by itself; because the common people lacked self-awakening capacities, they could not be good without being "taught."

As for "learning," its scope was even more elastic, the definition of its content even more dynamic. Tu Wei-ming has pointed out that "learning," to medieval Confucians, involved at least five "interrelated visions" (poetic, political, social, historical, and metaphysical); Wm. T. de Bary has shown that even a Chu Hsi disciple such as Ch'eng Tuan-li (1271–1345), when he attempted to create a curriculum of "learning" that could be linked to the Sung civil examination system, could not help narrowing, if not actually falsifying, Chu Hsi's original sweeping conception of what "learning" should be.[3] In the Ch'ing period, even if the classically educated were marked by a characteristic set of moralistic predispositions, differently shaded definitions of "learning" proliferated. Tseng Kuo-fan (1811–72) was not the only high official to write private letters to his sons about their reading even while he was politically preoccupied; indeed, there is a huge unstudied private gentry correspondence about the proper uses of advanced literacy that is every bit as much of a concealed iceberg in our understanding of the subject as unstudied evidence about the reading abilities of commoners.

"Learning" to Ch'ing Confucians therefore could mean something as narrowly technical as the verification of whether there were 34,685 words or 35,410 words in the original of the *Mencius*, or something as messianically broad as Ku Yen-wu's (1613–82) statement that everything from oneself to the vicissitudes of the empire was an appropriate subject for study. Even emperors complained, as did the Yung-cheng emperor (r. 1723–35) in 1733, that China needed more "practical learning" that was broad enough to "manage the age and help the people."[4] The abbreviation of the last phrase, *ching-chi*, had its meaning narrowed at the end of the Ch'ing to mean "economics." Most definitions agreed that "learning" was a social act guided by examples of past worthies and sages and encouraged by good companions. In Ch'ing schools, this preordained sociability of "learning" led to far more regimentation than the founders of Neo-Confucianism might have wished. When the eighteenth-century academician Pi Yuan (1730–97) produced a "Continuation" of Chu Hsi's famous twelfth-century "White Deer Hollow Academy Articles for Learning," his added rules, not to be found in Chu Hsi, required Ch'ing academy students to hold five-hour collective discussions four days a month, at which time students would divide themselves into five-person groups in which each student expounded one section of a text. Wing-tsit Chan suggests that Chu Hsi himself would have regarded such patronizing behavioral regulations as antithetical to real "learning" motivation that supposedly came from within.[5]

Finally, the whole web of meanings of "education" included the claims of culture as written literature. Anxiety about modes of writing was part of the historical consciousness of scholar-officials. Indeed, the relationship between words and thought was a major educational issue in this period. Many members of the T'ung-ch'eng school, for example, held that because literature and governing oneself were not separate things, writers should avoid Buddhist and Taoist vocabulary, rustic and colloquial phrases, and the stylistic anarchy of popular novels. They also maintained that the vital spirit of the ancient literature they admired could not be recaptured unless that literature was loudly chanted or hummed, rather than just silently read. Others mourned what they considered the literary vulgarity of late imperial China from a different angle, seeing decline where we might see incipient cultural democratization. Han Learning scholars such as Sun Hsing-yen (1753–1818) enviously recreated the memory of a vanished early medieval aristocratic world in which government clerks were tested for their positions in eight different kinds of written graphs and elite students commanded a literacy of more than ten thousand graphs, not the two thousand or so that Sun ascribed to students in his own day. Because written documents held their empire together, emperors also fretted about literature, particularly concerning overwrought or opaque writing styles. In 1779, the Ch'ien-lung emperor (r. 1736–95) insisted that Manchu and Mongol dignitaries outside Peking could not read the Manchu and Mongol court translations of his edicts because the translations had become arbitrarily infected with the mannerisms of Chinese examination essay prose; he complained that he himself could not understand many of the eight-legged essays that his own examinations produced. So dissatisfaction with literary behavior was part of the endemic—but creative—dissatisfaction with education itself.[6]

Our conference was compelled to limit itself to the examination of only a small part of what "education" meant to Ch'ing educators. The strategic enterprise of "teaching"—the reproduction of culturally and socially fit individuals—received priority. Nonetheless, our research focus allows each chapter in the volume to shed light on disparate aspects of Chinese state and society. The state is revealed as an asymmetrical overlapping of interests of both the ruling house and the state bureaucracy. Chinese society reflects domination by elites, whose local obligations to family, kin, and home increasingly involved them in delivering social and educational services to commoners and women. These aspects of daily practice have been overlooked or forgotten in recent studies of late imperial China, which have tended either to dismiss premodern Chinese education as a dismal exercise in rote learning before the coming of the West or to overdetermine the educational ideals of Neo-Confucian philosophy as the cultural basis for the evolution of modern Chinese history.[7] Overall, the chapters of this volume reveal the limitations in both of these lines of argument.

Part One brings together essays on education, family, and identity. In Part Two, we turn to examinations and curricula. Part Three addresses the scope and limits of technical learning and intellectual challenge in Ch'ing educational life. In Part Four, the focus is on the theory and practice of schools and community education. In a concluding afterword, the editors try to fill out some areas that are left unexplored in the preceding essays while at the same time introducing some guidelines to what they hope will be productive future research on the history of education in China.

PART ONE: EDUCATION, FAMILY, AND IDENTITY

Susan Mann links the history of women's formal education and the increasing number of literate women after the middle empire to the larger context of the symbolic and practical ways for defining the role of women in Chinese society. She demonstrates that nonliterate and literate education went together and that the limits on the latter were not in anticipation of the effects of women's literacy but in response to those effects. Literary activity among women was spreading among married women, who as writers during the Ch'ing dynasty gained a greater public voice formerly limited in medieval times to courtesans.

Allan Barr introduces a novel by Li Hai-kuan that is probably unknown to most Western readers. His analysis of the novel and its four different kinds of eighteenth-century schoolteachers illuminates the complexity of attitudes toward the examination system and gives us insights into the culture of schoolteachers and the importance of personality in teacher-student relations. At the conference, discussants were most struck by the contrast between official Ch'ing efforts to standardize school education, as in the creation of Fang Pao's (1668–1749) imperially sponsored anthology of examination essays, and this novel's conflicting suggestion that there was no evident standardization in what teachers taught at the village level.

Using Tseng Kuo-fan's family letters, Kwang-Ching Liu shows the influence of the various schools of learning, methods of study, and literary styles as they operated in the very human historical context of one of nineteenth-century China's greatest literati. We gain a sense of the balance between the moral and scholarly issues in the mind of one particular Ch'ing dynasty statesman, as well as a sense of the balance between personal development and examination competition as a goal. Tseng Kuo-fan represented the revival of an integrative Confucian vision in the middle of the nineteenth century that was far more vital and resourceful than the rigid Neo-Confucian moralism so commonly portrayed in textbooks; his thought enables us to appreciate the genuine breadth of the educational traditions to which a successful nineteenth-century scholar might offer homage.

PART TWO: EXAMINATIONS AND CURRICULA

Benjamin Elman describes in detail the civil service examination process and state curriculum during the Ming and Ch'ing dynasties, and then demonstrates that during the eighteenth and nineteenth centuries evidential research and Han Learning successfully penetrated the examination curriculum. Drawing on examples of both provincial and metropolitan policy questions and answers preserved in examination archives rarely studied before, Elman reveals how essential Neo-Confucian doctrines beginning in the late eighteenth century were increasingly reinterpreted in policy questions prepared by evidential research scholars serving as examiners outside their home area of the Yangtze Delta. They thereby brought the examinations into closer touch with the changing intellectual context of the late Ch'ing period.

R. Kent Guy provides new information concerning civil examinations with a close reading of two examination essays that Fang Pao selected and commented on in the imperially sponsored anthology of essays on the Four Books that Fang prepared. Guy integrates this close reading into a careful argument concerning the complex intentions and processes involved in Fang's production of what he hoped would be the standard guide to examinations in the Ch'ien-lung reign. Fang was a champion of Sung Learning who later became the doyen of the staunchly Neo-Confucian T'ung-ch'eng school, which Kai-wing Chow also discusses in this volume. Fang tried to gain imperial support for his views at a time when Neo-Confucian orthodoxy was increasingly challenged — even in the examinations, as Elman shows — by advocates of Han Learning. The emperor gave the collection his approval, suggesting that Fang Pao's initiative could not be shunted aside. Neo-Confucian values tested in the examination system were not simply the emperor's to do with as he pleased: he had to accommodate literati concerns.

Kai-wing Chow argues that the T'ung-ch'eng school was not the localized continuation of a Sung tradition but was invented by Yao Nai (1732–1815) in response to the rise of evidential research in the examination curriculum. This development had had the effect of disadvantaging such areas as T'ung-ch'eng that were less wealthy than the Yangtze Delta cities where Han Learning flourished and thus less competitive in developing the cultural resources (such as libraries and academies) that were required to master evidential studies. Hence, the T'ung-ch'eng appeal to Neo-Confucian orthodoxy, widely heralded in the mid-nineteenth century, was itself an ideological construction reflecting the complex social history of the Han Learning versus Sung Learning debate in the late eighteenth century.

PART THREE: TECHNICAL LEARNING AND INTELLECTUAL CHALLENGE IN CH'ING EDUCATIONAL LIFE

Catherine Jami effectively establishes an intersection between the history of science and the social, cultural, and political aspects of education. Chinese mathematicians, and the K'ang-hsi emperor (r. 1662–1722) who sponsored them, are shown as agents of technical knowledge and education outside the civil examination curriculum. The teaching of science in the Imperial Board of Astronomy and Imperial College, Jami suggests, was almost completely divorced from the larger community of literati in the Yangtze Delta interested in the natural sciences. Despite the K'ang-hsi emperor's temporary patronage of Jesuit science, the educational training of native astronomers showed little more than superficial influence.

Cynthia Brokaw clarifies for us the redefinition of literati learning that the polymath Tai Chen (1724–77) offered in the late eighteenth century. Resisting both the metaphysical pretensions of Chu Hsi-style Neo-Confucianism, which he traced to Ch'an Buddhist inroads in Confucian discourse, and the nominalist vogue of Han Learning, Tai Chen proposed a learning agenda for literati that was to first decipher the ancient language of the Classics and thereby reveal the true Way of the sages. Brokaw's exposition delineates the way in which Tai Chen's recommendations for specialized learning in classical studies (phonology, paleography, and etymology) incorporated the major philological agendas associated with Han Learning. Yet, as Brokaw demonstrates, Tai was fearful of the "decentering" possibilities of a technical research that could take on a life of its own ("knowledge for its own sake") and betray the unified Confucian moral vision that Tai still deemed essential to inform literati learning. We see in the end a Tai Chen vainly trying to hold the Confucian vision together in the 1770s (something that Tseng Kuo-fan had a much easier time with in the post-Taiping era), attacked by Han Learning scholars for his excursion into airy speculation on the one hand and derisively dismissed on the other by Sung Learning scholars for his heterodox pretenses vis-à-vis Neo-Confucian orthodoxy.

Wejen Chang challenges our conventional notions of the Confucian "amateur ideal" by describing the education of legal specialists such as the heralded legal secretary Wang Hui-tsu (1731–1807). He also challenges recent claims concerning the increasingly litigious nature of Ch'ing society, revealing both the popular sources of legal amateurism and the professionalized legal education of expert legal secretaries who served on the official staffs of magistrates and prefects. Chang shows us that although the dominant literati view of such specialists remained condescending into the nineteenth century, the latter's technical training nonetheless was often a marriage of legal expertise and ethical integrity, reinforced by a culture of apprenticeship and an institutionalized requirement of self-education (perhaps akin to on-the-job training). Wang Hui-tsu's sense of justice belies the usual picture of opportunistic yamen functionaries dependent on their Confucian superiors for overall guidance. Along the way, Chang reveals how vestiges of the T'ang-Sung legal examinations remained in Ch'ing examinations until their complete abrogation in the mid-eighteenth century.

Pamela Crossley presents us with a wealth of fascinating detail concerning education in the Manchu language and of Manchus. She relates the Ch'ien-lung emperor's insistence on Manchu language training not to a concern for subcultural identity, for which it was not essential, but to the emperor's ideology, which represented his empire as a universalist cultural mosaic with well-constructed archetypes of particular cultures. Confucianism became both Manchu and Chinese through a system of dual official languages in the empire. Education of Manchu bannermen in their own cultural heritage and education of Chinese in Manchu language became important cultural measures of Manchu political legitimacy and Chinese competence in the imperial bureaucracy. As state inventions, the Manchu "people" and a Manchu "language" became ideological tools; but, ironically, Manchu banners showed little enthusiasm in the emperor's Manchu revivalism.

PART FOUR: THE THEORY AND PRACTICE OF SCHOOLS AND COMMUNITY EDUCATION

Angela Leung traces the shift from state to community support for schools in the Yangtze Delta in the seventeenth and eighteenth centuries. She argues that, while charitable schools there were regarded as important instruments in the war against subversive popular culture, the state was not in direct control of this war and merely watched it after the 1500s with condescending approval. The Ch'ing state faded out of direct involvement with elementary education, and there were no major conflicts of interest or of aims in elementary education among the state, the community, and the family. Community schools for the poor depended on the charity of gentry, merchants, and the leading clans in local society; the goal of mass literacy was never entertained because the concern underlying such schools was the proper disciplining of commoners —physically, mentally, and socially—to resist the temptations of the emerging urban popular culture of the late Ming and Ch'ing periods.

William Rowe paints a provocative and paradoxical portrait of minority schooling under Manchu imperial domination and Chinese cultural hegemony in his account of Ch'en Hung-mou, a zealous eighteenth-century civilizer of Han and non-Han peoples in southwestern China. Part of a Ch'ing program in the incorporation of minorities into an enlarged, multiracial society, Ch'en's

educational plans revealed a linguistic and imagistic repertoire that presupposed an inevitable Chinese cultural conquest of tribal peoples. Confucian
rituals and Chinese marriage practices were even recommended in Ch'en
Hung-mou's nonliterary educational measures to reduce the level of violence
in tribal society. Ch'en also promoted community schools among the minorities
as venues for teaching the Confucian classical texts required for proper moral
training. Ch'en's "colonial" Confucian policies in the southwest clearly contrast
with the less assertive state policies toward Manchus in the northeast described by Crossley, where the latter were encouraged to recover their cultural
heritage.

Alexander Woodside argues that schools embody a society's collective
dreams, rather than just serving as agencies of socialization and deparochialization, and that the growing insecurity of the expanding numbers of
Chinese students and degree-holders in the late empire forced many of them
to reconsider the school system as a whole, and its weak and subordinate relationship to the political center. In doing so, some took an unprecedentedly
detailed interest in the reconceptualization of ancient ideals of school education in which the central government supposedly had a commanding position, rather than abandoning schools to provincial or private interests, and
used that position to uphold the dignity and the communal solidarity of the
educated class. Woodside shows that this interest collided with the late imperial reality that creative development of schools occurred for the most part
only on the periphery, but that it nevertheless ultimately coincided with the
late Ch'ing government's educational reform program, which dreamed of restoring some of the power of the centrally run state in education.

Finally, with his study of the Lung-men Academy in Shanghai, Barry
Keenan gives us a close-up portrait of what Confucian academies were like in
the post-Taiping era as they evolved from earlier private academies to later
"modern" normal schools. Keenan thereby completes for this volume the discussion of schools and schooling in the late Ch'ing and gives us a precise
example of the reform energies in this realm whose accumulation was outlined
by Woodside. Keenan argues that there was a linear development from the
founding of Lung-men in 1865 to the end of the Ch'ing that can best be described as a quest for autonomy in educational matters. The conservative
founders were steeped in ecumenical efforts to unite the best of Sung Learning
with the best of Han Learning as a framework to transmit Confucian moral
and political ideals in the last decades of the dynasty. As the last author to appear, Keenan fittingly challenges the notion that modern educators in China
emerged directly from those who rejected China's educational traditions and
were attracted to Western learning. Teachers at the Lung-men Academy saw,
as had Tseng Kuo-fan, the means in Confucian education to educate a new
generation of Chinese after the mid-century holocaust. Such authentic efforts
have been largely forgotten by most earlier scholarship.

MAJOR ISSUES AMONG THE CONFEREES

One major issue that emerged at the conference was the relationship of the late imperial state to education. Angela Leung's chapter took what might be called the minimalist position: it argued that while charitable schools were regarded as important instruments in the war against "subversive" popular culture, the state was not in direct control of this war and merely watched it, after 1500, with condescending approval. This viewpoint stimulated a great deal of debate. Some discussants agreed that the Ch'ing state's role in elementary education had receded when compared to that of the early Ming state. Others such as William Rowe disputed this, suggesting instead that given the expansion of Chinese society the Ch'ing state was actually doing more in education and other so-called "public spheres" in absolute terms than previous dynasties but still had a lesser share in such public services compared to the past. Moreover, many pointed out that state involvement in education in Ch'ing China differed greatly by region. Rowe and Alexander Woodside in particular demonstrated that the state's role in education was much more considerable on the frontiers than elsewhere and especially among minorities of the southwest. Even so, the general conclusion reached by Jack Goody was that the great importance of family and lineage schools in China did differentiate China sharply from premodern Europe and the Islamic world, where education had a nonfamilial "ecclesiastical" sponsorship that cut across kinship lines.

A second big issue, related to the first, was the totality of the civil examination experience, which the conference examined from many angles. Among other things, there was a debate over the relative educational importance of the examinations. Some conferees saw them as the means by which the late imperial state enforced political loyalty and standardized the content of learning, making direct state control of most schools unnecessary. Others such as Yü Ying-shih, Allan Barr, and Peter Bol came close to dismissing the examinations as a "lottery" whose essays were quickly forgotten and whose practices were marked by dissent and tension with "genuine" Confucian education. But Chow Kai-wing, Benjamin Elman, and R. Kent Guy agreed that the examinations were an institutional arena in which Manchu rulers and Han Chinese intellectuals negotiated the definition of orthodoxy and incorporated changes from the literati community into the official curriculum.

In a characteristically spirited dissent, Chang Wejen suggested that the Manchu emperors were much less interested in using the examinations to cultivate political loyalty, or moral orthodoxy, than many assumed. But Tetsuo Najita discoursed on the Chinese examinations from the perspective of a historian of Japanese Confucianism with an eloquence that made skepticism about their utility generally unfashionable at the conference. Najita supposed that—unlike Japan, where civil examinations were never adopted until the

Meiji era—the massive memorization in Ming-Ch'ing China that the examination system required reflected enormous cultural anxiety. The seemingly mindless rote memorization, which was integral to the civil examinations, has often been mocked by critics applying standards of twentieth-century progressive educators as a violation of sound pedagogical procedures; the conferees were intrigued by this suggestion that if it were seen instead as part of a collective mission to create an identity, the memorization process would gain a new historical significance.

Indeed, the creation of forms of identity through education became a third major issue that the conference considered. Susan Mann's paper raised the issue of the imposition of Confucian norms on women in the eighteenth century and looked at the debate about female socialization. Mann argued that "nonliterate" or informal instruction of women by signs and symbols was more potent than textual instruction. Some conferees reacted by focusing on the question of whether there was a "change of mood" in, and concerning, women's education in the eighteenth century. Chang Hsueh-ch'eng's famous essay "Women's Learning," which Mann discussed, was said by some to be an historical watershed, despite Chang's own conservative intentions in writing it. Never before had a supposed lost world of female cultural achievement been described so cogently, and in such detail, by a major male literatus; Woodside suggested that it was not surprising that this eighteenth-century text should later have served as a reference point for Chinese feminists of both sexes at the outset of the twentieth century.

Pamela Crossley enlarged on the "identity" issue when she treated the Manchu language as an "invention" of the Ch'ing state, whose early emperors were bent on using education in the Manchu language as part of an unsuccessful identity-creating effort for their governing elite. But Cynthia Brokaw suggested instead that the Manchus ultimately lacked faith in the viability of their language, which had always been more of an "ideological construct" than a living system of speech. As yet another example of education in late imperial China as an effort to impose new identities, Rowe studied the state's role in establishing elementary schools among minority groups in the southwest in the 1730s, which were created in the teeth of racist resistance by Chinese settlers. The chief effect appeared to be not successful Confucianization but demoralization comparable, as Chang Wejen put it, to that suffered by Taiwanese and Australian aborigines in the twentieth century.

A fourth major issue that the conference considered, though in less depth, was the accumulation and use of knowledge within the framework of late imperial education. Frederic Wakeman observed that the conference could have done more with "the question of the output of knowledge in this period." Jack Goody noted that the rapid growth of new kinds of knowledge in Europe after 1600 did not appear to have any parallel in China, whatever the claims made by others about educational changes in Chinese schools. The editors have further considered this issue, among others, in their afterword, which focuses on "The Expansion of Education." Moreover, Catherine Jami's essay on mathematics provoked a debate over whether Chinese mathematicians during the early Ch'ing should be called "scientists" or merely "technicians" or "historians of mathematics," as Peter Bol indicated. Harriet Zurndorfer suggested that the Ch'ing revival of interest in mathematical education in commercial centers such as Hui-chou prefecture, for example, had complex causes, representing the changing literati fashions in Confucian learning that reinforced the rise of evidential learning, but also resulting in part from the needs or the general predispositions of the buoyant and growing Yangtze Delta merchant community.

The conference recognized that there was a growing pressure in late imperial China to take law seriously as an educational subject. Beyond that, there were interesting disagreements. Chang Wejen's paper on Ch'ing legal education raised the issue of whether Chinese knowledge of law had really expanded significantly before the nineteenth century. On the one hand, Yü Ying-shih suggested that the upsurge of evidential research studies among literati originated in the expansion of legal training and the demand for this, and that we may also witness the expansion of a more popular familiarity with law in the Peking operas and vernacular novels of the time. Chang proposed, on the contrary, that all this was really just the expansion of a popular awareness of norms and perhaps regulations, and in fiction of an awareness of the clever maneuvers of judges, and that there were fewer grounds for assuming a widening popular consciousness of "basic legal principles" or their "strategic nature."

Finally, conferees considered changes in educational theory as exemplified by literati such as Tai Chen, Yao Nai, Tseng Kuo-fan, and those involved with the Lung-men Academy in Shanghai, who were active participants in the shifting nature of the Han versus Sung Learning debates in the late eighteenth and nineteenth centuries. Cynthia Brokaw described Tai Chen's program of learning, which shared some assumptions with earlier Neo-Confucian education, as paternalistic and elitist, while Yü Ying-shih added that Tai's views were complicated and characterized by several layers of meaning that historians of education had to distinguish. While some have read Tai's attacks on the Ch'eng-Chu orthodoxy as a framework for "human rights," he also had a far less simple view of the supposed goodness of human nature than Mencius, the thinker Tai celebrated in his own major work. As K. C. Liu and Chow Kai-wing demonstrated, Yao Nai and Tseng Kuo-fan were fearful of the more radical implications in Tai's program, but each included a portion of the evidential research agenda in their own more conservative efforts to revive Sung Learning. That these scholarly debates had penetrated into the curriculum of nineteenth-century Confucian academies, as Barry Keenan showed, and that of the civil service examinations, as Elman's chapter demonstrated, suggested that simplistic conclusions drawn in the past about the lack of flexibility in the orthodox curriculum require substantial revision.

In the discussion of these topics, there was disagreement as to whether the era before the Opium War (1839–42) was full of tension and self-doubt, as Najita observed, or had a more serene sense of completion, as Wakeman suggested. Conferees agreed that it was important to define the different sorts of audiences that Confucian educators—from Ch'en Hung-mou to Tai Chen and Tseng Kuo-fan—were addressing and hoping to reach. For future research on Chinese education and society, for which some suggestions are presented in the afterword, we generally agreed that more comprehensive contextualization of the educational debates of the late empire was the key to further improvement of our understanding of their actual historical significance and to the avoidance of the rhetorical teleologies of past interpretation.

As the editors, we hope that the conference lived up to its promise; we think that the chapters in their final form have largely sustained the sense of discovery that made the conference enjoyable to those who were there. Yet, as Peter Perdue noted in his closing remarks at the conference, we caught more of the "outer experience" of late imperial education than of the "inner experience." Still, conferees did enjoy using education as a window through which social and intellectual historians both could examine, in collaboration, some of the ferment and achievement of a sprawling, multiethnic empire. We are convinced that the future prosperity of Chinese studies rests on closer collaboration between social and intellectual historians and their specializing counterparts in other disciplines, and we would like to think that this volume, however insufficient, helps to encourage a more satisfying association of social and intellectual history.

NOTES

1. Wm. T. de Bary and John Chaffee, eds., *Neo-Confucian Education: The Formative Stage* (Berkeley: University of California Press, 1989). See also the review by Benjamin A. Elman, "Education in Sung China," *Journal of the American Oriental Society* 111, no. 1 (Jan.–Mar. 1991): 83–93.

2. *Ta-Ch'ing Jen-tsung Jui huang-ti shih-lu* 大清仁宗睿皇帝實錄 (Veritable records of the Chia-ch'ing reign) (Tokyo: Okura Press, 1937–38), 292: 13b–15a.

3. Tu Wei-ming, "The Sung Confucian Idea of Education: A Background Understanding," 142, and Wm. T. de Bary, "Chu Hsi's Aims as an Educator," 212ff., both in de Bary and John Chaffee, eds., *Neo-Confucian Education.*

4. *Ta-Ch'ing Shih-tsung Hsien huang-ti shih-lu* 大清世宗憲皇帝實錄 (Veritable records of the Yung-cheng reign) (Tokyo: Okura Press, 1937–38), 127: 12–13.

5. Wing-tsit Chan, "Chu Hsi and the Academies," 396–98, in de Bary and Chaffee, *Neo-Confucian Education.*

6. *Ta-Ch'ing K'ao-tsung Ch'un huang-ti shih-lu* 大清高宗純皇帝實錄 (Veritable records of the Ch'ien-lung reign) (Tokyo: Okura Press, 1937–38), 1088: 3–6.

7. A major exception to both these trends is Evelyn S. Rawski, *Education and Popular Literacy in Ch'ing China* (Ann Arbor: University of Michigan Press, 1979).

GLOSSARY

Ch'eng-Chu	程朱	*hsueh*	學
Ch'eng I	程頤	Hsun-tzu	荀子
Ch'eng Tuan-li	程端禮	Ku Yen-wu	顧炎武
chiao	教	Mo-tzu	墨子
Chiao Hsun	焦循	Pi Yuan	畢沅
Chien-yang	建陽	Sun Hsing-yen	孫星衍
ching-chi	經濟	*Tao-hsueh*	道學
Chu Hsi	朱熹	*wen*	文

PART ONE

Education, Family, and Identity

ONE

The Education of Daughters in the Mid-Ch'ing Period

Susan Mann

One of the best-loved and most-performed operas of the southern stage tells the romance of Liang Shan-po and Chu Ying-t'ai. In the story, Chu Ying-t'ai persuades her father to let her dress up like a boy and enroll in an academy in Hangchow, where — studying the classics and histories — she befriends and falls in love with a handsome classmate. The lovers' tragic end, celebrated in a Hong Kong film that ranks as China's *Gone with the Wind*, still draws sobs and sighs from Chinese audiences, who sing along with the ill-fated heroine as she goes to her grave to consummate her love, defying her parents' wishes.

The opera, which celebrates love matches, also dramatizes the consequences of sending a young woman outside the home for schooling. Chu Ying-t'ai was no anomaly in the Chinese cultural repertoire: she was a *nü-shih*, a female scholar. However, her ill-fated romance, her suicide, and even her cross-dressing are emblems of the contradictions the *nü-shih* role encompassed for Chinese women. Chu Ying-t'ai captures in full the tensions implicit in the ideal for upper-class women in mid-Ch'ing times, when *nü-shih* were drawing unprecedented attention. Independent in her intellectual quest, Chu Ying-t'ai's experience outside the home exposed her to independent choices about love. In her story, passion for learning conflates with passion for her lover. Concern about this confusion of passions was one root of intellectuals' debates about women's education during the eighteenth century.

The story of Liang Shan-po and Chu Ying-t'ai is a fitting introduction to a chapter on women's education in more ways than one. As opera that could be read, sung, or seen, it occupies the "interface between the written and the oral."[1] Like the opera's libretto, the literate world of the *nü-shih* represents only one part of the "education" of daughters this chapter examines. Myths, stories, and symbols formed a cultural matrix prescribing gender roles for all women, whether they could read or not. Because the "education" of daughters described here encompassed more than written words, I have juxtaposed literate and nonliterate forms of education to show how they overlapped, conveying the complex and sometimes contradictory messages that shaped women's behavior. To do this, I have used an unconventional combination of sources. I have extrapolated freely— some may judge too freely—from oral histories and modern memoirs and stories to suggest the scope and range of the symbolic world accessible to eighteenth-century women, literate or not. I hope that the reader will conclude, as I have, that we can understand a great deal more about even the distant past if we avail ourselves of living memories.

Marriageable daughters in Ch'ing times received different types of education, depending on the class and the means of their families.[2] At the highest level of the elite, sons and at least some daughters undertook classical learning (*hsueh*) with the aim of becoming cultured (*wen*). A somewhat larger female audience received formal instruction (*chiao*) from special didactic books for women. Though the distinction between a woman who had studied the Classics (*hsueh*) and a woman who had merely received moral instruction (*chiao*) may seem a subtle one in the context of Chinese culture, in which virtually all learning was considered to convey moral values, it was in fact clear and highly self-conscious. The didactic instructional literature compiled for women in Ch'ing times was a genre in its own right, separated by its single-sex audience and its subject matter from the larger field of learning shared with men by some women of the upper classes. Only the *nü-shih*, the truly learned female, studied the same classical canon as her brothers.

Even classically educated daughters, however, were set apart from sons by their place. Whereas boys moved as quickly as possible out of home tutorials into lineage- or community-sponsored schools, private local academies, or government schools, women in Ch'ing times were required to study at home. The gendered segregation of higher learning began to break down during the nineteenth century, but in high Ch'ing times it was de rigueur.

Whether learned or merely instructed, literate women were still only a tiny proportion of the female population in mid-Ch'ing times. Education for the majority of women was nonliterate. Some nonliterate education took place on a grand public scale, when monumental arches (*p'ai-lou*) erected with government support celebrated a maiden's chastity or a widow's fidelity, or when a chaste woman's tablet was installed in the shrine adjacent to the county school.[3] Nonliterate education of a more modest sort took place in home apprenticeships. Apprenticeship for a girl sometimes involved conscious learning, as when a mother taught her daughter how to behave or how to sew. Still another kind of nonliterate education took the form of unconscious role modeling, as when a young girl watched her mother assemble her dowry and attended to conversations among the older women present.

Examining these dimensions of female education will show that, though most women were denied access to literate education in the late imperial period, a rich repertoire of nonliterate forms of education conveyed to them clearly the orthodox family values of the literate elite. To be sure, both literate and nonliterate education for women nurtured possibilities for subverting and contesting elite values. For example, passion challenged the notion that parents must select one's spouse. But the general effect of all forms of women's education was to silence subversives and convert them into part-icipants in the dominant discourse. It has been observed that the lonely, dis-affected young bride became the pillar of the joint family as a mother-in-law,[4] and that the girl who shrieked her childhood away in agony as her foot bones were crushed grew up to insist on binding her own daughter's feet.[5] A close examination of the education of daughters makes these transformations much less surprising. From her first birthday to her last breath, a woman was taught *fu-tao*: how to be a wife.

DIDACTIC INSTRUCTION

We know that women made up an increasingly important part of the literate audience for education in late imperial times because of the range of didactic books published specifically for them. The Ch'ing period saw an explosion of such handbooks offering moral instruction for women.[6] These works, addressed to daughters, wives, and mothers from literati families, included Lan Ting-yuan's *Women's Learning* (*Nü hsueh*, preface dated 1712–13) and Ch'en Hung-mou's *Bequeathed Guidelines for the Education of Women* (*Chiao-nü i-kuei*), comprising one section of his *Bequeathed Guidelines of Five Kinds* (first preface dated CL 37 (1772)). They exemplify the two main approaches to women's in-struction current in Ch'ing times.

Lan Ting-yuan's text is a series of chapters illustrating the "four attributes" (*ssu-te*) singled out in Han times by Pan Chao (citing the *Chou li*) as those attributes all women must cultivate: womanly virtue (*te*), womanly speech (*yen*), womanly conduct (*jung*), and womanly work (*kung*). It includes quotations from the classics, philosophy, and history, along with exemplary biographies following the style in Liu Hsiang's (c. 77–6 B.C.) first classic collection. The biographies are idealized brief lives of women, often dramatic, always moral-istic, sometimes either precious or perverse.[7]

Ch'en Hung-mou's rules for educating daughters, by contrast, are more wide-ranging and practical (on Ch'en, see also Rowe, chap. 12 of this volume). He reprints some of the "classics" for women from earlier periods, along with a series of shorter pieces that more closely resemble the genre called "family instructions" or rules for living, such as those of Yuan Ts'ai.[8] In keeping with this tradition, Ch'en's work includes practical advice about such matters as how to dower a daughter, how to handle the servants, and how to cope with conflicts with in-laws. [9]

Whatever their differences, writers of these handbooks were explicit about their motives. As "wise mothers," educated women could be counted on to rear loyal subjects. This attitude may seem to mark a sharp departure from the view widely ascribed to Ming thinkers: "A good woman is a woman without [literary] talent" (nü-tzu wu ts'ai, shih te).[10] But the cultivation of female talent was not the goal of these educators. More important, in the view of Lan Ting-yuan and Ch'en Hung-mou, was the vital link between women's education, domestic harmony, and political order. Here, for instance, is Ch'en Hung-mou, explaining the rationale for improving women's literacy throughout the realm:

> The girl who begins as a daughter in your family marries out and becomes a wife; she bears a child and becomes a mother. A wise daughter will make a wise wife and mother. And wise mothers rear wise sons and grandsons. The process of kingly transformation [lit. wang-hua, "the transformative influence of the ruler on his subjects"] therefore begins in the women's apartments, and a family's future advantage is tied to the purity and the education of its women. Hence education is of the utmost importance.[11]

In a similar vein, Lan Ting-yuan prefaced his textbook *Women's Learning* with the following remarks: "The basis of the government of the empire lies in the habits of the people. The correctness of the habits of the people depends upon the orderly management of the family. The Way (tao) for the orderly management of the family begins with women."[12]

CLASSICAL LEARNING

Regardless of the writers' aims, and however narrowly they construed the goals of educating women, we know that these texts were not the sum total, or even the main body, of the curriculum many literate women actually studied.[13] First of all, a "wise mother" properly instructed had to learn the Classics so that she could personally attend to her sons' early education.[14] Mothers who taught their sons did not use women's instruction books; they used the classics and the histories.[15]

Well-educated women in Ch'ing times were also expected to compose elegant verse, as numerous literary collections of the period attest.[16] But neither Lan's nor Ch'en's text includes examples of good poetry or even good poetesses. The skills required for the genre we know Ch'ing women preferred —especially long poems or ballads—must have been garnered elsewhere. In fact, when all is said and done, it appears that the most highly educated women—Lin Tai-yü in *Dream of the Red Chamber* is a good example—read precisely the same texts their brothers read, including a good smattering of poetry and novels.[17]

Special didactic works "for women" were doubtlessly purchased and also read by fathers. We can infer this from one telling feature of the didactic works: their instructions focus on guiding young women, especially young married women. Conspicuously absent from every didactic text for women that I have consulted is any discussion of, say, how to be a good mother-in-law. On the contrary, the texts appear to have been written with the express purpose of controlling younger, sexually active women. They taught not literary arts, but behavior. In sum, the content of these hortatory texts suggests that they were not written simply to educate women; they were written in response to problems that arose as a **result** of educating women.[18]

The first problem was how to prescribe limits on the activities of educated daughters. Paradoxically, even the most extreme of the didactic texts implicitly offered elite women two contradictory classical ideals of womanhood—the *nü-shih* (female scholar) and the *chen-nü* (virtuous woman). Pan Chao and Sung Jo-chao, authors of the two earliest and most famous didactic women's texts, which were often cited and reprinted in Ch'ing instruction books for women, were scholarly women whose very act of writing posed a contradiction with what they wrote. As *nü-shih* they played men's roles. Pan Chao had stepped into her brother's shoes to compose significant chapters of the official Han history. Sung Jo-chao, one of five erudite sisters, refused to marry and instead accepted a position as "palace instructress" (*kung-shih*) in the T'ang court.[19] Educated women, in other words, always threatened to cross gender boundaries, defying their destiny as wives and mothers.

In addition, the ideal of woman-as-scholar—popularized in the opera that retold the story of Chu Ying-t'ai—conflated scholarship and romance, and held out the possibility, very much alive during the Ch'ing period, of a companionate marriage that included intellectual exchange and shared aesthetic experiences as well as household management and reproduction. So fathers interested in educated women were also concerned about wives for their sons and husbands for their daughters: a good education for one's child, regardless of gender, was a key to successful matchmaking in the upper classes.

Finally, of course, educated women of the eighteenth century did not confine themselves to teaching their children. Individual women writers won fame, especially for their poetry. They excelled in the long poem or ballad called the *t'an-tz'u*, written in the "southern style," using seven characters in a line.[20] Women wrote songs they could sing and play in solitude, in the confines of a garden or courtyard. Since they did not write for the stage, they even won the approval of moralistic literary critics who frowned on what they considered the vulgar performance style.[21]

These women writers have become historically visible through collections of women's writing that reveal not only numerical but also regional patterns of female erudition.[22] The core areas surrounding Hangchow and Soochow, capitals of the top two prefectures in total number of *chin-shih* (lit., "presented literati") during the Ch'ing period, and the two cities at the peak of the urban hierarchy in the Lower Yangtze macroregion, were home to the leading female artists and writers in Ch'ing times. [23] In the province of Kwangtung, where the development of local academies has been traced in some detail by both Chinese and Western scholars, there is evidence of educational opportunity for women well before the entry of foreigners who sponsored such activities. Canton — the site of Juan Yuan's Hsueh-hai T'ang — appears to have become a secondary center for women's art and letters: Juan Yuan himself is known to have taken a personal interest in the education and training of his own daughters.[24] Noted female artists and writers in Ch'ing times, in other words, seem to have built their careers in centers where men were also academically successful, at the peak of the urban hierarchy.

Equally striking, as seen in a recent survey of 32 famous women painters of the late imperial period, is not only the diffusion of women's artistic activity away from Yangchow and Nanking (the centers of Ming women's literary arts), but also an apparent shift in the marital status of famous women painters between the late Ming and the high Ch'ing periods.[25] Perhaps the latter is an emblem of the former: Nanking and Yangchow were cities renowned for courtesans, whereas the Ch'ing centers of women's literary activity were dominated by married women. The majority of famous women painters active after 1700, in fact, were married women with children (including a few chaste widows — that is, women widowed as young brides or even fiancées).[26]

A similar shift may have occurred, from late Ming to mid-Ch'ing times, in the marital status of educated women writers. Of the more than sixty-seven noted women writers mentioned in *Eminent Chinese of the Ch'ing Period*, eleven were concubines and none courtesans; the rest were all wives of noted scholars, including such major figures as Sun Hsing-yen and Ts'ui Shu.[27]

WOMEN'S LEARNING: TO WHAT END?

These genteel, learned wives of the eighteenth century personified the tension between the *nü-shih* and the *chen-nü* ideals. A long treatise reviewing the history of formal schooling for women — *Fu hsueh*, or "Women's Learning," by Chang Hsueh-ch'eng (1738–1801) — explores the tension in detail.[28] The treatise is part of a well-known debate provoked by the poet Yuan Mei's patronage of women's learning.[29] Yuan Mei (1716–98), a brilliant literary critic and iconoclastic scholar, made his Sui Garden a gathering point for talented women poets, including three of Yuan's own younger sisters. Yuan Mei also counted among his "pupils" the mothers, wives, and nieces of other prominent scholars.[30] The difficulty with Yuan Mei's role as patron of women's letters, in the eyes of Chang Hsueh-ch'eng, lay in his transgression of fundamental principles of the human moral order, especially the strict separation of the sexes, in the name of an aesthetic ideal that Chang considered frivolous: the writing of spontaneous and impassioned verse.[31] Chang insisted instead that women's learning should focus on "ritual." Just as Chang accused Yuan Mei of trivializing the proper substance of learning for educated women, Chang himself trivialized female education focused exclusively on literary art. In his view, women in literary relationships with men were themselves trivialized, reduced from their status as truly cultivated persons to mere entertainers and social companions for men. We might even say that in Chang's view Yuan's patronage transformed women from literary subjects into objects. Yuan, of course, would have said precisely the opposite.

The facts of the controversy aside, Chang's essay on women's learning is an erudite reflection on the historical decline of women's higher education centered in the domestic realm, disciplined by ritual practice and free from the quest for fame that corrupted the public world of men's letters. Chang had his own view, in other words, of a separate moral sphere much like that invoked for respectable women in debates about European women's status during the sixteenth and seventeenth centuries.[32]

Chang's essay—said by David Nivison to be the first of his works to attract a wide audience[33]—describes the separation of women's learning from the public sphere and the long slow process of privatization that followed, in the course of which women's learning was first transmitted through families and finally became the exclusive domain of individual persons:

> Some women's learning of ancient times, such as the learning of the Woman Historian, the Woman Libationer, the Woman Seer, was associated with a particular government office. In that respect, women's learning was like men's: both men and women specialized in a particular art in order to hold a particular official post. The general learning required of all women, on the other hand, was not prescribed by an office, but was encompassed in the four attributes of "virtue, speech, conduct, and work" [set forth for the first time in Pan Chao's *Instructions for Women.*] Of the four, virtue is elusive and difficult to call attention to; work is crude and easily flaunted. But the other two aspects of women's general learning are very close to literary art: they are speech and conduct, and they are the most important.
>
> So it was that in those days, from the individual household with its rules for living to the imperial court and all the high officials, not a woman could be found who had not been schooled in proper ritual conduct. Therefore, when a court audience was held, when a guest was received, when a funeral took place, when the sacrifices were performed, the empress, the imperial concubines, and the wives of the various high officials all had specific duties. If they did not prepare for this through regular lectures or discussions, how could they have mastered these arts when the time came to use them? The Erudites who discoursed on the classics in Han times generally used quotations and excerpts to talk about the rites, but they also depended on Hsu Sheng because he was so good at actually performing those rituals.[34] In this way the ancients achieved the fullest possible realization of dignity and decorum in ritual, which would have been impossible had they merely recited and repeated texts. In the same way we see that what is called women's conduct must include actual ritual practice ....

As for women's speech, its most important quality is deferential obedience. In ancient times, words were not to pass from the women's quarter to the outside world. What was called "deferential obedience" was also an essential character- istic of ritually correct literary art. Confucius once said: 'The person who has not studied the Odes is ill-equipped to speak.'[35] This means, of course, that any woman who was accomplished in proper speech — in other words, who could speak with deferential obedience — must have also been well versed in the Odes.

Thus it is clear that in women's learning of ancient times, ritual had to be mastered before one could understand poetry. But in the centuries since then, women's learning has ceased to be transmitted. There are some women who are accomplished and elegant and who know literature, and who on that basis claim to be women who can also do scholars' work. They wear their virtue, like their beauty, on their faces. Such women do not know that women originally had their own learning and that this learning always took the rites as its foundation. Since they have abandoned the instruction basic to their calling and wantonly flung themselves into poetry, the poems they write are not characterized by what the ancients would have called practiced deferential obedience or fine womanly speech. To study language under these conditions is like being a farmer who abandons his fields or an envoy who neglects to take a ceremonial gift when he leaves the country. How can their writing seriously be counted as women's learn- ing? This is pathetic!

The women's learning of ancient times always began with the rites as a foun- dation for mastering poetry. The women's learning of today is just the opposite: it uses poetry to destroy the rites. If the rites are cut off, we will no longer be able to speak of the human heart and mind or even of human behavior. Without ques- tion, certain literati with no character have perpetrated their heretical teachings to entice women to become their followers. Those of us who truly understand women's learning look on these men as so much excrement. We shall never be deceived!"[36]

Leading Female Scholars of the Eighteenth Century

It is ironic that Chang's polemic conflated women's literary achievements with a lapse from virtue, when some of the most outstanding female literary artists of his day were respectable married women who built their literary circles within the context of the family and not in the salons of patrons like Yuan Mei. To be sure, even within the home these women crossed the boundaries prescribed for them by Confucian convention and by family instruction books. Consider, for example, the case of Wang Tuan. One of the famous poets of the Ch'ing period, she was a daughter-in-law of the official and poet Ch'en Wen-shu (1775–1845), known for his liberal attitudes toward women, and him- self a patron of two accomplished concubines. Born and reared in Hangchow as the daughter of distinguished parents (her father was a bibliophile of some re- pute), Wang Tuan began reading "as an infant" and was writing poetry by the age of seven *sui*. Orphaned as a young girl, she was educated by her maternal aunt, Liang Te-sheng (1771–1847), who herself came from a family of highly educated women and reared two talented daughters of her own. Later, as the wife of Ch'en P'ei-chih, Wang Tuan collaborated with her husband in writing poetry. After P'ei-chih's untimely death, her only son developed a mental illness, and Wang Tuan, sorrowing over her losses, became a recluse, adopting two Taoist names.

After she married, Wang's literary interests drew her to cross Confucian boundaries twice. First, she developed a close relationship with her father-in-law, who was her patron during her years of widowhood. He shared her devotion to Taoism and is said to have greatly admired her poetry. With his collaboration and assistance, Wang edited and published her husband's collected works, including his most famous memoir, an account of the life of his talented concubine Wang Tzu-lan (1803–24). Wang Tuan herself composed a eulogy for this work, which father-in-law and daughter-in-law reprinted separately in a special edition.[37] Shared literary interests, then, even if safely confined within the domestic realm, had the effect of blurring the boundaries between the sexes—violating the taboo that separated daughter-in-law and father-in-law and collapsing the strict ritual hierarchy that distanced wives from concubines.[38]

By examining female literary circles, some of them clustered around men, we can see how women as well as men acted as patrons to each other through agnatic and affinal networks of birth and marriage.[39] Ch'en Wen-shu and Yuan Mei, the most renowned male patrons of women's arts in the mid-Ch'ing era and themselves influenced by role models at home (in the case of Yuan Mei, sisters and his aunt were critical), supported educated daughters, concubines, and wives.[40] The literary lineage centered on Ch'en Wen-shu is one example. It included not only his daughter-in-law, Wang Tuan, but also two concubines (Kuan Yun and Wen Ching-yü) and two daughters (Ch'en Hua-ch'ü and Ch'en Li-ch'ü). Ch'en made himself a local historian of women's achievements. A posthumous collection of his poems and articles about three women whose tombs on West Lake he had restored was published in 1881.[41]

Despite their close association with male patrons, however, successful female poets in the Ch'ing period remained carefully circumscribed in their role as writers, and most of them remained respectably cloistered. In that sense, they shared with illiterate women a common background—a childhood education grounded in signs and symbols that limited their role as "women scholars."

FU-TAO, THE WAY OF THE WIFE: THE WORLD OF SIGNS AND SYMBOLS

The world of signs and symbols that surrounded a young girl from birth conveyed more powerfully than any text the core values of what Chang Hsueh-ch'eng marked as true women's learning: her destiny and duties as a wife. Nowhere was this more true than in work. The practice and the ideology surrounding women's work must be the departure point for a larger discussion of the symbolic world that shaped women's consciousness, whether they were literate or not.

Nonliterate education began with an only partly playful ceremony of early childhood, when a tray containing various objects was presented to every child at the age of one year. The first object the child picked from the tray was thought to augur her future. A daughter was commonly offered a concave clay tile—the weight for a spindle—in token of her future role as a spinner-weaver, a handworker, in the household economy. The tile was the counterpart for her brother's brush and inkslab, or abacus, or tool. Unlike men, some of whom could hope to be free from manual labor, women regardless of class were expected from birth to work with their hands. While boys were presented with a range of career options in respectable families, including the possibility of becoming a scholar, merchant, or artisan, girls had only one route to take: toward the wifely womanly roles prescribing handwork.[42]

The second great rite of passage in a young girl's nonliterate education was the binding of her feet, essential to her desirability as a marriage partner.[43] In upper-class households, this might begin as early as age five; the most cloistered women had the tiniest feet. Poorer families waited longer and bound less tightly, in order to enhance their daughters' productivity;[44] but evidence suggests that marriageable daughters of Han Chinese families in the eighteenth century could expect their feet to be bound. The immediate excruciating pain of the bone crushing was supplanted in later life by a permanent handicap that made walking difficult and heavy labor nearly impossible.

The preferred forms of women's work, accordingly, were done in the home sitting on a chair or stool (the poor knelt or squatted on the floor). Initiation into the world of women's handwork came at home under mother's tutelage, but women's work was celebrated in the community as a whole once a year during the Double Seven Festival—the seventh day of the seventh lunar month. On this day, the star Vega (the Weaving Maid) was united with three stars of the constellation Aquila known as the Herd Boy. The festival confirmed the basic division of labor in peasant society: men plow with draft animals, women weave with their hands. Double Seven was about work and rest, for the Herd Boy and the Weaving Maid were separated in the heavens because their love for each other led them to abandon their labors when they tarried together. The festival was also about those emotions so often explored in women's poetry: love, separation, and reunion. But in the preparations for the festival and in the rituals themselves, the focal point of Double Seven was made clear. The seventh lunar month initiated the period of *li-ch'iu* (the beginning of autumn). It was the start of the sewing season, when winter garments had to be fashioned or mended before the cold weather set in.[45] The celebrations of Double Seven accordingly centered on women and their work and on the Weaving Maid (Chih-nü) herself, patron goddess of women's hand-work and ruler of the fecund female world of seedy melons and fruits, sericul-ture, and the gathering and storing of precious things.[46]

Rituals from different parts of China reveal the rich meanings of this festive women's holiday. For example, in Ningpo:

> On the seventh day of the seventh month, women wash their hair in water pre-pared by soaking hibiscus leaves. On the evening of the same day, they spread out melons and fruits and 'test for skill' (ch'i-ch'iao). In the light of the moon they try to thread a needle, and if the thread goes through, they will be skillful (te-ch'iao).[47]

In North China,

> In the homes at this time the people drop tiny cambric needles upon the surface of basins of water in which the sun is shining. These cast shadows across the bot-tom of the basin. The shadows take different forms according to the positions of the needles. If they take certain prescribed forms, the person casting the needles is supposed to be both clever and lucky. While if they take other forms, they are supposed to be despised by the gods as being ignorant.[48]

According to a missionary account,

> In Foochow the women make a special offering to the spinning maiden consisting of seven bowls of various kinds of melons, seven bowls of food, the usual candles, incense and idol paper. Frequently on a table near by are placed needles, thread, scissors, and other articles used by women in their work. After the incense has been kindled and each of the women has bowed thrice, the idol paper money is lighted and while it flickers the women try to thread seven needles. Their skill is judged by the number they succeed in threading. In some localities they put a spider in a box, and if he makes a web, this is regarded as a promise of skill in weaving and sewing.[49]

In certain parts of China, the Double Seven festival was managed — organized, conducted, and financed — by local women:

> Only women take part in the services appropriate to the day, and no males are present, except little boys still under their mother's wing. The ladies, formerly, went in for needlework contests with prizes for those who excelled in embroidery, or amused themselves, in gay rivalry, with needle-threading competitions. Humbler maidens still try to thread needles either by moonlight or beside a glowing incense-stick. In Kiangsu province, they thread a seven-eyed needle with red silk, almost without the aid of a light — under a table, for example. Such as succeed are sure to be good needlewomen.[50]

Festival celebrations in the Canton area were on a grand scale. An account of the festival in Canton around 1900 reported that "women, especially unmar-ried women, embroider shoes and silk garments as offerings for this anniver-sary. Flowers, sweetmeats, and preserved fruits, are also presented to the

Weaving Lady, and amongst these are placed basins containing shoots of the young rice-plant; they are so arranged as to appear as if they are growing, and in the centre of each cluster a little lamp is placed whose spark of light reminds one of a glow-worm or a firefly. Miniature bridges, formed of flower garlands, grains of boiled rice, and almonds cemented by gum, connect the various offering-tables."[51] Some women took a few stitches just after presenting this offering "to consolidate, as it were, the benediction which they have asked on their work." Others laid a threaded needle among the flowers.[52] The ritual burning of richly embroidered garments concluded the ceremony, which was capped by a midnight drawing of water from household wells. The blessing of the goddess and her six heavenly sisters assured that this water would cure family illness in the year ahead.[53]

Lessons about women's work—its value, its purpose, and its importance to the community as a whole— seem transparent in descriptions of the Double Seven festival. They may also seem at first glance a step removed from the Confucian discourse of the educated elite. But folk festivals, especially women's festivals, represented a world and a language with which the high culture of the elite was closely identified. First, it should be remembered that womanly work was one of the four quintessential female attributes. Women's handbooks —beginning with Pan Chao—and biographies of model women continually stressed a common theme: all women must be frugal (chien), they must be vigilant in managing household affairs (ts'ao), and they must be diligent (ch'in) in their labors. Tales of youthful chaste widows and fiancées celebrated the young women's resourcefulness in earning a living that, in the present, supported their aging in-laws and provided for their children and, in the future, would supply precious coffins for ritual burials, together with the income to educate sons who would bring honor to their ancestors.[54] Every son acknowledged his debt to his mother's industry in mourning rituals, as when at her funeral he carried in one hand a staff made from mulberry, emblem of the woman's work world of sericulture. Mulberry remained one of the symbols of filial piety found in decorations and drawings.[55]

A good example of the valorization of women's work in Confucian theories of political economy is found in the Ming dynasty agricultural handbook by Hsu Kuang-ch'i, Nung-cheng ch'üan-shu, a classic work reprinted seven times following its publication in the seventeenth century. The text continually stresses the intimate relationship between farming and handicraft industry, plowing and weaving—that is, the mutual dependency of men's and women's work. Moreover, the text explicitly draws a connection not only between women's handicraft work and the agricultural household economy, but also between women's handicraft work and the health of the body politic:

> Now if one woman does not spin, someone in the realm will suffer cold as a result (fu i-nü pu-chi, t'ien-hsia pi yu shou ch'i han-che); how much worse it will be if half the

women don't spin! And if they pass the years until they are fifty years old with no source of income, if they don't spin they will be idle; if they are idle they will become decadent; if they are decadent they will sink into debauchery and moral standards will collapse. Today the virtues cultivated in the home do not build strong moral character in women. A large number of the edicts and official announcements issued every year express concern about women's licentious behavior....[56]

Finally, the court's own imprimatur was stamped on women's work in the annual sacrifices to Lei Tsu, goddess of sericulture, conducted by the empress herself.[57] Each year the empress went in person to a special altar outside the Forbidden City, on a date specially chosen by the court astronomers, to sacrifice to the goddess and to assist in the gathering of mulberry leaves for the feeding of the silkworms. Elite women as workers, including the empress herself, were expected to set the example for their lesser sisters, whether rural peasant, domestic servant, or subject.

If work itself was education for women, this was nowhere more true than in needlework. Girls learned to embroider for two purposes: to prepare their own dowries and to meet the exacting demands of being a daughter-in-law. Each young girl was responsible for embroidering all the bedding and the shoes and so forth for her dowry. Embroidery was an emblem of virtue and a mark of class. To embroider, one must have leisure, long years of training, and all those amenities that accompany privileged living: a clean room, a fan when it's hot, fine silk thread and needles, space for the frame. Yet embroidery could be attempted by young women of modest means, as we learn from a pair of Ningpo conundrums describing a rich girl and a poor girl at work:

Embroidery (rich ladies' version)

On a stage framed in gold
Sits a rosy-cheeked maiden
A red flower, green leaves,
Slowly unfold.

Embroidery (poor girls' version)

A stage framed in purple bamboo
Invites a girl to come out
Only the needle sounds — *te-p'o-te-p'o*
A fresh flower slowly opens.[58]

Poor girls created simple designs framed in bamboo; rich girls, resplendent ones framed in gold. But any young woman who could manage it learned to embroider. Embroidering her pillowcases and quilts or bed hangings, each young girl, consciously or no, prepared for the day of her wedding. Phoenix and dragon, duck and butterfly, every design was a symbol of conjugal bliss.

Ling Shu-hua's modern short story "Embroidered Pillows" delicately reveals the connections between a young girl's hopes for marriage and her fine embroidery work, between embroidery and purity and class.[59] In the story, a servant's dirty child peers eagerly, but from the necessary safe distance, at the spectacular phoenix her mother's young mistress has embroidered. The single bird, in thirty to forty colors, took six months to work. In the heat, the young woman's maid fans her as she stitches, for if perspiration soaks the threads, she must rip out hours of work. She washes her hands frequently and rubs them with talcum powder afterward. The embroidery, we learn, will be sent as a gift to the family of a promising young man as a sign of her talent and assurance of her marriageability.

Then the scene shifts: it is years later. The same piece of embroidery, sent out as a gift long ago, appears once again in the room of the same woman, no longer young and still unmarried. Its soiled phoenix now adorns the same servant girl's own pillowcase. The very day the gorgeous creation was received in the home of the promising young man, we are told, someone spilled a drink on it. It slipped to the floor unnoticed, to be trampled and discarded. The serving girl, who had never learned embroidery, was only too happy to have the piece for her own nuptial bed. As the embroideress slowly recognizes the phoenix on the pillowcase, she relives every stitch she took so long ago and recalls painfully her hopes for a brilliant match, hopes now ruined like her handwork.

Needlework was only one aspect of a young woman's prolonged preparation for marriage, which began with the assembling of her dowry, often at a very young age. Dowry in turn became a kind of public education when it was paraded through the community en route to the bride's new home. Here, for example, is a detailed description of a dowry procession from Ningpo, Chekiang province, around the turn of the twentieth century:

Before the founding of the Republic [i.e., before 1911], it was customary for most girls in my area to marry between the age of eighteen and twenty *sui*, which is in accordance with the ancient injunction that a man should wed at thirty and a woman at twenty. When a daughter reached the age when she could wear her hair in tufts [i.e., about seven *sui*], even though her wedding was still some years away, her parents would frantically begin to prepare a dowry for her, as if they were birds rushing to build a nest before it rained. They would hire a dressmaker, a carpenter, a bamboo craftsman, a tinsmith, and a lacquerware maker to fashion her clothes and dishes and so on. And to make sure that her dowry was spectacular, they'd send one man to Hankow to buy copperware, and another to Chiu-chiang to pick out porcelain, and still another to Foochow for leather goods, and one to Changsha for embroidered linens. Meanwhile, the future bride would be instructed in embroidery by a skilled female relative invited to the home especially for that purpose. Each girl was expected to embroider all her own pillowcovers, quilts and bed covers, mirror cases, and flowered shoes; this demonstrated her mastery of the last of the Four Womanly Virtues. And so they all stretched themselves taut, working constantly, throwing their lives into confusion for years....

Then three days before the wedding, a hired laborer and his friends sent from the bride's household would carry the dowry gifts to the household of the groom: this was called the "dowry procession" (*fa-chia-chuang*). The boxes the dowry was carried in were called "swinging chests" (*k'ang-hsiang*), because they were hoisted on a bamboo pole balanced on the shoulders of two men. The chests were made of wood, ranging up to five feet high, three feet long, and four feet deep.... There were two types of chests: "soft" and "hard." The best quality soft chests had wooden frames no more than one foot across, while the hard boxes had four- foot frames. So you could tell how much a family had spent on a match by observing the size of the dowry chests. The chests were covered with red lacquer and had carved designs on every side, sometimes inlaid with gold leaf—the glitter and the color drew great crowds. Then on the top of the chests you'd see bundles full of satin sashes and silk streamers, of tassels embroidered with silk and pearls, all shining in every color of the rainbow. What a brilliant spectacle —it dazzled your eyes! Among the richest families, it was not unusual to have more than twenty chests, and all along the route crowds of onlookers would block the way, shouting out their admiration and envy.[60]

Dowry processions ensured that dowry remained a fact of life for families with daughters in Ningpo city; without a dowry, a respectable young woman could not marry.

The dowry of the rich young girl was not limited to what people saw passing down the street. Her parents might deposit money in a local native bank account, or they could present the new couple with the deed to a house or a piece of land. By contrast, dowry in families of modest means was no load of present wealth and consumer goods. Its value lay not in material wealth, but in the signs and symbols it conveyed to and for the bride. Even a few objects in the dowry could carry a heavy load of messages telling the bride, and the families that received and sent her, the significance of her passage.

In Ningpo, for instance, the minimum dowry consisted only of one pair of quilts (one heavy, one light), one chest, a chamberpot, and a birthing pot. But each item carried potent messages. Each was a rebus, explicating the bride's fate and her charge as a wife. The birthing pot, the most laden item in the dowry, went to the bride's new home heavy with peanuts, dates, red eggs, and cassia fruits. The word for peanuts, *hua-sheng*, is a homonym for *sheng*, which means "childbirth." The peanuts had to be be raw, not roasted, so that the person who bit into one would exclaim *sheng! sheng!* ("raw! raw!"—or "give birth! give birth!") to emphasize the point. Peanuts, moreover, had to be of two kinds —one shelled, the other still in the shell—because Ningpo people called peanut shells *ch'ang-sheng-kuo*, which means "everlasting descendants." Dates were called *tsao*, a homonym for "early," instructing the bride to *tsao sheng* ("give birth early"); red eggs were dyed the celebratory color marking propitious births (i.e., male births); and cassia fruits, pronounced *kuei-tzu*, were a homonym for "wealthy sons"—sons successful as merchants or officials. Inside the birthing pot, in other words, were the messages that told the new bride's future and prescribed her role: she was to bear sons, the future wealth of her new family.[61]

The load of messages continued inside the chests, into which were stuffed the quilts, pillowcovers, and other items. This store of wealth too was metaphorical, encoded in signs representing reproduction, not production. At the bottom of each chest, wrapped in red paper, the bride's family would place a single copper coin. Worthless as currency in the marketplace, it was priceless as the currency of reproduction and fertility. *Ya-hsiang-ch'ien*, the "money at the bottom of the box," ensured that *ts'ai-ch'i*, "wealth-energy," would be trapped beneath the quilts of the new couple to be released in the conjugal bed, site of procreation.

As for the dowry's basins, bowls, and other vessels for washing and serving, they too conveyed messages. Every morning the new bride knew she must rise at the crack of dawn, stoke the kitchen fire, and boil water for her mother-in-law. First the washing basin, then the teacup; vessels of every kind implied service to the lineage of the new family, especially to the mother-in-law. Serving dishes laden with food would be watched carefully by the daughter-in-law as she ate, for she must keep the bowl of each person at the table constantly filled.

Dowry objects, then, instructed the bride on two levels: they foretold her fertility and they tempered her fecundity with service, reminding her that the *fu-tao*, the wifely way, required her manual labor.

The bride's own mother sent her off with a sorrowful message that reaffirmed the signs in the dowry:

Kung huan-hsi	May your father-in-law be pleased,
P'o tsung-i	May your mother-in-law approve,
Chiao-t'a lou-t'i	May each step you take on the stairs
Pu-pu kao.	Bring you higher and higher.
Tu-jen ch'ü	You leave alone—
Man-chiao hui.	May you return, sedan-chair full of children.

These artifacts, signs, and messages were the culmination of a lifelong "education" that prepared a young woman to accept her role as procreator, to understand that riches come only through sons. And the signs continued after the bride's arrival at her husband's home. As she left her natal family, she would have been lifted into the sedan chair by a brother, on her feet embroidered shoes that must never touch the ground until she reached her destination. Alighting at her husband's home, she would find five empty sacks (*tai*) spread in a line on the ground leading from the sedan chair to the threshold of the house. Each step on this new ground signified once again the wealth she brought, for *wu-tai* (five bags) is a rebus for "five generations."

Young girls of mid-Ch'ing times may not have received any sex education from mothers or peers, but no young girl receiving these messages could be in doubt about the purpose of her marriage. In fact, as we have seen, since girls were betrothed as early as age eight, and dowry was assembled from the time of betrothal, learning about marriage through the dowry was a nearly lifelong process for some women. For girls betrothed in childhood, the process began precisely as they started to assume other responsibilities preparing them for adult life: work at home to help mother or to provide income, footbinding, segregation from boys and play groups outside the home.

The long, lurching ride of every Chinese bride from her house to his was the culmination of her family's effort to prepare her (and themselves) for her future. Each literal step she took, each object loaded onto the shoulders of the porters sent to bear her to her new home, educated her about her position, and about what she would be expected to do from the moment of her marriage onward.

Education of Daughters in the Renaissance

This chapter has already alluded to striking similarities between the mid-Ch'ing crisis and the Renaissance crisis over women's education. As in China, in Renaissance Europe women's education was centered on a classical ideal of virtue that encompassed practical skills. Women of upper-class families learned to sew and to manage the home, beginning their training as early as six years of age. They were expected to know how to brew herbal medicines and treat simple ailments and even broken limbs. Practical skills aside, young women of the Renaissance, like their Chinese counterparts, had to be the embodiment of all virtues: charm, chastity, modesty, reserve, and composure.[62]

At the same time, slight discrepancies point to critical differences between the European Renaissance ideal and the high Ch'ing norm. For instance, like young Chinese women of Ch'ing times, girls in the Italian Renaissance studied musical instruments (zither, harp, and lute were the favorites) and learned to sing. But unlike their Chinese counterparts they also learned to dance. Young women of the Renaissance cooked, practiced good manners, and knew how to apply makeup. But again, unlike their Chinese counterparts, they also studied how to flirt during courtship. Ladies in the Renaissance, like upper-class women of the Ch'ing, read the same classical works men studied—Dante, Virgil, Petrarch, and Horace; the Book of Odes, the Book of Rites, the Four Books, and T'ang poetry. Like Ch'ing women, Renaissance women used their reading skills to expand their horizons: they threw caution to the winds, consuming the *Decameron* as avidly as Lin Tai-yü read *Hsi-hsiang chi*.[63] But Renaissance women might also learn a foreign language, Greek. They did outdoor exercises to promote physical fitness. And though men alone were trained to be citizens while women were taught to serve in the home, Leonardo Bruni, the author of a treatise on women's education, argued that women should learn the history of their own country so that they would take an interest in current events.[64]

How far was that interest to go? Here Bruni was troubled by the same questions that plagued Chang Hsueh-ch'eng. What and how should women write, and where would they find an appropriate voice? Bruni was adamant that women should not study rhetoric, for that would enable them to participate in public intellectual discourse.[65] Like Chinese women of the eighteenth century, Renaissance women were not supposed to apply their knowledge outside the home. Only courtesans did that, with the predictable results. In fact, as Natalie Davis has pointed out, Renaissance women writers were constrained by the same domestic limits that confined eighteenth-century Chinese women and circumscribed the subjects of their writing. They had limited access to materials, few genres that might serve as models, and no connections with relevant areas of public life that would have enabled them to move into spheres of historical or political writing dominated by men.[66]

A comparison of the Renaissance with the high Ch'ing can only underscore the magnitude of the silence imposed on women by the combined pressures that confined them to the home. And it can only illuminate more sharply the anxiety men experienced as they watched respectable wives move out into the gardens where "public" conversations occurred. These wives were too much like the courtesans who, in Ch'ing China as in Renaissance Europe, violated all taboos on public status and public speech. The courtesan embodied a female intellectual capacity unchecked by the constraints of domestic life. And her unchecked intellect always carried overtones of unchecked sexuality.[67]

Although high Ch'ing and Renaissance educational institutions had much in common where women were concerned, there were slight but important differences between them. These differences signaled a greater degree of seclusion and segregation for Ch'ing women, both physically (as in their bound feet and sedentary life) and culturally (as in their exposure to only one language and one country). Far from being the norm for Ch'ing females, physical exercise and movement were anathema. Equestrian skills cultivated by women of earlier dynasties had long since disappeared from the female regimen. Being sickly or physically weak was admired as a mark of sensitivity and seductiveness, as we see so clearly in the character of Lin Tai-yü.[68] Nor was formal training in history or contemporary affairs a part of China's classical ideal for female education.[69] Statecraft writers of the early nineteenth century, harking back to ancient classical texts, placed women and their education firmly in the home, centered on ritual and domesticity.

WOMEN'S EDUCATION IN CH'ING CHINA AND TOKUGAWA JAPAN

In Japan, where women held the central place in the world of letters in medieval times, the rise of the warrior class after the thirteenth century reduced the importance of literary arts in court politics. Nonetheless, women continued to appear in roles suggesting a fair degree of literacy, despite the decline of interest in Chinese poetry and prose. The female storytellers, *bikuni*, shopkeepers' wives, and geisha entertainers of the late Muromachi and the Tokugawa periods all show that education of various kinds was available to women as well as men in the post-Heian period.

The Tokugawa state embraced Confucian norms for state and society, but it appears to have been least successful in foisting them on the domestic realm.[70] Scholars in fact present sanguine assessments of female literacy rates in the Tokugawa period. Passin estimates that boys averaged four years of schooling, girls five! Dore guesses that about 40 percent of males and 10 percent of females got some type of formal education outside the home at the end of Tokugawa.[71] Women in urban centers attended private schools (*terakoya*) for girls; in the countryside, where the curriculum was apparently more conservative, they nonetheless were tutored at home. In Tokugawa times, a special vocational system for women, the *ohariya* (sewing school), taught girls sewing and etiquette; and domestic service to samurai families was considered an appropriate form of premarital apprenticeship for the daughters of well-to-do townsmen. Townsmen, in turn, received daughters from farm families for the same purpose. The remarkable rise of economic opportunities for women during the protoindustrial revolution of the eighteenth century clearly raised the value of daughters in farm families and may have contributed significantly to the mobility and practical learning available to Tokugawa women outside the samurai class.[72]

During the late nineteenth century, when both China and Japan attempted reforms that aped European and North American practices, educational policies for women (centered on the training of "good wives, wise mothers") converged.[73] But the differences in historical precedent in these two "Confucian" cultures warrant more attention as we examine the modern era.

Conclusion

Considering the full scope of the education of daughters in mid-Ch'ing times — if we may infer from contemporary memories about the world of signs and symbols transmitted through oral culture — we can point to clear contrasts between the education of sons and the education of daughters in a world of strict gender segregation.

First, all daughters, regardless of class, were educated to work and to procreate in the service of a male line. Bound feet, reproduction, and work kept daughters close to home. Work in the home centered on service to the family. A young girl first served her mother, training to be a future daughter-in-law. Then she served her mother-in-law by waiting on the older woman's personal needs and bearing the sons of the next generation. A different kind of work — ritual work — also followed marriage. Women who became brides and mothers entered a descent group in which they were expected to prepare the rites of ancestor worship in the home; as wives, they looked forward in turn to the enshrinement of their own tablets in an ancestral hall.[74]

Second, as a result of their wifely obligations, women's literary productivity varied with the life cycle. Before marriage, upper-class young women had plenty of time for writing, as we see in *Dream of the Red Chamber*. But once married, young women who were fully active as "working mothers"—those who conformed to Chang Hsueh-ch'eng's ideal—had to postpone or curb their creative, intellectual, and aesthetic efforts throughout their child-rearing years.[75]

Thus, though in upper-class families scholarship was part of the process of educating a daughter to enter a new descent group, the most impassioned female writers and artists may have been those denied the wife-mother role.[76] Indeed, as Lan Ting-yuan pointed out in his preface to *Women's Learning*, the sad difference between the educational achievements of men and women resulted not from women's inferior intellectual capacity, but from the steady diversion of women's talent into the work and rituals of domestic life after marriage:

> A man can study during his whole life; whether he is abroad or at home, he can always look into the classics and history, and become thoroughly acquainted with the whole range of authors. But a woman does not study more than ten years, before she takes upon herself the management of a family, where a multiplicity of cares distract her attention. Having no leisure for undisturbed study, she cannot easily understand learned authors. Not having obtained a thorough acquaintance with letters, she does not fully comprehend their principles. And like water that has flowed from its fountain, she cannot regulate her conduct by their guidance.[77]

Still, limited as it was, the education described in this chapter left a legacy. The legacy is evident in the late Ch'ing reform proposals, in which "wise mothers" for the home and "industrious workers" for the factories became new goals for the education of China's daughters.[78] And though most women were illiterate, even the legacy of nonliterate women's education gave them powerful resources.

Mary Anderson took note of this paradox in the 1930s when she surveyed data on the appalling state of female literacy in Kwangtung province during the nineteenth century. She found rates ranging from 10 percent (Dr. William Milne, c. 1827) to 1 percent (Morrison Education Society, 1837) to 0.1 percent: "Aside from nuns and actresses, taking city and country together, I think the average would be about one woman in a thousand who could read at all," wrote Adele Fielde in Swatow in 1873. (In North China at about the same time, W.A.P. Martin had pronounced that "not one woman in 10,000 can read.")[79] Nevertheless, Anderson observed, "The education of women in [Ch'ing] China far exceeded their ability to read. In the middle and lower classes of society, training in the home often included field labor or experience in certain types of industry. Under the handicraft system there were many occupations in which a girl could take part without going beyond the walls of her home."[80] She singled out women's festivals, which encouraged "initiative and creative work that would do credit to a progressive school of today." And she astutely concluded, "Although in ancient times Chinese women could not read, their training for practical efficiency in life situations often produced strong and able leaders."[81]

Disciplined manual labor, stoicism in the face of pain, devotion to service, potency through fecundity, high standards for the education of their sons— these values lay at the heart of the education of daughters in Ch'ing times. Most values were transmitted orally through role modeling, signs, and symbols. To this repertoire of early childhood training, highly literate women added the classics, novels, drama, poetry, and a private world of passion and longing that explored the interface between the written and the oral, that world celebrated in the Double Seven festival and exemplified by the tragic death of Chu Ying-t'ai.

This was the tension in mid-Ch'ing women's education as opportunities for literate women expanded. It was precisely the tension tapped in the debate between Yuan Mei and Chang Hsueh-ch'eng. Women's passionate heterosexual love had to be captured in the service of the family; talented women writers had to marry and bear children. In Ch'ing China, the "book-lined cell"[82] of the celibate female scholar was accessible only to widows. The best hope for the highly educated woman of the Ch'ing period was that her parents might select a spouse who could share and support her talent, or that she might bear a son whose talent she could nurture. Those exceptional wives whose marriages did combine physical passion with intellectual expression, like those unusual mothers who shared manuscripts with their sons,[83] challenge our conventional views of women and the family in late imperial times, as they themselves challenged convention. In that sense, the changing gender relations of the mid-Ch'ing period owe much to the education of daughters.

NOTES

Judith Brown, Paula Findlen, Gail Hershatter, Ann Waltner, and Marilyn Young all made comments that helped to shape this chapter. I also wish to thank the conference participants, especially William Rowe and Kent Guy, and the editors for their insightful criticisms. Anonymous readers' perceptive comments helped focus the revisions, though I have been unable to do justice to all of their criticisms here. Part of the research on which this chapter is based was conducted under a grant from the Committee on Scholarly Communication with the People's Republic of China, of the National Academy of Sciences. I thank the Shanghai Academy of Social Sciences for its sponsorship. I owe a special debt to my research associate in Shanghai, Yao Xinrong, who helped me conduct the interviews that revealed the dowry as sign and symbol.

1. See Jack Goody, *The Interface Between the Written and the Oral* (New York: Cambridge University Press, 1987).

2. The term *daughters* in this chapter refers specifically to females reared in their natal families for the purpose of marriage (as distinguished from females who were sold or adopted out).

3. See Mark Elvin, "Female Virtue and the State in China," *Past and Present* 104 (1984): 111–52; Susan Mann, "Widows in the Kinship, Class, and Community Structures of Qing Dynasty China," *Journal of Asian Studies* 46, no.1 (1987): 37–56.

4. Illuminated by Margery Wolf's study *Women and the Family in Rural Taiwan* (Stanford: Stanford University Press, 1972).

5. Howard S. Levy, *Chinese Footbinding: The History of a Curious Erotic Custom* (New York: Walton Rawls, 1966), 249–50 et passim.

6. Joanna F. Handlin, "Lü K'un's New Audience: The Influence of Women's Literacy on Sixteenth-Century Thought," in *Women in Chinese Society*, ed. Margery Wolf and Roxane Witke (Stanford: Stanford University Press, 1975), 13–38, shows that this trend was well under way in the late Ming period. Liu Chi-hua 劉紀華, "Chung-kuo chen-chieh kuan-nien ti li-shih yen-pien" 中國貞節觀念的歷史演變 (Historical evolution of the Chinese concept of chastity), *She-hui hsueh-chieh* 8 (1934): 29–30, singles out three key didactic texts in the Ch'ing period. The first was Lan Ting-yuan's *Nü hsueh*. The second was titled *Nei-tse yen-i* (Rules for the inner quarters, fully explicated), compiled in 1656 under imperial auspices. The third, Wang Hsiang's *Nü-fan chieh-lu* (Concise guide to women's deportment), was bound together with three other classics to form the so-called "Four Books for Women" (*Nü ssu-shu*): Pan Chao's *Nü chieh*, Sung Jo-chao's *Nü lun-yü* (Analects for women), and the *Nei-hsun* (Precepts for the inner quarters) compiled early in the fifteenth century by a Ming empress. A *Classic of Filial Piety for Girls* (*Nü hsiao-ching*) composed in the T'ang period was reprinted in widely available compendia six times in the Ming period and three times in the Ch'ing. These works, together with Lu Chi's *Hsin-fu p'u* (Standard guide for the new wife), compiled 1656–57, are the subject of Yamazaki Jun'ichi's 山崎純一 comprehensive research on women's didactic texts, published in one volume titled *Chūgoku joseishi shiryō no kenkyū: Nyo shi sho to Shinfu fu sambu sho* 中國女性史資料の研究：「女四書」と「新婦譜」三部書 (Researches in materials on Chinese women's history: the *Nü ssu-shu* and the three editions of the *Hsin-fu p'u*) (Tokyo: Meiji sho-in, 1987).

7. For example, Lan approvingly reproduces Liu Hsiang's tale of the woman who perished in the flames of her burning house, ignoring the pleas of relatives and servants, because it was improper for a widow to go outside the home (*chüan* 2:3b–4b), without the reservations about the wisdom of this decision expressed in Ming times by the more practical Lü K'un. On Lü K'un's editorial comments on the same story, see Handlin, "New Audience," 19–20. For the original story, see Liu Hsiang, 劉向, *Ku lieh-nü chuan* 古列女傳 (Original biographies of exemplary women) (Ts'ung-shu chi-ch'eng edition, Shanghai: Commercial Press, 1938), 4:95–96.

8. See Patricia Buckley Ebrey, *Family and Property in Sung China: Yuan Ts'ai's Precepts for Social Life* (Princeton: Princeton University Press, 1984), for a translation and comments on the genre.

9. Such advice books were extraordinarily popular in the Ch'ing period, when the genre reached its apogee. See Hui-chen Wang Liu, "An Analysis of Chinese Clan Rules:

Confucian Theories in Action," in *Confucianism in Action*, ed. David S. Nivison and Arthur F. Wright (Stanford: Stanford University Press, 1959), 70–71. On the treatment of women in these books, see Charlotte Furth, "The Patriarch's Legacy: Household Instructions and the Transmission of Orthodox Values," in *Orthodoxy in Late Imperial China*, ed. Kwang-Ching Liu (Berkeley: University of California Press, 1990), 196–98.

10. See Ch'en Tung-yuan, 陳東原 *Chung-kuo fu-nü sheng-huo shih* 中國婦女生活史 (History of the lives of Chinese women) (1928; reprint, Taipei: Shang-wu yin-shu-kuan, 1977), 198–99; Handlin, "New Audience," 29.

11. Ch'en Hung-mou 陳宏謀, *Chiao-nü i-kuei* 教女遺規 (Bequeathed guidelines for the education of women), printed in *Wu-chung i-kuei* 五種遺規 (Bequeathed guidelines of five kinds), preface dated 1742 (Nanking: Kuang-i shu-chü, 1937).

12. Lan Ting-yuan 藍鼎元, *Nü hsueh* 女學 (Women's Learning), preface dated 1712-13 (Taipei: Wen-hai ch'u-pan-she, 1977), 1a. The entire preface is translated in S. Wells Williams, *The Middle Kingdom* (New York: Charles Scribners Sons, 1900), 1:574–76.

13. In *Dream of the Red Chamber*, the author explains with veiled sarcasm that the young widow Li Wan was able to keep herself like the "withered tree and dead ashes" prescribed for women of her lot precisely because she was allowed to read only didactic texts for women; she did not receive a "first-class" education. See David Hawkes, trans., *The Story of the Stone* (Harmondsworth, Middlesex: Penguin Books, 1973) 1:108; the original text is Ts'ao Hsueh-ch'in 曹雪芹, *Hung lou meng* 紅樓夢 (Dream of the red chamber) (Peking: Jen-min wen-hsueh ch'u-pan-she, 1973), 1:41. For other examples, see Hawkes, trans., *Stone*, 2:337, 385; Ts'ao, *Hung lou meng*, 2:585, 616-17.

14. In *Dream of the Red Chamber*, Lin Tai-yü amazes her grandmother when she reports that she is studying the Four Books, but her pursuits must not have been so unusual in the households of upper-class Han Chinese families. See Hawkes, trans., *Stone*, vol.1, ch. 3, 100; Ts'ao, *Hung lou meng*, 1:34.

15. Well-known examples of sons whose mothers started them up the ladder of success by teaching them the classics and the histories are Ch'ien Ch'en-ch'ün (mother Ch'en Shu), Fa-shih-shan (mother née Han), Chang Ch'i and Chang Hui-yen (mother née Chiang), Ts'ui Shu (mother née Li), Lin-ch'ing (mother Yun Chu), Ku Kuang-ch'i (mother née Cheng), Cha Shen-hsing and Cha Ssu-t'ing (mother Chung Yun), and Liu Feng-lu (mother née Chuang). See *Eminent Chinese of the Ch'ing Period* (hereafter *ECCP*), ed. Arthur W. Hummel (Washington, D.C.: U.S. Government Printing Office, 1943; reprint, Taipei: Literature House, 1964), 99, 227, 25–26, 42–43, 771, 507, 418, 21, 518.

16. See Hu Wen-k'ai 胡文楷, *Li-tai fu-nü chu-tso k'ao* 歷代婦女著作考 (A survey of women's writings through the ages) (Shanghai: Ku-chi ch'u-pan-she, 1985).

17. See Ann Waltner, "On Not Becoming a Heroine: Lin Daiyu and Cui Yingying," *Signs* 15, no.1 (1989): 61–78.

18. On family instruction books and control of women, see Furth, "Patriarch's Legacy," 196–97, 202. Women's ability to read Buddhist texts, she implies (202), may have represented one source of their potential "heterodoxy" in the family.

19. On Pan Chao, see Nancy Lee Swann, *Pan Chao: Foremost Woman Scholar of China* (New York: Century Company, 1932). On Sung Jo-chao, see Ch'en Tung-yuan, *Chung-kuo fu-nü*, 114-15.

20. Paul Ropp, "The Status of Women in Mid-Qing China: Evidence from Letters, Laws and Literature," (Paper delivered at the Annual Meeting of the American Historical Association, 1987), presents an analysis of women's ballads, with beautiful translations.

21. See T'an Cheng-pi 譚正璧, Chung-kuo nü-hsing ti wen-hsueh sheng-huo 中國女性的文學生活 (Literary life of Chinese women) (Shanghai: Kuang-ming shu-chü, 1935), 2: 383–466, where he also observes that during this period women began to write in the vernacular. Dorothy Ko's research shows that many women were not as cloistered as they appeared. They developed networks for reading and publishing each others' work, so that women's words traveled well beyond the inner chambers of individual writers. See Dorothy Ko, Teachers of the Inner Chambers (Stanford: Stanford University Press, forthcoming, 1994).

22. One survey of female writers listed in two major compendia found that the majority came from four provinces: Kiangsu, Chekiang, Anhwei, and Kiangsi and were concentrated in Kiangsu and Chekiang. See Mary Backus Rankin, "The Emergence of Women at the End of the Ch'ing: The Case of Ch'iu Chin," in Women in Chinese Society, ed. Margery Wolf and Roxane Witke (Stanford: Stanford University Press, 1975), 41n. See also comments on regional variation in female literacy in David Johnson, "Communication, Class, and Consciousness in Late Imperial China," in Popular Culture in Late Imperial China, ed. David Johnson, Andrew J. Nathan, and Evelyn S. Rawski (Berkeley: University of California Press, 1985), 70–71.

23. A computer analysis of data in Hu, Li-tai fu-nü, confirms this regional concentration of female talent, showing that 70 percent of the 3,184 Qing women writers whose native place is known were active in the Lower Yangtze macroregion as defined in G. William Skinner, ed., The City in Late Imperial China (Stanford: Stanford University Press, 1977), 214–15. On chin-shih quotas, see Ho Ping-ti, The Ladder of Success in Imperial China (New York: Columbia University Press, 1962), 247; on the rank-size distribution of urban central places in the Lower Yangtze, see G. William Skinner, "Regional Urbanization in Nineteenth-Century China," in Skinner, City, 238.

24. Based on data on native place origins in Views from Jade Terrace: Chinese Women Artists, 1300–1912 (Indianapolis: Indianapolis Museum of Art, 1988). On Juan Yuan as a patron of women's education, see Williams, Middle Kingdom 1:573, and Liang I-chen 梁乙真, Ch'ing-tai fu-nü wen-hsueh shih 清代婦女文學史 (History of women writers in the Ch'ing period) (Taipei: Chung-hua shu-chü, 1968), 146–47. Juan Yuan's second wife, K'ung Lu-hua, was a poet who left her own collection of verse. See ECCP, 402. Canton, of course, was at the pinnacle of the urban hierarchy in the Lingnan macroregion. See Skinner, "Regional Urbanization," 238.

25. Listed in Views from Jade Terrace. The statement refers to all women painters from late Ming times through the late nineteenth century listed in the catalog, excluding painters who were active after 1900 because of the high probability of Western influence in their work and on their careers.

26. According to the data in Views from Jade Terrace (see n. 25, above), ten of sixteen famous women painters of the late Ming period were courtesans or concubines, three were wives; in Ch'ing times (to 1900), thirteen of sixteen famous women painters were wives, while only three were courtesans or concubines. Ellen Laing cites noted examples of companionship based on a shared interest in painting that included both wives and

concubines, but suggests that concubines were even more likely than wives to share this interest with their partners. See Ellen Johnston Laing, "Women Painters in Traditional China," in *Flowering in the Shadows: Women in the History of Chinese and Japanese Painting*, ed. Marsha Weidner (Honolulu: University of Hawaii Press, 1990), 87–88. For an account of a painterly marriage, see also Marsha Weidner, "The Conventional Success of Ch'en Shu," in *Flowering*, 126–9. Weidner explores the relationship between Ch'en Shu's success as a painter and her family roles as wife, mother, and daughter-in-law.

27. My survey of *ECCP* includes every female poet mentioned in the text. I say "more than sixty-seven" because many individuals had daughters or sisters who were also active as writers and poets. The concubines mentioned are Ts'ai Han (p. 566), Kuan Yun (p. 104), Wen Ching-yü (p. 104), Tung Po (p. 566), Ku Mei (p. 431), Ku-t'ai-ch'ing (pp. 386–7), Chin I (p. 956), Chin Yueh (p. 566), Liu Shi (pp. 529–30), Ch'iao-chi (p. 496), and Hsiang-fei (p. 74). Only Hsiang-fei, Kuan Yun, and Wen Ching-yü were active during the eighteenth century. This may lend some support to the notion that companionate marriage was gaining currency among the elite in the same period. The most commonly cited example of this ideal comes from the widely read memoirs of erstwhile yamen secretary and traveler Shen Fu and his beloved Yun. See Shen Fu, *Six Records of a Floating Life*, trans. Leonard Pratt and Chiang Su-hui (Harmondsworth, Middlesex: Penguin Books, 1983.) Shen Fu (1763–?) himself was not a degree-holder, and his wife, while literate, was self-taught. But examples of companionate marriage appear among the most eminent scholars and officials. In *ECCP* alone, see accounts of the marriages of Sun Hsing-yen to Wang Ts'ai-wei (p. 675), Kao Ch'i-cho to Ts'ai Wan (p. 735), Ts'ui Shu to Ch'eng Ching-lan (p. 771–2, 775), Li Hsing-yuan to Kuo Jun-yü (p. 458), Hsu Tsung-yen to Liang Te-sheng (pp. 82, 824), Ch'en P'ei-chih to Wang Tuan (pp. 839–40), Ch'ü Ta-chün to Wang Hua-chiang (p. 202), Hao I-hsing to Wang Chao-yuan (p. 278), Sun Yuan-hsiang to Hsi P'ei-lan (pp. 685–6), Wang Shih-tuo to Tsung Chi-lan (pp. 834–5). Note that in Ts'ui Shu's case, a highly educated mother selected for her son a well-educated wife; for Sun Hsing-yen, a highly educated wife set the example for an accomplished daughter (p. 677). Since mothers generally had the final say in the selection of their sons' wives, and mothers took primary responsibility for the education of their own daughters, we would expect generations of educated women in a single family to reproduce themselves through the common standards set by the matriarch for both out-marrying daughters and in-marrying brides. (I mention here only those women who are said specifically to have collaborated with their husbands on literary works; there are numerous other examples of cultivated wives and famous husbands, but these were not necessarily collaborative marriages.) See also *Views from Jade Terrace* for numerous additional examples and Ropp, "The Status of Women," for further discussion.

28. The roots of this tension have already been examined by Handlin, "New Audience," and Paul Ropp, *Dissent in Early Modern China: Ju-lin Wai-shih and Ch'ing Social Criticism* (Ann Arbor: University of Michigan Press, 1981). For more recent studies, see Ellen Widmer, "The Epistolary World of Female Talent in Seventeenth-Century China," *Late Imperial China* 10, no.2 (1989): 1–43; Ko, *Teachers of the Inner Chambers*; and Ropp, "Status of Women." Classical revival also played a role. See Susan Mann, "*Fuxue* (Women's Learning) by Zhang Xuecheng (1738–1801): China's First History of Women's Culture," *Late Imperial China* 13, no.1 (1992):40–62; and Mann, "Grooming a

Daughter for Marriage: Brides and Wives in the Mid-Ch'ing Period," in *Marriage and Inequality in Chinese Society*, ed. Rubie S. Watson and Patricia Buckley Ebrey (Berkeley: University of California Press, 1991), 204–30.

29. Accounts of this controversy may be found in David S. Nivison, *The Life and Thought of Chang Hsueh-ch'eng, 1738–1801* (Stanford: Stanford University Press, 1966), 133–38; see also Chou Ch'i-jung 周啟榮 and Liu Kuang-ching 劉廣京 (Chow Kai-wing and K. C. Liu), "Hsueh-shu ching-shih: Chang Hsueh-ch'eng chih wen-shih lun yü ching-shih ssu-hsiang" 學術經世：章學誠之文史論與經世思想 (Chang Hsueh-ch'eng's theories of literature and history and statecraft thought), in *Chin-shih Chung-kuo ching-shih ssu-hsiang yen-t'ao-hui lun-wen chi* 近世中國經世思想研討會論文集, ed. Chung-yang yen-chiu-yuan chin-tai-shih yen-chiu-so (Taipei: Academia Sinica, 1984), 142–45.

30. Widmer, "Epistolary World," 33, cautions that many of Yuan's female "pupils" seem to have had their own independent literary lives centered not on his salon but on their own quarters. The collected works of Yuan Mei's female "disciples" were published as *Sui-yuan nü ti-tzu shih* 隨園女弟子詩 (Collected poems of the disciples of the Sui Garden), preface dated 1796.

31. Yuan Mei was known for stressing the "spiritual power" (*hsing-ling*) of poetry rather than the rules of meter and rhyme (*ko-tiao*). See Liang, *Ch'ing-tai fu-nü wen-hsueh shih*, 61–132. Irving Yucheng Lo and William Schultz, eds., *Waiting for the Unicorn: Poems and Lyrics of China's Last Dynasty, 1644–1911* (Bloomington: Indiana University Press, 1990), 20, translate *hsing-ling* as "native sensibilities" and note that *ko-tiao* may refer either to rules or to high standards of excellence. I have rendered *hsing-ling* "spiritual power" because it conveys the sense of passion that animated the debate over the purpose and meaning of a good poem.

32. Literature on this subject is abundant, but see Carolyn C. Lougee, *Le Paradis des Femmes: Women, Salons, and Social Stratification in Seventeenth-Century France* (Princeton: Princeton University Press, 1976); Anthony Grafton and Lisa Jardine, *From Humanism to the Humanities* (London: Gerald Duckworth and Co., 1986), 29–57; Margaret L. King, "Book-lined Cells: Women and Humanism in the Early Italian Renaissance," in *Beyond Their Sex: Learned Women of the European Past*, ed. Patricia H. Labalme (New York: New York University Press, 1980); Ann Rosalind Jones, "City Women and Their Audiences: Louise Labé and Veronica Franco," in *Rewriting the Renaissance: The Discourses of Sexual Difference in Early Modern Europe* (Chicago: University of Chicago Press, 1986); and Margaret F. Rosenthal, "Veronica Franco's *Terze Rime*: the Venetian Courtesan's Defense," *Renaissance Quarterly* 42 (1989): 227–57. See also the discussion of women's education in Renaissance Europe, below.

33. Nivison, *Life and Thought*, 274–75. See also Ch'en Tung-yuan, *Chung-kuo fu-nü*, 270. An excerpt from the essay was reprinted in the standard mid-Ch'ing compendium of statecraft writings, the *Huang-ch'ao ching-shih wen-pien* 皇朝經世文編 (Collected writings on statecraft of our august dynasty), comp. Ho Ch'ang-ling, 賀長齡, preface dated 1826 (Taipei: Kuo-feng ch'u-pan-she, 1963), 60:11a–12b. It was reprinted twice in mid-Ch'ing collectanea.

34. Hsu Sheng was minister of rites (*li-kuan tai-fu*) during the reign of Han Emperor Wen (179–156 B.C.E).

35. *Analects* 16:13. Translation from D.C. Lau, trans., *The Analects (Lun yü)* (New York: Penguin Books, 1979), 141.

36. See *Chang Shih I-shu* 章氏遺書 (Bequeathed writings of Master Chang), ed. Liu Ch'eng-kan (Chia-yeh-t'ang blockprint ed., 1922), 5:37a–38a. For a modern punctuated text, see Chang Hsueh-ch'eng, *Wen-shih t'ung-i* 文史通義 (Comprehensive meaning of literature and history) (Hong Kong: T'ai-p'ing shu-chü, 1964), 174.

37. On Wang Tuan, see *ECCP*, 839–40.

38. On the segregation of the sexes, see Furth, "Patriarch's Legacy," 196. On the ritual subservience of concubines, see Patricia Ebrey, "Concubines in Song Chin," *Journal of Family History* 11, no.1 (1986):1–24. Less problematically, brothers could be patrons as well. The poems of Chang Ch'i's (1765–1833) four daughters, for example, were edited and published by one of their brothers. See *ECCP*, 25–26. In the case of Yun Chu, compiler of a collection of women's poetry titled *Kuo-ch'ao kuei-hsiu cheng-shih chi* 國朝閨秀正始集 (Correcting the source: collected women's poetry of our dynasty; hereafter *KCKHCSC*) preface dated 1829 (1833), an eldest son arranged for the publication of her anthology. See *KCKHCSC*, preface 1a–b.

39. The best published work on this subject is Widmer, "Epistolary World." See also Ko, *Social History*.

40. See T'an, *Chung-kuo nü-hsing ti wen-hsueh sheng-huo*, 2:391. On Yuan Mei's "Aunt Shen," who taught him his first texts, and his sisters, see Arthur Waley, *Yuan Mei: Eighteenth Century Chinese Poet* (New York: Grove Press, 1956), esp. 36–37, an account of the tragic ruin of Yuan's talented sister as a result of an arranged marriage, and 189, on the marriage of his untalented son to a gifted poetess from Ningpo. See also *ECCP*, 956, and Liang, *Fu-nü wen-hsueh*, 165–92.

41. *ECCP*, 103–5. See also Liang, *Fu-nü wen-hsueh shih*, 165–92.

42. Isaac Taylor Headland, *Home Life in China* (1914; reprint, Taipei: Ch'eng-wen ch'u-pan-she, 1974), 139, notes that boys were offered pen, inkstone, or book; abacus; and tool. Girls found "a different class of things" on their trays — scissors, thimble, and so forth. See also Lewis Hodous, *Folkways in China*; (1929; reprint, Taipei: Orient Cultural Service, 1984), 56. Hence the family's dismay in *Dream of the Red Chamber* when the baby Pao-yü grabs "combs, bracelets, pots of rouge and powder and the like" at his first twelve-month ceremony. See Hawkes, trans., vol. 1, ch. 2, 76; Ts'ao, *Hung lou meng*, 1:19.

43. The best study of footbinding remains Levy, *Footbinding*.

44. See Levy, *Footbinding*, 274, for a discussion of class variation in the severity and age of footbinding.

45. Juliet Bredon and Igor Mitrophanow, *The Moon Year: A Record of Chinese Customs and Festivals* (1927; reprint Taipei: Ch'eng-wen, 1972), 369.

46. Hodous, *Folkways*, 176.

47. *Hsin-hsiu Yin hsien chih* 新修鄞縣志 (Gazetteer of Ningpo county, newly revised) (1877), *chüan* 2:12b.

48. Headland, *Home Life*, 136–37.

49. Hodous, *Folkways*, 176.

50. Bredon and Mitrophanow, *Moon Year*, 374.

51. Ibid., 374–5, citing Gray.

52. Ibid., 375.

53. Ibid. In Canton, the Weaving Maid was thought to be one of the seven daughters of the Stove God, and the festival there was sometimes called the Seven Sisters festival. See also Janice E. Stockard, *Daughters of the Canton Delta: Marriage Patterns*

and Economic Strategies in South China, 1860–1930 (Stanford: Stanford University Press, 1989), 41–44.

54. See Mann, "Widows," and Elvin, "Female Virtue."

55. C.A.S. Williams, *Outlines of Chinese Symbolism and Art Motives,* 3d rev. ed. (1941; reprint, New York: Dover, 1976), 282–8.

56. *Nung cheng ch'üan-shu* 農政全書 (Complete writings on the administration of agriculture), comp. Hsu Kuang-ch'i 徐光啟, preface dated 1639–40, vol. 1, *chüan* 31, 615-16.

57. See Edward T. Williams, "The Worship of Lei Tsu, Patron Saint of Silk Workers," *Journal of the North China Branch of the Royal Asiatic Society*, n.s. 66 (1935):1–14.

58. "Ning-po mi-yü 寧波謎語 (Ningpo riddles), in *Ning-po i-wen shih-chih*, 寧波藝文什誌 (Collected studies of the arts in Ningpo), ed. Chang Hsing-chou 張行周 (Taipei: Min-chu ch'u-pan-she, 1978), 185.

59. Jane Parish Yang, trans., "Embroidered Pillows," in *Modern Chinese Stories and Novellas, 1919–1949* (New York: Columbia University Press, 1981), 197–99. The original story, first published in the 1930s, is reprinted in Lin Hai-yin 林海音 et al., *Chin-tai Chung-kuo tso-chia yü tso-p'in* 近代中國作家與作品 (Modern Chinese writers and their works) (Taipei: Ch'un-wen-hsueh yueh-k'an she, 1967), 1:95–100.

60. The dowry description appears in T'ang K'ang-hsiung 湯康雄, "P'ei-chia chuang-lien" 陪嫁粧奩 (Dowry), in *Ning-po hsi-su ts'ung-t'an* 寧波習俗叢談 (Collected folkways and customs of Ningpo), ed. Chang Hsing-chou, 張行周 (Taipei: Min-chu ch'u-pan-she, 1973), 212–13.

61. This account and what follows is based on interviews with older women from Ningpo conducted in Shanghai and Ningpo in autumn 1988.

62. See Melinda K. Blade, *Education of Italian Renaissance Women* (Mesquite, Tex.: Ide House, 1983).

63. See Blade, *Education.* and Waltner, "Heroine."

64. Blade, *Education,* 29–38.

65. See King, "Book-lined Cells," 77; and Grafton and Jardine, *From Humanism to the Humanities,* 32–33.

66. See Natalie Zemon Davis, "Gender and Genre: Women as Historical Writers, 1400–1820," in *Beyond Their Sex: Learned Women of the European Past*, ed. Patricia H. Labalme (New York: New York University Press, 1980), 153–82.

67. See Rosenthal, *"Terze Rime"*; Lougee, *Le Paradis.*

68. See also Charlotte Furth, "Blood, Body and Gender: Medical Images of the Female Condition in China," *Chinese Science* 7 (1986): 43–65.

69. On Renaissance education, see Blade, *Education*, especially 29–38. Blade points out that the example set by Sir Thomas More influenced noble families of the late fifteenth century to educate their daughters (p. 37).

70. I owe this observation to comments by Robert J. Smith at a panel on "Widowhood in Three Asian Societies," Association for Asian Studies annual meeting, Washington, D.C., 23–25 March 1984.

71. Evidence is reviewed by Kumiko Fujimura-Fanselow, *Women and Higher Education in Japan: Tradition and Change* (Ph. D. diss., Columbia University, 1981), 27–28.

72. Whether or not the education of girls in Tokugawa Japan was significantly different from the education of women in Ch'ing times—and if so, how and why—is

not a question this essay can directly address. I would argue, however, that the differences were significant because of (1) differences in kinship and inheritance practice in Tokugawa families, in which only one male was expected to marry and claim the headship (reducing the proportion of the population that was ever married, and thereby the demand for brides); (2) higher levels of commercialization across the board in Japan, which raised the status of women by increasing their economic value to the household; and (3) the extraordinary demand for consumer services and entertainment in Japanese cities, especially in Edo and Osaka, but in fact in all castle towns created by the Tokugawa conquest. On the economic value of daughters, see Thomas C. Smith, *Nakahara: Family Farming and Population in a Japanese Village, 1717–1830* (Stanford: Stanford University Press, 1977), 154–55. Clearly these circumstances dampened the appeal of Neo-Confucian doctrines calling for the seclusion of women. Footbinding, the cruelest manifestation of the Chinese concern for cloistering women, became customary practice in China during a period when Japan was not in a sinophile phase, and to my knowledge the Japanese never developed any interest in this perverse feature of China's high culture.

73. See Fujimura-Fanselow, *Women and Higher Education*, 29–31; Ono Kazuko, *Chinese Women in a Century of Revolution, 1850–1950*, trans. and ed. Joshua A. Fogel (Stanford: Stanford University Press, 1989) 23–46, 54–59.

74. On the ritual role of wives in the mid-Ch'ing era, see Mann, "Grooming a Daughter."

75. As in the career of the artist Ch'en Shu. See *Views from Jade Terrace*, 117. See also comments by Yun Chu, *KCKHCSC*, preface dated 1829.

76. Examples are Liu Shih, concubine of Ch'ien Ch'ien-i, who committed suicide out of humiliation after being reduced to an outcast following his death, and Wang Tuan, whose own writings respond so directly to her bereavement. Widows are prominent in the ranks of creative women, both writers and painters, during Ch'ing times.

77. Lan Ting-yuan, *Nü hsueh*, preface, 1b–2a; translation adapted from Williams, *Middle Kingdom*, 1:575.

78. See Ono, *Chinese Women*, 23-29, 54–59.

79. Cited in Mary Raleigh Anderson, *Protestant Mission Schools for Girls in South China (1827 to the Japanese Invasion)* (Mobile, Alabama: Heiter-Starke Printing Co., 1943), 27–28.

80. Ibid., 28.

81. Ibid., 29.

82. King, "Book-lined Cells."

83. See n.39 on Yun Chu.

GLOSSARY

This glossary includes all names and terms in the text except names from notes with page references to *ECCP* or *Views from Jade Terrace*.

bikuni	比丘尼	*ch'ang-sheng-kuo*	長生果
Chang Ch'i	張琦	*chen-nü*	真女
Chang Hsueh-ch'eng	章學誠	Ch'en Hua-ch'ü	陳華姁

Chen Li-ch'ü	陳麗娕
Ch'en P'ei-chih	陳裴之
Ch'en Shu	陳書
Ch'en Wen-shu	陳文述
ch'i-ch'iao	乞巧
chiao	教
chien	儉
Ch'ien Ch'ien-i	錢謙益
Chih-nü	織女
chin-shih	進士
ch'in	勤
Chu Ying-t'ai	祝英台
chüan	卷
Cui Yingying	崔鶯鶯
(Ts'ui Ying-ying)	
fa chia-chuang	發嫁粧
feng-chiao	風教
Fu hsueh	婦學
fu i-nü pu chi,	夫一女不績
t'ien-hsia pi yu	天下必有
shou ch'i han-che	受其寒者
fu-tao	婦道
Fuxue (see *Fu hsueh*)	
Hsi hsiang chi	西廂記
Hsin-fu p'u	新婦譜
hsing-ling	性靈
Hsu Kuang-ch'i	徐光啟
Hsu Sheng	徐生
hsueh	學
Hsueh-hai T'ang	學海堂
hua-sheng	花生
Ju-lin Wai-shih	儒林外史
Juan Yuan	阮元
jung	容
k'ang-hsiang	扛箱
ko-tiao	格調
Kuan-yin	觀音
Kuan Yun	管筠
kuei-tzu	貴子(桂子)
kung	工(功)
kung huan-hsi, p'o tsung-i,	公歡喜婆縱意
chiao-t'a lou-t'i pu-pu kao;	腳踏樓梯步步高
tu-jen ch'ü, man-chiao hui	獨人去滿轎回
kung-shih	宮師
Lan Ting-yuan	藍鼎元
Lei Tsu	嫘祖

li-ch'iu	立秋
li-kuan tai-fu	禮官大夫
Li Wan	李紈
Liang Shan-po	梁山伯
Liang Te-sheng	梁德繩
Lin Daiyü (see Lin Tai-yü)	
Lin Tai-yu	林黛玉
Ling Shu-hua	凌叔華
Liu Hsiang	劉向
Liu Shih	柳是
Lu Ch'i	陸圻
Lü K'un	呂坤
Nei-hsun	內訓
Nei-tse yen-i	內則衍義
Nü-chieh	女誡
Nü-fan chieh-lu	女範捷錄
Nü hsiao-ching	女孝經
nü hsiu-ts'ai	女秀才
Nü hsueh	女學
Nü lun-yü	女論語
nü-shih	女士
Nü ssu-shu	女四書
nü-tzu wu ts'ai,	女子無才
shih te	是德
Nung-cheng ch'üan-shu	農政全書
ohariya	よ針屋
p'ai-lou	牌樓
Pan Chao	班昭
Pao Yü	寶玉
P'u-t'uo Shan	普陀山
Shen Fu	沈復
sheng	生
Shih ching	詩經
ssu-te	四德
Sun Hsing-yen	孫星衍
Sung Jo-chao	宋若昭
tai	代(袋)
t'an-tz'u	彈詞
T'an-yang-tzu	曇陽子
tao	道
te	德
te-ch'iao	得巧
terakoya	寺子屋
ts'ai-ch'i	財氣
tsao	早(棗)
tsao sheng	早生

ts'ao	操	Wen Ching-yü	文靜玉
Ts'ui Shu	崔述	*wu-tai*	五代(袋)
tz'u-t'ang	祠堂	*ya-hsiang-ch'ien*	壓箱錢
Wang Hsiang	王相	*yen*	言
wang-hua	王化	Yuan Mei	袁枚
Wang Tuan	汪端	Yuan Ts'ai	袁采
Wang Tzu-lan	王子蘭	Yun Chu	惲珠
wen	文	Zhang Xuecheng	
		(see Chang Hsueh-ch'eng)	

TWO

Four Schoolmasters

Educational Issues in Li Hai-kuan's *Lamp at the Crossroads*

Allan Barr

Studies of education in late imperial China have often drawn upon literary works to provide human perspectives and social nuances not always manifested in conventional historical sources. Some scholars have delved into the rich treasury of classical anecdotes to document the widespread belief in the power that fate and the spirits exerted over the civil service selection process.[1] Others have examined the tales of P'u Sung-ling, (1640–1715) and shown how one author responded to his failed candidacy with a mixture of rancor and resignation.[2] Most frequently cited, perhaps, is the novel *Ju-lin wai-shih* (The scholars), in which Wu Ching-tzu (1701–54) castigates the examination system for its corrosion of Confucian values.[3] Although these works help to illuminate the tensions and textures of traditional education, they of course constitute a mere sample of intellectual opinion and represent only a small portion of the enormous body of informal literature that has a bearing on the subject.

This chapter attempts to broaden the range of discussion by drawing attention to educational themes in other literary works, focusing primarily but not exclusively on the eighteenth-century novel *Ch'i-lu teng* (Lamp at the crossroads). The relevance of this book to the history of Chinese education was pointed out by Fung Yu-lan as early as 1927, but it is only since 1980 that the novel has begun to receive the attention it deserves.[4] By introducing in particular four schoolmasters who appear in the novel and placing them in their historical and literary context, this chapter seeks to explore certain enduring issues in the Ch'ing educational scene.

LI HAI-KUAN AND *LAMP AT THE CROSSROADS*

Li Hai-kuan (1707–90) differs from P'u Sung-ling and Wu Ching-tzu in that he experienced a considerable measure of upward mobility during his lifetime.

This success may account in part for the more positive response to the examination system that is exhibited in his work. Both his grandfather and father were licentiates and acquired distinction in their home district in Honan chiefly for their filial piety. Li's grandfather (and, most likely, his father) earned a living as a schoolmaster. A dedication to Confucian values was thus something of a family tradition.[5]

The image of Li Hai-kuan projected in biographical sources is that of an energetic, articulate man with a strong sense of mission. Liu Ch'ing-chih (chin-shih 1727), who met Li soon after he passed the Honan provincial examination in 1736, found him eager to eradicate "vulgar studies" (su-hsueh) and pursue a program of extensive reading.[6] One biography says of him: "His scholarship was wide-ranging. He possessed a thorough knowledge of classical studies, philosophers, and histories alike and had an exceptional insight into human behavior. In his late years, when flushed with excitement from drinking, he would often describe himself as a consummate Confucian."[7] Failures in the metropolitan examination denied Li the opportunity to gain a prompt appointment in the civil service, and it was not until 1772 that he was belatedly selected to serve as district magistrate in remote Kweichow. At least two periods of his life, in the early 1750s and the late 1770s, were devoted to teaching.[8]

From the anthology of sayings collected by Li's pupils under the title Chia-hsun ch'un-yen (Family instructions and earnest words), one gains a fairly clear picture of Li's views on education. The opening statement defines his curricular priorities: "One must first study the Classics and histories and turn to examination essays later. If one lacks an understanding of the Classics and histories and dedicates oneself exclusively to the eight-leg [essays], then in the absence of firm roots, it will be hard to imagine the boughs and leaves flourishing."[9]

As this remark suggests, Li did not regard examination essays with the same distaste that is apparent in the work of Wu Ching-tzu. He seems to have been rather proud of his own collection of examination essays, soliciting a preface to them from a distinguished Honan scholar.[10] But he believed strongly that a study of eight-legged essays could not be pursued without a close familiarity with the whole range of classical texts. This view, of course, was widely shared among members of the intellectual elite (see also Guy, chap. 5 of this volume). Cheng Hsieh (1693–1765), for example, rated the examination essays of Fang Chou (1665–1701) as the finest literary achievement of the dynasty but at the same time cautioned his young son to engage in wider reading: "Simply to study examination essays is of no practical value—you should devote more time to reading, and peruse the Classics, histories, philosophers, and literary collections."[11]

At the elementary level, Li held as particularly vital a thorough understanding of the Hsiao-hsueh (Elementary education), which he likened to a wall's foundation. Of the Five Classics, he attached special importance to the *Spring and Autumn Annals* and recommended it for specialization. This preference no doubt reflects a conviction that the *Annals*, by drawing moral lessons from historical incidents, constituted an indispensable guide to the application of Confucian ethics in social and political affairs.[12] Like a number of other scholars, Li objected to the tendency among "philistine teachers" to rely on abridged versions of the canonical texts and largely ignore the appended commentaries. Above all, Li sought to inculcate in his students his own educational values. The purpose of study, he argued, is not simply to familiarize oneself with abstract principles, much less to equip oneself to compete for examination honors, but rather to put into practice the ethical imperatives embodied in the Classics.[13] In this respect also Li was fully in agreement with fellow critics, disturbed by the utilitarian objectives of contemporary education, who insisted that upright conduct was the primary goal of classical studies. As one put it, "To study and pass examinations and become an official — these are trivial matters; the most important thing is to acquire a clear understanding of moral principles and be a good person."[14]

Li Hai-kuan may well have felt that the achievements of his son Li Ch'ü (1743–1816) demonstrated the soundness of his educational philosophy. Li Ch'ü, whom Hai-kuan himself had tutored, graduated as a *chin-shih* in 1775 and became known as a model official, impressing his contemporaries with his wide learning and proficiency in both poetry and prose. Li Ch'ü's son Li Yü-huang (1796–1835) was to carry on the tradition of scholarship and literary talent, acquiring a considerable reputation as a poet.[15]

Li Hai-kuan's educational concerns also find clear expression in *Lamp at the Crossroads*, which he began to write after the death of his father in 1748 and completed in 1777. In his preface, Li makes a strong case for the effectiveness of moral instruction presented in the form of fiction and drama. Quoting Chu Hsi (1130–1200), Li affirms, "The good will inspire people's virtuous instincts, and the wicked will chastise their wayward tendencies." Disdainful of Ming fiction, Li claimed to be influenced rather by plays such as K'ung Shang-jen's (1648–1718) *T'ao-hua shan* (Peach blossom fan). To such dramas he attributed the power to stir a simple audience of "woodcutters and shepherds, cooks and kitchen maids."[16] Through his novel, a 108-chapter saga of provincial life, he sought likewise to move the consciences of his readers and guide them toward an appreciation of Confucian values.

A scene in *Lamp at the Crossroads* reflects the author's confidence in the potency of ethical precepts conveyed in an accessible medium. When Su Lin-ch'en completes his vernacular translation of the *Classic of Filial Piety*, his friend Ch'eng Sung-shu pays him the following tribute:

> You have rewritten the Classic in plain and simple language, so that a young boy needs only to recognize the characters to be able to read it aloud, understanding

every sentence as he goes. It would seem then that to compose an erudite work that wins the acclaim of the learned is a simple matter. To present the enduring ethical principles in words that are easy to follow, enlightening to women and children alike, this is a rare feat.[17]

When Su's colloquial adaptation immediately wins an enthusiastic reception among all members of the household, the narrator comments, in words that are surely the author's, "It is not that Su Lin-ch'en's book was so exceptional, simply that a moral sense is common to all humanity, and when one appeals to it through everyday language, it moves people all the more rapidly and makes a deeper impact, much like the poetry of Po Lo-t'ien, which even an old cook could understand" (91:854).

One might infer from passages such as this that Li Hai-kuan intended his novel's readership to extend beyond the educated elite. If such were his expectations, they were probably unrealistic, for the many Classical elements and canonical allusions embedded in the narrative would have posed considerable difficulties for a popular audience.[18] It seems more likely that Li saw other literati families as his chief audience, hoping to impress upon them the need to ensure that their sons received the right kind of education. One of the novel's earliest admirers, a student of Li's, indicated that the manuscript should be shared only with discriminating and cultured readers like himself, and the book appears never to have enjoyed wide circulation.[19]

The theme of *Lamp at the Crossroads*, announced at the outset, is the decisive influence on a young man's development of his early education and upbringing. To illustrate this process, the author presents for our edification a detailed case-study, the life of T'an Shao-wen from ages six to thirty-five. Through the example of T'an's degeneration and subsequent redemption, Li Hai-kuan highlights three key aspects of a young man's education: his scholastic training, the guidance of his parents, and the influence of his peers. For Li, as for other Chinese educators, the lasting benefits of a rigorous academic training are contingent upon a healthy family and social environment.[20] This point is worth examining in more detail before we go on to explore Li Hai-kuan's notion of proper scholastic instruction.

The importance of parental example is made very clear in *Lamp at the Crossroads*. In the opening chapters, T'an Shao-wen makes sound progress in his studies under the watchful eye of his stern Confucian father, T'an Hsiao-i. After Hsiao-i's untimely death in Chapter 12, paternal severity is replaced by maternal indulgence and, all restraints removed, Shao-wen begins his long descent into perdition. Shao-wen's mother Wang-shih has little sympathy for study, convinced by her younger brother's successful career as a merchant that there is no particular value in conventional scholarship. From very early on she objects to the subjection of her only son to an intensive regimen of study and later sums up her basic philosophy in blunt terms: "What you need in the world today is money, not books" (74:718). Throughout the novel her scepticism toward formal education is shown to have a detrimental impact on Shao-wen's own attitudes.

Shao-wen's moral fiber is also weakened through exposure to the dissolute life-style of the playboys and wastrels with whom he begins to associate in his teenage years. An unashamedly hedonistic outlook entirely new to Shao-wen is articulated by his companions:

> All that really matters in life is having fun. Whether you spend your days carousing in the gay quarters or whether you sentence yourself to a life of straitlaced inhibition, you are going to die all the same. If you perform acts of saintly virtue, there's no guarantee that you'll find a place in a corner of the shrine to local worthies. If you accomplish some remarkable feat of loyalty, there's no certainty that your name will be recorded in the history books. Even if you were remembered, what good would it actually do you? As somebody who saw through everything once said, "The pursuit of pleasure is all there is to life." (21:209)

To Shao-wen, impressionable and inexperienced, this carpe diem credo offers an almost irresistible appeal and he soon becomes a convert. In subsequent chapters, Li Hai-kuan graphically demonstrates the role of peer pressure and group behavior in shaping the orientation of the young adolescent.

In assigning such prominence to the social environment, Li's position is reminiscent of the view expressed a century earlier by Lu Shih-i (1611–72). In a passage that may have struck a chord in Li Hai-kuan, Lu had also identified the teenage years as a particularly critical period in moral development:

> My friend Chiang Yü-chiu has said: "The individual takes shape for the first time within the mother's womb. When one reaches the age of fourteen or fifteen and comes into contact with teachers and friends, one's character is formed on a second level. If there are any shortcomings in one's upbringing at this point, then one will become an entirely different person." As I see it, great as a teacher's powers may be, he is likely to be severe and detached. These days a teacher's appointment tends not to last more than two or three years. Virtuous though a teacher may be, he is not going to transform radically the student in his charge. And conversely, even if a teacher is not exemplary, the pupil will not suffer permanent damage. It is friends alone who are close and intimate, and it is their habits which are easily adopted. If you get on well with them, then you will find yourselves inseparable for life. When you first go out into society, it is imperative that you exercise caution.[21]

Li Hai-kuan agreed with Lu that one must be discriminating in choosing one's friends. "A student would do better not to read books than to spend a day in the company of a scoundrel" (17:182, 21:210) is a remark he makes more than once. But he also attached a high priority to schooling and clearly subscribed to the sentiment expressed by one of his characters that "taking a teacher is like being born a second time" (86:817). By examining his portrayal of several schoolmasters in the novel, we will gain a further insight into his views on education. Let us introduce the cast in order of appearance.

THE MODEL TUTOR

There is nothing easier than engaging a schoolmaster, but if you want to select an able teacher who strikes the proper balance between leniency and severity, who is untiring in his explanations, and who possesses wide learning, that is difficult.
Cheng Hsieh, "Wei-hsien shu-chung chi ssu-ti Mo," in *Cheng Pan-ch'iao wai-chi*, 1751.

When first introduced in Chapter 1, T'an Hsiao-i has already lost interest in examination competition after several unlucky failures in the provincial examination and, now in his forties, devotes himself to literary pursuits in the company of his licentiate friends. Under his tutelage, Shao-wen has committed to memory the bulk of the *Analects* and the *Classic of Filial Piety* but does not yet attend regular classes. Impressed by the quality of education offered in the clan school of another branch of the T'an lineage, T'an Hsiao-i resolves on his return to Kaifeng to delay no longer in appointing a tutor.

His choice is a friend of his, a licentiate named Lou Ch'ien-chai, who throughout the novel sets the standard by which other scholars are judged. On the way to Lou's house, Hsiao-i explains to his companion Lou's qualifications: "I think that Ch'ien-chai is upright, principled, and learned, in all respects the perfect exemplar for a young pupil. If my son takes instruction from him, then he'll establish a firm footing not just in study but in learning how to conduct himself" (2:13).

In the following scene, Li Hai-kuan takes pains to depict the prospective tutor as a man of great integrity. The studious, deferential manner of Lou's son and the firm bond between Lou and his elder brother are clear indicators of Lou's rectitude. For the author, as for other commentators, virtuous character is one of the prime desiderata in a schoolteacher.[22]

Erudition is the other prerequisite for effective teaching in Li's view. This too Lou Ch'ien-chai possesses in full measure. Lou is thoroughly conversant with all of the Five Classics and at one stage entertains the notion of preparing a textual commentary on the whole canon. Lou's expertise in the Five Classics may initially seem unremarkable—familiarity with the Confucian canon was after all a fundamental goal of traditional education. In the context of the novel, however, Lou's scholarship is exceptional. A brief review of academic standards prevailing in eighteenth-century China will explain why this should be so.

Until 1753, candidates in the provincial examination could choose to be examined on all the Five Classics, but very few selected this option, for if taken seriously it entailed an enormous amount of preparation.[23] The vast majority of

scholars preferred to specialize in one of the Five Classics in order to minimize
the extent of memorization required and tended to opt for the more manageable texts — the *Poetry*, *Changes*, and *Documents* Classics, in descending order of
popularity. [24] The format of the examination curriculum (see also Elman, chap.
4 of this volume) thus encouraged candidates to concentrate narrowly on their
own specified text and largely ignore the rest of the Confucian corpus, a trend
deplored by early Ch'ing commentators such as Ku Yen-wu (1613–82), who
observed: "When people these days exchange information, they refer to the
other person's specialization as 'your honorable Classic' and to their own as
'my humble Classic.' How absolutely ludicrous!"[25] Corrective measures were
introduced in 1787 and requirements tightened in order to compel scholars to
widen their repertoire.[26] Until then scholars were free to confine themselves to
their own favored Classic.

Many, of course, sought to lighten their burdens still further by identifying
the themes from their specializations most likely to be set in the examination
and memorizing appropriate essays ahead of time. Tai Ming-shih (1653–1713)
makes a revealing observation on this score:

> There is no pest more damaging to the Four Books and Five Classics than exam-
> ination essays. The threat that they pose to the Five Classics is particularly
> severe. Everybody studies all the Four Books, but people specialize in just one of
> the Five Classics. It is true that some essays on the Four Books are penned by the
> inept, but at least they make some effort in this field; with essays on the Classics,
> even competent scholars frequently complete the assignment in desultory
> fashion. Why so? The examiners do not attach great importance to the expli-
> cation of the Classics, and candidates respond *collectively* by simply going through
> the motions. It reaches the point where scholars pay no notice whatsoever to
> sections of the texts to which the examination questions make no allusion. There
> are passages which they would not even know how to punctuate — it is not just
> that they do not understand the meaning of the whole Classic! In the years when
> the provincial examination is held, candidates regularly pick up their chosen
> Classic and study an abridged version, select the passages that lend themselves
> to inclusion in the examination; compose familiar, formula-ridden essays; and
> exchange copies with other people, convinced that without this kind of prep-
> aration they will have no chance of passing. Northern scholars have unrestricted
> movement during the Classics session of the examination, and among every
> group of four candidates each shares with his neighbors an essay of his own, and
> they all then transfer the copies to their own scripts. When academic trends
> reach the point of endorsing such a perfunctory approach, it is a rare scholar who
> has more than a cursory acquaintance with the Five Classics.[27]

Edicts urging examiners to forestall such practices by avoiding predictable
topics were issued in 1713, 1715, 1735, 1764, and 1796, their very regularity
betraying their failure to stem the tide.[28] With the relegation of the Five
Classics questions to the second session of examinations in 1757, the tendency

of examiners to focus their attention almost exclusively on the Four Books topics became all the more pronounced.[29] In the view of Ch'ien Ta-hsin, writing in 1799, the only way to reassert the importance of genuine scholarship was to reverse this policy and devote the first session entirely to the Five Classics—a recommendation, however, that fell on deaf ears. Throughout the eighteenth century, therefore, examination candidates lacked a strong practical incentive to master the whole Confucian curriculum (on curriculum reforms, cf. Elman, chap. 4 of this volume).[30]

In *Lamp at the Crossroads*, a clear contrast is thus drawn between Lou Ch'ien-chai, who goes on to pass the Honan provincial examination as a Five Classics candidate, and run-of-the-mill scholars such as Ch'en Ch'iao-ling, the instructor in the prefectural school, who makes the following admission:

> In the days when I was a licentiate, I used to write on the covers of my scripts that I was practiced in the *Book of Poetry*, but in fact I had just read the first three volumes and never actually finished it. My teacher used to say that one needed to know only eighty essays to be able to anticipate all the conceivable themes for the Classics questions. I had a crib, too, and when faced in the examination with the four Classics questions, I simply copied the answers that other people had written. Once I left the examination hall I forgot even the topics set. (7:78–79)

In much the same vein, the licentiate Chang Lei-ts'un acknowledges that he had passed the examination by simply familiarizing himself with the panegyric themes that examiners favored, had not read any of the other Classics apart from his own, and had a grounding in history only as far as the T'ang dynasty (77:752–53).

Lou Ch'ien-chai acts as a spokesman for the author's own educational philosophy: a number of his comments replicate Li Hai-kuan's pronouncements in his *Family Instructions*. His approach to the curriculum in particular mirrors that of the novelist: a solid grasp of the Five Classics comes first, examination essays later. After several years of schooling, T'an Shao-wen, now eleven years old, greatly impresses the provincial director of education by his capacity to recite from memory any passage from the Five Classics, a feat equaled by only twelve other pupils (t'ung-sheng) in Kaifeng prefecture. At the same time, T'an is quite unable to complete the eight-legged essays assigned in the qualifying examination itself. When asked to account for this apparent anomaly, the young student explains: "We have not studied essays and do not know how to write them. Our teacher also told us that when reading the Five Classics one must be able to give a clear explanation of their meaning. In addition to the Five Classics, there are a number of other books that we must read before he will instruct us in the study of essays" (7:81–82).

During his period as a tutor in the T'an household, Lou proves himself a demanding taskmaster but also at times surprises Shao-wen's father by adopting a flexible attitude toward his pupil's extracurricular activities. He prevails on the more rigid T'an Hsiao-i to allow his son to visit the Kaifeng spring fair, arguing that no harm can be done if boys are accompanied by their fathers on such an outing:

> If you insist on cooping up a student in a room and spend every day lecturing him on moral precepts, the dull-witted pupil will end up as wooden as a dummy, while the clever one is bound to discard these injunctions as soon as he steps out of the study and leaves his books behind. This may all sound a little extreme, but when educating young pupils, you cannot afford to be too slow nor too quick, neither too slack nor too strict. In a nutshell, it is difficult, that's all. (3:22)

Lou's academic qualifications are thus accompanied by an awareness of the role in a student's development of healthy diversions enjoyed under parental supervision. For Li Hai-kuan, who encouraged his own pupils to involve themselves in agricultural chores, this appreciation of the need for occasional variety in the scholastic routine seems to have been an important virtue of the model teacher.[31]

Unfortunately for Shao-wen, Lou's tenure as schoolmaster is relatively short. To an eminent scholar, a teaching appointment in a prestigious academy might offer an attractive alternative to an official career, but for most licentiates a tutorial post was often little more than an expedient way of supporting oneself and one's family while awaiting the next provincial examination.[32] There was thus a widespread tendency among teachers to relinquish their jobs whenever better prospects beckoned. Cheng Hsieh, commenting on the resignation of his son's tutor, attributed it to the limited appeal that teaching offered to talented and ambitious scholars.[33] It therefore comes as no surprise that Lou Ch'ien-chai resigns from his post as soon as he is awarded the provincial degree, setting off for Peking soon afterward to try his luck in the metropolitan examination.

In the wake of Lou's departure, T'an Shao-wen is left without a tutor, a problem aggravated by his father's removal to Peking. The selection of Lou's replacement is left in the hands of Shao-wen's mother. Her decision and its dire repercussions are examined below.

THE PHILISTINE

Academic standards have recently been deteriorating steadily. Those who study examination essays seek only to accelerate their promotion and do not follow the proper path. Quite apart from their neglect of the classical canon, they do not even take the time to study the commentaries and annotations of earlier scholars. They simply use hackneyed phraseology and resort to plagiarism in their quest for success. Teachers make this their principle of instruction and pupils apply it in their studies. Candidates model their compositions according to this standard and officials base their selections on it. Today's candidates are tomorrow's examiners—if this practice is perpetuated, where is it all going to end?

Imperial Edict, *Ch'in-ting Ta-Ch'ing hui-tien shih-li,* 1779

Lou's successor is Hou Kuan-yü, formerly a schoolmaster at a neighborhood school. He is chosen for all the wrong reasons. Wang-shih hears his name mentioned in a casual conversation and, without making any effort to ascertain his scholarly credentials or personal merits, decides to hire him on the spot. For her, the decisive factor is practical convenience. She need not provide Hou with cooked meals: basic foodstuffs will be issued to the teacher and Hou's wife will attend to the rest. In Wang-shih's eyes, the effort-saving aspects of this arrangement entirely eclipse any other considerations.

Hou, we soon learn, is in moral terms exactly the reverse of Lou Ch'ien-chai:

Because he had disgraced himself by creating some scandal at home and was being pressed on all sides for payment of his gambling debts, he had had no option but to flee to the provincial capital with his wife in tow and seek refuge at the home of a relative, Liu Wang the flour merchant. Liu Wang had arranged for him a two-year teaching post at the local school in the Temple of Three Officials. When celebrating a birthday, he had allowed one of his young pupils to drink so heavily that he had collapsed in a stupor. The boy's mother kicked up a big fuss in the temple and such an outcry was raised that Hou was forced to call the proceedings to a halt. When Liu Wang and Wang Ch'un-yü tried to placate the outraged parents, one family after another blamed Hou for "spoiling the students" or "violating academic standards." After two or three days of adjudication, it was decided that as soon as the school year ended the appointment would be terminated. (8:88)

This depiction of a schoolmaster as a disreputable individual with no real interest in his job apart from its financial rewards is by no means unique to *Lamp at the Crossroads*. The seventeenth-century novel *Hsing-shih yin-yuan chuan* (Marriage destinies to awaken the world) chronicles in lurid detail the career of a schoolmaster who is motivated solely by mercenary concerns. Mendacious, belligerent, and sexually perverted, he is perhaps the most repellent character in a book stocked with unpleasant personalities. The novel's anonymous author evidently believed that such behavior was symptomatic of a general trend, for he offers the following commentary:

Teachers these days have the same mentality as officials. Officials in the old days sought to serve their emperor and succor the people, while today's officials simply aim to enrich themselves at the expense of the populace, and so if they do not win the emperor's special favor they are bound to channel their energies in this direction. The teachers of old sought to transmit learning to the younger generation, whereas teachers today are interested only in making a living. The result is that if they fail to receive their wages, they act just like some district magistrate outraged by residents who cannot afford to pay their taxes. If a student terminates their appointment in favor of another tutor, they react just like an army officer as he chastises a deserter.[34]

Academically as well, Hou is the antithesis of Lou:

> He too was a licentiate and had once or twice been placed in the first or second rank. If it was a question of the eight-leg, he was extremely conversant with the rules of the explanation, amplification, transition, and synthesis; if it was a matter of the Five Classics, he was perfectly capable of listing the titles of the *Poetry*, *Documents*, *Changes*, *Rites*, and *Spring and Autumn Annals*. (8:88)

Hou is an outspoken proponent of the exclusively examination-oriented program of study that was prevalent in the eighteenth century. Critiques by the Ch'ien-lung emperor and others of such an approach are familiar; observe how it is defended:

> As one might expect, "a new monk is fond of beating the gong," and [Hou] never left the study the whole day through. Finding that the texts that T'an Shao-wen had been reading presented too many difficulties in comprehension, he cast them all aside and instead made a trip to the bookstore to buy a couple of volumes of elementary-level examination essays and had Shao-wen start reciting them. As he explained to Shao-wen: "If you had started studying eight-legs earlier, and produced two decent essays in the examination last year, the director of education would most likely have passed you. Though you could recite the Five Classics, it turned out in the end to be of no use. You can see for yourself now that it's only essays that can get you anywhere, and the Five Classics are of no real consequence. Take even Mr. Lou, who I hear knows by heart the Classics and histories — if you look at the essays that got him a pass, you'll see that they were written in a very clear style — not only did he not need to know those books, but he couldn't afford to make very much reference to them. I once happened to glance at the paper that got K'ung Yun-hsuan his place on the supplementary list and, sound though it was, it erred a bit on the dense side, thus denying him a place in the first rank. In short, a student's goal in reading is to attain honor and fame; if a book is not conducive to the achievement of such goals, you are better off not reading it. If you argue that learning the Classics and histories better equips you to emulate great writers, this is an even greater blunder. Think about it: among the famous writers of past or present, how many are *t'ung-sheng*? They are all either grand secretaries or Hanlin academicians — if they weren't so eminent, their writings would never have been transmitted. Besides, their essays are all simple and straightforward and really have nothing to do with Classics and histories. Why bother to squander your valuable energies on something that will not generate honor and fame? All you need to do is study over and over again these two collections I've just bought, learn the formula that they follow, and you can rest assured that success will be yours. (8:88–89)

Those familiar with *The Scholars* may be struck by certain similarities between this extract and passages in Wu Ching-tzu's novel in which such loyal devotees of the examination essay as Compiler Lu and Ma Ch'un-shang wax lyrical in its praise. Hou's suggestion that literary distinction is determined more by one's examination career than by one's artistic achievement finds a particularly close parallel in the rhetorical question posed by Compiler Lu's daughter in Chapter 11 of *The Scholars*: "Listen, mother, do you know anyone, past or present, who is entitled to be called a brilliant young scholar without having passed the examinations?"[35]

These superficial correspondences do not conceal a more significant difference. In *The Scholars*, the views of the essay aficionados are deliberately exaggerated and presented in such an extreme form as to seem preposterous. In *Lamp at the Crossroads* a much more plausible case for the examination essay is made. The limited practical application of a thorough knowledge of the Five Classics and the need to subordinate one's learning to the dictates of the eight-legged format have rarely found such forceful expression as here. When T'an Shao-wen promptly succumbs to the seemingly incontrovertible logic of Hou's argument, we have a glimpse of an educational trend in miniature. By the end of the eighteenth century, many young students were following similar advice from their teachers, to the alarm of some examiners. Wang T'ing-chen (1757–1827), Education Intendant in Kiangsi from 1807 to 1810, was shocked to find among his examinees boys of ten or eleven who were proficient in examination essays but had never opened a copy of the Five Classics.[36]

Hou Kuan-yü claims an expertise in prognostication among his accomplishments and soon endears himself to Shao-wen's mother by forecasting a glorious future for her darling son. Securely ensconced in his position, he then renews his old vices, loafing, drinking, gambling, and engaging in various lucrative sidelines, while Shao-wen is left largely to his own devices.

T'an Hsiao-i's return home after a two-year stay in the capital brings about a dramatic confrontation with his son's tutor:

"Does Shao-wen know the Five Classics by heart now?" Hsiao-i asked. "How many has he learned?"

Hou Kuan-yü replied: "In the examination these days there's only the one question on the Classics. So long as you know seventy or eighty essays, you will have all the themes covered; even if a different topic is set, you can always swap with somebody specializing in the same classic. If you're in a hurry to graduate or want to be placed in the top rank, all you have to do is study essays more intensively. If you have a few hundred on call, then you'll have plenty of models to utilize."

"One acquires an exhaustive knowledge of the Classics in order to apply their truths in practice," Hsiao-i responded. "Rank and fame are not the sole objectives. Even if rank and fame are what you're aiming for, your views will lack substance if you ignore the Classics." (11:120)

T'an's position here recalls Li Hai-kuan's strictures at the beginning of his *Family Instructions*. Shao-wen's father amplifies the point on another occasion:

Wang Po-hou's *Trimetrical Classic* explains it clearly:

When the *Elementary Education* is finished,
You come to the Four Books.

> When the *Classic of Filial Piety* is mastered,
> And the Four Books are known by heart,
> The next step is to the Six Classics
> Which may now be studied.

This sequence may serve permanently as the basis for primary education. If you follow this program of study, then as a licentiate you will be a scholar of integrity and sound learning, and as an official you are bound to be a capable administrator; the very least you can be is a cultured man of letters. If you spend all your time on the eight-leg, this will actually retard your progress towards the rank and fame you are so eagerly seeking; even if you are lucky enough to be awarded the first degree, you'll end up as a licentiate all your life and nothing more.(11:122)

In this debate, Li Hai-kuan's sympathies clearly lie with T'an Hsiao-i, but he acknowledges the strength of Hou's convictions by allowing him the last word in the argument:

> All you need to do is read more essays. As the saying goes, 'If you've read three thousand good poems, you can always steal a line if you can't think of one.' If you've read a lot, you'll have no trouble in following the formula. 'What's hewn with an axe is never as round as what's crafted by a lathe'; why scorn the ready-made and go to all the bother of starting from scratch? (11:120)

Hou further discredits himself in the eyes of T'an Hsiao-i by recommending as reading matter for Shao-wen the drama *Hsi-hsiang chi* (Romance of the western chamber) and the novel *Chin p'ing mei* (Golden lotus). T'an's horror at the sight of the latter book causes a relapse of an old illness and hastens his death in the following chapter. In terms of Shao-wen's personal development, Hou's intellectual mediocrity and moral turpitude set in motion the opening stages of the young man's degeneration. By Chapter 14, when Shao-wen is fifteen years old and Hou's appointment is finally terminated, Shao-wen's decline is obvious to all his father's friends.

THE HYPOCRITE

Two schoolmasters lived in neighboring villages. Both prided themselves on their dedication to moral teaching. One day they met for a colloquium attended by a dozen or so students. Just as they were engaged in discussion of nature and Heaven and analysis of principle and desire, expounding their views with weighty phrase and solemn expression as if in the presence of the sages, a breeze suddenly wafted a slip of paper to the foot of the steps and blew it round and round. One of their pupils picked it up, only to find that it was a letter sent from one teacher to the other, secretly discussing their plan of robbing a widow of her land.

Chi Yun, *Yueh-wei ts'ao-tang pi-chi*, 1789

T'an Shao-wen's education is entrusted to a third tutor in Chapter 38. Hui Yang-min, a licentiate in his early fifties, has hitherto been teaching young pupils at a neighborhood temple; his invitation to teach in the T'an household is an unexpected promotion. Hui Yang-min sets before us yet another image of the schoolmaster, in this case the pedantic devotee of the Ch'eng-Chu "study of principle."

Hui presents an interesting contrast to his predecessor. Unlike Hou Kuan-yü, Hui disparages eight-legged essays and professes a distaste for examinations, arguing that they divert one from the more vital task of self-cultivation. As he defines it, his chief concern in instructing T'an Shao-wen "lies not in the attainment of success and fame but in the correctness of his studies" (38:355). At the same time, Hui shares with Hou Kuan-yü a complete indifference to any program of wide-ranging study and confines himself to a very limited range of readings, primarily the *Ta-hsueh* (Great learning). He has no interest in poetry of any kind and displays an intolerance for works of "heterodox" tendency (38:356). This intellectual narrowness, we are expected to infer, accounts for his lackluster academic performance: he is a permanent fixture in the third rank of licentiates in the "annual" examination.

Hui Yang-min is given to quoting from the Four Books and extolling the principles of the Supreme Ultimate and the values of self-improvement, but this thin veneer of learning does little to conceal the lack of any real intellectual substance in him. He has nothing of practical benefit to offer to his student. Denouncing examination essays as superficial trimmings but dismissing in the same breath the study of the Classics and histories, he leaves Shao-wen with no clear direction to follow.

Subsequent events discredit Hui and expose him as a sham. Despite his much-publicized adherence to Neo-Confucian orthodoxy, he proves quite incapable of living up to one of its key tenets: the proper management of one's family. He spinelessly yields to the selfish interests of his wife and takes no action to rescue his elder brother from debt, eventually capitulating to her demand that he and his brother divide the family property.

The contrast between Hui Yang-min, the hypocritical moralist, and Lou Ch'ien-chai, a true Confucian, is made explicit in a discussion in Chapter 39. Ch'eng Sung-shu, a character who often seems to articulate the author's own view, is the speaker:

> It is Ch'ien-chai who is the true practitioner of the study of principle. When he speaks it is always in simple but pertinent comments, and when you visit his home you sense immediately an atmosphere of order and discipline. This is why he and his brother have always been inseparable, and why their sons are so well-behaved.... Just think, in the twenty or so years we have known him, has Ch'ien-chai ever spouted any of that *li-hsueh* theory? But has not everything he has done accorded with *li-hsueh*? It's precisely those people who are always talking about *li-hsueh* who as poor licentiates are utterly unable to maintain order in their family, and if they happen to strike it lucky in the examinations, all they think about is getting a promotion and making money.... What's even more despicable

is that this man Hui hardly says anything that is not a quotation from K'ung or Meng, Ch'eng or Chu, but in fact he has no real understanding of what he is saying! He makes a living out of teaching, but actually he is a subverter of the Classics! (39:359)

As this passage suggests, Li Hai-kuan was far from being a critic of the Ch'eng-Chu school itself but simply deplored the insincere espousal of Neo-Confucian ideals. In the 1744 postface to an anthology of Sung and Ming Neo-Confucian thought, *Hsing-li ts'ui-yen lu* (Quintessential sayings on nature and principle), Li lamented the indifference of many of his contemporaries to the central core of Neo-Confucian philosophy.[37] At the same time, he clearly regarded with aversion those who made an ostentatious show of dedication to Ch'eng-Chu thought while in reality betraying its moral injunctions. Just as Hou Kuan-yü champions a philistine version of the examination curriculum, so too Hui Yang-min represents a debased form of Neo-Confucianism. For Li Hai-kuan, both men pose a grave threat to Shao-wen's development, and in order to demonstrate the danger of giving credence to their values, their intellectual and moral failings are fully exposed in the pages of his novel.

The unmasking of schoolmasters as pedants and hypocrites was a popular theme of Ch'ing anecdotal literature. Perhaps no author satirized such men with greater relish than Chi Yun (1724–1805). Chi was a friend of Tai Chen (1724–77) and sympathetic to Tai's critique of Neo-Confucian philosophy (see also Brokaw, chap. 8 of this volume). He made his own contribution to the eighteenth-century reaction against the Ch'eng-Chu school in the form of brief tales of the supernatural that offer a trenchant commentary on the intellectual and moral failings of Ch'eng-Chu practitioners.[38] The excerpt that opens this section is just one of many exposés in the collection. Chi Yun, like Li Hai-kuan, takes as his theme the pedant's complacency and mediocrity and, like Li, shapes his narrative to puncture the moralist's pretensions. In one story, a self-righteous lecturer on Neo-Confucian thought appears ridiculous when his acquisitive instincts are exposed by a Buddhist monk. A second pedant is reduced to speechless embarrassment when his egotism and shallow understanding are challenged by a hostile ghost. Yet another teacher is presented as an intransigent and callous arbiter on moral issues, whose apparent rectitude disguises prurient motives. In one of his later stories, Chi pursues this theme to its logical conclusion. Here, a strict Neo-Confucian disciplinarian falls far short of the exacting standards he demands of others when he responds eagerly to a prostitute's invitation. Chi Yun's judgment on this teacher could be said to apply to all these individuals: "How true it is that an external superfluity reflects an inner insufficiency!"[39]

This tradition of scepticism toward a teacher's character was to be sustained well into the twentieth century. In "The White Light," drawing perhaps equally on childhood memories and literary convention (for he was a keen reader of Chi Yun's fiction), Lu Hsun (1881–1936) offers an ironic portrait of a schoolmaster in the dying years of the Ch'ing dynasty. The subject of this short story, Ch'en Shih-ch'eng, sixteen times a failure in the county examination, is a tutor in the Confucian classics, but he privately indulges in elaborate fantasies of self-gratification:

> He had won his first degree in the county examination and taken his second in the provincial capital, success following success.... The local gentry were trying by every means to ally with him by marriage; people were treating him like a god, cursing themselves for their former contempt and blindness.... The other famil-ies renting his tumble-down house had been driven away—no need for that, they would move of their own accord—and the whole place was completely renovated with flagpoles and a placard at the gate.... If he wanted to keep his hands clean he could be an official in the capital, otherwise some post in the provinces would prove more lucrative.[40]

THE VILLAGE SCHOOLMASTER

> *On making a million your heart is set?*
> *Teach school for a thousand years.*
> *And you'll just about reach your target.*
> T'ang Hsien-tsu, *Mu-tan t'ing*, 1598

In Chapter 44 of *Lamp at the Crossroads*, T'an Shao-wen has a brief encounter with another schoolmaster. Fleeing from his creditors, T'an has been robbed en route of all his baggage and traveling expenses and is desperate with hunger. In a dilapidated temple he comes across a bespectacled, elderly schoolteacher and, appealing to his Confucian generosity, begs him for a meal. The tutor is compelled to turn him away:

> Haven't you noticed that the whole class is made up of village youths? My sole compensation here is room and board, and I have no freedom to decide things for myself. When farming families appoint a teacher, every single meal is fixed well beforehand, and allowance is made for me alone—how could I possibly cater to someone else's needs?" (44:408)

After this rebuff, T'an Shao-wen can do nothing except struggle on, his hunger unabated, and we see no more of the anonymous schoolmaster, eking out the most meager of livings in rural Honan. Despite his minor role in the novel, this tutor merits closer study as a character-type who features prominently in Ch'ing literature, the impecunious village schoolmaster.

"The poor do not study, the rich do not teach," a common saying in eight-eenth-century China, encapsulates the notion that, as in other early modern societies, teaching was often regarded as "the refuge of men without other prospects and was generally ill-paid."[41] In China at large, it tended to be the preserve of that perennial examination failure, the lowly licentiate.

Although Chung-li Chang has estimated that teachers' average income was about one hundred taels, evidence suggests that most schoolmasters were paid much less.[42] To Arthur H. Smith, surveying Shantung village life in the nineteenth century, it seemed that many teachers were "chronically on the verge of starvation."[43] He acknowledged that "teachers of real ability, or who have in some way secured a great reputation, are able to command salaries in proportion," but found the country schoolmaster more typically to be "remunerated with but a mere pittance."[44] The data collected from gazetteers by Evelyn Rawski indicate that salaries ranged from five to eighty taels, with most incomes in the twenty to thirty tael range.[45] Literary materials confirm that ordinary schoolmasters could not expect a salary much above fifty taels. In *Lamp at the Crossroads,* Lou Ch'ien-chai receives a total of forty-eight taels a year (2:18), while Hui Yang-min is offered about twenty-eight taels (38:352). In a seventeenth-century novel, the licentiate Ch'eng Ying-ts'ai accepts a tutorial position at a salary of twenty-four taels, with seasonal supplements.[46] In *The Scholars,* the licentiate Yü Yü-te receives a salary of thirty taels, and Yü Yü-ta, a senior licentiate, is offered an income of forty taels plus bonuses.[47]

It is in *The Scholars* also that we encounter, near the bottom of the pay scale, the archetypal village schoolmaster in the form of the half-pathetic, half-ridiculous Chou Chin. In his sixties, yet still a mere *t'ung-sheng,* Chou is despised by young licentiates, cold-shouldered by provincial graduates, and treated with scant respect by the villagers who employ him to teach their sons. Although promised an annual stipend of twelve taels, the money actually received falls so far short of this figure that he cannot afford even a month's meals. His position becomes all the more precarious as he inadvertently offends the villagers and his contract is terminated at the end of the year.[48] This depiction of Chou Chin's plight is clearly designed to illustrate the very lowest depths to which a scholar might sink — Chou's miraculous rise in the following chapter maps out the opposite extreme.

Thus, in late imperial China there existed a stereotype of the schoolmaster that has much in common with the tragicomic image of the schoolteacher in eighteenth-century Germany, "a caricature of servility and impotence."[49] Just as Prussian schoolteachers found themselves in "a tangle of frustrating, often humiliating dependencies" and bitterly resented the terms and conditions of their employment, so too did Chinese schoolmasters at the village level chafe at the demeaning bondage to their employers to which they felt confined.[50]

> Half hungry, half full, the unhappy sojourner,
> No cangue, no locks, but just the same a prisoner[51]

In such terms was the plight of the village teacher described by P'u Sung-ling, perhaps the most acerbic commentator on this facet of education. P'u was well qualified to comment, for he spent almost his entire adult life teaching school in rural Shantung. The theme common to a number of his works is the yawning gap that lies between a schoolmaster's theoretical status and his actual position in society. As P'u Sung-ling puts it, "People think only of the honor accorded to a teacher, little knowing how cheaply he is valued."[52]

P'u's vernacular ballad *The Pedant's Lament* follows a teacher's progress through the course of a year: his initial apprehension as to how his new employer will treat him, his pleasure at the quality of the first welcoming dinner, his disillusionment when he is reduced to a simple diet the next day, the discomfort of his living quarters and the loneliness of separation from his family, his dismay at the unwillingness of his employer to pay him the promised seasonal bonuses, and the relief he feels at the end of the year, knowing he will not have to see his pupils again.[53]

In P'u's play *Begging to Teach*, a penniless schoolmaster, drifting far from home in search of a job, has no choice but to accept the outrageous terms of employment which a miserly patron offers him. Not only will his meals be rudimentary, his living arrangements primitive, and his salary subject to unfavorable conversion rates, but he will even be expected to pay for the writing materials used in class and carry the boys to school on his back if the road is muddy. The play closes with the teacher consenting to yet more absurd conditions in his desperation to be hired:

> After school and before dinner I'll shovel soil in the pig-sty, in the evening I'll fetch water from the well, if you're busy I'll look after the children and get the fire started, if you're out of flour and the mule is not available I'll grind the mill, I'll sweep the yard and carry firewood and pick up droppings on the way, and when you have company I'll wipe the table and bring in dishes.[54]

Although passive resignation seems to have been the most common response of teachers to their adverse working conditions, isolated acts of protest also took place, as P'u again records:

> An old man of Ch'ang-shan, when appointing a teacher each year, followed the practice of computing the tutor's daily wage by dividing his salary among the total number of calendar days. He would then keep a detailed record of the teacher's absences. At the end of the term of appointment he would deduct from the salary accordingly. A licentiate named Ma was teaching at this man's house and was utterly appalled when he realized why it was his patron had come to see him with abacus in hand. Soon, however, a devious form of reprisal occurred to him, and he concealed his resentment under a show of cheerful indifference, allowing his employer to make his deductions without the slightest dissent. Delighted, the old man made every effort to confirm Ma's appointment for the next year. Ma declined on the grounds that he had other commitments. Instead he recommended a licentiate notorious for his obstreperous character as his replacement.
>
> Once his successor was established, he would regularly revile his employer in the foulest language, and the old man had no option but to endure these insults. At the end of the year he called on the tutor, clutching his abacus. Although

outraged, the licentiate initially offered no resistance. When the old man proceeded to deduct from his pay the days he spent traveling to and from his post, the tutor would have none of it, and flicked the balls back to the other side of the board. After much inconclusive argument, they seized whatever weapon came to hand and threatened each other. In the end, bruised and bleeding, they took the case to court.[55]

Judging from their popularity in the Ch'ing period, such anecdotes seem to reflect a widespread awareness of the deprivations suffered by schoolteachers. Arthur Smith, who saw *Begging to Teach* performed in the late nineteenth century, reports that it was enormously popular.[56] Showdowns between stingy employers and abused schoolmasters were a staple ingredient of Chinese joke books. Typical is the following example, from a compilation edited by Yü Yueh (1821–1907):

> A man engaged a teacher to instruct his sons. The food provided was paltry in the extreme, meal after meal consisting of winter melon and nothing else. The teacher said to his employer, "You are very fond of winter melon, are you?"
>
> "That's right," was the answer. "Not only does it taste good, but it does wonders for one's eyesight."
>
> A few days later, when the master of the house dropped by the schoolroom, the teacher was leaning against the window and gazing far off into the distance, seemingly unaware of the other's arrival. Only when called did he turn around and say apologetically, "I'm afraid I failed to greet you—I was just watching the opera in town."
>
> His host, quite taken aback, asked him: "How could you possibly see a play in town?"
>
> Replied the teacher, "Ever since I started eating your winter melon, my vision has been enormously enhanced."[57]

Whereas in Europe a movement developed to emancipate and modernize the teaching profession, no comparable change occurred in the working conditions of rural schoolmasters in China. It was clear to some observers, however, that by taking care not to relinquish his autonomy or compromise his standards, a teacher might reasonably hope to escape the worst abuses. To operate one's own school, independently of any particular family, was seen as the best guarantee of satisfactory employment. A seventeenth-century novelist thus stresses the importance of reserving the right to pick and choose one's own students:

> Be sure to run your own school—don't accept other people's invitations. If you run your own school and people send their sons to you, you can accept the good students and tactfully turn away the bad ones. If you want to teach more pupils, nobody is going to stop you from enrolling a hundred; if you want to teach fewer, no one is going to force you to teach even one. If you get on well with your students, you need not turn down the application of new arrivals; if you have problems with them you have no reason to worry if they leave. Even if you lose

two out of ten, you'll still have four pairs; even if eight leave, you'll still have a couple. Then if you advertise again, there are bound to be more takers.

If you teach at someone else's behest, then after teaching for a year you still won't know whether they are going to employ you for the next. If you are given notice at the very end of the year, other families will already have made their arrangements, and you'll be stuck at home for a year with no money coming in.

What's more, if you go to someone else's house, there's the whole question of getting on with them. If your employer values teachers and honors friends, and you can establish a close rapport, maintaining amicable ties from start to finish, that rates as excellent. If you also have several attentive pupils who live up to their fathers' and brothers' hopes and reward their tutor's efforts, so that the teacher-student relationship is imbued with the spirit of the father and son bond, that counts as exceptional.

If the father or brother in question is unbearably vulgar and subjects you to indignities, so that proper standards of hospitality and courtesy are ignored, but you have brilliant students, and so can make some adjustment, this may be considered second-rate.

If your patron treats you with the greatest respect but your pupils are wayward, then "you can't make gold out of iron, and you won't change an eel to a dragon," and you'll be drawing your salary with nothing to show for it. Dismayed by your pupil's mediocrity, you'll be all the more shamed at the prospect of being blamed for your protégé's misdeeds — this is the worst kind of teaching post. If you run your own school and happen to run into this kind of student, there's a simple solution: just send him packing! But if you run into this kind of obnoxious student when hired by a family, what can you do about it? You just have to put up with him for a whole year![58]

CONCLUSION: LI HAI-KUAN IN PERSPECTIVE

On his deathbed, T'an Hsiao-i urges his son to commit to memory the following injunction: "Apply yourself to study, befriend men of honor" (12:130). This precept becomes the novel's leitmotif, its simple message reiterated at critical moments and hailed in the closing chapters of the book as "an eight-word *Elementary Education*, a miniature *Classic of Filial Piety*" (95:894). The author's confidence in the efficacy of this maxim is rooted in his faith in the potential of the educational system to reward true scholarship and recognize moral integrity.

Although Li Hai-kuan was fully aware of the pervasiveness of a purely examination-oriented curriculum and draws attention to corrupt practices such as illicit collusion between candidates and examiners (68:655), the image of the examination system projected in his novel is on the whole a positive one. The examiners who appear in *Lamp at the Crossroads* are uniformly capable and conscientious. They include the erudite provincial director of education who lays so much stress on the Five Classics (7:78–82) and his successor who aspires to select only candidates who demonstrate evidence of solid learning and who show outstanding potential for practical government service

(93:872–74). This dedication to high academic standards is shared by the painstaking Hanlin compiler who perceives the talent of Lou Ch'ien-chai's son and recommends him for the *chin-shih* degree (102:951) and the metropolitan examiners who scrutinize the papers of T'an Shao-wen's son in the book's final pages (108:1012).

Li's position invites comparison with that of his contemporary, Wu Ching-tzu, who presents in *The Scholars* "the emphatic affirmation of the idealistic side of orthodox Confucianism" and, adopting a detached stance, rejects wholesale the traditional examination system.[59] Li Hai-kuan, in contrast, advocates a more sanguine, socially engaged role. Li's confidence in the human potential for regeneration and self-renewal clearly shaped his views on the life of the individual: by the end of the book, T'an Shao-wen has transformed himself from a prodigal son to a devoted family man, war hero, and district magistrate of distinction. Li's depiction of the examination system at work also reflects a faith in the capacity of cultural and political institutions to direct ideology and correct deviant trends in society. *Lamp at the Crossroads*, conceived as a prescriptive yet readable study guide, is itself a monument to Li's reformist goals.

Li's presentation of the teaching fraternity is shaped to some extent by his didactic purposes, that is, his interest in demonstrating the influence that a teacher exerts upon his pupil's moral and academic development. The various images of the schoolmaster that appear in *Lamp at the Crossroads* also reflect Li Hai-kuan's observation of the society around him.[60] There are signs that portrayals such as that of Hou Kuan-yü are a projection of educational practice in the northern provinces of China where, according to several witnesses, teaching standards were generally lower than in the culturally more advanced Kiangnan region.[61] When a character in Li's novel declares that he has striven to secure the best possible education for his younger brother, he puts it in these terms: "Provincial graduates from Kiangnan, metropolitan graduates from Chekiang, senior licentiates, and supplementary graduates, renowned scholars from far and wide—I've engaged them all as tutors. When have I spent less than two or three hundred taels a year?" (68:654) It is thus suggested that a superior quality of teaching and correspondingly higher salaries were characteristic of education in the southern provinces. But the elite world of eminent teachers and distinguished academies is remote from the provincial educational scene portrayed in Li's novel as it was, indeed, from the experience of a great many students. Although selective and incomplete in its presentation of education, *Lamp at the Crossroads* remains a valuable document, depicting in vivid detail the interaction of education and society in eighteenth-century Honan.

NOTES

1. See Ichisada Miyazaki, *China's Examination Hell: The Civil Service Examinations of Imperial China*, trans. Conrad Schirokauer (New Haven and London: Yale University Press, 1981), passim; John W. Chaffee, *The Thorny Gates of Learning in Sung China: A Social History of Examinations* (Cambridge: Cambridge University Press, 1985),169–81.

2. See Allan Barr, "Pu Songling and the Qing Examination System," *Late Imperial China* 7, no.1 (June 1986): 87–111.

3. See Paul S. Ropp, *Dissent in Early Modern China: Ju-lin wai-shih and Ch'ing Social Criticism* (Ann Arbor: University of Michigan Press, 1981); Timothy C. Wong, *Wu Ching-tzu* (Boston: Twayne, 1978).

4. See the preface by Fung Yu-lan 馮友蘭 to the 1927 edition, *Ch'i-lu teng yen-chiu tzu-liao* 歧路燈研究資料 (Research materials on *Lamp at the Crossroads*), ed. Luan Hsing 欒星 (reprint, Honan: Chung-chou, 1982) (hereafter *YCTL*), 109.

5. *YCTL*, 1–4.

6. See Liu Ch'ing-chih 劉青芝, "*Li K'ung-t'ang chih-i hsu*" 李孔堂制義序(Preface to Li K'ung- t'ang's examination essays), reprinted in *YCTL*, 135.

7. Yang Huai 楊淮, ed., *Kuo-ch'ao Chung-chou shih-ch'ao* 國朝中州詩鈔 (Selections from Honan poets of the Ch'ing dynasty), reprinted in *YCTL*, 102.

8. *YCTL*, 27–29; Luan Hsing, "Li Lü-yuan chia-shih sheng-p'ing tsai-pu" 李綠園家世生平再補 (Further supplement to the biography of Li Lü-yuan), in *Ming Ch'ing hsiao-shuo yen-chiu* 明清小説研究, 3 (1986): 258–60.

9. See *Chia-hsun ch'un-yen* 家訓諄言, reprinted in *YCTL*, 141.

10. See "*Li K'ung-t'ang chih-i hsu*" in *YCTL*, 135.

11. See "Wei-hsien shu-chung yü she-ti ti-wu shu" 濰縣署中與舍弟第五書 (Fifth letter to my brother from the magistracy of Wei-hsien), in Cheng Hsieh 鄭燮, *Cheng Pan-ch'iao chi* 鄭板橋集 (Collected works of Cheng Hsieh), (reprint, Hong Kong: Chung-hua, 1979, 19; "Wei-hsien shu-chung yü Lin-erh" 濰縣署中諭麟兒 (Instructions to my son Lin, from the magistracy of Wei-hsien), in *Cheng Pan-ch'iao wai-chi* 鄭板橋外集 (Supplemental collection of works by Cheng Hsieh), comp. Cheng Ping-ch'un 鄭炳純 (Taiyuan: Shan-hsi jen-min, 1987), 38. Cf. the recollections by Chao I 趙翼 (1727–1814) of his father's admonitions, in *Yen-p'u tsa-chi* 簷曝雜記 (Miscellaneous notes of Chao I), (reprint, Peking: Chung-hua, 1982), 2:22.

12. Eighteenth-century editions of the *Annals* gave special prominence to the remarks of Ch'eng I 程頤 (1033–1107) on this score: "The Five Classics resemble medical prescriptions; the *Spring and Autumn Annals* is comparable to the application of medicines in the treatment of illnesse.... If scholars simply read the *Annals* they will still be able to master the Way. It is not that one will fail to gain full understanding of the principles from the other Classics, but they merely discuss moral concepts. Because the *Annals* deals with actions, it makes the rights and wrongs all the more evident." See "Kang-ling," 綱領 (Introductory principles), p. 4a, in *Ch'un-ch'iu ssu-chuan* 春秋四傳 (Four commentaries to the *Annals*), (reprint, 1726), Bodleian Library, Oxford; "Kang-ling," p. 31b, in *Ch'in-ting Ch'un-ch'iu chuan-shuo hui-tsuan* 欽定春秋傳説彙纂 (Imperially commissioned compilation of commentaries on the *Annals*), (1721), Bodleian Library, Oxford.

13. *YCTL*, 141–12.

14. "Wei-hsien shu-chung yü she-ti Mo ti-erh shu" 墨第二書 (Second letter to my brother Mo from the magistracy of Wei-hsien), *Cheng Pan-ch'iao chi*, 19.

15. *YCTL*, 4–6, 122–26.

16. *Ch'i-lu teng tzu-hsü* 歧路燈自序 (Author's preface to *Lamp at the Crossroads*), reprinted in *YCTL*, 94.

17. Li Lü-yuan 李綠園, *Ch'i-lu teng*, ed. Luan Hsing (Honan: Chung-chou, 1980), ch. 90, p. 850. References to the novel will hereafter be incorporated in the text.

18. For a fuller study of the disjunction between Li's avowed purpose and his written style, see Chang Hung-k'uei 張鴻魁, "Tsai chang-man ching-chi ti lu-shang mai-chin: Li Lü-yuan ti pao-shou ssu-hsiang tui *Ch'i-lu teng* yü-yen ti hsiao-chi ying-hsiang" 在長滿荊棘的路上邁進—李綠園的保守思想對《歧路燈》語言的消極影響, (Advancing along a thorny path—the negative effect of Li Lü-yuan's conservative ideology on the language of *Lamp at the Crossroads*), in *Ch'i-lu teng lun-ts'ung* 歧路燈論叢 2(1984): 256–62.

19. See the anonymous preface to the 1780 manuscript of *Ch'i-lu teng*, reprinted in *YCTL*, 101.

20. See Charles P. Ridley, "Theories of Education in the Ch'ing Period," *Ch'ing-shih wen-t'i* 3, no. 8 (Dec. 1977): 35–39.

21. Lu Shih-i 陸世儀, *Ssu-pien lu chi-yao* 思辨錄輯要, (Abstracts from Ssu-pien lu), reprinted in *Ssu-k'u ch'üan-shu chen-pen ssu-chi* 四庫全書珍本四集 (Rare books from the *Ssu-k'u ch'üan-shu*, fourth series), 2:9a–b.

22. Cf. Hsi Chou Sheng 西周生, *Hsing-shih yin-yuan chuan* 醒世姻緣傳 (Marriage destinies to awaken the world), (reprint, Shanghai: Shanghai ku-chi, 1981), 35:510.

23. See *Ch'in-ting Ta-Ch'ing hui-tien shih-li* 欽定大清會典事例 (Collected statutes and precedents of the Ch'ing dynasty), (1899; reprint, Taipei: Tai-wan Chung-wen, 1963) (hereafter abbreviated to *HTSL*), 348:11b–12a.

24. *HTSL*, 348:1b. The *Book of Rites* and the *Annals* (with commentary) were the most voluminous of the Five Classics and may well have been avoided for precisely this reason. Other factors no doubt also had a bearing on candidates' choices: the *Poetry Classic*, for example, would have appealed to those with a particular interest in verse.

25. Ku Yen-wu 顧炎武, "Ni-t'i" 擬題 (Practice essays), in *Jih-chih lu chi-shih* 日知錄集釋 (Record of daily knowledge, with collected annotations), (*Ssu-pu pei-yao* ed.), 16: 17b.

26. *HTSL*, 331:13b.

27. Tai Ming-shih 戴名世, "Ssu-chia shih-i he-k'e hsu" 四家詩義合刻序, (Preface to the combined publication of essays by four scholars), in *Tai Ming-shih chi* 戴名世集 (Collected works of Tai Ming-shih), (Peking: Chung-hua, 1986), 2:35. For other similar comments, see Yeh Meng-chu 葉夢珠 (1624–92), *Yueh-shih pien* 閱世編 (Perspectives on society), (Shanghai: Shang-hai ku-chi, 1981), 4:85; Tai Chen (1724-77), "Chi-wu Wang hsien-sheng mu-chih-ming." 輯五王先生墓誌銘 (Epitaph for Mr. Wang Chi-wu), in *Tai Chen chi* 戴震集 (Collected works of Tai Chen), (Shanghai: Shang-hai ku-chi, 1980), 12:249–50. Fraternization and collaboration with examination candidates in adjacent cells appear to have been not unusual. See, for example, *Hsing-shih yin-yuan chuan*, 37:540–50, 38:557; Lu Ta-huang 路大荒, ed., *P'u Sung-ling chi* 蒲松齡集 (Collected works of P'u Sung-ling), (reprint, Shanghai: Shang-hai ku-chi, 1986), 1492–96; *Ch'i-lu teng*, 102:950.

28. *HTSL*, 331:3b-15a.

29. *HTSL*, 331:8a–b.

30. Ch'ien Ta-hsin 錢大昕 (1728–1804), *Shih-chia chai yang-hsin lu* 十駕齋養新錄 (Miscellaneous notes by Ch'ien Ta-hsin), (reprint, Shanghai: Shang-wu, 1957), 18:431.

31. See *YCTL*, 142.

32. See Benjamin A. Elman, *From Philosophy to Philology: Intellectual and Social Aspects of Change in Late Imperial China* (Cambridge, Mass.: Harvard University Press, 1984), 129–33.

33. *Cheng Pan-ch'iao wai-chi*, 31–32.

34. *Hsing-shih yin-yuan chuan*, 35:510–51.

35. Wu Ching-tzu 吳敬梓, *Ju-lin wai-shih* 儒林外史 (Peking: Tso-chia, 1955), 11: 112. The translation is that of Yang Hsien-i and Gladys Yang in *The Scholars* (Peking: Foreign Languages Press, 1957), 11:173. A more subtle form of the same argument is found in the letters of Yuan Mei 袁枚 (1716–98). Yuan, himself no admirer of the examination essay, still stressed the importance of mastery of the essay format, pointing out that success in the examinations was a prerequisite for greater scholarly achievement and lasting fame. See "Yü Fu-chih hsiu-ts'ai ti-erh shu" 與傅之秀才第二 書, (Second letter of licentiate Fu-chih), in *Hsiao-ts'ang shan-fang wen-chi* 小倉山房文集 (Prose works of Yuan Mei), (Shanghai: Shang-hai ku-chi, 1988) 31:1860–61.

36. See Wang T'ing-chen 汪廷珍, "Hsueh-yueh wu-tse" 學約五則 (Five examination protocols), in Sheng K'ang 盛康, comp., *Huang-ch'ao ching-shih wen-pien hsu-pien* 皇朝經世文編續編 (Continuation of the compilation of Ch'ing dynasty essays on statecraft), (reprint, Taipei: Wen-hai, 1972), 4:15a.

37. *"Hsing-li ts'ui-yen lu* pa-yü" 性理粹言錄跋語 (Colophon to Quintessential Says on Nature and Principle), reprinted in *YCTL*, 92.

38. For another contemporary criticism of their blinkered vision and pedestrian scholarship, see Yuan Mei, "Ta Yin Ssu-ts'un shu" 答君似村書 (Letter in reply to Yin Ssu-ts'un), in *Hsiao-ts'ang shan-fang wen-chi*, 19:1560–61.

39. *Yueh-wei ts'ao-t'ang pi-chi* 2:34, 4:78, 15:362, 16:403.

40. See "Pai-kuang" 白光 (White light), in *Lu Hsun ch'üan-chi* 魯迅全集 (Complete works of Lu Hsun), (Peking: Jen-min wen-hsueh, 1956), 1:124. The translation is that of Yang Xianyi and Gladys Yang in *The Complete Stories of Lu Xun* (Bloomington: Indiana University Press, 1981), 123.

41. For adage, see Wang Yu-kuang 王有光, ed., *Wu-hsia yen-lien* 吳下諺聯 (Proverbs and verses of the Wu region), (reprint, Peking: Chung-hua 1982), 2:53. The saying was still current in the late nineteenth century; see Arthur H. Smith, *Village Life in China* (New York: Fleming H. Revell, 1899), 74. On teaching as the refuge of men without prospects, see Anthony J. La Vopa, *Prussian Schoolteachers: Profession and Office, 1763–1848* (Chapel Hill: University of North Carolina Press, 1980), 3.

42. Chung-li Chang, *The Income of the Chinese Gentry* (Seattle: University of Washington Press, 1962), 101.

43. Smith, *Village Life*, 94.

44. Ibid., 74.

45. Evelyn S. Rawski, *Education and Popular Literacy in Ch'ing China* (Ann Arbor: University of Michigan Press, 1979), 54–61.

46. *Hsing-shih yin-yuan chuan*, 33:486.

47. *Ju-lin wai-shih*, 36:353, 46:453.

48. *Ju-lin wai-shih*, 2:16–22. The scholar Hsu P'eng-tzu finds himself in a similar predicament in the seventeenth-century short story collection *Yuan-yang chen* 鴛鴦針 (Embroidery needle), (reprint, Shen-yang: Ch'un-feng wen-i, 1985), 24–26.

49. La Vopa, *Prussian Schoolmasters*, 3. This image of the teacher in China was not of course uniquely a Ch'ing phenomenon. As Wu Pei-yi has noted, the stereotype was already taking shape during the Sung period. See Wu's "Education of Children in the Sung," in *Neo-Confucian Education: The Formative Stage*, ed. Wm. Theodore de Bary and John W. Chaffee (Berkeley: University of California Press, 1989), 317–18.

50. Ibid., 88.

51. See P'u Sung-ling 蒲松齡, *Hsueh-chiu tzu-ch'ao* 學究自嘲, in *Liao-chai li-ch'ü hsuan* 聯齋俚曲選 (Selected dramas of P'u Sung-ling), (Chi-nan: Ch'i-lu, 1980), 9. Identical lines are found in a poem entitled "Chiao-kuan shih" 教館詩 (Poem on tutoring) that has been attributed to Cheng Hsieh and which is included in *Cheng Pan-ch'iao chi*, 209. This ascription lacks support, however, and has been largely discredited: see *Cheng Pan-ch'iao wai-chi*, 349–50. The poem is omitted from *Cheng Pan-ch'iao ch'üan-chi* 鄭板橋全集 (Complete works of Cheng Hsieh), ed. Pien Hsiao-hsüan 卞孝萱 (Chi-nan: Ch'i-lu, 1985).

52. Ibid. In addition to the works by P'u cited in this paper, see also his "Liao-chai i-wen 'Chiao-shu tz'u' 'Tz'u-kuan ko' 'Hsien-sheng lun' 'T'ao ch'ing-ying wen'" 聊齋遺文《教書詞》《辭館歌》《先生論》《討青蠅文》 (Rediscovered writings by P'u Sung-ling), in *Wen-hsien* 文獻 31, no. 1 (1987: 81–85; and "P'u Sung-ling i-wen 'Shu-shih ssu-k'u' 'Hsun meng chüeh' 'Chüan-t'ang wen'" 蒲松齡遺文《塾師四苦》《訓蒙訣》《卷堂文》 (Rediscovered writings by P'u Sung-ling), in *Wen-hsien* 38, no. 4 (1988): 59–63. Urban schoolteachers sometimes suffered similar indignities. See, for example, the set of ten poems on the teacher's fate in early nineteenth-century Peking in the anonymous *Tu-men chu-chih tz'u* 都門竹枝詞 (Bamboo-branch lyrics of the capital), in Lu Kung 路工, ed., *Ch'ing-tai Pei-ching chu-chih tz'u* 清代北京竹枝詞 (Bamboo-branch lyrics of Ch'ing dynasty Peking), (reprint, Peking: Pei-ching ku-chi, 1982), 43–44.

53. *Hsueh-chiu tzu-ch'ao*, 9–13.

54. *Nao-kuan* 鬧館, in *Liao-chai li-ch'ü hsuan*, 99.

55. *Liao-chai chih-i: hui-chiao hui-chu hui-p'ing pen* 聊齋志異會校會注會評本 (Strange tales from Makeshift Studio, varorium edition), ed. Chang Yu-he 張友鶴 (1962; reprint, Shanghai: Shang-hai ku-chi, 1978), 9:1195–96.

56. Smith, *Village Life*, 66–68.

57. Yü Yüeh 俞樾, *I-hsiao* 一笑 (Just for a laugh), reprinted in Wang Li-ch'i 王利器, ed., *Li-tai hsiao-hua chi* 歷代笑話集 (Jokebooks of the imperial past), (Shanghai: Shanghai ku-chi, 1981), 574.

58. *Hsing-shih yin-yuan chuan*, 33:482–83.

59. Wong, *Wu Ching-tzu*, 77.

60. It should be added that a fifth schoolmaster, Chih Chou-wan 智周萬, assumes teaching duties in Chapters 55–56. He is an instructor in the same mould as Lou Ch'ien-chai, and his brief term as tutor does not call for extensive discussion.

61. See, for example, "Pei-chüan" 北卷 (Northern exam books), in *Jih-chih lu*, 17: 16b–17a; *Hsing-shih yin-yuan chuan*, 35:511–12.

GLOSSARY

Chang Lei-ts'un	張類村	Li Ts'un-ch'i	李存其
Ch'en Ch'iao-ling	陳喬齡	Li Yü-huang	李于潢
Ch'en Shih-ch'eng	陳士成	Lou Ch'ien-chai	婁潛齋
Ch'eng Sung-shu	程嵩淑	Ma Ch'un-shang	馬純上
Ch'eng Ying-ts'ai	程英才	Po Lo-t'ien	白樂天
Chin p'ing mei	金瓶梅	*su-hsueh*	俗學
Chou Chin	周進	Su Lin-ch'en	蘇霖臣
Compiler Lu	魯編修	T'an Hsiao-i	譚孝移
Fang Chou	方舟	T'an Shao-wen	譚紹聞
Hou Kuan-yü	侯冠玉	*T'ao-hua shan*	桃花扇
Hsi-hsiang chi	西廂記	*t'ung-sheng*	童生
Hui Yang-min	惠養民	Wang Po-hou	王伯厚
K'ung Shang-jen	孔尚任	Wang-shih	王氏
K'ung Yün-hsüan	孔耘軒	Yü Yu-ta	余有達
Li Ch'ü	李蘧	Yü Yü-te	虞育德
Li Hai-kuan	李海觀		

THREE

Education for Its Own Sake
Notes on Tseng Kuo-fan's *Family Letters*

Kwang-Ching Liu

The importance of Tseng Kuo-fan in modern Chinese history is well known. It is also well known that he believed in the intellectual and moral influence of the elite — the influence of "one or two who are both good and wise" in shaping the customs and standards of an age. His short essay "On the Origins of Talent" (*Yuan ts'ai*), which has been assigned for memorization by students in contemporary Taiwan and Hong Kong, testifies to his belief in goodness and intellectualism, in ethical teaching and statecraft, in the Classics and literary writing.[1] Tseng held strongly and persuasively to standards for all three areas of concern defined by the northern Sung Confucian Liu I (1017–86) —*t'i* (substance), *yung* (function), and *wen* (literature).[2] He was a Confucian of great stature; his devoted service to the state was outstanding. His ideas on education were only partly determined by the existing institutions of his time. His views on the training of the young and of those in early adulthood stemmed from his own scholarship and literary taste and from Confucian social ethics, of which Tseng's entire career was an eloquent confirmation.

This chapter presents an analysis of Tseng's ideas on education, as shown especially in his letters to his brothers and sons.[3] These letters are important not only as the record of a major intellectual and political figure of the nineteenth century but also as writings that had a widespread influence in the late Ch'ing period and on into Republican times. Tseng's family letters and instructions (*chia-shu* and *chia-hsun*), as part of Tseng's *Collected Writings*, first published in 1879, were reprinted in several later editions. The biographical chronicle of Tseng, first published with *Collected Writings*, was set in movable type by a Shanghai publisher and went through six editions by 1924. The *Family Letters* (including *Family Instructions*) were available in popular editions dated, for example, 1905 and 1943. Short extracts from *Family Letters* were published in the *Selected Good Words of Tseng Kuo-fan* (*Chia-yen ch'ao*), compiled by Liang Ch'i-ch'ao in 1927 and available, for example, in a 1935 edition.[4]

TABLE 3.1   Tseng Kuo-fan's Brothers and Sons

Brothers

Tseng Kuo-fan, 1811–72
Tseng Kuo-huang, 1820–85 ("fourth brother," ranked among a larger group of
   cousins)
Tseng Kuo-hua, 1822–58 ("sixth brother")
Tseng Kuo-ch'üan, 1824–90 ("ninth brother")
Tseng Kuo-pao (renamed Chen-kan), 1828–63 ("The youngest brother")

Sons

Tseng Chi-tse, 1839–90
Tseng Chi-hung, 1848–81

SOURCES: *Hsiang-hsiang Tseng-shih wen-hsien* (Documents of the Tseng Family of Hsiang-hsiang, Hunan) (Taipei: Hsueh-sheng, 1965) 1: Front matter, 10; *Tseng Kuo-fan chia-shu* (Family letters of Tseng Kuo-fun) (Changsha: Yueh-lu shu-she, 1985) 2:905; *Tseng Kuo-fan jih-chi* (Diaries of Tseng Kuo-fan) (Changsha: Yueh-lu shu-she, 1986) 2:832.

Readers of Tseng's *Family Letters* will find an infinite concern for details of family life and an inexhaustible solicitude. Yet a few of Tseng's intellectual and literary concerns stand out. This chapter explores the area between Tseng's intellectual biography and his family history. Briefly analyzed here are Tseng's letters to his four brothers, especially in the period 1840–51, and his letters to his two sons, especially those written in the period 1856–66 (table 3.1). So much material exists on Tseng and his family that this chapter can serve only as a preliminary survey. The attention Tseng paid to the education of his daughters is discussed elsewhere and is touched upon only incidentally here. [5]

THE HANLIN SCHOLAR AND HIS BROTHERS

The early life of Tseng Kuo-fan (1811–72) up to the time he was thirty years old was distinguished chiefly by his examination success and by his concern for family affairs. He passed the prefectural examination and earned the *sheng-yuan* degree in 1833; it was only in the preceding year that his father had received the same degree. Tseng Kuo-fan went on to pass the provincial examination and obtained the *chü-jen* degree in 1834, after a brief period of study at the Yueh-lu Academy in Changsha. In 1838 he passed the metropolitan examination at Peking and was awarded not only the *chin-shih* degree but also Hanlin Academy status. He stayed for a time at his home in Hsiang-hsiang, Hunan, before returning to Peking in late 1839 to take the examination that qualified him as a resident bachelor (*liu-kuan shu chi-shih*) at the Hanlin Academy.[6]

Tseng's extant diaries, which begin in February 1839, reflect his lifelong devotion to poetry and calligraphy and concern with family and friends. While at home as a nonresident bachelor of the Hanlin Academy, he trained himself further in the writing of eight-legged essays and participated in the plans to found a new ancestral hall. He made trips to see his relatives in Hsiang-hsiang county and beyond to collect materials for a new genealogy and to request a loan to finance his trip back to Peking. With his Hanlin Academy status, he was welcome everywhere and was consulted on such matters as purchase of land, the contracting of new tenants, and bringing lawsuits before the magistrate.[7] Tseng's youngest sister and his infant son died of smallpox in 1839. His wife gave birth to another son in December—who was to be Tseng Chi-tse—but Tseng had to leave for Peking later on the same day.[8] He passed the Hanlin Academy examination giving him the status of bachelor in residence in May 1840. He looked for a spacious residence in town and sent for his family. His wife, son, father, and younger brother Kuo-ch'üan were to join him before the New Year. His father returned to Hunan in May 1841.[9] Meanwhile, Tseng Kuo-fan had taken on the duty of the instruction of Kuo-ch'üan (1824–90).

Tseng Kuo-fan himself may have been exposed to the influence of Ch'eng-Chu Neo-Confucianism at an early age. Two friends that he met in Hunan in the mid-1830s, Liu Jung and Kuo Sung-tao, were later to take the Ch'eng-Chu Neo-Confucian position in philosophy.[10] But Tseng Kuo-fan seriously considered the Neo-Confucian formula for self-cultivation only in 1842, when he came under the influence of several high-minded scholars in Peking. One was T'ang Chien, an official originally from Shan-hua, a county of the Changsha prefecture in Hunan, who had served in important provincial posts and was in Peking as a director of the Court of Sacrificial Worship before he retired and returned to Hunan in 1846. Tseng's diary entry for 27 August (11th day of the 7th month) 1841 notes that he bought a copy of Chu Hsi's complete works; on the next day, he read some dozen pages of it. His diary of 30 August describes his meeting with T'ang:

> Mr. T'ang Chien said of himself that he likes to read the *I ching* best. He also said that there are only three branches of learning, namely moral principles (*i-li*), evidential criticism (*k'ao-ho*), and literature (*wen-chang*). Evidential learning often seeks the coarse and misses the refined, taking a narrow viewpoint and engaging in speculation. Literary learning can only be attained by those who are excellent in moral learning. The learning of statecraft (*ching-chi*) is inherent in the learning of moral principles. Mr. T'ang was asked: How is one to begin one's effort at the learning of statecraft? His reply: The learning of statecraft is no more than reading history.[11]

T'ang advised Tseng to read the complete works of Chu Hsi (*Chu-tzu ch'üan-shu*) and to follow a regime of self-cultivation that included control of selfish desires (*ssu-yü*). Tseng notes in his diary that upon hearing T'ang's words, he was suddenly illuminated (*chao-jan jo fa-meng*).

In October of the same year Tseng resolved to put an end to his habit of tobacco smoking at the same time that he persevered in reading Chu Hsi on the subject of self-cultivation. He did not succeed in giving up smoking until a year later, when his extant diaries show him becoming more introspective and critical, under the influence of Wu T'ing-tung (1793–1873), a friend known for his Neo-Confucian attainments, and of Wo-jen (d. 1871), a revered senior colleague.[12] Wo-jen had a distinguished career at the Hanlin Academy. He had served as examiner for the metropolitan examinations and was in 1844 director of the Court of Judicature and Revision. Wo-jen was especially respected for his exemplary self-effacing life-style and he taught Tseng the use of the diary as a means of self-criticism with the aim of moral attainment. Tseng began to criticize his own habits and words and indeed submitted his diaries for Wo-jen's inspection, on the top margins of which the latter wrote terse comments. Wo-jen in turn showed Tseng his own journal and Tseng noted in his diary that he was "overwhelmed with admiration for Wo-jen's overflowingly sincere sentiment of filiality and fraternal respect (hsiao-t'i)."[13] Tseng committed himself to a moral purpose in life (li-chih). He set for himself a regime of getting up early, reading the Classics or history, practicing calligraphy, and being modest and sincere in his contacts with people.[14] Tseng did not succeed in all his goals. He tried quiet-sitting but found that he became weary and fell asleep. He tried to adopt the perspective that principle or attitude was more important than practical advantage or profit yet, as he admitted to himself, he could not suppress his concern for practical gain or loss (huan-te huan-shih) and for his status and reputation. Tseng liked to make his presence felt in literary and bureaucratic circles. He was conscious of the material reciprocity in social life and engaged in flattery of his superiors. Tseng never seems to have taken up seriously the struggle between principle and desire; he never seems to have suppressed the latter.[15] Yet the fact that he would criticize himself for being hypocritical indicates that his self-training had realized some of the Ch'eng-Chu goals. Tseng was probably never a succesful mystic, yet he was able to affirm with the force of a deepened conviction the rituals and ethics with which he was brought up and which his office in the Hanlin Academy further sanctified. He continued, moreover, to assign very high value to good literature and take seriously the aims of Confucian education.[16]

For more than a year in 1841–42, he took on the tutoring of his brother Kuo-ch'üan whom he addressed sometimes as "ninth brother." Kuo-ch'üan, now eighteen, had had considerable schooling at home in Hsiang-hsiang. He stayed with his elder brother in Peking until September 1842 and was taught some fu rhyme prose and poetry as well as model essays of the eight-legged style, chosen from such anthologies as Erh-shih-ssu chia shih-wen (Composition of the examination style by twenty-four writers) and Chih-i ts'un-chen chi (A collection of authentic examination compositions). Kuo-ch'üan was asked to review Shih-ching (Book of poetry), Li-chi (Book of rites) and Chou-li (Rites of Chou). For history he was taught Kang-chien i-chih lu, a simplified version of Tzu-chih t'ung-chien (Complete mirror for aid in government), in addition to Han-shu

(History of the Han dynasty) and *Hou-Han shu* (History of the later Han dynasty). An anthology of prose and poetry of the ancient style, including those of Tu Fu, Han Yü, and Su Shih, entitled *Ssu-wen ching-hua* (Essential anthology of refined literature) was also taught.[17] A few pages from these works would be marked out by Tseng Kuo-fan every morning for his brother to read. A principal goal was the ability to write the eight-legged essay (see also Guy, chap. 5 of this volume). Tseng Kuo-fan would assign the topics, usually a phrase from the Four Books, and would edit the essays Kuo-chüan produced with only occasional praise.[18]

Kuo-fan's personal instruction of Kuo-ch'üan was not altogether successful. According to Kuo-fan, during the time that his brother lived with him in Peking, Kuo-ch'üan seems to have made progress only in calligraphy. He was often sulky, quarreled with the servants, and expressed his wish to return to Hunan. Kuo-fan finally consented to let him go, confessing to his other brothers, who were at home in Hunan, that among the Five Relations (*wu-lun*) he himself had failed in his duty as a brother. "Father has taught me all that he knows, but I am unable to teach all that I know to my brother; this is grossly unfilial."[19]

Although apologetic, Tseng was also didactic. All four of his brothers in Hunan, including Kuo-ch'üan, were preparing for examinations. Kuo-fan encouraged them to do so, but beginning in October 1842, at about the same time that he himself was making a serious effort at self-cultivation in the Ch'eng-Chu mode, a new theme emerges in his letters to them: the value of study as an end in itself, not simply as a means of success in the examinations.

Tseng shared with his brothers his new realization that one should establish a purpose for one's life (*li-chih*) and that one should develop insights (*shih*) as well as constancy and perseverance (*heng*). Moreover, the fulfillment of filial and fraternal responsibilities was the overriding consideration. Addressing himself especially to Kuo-ch'üan, the oldest brother wrote, "to read only anthologies of examination essays is to allow one's inner spirit to be suffocated (*ku-mo hsing-ling*)."

Tseng repeatedly wrote to his brothers that studying had two purposes — to advance virtue (*chin-te*) and to prepare for a vocation (*hsiu-yeh*). The civil service examination would lead to a vocation, of course, but it was not the only one. The scholar's vocation could secure livelihood not only through an official career but also as a local teacher or as a staff member of an official (*ch'uan-shih chih k'e, ju-mu chih pin*).[20] The official career was to be preferred, but whether one passed the examination was a matter for Heaven to decide. What one could count on was the effort one made and the proficiency one acquired. Such ability and skill would enable one to earn degrees if such was Heaven's will. If not, such training would still enable one to earn a livelihood.

If the farmer works hard at plowing, there may still be famines, but there will surely be years of good harvest. If the merchant adds to his stock of merchandise, there may be times when sales are slow, but there will surely be times when the market is unimpeded. If the scholar is excellent in his vocation (*yeh*), how could it be that he will never obtain a degree? Even if he never obtains one, are there not other paths to livelihood? Therefore, the problem lies in one's not being excellent in work (*yeh*).[21]

In what way can the scholar attain excellence? The advice Tseng Kuo-fan gave his brothers in 1842 was to concentrate (*chuan*, i.e., "specialize") in one thing at a time. In the case of Tseng Kuo-ch'üan, who was very interested in calligraphy, he should pay special attention to that without abandoning other studies. While concentrating on calligraphy, he might receive "inspiration at any time and on any subject." He who was interested in the Classics should specialize in one Classic. If one was especially interested in the eight-legged essay, one should read such essays by one author; if interested in prose of the ancient style (*ku-wen*), one should read the collected works of a single author of prose in that style. Kuo-fan asked his brothers to write him about their respective special interests and send him their compositions.[22] Kuo-fan's letters to his brothers were always addressed to all those who were at home in Hsiang-hsiang — in the instance quoted above, all four of them. Tseng wrote in this letter, dated 21 October 1842, that thenceforth he would write them on uniform stationery so that the letters could eventually be bound in volumes neatly.

Kuo-fan was also concerned about the instruction his brothers were receiving and the friends with whom they associated. Their father, Tseng Lin-shu (1790–1857), had been tutoring his sons through the 1840s, but should not the help of other tutors be enlisted? Should one or more of the brothers go to the urban centers of Hengyang or Changsha for schooling, perhaps seeking employment as a tutor at the same time? When such questions were raised, Kuo-fan would offer advice and help, but he would also raise the question of each brother's life purpose. He would remind his brothers that in Hengyang, for example, one was likely to meet friends with evil habits who would exert a harmful influence. In any case, it was one's own sense of purpose that was important, wherever one might be. Citing Mencius and the Sung Neo-Confucians, Tseng expounded on the importance of broad concern for humanity and of combining sagehood with service to the state — such were the high purposes of the gentleman. One should always aim at making one's parents happy and spreading moral influence to every community.[23] Referring especially to the sense of grievance of Kuo-hua (1822–58), "the sixth brother," who had failed in his recent try for the prefectural examination, Kuo-fan urged introspection on Kuo-hua's part; he should improve himself before the next try so that he would become truly worthy. Tseng stressed the moral purpose of the civil service examination system:

> The court selects scholars according to their examination essays (*chih-i*). Because they are to speak on behalf of the sages and worthies, they must know the principles of the sages and worthies and act according to the conduct of the sages and worthies. As officials, they govern the people; they rectify themselves and they lead others. If one should regard the "manifestation of virtue" and the "renovation of the people" as beyond one's own capacity, then even though one can write prose and poetry, one is still quite hazy and ignorant of the way of cultivating oneself and governing others. If the court should employ such persons as officials, how would this differ from employing swineherds instead?[24]

Although defending the examination system, Tseng nevertheless felt that the eight-legged essay was limited as a vehicle for self-cultivation. He advised his brothers to heed the importance, above all, of filial and fraternal respect:

> The greatest knowledge lies nowhere but in the daily conduct of the family (*chia-t'ing jih-yung chih chien*). If one fulfills 10 percent of one's filial and brotherly duties, 10 percent will be gained; if one fulfills 100 percent of such duties, then 100 percent will be gained. People today study only for the sake of the examination degrees; it seems that the major concerns of filiality and brotherly respect and of personal relations and bonds (*lun-chi*) have nothing to do with the books. It is not realized that what the books have recorded and what one says on behalf of the sages and worthies in one's literary compositions are none other than the exposition of such principles.[25]

Again, although Tseng defended the examination system, he told his brothers that from the standpoint of moral self-cultivation the ancient prose style (*ku-wen*) was of greater value than the eight-legged essay. In 1844, Tseng advised Kuo-hua, who continued to aspire to win examination degrees at more than twenty years of age, that he should broaden his studies beyond the eight-legged essay to include writers of the ancient prose style:

> It would be wonderful if you, the sixth brother, should be enrolled in the county school (*ju-p'an*), but if by any small chance you are not admitted, you should give up all that you have previously learned and concentrate on studying the prose of the great authors of an earlier generation (*ch'ien-pei ta-chia*). Age twenty is not young. If you continue to lean on the familiar and dissipate all effort on small and truncated themes, time will pass and still you will not be excellent in your work (*yeh*); you will regret that you have been ill advised. You must make plans early. [26]

Tseng's letters in the mid-1840s show that he increasingly regarded studying the Classics and history and composing essays and poetry to be ends in themselves. He believed that in studying the Classics it is of primary importance to seek moral truth, not simply to interpret every passage according to the commentaries. He felt that one must try to grasp the meaning of each passage in the Classics before going on to the next:

In the pursuit of the Classics it is necessary to concentrate on one Classic and not to be spread thin. In studying the Classics, the fundamental is to seek the moral truth (*i-li*); the evidential research of names and things (*k'ao-chü ming-wu*) is secondary. In studying the Classics, the secret is to be patient. Until one understands one sentence, one will not read the next. If one does not understand it today, one reads it again tomorrow. If one is not refined in understanding this year, one reads it again next year.[27]

As for history, the secret is to specialize in the history of one period or dynasty and to immerse oneself in the specific human situation of the time studied:

> The most wonderful method of reading history is to put oneself in the specific situation (*she-shen ch'u-ti*). When one reads about one situation, it seems as if one were conversing and joking with the people of the time. It is not necessary to remember what everybody said; just remember what one of them said and it will be as if one were in contact with that person. It is not necessary to remember all events; just remember one of them and it will be as if one were part of it oneself.[28]

In addition to the Classics and history, it is also important to study the philosophers and the literary writers. Here again one must specialize, concentrating at any given time on one author. One should not open one book here and another one there: "For example, if one reads the collected writings of Han Yü, then what one sees with one's eyes and hears with one's ears should be Han Yü and him alone, as if between heaven and earth there is no book except for Han Yü's collected writings. Until one completes the reading of this collection, one should not read the works of other writers."[29]

For eight years beginning in 1843, Tseng Kuo-fan was very successful in the imperial bureaucratic world of Peking. He was given a position in the Grand Secretariat in 1843 and also acted as an expositor (*shih-tu*) of the Hanlin Academy; he read examinations given at the academy and traveled to Szechwan as imperial commissioner for the provincial examination that autumn.[30] In 1844, he participated in the imperial seminar (*ching-yen*) and was formally appointed expositor of the Hanlin Academy. In 1845 he was made a deputy supervisor of instruction at the Supervisorate of Imperial Instruction and a diarist in the Office of the Emperor's Daily Schedule. In 1847, he received the unusual promotion to subchancellor of the Grand Secretariat with the title of junior vice president of the Board of Rites. This was followed in 1849 with appointment as junior vice president of the Board of Rites, concurrently acting junior vice president of the Board of War. Meanwhile, in accordance with a carefully planned schedule, he continued his daily reading of the Classics, history, and literature. The introspective, self-critical tone had, however, all but disappeared from his diary. He seems to have achieved greater self-confidence and equilibrium in his intellectual and moral quest.

Writing to his brothers in 1844, Tseng said that he had confidence in his own attainments in poetry and prose and regretted only that there was no one "of the caliber of Han Yü and Wang An-shih among the contemporaries who can test me out."[31] He sent to his brothers a copy of the *Five Admonitions* (*Wu chen*), written by him in early 1844, which urged the Ch'eng-Chu procedure of self-cultivation—setting oneself a purpose in life, maintaining a mental state of reverence and of tranquility, being careful in choosing what one said, and adhering to daily routine.[32] But he did not elaborate on such matters. Instead, he merely advised the brothers to read more broadly and to follow the norms of rituals.

In apparent contradiction to his earlier advice on the need to specialize, Tseng stressed repeatedly that reading widely would not hurt and could only contribute to one's ability to write the eight-legged essay. Whether one passes the examination, he repeatedly said, is for Heaven to decide.[33] Yet one can help oneself by expanding one's knowledge as well as writing skills, for otherwise "as one grows older, one not only does not attain an examination degree, but there is no real knowledge to rely on; in the future one cannot even be a private tutor (*shu-shih*). Whether it be the Classics, history, or collections of poems or prose, one should read some twenty pages a day."[34]

Tseng often returned to the theme of providence in the examinations. But he also argued sometimes that those whose essays were "excellent" would in time be recognized. He gave himself as an example of one who had been lucky in being chosen.[35] There is perhaps an element of Calvinist ethic in Tseng's belief that "in the examination hall there are those whose essays are inferior and who are fortunate to pass but there is never someone whose essay is excellent and who is never to be recognized."[36] Destiny is predetermined, yet excellence in work (*yeh*) must be proven. Tseng asked his brothers to report to him how many essays and poems each had written every month and asked them to send him their work so that he could have a good teacher in Peking go over them.[37]

Tseng kept his brothers up to date on his own thinking on intellectual issues. In late October 1844, Tseng asked his family to deliver to his old Hunanese friend Liu Jung a letter in which he discussed his positions regarding the scholarly and literary tendencies of his time. Tseng asked his brothers to make copies of the letter and to study it.[38] In literary matters, Tseng acknowledged that he was following the lead of Yao Nai (1732–1815) in his preference for prose writers such as Ssu-ma Ch'ien and Han Yü and poets like Tu Fu and Su Shih. Like Yao Nai, Tseng believed in the importance of self-cultivation yet argued that literary cultivation is a part of the larger process; one needs to understand the written language of the ancient sages to come closer to knowing what they meant. Tseng wanted to combine the essences of the Sung and Han Learning by understanding and capturing the subtleties of tone, rhythm, and rhyme in the ancient literary heritage. He insisted on a unity between literary quality and moral content in each piece of writing, and indeed unity between writings and the writer's conduct in life. Stressing literature more than philosophy, Tseng declared that he "especially cannot agree with those Confucians who exalt the Way at the expense of literature (*ch'ung-tao pien-wen*)." Literature is indeed the "vehicle of the Way" (*wen i tsai tao*), now as in the past:

> Chou Tun-i (1017–73) believes that literature is a vehicle of truth, but he criticizes the vulgar scholars as having only empty vehicles. Indeed one must not have empty vehicles, but without any vehicle, can one go far? That the Way has been preserved to the present, long after the death of Confucius and Mencius, is thanks to the vehicle's going far. If we have some insights today and want them to go a long way, should we not try to build sturdy vehicles right away?[39]

Tseng felt that the ancient prose style that was exemplified in the Classics and histories and continued by such T'ang writers as Han Yü was unquestionably superior. Despite his earlier advice to concentrate their reading on one author only, in 1845 we find Tseng sending copies of a number of anthologies to his brothers. These included *Tzu-shih ching-hua* (Selections from philosophical and historical works), *Han-Wei pai-san chia wen-chi* (Anthology drawn from 103 authors of Han and Wei times), and *Ku wen-tz'u lei-tsuan* (Classified anthology of ancient prose style), compiled by Yao Nai.[40]

Tseng's letters to his brothers show his concern not only for their literary training but also for family affairs. He wanted his brothers and their wives to observe rituals and rules of behavior meticulously.[41] They must rise early, work hard, and be in general respectful and serious (*ching*). Tseng enthusiastically recommended Ch'en Hung-mou's *Wu-chung i-kuei* (Inherited rules and regulations in five categories) as required reading for all the brothers and especially Kuo-huang ("the fourth brother"), who was to take over the management of the household from their father in 1847 (see also Rowe, chap. 12 of this volume). Tseng wrote to Kuo-huang:

> At present I am not at home and hope that you will be in charge (*tso-chu*) of everything. Disharmony among brothers will be your fault, differences among sisters-in-law will be your fault, overbearing demeanor and breaches of rule among the younger generation will be your fault. I have three recommendations: First, be industrious; second, rise early in the morning; and third, study *Wu-chung i-kuei*. If you will abide by such advice you will be loving and respecting me. If you do not, you will be rejecting and trivializing me.[42]

In 1845, all four brothers—Kuo-huang, Kuo-hua, Kuo-ch'üan, and Kuo-pao— passed the county examination. In this test, Kuo-ch'üan earned the third highest score, and the other three brothers were among the top twenty. But the next step, the prefectural examination, was far more difficult. In 1846, first Kuo-hua and then Kuo-huang traveled to Peking and purchased the *chien-sheng* degree. In 1847, Kuo-ch'üan ("the ninth brother") passed the prefectural examination that enabled him to enroll in the county school; in the following year, he passed a further examination and became a salaried licentiate (*lin-sheng*). In 1849, Kuo-pao ("the youngest brother") passed the prefectural examination. The brothers were now all grown up; the youngest, Kuo-pao, was twenty-one. Instead of stressing studying, Tseng's letters to the brothers now dwelt more often on questions of lineage relationships, marriage plans for the younger generation, and the appropriate rituals and family rules.[43] In addition to *Wu-chung i-kuei*, he recommended Lü K'un's *Shen-yin yü* (Groaning words) as containing valuable advice on family affairs. Undoubtedly reflecting his increasing interest in the exegesis of passages in the Classics, Tseng arranged in 1849 to have a copy of Juan Yuan's *Huang Ch'ing ching-chieh* (Ch'ing exegesis of the Classics) delivered to his brothers. Tseng wrote them that they would do well to "dip into the work and look through it" (*lueh-i she-lieh*).[44]

Tseng was rising to important posts at court. In 1850, he was promoted to acting senior vice president of the Board of Works and, concurrently, acting senior vice president of the Board of War. In 1851, he was made acting senior vice president of the Board of Punishments, and in early 1852 he became acting senior vice president of the Board of Civil Office. Amidst all these duties, he managed to find time to compile an anthology of eighteen poets from Ts'ao Chih to Lu Yu.[45] He began to compile a compendium on institutions relating to economic statecraft that would supplement the great *Wu-li t'ung-k'ao* (Compendium on rituals in five categories) by Ch'in Hui-t'ien (1702–64), but it was never completed.[46]

Perusal of Ch'in's work convinced Tseng of the importance of ritual in binding together state and family, moral aspiration and practice. He was pleased when in 1851 his youngest brother, Kuo-pao, wrote that he was interested in moral and introspective studies (*tao-i shen-hsin chih hsueh*).[47] Tseng commended his brother for his aspiration to become sage and worthy, yet the reading he prescribed for the attainment of this goal consisted of two works that especially emphasized ritual and ethics — Chu Hsi's *Hsiao-hsueh* (Elementary learning) and *Wu-chung i-kuei*. In Tseng's view, a requirement of sagehood is the internalization of the proper rituals and rules of behavior. Despite his earlier advice to his brothers that they should read widely, he now counseled concentration on the ritual handbooks:

I am so happy to have received Kuo-pao's letter. There is no one who cannot be sage and worthy; this does not depend on the number of books read. If such indeed is your purpose, you should read thoroughly both *Hsiao-hsueh* and *Wu-chung i-kuei*. In addition, it would be good if you could read other books, but there will be no immediate loss if you do not read other books. One can be a perfect person between Heaven and Earth (*t'ien-ti chih wan-jen*) and a good son to one's parents; it is not necessarily true that reading books will add anything to this. Not only does one not have to read prose of the parallel style (*ssu-liu*) and poetry in the ancient style, even not reading prose in the ancient style which you want to learn will not really matter. What is important is to abide by the two books *Hsiao-hsueh* and *Wu-chung i-kuei*.[48]

THE STATESMAN-COMMANDER AND HIS SONS

Tseng Kuo-fan's effort to educate his brothers for greater examination success did not end as expected. The two older brothers, Kuo-huang and Kuo-hua, could boast only of the purchased *chien-sheng* degree. Kuo-hua, especially, was melancholic after repeated failures in the prefectural examination. The two younger brothers, Kuo-ch'üan and Kuo-pao, did pass the prefectural examination and win the *sheng-yuan* degree, but their aspirations, too, remained frustrated until the Taiping rebellion presented the Tseng family with new opportunities. As is well known, in 1852 Tseng Kuo-fan abandoned his journey to Kiangsi, where he was to serve as the provincial examiner, to return home to mourn his mother—only to find that Changsha, the provincial capital of Hunan, was being threatened by the Taipings. In their native county of Hsiang-hsiang, all his brothers now practiced martial arts and were involved in the organization of local defense forces, at least for a few months in 1852–53. Kuo-fan himself, with the support of Chang Liang-chi, governor general of Hupei and Hunan, and the authorization of the throne, now emerged as a principal organizer of the new Ch'ing forces that turned the tide in the war against the rebels. Three of Tseng's brothers—Kuo-ch'üan, Kuo-hua, and Kuo-pao—were to join the war effort, the latter two losing their lives before the war's end, while Kuo-ch'üan commanded the army that marched into Nanking in 1864 under the direction of Tseng Kuo-fan himself.[49]

The story of the Tseng brothers as enemies of the mid-nineteenth-century rebellions remains to be thoroughly researched. The role of the Tseng family as local gentry also deserves further study. Beginning in the mid-1840s, Tseng Kuo-fan's letters repeatedly urged his father and uncle as well as his brothers to pay taxes dutifully and not to interfere in lawsuits and other local affairs. Tseng's father negotiated with the local officials in 1851 for fair tax rates for large areas of the county, apparently at the expense of the yamen clerks and runners. Later in the same year, Kuo-fan himself sought to influence "the higher reaches" of bureaucracy to prolong the tenure of a local official of prefectural rank. Evidence indicates that Tseng's interest in the affairs of his home county continued long after he took up military leadership; this story also awaits further research. The account of Tseng's war years in the following pages focuses on his continuing intellectual interests and the requirements he made of his sons as shown in his regular correspondence with them.

Because Tseng's diaries for the period 1845–58 have not been fully preserved, it is difficult to trace precisely changes in his views on scholarship and education during this period. It is safe to say, however, that after he wrote his famous letter to Liu Jung in October 1844, in which he protested against those of the Ch'eng-Chu school who would pursue philosophical truth without a commensurate emphasis on literature, his own views on literature developed further. He had begun to read the philological studies of Wang Nien-sun (1744–1832) and others with great admiration. He even tried his own hand at evidential research regarding *I ching* (Book of changes), *Shih-ching* (Book of poetry), *Shih-chi* (Historical record), and *Han-shu* (History of the former Han dynasty), projects which he did not pursue for long.[50] While his endorsement of Ch'ing philological studies was not unreserved, he held the Han-hsueh discipline in high esteem and found that both it and the Ch'eng-Chu moral message had contributed to the preservation of proper ritual and institutions to which he would dedicate his life.

Tseng's writings in the late 1840s indicate that he was critical of the evidential scholars who merely did "fractured studies" (*p'o-sui chih hsueh*), some even tendentiously aiming at dismantling the Ch'eng-Chu metaphysical edifice. Like his friend Liu Ch'uan-ying, upon whose death in 1848 he wrote several commemorative essays, Tseng continued to respect the introspective Ch'eng-Chu approach and its emphasis on moral action and self-cultivation. He also respected evidential research, not only as a discipline in itself, but also as a way to affirm the correctness of ancient ritual that constituted a source of moral life. Despite the fragmentary nature of Han Learning as practiced in the mid-Ch'ing period, it had contributed to the clarification of ritual practices that were essential to the "daily conduct of Five Relations and Five Constant Virtues (*lun-ch'ang jih-yung*)." Tseng agreed wholeheartedly with Liu Ch'uan-ying's statement that "rituals are clearly established only through evidential research, while learning is not accomplished until there is insight (*hsin-te*, lit., "what the heart-and-mind attains").[51] What Tseng himself added to this dual emphasis on evidential and moral learning was a concern for good literature. Amidst his arduous and often perilous life during the military campaigns, Tseng was often able to maintain a program of daily reading that included the familiar Classics, historical works, prose, and poetry, especially writings in the ancient style.[52] The belief system to which Tseng adhered and his literary tastes are reflected in his regular correspondence with his son Chi-tse, who lived with his mother in the family home in Hsiang-hsiang.

Chi-tse (1839–90) had started his schooling at the age of five in 1844, when his parents lived in Peking.[53] By 1856, when Kuo-fan's regular correspondence with him began, Chi-tse was seventeen and had studied the basic Classics and history, including *Shih-chi*. Tseng brought essentially the same message to his sons — some letters were also addressed to his second son, Chi-hung, who was born in 1848 — that he did to his brothers: One must be virtuous, beginning with the performance of family duties, being at all times industrious and frugal. One must rise early and work hard. One must strive for literacy and knowledge and for the scholarly vocation of service to the state. "Wealth and honor and degree-holding are statuses controlled by destiny (*ming*)," he wrote in a letter in October 1856, yet human effort accounts for "one half" of the possibility of success. Moreover, to be a sage or worthy is a matter entirely of human effort and "has nothing to do with Heaven's will (*t'ien-ming*)."[54]

Chi-tse was then about to be married to the daughter of Ho Ch'ang-ling, a fellow Hunanese who was a former governor of Kiangsu. Kuo-fan wrote Chi-tse on 30 October that he wanted Chi-tse's bride to go personally to the kitchen to make soup and to practice spinning and weaving. Just as he would ask his sons to send their essays to be checked by him, he expected his daughter-in-law as well as his daughters at home each to send him a pair of cloth shoes every year, as well as the cloth and socks woven by them.[55]

Chi-tse, having recently read *Shih-chi*, was reading *Han-shu* in early 1857. Kuo-fan was very glad that he seemed to enjoy it but wrote him that to read *Han-shu* properly one must first be versed in philology and scholia (*hsun-ku*). Tseng asked Chi-tse to familiarize himself with Tuan Yü-ts'ai's *Shuo-wen chieh-tzu chu* (Notes to *Shuo-wen chieh-tzu*) and Juan Yuan's *Ching-chi tsuan-ku* (Compendium of scholia to the Classics) and especially *Tu-shu tsa-chih* (Random reading notes) by Wang Nien-sun. In order to understand the prose of the ancient style, of which *Han-shu* is a prime example, one should also read *Wen-hsuan* (Selections of refined literature) as well as Yao Nai's *Ku wen-tz'u lei-tsuan*.[56] Kuo-fan set a syllabus for Chi-tse as follows:

Works that are to be read aloud (*tu*):
    Four Books
    Book of Poetry
    Book of Documents
    Book of Changes
    Tso-chuan
    Wen-hsuan
    Poetry by Li Po, Tu Fu, Han Yü, and Su Shih
    Prose by Han Yü, Ou-yang Hsiu, Tseng Kung, and Wang An-shih
Works that are to be read comparatively rapidly (*k'an*) — examples only:
    Shih-chi
    Han-shu
    Han Yü's prose
    Chin-ssu lu (Reflections on things at hand)
    Chou-i che-chung (Equitable interpretation of *I-ching*)[57]

This was only a partial syllabus, for Kuo-fan wanted Chi-tse to read with his tutor all thirteen of the Classics. In addition he should explore such writings as *Chuang-tzu* and *Sun-tzu* and be familiar with the following reference works and anthologies:

    T'ung-tien (Encyclopedia), by Tu Yu
    Shuo-wen (Analysis of characters), by Hsü Shen
    Tu-shih fang-yü chi-yao (Concise historical geography), by Ku Tsu-yü

Ku wen-tz'u lei-tsuan
Shih-pa chia shih-ch'ao, compiled by Tseng himself[58]

Toward those works to be read aloud, Kuo-fan especially wanted Chi-tse to adopt a humble attitude, soaking himself in each work, submerging and swimming in it (*han-yung*). In reading aloud, one should see that the tones are always very musical (*sheng tiao chieh-chi k'eng-ch'iang*), for the ancient poets always worked hard to get the tones just right. One of them wrote this:

> After I have edited my poem, I sing it long and aloud.

And this:

> I have not succeeded in recasting my poem, yet I sing it long and aloud anyway.[59]

Kuo-fan exhorted Chi-tse not only to practice calligraphy regularly but also to try the various styles of composition — the eight-legged essay on a topic from the Four Books, and poetry in the form required by the examinations, regulated rhapsody (*lü fu*), poetry in the ancient and latter-day styles, prose in the ancient style, and parallel prose.[60]

Despite the plan Tseng had made earlier for Chi-tse not to take the examination until he was twenty-four by Chinese reckoning (see n. 53), he encouraged the latter to take the provincial examination in Changsha in 1858, when he was only twenty by the same reckoning. Chi-tse had the *yin-sheng* status by virtue of his father's high official position; this made it unnecessary to take the "small examinations" (*hsiao k'ao*) at the local level. Kuo-fan told Chi-tse that it did not really matter whether he passed. He failed and afterward wrote his father to ask whether he could put aside the practice of the eight-legged essay. Kuo-fan could only consent, initially, but he told Chi-tse to concentrate on the *fu* rhapsody style, for this style could "transport one to the ancient age and it also fits in with the present times." He made a selection from the *Wen-hsuan* and from the Ch'ing dynasty rhapsodists for Chi-tse to study.[61] Continuing the practice of the examination essays was, however, what Chi-tse's tutor and at least one of his uncles at home had urged him to do, and this requirement was confirmed by Kuo-fan, who wrote Chi-tse in January 1859 that he should send him three eight-legged essays per month through his military courier.[62] Chi-tse's tutor was known to be an expert on the eight-legged essay. Kuo-fan also got a very able essayist who was on his staff, Li Yuan-tu, to edit Chi-tse's essays.

With all this help, Chi-tse was still not enthusiastic. Kuo-fan was disappointed by what he saw of Chi-tse's eight-legged essays. In any case, he avoided the subject and instead wrote to him on such subjects as calligraphy (Chi-tse was often praised for his skill in this), classical studies, and the beauty of *fu* rhapsody of the Han period.[63] Kuo-fan further relented when in March 1860 he wrote Chi-tse that perhaps there was no point in doing the eight-legged essays "heroically." Instead of requiring three eight-legged essays per month, Kuo-fan now asked for only one essay in such form, along with one in the rhapsody form and one in the ancient prose style.[64] Kuo-fan regarded his son as gifted but weak in literary composition. In February 1861, Kuo-fan wrote Chi-tse:

> Your talent for writing poetry and prose is somewhat small. If you had been taught right when you were fifteen or sixteen, it would probably not be this way. This year you are already twenty-three. All depends on your own struggle and drive; your father and your tutor will not be able to help. Poetry and prose are your weak areas and you must make a strong effort to improve them.[65]

Chi-tse continued to find the eight-legged essays repugnant and showed no intention to participate in the examinations again. He had not been idle, however. He had been reading prose in the ancient style and in letters to his father asked questions about that style and about the textual study of the Classics, showing genuine interest.[66] Kuo-fan, who had meanwhile weathered serious military crises, now showed more understanding of Chi-tse and accommodated his new interests.

It is necessary to pause, if briefly, in this narrative and shift the focus back to Tseng Kuo-fan's own intellectual concerns. He seems to have led more than one life. Amidst his arduous and perilous work as commander of a major force against the Taipings, he found time for reading and writing in order to clarify his own thoughts and beliefs while maintaining an extensive correspondence with his family and friends. It seems that there was in him a compulsion to affirm his faith anew. In the winter of 1858–59, in the aftermath of the crisis created by the Taiping victory at San-ho, Anhwei, he made a list of thirty-two sages and worthies and asked Chi-tse to find portraits of them for an album that would also include an essay by Kuo-fan. The thirty-two venerated figures were drawn from China's entire history.[67]

For their sageliness and advocacy of the Way	King Wen
	The Duke of Chou
	Confucius
	Mencius
For their literary or historiographical excellence	Tso Ch'iu-ming
	Chuang-tzu
	Ssu-ma Ch'ien
	Pan Ku
For statecraft	Chu-ko Liang
	Lu Chih
	Fan Chung-yen
	Ssu-ma Kuang
For Confucian philosophy	Chou Tun-i
	Chang Tsai
	Ch'eng I
	Chu Hsi

For achievements in prose	Han Yü Liu Tsung-yuan Ou-yang Hsiu Tseng Kung
For poetry	Li Po Tu Fu Su Tung-p'o (Su Shih) Huang T'ing-chien
For philology	Hsu Shen Cheng K'ang-ch'eng
For scholarship regarding ritual and institutions	Tu Yu Ma Tuan-lin Ku Yen-wu Ch'in Hui-t'ien
For literary and textual criticism	Yao Nai Wang Nien-sun

In an essay entitled "Sheng-che hua-hsiang chi" (Preface to *Portraits of sages and worthies*), which he produced over a three-day period in 1859, he explained the categories according to which the selection of the thirty-two figures had been made—and which have been rephrased in the above list.[68] Tseng admitted that the Sung Neo-Confucian philosophers, including Chu Hsi, were the successors of Confucius and Mencius.[69] He wished to affirm, however, that the study of *li* (ritual and institutions) was the major development since antiquity, reinforced in scholarly works since Tu Yu's *T'ung tien* (Encyclopedia of institutions) in the T'ang dynasty. In these remarks, Tseng offered for the first time his concept of the learning of ritual and institutions (*li-hsueh*). Such learning was inherent, Tseng declared, in all the teachings from the sages of antiquity through the Sung philosophers to the philologists of the Ch'ing dynasty. This continuity was indeed the great achievement of the Ch'ing Confucians:

> Among the scholars of the present dynasty, the preeminent one was Ku Yen-wu [1613–82]. Should the biographies of scholars of the present dynasty be compiled, his will be the first. While reading his works, I have found that whenever he speaks of rituals, customs, and morally transforming influences (*li shu chiao-hua*), he always wants to be the first to go forward and lead others, as if announcing, 'If not myself, then who?' How gallant he was! Later Chang Erh-ch'i [1612–78] wrote his treatise on the *Doctrine of the Mean*, and Chiang Yung [1681–1762] and Tai Chen [1724–77] especially regarded ritual and institutions (*li*) as matters of utmost importance. Thereafter, Board President Ch'in Hui-t'ien [1702–64] wrote *Inquiry into Ritual and Institutions in Five Categories* (*Wu-li t'ung-k'ao*). He has synthesized all the myriad matters under Heaven in ancient

and modern times, whether spiritual or mundane—indeed his work is comprehensive in structure and refined in thought![70]

While Ch'in Hui-t'ien was undoubtedly preeminent, Tseng also praised Yao Nai and Wang Nien-sun, who were not necessarily "perfect" in their scholarship on ritual and institutions. Yao had the broadest vision of the literary heritage, Tseng felt; he had inspired students of literature including himself. Wang, unsurpassed in philology and scholia, was important to the understanding of the Classics. Both deserved to be ranked with the sages and worthies.[71]

Undoubtedly for his own satisfaction and not simply for the sake of his sons' education, Tseng spent most of the time he allotted to reading and writing daily during 1859–60 in preparing a new anthology, *Ching-shih pai-chia tsa-ch'ao* (Random selections from the Classics, history, and various writers).[72] He explains in the preface to this work that although the categories used in his anthology differ from those of Yao Nai's *Ku wen-tz'u lei-tsuan* only slightly, there is nonetheless a substantial distinction in that Tseng includes selections from both the Classics and historical works within each category of ancient prose style. Although Yao's anthology does include excerpts from *Han-shu* under the categories of "Memorials" and "Edicts and Decrees," Yao seems to have set such material apart from the historian's own work.[73] In 1861 Tseng produced a further selection of only forty-eight items from his anthology under the title of *Ching-shih pai-chia chien-pien* (Short anthology of selections from the Classics, history, and various writers). Tseng and his brother Kuo-ch'üan went over the texts in the light of the Ch'ing dynasty scholarship regarding ancient texts. The shorter anthology was meant to be read by "sons and nephews of the whole family."[74]

The works "Sheng-che hua-hsiang chi" and *Ching-shih pai-chia tsa-ch'ao* were to inspire a revival of Confucian scholarship and of ancient prose style of the T'ung-ch'eng school.[75] Yet their immediate effect on Tseng's sons would be impossible to evaluate. Tseng still urged Chi-tse to prepare for the examinations. Although Chi-tse did not respond favorably to the eight-legged essays, he became interested in the commentaries on the Classics, especially Wang Yin-chih's *Ching-i shu-wen* (Report on the meaning of the Classics). However, in April 1859 his father advised him not to read more of this book, since Chi-tse was apparently admiring Wang Yin-chih's evidential research without knowing the texts of the Classics themselves:

I wrote you that it is not necessary to read *Ching-i shu-wen*. Your present letter [of March 1859] says that you have read three volumes (*pen*) of *Ching-i shu-wen*. If you find it interesting and would go on reading it instead of taking something up and then leaving it, it would be good. But you have not yet read the texts of such works as *Chou-li, I-li, Ta-Tai li-chi, Kung-yang, Ku-liang, Erh-ya, Kuo-yü* and *T'ai-sui k'ao*. You may temporarily set aside Wang Yin-chih's *Ching-i shu-wen*.[76]

Although he continued to encourage Chi-tse to work on the eight-legged essay, Kuo-fan seems to have been pleased by Chi-tse's newly awakened scholarly interest. He advised him to keep a journal of reading notes (*tsa-chi*), doing so especially for the Four Books, the Five Classics, and eight works that Kuo-fan himself favored most:

> *Shih-chi*
> *Han-shu*
> *Chuang-tzu*
> Han Yü's prose
> *Tzu-chih t'ung-chien*
> *Wen-hsuan*
> *Ku wen-tz'u lei-tsuan*
> *Shih-pa chia shih-ch'ao*[77]

Chi-tse was also advised to compile a classified list of elegant words and phrases taken from his readings, including the parts of *Shuo-wen* and *Ching-i shu-wen* that he had read. Such a thesaural list would be useful, Kuo-fan said, not only in writing the eight-legged essays but also "as a shortcut to scholarship."[78] Evidently, Kuo-fan still wanted to influence Chi-tse in the direction of further effort regarding examination essays without entirely giving up his interest in philology and textual research.

Chi-tse persisted in being uninterested in the examinations. There was nothing that Kuo-fan could do except accommodate his interest and discuss with him Ch'ing scholarship on the *Book of Documents* (of which Sun Hsing-yen's works were preferred) and on *Tso-chuan* (on which the writings of Ku Yen-wu, Hui Tung, and Wang Yin-chih were considered excellent). Of the notes and commentaries on the Classics in Juan Yuan's edition, Kuo-fan considered those on the three ritual Classics the best and those on the *Book of Poetry* second best; those on the other Classics were of mixed quality.[79] Chi-tse, whose first wife had died in 1857 in childbirth, married again in 1859 when he was twenty. (His new bride was a daughter of Liu Jung, Tseng's old friend.)[80] In addition to routine advice about family life, Kuo-fan exhorted him to read more of *Wen-hsuan*. From the research of Tuan Yü-ts'ai and Wang Nien-sun, Kuo-fan found that characters that were mistakenly employed by the T'ang and Sung authors were used correctly and consistently in the ancient Classics and in *Wen-hsuan*. This had prompted him to include selections from the Classics in his *Ching-shih pai-chia tsa-ch'ao*, compiled in 1860. Kuo-fan was pleased that Chi-tse sent him compositions in the rhapsody style, but that was as far as Chi-tse accommodated Kuo-fan's expectations.[81] At his father's repeated urging, he did come forth in October 1861 with an outline for a classified compilation, but it was not to be a thesaurus. Chi-tse entitled his outline "Shuo-wen fen-yun chieh-tzu fan-li" (Editorial rules regarding analysis of characters according to the rhymes as an explanation of writing). Chi-tse had become an aspiring etymologist and phonologist. Kuo-fan complimented him by saying that beginning in the Sung dynasty writers versed in literature (*wen-chang*) did not know philology, while the philologists of the Ch'ing dynasty were without literary grace. Kuo-fan hoped that Chi-tse would be interested in literature as well as textual studies.[82]

In 1863, Kuo-fan's fifteen-year-old son Chi-hung passed the county examination, ranking first in the list of candidates. (As the second son, Chi-hung did not have the *yin-sheng* status and had to sit for the local examinations.) Kuo-fan praised the winning essay Chi-hung sent him but corrected a few erroneous uses of words representing even or oblique tones (*p'ing-tse*).[83] By this time Kuo-fan realized that Chi-tse, who still refused to take the examinations, probably never would. These were consoling words from a patriarch who was otherwise stern:

> Since you are not interested in degrees and positions with emolument, you must read more of the ancient books. You should frequently hum verses and practice calligraphy so as to foster character and sentiment; there will be enjoyment in store for your lifetime and to spare.[84]

While his studies had been guided by tutors and by his father, what Chi-tse had accepted—and what Kuo-fan now conceded—was education for its own sake, which was after all what Chi-tse enjoyed. Extant samples of his writings are lucid and competent; his poetry of the ancient style is often praised by his father as excellent.[85] The father continued to want him to improve, however. Kuo-fan wrote in the fall of 1862, "If you can understand the scholia of *Han-shu* and combine them with the humor and irony of *Chuang-tzu* in your writings, I shall be satisfied."[86] Whether Chi-tse achieved this is hard to say; he was in any case happy with his own blend of learning and literary tastes.

With his father's encouragement, Chi-tse took on the management of family affairs at home. Although Kuo-fan seems to have sent only moderate sums home to his wife and children, his brothers who had joined the war against the Taipings were able to remit a considerable amount. New houses were built and uncles and cousins moved into them.[87] Kuo-fan had been home for nearly a year in 1857–58 mourning his father and had set the rules for his household. Beginning in April 1860, Chi-tse was the head of his house in Hsiang-hsiang and oversaw finances and other affairs in consultation with his mother and with a household bursar who was referred to as Mr. Chu Yun-ssu. Kuo-fan urged Chi-tse to see to it that the farms be tended, bamboo groves planted, and pigs raised.[88] He asked Chi-tse to be polite and kind to the lineage relatives and to help his mother conduct the annual sacrifices: "Regarding the sincere preparation for sacrifices (*ch'eng hsiu chi-ssu*), your mother needs to give attention at all times. The best of the utensils should be reserved for use at the sacrifices; the best of food and drink should be saved for the needs of the sacrifices. Families that do not do their best in sacrifices, even though prosperous, will not be so for long. This is of the utmost importance!"[89]

As household head, Chi-tse helped to prepare for the weddings of his sisters
(see also Mann, chap. 1 of this volume). He had five sisters who lived to be
adults and the first three were married in 1862. The engagement of the two
eldest daughters had been arranged by Tseng and his wife back in 1847, when
they were little; the third sister's fiancé seems to have been chosen in consultation with two uncles who were at home in 1858–59.[90] At least two of these
marriages did not turn out to be happy. Within six months of the eldest sister's
marriage, Chi-tse reported to his father that her husband, Yuan Ping-chen had
"learned bad ways" (*hsueh huai*), and Kuo-fan wrote to reprimand his
son-in-law.[91] In early 1863 Chi-tse reported that the husband of the third sister,
Lo Chao-sheng, was unruly and perverse in his behavior (*kuai-li*). Kuo-fan was
concerned as to whether he had been violent to his daughter but said that
there was nothing one could do (*wu-k'o ju-ho*). Kuo-fan wrote as a patriarch:

> Please advise your third sister to be yielding, obedient, careful, and respectful
> and that she should not say a word that is unseemly. Of the three bonds, mon-
> arch controls ministers, father controls sons, and husband controls wife; the earth
> stands on these bonds and the pillars of the sky are thus bolstered.... Ours is a
> family of scholars and officials that observes ritual and duty (*li-i*) from one gener-
> ation to the next. Please admonish your first sister and third sister to be patient
> and to suffer obediently.[92]

TSENG KUO-FAN AND HIS FAMILY LEGACY

So much material is available regarding Tseng Kuo-fan's intellectual background and family history that it is difficult to do justice to the subject.[93] This
chapter has merely discussed aspects of one primary source, Tseng's *chia-shu*
and *chia-hsun*, that may contribute to an understanding of education and society in the Ch'ing period. Only occasional references have been made to
Tseng's published diaries and to other of his works. Tseng was a gifted if pon-
derous patriarch who had such energy that he could attend to details of the
education of his brothers and his sons by correspondence. His concern for the
choice of tutors for his brothers, nephews, and sons is documented throughout
the correspondence. This is surely not a singular case. Throughout the length
and breadth of China, there were tutors teaching boys and young men
preparing for the civil service examinations (see also Barr, chap. 2 of this volume). Fathers often participated in this educational process. The potential of
scholars as officials — indeed, as gentry — was important in determining the
quality of education the young men received. In the background there were
also the deeply rooted social ethics that sometimes had the effect of a religion.

This chapter has also shown that Tseng Kuo-fan encouraged his brothers
and sons to seek success through taking civil service examinations. Tseng's
Family Letters embody a view of human effort as a means through which
Heaven's will is fulfilled. One can not only aspire to become sage and worthy

but also hope to insure the success of one's own career through proper and industrious preparation for the examinations. Tseng's letters demonstrate that he used his authority as patriarch to urge his brothers and sons toward such success, yet he was practical enough to see the limitations of this approach. When his brothers and his son Chi-tse either failed to measure up to his expectations or lacked interest in the examinations as a ladder of success, Tseng sensibly although reluctantly allowed them to pursue their own interests within the framework of propriety and rituals. This attitude, along with his intellectual interest in literature of the ancient prose style, may be seen as indicating a human and humanist concern compatible with his socio-ethical premises but exceeding the stuffy Neo-Confucian moralism portrayed in textbooks.

While he urged on his brothers and sons, Tseng pursued his own lifelong self-education. From the letters and essays reviewed here, one gains a sense of the breadth of the intellectual tradition with which a successful nineteenth-century Chinese literatus could identify without reference to the West that was then only beginning to make its presence felt in China. In its own terms, Tseng's canon was broad. For him great literature and scholarship possessed value down through the ages, as the essence of an entire civilization. Education—immersion in the best of the cultural experience—was an end in itself, even as it enhanced a person's social and moral worth.

The results of Tseng's educational efforts were not always those intended. His brother Kuo-ch'üan did win the *sheng-yuan* degree by examination in 1847 and advanced to the status which carried a stipend (*lin-sheng*) the following year. Although his calligraphy was excellent, Kuo-ch'üan was not deeply interested in literature as such and had an opportunity to become a high official thanks only to the unusual opportunities that arose during the period of the Taiping Rebellion.[94] The present evidence points to the fact that he did very well as an official on behalf of his family and lineage. It was in the intervals of his military and administrative service when he returned to Hsiang-hsiang that his family properties expanded the most rapidly.[95] Earlier, Kuo-ch'üan had gone through a self-righteous phase and had been defiant toward and critical of his eldest brother.[96] He was, however, to be the triumphant general who recovered Nanking from the Taipings in 1864. He fought the Niens as governor of Hupeh (1866–67), stayed in Hunan as an eminent member of the gentry (1868–75), built hostels for Hsiang-hsiang candidates taking the examination in Changsha, and donated to the community and charitable granaries in his home county. As governor of Shansi (1877–80), he made an energetic if inadequate effort on behalf of relief work in the great North China famine. He reprinted such books as Chu Hsi's *Elementary Learning* and *Reflections on Things at Hand*, Lü K'un's *Groaning Words*, and Ch'en Hung-mou's *Wu-chung i-kuei*. He served as governor general of Liang-kuang (1882–83) and of Liang-chiang from 1883 to his death in 1890.[97]

His success in official life rivaled that of Tseng Kuo-fan and his solicitude as head of the extended family after Kuo-fan's death in 1872 was to be remembered by his relatives. But how is the elder brother's educational influence on him to be evaluated?

Tseng Kuo-fan's hopes for his sons were at least partly fulfilled. Chi-tse grew up to be a Confucian gentleman, attending to all his duties and intellectual in outlook. His refusal to take the examinations after the first failure showed his strength of character. He regarded education as an end in itself and he was open-minded enough to turn his attention from the phonology of the Chinese tradition to an unusual interest in Western matters and in the English language. Kuo-fan had been impressed by a work on astronomy in *Wu-li t'ung-k'ao* and as early as 1858 had written Chi-tse about his own regret at not being able to pursue this subject. Chi-tse took this up and reported to his father the "planets" (*heng hsing*) he observed in the night sky.[98] In the fall of 1863, while he was with his father in An-ch'ing on the Yangtze, he met Hua Heng-fang, Hsu Shou, and Li Shan-lan, mathematicians and scientists who helped design the first Chinese-built steamship, the *Huang Ku* (Yellow goose).[99] In 1865, Chi-tse arranged for the publication of a complete translation of Euclid's *Elements of Geometry* (*Chi-ho yuan-pen*), including the last nine chapters of the work, which had earlier been translated and published separately by Alexander Wylie and Li Shan-lan (see Jami, chap. 7 of this volume). The prestige of Western mathematics was enhanced by a preface signed by Tseng Kuo-fan and drafted by Chi-tse.[100] Chi-tse met Halliday Macartney, who worked for the Nanking Arsenal from 1865 on, and from him learned "a smattering of English." Chi-tse later wrote that he tried to apply Chinese phonetic and rhyming principles to the study of English.[101]

Chi-tse did take an examination in Peking in 1870 — the competition for positions in the metropolitan bureaucracy among applicants who had the *yin-sheng* status. He passed the test and was appointed to a sinecure on the Board of Revenue, but he took a prolonged leave from this position, since his assistance was needed by the ailing Tseng Kuo-fan, who was governor general of Chihli in 1870 and then fufilled the same office at Nanking. Tseng Kuo-fan died in 1872. Chi-tse accompanied the catafalque to Hunan, where he mourned his father and mother, who died two and a half years after her husband. Chi-tse's interest in things Western stood him in good stead when he emerged from mourning and returned to Peking in 1877 with the rank of marquis (*hou*) inherited from his father. In 1878, he was appointed minister to Britain and France and for more than eight years was the outstanding Ch'ing diplomat in Europe.[102] In February 1881 in St. Petersburg, he ably renegotiated the draft Sino-Russian treaty of 1879 and recovered Ch'ing sovereignty over Ili. Among Tseng Chi-tse's lasting contributions is the journal kept during his diplomatic service in Europe (1878–86).[103]

Compared with Chi-tse's, the achievements of his brother Chi-hung were less apparent. Chi-hung passed the county test in 1862, ranking first on the list, and went on to pass the prefectural examination and earn the *sheng-yuan* degree in 1863. For years, he took his father's advice and concentrated on practicing eight-legged essays and the style of poetry required for the examinations.[104] Chi-hung, in his turn, became interested in mathematics at about the same time that the complete translation of Euclid's *Geometry* was published. But Kuo-fan wrote both him and Chi-tse repeatedly:

Please do not read more of mathematics. (17 Nov. 1865).[105]

Even the *T'ung-chien*, calligraphy, and mathematics must be interrupted. You must concentrate on the eight-legged essays and the style of poetry required for the examinations. (10 Mar. 1866).[106]

Chi-hung was asked to learn from an especially recommended book of model eight-legged essays, "to concentrate on them (*chuan kung*) yet study classical themes as well (*chien-hsueh ching-ts'e*)." He was expected to send his father six exercises each month.[107]

Chi-hung twice tried taking the provincial examination in the latter part of the 1860s but never passed it. Kuo-fan, who went over some of his examination papers, was frankly disappointed.[108] It was only on Kuo-fan's death that Chi-hung came to possess a *chü-jen* degree, awarded by the throne by virtue of his being a son of the deceased statesman.[109]

After the period of mourning for his father and mother, Chi-hung tried taking the metropolitan examination for the *chin-shih* degree but without success. He died in Peking in 1881 at the age of thirty-three.[110] His life, however, had not been a barren one. Between the examinations he had continued to study mathematics and learn English. He had authored a work in Chinese on the relation between circumference and diameter and enjoyed chess and music. He was evidently an introspective person of talent who tried in vain to comply with his father's wishes.[111]

Tseng Kuo-fan's hopes for the examination and educational success of his family were to be fulfilled. Chi-hung married in 1865 and his wife, née Kuo, raised their three sons and one daughter.[112] Of the sons, Tseng Kuang-chün (1867–1929) had the good fortune to be awarded a *chü-jen* degree by imperial grace after Tseng Kuo-fan's death, then went on to capture the prize of the examination system on his own merit. In 1889, at the age of twenty-three, he won the metropolitan *chin-shih* degree and was appointed a Hanlin academician, as had Tseng Kuo-fan a half century before.[113] One of Kuang-chün's daughters was Tseng Pao-sun (1893–1978) who, thanks to the broad-mindedness of her father and grandmother, was allowed to enter Protestant missionary schools in Hangchow and Shanghai and to go to England for further study.[114] She founded in 1918 the I-fang Women's School in Changsha and was assisted in this work by her first cousin, Tseng Yueh-nung (1893–1986), who also went to England for college. After some thirty years of teaching at the Women's School, Yueh-nung accompanied Pao-sun to Taiwan. He was a founder of Tung Hai University in Taichung in 1956.[115]

The long and rich experience of Tseng Kuo-fan's fifth and youngest daughter, Tseng Chi-fen (1852–1941), who wed Nieh Chi-kuei (1855–1911) in 1875 in what was then considered a late marriage, has been the subject of recent research.[116] The memoir that she wrote at her eightieth birthday deserves further study, especially since the facsimile copies of some letters by her sisters and other relatives have been preserved and are published.[117] While the present chapter has offered glimpses of the part Tseng Kuo-fan played in the education of his brothers and sons, the effectiveness of Tseng's influence on his younger relatives through his writings and personal example can be more fully measured only when the family history of his descendants is more fully explored.

NOTES

Abbreviations

HHTS *Hsiang-hsiang Tseng-shih wen-hsien* 湘鄉曾氏文獻 (Documents of the Tseng family of Hsiang-hsiang, Hunan). A collection of manuscripts photographically reproduced. 10 vols. Taipei: Hsueh-sheng, 1965. Supp. vol. 1975.

TKFCS *Tseng Kuo-fan chia-shu* 曾國藩家書 (Family letters of Tseng Kuo-fan). 2 vols. Changsha: Yueh-lu shu-she, 1985.

TKFJC *Tseng Kuo-fan jih-chi* 曾國藩日記 (Diaries of Tseng Kuo-fan). 3 vols. Changsha: Yueh-lu shu-she, 1987–89.

TKFNP *Tseng Kuo-fan nien-p'u* 曾國藩年譜, (Biographical chronicle of Tseng Kuo-fan). Changsha: Yueh-lu shu-she, 1986.

TWCK *Tseng Wen-cheng kung ch'üan-chi* 曾文正公全集 (Complete papers of Tseng Kuo-fan). Nanking: Ch'uan-chung shu-chü, 1879. Reprint. 38 vols., Taipei: Wen-hai, 1974.

CH *Chia-hsun* 家訓 (Family instructions).

CS *Chia-shu* 家書 (Family letters).

NP *Nien-p'u* 年譜 (Biographical chronicle).

SC *Shu-cha* 書札 (Letters to friends and colleagues).

WC *Wen-chi* 文集 (Collected essays).

1. *TWCK: WC*, 2:2–3.

2. Cf. Wm. Theodore de Bary et al., comps., *Sources of the Chinese Tradition* (New York: Columbia University Press, 1960), 384.

3. *TWCK: CS* and *CH* have been supplemented by *HHTS*, vols. 1, 2.
These sources, as well as a few hitherto unpublished letters,
are now in the punctuated edition in simplified characters, *TKFCS*.

4. Publication data given here are based on the printed catalogs in the Library of
Congress and the Harvard-Yenching Library. See also Liang Ch'i-ch'ao 梁啟超, *Yin-ping
shih wen-chi* 飲冰室文集 (Collected essays from the Ice-drinker's Studio) (Taipei:
Chung-hua, 1960), 34:1; cf. front matter in vol. 1, 70.

5. Sources on Tseng Kuo-fan and his family include the extensive papers in *TWCK*
and *HHTS*. In addition, extensive papers of Tseng Kuo-ch'üan and Tseng Chi-tse have
been published, as well as the memoirs of two women among Tseng's descendants. See
nn. 93, 94, 110, 111. For original manuscript papers see *Hsiang-hsiang Tseng-shih
wen-hsien mu-lu* 湘鄉曾氏文獻目錄 (Catalog of the papers of the Tseng family of
Hsiang-hsiang) ed. Kuo-li ku-kung po-wu yuan 國立故宮博物院 (Taipei, 1982 postscript). For an excellent recent study of the Tseng family history see Li Jung-t'ai 李榮
泰, *Hsiang-hsiang Tseng-shih yen-chiu* 湘鄉曾氏研究 (Study of the Tsengs of
Hsiang-hsiang) (Taipei: National Taiwan University, 1989). For a brief treatment of the
experiences of the Tseng daughters, see my article "Ts'ung Tseng Kuo-fan *chia-shu
shuo-ch'i* 從曾國藩家書說起 (Reflections on Tseng Kuo-fan's *Family Letters*), in
Chin-shih chia-tsu yü cheng-chih pi-chiao li-shih lun-wen chi 近世家族與政治比較歷史論文
集 (Family process and political process in modern Chinese history) (Taipei: Institute of
Modern History, Academia Sinica, 1992), 1:97–118, esp. 107–18.

6. Data on Tseng's biography, unless otherwise stated, are based on *TWCK: NP*,
Also available in *TKFNP*.

7. *TKFJC*, 1:2, 4, 8, 10, 15, 18, 22.

8. *TKFJC*, 1:5–6, 34.

9. Ibid., 42–76.

10. Lu Pao-ch'ien 陸寶千, *Liu Jung nien-p'u* 劉蓉年譜 (Biographical chronicle of Liu
Jung) (Taipei: Institute of Modern History, Academia Sinica, 1979), 4–20; Kuo T'ing-i
郭廷以 and Lu Pao-ch'ien, *Kuo Sung-tao hsien-sheng nien-p'u* 郭嵩燾先生年譜 (Biographical chronicle of the honorable Kuo Sung-tao) (Taipei: Institute of Modern History,
Academia Sinica, 1971), 1:13–33.

11. *TKFJC*, 1:92.

12. Ibid., 100, 108, 113–15. In December 1842 Tseng was still smoking; see 115, 121
–122, 130.

13. Ibid., frontispiece, 113–15, 119, 122–23, 125, 127, 133–34.

14. Ibid., 113, 130, 138, 152; *TKFCS*, 1:38–41, 46–49.

15. See esp. *TKFJC*, 1:114–16, 119, 128–29, 131, 133, 136–37, 148, 153, 155–57,
160, 165. For Tseng's self-denunciatory references to "great disrespect in the bedroom",
see 125, 130, 141–42, 162–63, 165.

16. Some of Tseng's writings in the mid-1840s clearly indicate Chu Hsi's influence;
see *TWCK: WC*, esp. 1:20–21, 26–27, 32–33. Tseng took exception to quiet-sitting as
practiced by such late-Ming Confucians as Kao P'an-lung and Ku Hsien-ch'eng because
"its emphasis was still on consciousness (*chih-chueh*)." It was Tseng's belief that one
could "dwell in reverence without falling into quietude." *TWCK:WC*, 1:49–50.

17. *TKFJC*, 1:59–62, 70, 73, 78, 106, 109; *TKFCS*, 1:5, 29. Tseng Kuo-fan purchased
Ssu-wen ching-hua in late March or early April 1841.

18. *TKFJC*, 1:71, 90, 110.

19. Ibid., 1:106, 110; *TKFCS*, 1:29–30, 36, 95.

20. *TKFCS*, 1:35, 108.

21. Ibid., 35–36; see also 38–41, 46–48, 52–56, 67–68, 80, 87, 92–94, 98–99.

22. Ibid., 36.

23. Ibid., 38–39, 51–58, 71.

24. Ibid., 38–39.

25. Ibid., 67–68. See also 42, 52–54, 59.

26. Ibid., 87.

27. Ibid., 55.

28. Ibid.

29. Ibid.

30. This and other information on Tseng's career is drawn from *TKFNP* under the appropriate year.

31. *TKFCS*, 1:80.

32. Ibid., 81–82; see also *TWCK: WC*, 1:20–21.

33. *TKFCS*, 1:35, 92.

34. Ibid., 93.

35. Ibid., 96, 98. Tseng also ascribed his good fortune to the "heritage left by the ancestors" (*tsu-tsung i-tse*).

36. Ibid., 54, 92, 96. The phrase for predestination Tseng used is *ch'ien-ting* or *ming-ting*. He was probably quoting from a proverb when he said, "It is up to me to do my best and let Heaven have its say" (*Chin-chih tsai wo, t'ing-ch'i tsai t'ien*), ibid., 92. Later, in 1851, he wrote of his brother Kuo-hua's blaming misfortune for failing in an examination: "If one blames Heaven without reason, Heaven will disapprove; if one blames a person without reason, the person will have a sense of grievance. The principle of response and retribution naturally applies here." Ibid., 223.

37. Ibid., 99, 106.

38. Ibid., 94–95; *TWCK: SC*, 1:2–5.

39. *TWCK: SC*, 1:1–5. That Tseng's view of self-cultivation was considerably different from that of the more rigorous followers of Chu Hsi can be seen by comparing this letter with what Liu Jung was writing in the same year. Cf. Lu Pao-ch'ien, *Liu Jung nien-p'u*, 48–50.

40. *TKFCS*, 1:108–10.

41. Ibid., 101–2, 107, 112, 144, 153.

42. Ibid., 154–55; see also 147.

43. Ibid., 150, 152, 155–56, 159–60, 177, 183–84, 186–87, 197.

44. Ibid., 168, 197.

45. See *TKFNP*, under Hsien-feng 1 (1851). This anthology was later published in 1870 as part of *TWCK*.

46. See *TWCK: NP*, under Tao-kuang 28 (1848). Tseng used the phrase *shih-huo* (lit., "food and money") or *ching-chi* (economic matters) for what, following Helen Dunstan, I have translated as "economic statecraft." (Tseng's usage of this narrow sense of statecraft includes the military aspects of public finance.) Tseng preferred to use the term *ching-shih* (commonly rendered as "statecraft") to represent a broader category including ritual and institutions. See *TWCK: WC*, 3:33–34. For a general analysis of the con-

cept of *ching-shih* as found in the works of Wei Yuan et al., see the paper by Kai-wing Chow and myself, now available in Liu Kuang-ching 劉廣京, *Ching-shih ssu-hsiang yü hsin-hsing ch'i-yeh* 經世思想與新興企業 (Statecraft thought and the newly arisen enterprises) (Taipei: Lien-ching, 1990), ch. 2. Cf. Helen Dunstan, *An Anthology of Chinese Economic Statecraft, The Sprouts of Liberalism* (Hong Kong: Chinese University Press, forthcoming).

47. *TKFCS*, 1:220.

48. Ibid. See also M. Teresa Kelleher, "Back to Basics: Chu Hsi's Elementary Learning *(Hsiao-hsüeh)*," in Wm. Theodore de Bary and John W. Chaffee, eds., *Neo-Confucian Education: The Formative Stage* (Berkeley: University of California Press, 1989), 219–51. On Ch'en Hung-mou, see Rowe, chap. 12 of this volume.

49. For nearly four years the brothers complained of Kuo-fan's reluctance to recommend them for military work. It was not until the spring of 1856 that Kuo-hua joined the war effort under the famous commander Li Hsu-pin with a force of 500 men recruited in Hunan. It was not until autumn of that year that Kuo-ch'üan raised fifteen hundred men who were welcomed by Kuo-fan in Kiangsi. Kuo-pao, the youngest brother, had been with the Hunan Army's naval force in 1853–54. In late 1858, he rejoined the war under Hu Lin-i's command. Kuo-huang, the "fourth brother," stayed behind to tend to family affairs through these years; however, he was involved in militia activities in nearby localities on occasion. *TKFCS*, 1:303–4, 318–19, 322–26, 542, 554, 743. *TWCK: WC*, 3:56–57.

50. These interests were recalled by Tseng later in his letters to Chi-tse; see *TKFCS*, 1:331–32; 2:808.

51. *TWCK: WC*, 2:46–47, 48–49; 3:34.

52. See *TKFJC*, 1:24lff. and 2, passim.

53. *TKFJC*, 1:186, *TKFCS*, 1:85, 97, 117, 124–25, 143, 152 et passim. Tseng wrote his brothers in 1852 that he had a plan for Chi-tse's education. Chi-tse would be taught the Classics and history and literature in general and not be taught the writing of the eight-legged essay until he was fourteen years old by Chinese reckoning. Chi-tse already had the *yin-sheng* status by virtue of Kuo-fan's high official status. It would be unnecessary for him to attempt the low-level examinations *(hsiao-k'ao)*; he could go directly to the provincial examination when he was twenty-four. "Having been trained in the eight-legged essay for ten years, if he is at all intelligent, how can he not be well-versed in it?" *TKFCS*, 1:230.

54. Ibid., 324–25.

55. Ibid., 327.

56. Ibid., 331–32.

57. Ibid., 406.

58. Ibid., 430.

59. Ibid., 406, 409, 418; see also 533.

60. Ibid., 406.

61. Ibid., 437, 451–52.

62. Ibid., 451, 472.

63. Ibid., 468, 480–81, 488 et passim.

64. Ibid., 527, 537.

65. Ibid., 634; see also 597.

66. Ibid., 540–41, 629, 639.

67. *TWCK: WC*, 3:22–27.

68. *TKFJC*, 1:350–51; *TKFCS*, 1:460.

69. *TWCK: WC*, 3:23b.

70. Ibid., 24b–25.

71. Ibid., 25.

72. This has been published as part of *TWCK* (1874).

73. *TWCK: WC*, 41. The sources Tseng used for his anthology included not only Yao's work but also *Han-Wei pai san chia wen-chi* 漢魏百三家文集 (Collected essays of 103 authors of the Han and Wei periods) and *Wen-hsuan*; see *TKFCS*, 1:637 (slight adjustment made in the former book title).

74. *TWCK: WC*, 48. The shorter anthology has also been published in *TWCK*.

75. See Ch'ien Mu 錢穆, *Chung-kuo chin san-pai nien hsueh-shu shih* 中國近三百年學術史 (Intellectual history of China over the last three hundred years), 2 vols. (1937; reprint, Taipei: Commercial Press, 1987), esp. 583–91; Ho I-k'un 何貽焜, *Tseng Kuo-fan p'ing-chuan* 曾國藩評傳 (Critical biography of Tseng Kuo-fan) (1937; reprint, Taipei: Cheng-chung, 1972), 470–75. For a recent appraisal, see Chang Chi-kuang 章繼光, *Tseng Kuo-fan ssu-hsiang chien-lun* 曾國藩思想簡論 (Short intellectual history of Tseng Kuo-fan) (Changsha: Hunan Jen-min, 1988).

76. *TKFCS*, 1:469; cf. 452–53.

77. Ibid., 472, 476–77.

78. Ibid., 480–81, 527.

79. Ibid., 488–89, 498.

80. Ibid., 462, 469. Li En-han 李恩涵, *Tseng Chi-tse ti wai-chiao* 曾紀澤的外交 (Diplomacy of Tseng Chi-tse) (Taipei: Institute of Modern History, Academia Sinica, 1966), 6.

81. *TKFCS*, 1:527, 532–33, 540–41.

82. Ibid., 764, 772–73 and esp. 786; 2:809, 831–32.

83. Ibid., 2:836–37.

84. Ibid., 849.

85. See Tseng Chi-tse, *Tseng Hui-ming kung i-chi* 曾惠敏公遺集 (Collected writings of the late Tseng Chi-tse) (Shanghai: The Kiangnan Arsenal, 1893); also available as *Tseng Chi-tse i-chi* 曾紀澤遺集 (Collected writings) (Changsha: Yueh-lu shu-she, 1983). Tseng Kuo-fan's comments were published along with Chi-tse's poems. See, for example, *TKFCS*, 1:237–42, 245–47.

86. *TKFCS*, 2:853.

87. Ibid., 1:313, 356, 377, 420, 456, et passim. The family property of Tseng's father, Tseng Lin-shu, remained undivided after the latter's death. Ibid., 444, 450, 521.

88. Ibid., 532

89. Ibid. For the role of Chi-tse's mother in making decisions with Kuo-huang ("the fourth uncle") on the appropriate gifts for relatives on the occasions of weddings and funerals, see 502. She was also consulted about such financial matters as the salary for Chi-tse's tutor; see 798.

90. Ibid., 150–51, 439, 503, 792, 801; 2:815, 819.

91. Ibid., 835.

92. Ibid., 936–37.

93. See the extensive sources in *HHTS*; also photographically reproduced is Tseng Chi-tse, *Tseng Hui-min kung shou-hsieh jih-chi* 曾惠敏公手寫日記 (Manuscript diaries of Tseng Chi-tse), 8 vols. (Taipei: Hsueh-sheng, 1965). See also n. 94, on Tseng Kuo-ch'üan's published papers. For a catalog of original manuscripts, see n. 5. Li Jung-t'ai's *Hsiang-hsiang Tseng-shih* is a valuable guide.

94. These generalizations are tentative. Kuo-ch'üan's extensive published papers remain to be studied: *Tseng Chung-hsiang kung (Kuo-ch'üan), Shu-cha fu wen-chi* 曾忠襄公（國荃）書札附文集 (Letters to friends and colleagues, with collected essays); *Tseng Chung-hsiang kung (Kuo-ch'üan), P'i-tu; Nien-p'u* 批牘年譜 (Comments on official communications; Biographical chronicle); *Tseng Chung-hsiang Kung (Kuo ch'üan) tsou-i* 奏議 (Memorials), 14 vols. (1903 et seq.; reprint, Taipei: Wen-hai, 1967–69).

95. He was often criticized by Tseng Kuo-fan for his acquisition of property. See *TKFCS*, 1:456, 462, 474, 514, 592, 795.

96. Tseng Kuo-ch'üan left Peking (where he had lived with his brother and been tutored by him) in an unhappy mood in 1844. After staying home for a while, he went to study in Changsha and became friendly with Lo Tse-nan (1808–56) and Liu Jung. Kuo-ch'üan had developed his own version of Ch'eng-Chu Neo-Confucianism and wrote to criticize Kuo-fan on the latter's conduct of his household in Peking and even on his attitude as an official. See Ibid., 1:52, 57, 92, 141, 143. For an example of a letter in Kuo-ch'üan's handwriting (dated March 1852 from internal evidence) in which he criticized his elder brother in the name of the "spirit of rectitude" (*cheng-ch'i*) and the distinction between "commonweal and private interest" (*kung-ssu*), see *HHTS*, supp. vol., 475–81. Kuo-ch'üan also blamed Kuo-fan for not always answering letters he received from friends: "If you are still this way, then I think this is also a fault." Ibid.

97. *Tseng Chung-hsiang kung (Kuo-ch'üan), P'i-tu; Nien-p'u*, esp. for the years 1877–80.

98. *TKFCS*, 1:418, 441. Kuo-fan made a distinction between astronomy (*t'ui-pu*) and astrology (*chan-yen*). He also referred to *Huang Ch'ing ching-chieh* (Ch'ing dynasty commentaries on the Classics) as a source on the "planets."

99. See the sources cited in Li En-han, *Tseng Chi-tse*, 18–20.

100. "Wen-chi" (Essays), in *Tseng Chi-tse i-chi*, 133–34. The preface drafted by Chi-tse in his father's name was approved by Kuo-fan on 3 Aug. 1865. *TKFJC*, 2:1164. Kuo-fan suggested a printing of "one hundred copies at first." *TKFCS*, 2:1203, 1213.

101. Macartney is cited in Li En-han, *Tseng Chi-tse*, 21. For Chi-tse's approach to the English language through Chinese phonology, see "Wen-chi," in *Tseng Chi-tse i-chi*; 158–59.

102. Li En-han, *Tseng Chi-tse*; see also Chung Shu-ho's 鍾叔河 introduction to the 1985 republication of Tseng's diaries cited in n. 103.

103. The earliest abridged version of Tseng's diaries, unauthorized, appeared in 1882; a more ample version was first published in 1893. Chi-tse's complete diaries appeared in the photographically reproduced version in eight volumes published in Taiwan in 1965; see n. 93. A typeset edition of Chi-tse's diaries for his years as a diplomat, 1878–86, has appeared more recently as *Ch'u-shih Yin-Fa-O kuo jih-chi* 出使英法俄國日記 (Diaries of the missions to Britain, France, and Russia), ed. Chung Shu-ho (Changsha: Yueh-lu shu-she, 1985).

104. *TKFCS*, 2:812, 836–37, 988–89, 1238, 1247, 1259–60. To Chi-hung too Kuo-fan had stressed that literature is an end in itself and that philology is important; see 1204–05, 1243–44.

105. Ibid., 1220–21.

106. Ibid., 1238.

107. Ibid., 1259–60, 1263.

108. Ibid., 1266–67, 1278–79, 1301, 1327, 1342.

109. *TWCK: NP*, for the year 1872.

110. *HHTS*, 10:6284–85. See 1881 entry in Nieh Tseng Chi-fen 聶曾紀芬, *Ch'ung-te lao-jen tzu-t'ing nien-p'u* 崇德老人自訂年譜 (Autobiographical chronicle of Nieh Tseng Chi-fen), printed with *Ch'ung-te lao-jen chi-nien ts'e* 紀念冊 (Memorial volume for Nieh Tseng Chi-fen, with illustrations, ed. Nieh Ch'i-chieh, 1935). This source is also available as an appendix to the 1986 edition of Tseng Pao-sun's memoirs; see n. 111.

111. Tseng Pao-sun, *Tseng Pao-sun hui-i lu* 曾寶蓀回憶錄 (Memoirs of Tseng Pao-sun), in *Tseng Pao-sun chi-nien chi* 曾寶蓀紀念集 (Memorial volume) (Taipei, 1978); reprinted as *T'seng Pao-sun hui-i lu*, ed. Chung Shu-ho (Changsha: Yueh-lu shu-she, 1986), esp. 177. The mathematical publication Tseng Pao-sun cited as evidence of Chi-hung's contribution, *Pai-fu t'ang shuan-hsueh ts'ung shu* 白芙堂算學叢書 (Mathematical series of Pai-fu t'ang), ed. Ting Ch'ü-chung 丁取忠 (1875) is mentioned in Joseph Needham, *Science and Civilization in China*, 3 (1959):48. Chi-hung's English notebooks are reproduced in *HHTS*, 10:6305–47, and a mathematical essay appears on 6048–54.

112. *TKFJC*, 2:1134; Chi-hung's wife, according to her daughter, studied the Thirteen Classics and *T'ung-chien* after her marriage and also learned to write poetry. *Tseng Pao-sun hui-i lu*, 2–3.

113. Ibid., 2–4, 117–80.

114. Ibid., esp. 18ff., 180–82.

115. Ibid., 70ff., 226.

116. See Thomas L. Kennedy, *Testimony of a Confucian Woman: The Autobiography of Mrs. Nie Zeng Jifen, 1852–1942* (Athens: University of Georgia Press, 1993).

117. See n. 93. Chung Shu-ho's preface to a popular edition of Tseng Kuo-fan's letters to his sons has stressed the effectiveness of Tseng's educational influence on his descendants, emphasizing the fostering of intellectual interest as well as self-discipline. See *Tseng Kuo-fan chiao-tzu shu* 曾國藩教子書 (Tseng Kuo-fan's letters to his sons), ed. Chung Shu-ho (Changsha: Yueh-lu shu-she, 1986), front matter, 1–5.

GLOSSARY

chan-yen	占驗	*chia-hsun*	家訓
Chang Erh-ch'i	張爾岐	*chia-shu*	家書
Chang Liang-chi	張亮基	*chia-t'ing jih-yung chih-chien*	家庭日用之間
Chang Tsai	張載	Chiang Yung	江永
chao-jan jo fa-meng	昭然若發蒙	*chien-hsueh ching-ts'e*	兼學經策
Ch'en Hung-mou	陳宏謀	*ch'ien-pei ta-chia*	前輩大家
cheng-ch'i	正氣	chien-sheng	監生
Cheng K'ang-ch'eng	鄭康成	*ch'ien-ting*	前定
ch'eng-hsiu chi-ssu	誠修祭祀	*chih-chueh*	知覺
Ch'eng I	程頤	*chih-i*	制藝
Chi-ho yuan-pen	幾何原本	*Chih-i ts'un-chen chi*	制藝存真集

Chin-chih tsai-wo,	盡之在我,	Hu Lin-i	胡林翼
t'ing ch'i tsai-t'ien	聽其在天	Hua Heng-fang	華蘅芳
Chin-ssu lu	近思錄	*huan-te huan-shih*	患得患失
chin-te	進德	*Huang Ch'ing ching-chieh*	皇清經解
Ch'in Hui-t'ien	秦蕙田	*Huang Ku*	黃鵠
ching	敬	Huang T'ing-chien	黃庭堅
ching-chi	經濟	Hui Tung	惠棟
Ching-chi tsuan-ku	經籍纂詁	I-fang	藝芳
Ching-i shu-wen	經義述聞	*i-li (philosophy)*	義理
ching-shih	經世	*i-li (ritual)*	儀禮
Ching-shih pai-chia chien-pien	經史百家簡編	*ju-p'an*	入泮
Ching-shih pai-chia tsa-ch'ao	經史百家雜鈔	Juan Yuan	阮元
ching-yen	經筵	*Kang-chien*	綱鑑
Chou-i che-chung	周易折中	*i-chih lu*	易知錄
Chou Tun-i	周敦頤	Kao P'an-lung	高攀龍
Chu Hsi	朱熹	*k'ao-ch-ü ming wu*	考據名物
Chu-tzu ch'üan-shu	朱子全書	*k'ao-ho*	考核
Chu Yun-ssu	朱運四	Ku Hsien-ch'eng	顧憲成
chuan	專	Ku-liang	穀梁
chuan-kung	專攻	*ku-mo hsing-ling*	泪沒性靈
ch'uan-shih chih k'e,	傳食之客,	Ku Tsu-yü	顧祖禹
ju-mu chih pin	入幕之賓	*ku-wen*	古文
ch'ung-tao pien-wen	崇道貶文	*Ku wen-tz'u*	古文辭
Erh-shih-ssu chia shih-wen	二十四家時文	*lei-tsuan*	類纂
Erh-ya	爾雅	Ku Yen-wu	顧炎武
Fan Chung-yen	范仲淹	*kuai-li*	乖戾
fu	賦	*kung-ssu*	公私
Han-hsueh	漢學	Kung-yang	公羊
Han-shu	漢書	Kuo shih	郭氏
Han-Wei pai-san chia wen-chi	漢魏百三家文集	Kuo Sung-tao	郭嵩燾
Han Yü	韓愈	*Kuo-yü*	國語
han-yung	涵泳	*li-chih*	立志
heng	恒	Li Hsu-ping	李續賓
heng-hsing	恒星	*li-i*	禮義
Ho Ch'ang-ling	賀長齡	Li Po	李白
hou	侯	Li Shan-lan	李善蘭
Hou-Han shu	後漢書	Li Yuan-tu	李元度
Hsiao-hsueh	小學	*lin-sheng*	廩生
hsiao k'ao	小考	Liu Ch'uan-ying	劉傳瑩
hsiao-t'i	教悌	Liu Jung	劉蓉
hsin-te	心得	*liu-kuan shu*	留館庶
hsiu-yeh	修業	*chi-shih*	吉士
Hsu Shen	許慎	Liu Tsung-yuan	柳宗元
Hsu Shou	徐壽	Lo Chao-sheng	羅兆升
hsueh huai	學壞	Lu Chih	陸贄
hsun ku	訓詁	*lü-fu*	律賦

Lu Yu	陸游	Tseng Chi-fen	曾紀芬
lueh-i she-lieh	略一涉獵	Tseng Chi-hung	曾紀鴻
lun-ch'ang jih-yung	倫常日用	Tseng Chi-tse	曾紀澤
lun-chi	倫紀	Tseng Kuang-chün	曾廣鈞
Ma Tuan-lin	馬端臨	Tseng Kung	曾鞏
ming	命	Tseng Kuo-ch'üan	曾國荃
ming-ting	命定	Tseng Kuo-fan	曾國藩
Nieh Chi-kuei	聶緝槼	Tseng Kuo-hua	曾國華
Ou-yang Hsiu	歐陽修	Tseng Kuo-huang	曾國潢
Pan Ku	班固	Tseng Kuo-pao	曾國葆
pen	本	Tseng Lin-shu	曾麟書
p'ing-tse	平仄	Tseng Pao-sun	曾寶蓀
p'o-sui chih hsueh	破碎之學	Tseng Yueh-nung	曾約農
she-shen ch'u-ti	設身處地	Tso Ch'iu-ming	左邱明
Shen-yin yü	呻吟語	*tso-chu*	作主
sheng tiao chieh-chi	聲調皆樞	*tsu-tsung i-tse*	祖宗遺澤
k'eng-ch'iang	鏗鏘	*Tu-shu tsa-chih*	讀書雜誌
shih	識	Tuan Yü-ts'ai	段玉裁
shih-huo	食貨	*t'ui-pu*	推步
Shih-pa chia shih-ch'ao	十八家詩鈔	Tung-hai	東海
shih-tu	侍讀	*T'ung tien*	通典
shu-shih	塾師	*Tzu-chih t'ung-chien*	資治通鑑
Shuo-wen	說文	*Tzu-shih ching-hua*	子史精華
Shuo-wen chien-tzu chu	說文解字注	Wang An-shih	王安石
Shuo-wen fen-yun	說文分韻	Wang Nien-sun	王念孫
chieh-tzu fan-li	解字凡例	Wang Yin-chih	王引之
ssu-liu	四六	Wei Yuan	魏源
Ssu-ma Ch'ien	司馬遷	Wen (King)	文
Ssu-ma Kuang	司馬光	*wen* (literature)	文
Ssu-wen ching-hua	斯文精華	*wen-chang*	文章
ssu-yü	私欲	*wen i tsai tao*	文以載道
Su Tung-p'o	蘇東坡	Wo-jen	倭仁
Sun Hsing-yen	孫星衍	*wu chen*	五箴
Sun-tzu	孫子	*Wu-chung i-kuei*	五種遺規
Ta-Tai li-chi	大戴禮記	*wu-k'o ju-ho*	無可如何
Tai Chen	戴震	*Wu-li t'ung-k'ao*	五禮通考
T'ang Chien	唐鑑	*wu-lun*	五倫
tao-i shen-hsin chih hsueh	道義身心之學	Wu T'ing-tung	吳廷棟
T'ai-sui K'ao	太歲考	Yao Nai	姚鼐
t'i	體	*yeh*	業
t'ien-ming	天命	*yin-sheng*	蔭生
t'ien-ti chih wan-jen	天地之完人	Yuan Ping-chen	袁秉楨
tsa-chi	札記	Yuan ts'ai	原才
Ts'ao Chih	曹植	Yueh-lu	岳麓
Tseng Chen-kan	曾貞幹	*yung*	用
	(Tseng Kuo-pao)		

PART TWO

Examinations and Curricula

FOUR

Changes in Confucian Civil Service Examinations from the Ming to the Ch'ing Dynasty

Benjamin A. Elman

The goals of this chapter are to summarize the external structure and process of civil service examinations in late imperial China, address the intellectual aspects of the examination process, and evaluate the degree of change in the internal content of the examinations tolerated by the state structure in the eighteenth and nineteenth centuries when the state's Sung Learning orthodoxy was decisively challenged by the rise of Han Learning in the Yangtze Delta. This chapter attempts to show how the late imperial state successfully incorporated both Sung Learning moral philosophy and Han Learning classical scholarship into the civil service examination system to enhance its larger agenda of selecting loyal officials to share power with the ruler.

The terms "orthodoxy" and "ideology" occur frequently in this chapter. "Orthodoxy" is that which the late imperial state, represented by the overlapping but asymmetrical interests of the bureaucracy and the throne, publicly authorized and which became the core of the civil service examination curriculum. Perennial in public and private life as a variegated form of elite discourse, Confucian moral philosopy was endorsed by the bureaucracy and the throne as the core of the education of a literatus during the Ming (1368–1644) and Ch'ing (1644–1911) dynasties. When moral philosophy entered the political arena of state examinations, however, its intellectual life was constricted into a system of concepts, arguments, and beliefs endorsed by the state for larger political purposes. The educational content of civil examinations resulting from that process of restrictive manipulation, by which concepts, arguments, and beliefs selectively served to legitimate political sovereignty and create a Confucian mind-set, is what this chapter refers to as imperial "ideology."

The political coherence of imperial ideology derived from its selective reproduction of Confucian philosophy. State ideology may have had many "elective affinities" with Confucian moral philosophy, but the political purposes to which those affinities were applied were determined by the needs of the state rather than the integrity of the philosophy. The emperor (or the bureaucracy that spoke for him), not the philosopher, had the final say on how Confucian concepts, arguments, and beliefs were put into educational practice via examinations. As a carefully crafted Confucian "disguise" worn by an autocratic but not yet totalitarian state, imperial ideology successfully Confucianized the bureaucratic and military forms of power on which the late empires of Ming and Ch'ing were based. This chapter, then, seeks to identify the political and cultural uses of Confucianism in the required educational curriculum of civil service examinations.

THE EVOLUTION OF MING CIVIL SERVICE EXAMINATIONS

Imperial institutions for testing and selecting candidates for the Chinese civil service took their final form during the Ming dynasty. In an effort to bridge the civilian, cultural, and racial gaps in the Chinese imperial system that had emerged under alien Mongol militarization of state governance during the Yuan dynasty (1280–1368), Chu Yuan-chang (1328–98), the founding emperor of the Ming, in 1368 invited Confucians to recommend local talents for appointment as prefects and magistrates. An early adept of the millenarian White Lotus Buddhist sects that had revolted against Mongol rule, the Hung-wu emperor (r. 1368–98) was persuaded by Confucianized elites to don the ideological garb of a Confucian sage-king to reunify the empire and rekindle the orthodox legacy of the Sung dynasties (960–1279).

Central to this enterprise of political legitimation was the ability to recruit talented men and assign them positions in state and local governance. Under Mongol rule, the Chinese had been treated as "third-class citizens" in their own land, continually subjected to arbitrary decisions that granted Mongols, Muslims, Tibetans, and other Central Asian peoples privileged status in the Pax Mongolica of the day. Chinese chafed under the symbolic and material forms of violence used by the Mongols to maintain control as a minority over the massive numbers of Han people in North and South China. Confucian eremitism, a legitimate response to alien rule, meant that when the Ming dynasty replaced the Yuan, the new ruler would have to find ways to attract such Confucians into government service.[1]

Following the Sung model for civil and military service, the first Ming emperor reconstituted a selection and appointment process that governed the civilian and military bureaucracies and enabled the imperial state to control its human resources. Chu Yuan-chang effectively replaced Mongol rule with his own and established bureaucratic channels that penetrated fairly efficiently down into counties and prefectures in search of classically literate men to enter the elite world of officialdom.[2]

The civil service process, with its curriculum, forms of testing, and routines for official appointment, became one of the key institutions to bridge the

Mongol era and permit Sung cultural values to flourish in late imperial China. The curriculum of Sung moral philosophy that had been forged in the pre-Mongol era achieved orthodoxy briefly just before the southern Sung dynasty (1127–1279) was extinguished by Mongol armies. Later, Sung moral philosophy was assimilated into the repertoire of ideological devices used by the Yuan when in 1313 the alien dynasty decreed that civil service examinations stressing the Ch'eng-Chu "school of principle" (developed by Ch'eng I, 1033–1107, and Chu Hsi, 1130–1200) were required of all Chinese officials serving in the bureaucracy.[3]

The Ming state bureaucracy reproduced itself through a selection and appointment system that had four major components: schools, examinations, recommendation, and appointment. This organization represented a modification of the Sung selection and appointment process: (1) examinations; (2) schools; (3) appointment; (4) protection privilege for heirs; (5) sponsored appointment; and (6) evaluation. During the Ming dynasty, those that held office by virtue of their degrees were part of a larger administrative process involving the Ministry of Rites for education and the Ministry of Personnel for appointment and evaluation.[4]

The degree curriculum became the basis for the public school system that extended down from the National University to state-run schools at the prefectural and county levels of administration. Although Chinese candidates continued to take advantage of the recommendation, inheritance, and purchase provisions of the selection and appointment process, most high-level civil officials in Ming and Ch'ing China were selected on the basis of their success on local, provincial, and metropolitan examinations.[5]

Accordingly, state examinations in late imperial China were part of the larger administrative process of selecting, evaluating, promoting, and punishing officials. Viewed in isolation, the Sung Confucian curriculum of the Ming and Ch'ing dynasties is often misperceived as a cultural field of philosophical and historical discourse tied simply to the Four Books, Five Classics, and Dynastic Histories. The "examination life," its rituals of preparation, and its stages of success were intimately tied to the complex and interrelated processes of political, social, and cultural reproduction.[6]

Education in the state schools counted for little if a student failed to pass the state examinations. Doomed to lives as minor functionaries, students who remained in state schools too long had little chance of success in imperial politics. In fact, by the late Ming it became difficult to gain reputable government positions for candidates who got only as far as the provincial chü-jen (lit., "raised candidates") degree. Earlier in the dynasty, provincial degree-holders were conspicuous in state administration, but they were eventually displaced by increasing numbers of metropolitan chin-shih (lit., "presented literati") degree-holders. Of the three routes of career advancement — namely metropolitan graduates, provincial graduates, and clerical officials — the chin-

TABLE 4.1   Format of Provincial and Metropolitan
Civil Service Examinations during the Ming Dynasty

Session No.	No. of Questions
One	
1. Four Books 四書	3 quotations
2. Change 易經	4 quotations
3. Documents 書經	4 quotations
4. Poetry 詩經	4 quotations
5. Annals 春秋	4 quotations
6. Rites 禮記	4 quotations
Two	
1. Discourse 論	1 quotation
2. Documentary style 詔誥表	3 documents
3. Judicial terms 判語	5 terms
Three	
1. Policy questions 經史事務策	5 issues

shih degree became the sole guarantee of high political position and elite social esteem.[7]

Until state examinations displaced other mechanisms for career advancement, the Confucian curriculum in state schools stressed moral philosophy, classical studies, and history. Mastery of moral philosophy was measured by examination questions based on the Four Books, which required an essay answer of at least 200 written graphs in length. An essay of at least 300 graphs elucidating the "meanings" of one of the Five Classics was the standard for classical studies. History questions stressed early dynastic histories such as the *Han-shu* (History of the former Han dynasty) and the *Shih-chi* (Records of the Grand Historian), as well as Confucius's *Spring and Autumn Annals,* one of the Five Classics but essentially a historical chronicle.[8]

Provincial and metropolitan examinations during the early Ming mirrored the education administered in state schools. The first high-level state examinations were in three parts, administered together on the same day. First, candidates were required to prepare two essays based on quotations from the Five Classics and one essay on the Four Books. Next, a discourse based on a text from the *Classic of Filial Piety* was required. Finally, the candidate had to prepare an answer to a practical question on public policy. Those who passed this stage were tested again in ten days for their physical prowess in horsemanship and archery and their mental prowess in calligraphy, mathematics, and penal law.[9]

This more technically oriented arrangement was subsequently changed into the more formalist, three-tiered format for provincial and metropolitan examinations outlined in table 4.1. Priority was given to the Four Books over the Five Classics in session one, legal and documentary requirements were added for session two, and the number of required policy questions was increased to five in session three. Moreover, students were required to answer three questions from the Four Books, but they could specialize in one of the Five Classics and elect to elucidate only quotations from that Classic.

These three testing sessions were administered triennially over a period of several days with three days between sessions to give examination officials time to rank the papers handed in. Candidates had one full day to complete answers for each session. Normally, candidates would take the provincial examinations in the fall and if successful move on to the metropolitan examinations in Peking and Nanking in the spring of the following year. A final palace examination for all metropolitan graduates was administered by the emperor himself as a personal litmus test to ensure political loyalty to him and fair and impartial final rankings. In general, this three-tiered arrangement remained in force until 1905, although the questions for each session were frequently changed during the Ch'ing period (see below).

In time, stylistic answers written in eight-legged essay forms, which were derived from early Ming standardized essays selected as models for emulation, became expected of all candidates. The essays that dealt with quotations from the Four Books were read with extreme care, and frequently the questions from sessions two and three were viewed as merely confirming the initial standings of the candidates after session one. Policy questions during session three, for example, became especially undervalued in the grading process. The result was that students often merely "went through the motions" in preparing these answers, realizing full well that their standing had already been determined based on earlier sessions.[10]

Sung dynasty interpretations of the Four Books and Five Classics were chosen by the Hung-wu emperor and his successors as the orthodox curriculum. On the Four Books, candidates were expected to have mastered the relevant materials in Chu Hsi's *Chu-tzu chi-chu* (Collected notes by Chu Hsi). For the Five Classics, Chu Hsi's views were also favored. On the *Change Classic*, Ch'eng I's commentary and Chu Hsi's "Original Meanings" were required. Ts'ai Shen's (1167–1230) commentary on the *Documents Classic*, which Chu Hsi had directed Ts'ai to compile, was emphasized. Similarly, for the *Poetry Classic*, Chu's "Collected Commentaries" were required.

For the *Spring and Autumn Annals* and *Record of Rites*, for which Chu Hsi had not prepared commentaries, the views of other Sung Confucians were used for examination standards. In addition to the ancient "three commentaries"—that is, the *Tso*, *Kung-yang*, and *Ku-liang* commentaries—for the *Spring and Autumn Annals*, Hu An-kuo's (1074–1138) and Chang Hsia's (1161–1237) commentaries were also chosen for testing (Chang's was later dropped). Like Ts'ai Shen, Chang had studied under Chu Hsi. For the *Record of Rites*, ancient

Han commentaries and T'ang subcommentaries were at first required although, later in the Ming, Ch'en Hao's (1261–1341) "Collected Sayings" was singled out for attention.

Under the Yung-lo emperor (r. 1403–24), the championing of state orthodoxy drew attention away from the emperor's usurpation of power from the Chien-wen emperor (r. 1399–1402). Sung Confucian interpretations of the Classics were for the first time collected together in definitive editions for the civil examinations and entitled *Complete Collection [of commentaries] for the Four Books and Five Classics* and *Great Collection of Works on Nature and Principles*. Thereafter, this *Complete Collection* alone was used for the questions on the Four Books and Five Classics administered during the first sessions of the provincial and metropolitan examinations. All Han and T'ang dynasty commentaries and subcommentaries were made secondary, leaving the orthodox Ch'eng-Chu school in a bittersweet ideological marriage with late imperial autocratic government.[11]

THE EVOLUTION OF CH'ING CIVIL SERVICE EXAMINATIONS

Under Manchu military and political control, the Ming civil and military service system was reinstated soon after the Ch'ing dynasty was formed in Peking in 1644. The fourfold division of the selection and evaluation process for officials remained: (1) schools; (2) examinations; (3) recommendation; and (4) appointment. However, important changes, especially in the schooling system, were made. For example, in addition to the national university system of schools, special state schools were also established for the eight military banners (composed of Manchus, Mongols, and Chinese military families) as well as a school for the Manchu imperial family.[12]

Special examinations for Manchu tribesmen were also established in 1651. Those who did not know classical Chinese were permitted to take the tests in their native language. During the K'ang-hsi reign, such examinations were formalized into translation examinations at the provincial level. Such privileges were extended to Mongol tribesmen in 1735. Later, during the Ch'ien-lung reign (1736–95), the requirements were tightened, and Manchus and Mongols were encouraged to take examinations in classical Chinese in an effort to unite civilian and military training. Questions in Chinese based on Sung dynasty Confucianism and philology were introduced, but most Manchus still did not compete with the Chinese in provincial and metropolitan examinations.

In addition, Chinese who passed the metropolitan examinations with highest honors and entered the Hanlin Academy, where they served as imperial secretaries, were required to learn Manchu. Special essay tests in Manchu and translation questions from classical Chinese to Manchu were administered to Hanlin academicians in the palace to ensure that documents and memorials were accurately recorded in the dual official languages.[13]

Early Manchu rulers deliberately set lower quotas for local and provincial examinations in Han Chinese provinces, perceiving that late Ming high quotas contributed to the state's loss of control over gentry in local society. In addition, because of the large number of Manchus in the central bureaucracy, fewer positions were now available for Han Chinese to hold, although Manchu appointments were less conspicuous in provincial and local administration. Provincial quotas were somewhat more generous in number during the Shun-chih reign (1644–61), but in 1660 provincial quotas were more drastically cut. Although gradually increased during the K'ang-hsi reign (1662–1722), the numbers remained far below late Ming quotas even though by 1700 the population of the empire reached over 150 million.[14]

In 1400, for example, it is estimated that there were thirty thousand licentiates out of an approximate population of 65 million, a ratio of almost one licentiate per 2,200 persons. In 1700, there were perhaps 500,000 licentiates in a total population of 150 million, or a ratio of one licentiate per 300 persons. While the ratio of licentiates to population became lower and thus less competitive over time, the likelihood of licentiates passing the higher examinations that would entitle them to civil appointments also decreased. In fact, by Ch'ing times licentiate status was much less rare and had become a social necessity.[15]

By 1850, approximately two million candidates sat for licensing and county examinations held annually and biannually. Of these only thirty thousand (1.5 percent) achieved licentiate status. Fifteen hundred of the latter (5 percent) passed the triennial provincial examinations, and of these only 300 (20 percent) would pass the triennial metropolitan examinations. Each stage eliminated the vast majority of candidates, and the odds for success in all stages of the selection process was one in six thousand (.01 percent).[16]

The number of metropolitan graduates tended to be around 300 for the triennial examinations, with a low of 110 in 1789 and a high of 406 in 1730. Ping-ti Ho has calculated that for the Ch'ing period as a whole there were 239 graduates per examination (down 50 from the Ming) or approximately 100 per annum (up 10 from the Ming). The number of per annum graduates was actually higher during the Ch'ing because of the frequent use of special examinations such as those in 1679 and 1736.[17]

Table 4.2 indicates that the format for provincial and metropolitan examinations during the early Ch'ing remained the same as during the Ming. Similarly, the curriculum for state schools and public examinations continued to emphasize the Four Books, Five Classics, and Dynastic Histories. In addition to the *Complete Collection [of commentaries] for the Four Books and Five Classics* and *Great Collection of Works on Nature and Principle* used during the Ming, the Ch'ing state also promoted compilation of the *Essential Meanings of Nature and Principle* as a convenient compendium of orthodox philosophical and moral teachings.

TABLE 4.2   Format of Provincial and Metropolitan
Civil Service Examinations during the Early
Ch'ing Dynasty, 1646–1756

Session No.	No. of Questions
One	
1. Four Books 四書	3 quotations
2. Change 易經	4 quotations
3. Documents 書經	4 quotations
4. Poetry 詩經	4 quotations
5. Annals 春秋	4 quotations
6. Rites 禮記	4 quotations
Two	
1. Discourse 論	1 quotation
2. Documentary style 詔誥表	3 documents
3. Judicial terms 判語	5 terms
Three	
1. Policy questions 經史事務策	5 issues

Essays for the examinations were still required in eight-legged essay form (see also Guy, chap. 5 of this volume). In the early Ch'ing, a maximum of 550 graphs was required for each of the first session examination essays dealing with the Four Books and Five Classics. The maximum was raised to 650 in 1681 and again to 700 in 1778, a number that remained in effect until the end of the dynasty. Models for the essays based on ancient-style prose were collected together under imperial auspices in 1753 by the Sung Learning partisan and T'ung-ch'eng classicist Fang Pao (1668–1749) (see also Guy, chap. 5 of this volume). Again in 1814, officials asked that model examination essays prepared since Fang Pao's collection be issued to the public.

As a result of these increases in maximum essay length, however, the task of grading papers by readers and examiners increased proportionally. Despite added numbers of examiners, their increased reading load prevented them from paying adequate attention to essays prepared during the second and third sessions. Especially overlooked were the last session's five policy questions. By 1786, regulations had to be enforced requiring a minimum of 300 graphs for each answer to a policy question, indicating that candidates were preparing short replies to the questions. In many cases, the policy questions themselves contained some 500 to 600 graphs, frequently double those in the answer, although in 1735 examiners were asked to curtail their rhetoric.[18]

As in the Ming, examination candidates were expected to master the orthodox interpretations of the Ch'eng-Chu school for their essays. Chu Hsi's "Col-

TABLE 4.3   Format of Provincial and Metropolitan
Civil Service Examinations during the Early
Ch'ing Dynasty Reform of 1663 (Rescinded in 1667)

Session No.	*No. of Questions*
One	
1. Policy questions 經史事務策	5 issues
Two	
1. Discourse 論	1 quotation
2. Four Books 四書	1 quotation
or Five Classics 五經	
Three	
1. Documentary style 表	1 document
2. Judicial terms 判語	5 terms

lected Notes" was again required for questions from the Four Books. For the
Change and *Poetry* Classics, Chu Hsi's commentaries were also chosen, along
with Ch'eng I's commentary for the *Change*. On the *Documents*, once again the
commentary by Chu's student Ts'ai Shen was required. In the early Ch'ing,
the Hu An-kuo commentary was singled out for students specializing in the
Spring and Autumn Annals, although later in the dynasty, when Han Learning
became popular in the eighteenth century, the Hu commentary was replaced
by the three commentaries of the Han dynasties as the proper guides to the
Annals. Finally, for the *Record of Rites*, Ch'en Hao's "Collected Sayings"
remained orthodox.[19]

In 1663, under the Oboi regents, who as Manchu military men were sceptical of the efficacy of purely literary qualifications for office, extensive changes
in the format of the examinations were introduced. The requirement that all
examination essays be prepared in rigorous eight-legged essay form was ab-
ruptly rescinded. To devalue literary exercises, quotations based on the Four
Books and Five Classics were relegated to the second session and limited to
one question for each. In effect, the entire first session of the Ming and early
Ch'ing provincial and metropolitan examinations, which had been the most
important determinant in the final rankings of candidates, was jettisoned. To
stress practical questions of government policy and concrete themes dealing
with state institutions, the regents moved the five policy questions from the
third session of the examination proceedings to the first. As table 4.3 reveals,
the second session now also included a single discourse essay based on a quotation from the *Classic of Filial Piety*, while the third session required a single
documentary question and identification of five legal terms.[20]

These innovative reforms, which removed memorization of the Five Classics
and Four Books from the core of skills tested in the selection process, produced

TABLE 4.4　Format of Provincial and Metropolitan
Civil Service Examinations during the Mid-Ch'ing
Dynasty, 1757–87

Session No.	*No. of Questions*
One	
1. Four Books 四書	3 quotations
2. Discourse 論	1 quotation
Two	
1. Change 易經	4 quotations
2. Documents 書經	4 quotations
3. Poetry 詩經	4 quotations
4. Annals 春秋	4 quotations
5. Rites 禮記	4 quotations
6. Poetry question 詩題	1 poetic model
Three	
1. Policy questions 經史事務策	5 issues

an uproar among Han Chinese. Understandably, many Chinese preparing for the rigorous Ming-style examinations felt that their financial sacrifices and memorization efforts had been compromised. Moreover, in an era when Ming loyalism was still a potent political and military force in the Yangtze Delta, many dissenters could point to these examination reforms as an example of the betrayal of Confucian orthodoxy by ignorant Manchu usurpers. To avoid a potentially damaging clash between Chinese and Manchus, the Oboi regents yielded and, after two metropolitan examinations, the reformed format was ended and the Ming format stressing memorization and literary style restored.[21]

After the K'ang-hsi emperor himself took full control of his reign in the 1680s, further efforts to reform the examination process were made. In 1687, for example, requirements to prepare state documents in "decree" and "bestowal of title" forms were briefly dropped. Not until 1756 were these changes reintroduced (see table 4.4). The discourse essay was also subjected to change. In 1690, *Essential Meanings of Nature and Principle, Theories of the Great Ultimate in Diagram Form*, and other Sung writings were added to the *Classic of Filial Piety* as possible sources of quotations requiring discourse essays. In 1718, *Essential Meanings* was alone designated for discourse essays and all other sources were dropped. In 1723, however, uproar over dropping the *Classic of Filial Piety* forced the state to reinstate it for the discourse question. From then until 1787, the *Classic of Filial Piety* and *Essential Meanings* were equally stressed.[22]

Suspicious of the extent of corruption among Chinese competing in the selection process, the Manchus had already instituted in 1658 a confirmation

TABLE 4.5   Format of Provincial and Metropolitan
Civil Service Examinations during the Late Ch'ing
Dynasty, 1787–1901

Session No.	*No. of Questions*
One	
1. Four Books 四書	3 quotations
2. Poetry question 詩題	1 poetic model
Two	
1. Change 易經	1 quotation
2. Documents 書經	1 quotation
3. Poetry 詩經	1 quotation
4. Annals 春秋	1 quotation
5. Rites 禮記	1 quotation
6. Discourse 論	1 quotation
(removed 1787)	
Three	
1. Policy questions 經史事務策	5 issues

examination for provincial graduates to be administered in Peking before the triennial metropolitian examinations began. Examination officials in the capital region and the Yangtze Delta in particular were singled out for laxness in supervising provincial examinations. This process of reexamination was later extended to include the metropolitan examination. In 1723, the Yung-cheng emperor (r. 1723–35) added a "court examination" (*ch'ao-k'ao*) of four questions (later lowered to three) to the examination process in order to corroborate the final bureaucratic appointments for those who had passed the palace examination. In effect, the capital selection process now had five separate examination hurdles.[23]

Although attacks on examination essays increased after 1738, little was accomplished to answer the charges that "contemporary-style essays," as eight-legged essays were called, were "noninnovative" and "impractical." Again, there were frequent calls to emphasize the policy questions in session three and increase attention paid to current affairs. As a result, after 1756 extensive changes were made in the provincial and metropolitan examinations, as table 4.4 shows. The Four Books remained in session one, but in deference to the popularity of Han Learning the Five Classics became the core of the second session and were replaced in the first session by a discourse essay stressing the *Essential Meanings*. Along with quotations from the Classics, students were also expected to compose during session two a poem in eight-syllable regulated verse, indicating revival of interest in T'ang-Sung poetry as a testable measure of cultural attainment. As before, however, the policy questions remained relegated to the last session.[24]

TABLE 4.6   Format of Provincial and Metropolitan
Civil Service Examinations during the Late Ch'ing
Dynasty, after the 1901 Reform
(Abolished in 1905)

Session No.	No. of Questions
One	
1. Discourses on the history of Chinese politics 中國政治史事論	5 essays
Two	
1. Policy questions on world politics 各國政治藝學策	5 questions
Three	
1. Four Books 四書義	2 essays
2. Five Classics 五經義	1 essay

In addition, the requirement that candidates specialize in one of the Classics for session two was changed. Beginning in 1787, again reflecting the influence of Han Learning, degree candidates were expected to study all of the Classics for each of the triennial provincial and metropolitan examinations. (table 4.5). The poetry requirement was moved from session two to the first session, immediately after quotations from the Four Books. The discourse essay based on the *Essential Meanings* was moved to the second session, following quotations from each of the Five Classics. Policy questions remained last and least important. Later modifications were introduced in which the discourse requirement was removed entirely (a different sort of discourse question had been included since 1723 in the court examination), and the examination format remained unchanged until 1901, when more radical reforms were promulgated (see table 4.6).[25]

Despite these changes in the examination process, China's demographic realities, to which the reform of requirements was addressed, meant that as the examinations became more streamlined in content the odds of passing them became increasingly steep. The population of the empire had reached 300 million in 1800 and then 450 million in 1850 with no commensurate increase in the number of government positions available to deal successfully with the increase in graduates. The odds against attaining *chü-jen* status on the provincial examinations and succeeding on the metropolitan examinations soared.[26]

During the Taiping Rebellion (1850–64), provincial examinations in many provinces were brought to a halt, although the Taipings held their own civil examinations. Particularly hard hit because the Taiping rebels made Nanking their capital, Kiangnan ceased holding Ch'ing examinations in 1859. The

Yangtze Delta had dominated imperial examinations since the Ming dynasty, but after the devastation of the Taiping Rebellion sons of Kiangnan families no longer went unchallenged in the national examination competition. Provinces such as Hunan in the central Yangtze region and Kwangtung in the southeast increasingly placed their candidates among metropolitan graduates.

During and after the rebellion, examination quotas were drastically increased, recommendation again became an important means of selecting officials, and sales of degrees and official positions encouraged by the state to raise funds for military campaigns reached unprecedented levels. Overworked examiners frantically asked for increases in personnel when increases in the numbers of candidates meant reading twice as many papers. Corruption became endemic. Despite efforts during the T'ung-chih Restoration (1862–74) to rectify the breakdowns in the selection process, the state in effect lost control over its human resources.[27]

By the time the civil service selection process was completely revamped in 1901 under the leadership of Chang Chih-tung (1837–1909) and other reformers, who were inundated with Western and Japanese models of education for nation-building, it was too late. Table 4.6 reveals that the 1901 reforms repeated one of the changes initially carried out in 1663 but then quickly repealed, namely stressing policy questions for testing. Session one of the new proceedings focused on Chinese political history, while session two required five answers to questions dealing with world politics. The Four Books and Five Classics were relegated to the last session. Such changes, however, were by now insufficient.[28]

As a system of education, the late imperial Chinese civil service examinations had prescribed forms of reasoning with a corresponding hierarchy of legitimate subjects. Ming and Ch'ing rulers perceived in state examinations a useful ideological tool to extract political loyalty from their influential gentry elite. Monolithic as a political and social structure, the Confucian examination system had at its heart classical content and epistemological forms of expression that were nonetheless subject to change as mental exercises and as public curricula. In the eighteenth century, the examination system began to reflect Han Learning debates among Confucian scholars questioning the nature and legitimacy of Sung Learning as orthodox Confucianism, and the system's intellectual content began to change.[29]

CIVIL EXAMINATIONS AND CLASSICAL ORTHODOXY

The Five Classics and Four Books, as interpreted by Sung Confucians, became the core of the civil service educational curriculum during the Yuan, Ming, and Ch'ing dynasties. Because of the centrality of classical studies to political discourse, the examination process emphasized allegiance to the Ch'eng-Chu school in addition to dynastic loyalty. Session one and later session two questions based on quotations selected from the Four Books and Five Classics elicited from students their knowledge of Confucian orthodoxy. For instance, one of the most telling classical passages for both orthodox philosophy and imperial ideology was drawn from Confucius's response to his disciple Yen Yuan's query concerning the moral doctrine of benevolence. Confucius responded: "*To return to the observance of the rites through overcoming the self constitutes benevolence.* If for a single day a man could return to the observance of the rites through overcoming himself, then the whole Empire would consider benevolence to be his. However, *the practice of benevolence depends on oneself alone,* and not on others." (emphasis added) [30]

In his commentary on this passage, Chu Hsi gave the following glosses: "*K'e* means to conquer (*sheng*). *Chi* refers to one's selfish desires." According to Chu Hsi, this meant that "to practice benevolence, one must conquer one's selfish desires and return to the observance of the rites." In this manner, the "perfect virtue of the original mind," which Chu equated with heavenly principle, could be attained.[31]

The 1465 Shantung provincial examination demonstrates how prominent such views became when they were required on state examinations. The first quotation from the Four Books for session one of the Shantung examination proceedings, drawn from the passage in the *Analects* cited above, required that all candidates have mastered Chu Hsi's views on the practice of benevolence and the return to ritual. Ranked second of all candidates in Shantung who took the 1465 examination, Wang Lun's (fl. 1465–87) essay for this passage from the *Analects* was judged the best and included in the official records of the proceedings. One of the examiners wrote that "the words in this essay were well-ordered and comprehensive, indeed they were worthy of revealing the essential thread in [Confucius's] teachings."[32]

In his essay, Wang Lun emphasized Chu Hsi's gloss for the benevolence passage, in which Chu claimed that the "perfect virtue of the original mind" was not derived from external forms but instead emanated from the "heavenly principles of the individual mind." In his eight-legged essay, Wang neatly reproduced for the examiners the orthodox bifurcation of heavenly principles from human desires, contending that the "transmission of the mind-set of the sages was the gate to their vision." Confucius's "theory of the four renunciations" was defended by Wang Lun in light of the constant struggle required to enable heavenly principles to prevail over wayward desires.

Immediately following the benevolence passage in the *Analects,* Confucius had said: "Do not look unless it is in accordance with the rites; do not listen unless it accords with the rites; do not speak unless it accords with the rites; do not move unless it is in accordance with the rites." Because Chu Hsi's interpretation of this passage was orthodox, candidates like Wang Lun were expected to demonstrate that they had mastered what Confucius had meant about benevolence and the four renunciations by reproducing the essentials of

Chu Hsi's dualistic position on the antagonism between moral principles and human desires. No leeway was permitted to question whether Chu Hsi's views were appropriate to the passage in question. In the pages of examination questions and answers, the students were expected to confirm correct views, not stray into textual debates that might cloud the moral issues at stake in the passage.[33]

Outside the precincts of civil examinations, many late Ming Confucians had objected to Chu Hsi's gloss "to conquer one's selfish desires" for Confucius's, notion of "overcoming the self." Members of the T'ai-chou school (in Yangchow prefecture), a radical group of Wang Yang-ming's followers, saw in this gloss confirmation of what they considered the absolutism of Chu Hsi's bifurcation of human desires from heavenly principle. Chu Hsi, they thought, was in effect reading into this passage from the *Analects* Chu's distinction between *li* (moral principles) and *ch'i* (variously rendered as "material force," "ether," "stuff," "energy," "matter"). Despite such disagreements in interpretation during the Ming, however, Chu Hsi's views continued to prevail in the important arena of provincial and national examinations whenever examiners picked the benevolence passage for a quotation from the Four Books in the first session.[34]

Questions dealing with the benevolence passage in the *Analects* were repeated during the Ch'ing dynasty. In the 1685 metropolitan examination, the first quotation from the Four Books selected was this passage recording the exchange between Yen Yuan and Confucius. The prize essay, which was rated as "orthodox principle" by the examiner Wang Hung-hsu (1645–1723), was prepared by the eventual optimus for the competition, a southern literatus from Soochow prefecture in the Yangtze Delta heartland, Lu K'en-t'ang (1650–96). Lu's eight-legged essay presented the orthodox Ch'eng-Chu position on the importance of "overcoming the self" and "returning to the rites" outlined above. Between 1465 and 1685, the acceptable interpretation of this passage had not changed.

For emphasis, Lu K'en-t'ang's essay on "benevolence" focused on the tension between human desires and moral principles. To "bring order to one's selfish interests," Lu noted, one had to "recognize that the inception of selfishness begins in desires." If personal desires could be overcome, there were no limits to what could be achieved. To manifest benevolence in one's behavior demanded that "each affair be cleansed by principles." Perhaps the most adulated essay for the entire examination, this eight-legged masterpiece affirmed the cultural values of Sung Confucianism and divided the world according to orthodox philosophical categories acceptable to the political authorities.[35]

Differing interpretations of this celebrated passage reemerged in the late eighteenth century, however, when Han Learning and evidential research (*k'ao-cheng-hsueh*) became popular among Ch'ing scholars. The polymath Tai

Chen (1724–77) explicitly attacked the orthodox position, although little impact was felt in the examination process itself (see also Brokaw, chap. 8 of this volume). Chu Hsi's rigorous definition of human desires was the key issue for Tai Chen. In his discussion of the *Analects* passage, Tai noted: "Lao-tzu, Chuang-tzu, and the Buddha [spoke of] 'having no desires,' not of 'having no selfishness.' The way of the sages and worthies was 'to have no selfishness' and not 'to have no desires.' To equate [the self] with selfish desires is therefore a notion the sages totally lacked."[36]

The theoretical debate was drawn over the affirmation or negation of human desires. For Tai Chen, the Chu Hsi line of inquiry had scorned the essential characteristics of humanity in favor of attention to heavenly principles:

> The sages ordered the world by giving an outlet to people's feelings and by making it possible for them to realize their desires. In this way, the Way of the sages was brought to completion.... With regard to the Sung Confucians, however, [the people] believe in them, thinking that they are the equivalent of the sages. Everyone can talk about the distinction between moral principles and human desires. Therefore, those who control the people today pay no attention to the sages giving an outlet to people's feelings and making it possible for them to realize their desires.[37]

Tai's political criticism of the way in which classical values had been used to stifle the interests of the people was a direct result of his reevaluation of the Chu Hsi interpretation of classical terms such as benevolence. Not until the last years of the dynasty did such views have more than interpretive impact.[38]

In addition to the passage in the *Analects* in which Confucius called for "overcoming the self," two passages from the *Documents Classic* added fuel to the orthodox Ch'eng-Chu position. In the chapter of that Classic entitled "Offices of Chou" ("Chou kuan"), the Chou dynasty king announced:

> Oh, all my officials and superior men, pay reverent attention to your charges, and be careful of the commands you issue. Once issued, commands must be put into effect and cannot be retracted. By your public-mindedness extinguish all selfish aims, and the people will have confidence.[39]

This was the locus classicus for the priority of the "public" domain over the "private" in Confucian discourse.

In another chapter in the *Documents Classic*, "Counsels of Yü the Great" ("Ta Yü mo"), the distinction between the "human" and "moral" minds was enunciated for the first time. The sage-king Shun admonished the soon-to-be-crowned Yü as follows: "The human mind is precarious. The moral mind is subtle. Have absolute refinement and singleness of purpose. Hold fast the mean."[40]

Taken together, these two passages from the *Documents Classic* became key pillars of the orthodox position during the Yuan, Ming, and Ch'ing dynasties.

In a culture that drew its ideals from a past golden age populated by sage-kings of unquestioned wisdom, orthodoxy required classical verifications for its present articulation. Accordingly, Ch'eng I had drawn the explicit bifurcation between the human and moral minds as uncontrolled desire versus heavenly principle: "The human mind equals human desires; therefore it is very precarious. The moral mind equals heavenly principle; therefore it is extremely subtle. Only through refinement can the [moral mind] be observed. Only through singleness of purpose can it be preserved. In this manner only can one hold to the mean. These words say it all."[41]

Chu Hsi, building on Ch'eng I's interpretation, gave the "human and moral minds" (*jen-hsin Tao-hsin*) passage a new theoretical twist by subsuming the distinction into his own philosophy of principle: "Those who speak of the precariousness of the human mind mean that it is the sprout of human desires. The subtlety of the moral mind is the place of honor for heavenly principle."[42]

Chu Hsi was suggesting that his bifurcation between *li* and *ch'i* had its counterpart in Shun's declaration of the distinction between the moral and human minds. The former could be described as moral, that is, the source of moral principles, and the latter as human, that is, the source of desires and hence evil. To the degree that Chu Hsi's concepts of *li* and *ch'i* were mutually exclusive and thus mutually irreducible, his position could be interpreted as introducing a profound antagonism between moral principles and the material world of human desires.[43]

In the 1189 preface to his "Phrases and Sentences in the Doctrine of the Mean," Chu made more explicit his reason for linking the distinction between the moral and human minds to his philosophy of *li-hsueh*. Moreover, he added to the distinction between the moral and human minds the parallel distinction between "public" and "private" as enunciated in the "Offices of Chou" chapter:

> All persons, however, have their material form. Even if they are endowed with superior intelligence, they therefore all have a human mind. Moreover, everyone has a [correct] nature. Even if they are endowed with the basest stupidity, they all have a moral mind. If one does not know how to control the mind, then it is precarious. The more precarious [the human mind becomes] the more subtle the subtle [moral mind] becomes. The public-mindedness of [universal] principles thus has no way to overcome the personal concerns of one's human desires. One must cause the moral mind always to be the master of the person and the human mind always to obey it. As a result, the precarious [human mind] will be pacified; the subtle [moral mind] will appear clearly, and all impulses, talk, and behavior will of themselves not reach extreme error.[44]

Chu Hsi moved freely between the Four Books and Five Classics, treating them holistically as the basis for the "thought-world" of the classical age. Chu's efforts culminated with his student Ts'ai Shen, who used the "human and moral minds" passage as the basis for a holistic interpretation of all the chapters in the *Documents*, which as we have seen became the required commentary in the examination curriculum. In the 1209 preface to his annotation of the *Documents*, Ts'ai wrote: "The world-ordering of the two emperors and three kings drew its roots from the Way. The Way of the two emperors and three kings drew its roots from the mind. If one recaptures their thought-world, the Way and world order can be gotten and articulated. What is [this mind]? It is 'absolute refinement and singleness of purpose [thereby] holding the mean.' These are the methods of mental discipline, which [the sage-kings] Yao, Shun, and Yü transmitted to each other."[45]

Referring specifically to the *jen-hsin Tao-hsin* passage in the "Counsels of Yü the Great" and the "public" versus "private" distinction in the "Offices of Chou" chapter, Ts'ai made his point even more explicit. Mental discipline was the essence of the tension between the moral and human minds. The sage-king became master of himself and forced his desires to obey his will:

> The mind is a person's knowledge and perception. It is controlled from within [the body] and responds to the outside. Pointing to its inception in material forms, it is called the "human mind." Pointing to its inception in moral principle, it is called the "moral mind." The human mind easily becomes selfish and is hard to keep public-minded. Therefore, it is precarious. The moral mind is hard to illuminate but easy to cloud over. Therefore, it is subtle.... If the moral mind is always made the master and the human mind obeys it, then the precarious [human mind] is pacified and the subtle [moral mind] manifests itself.... Probably, when the ancient sages were about to hand the empire over to a successor, they always brought together and transmitted their methods of world-ordering to [him].[46]

In addition, Ts'ai Shen made clear that the moral and human minds reflected the bifurcation between public and private. Commenting on the words "by your public-mindedness extinguish all selfish aims" in the "Offices of Chou" chapter, Ts'ai Shen wrote: "One uses public-minded principles in the world to extinguish selfish feelings."[47]

In his discussions with his students concerning the need "to overcome oneself," Chu Hsi had earlier put the final touches on his theoretical position. What emerged was a vision of human nature in which benevolence was the product of personal control through overcoming the self, public-minded behavior, and the elimination of selfish motives and desires:

> What is meant by 'returning to the observance of the rites through overcoming the self' is the elimination of selfish motives and that's all. If you can eliminate selfish motives, then heavenly principle will spread widely of itself.... Public-mindedness is the way of practicing benevolence. Man is the raw material for benevolence. When you have a [public-spirited] man, then you also have benevolence.... If there were no selfish interests, then the entire physical existence of

man would exhibit such benevolence.... The reason why men are not benevolent is because of their selfish interests. If one does not have a selfish mind, then this principle [of benevolence] will be prevalent.... Thus, without a selfish mind, benevolence will automatically appear.[48]

By equating public-mindedness with the chief Confucian virtue of benevolence, Confucius's admonition "to overcome the self" was placed within a theoretical framework in which personal emotions and aspirations were designated as selfish desires that required elimination. Furthermore, the public domain of benevolence included the practice of love and reciprocity precisely to the degree that the private domain of the self was curtailed.

In his effort to wed classical passages to his analysis of the public domain of heavenly principle and the private domain of human desires, Chu Hsi successfully developed a classical sanction for his philosophic ideas. What is not so apparent is how a humanistic philosophy such as the Ch'eng-Chu school of *li-hsueh* could readily serve as theoretical underpinning for the imperial state.

Sung Confucian ideals of the priority of "public" over "private" overlapped with appeals to the throne as the representative of public virtue and virtuous succession. The interpretation of "public" left no room for appeals to individual desires or private interests. Employing the image of "master" and "slave" in his theory of the mind and desires, Chu Hsi created sufficient ideological space in his political philosophy for unintended interpretive consequences that Ming spokesmen for the state would find useful.[49]

For example, during the 1516 provincial examination in Chekiang, the second policy question for session three of the proceedings focused on the issue of the "orthodox transmission of the Way" and the role of the "transmission of the mind" in enabling the moral mind to reach its goals of "absolute refinement, singleness of purpose, and allegiance to the mean." The examiners stressed in their question that spiritual and mental subtlety was the key to unraveling the ties between individual self-cultivation of the moral mind and public mastery of the comprehensive handles of government. Study of nature and principle was presented as the Sung dynasty reconstruction of the mind-set of the sage-king Yao, who had passed on the lesson of the middle way of governance to his chosen successor Shun. In fact, the candidates were asked to reconcile Chu Hsi's views with the classical doctrines of absolute refinement, singleness of purpose, and allegiance to the mean.[50]

Examiners chose as the most outstanding essay for this policy question the answer prepared by Wu Ch'in (fl. c. 1516–17), who finished third in the overall competition. One examiner rated Wu's essay as an exemplar for "studies of the Way" and explication of the *Tao-t'ung*. Another remarked that Wu was "one with whom one could discuss the Way." Wu's essay indeed confirmed the orthodox position on the nature of the mind and its transmission since the sage-kings of antiquity: "From antiquity to the present, through different periods, this mind-set has been unaltered." Chu Hsi's views were defended in the strongest terms; his efforts to encompass both morality and learning were praised. "Morality depended on the Doctrine of the Mean for its efficacy," Wu Ch'in wrote, and "learning must seek out benevolence as its goal."

To complete the exercise, Wu Ch'in incorporated into his answer the benevolence passage from the *Analects* (see above) to demonstrate the inner consistency between the classical teachings regarding the restraint of desires associated with the human mind and the mastery of the principles in the moral mind. "Different epochs all shared the same mind. Different [historical] traces all shared the same principles." The goal according to Wu was to "complete the original power" and "recapture the natural essence of one's mind."

Wu Ch'in's prize essay concluded with a twin assault on the Buddhist doctrines of "emptiness" and "extinction" and the Confucian predilection for the arid textual field of etymology and grammar and punctuation exercises associated with literary works. These were each pursuits in which the "human mind was daily buried and the Way was daily distanced." Such attacks on heterodoxy clarified for the examiners the doctrinal ground upon which Chu Hsi's orthodox position was constructed.

Wu Ch'in's writing ability carried him successfully through the metropolitan examination hurdle the following year, when he received his *chin-shih* degree in the third tier of graduates. Interestingly, however, Wu retired early to a life of scholarship, poetry, prose, and leisure, associating with many of the leading literary figures of his day (such as Li Meng-yang, 1473–1529). His well-thought-out attack on such pursuits in his youthful examination essay seemed to carry little weight. Perhaps he just changed his mind; perhaps the examination was a mere exercise for him; perhaps he became disenchanted with the harsh realities of the Cheng-te and Chia-ching reigns, particularly the Great Ritual Debate that rocked the court in 1522–24.[51]

Orthodox Sung Confucianism, although frequently criticized outside the examination cubicles, survived intact into the seventeenth century. During the late Ming, Ku Hsien-ch'eng (1550–1612), the influential leader of the privately endowed Tung-lin Academy in Wu-hsi county, agreed with Chu Hsi that evil was due to the inherent instability of the human mind, which if left unchecked could cloud the moral mind: "The moral mind has a master; the human mind does not. If there is a master [in charge], then everything in the world through its activity will be the epitome of sacred. This is called the gate of numerous subtleties. If there is no master, then everything in the world through its activity will reach extreme danger. This is the gate of numerous calamities." By appealing to the "commanding presence" of the moral mind, Ku was reaffirming in political terms the authority of the Ch'eng-Chu orthodoxy for classical discourse and gainsaying the views of Wang Yang-ming.

Similarly, the Changchow Tung-lin partisan Ch'ien I-pen (1539–1610) accepted Chu Hsi's bifurcation of the mind, but with an important political twist:

he equated the moral mind with the ruler and the human mind with the subject. Just as the moral mind was master in Chu Hsi's theory of mind, so the ruler was master of his subjects in Ch'ien I-pen's late Ming gloss of Ch'eng-Chu orthodoxy. The "descending" view of political power now operated in moral theory as well.[52]

Such interpretations in the hands of dogmatic Confucian moralists and formalistic political hacks provided state autocrats with the ideological weapons they would require to maintain the perennial goals of short-term gains based on political opportunism and long-term preservation of imperial power and prestige. After the Manchu triumph, Manchu rulers still accorded Ch'eng-Chu orthodoxy eminence of place in state ideology and examination requirements.[53]

During the 1685 metropolitan examination in Peking, the "moral mind" passage was again raised in the first policy question for session three. Referring to the passage in the *Documents* in which the distinction between the human and moral mind occurred, the examiners summarized Chu Hsi's and Ts'ai Shen's interpretations: "The rule of the ancient emperors and kings was based on the Way. The Way was grounded in the mind. After Yao instructed Shun to hold fast to the mean, Shun then expanded this lesson and passed it on to Yü."[54]

In essence, the examiners contended that the doctrines of "preserving sincerity" and "investigating things" depended on the "learning of the mind." Lu K'en-t'ang's prize essay opened with a summary of the centrality of the mind that corroborated the examiners' position: "All emperors and kings [of old] were men who through study governed effectively. Accordingly, they were all men who learned through the mind."[55]

During both the regular 1729 and special 1737 metropolitan examinations, policy questions raised in the third session dealt with the "human and moral minds" passage. For the first policy question of 1729, examiners explicitly brought up the distinction between the moral and human minds while asking candidates to discuss the metaphysical attributes of the Supreme Ultimate. The answer prepared by Shen Ch'ang-yü (1700–44), secundus for the entire competition, was reprinted in the official record and was described by one of the chief examiners as "learning having a basis." Shen's exemplary essay presented the Sung Confucian view of cosmology in which the Supreme Ultimate gave rise to yin and yang, which in turn produced the Five Phases and the world of myriad things.

Discussion of cosmology served as a prelude to explication of the metaphysical foundations of the "mind and nature." Nature, according to Shen Ch'ang-yü, "served as a standard for the mind." The essay then explored how the relation between nature and the mind corroborated the Ch'eng-Chu distinction between the human and moral minds. Without the moral categories derived from nature, the mind remained unaffected by its roots in the Supreme Ultimate. The practice of benevolence required "nurturing one's nature" by "having singleness of purpose and holding fast to the mean." Otherwise, Shen concluded, the "human mind" would reign and one's heavenly nature containing moral principles would be lost. Rhetorically presenting his answer to the Yung-cheng emperor, Shen appealed to the "orthodox studies" on which his essay was based.[56]

For the first policy question prepared during the 1737 special examination, which commemorated the recent coronation of the Ch'ien-lung emperor, the examiners repeated almost verbatim earlier questions dealing with correspondences between the doctrines of "orthodox statecraft" and "orthodox transmission of the Way." Claiming that these doctrines were the "unified Way" of governance, the examiners asked candidates to demonstrate their understanding of the Ch'eng-Chu agenda for "mental discipline" (*hsin-fa*) and "singleness of purpose and holding to the mean," which derived from the distinction between the moral and human mind.[57]

From Kiangsi, Ho Ch'i-jui (n.d.) prepared an answer that was selected as the best essay for this policy question. Although Ho was ranked first on the metropolitan examination, the Ch'ien-lung emperor, exercising his imperial prerogative, later had him demoted to the top of the second tier of graduates after the palace examination was held. Understandably, Ho's essay recapitulated the orthodox bifurcation between threatening human desires and saving moral principles derived from heaven. The Ch'eng-Chu program for mental discipline required allegiance to the doctrine of the mean and to the "esoteric words and great meanings" bequeathed by the sages.

The heart of Ho's essay defended the chief doctrines Chu Hsi had championed in the latter's quest to provide a framework for cultivation of the moral mind. "The extension of knowledge" and "residing in seriousness" are examples of Chu's doctrines that Ho Ch'i-jui covered. According to Ho, the goal Chu had demarcated was to "save people so they could become sages." Sageness and benevolence went hand in hand in orthodox moral theory. Self-cultivation based on mental discipline was the prerequisite for political order.[58]

The Ming and Ch'ing student essays examined above exemplify the general uniformity of views that appeared in the civil service selection process, which contrasted sharply with the diversity of opinions in the private domain (see also Guy, chap. 5 of this volume). During both dynasties there was a wide range of scholarly opinions and classical positions variously defended by Confucian literati. In the precincts of the examination system, however, diversity of opinion was for the most part not tolerated until the late eighteenth century. Unintentionally, the Ch'eng-Chu school's appeal to absolute and universal principles provided the Yuan, Ming, and Ch'ing imperiums with a system of theoretical devices, that is, an "ideology," to combat threats to the political and moral status quo.

Chu Hsi's views on the priority of public values over private interests dovetailed neatly in theoretical terms with his negative view of factional alignments in politics. The ideal of personal behavior and political action reduced to the same formula: affirm the public-minded principles of the moral mind and oppose the selfish tendencies of the human mind. To join a political faction was to follow one's personal interests, which would in the end be based on one's selfish desires. A faction or party conformed to the wayward tendencies of the "human mind"—in this case a number of human minds horizontally joined together—against the universal standards of the moral mind exemplified hierarchically by a steadfast minister who served the emperor with unswerving loyalty.[59]

As we will see below, the distance between official orthodoxy tested in state examinations and research findings in Ch'ing dynasty classical and historical studies began to widen so much in the eighteenth century, however, that the controversy over Sung versus Han Learning as Confucian orthodoxy began to impact upon the questions and answers administered in the provincial and metropolitan examinations. Sagehood might remain an orthodox ideal in eight-legged essays, but among empirically-minded *k'ao-cheng* scholars the Sung and Ming Confucian program for self-cultivation was increasingly deemed naive and impractical.

HAN VS. SUNG LEARNING IN LATE CH'ING EXAMINATIONS

The late imperial state in China encouraged the widespread publication and circulation of acceptable materials dealing with the Four Books and Five Classics because the latter were the basis of the civil service curriculum. Throughout the Ming and Ch'ing dynasties, more classically literate Chinese read or had access to the Five Classics and Four Books than literate Europeans had access to the Old and New Testaments.[60]

In the seventeenth and eighteenth centuries, for example, the Classics and Dynastic Histories were carefully scrutinized by a growing community of textual scholars in Yangtze Delta urban centers. The slow but steady emergence of evidential research studies in the Delta as a self-conscious field of academic discourse was predicated on the centrality of philological research to (1) determine the authenticity of classical and historical texts, (2) unravel the etymologies of ancient classical terms, (3) reconstruct the phonology of ancient Chinese, and (4) clarify the paleography of Chinese characters.[61]

The *k'ao-cheng* research agenda for accumulating verifiable knowledge represented a major reorientation in thought and epistemology among classical scholars in the Yangtze Delta. Evidential scholars there favored a return to the most ancient sources available, usually from the Han dynasties, to reconstruct the classical tradition. Because the latter were closer in time to the actual compilation of the Classics, Ch'ing scholars increasingly used Han works (hence "Han Learning") to reevaluate the Classics. Frequently, this change in emphasis also entailed a rejection of Sung and Ming sources (hence "Sung

Learning") to study the Classics because the latter were separated by over fifteen hundred years from the classical era and because many Ch'ing scholars were convinced that the schools of Chu Hsi and Wang Yang-ming had unwittingly incorporated heterodox Taoist and Buddhist doctrines and theories into the Confucian Canon.[62]

The Old Text Documents *Controversy*

Many *k'ao-cheng* scholars claimed, for instance, that the Old Text portions of the *Documents Classic* were forgeries from the third century A.D. and not the work of the sage-kings of antiquity. This textual controversy became a cause célèbre among Han Learning scholars at the same time that the examination system used Old Text passages on the "human and moral minds" to test candidates' knowledge of the Sung Learning orthodoxy. Students were expected to parrot the Ch'eng-Chu position on the Classics for state examiners, but even the latter increasingly recognized that many orthodox views were philologically untenable.

Since the Sung dynasty, doubts had been expressed concerning the provenance of the Old Text chapters of the *Documents,* but it was not until Yen Jo-chü's research (1636–1704) and the definitive conclusions he drew in his *Evidential analysis of the Old Text Documents* that the question was considered settled. Based on Yen's demonstrations that the Old Text portion was not authentic, proposals were sent to the throne in the 1690s and again in the 1740s calling for elimination of the Old Text chapters from the official text used in the examination system. Each time the proposals were set aside.

Hui Tung (1697–1758), the doyen of Han Learning in Soochow, had renewed Yen Jo-chü's attack on the Old Text chapters in the 1740s. Appending Yen Jo-chü's points of agreement, Hui noted that it had taken several centuries for suspicions concerning the Old Text *Documents* to lead anywhere conclusive. Hui Tung's Han Learning followers continued research on the Old Text chapters, picking up where their mentor had left off. Changchow's Sun Hsing-yen (1753–1818), with his definitive study of the Old and New Text *Documents*, brought to completion the attack on the spurious Old Text chapters. Sun's analysis of Later and Former Han sources marked the high point of Han Learning prestige during the Ch'ing dynasty.[63]

At the confluence of classical studies, legitimation of state power, and policy articulation, the conservative position vis-à-vis the Classics taken by Sung Learning advocates represented their ideological solidarity with the state orthodoxy of the Ming and Ch'ing dynasties. The Han Learning threat to the orthodox Old Text Classics threatened the shared consensus enshrined since the fifteenth century in the curriculum of the examination system. Many refused to accept the textual findings of evidential research scholars.

Chuang Ts'un-yü (1719–88), later a leader in the reemergence of New Text Confucianism in Changchow, noted while serving as a Hanlin secretary to the Ch'ien-lung emperor in the 1740s that if the long accepted Old Text chapter known as the "Counsels of Yü the Great" was impugned, then the cardinal doctrine of the "human mind and moral mind" — as well as the legal injunction of Kao Yao, minister to Emperor Shun, which stated "rather than put to death an innocent person, you [Shun] would rather run the risk of irregularity" — would be subverted. These were teachings, Chuang contended, that depended on their classical sanction. Accordingly, Chuang Ts'un-yü attempted on ideological grounds to set limits to the accruing *k'ao-cheng* research by scholars in the Han Learning mainstream.[64]

Changes in Examination Questions on the Documents Classic
Yet, as we have noted above, the metropolitan examinations of 1685, 1730, and 1737 continued to cite the passage on the human and moral minds from the Old Text "Counsels of Yü the Great" with no indication of the philological controversy surrounding its authenticity. Similarly, we have seen that student answers never mentioned such textual debates and that students faithfully recapitulated the Ch'eng-Chu interpretation of the transmission of the mind of the sage-kings. Whether as an oath of political loyalty to the reigning dynasty, or as confirmation of orthodox Confucian cultural values, the examination essay was not conceptually designed for rigorous textual analysis. To bring up philological issues when they were not broached by the examiners in their choice of quotations and questions was to run the risk of failing a selection process designed as a dual cultural and political litmus test.

Such predispositions began to change in the late eighteenth century, however, when in policy questions during session three of the provincial and metropolitan examinations examiners began to test on technical *k'ao-cheng* topics previously outside the state curriculum. In the 1810 Kiangnan provincial examination for candidates from Anhwei and Kiangsu, for instance, the first of the third session's policy questions straightforwardly raised the issue of the authenticity of portions of the *Documents Classic*.

The examiners opened their query by immediately raising the debate concerning the provenance of the "Preface" ("*Hsu*") to the original hundred-chapter version of the *Documents*, which had long been attributed to Confucius. The examiners asked, "Why wasn't the preface included in the [original] listing of the hundred chapters?" Next candidates were asked to explain why during the Former Han dynasty there were discrepancies in reports regarding how many chapters (twenty-eight or twenty-nine) of the New Text version of the *Documents* text had survived the Ch'in "burning of the books" policy. Following this, the candidates were required to explicate the perplexing circumstances in which K'ung An-kuo (156–74? B.C.), a descendant of Confucius and a Han erudite of the Classics, had prepared his own "Preface" for a version of the *Documents* that added twenty-nine more Old Text chapters from a recently discovered text of the *Documents* to the earlier New Text version. "Why," the examiners asked, "had fifty-nine chapters been listed for this version when there should have been only fifty-eight?"

After dealing with former Han sources, the examiners turned to the later Han dynasty (25–220) classicist Cheng Hsuan, the "patron saint" of Ch'ing dynasty Han Learning, whose scholia listed the one hundred chapters in the original but list *Documents* in a different order from K'ung An-kuo's version. "Why this discrepancy?" the students were asked. Subsequently, issues related to T'ang and Sung handling of the *Documents* text were raised. Why had K'ung Ying-ta (574–648), then in charge of T'ang efforts to settle on authoritative texts for the Confucian examination curriculum, labeled a third version of the *Documents* from the Han dynasty a forgery? Why had Chu Hsi voiced suspicions concerning the unusual phraseology (for Han dynasty writings) of K'ung An-kuo's commentary and preface to the *Documents*?[65]

The organization and content of this query reveal the degree to which the philological discoveries associated with Han Learning and evidential research had begun to filter into the examination system. Although still a test of cultural and political loyalty in which the Ch'ing reign was praised by the examiners for its nourishing of classical studies, this exploration of the textual vicissitudes surrounding the *Documents Classic* required precise information that would demonstrate to the examiners that the candidate was aware of the controversy surrounding this particular Classic. Rather than a test of cultural orthodoxy, however, the question raised potentially corrosive issues that could challenge orthodox "truths." One of the key Old Text chapters now thought by many Confucians to be a forgery was the "Ta Yü mo," which contained classical lessons on the basis of which the theories of "orthodox statecraft" and "orthodox transmission of the Way" had been constructed.[66]

Such textual concerns might be considered unique to the Yangtze Delta because the academic community there had been pioneers in reviving Han Learning concerns and appropriating *k'ao-cheng* research techniques for classical and historical studies. On the contrary, changes in examination questioning were occurring throughout the empire, principally as a result of the appointment of provincial examiners, who frequently came from the Yangtze Delta and thus were conversant with the latest research findings of classical scholars there. Yangtze Delta scholars had long been the most successful on the metropolitan and palace examinations in Peking and thus were most likely to gain appointment to the Hanlin Academy and the Ministry of Rites. Most of those who served as provincial examination officials were chosen from these two overlapping institutions in the metropolitan bureaucracy. Examinations held in the peripheral provinces of Shantung in the north, Szechwan in the southwest, and Shensi in the northwest all reveal the magnitude of the changes in examination mind-set that were appearing after 1750.[67]

Examinations in Shantung. Although not as directly stated as in the above 1810 question, the first policy question in the Shantung provincial examination of 1771 dealt with the philology of the Classics. By the mid-eighteenth century, the third session's policy questions for provincial examinations began to exhibit an irregular but somewhat common five-way division of topics, usually but not always in the following order: Classics, histories, literature, statecraft, and local geography.

For the policy question dealing with the Classics, examiners frequently explored textual issues, though themes pertaining to moral philosophy remained more common. The 1771 policy question, for example, raised the complicated divisions between the Old and New Text versions of the *Documents* in order to elicit from candidates their grasp of the lack of unanimity about the Classics and their sense of what sort of consensus was possible based on differing viewpoints. Why had even Chu Hsi and Ch'eng I failed to agree on certain issues?[68]

During the 1819 Shantung examination, the examiners specifically asked in the first policy question that candidates engage in a *k'ao-cheng* analysis of the New Text/Old Text provenance of the Classics:

> Wang Po-hou [Ying-lin, 1223–96] claimed that the "Offices of Chou" [chapter of the *Documents*] belonged to the New Text version, but he added that within the Classic many Old Text portions remained. Moreover, in his annotation Wang used New Text [sources] to change the latter. Why? Notes to the *Decorum Ritual* [*I-li*] in some cases follow Old Text [views], in others follow New Text [views], and in still other cases they combine New and Old Text [views]. Can you separate out these issues for clarification?

Later during the 1831 examination, Shantung students were required to answer two policy questions dealing with philology. The first asked specific information about the Old and New Text *Documents*; the second tested the students' knowledge of the paleographical origins of the distinctions between Old and New Text scripts. Students who had only mastered Ch'eng-Chu moral philosophy for sessions one and two were now hard-pressed to pass session three of the provincial examinations in Shantung.[69]

Other technical aspects of *k'ao-cheng* were also tested. In the 1807 provincial examinations held in Shantung, for example, the third policy question dealt with the field of ancient phonology. Inclusion of this question was due to the presence of Sun Hsing-yen as examiner, who as a distinguished *k'ao-cheng* scholar from Changchow prefecture in the Yangtze Delta made his influence felt among candidates preparing for the Shantung examinations. The examination question stressed the priority of ancient rhyme schemes in the *Poetry Classic* for the reconstruction of ancient phonology. Students were also expected to take into account the linguistic factor of the development of four tones in their explication of the classification of rhymes.[70]

Examinations in Szechwan. In Szechwan province, on the other hand, the 1738 examination there revealed that Sung Learning orthodoxy remained intact as the mind-set of examiners. Students were asked, for example, to prepare a policy question essay dealing with the Ch'eng-Chu agenda for mental discipline, which duplicated almost verbatim earlier questions on the metropolitan examinations that we have analyzed above. The first policy question of 1738 thus assumed a unified classical vision for the "orthodox transmission of the Way" that was based on the long-accepted distinction between the "human and moral minds" and the Ch'eng-Chu agenda for "absolute refinement, singleness of purpose, and allegiance to the mean."[71]

Although philological issues were sometimes raised—as in policy questions prepared for the Szechwan provincial examinations of 1741 and 1747, for instance—Sung Learning remained the dominant mind-set for questioning through the eighteenth century. In the 1800 provincial examinations, however, Han Learning issues were raised in policy questions. For the second policy question, students were asked to compare Han-T'ang scholia with Sung "meanings and principles" and to determine how the Ch'eng-Chu school differed from Han and T'ang Confucians. Examiners required for the third policy question an explicit "evidential" analysis to assess the accuracy of historical studies to date. To answer the fourth policy question, candidates had to demonstrate their understanding of the fields of ancient etymology, ancient phonology, and paleography, which the examiners defined as the key subdisciplines of philology.[72]

In subsequent Szechwan examinations, Han and Sung Learning issues were frequently raised. In the first policy question of 1832, for instance, examiners prepared a question focusing on the history of calligraphy and how Old Text (lit., "ancient script") forms of writing pertained to the Four Books. Later in 1846, the third policy question flatly granted one of the linguistic premises of evidential research studies: "The starting point for mastering the Classics is the knowledge of written graphs. To understand written graphs, nothing takes priority over the *Shuo-wen* (Explication of writing)." In the lead policy question of 1859, candidates were asked about doubts concerning the Old Text *Documents*: "Many who are fond of antiquity have supposed that the twenty-five Old Text chapters of the *Documents*, such as the "Counsels of Yü the Great," are forgeries. From what period do they come? Who transmitted them? Who were the first to question them?"

By 1860, then, the very texts upon which orthodox interpretation had been based were openly questioned in the precincts of provincial civil service examinations. Such developments were cumulative but not irrevocable. In 1885, the examiners raised issues pertaining to New and Old Text philology in the first policy question but for the second question prepared a typical query testing the students' knowledge of Sung Learning "orthodox studies." In fact, the juxtaposition of Han and Sung Learning on the same examination in different questions reflected the synthesis of the competing schools that became an important characteristic of the last century of Confucian classical thought.[73]

Examinations in Shensi. Similarly, in Shensi province provincial examination questions remained focused on Sung Confucian themes and issues for most of the first century of Ch'ing rule. In 1756, for example, examiners prepared the first policy question as a test of the students' knowledge of the by now standard doctrine of the "transmission of the mind-set of the sages and worthies," referring specifically to the passage in the "Counsels of Yü the Great" on the distinction between the human and moral minds. This question was repeated almost verbatim in 1788 when the centrality of the "Counsels" chapter was affirmed without any questioning of its Old Text provenance.

In 1759, however, the tenor of questions had already begun to change. The first policy question for the latter proceedings emphasized pre-T'ang classical traditions dating back to the "schools system" used in the Han dynasty Imperial Academy to teach the Classics. Students were asked to summarize the history of the transmission of the *Documents Classic* as well as the other Classics. In the first policy questions for both 1795 and 1800, examiners focused their queries dealing with the Classics specifically on the Han Learning of Cheng Hsuan.

Students were asked in 1795 to discuss the exemplary position Cheng Hsuan held in the "classical studies of Han Confucians." In 1800, the examiners again stressed Cheng Hsuan's contributions to classical studies and tested candidates about Cheng's explication of the Chou dynasty *Change Classic*, among other issues. For the third policy question of 1800, archaeology and paleography as fields of expertise were raised by the examiners when they asked students to demonstrate their knowledge of the characteristics of engraved monoliths from the Han dynasty that contained the "Classics carved onto stone tablets." Similarly, for the fourth policy question philological issues concerning the relationship between the present three-hundred-chapter version of the *Poetry Classic* and its numerous "missing poems" were tested.

Thereafter, Han Learning and *k'ao-cheng* themes became a regular feature of the Shensi examinations. In the 1825 examination, the first policy question queried students on the antiquity of the Five Classics. With regard to the *Documents*, for example, the examiners asked students to comment on the possible forgery of K'ung An-kuo's preface. Similar philological points were raised concerning the *Change* and *Poetry* Classics. In 1831, the Han dynasty "schools system" was tested in the first policy question. By 1833, provincial Shensi examiners were openly sceptical of the authenticity of the Old Text *Documents* and proudly announced in the first policy question that "classical studies under the sagely [Ch'ing] dynasty had been greatly illumined, doubts investigated, and forgeries ferreted out." Political legitimacy was now transmitted through evidential research as well as through the Ch'eng-Chu orthodoxy, indicating that students could demonstrate their loyalty to the dynasty by mastering *k'ao-cheng* techniques.[74]

Changes in Metropolitan Examination Questions. As might be expected of a dynasty that used Sung Confucian rhetoric to defend its political legitimacy, changes in questions for the metropolitan and palace examinations were slower in coming than in their provincial counterparts. Here we are witness to dynamic intellectual changes that began in the urban centers of the Yangtze Delta and first influenced local provincial examinations before these new developments filtered up into the capital selection process. Ch'ing currents of scholarship were ascending the examination ladder on the strength of those Han Learning and *k'ao-cheng* scholars who were themselves moving up the civil service ladder of success.

As noted above, the 1685 metropolitan examination was administered by officials who prepared questions that required mastery of Sung Confucian moral and political theory. Although classical issues dealing with texts and their transmission were tested, the overall Sung Learning mind-set did not change. In the metropolitan examination of 1729, for instance, the 1685 question on the "human and moral minds" had been repeated almost verbatim. In 1737, the question appeared again.

In the metropolitan examinations of 1739, 1742, 1748, 1751, and 1752, the first policy question for each characteristically dealt with the topic of "orthodox statecraft" and the "orthodox transmission of the Way." Examiners in Peking seemed intent on making sure that students got the message: the doctrine of "mental discipline" enabling students to "grasp the fundamentals of moral principles" was the sine qua non for discussing the "methods of governance of the [Three] Emperors and [Five] Kings." Ch'en Chin (1784–1843), a native of the Yangtze Delta, prepared the model answer for the 1739 policy question, which emphasized the dual roles of "external kingship" and "inner sagehood."[75]

In 1742 policy questions, the examiners expressly asked students to treat the Ch'eng-Chu position on human nature. The prize answer focused on "principles of the mind and nature," which were equated with the primacy of the "moral mind" over the "human mind." The "mind of the sages" was the key subject for the policy questions of the 1748 proceedings. Examiners asked: "Do the teachings of Confucius stress sincerity and seriousness? Before Confucius, in what Classic did the principle of sincerity first appear?" The most outstanding essay was prepared by Li Chung-chien (c. 1713–74), who traced the linkage between orthodox statecraft and the orthodox transmission of the Way to the teachings transmitted from Yao to Shun and from Shun to Yü.[76]

The first policy question in 1751 presented the view that "nature originated in the heavenly mind." To "return to one's nature" entailed "holding to the mean" and grasping the superiority of the "moral mind." This time, however, the examiners asked candidates to compare the positions held by Chu Hsi and Wang Yang-ming concerning the polarity between "honoring one's moral nature" and "inquiring into culture and study." In his answer, the Chekiang literatus Chou Li (1709–53) summarized the orthodox position in which Chu Hsi's equation of human nature and principle took precedence over Wang Yang-ming's equation of the mind with principle.[77]

Again in 1752, the "human and moral minds" were made the focus of the first policy question. "Mental discipline," according to the prize essay prepared by Chi Fu-hsiang (n.d.), was equated with "methods of governance." To perfect one's discipline, Chi contended, one had to "grasp the learning of the Way." Such training was premised on "residing in seriousness" and "fathoming principles."[78]

Although questions dealing with textual aspects of the Classics were presented in some of these metropolitan examinations, the mind-set the examiners sought to reproduce among the candidates was decidedly in favor of Sung Learning orthodoxy—so much so that in the 1754 metropolitan examination, which became famous as the one passed by five of the greatest Han Learning scholars of the late eighteenth century (Ch'ien Ta-hsin, 1728–1804; Chi Yun, 1724–1805; Wang Ch'ang, 1725–1807; Wang Ming-sheng, 1722–98; and Chu Yun, 1729–81), only one of the policy questions dealt with textual issues at all. The first policy question in fact required an orthodox restatement of the premises of the Ch'eng-Chu "school of principle," which the Han Learning scholars-to-be would later attack as "empty and unverifiable" rhetoric (*k'ung-t'an*).[79]

Ch'ien Ta-hsin's 1754 examination essay for the second policy question, which dealt with textual issues concerning the transmission of the Four Books and Five Classics, was selected as the most outstanding answer to the question. Although the examiners had stressed the importance of Chu Hsi's place in classical studies, particularly with regard to arranging the proper order of chapters in the *Great Learning* (one of the Four Books), their question did address technical issues surrounding the Four Books. Ch'ien Ta-hsin's extremely long model answer (indicating that unlike most other candidates he took this policy question on session three very seriously) deftly maneuvered through the complexities of classical studies. Without directly impugning Sung Learning orthodoxy, Ch'ien pointed out that the Four Books were never referred to as the "Four Books" until the Sung dynasty, when Chu Hsi and his followers brought the *Analects, Mencius, Great Learning*, and *Doctrine of the Mean* together as a special repository of classical teachings. Although the Four Books had since taken precedence over the Five Classics, Ch'ien Ta-hsin noted that originally the Four Books had been directly and indirectly derived from the Five Classics. Ch'ien said that "the six Classics were all definitively compiled by the sages," suggesting that the later Four Books had less classical authority.[80]

Policy questions dealing with the Confucian Canon increasingly moved from obligatory requests that candidates reproduce Sung Confucian moral discourse to tests of their mastery of classical information. In the 1766 metropolitan examination, for example, candidates were asked a policy question requiring mastery of the Han Learning field of phonology. The examiners pointed out in their question that "because the Han was not very far separated in time from antiquity," the initials and finals in Han versions of the *Poetry Classic* were likely to be the most accurate ancient pronunciations available.[81]

Later policy questions prepared during the 1793 and 1823 metropolitan examinations reveal the degree to which Ch'ing classical studies were impacting the examination process. In 1793, students were asked to deal with the controversies surrounding the three orthodox commentaries to Confucius's *Spring and Autumn Annals*, particularly the debate over the reliability of the *Tso-chuan* ("Tso's commentary"), whose author, Tso Ch'iu-ming, had been regarded as one of Confucius's direct disciples, although this Old Text claim had been challenged by eighteenth-century New Text scholars. In 1792, for instance, Chi Yun had memorialized the throne concerning the commentaries to the *Annals*, which had included since the Ming dynasty the Hu An-kuo commentary as one of the four required commentaries. Chi requested that this Sung commentary be removed from the curriculum because of its more than fifteen-hundred-year distance from the compiling of the Classic itself. Chi's request was granted—an event symbolizing the victory of Han Learning at court. Thereafter, only the three Han commentaries were regarded as orthodox, and the Hu commentary fell into oblivion.[82]

The 1823 examination, for which the distinguished *k'ao-cheng* scholar Wang Yin-chih (1766–1834) served as examiner, included three policy questions that queried students about classical studies. In the first, examiners asked candidates about the historical transmission of the Classics. The model answer by Chou K'ai-ch'i (n.d.), who finished fifty-sixth in the metropolitan examination but moved up to third in the palace examination, focused on the role Cheng Hsuan had played during the Later Han dynasty as the key transmitter of the meaning of the Classics to posterity.

For the second policy question, students were asked to describe the origins, evolution, and content of lectures to the emperor by prominent Confucians since the Han dynasties. Again, the best essay was by Chou K'ai-ch'i. The third policy question tested the role of Confucians in the imperial system. In his prize essay, Lin Chao-t'ang (n.d.), twenty-sixth on the metropolitan but optimus for the palace examination, noted how emperors had variously promoted the teachings of notable Confucians. Lin described how in 1242 the Ch'eng-Chu school was patronized, whereas Ming T'ai-tsu had for a time promoted the teachings of the former Han Confucian Tung Chung-shu, who had advised Emperor Wu on state policy.[83]

A Han Learning bent to policy questions was solidified in session three of the 1847 and 1852 metropolitan examinations. Prize essays for the initial policy questions by Hsu P'eng-shou (n.d.), first on the 1847 metropolitan

examinations, covered the fields of classical studies with an emphasis on etymology in the first question and poetic rhymes and cadences in the second. In
1852, examiners who prepared the first policy question for session three asked
students to present evidence (*cheng*) concerning textual issues related to the
Classics. In his prize essay, Hsu Ho-ch'ing (n.d.), who was ranked in the third
tier of graduates after the palace examination, summarized the contributions
made by earlier Han and T'ang Confucians to the study of the Classics. In a
closing rhetorical flourish, however, Hsu reveled in the research "exhausting
the Classics" by Ch'ing Confucians, research which candidates such as he
should emulate.[84]

Consequently, policy questions during the late eighteenth and early nineteenth centuries began to reflect the changing intellectual context within
which the Confucian civil service examinations were administered. Although
the quotations from the Four Books and Five Classics presented during
sessions one and two of the metropolitan examinations remained for the most
part unchanged and dominated by orthodox Ch'eng-Chu interpretations, Han
Learning trends and *k'ao-cheng* issues had successfully penetrated both provincial and metropolitan examinations through the policy questions of session
three. The Ch'ing dynasty continued to employ the civil service examinations
to legitimate itself politically and culturally. The cultural dimension, however,
increasingly reflected the debate then prominent among Ch'ing Confucians
between Han and Sung Learning, neither of which the Manchu rulers saw as
politically corrosive. Before the Taiping Rebellion (1850–64), then, there is evidence that the civil examination system was itself undergoing slow but
nonetheless important internal changes in content and direction, even as it
remained the key governmental institution for political and social reproduction
of Confucian gentry-officials.

CONCLUDING REMARKS

Scrutiny of the vicissitudes of linguistic structures and syllogistic chains of
moral argument commonly found in examination questions and answers during the Ming and Ch'ing dynasties reveals that the examination system in late
imperial China included an explicit logic for the formulation of examination
questions and an implicit logic for building semantic categorizations that
enabled examiners and students to mark and divide their cognitive world according to the moral attitudes, social dispositions, and political compulsions of
their day. The general analytic framework for moral reasoning in imperial
examinations presupposed powerful linguistic assumptions about the
behavioral consequences of examinations testing moral categories and
distinctions (see Afterword).

Before the impact of Western thought and the Taiping Rebellion, many
Confucians began to reevaluate their cultural tradition and the forms of edu-

cation through which native values were transmitted from the past and reproduced in the present. The cumulative effects of these new scholarly and educational initiatives eventually made themselves felt in private academies and state examinations at the provincial and national levels. Although the attitude-forming role of civil examinations remained central even after reforms were initiated, its content-expressing function took on increasing significance after 1750. If sessions one and two of the state examinations remained tied to the political and social effects of orthodox moral reasoning drawn from the Ch'eng-Chu school of *li-hsueh*, session three policy questions reveal that Confucian examiners in the late eighteenth and early nineteenth centuries had become very conscious of Han Learning contributions to Ch'ing classical studies. Confucian examiners, mirroring their larger community of scholar-officials, tried to bring Han and Sung Learning together in the nineteenth century to achieve a balance between moral training and classical erudition.[85]

Overall, however, the pedagogical role of Ch'eng-Chu Confucianism as state orthodoxy prevailed in preparation for late imperial civil examinations. Candidates were asked to demonstrate both their political loyalty to the reigning emperor and allegiance to the moral orthodoxy that legitimated the political status quo. Visible cracks that appeared in the moral orthodoxy, brought on by the eighteenth-century *k'ao-cheng* movement, surfaced during the nineteenth century and were worked into the examination system. The political implications of these classical tremors, however, were not felt fully until the twentieth century when Confucian intellectual hegemony was renounced.

NOTES

Research for this article was supported by grants from the UCLA Academic Senate and research assistance from the UCLA Center for Chinese Studies for the 1987–88 and 1988–89 academic years. Final revisions were completed while I was privileged to hold research fellowships from the Fulbright Foundation (Taiwan), Pacific Cultural Foundation (Taiwan), and Japan Foundation during the 1990–91 academic year.

1. *Ming-shih* 明史 (History of the Ming dynasty), comp. under the auspices of the Ch'ing dynasty, 12 vols. (reprint, Taipei: Ting-wen Press, 1982), 3:1686, 1711.

2. *Ming-shih* 3:1724–25; *Huang-ch'ao hsu wen-hsien t'ung-kao* 皇朝續文獻通考 (Comprehensive survey of state documents during the Ch'ing dynasty), comp. Liu Chin-tsao (Shanghai: Commercial Press, 1936), 8452–53.

3. James T. C. Liu, "How did a Neo-Confucian School Become the State Orthodoxy?" *Philosophy East and West* 23, no. 4 (1973): 483–505; Conrad Schirokauer, "Neo-Confucians Under Attack: The Condemnation of *Wei-hsueh*," in John Haeger, ed., *Crisis and Prosperity in Sung China* (Tucson: University of Arizona Press, 1975), 163–96.

4. *Sung-shih* 宋史 (History of the Sung dynasty) 10 vols. (reprint, Taipei: Ting-wen Press, 1982), 5:3604; *Ming-shih* 3:1675, 3:1719, *Ch'ing-shih kao* 清史稿 (Draft History of the Ch'ing dynasty) 40 vols. (Peking: Chung-hua Press, 1977), 12:3181–92;

Ming-Ch'ing chin-shih t'i-ming pei-lu suo-yin 明 清 進 士 題 名 碑 錄 索 引 (Index to commemorative rolls of presented scholars during the Ming and Ch'ing) 3 vols. (reprint, Taipei: Wen-shih-che Press, 1982), 3:2415–16.

5. *Ming-shih*, 3:1675–76, 1677–78, 1679, 1713; *Ch'ing-shih kao*, 11:3108.

6. See Benjamin A. Elman, "Political, Social, and Cultural Reproduction via Civil Service Examinations in Late Imperial China," *Journal of Asian Studies* 50, no.1 (Feb. 1991): 7–28 .

7. *Ming-shih*, 3:1680, 1715, 1717.

8. *Ming-shih*, 3:1689.

9. *Ming-shih*, 3:1694.

10. *Ming-shih*, 3:1685, 1688–89, 1693–94, 1698–99. See also *Ch'ing-shih kao*, 11:3149, 3152, for unsuccessful efforts to correct these problems.

11. *Ming-shih*, 3:1694.

12. *Ch'ing-shih kao*, 11:3099–3100.

13. *Ch'ing-shih kao*, 11:3169. See also *Huang-ch'ao hsu wen-hsien t'ung-k'ao* 1:8424–25, 8429, 8433, 8438–39, 8440, 8447, 8450. Manchu-language examinations administered to Hanlin members are part of the Han Yü-shan Special Collection in the UCLA University Research Library. Thanks are due Pamela Crossley, who identified the Manchu-language materials in the collection.

14. *Ch'ing-shih kao*, 11:3157–58.

15. Ping-ti Ho, *The Ladder of Success in Imperial China* (New York: Columbia University Press, 1962), 173–83; Mi Chu Wiens, "Lord and Peasant: The Sixteenth to the Eighteenth Century," *Modern China* 6, no. 1 (1980): 9–12.

16. See Frederic Wakeman, Jr., *The Fall of Imperial China* (New York: Free Press, 1975), 21–23; Miyazaki Ichisada, *China's Examination Hell* (New Haven: Yale University Press, 1981), 121–22; Allan Barr, "Pu Songling (P'u Sung-ling) and the Qing Examination System," *Late Imperial China* 7, no. 1 (1986): 92–103.

17. *Ch'ing-shih kao*, 11:3099, 3158–59. See also Ho, *Ladder*, 189.

18. *Ch'ing-shih kao*, 11:3101, 3115, 3152–53. See also *Huang-ch'ao hsu wen-hsien t'ung-k'ao*. 1:8442.

19. *Ch'ing-shih kao*, 1:3147; *Huang-ch'ao hsu wen-hsien t'ung-k'ao*, 1:8429.

20. *Ch'ing-shih kao*, 11:3148–49, 3161.

21. *Ch'ing-shih kao*, 11:3149.

22. *Ch'ing-shih kao*, 11:3149–50.

23. *Ch'in-ting k'e-ch'ang t'iao-li* 欽定科場條例 (Imperially prescribed guidelines for the civil examination grounds) (1834), 57:1a–9a .

24. *Ch'ing-shih kao*, 11:3150–51. See also James J.Y. Liu, *The Art of Chinese Poetry* (Chicago: University of Chicago Press, 1962), 26–29.

25. *Ch'ing-shih kao*, 11:3151–52; *Huang-ch'ao hsu wen-hsien t'ung-k'ao*, 1:8448.

26. *Ch'ing-shih kao*, 11:3193ff; Wakeman, *The Fall of Imperial China*, 21–23.

27. *Ch'ing-shih kao*, 11:3104, 3168. *Huang-ch'ao hsu wen-hsien t'ung-k'ao*, 1:8452–54.

28. *Ch'ing-shih kao*, 1:3153–54. See also *Huang-ch'ao hsu wen-hsien t'ung-k'ao*, 1:8455–60; Cyrus Peake, *Nationalism and Education in Modern China* (New York: Howard Fertig, 1970), *passim*.

29. For discussion, see Chung-ying Cheng, "Logic and Language in Chinese Thought," in Raymond Klibansky, ed., *Contemporary Philosophy, A Survey* (Firenze: La

nouva Italia, 1969), 335–44; Pierre Bourdieu, "Systems of Education and Systems of Thought," in Michael Young, ed., *Knowledge and Control: New Directions for the Sociology of Education* (London: Collier Macmillan, 1971), 190–94.

30. See *Lun-yü yin-te* 論語引得 (Concordance to the *Analects*) (Taipei: Ch'eng-wen, 1966), 22/12/1; D.C. Lau, trans., *Confucius: The Analects* (New York: Penguin, 1979), 112. For discussion, see Benjamin A. Elman, "Criticism as Philosophy: Conceptual Change in Ch'ing Dynasty Evidential Research," *Tsing-hua Journal of Chinese Studies*, n.s. 17 (1985): 165–98.

31. See Chu Hsi 朱熹, *Lun yü chi-chu* 論語集注 (Collected notes to the *Analects*) (Taipei: *Ssu-pu ts'ung-k'an*, 1980; reprint of Ming ed.) 6:10b–11a.

32. *Shan-tung hsiang-shih lu, Ch'eng-hua yuan nien*, 山東鄉試錄・成化元年 (Record of the Shantung provincial examination, 1465), in *Ming-tai teng-k'e-lu hui-pien*, 明代登科錄彙編 (Compendium of Ming civil service examinations) (Taipei: Student Bookstore, 1969), 2:68n, 719. Earlier in 1456, Wang had taken the equivalent of the provincial examinations in the capital region, where his father was a high official. When Wang Lun failed, his father charged the chief examiner with corruption, but the charges were dismissed. See *Dictionary of Ming Biography* (New York: Columbia University Press, 1976), 970, 1610.

33. *Shan-tung hsiang-shih lu Ch'eng-hua yuan nien*, 2: 719–22. See Lau, *Confucius*, 112.

34. Mizoguchi Yūzō 溝口雄三, "*Mōshi jigi soshō* no rekishi teki kōsatsu" 孟子字義疏證の歷史的考察 (Historical analysis of the evidential analysis of the meaning of terms in the *Mencius*), *Tōyō bunka kenkyūjo kiyō*, 48 (1969): 144–45, 163–65.

35. *Hui-shih lu* 會試錄 (Record of metropolitan civil examinations), 1685: 7a, 32a–34b.

36. Tai Chen 戴震, *Meng-tzu tzu-i shu-cheng* 孟子字義疏證 (Evidential analysis of meaning of terms in the Mencius) (Peking : Chung-hua Bookstore, 1961), 56.

37. Tai Chen, *Meng-tzu tzu-i shu-cheng*, 9–10.

38. See Elman, "Criticism as Philosophy," 191–97.

39. *Shang-shu t'ung-chien* 尚書通檢 (Concordance to the *Documents*) (Peking: Harvard-Yenching Institute, 1936), 40:0281–0313, p. 21. Cf. James Legge, *The Shoo King* (reprint, Taipei: Wen-shih-che Press, 1972), 531.

40. *Shang-shu t'ung-chien*, 03:0517–32, p. 2.

41. *Erh-Ch'eng ch'üan-shu* 二程全書 (Complete writings of Ch'eng Hao and Ch'eng I), in *Ho-nan Ch'eng-shih i-shu* 河南程氏遺書 (Bequeathed writings of Ch'eng I), *Ssu-pu pei-yao* 1966 ed. (Taipei: Chung-hua Bookstore, 1966), 19: 7a–7b.

42. *Chu-tzu ta-ch'üan* 朱子大全 (Master Chu [Hsi's] Great Compendium), *Ssu-pu pei-yao* ed. (Shanghai: Chung-hua Bookstore, 1937), 67:19a. Cf. Chu Hsi's answers about the passage to inquiring students in the *Chu-tzu yü-lei* 朱子語類 (Conversations with Master Chu [Hsi] classified topically) (1473; reprint, Taipei: Cheng-chung Bookstore), 78:26b–34a.

43. Huang Chün-chieh, "The Synthesis of Old Pursuits and New Knowledge: Chu Hsi's Interpretation of Mencian Morality," *Hsin-Ya hsueh-shu nien-k'an*, 3 (1982): 214, esp. 214n.

44. *Chu-tzu ta-ch'üan*, 76: 21a–22a.

45. Ts'ai Shen 蔡沈, "Hsu" 序 (Preface) to the *Shu chi-chuan* 書集傳 (Collected commentaries to the *Documents*) (Taipei: World Bookstore, 1969), 1–2.

46. Ibid., p. 14.

47. Ibid., p. 121.

48. *Chu-tzu yü-lei* 朱子語類 (Conversations with Master Chu classified topically) (1473; reprint, Taipei: Cheng-chung Bookstore), 95:32b–33a.

49. Mizoguchi Yūzō, "Chūgoku ni okeru kō shi gainen no tenkai" 中國における公私概念の展開 (Evolution of the concepts public and private in China), *Shisō* 669: 19–38.

50. *Che-chiang hsiang-shih lu, Cheng-te shih-i nien*, 浙江鄉試錄, 正德十一年 (Record of the Chekiang provincial examination, 1516), in *Ming-tai teng-k'e-lu hui-pien*, 5:2679–81.

51. *Che-chiang hsiang-shih lu, Cheng-te shih-i nien*, 5:2787–94. See Carney Fisher, "The Great Ritual Controversy in the Age of Ming Shih-tsung," *Society for the Study of Chinese Religions Bulletin*, 7 (Fall,1979): 71–87.

52. See Ku Hsien-ch'eng's 顧憲成 paraphrase of Chu Hsi's position in "Hsiao-hsin-chai cha-chi" 小心齋劄記 (Random notes from the Pavilion of Watchfulness) in *Ku Tuan-wen kung i-shu* 顧端文公遺書 (Bequeathed writings of Ku Hsien-ch'eng) (K'ang-hsi reign edition), 5:7a. See also Ch'ien I-pen 錢一本, *Kuei-chi* 龜記 (Records on tortoise shells) (c. 1613) 1:11a, and *Fan-yen* 範衍 (Exposition of models) (c. 1606) 1:9a–9b.

53. See Benjamin A. Elman, *Classicism, Politics, and Kinship: The Ch'ang-chou New Text School of Confucianism in Late Imperial China* (Berkeley: University of California Press, 1990), ch. 1.

54. *Hui-shih lu*, 1685: 11a.

55. *Hui-shih lu*, 1685: 71a.

56. *Hui-shih lu*, 1730: 41a–43a.

57. *Hui-shih lu*, 1737: 4a–5a.

58. *Hui-shih lu*, 1737: 38a–40a. See also *Ming-Ch'ing chin-shih t'i-ming pei-lu suo-yin*, 3: 2707.

59. *Chu-tzu ta-ch'üan* 朱子大全 (Great Collection of Master Chu [Hsi]), (*Ssu-pu ts'ung-k'an* ed., (Shanghai: Commercial Press, 1920–22), 11:9b–10a, 12:4b, 12:8b. Chu Hsi himself joined with fellow literati to promote his teachings. In fact, the early *Tao-hsueh* movement had some characteristics of a horizontal peer association of like-minded gentry and was condemned by its opponents for such behavior. Chu Hsi's own theories were later appropriated against forms of gentry solidarity he himself had engaged in but had never legitimated in his political theories. See James T.C. Liu, "How did a Neo-Confucian School Become the State Orthodoxy?" 483–505.

60. Benjamin A. Elman, *From Philosophy to Philology: Intellectual and Social Aspects of Change in Late Imperial China* (Cambridge, Mass.: Harvard University Press, 1984), 140–69.

61. On the emergence of evidential research to scholarly prominence, see Elman, *From Philosophy to Philology*, 38–54.

62. See Elman, *From Philosophy to Philology*, 26–36.

63. For discussion, see Benjamin A. Elman, "Philosophy (*I-li*) Versus Philology (*Kao-cheng*): The *Jen-hsin Tao-hsin* Debate," *T'oung Pao* 4–5 (1983): 175–222.

64. See Elman, *Classicism, Politics, and Kinship*, chs. 3–5.

65. *Chiang-nan hsiang-shih t'i-ming lu* 江南鄉試題名錄 (Record of successful candidates in the Kiangnan provincial examination), 1810: 9a–9b, in the No. 1 Historical Archives, Peking. For purposes of focus and because of the lack of space in this chap-

ter, I have chosen the relatively well-known and representative Old Text versus New Text *Documents* debate to summarize the changes in examination questions that were occurring in the eighteenth and nineteenth centuries.

66. For discussion, see Elman, *From Philosophy to Philology*, 177–80, 200–202, 207–12.

67. See Elman, *Classicism, Politics, and Kinship*, ch. 3.

68. *Shan-tung hsiang-shih t'i-ming lu* 山東鄉試題名錄 (Record of successful candidates in the Shantung provincial examination), 1771: unpaginated manuscript, in the No. 1 Historical Archives, Peking. Policy questions for the 1783, 1807, 1808, 1810, 1813, 1819, 1831, 1832, 1855, 1859, 1885, 1893, and 1894 Shantung examinations also contain significant philological queries.

69. *Shan-tung hsiang-shih t'i-ming lu*, 1819 and 1831: unpaginated manuscripts.

70. *Shan-tung hsiang-shih t'i-ming lu*, 1807: unpaginated manuscript.

71. *Ssu-ch'uan hsiang-shih t'i-ming lu* 四川鄉試題名錄 (Record of successful candidates in the Szechwan provincial examination), 1738: unpaginated manuscript, in the No. 1 Historical Archives, Peking.

72. *Ssu-ch'uan hsiang-shih t'i-ming lu*, 1800: unpaginated manuscript.

73. *Ssu-ch'uan hsiang-shih t'i-ming lu*, 1832, 1846, 1859, 1885: unpaginated manuscripts. In the 1885 examination, examiners faithful to Sung Learning were clearly in charge. See also Elman, *From Philosophy to Philology*, 245–48.

74. *Shan-hsi hsiang-shih t'i-ming lu* 陝西鄉試題名錄 (Record of successful candidates in the Shensi provincial examination), 1690, 1741, 1756, 1759, 1788, 1795, 1800, 1825, 1831, and 1833: unpaginated manuscripts, in the No. 1 Historical Archives, Peking.

75. *Hui-shih lu*, 1739: 4a–4b, 36a–38b.

76. *Hui-shih lu*, 1742: 4a–5b, 35b–39a; 1748: 4b–6a, 33a–35a.

77. *Hui-shih lu*, 1751: 4a–6a, 37a–41a.

78. *Hui-shih lu*, 1752: 4a–6a, 33b–36a.

79. *Hui-shih lu*, 1739: 6a–6b, 1748: 6a–7b; 1751: 6a–8a, 1754: 4a–5a.

80. *Hui-shih lu*, 1754: 39b–45b. Ch'ien also raised doubts concerning the authenticity of the Old Text portions of the *Documents Classic*.

81. *Hui-shih lu*, 1766: 3a–4b, 50a–53b.

82. *Hui-shih lu*, 1793: 15a–17a, 46a–50; *Huang-ch'ao hsu wen-hsien t'ung-kao*, 8429. See also Elman, *Classicism, Politics, and Kinship*, chs. 5-8.

83. *Hui-shih lu*, 1823: 16a–19b, 61a–72a.

84. *Hui-shih lu*, 1847: 17a–20a, 62a–70b; 1852: 17a–18a, 62a–65b.

85. Cf. Chad D. Hansen, "Ancient Chinese Theories of Language," *Journal of Chinese Philosophy* 2 (1975): 245–80.

GLOSSARY

Chang Chih-tung	張之洞	Cheng-te	正德
Chang Hsia	張洽	Ch'eng-Chu	程朱
ch'ao-k'ao	朝考	Ch'eng I	程頤
Ch'en Chin	陳晉	*chi*	己
Ch'en Hao	陳澔	Chi Fu-hsiang	紀復亨
Cheng Hsuan	鄭玄	Chi Yun	紀昀

ch'i	氣	Li Chung-chien	李中簡
Chia-ching	嘉靖	*li-hsueh*	理學
Chien-wen	建文	Li Meng-yang	李夢陽
Ch'ien I-pen	錢一本	Lin Chao-t'ang	林召棠
Ch'ien-lung	乾隆	Lu K'en-t'ang	陸肯堂
Ch'ien Ta-hsin	錢大昕	Shen Ch'ang-yü	沈昌宇
chin-shih	進士	*sheng*	勝
Chou K'ai-ch'i	周開麒	*Shih-chi*	史記
"Chou-kuan"	周官	Shun	舜
Chou Li	周澧	Shun-chih	順治
Chu Hsi	朱熹	Sun Hsing-yen	孫星衍
Chu-tzu chi-chu	朱子集註	"Ta Yü mo"	大禹謨
Chu Yuan-chang	朱元璋	Tai Chen	戴震
Chu Yun	朱筠	T'ai-tsu	太祖
chü-jen	舉人	*Tao-hsueh*	道學
Chuang Ts'un-yü	莊存與	*Tao-t'ung*	道統
Fang Pao	方苞	Ts'ai Shen	蔡沈
Han-shu	漢書	Tso Ch'iu-ming	左丘明
Ho Ch'i-jui	何其睿	*Tso-chuan*	左傳
"Hsu"	序	Tung Chung-shu	董仲舒
Hsu Ho-ch'ing	徐河清	Wang Ch'ang	王昶
Hsu P'eng-shou	許彭壽	Wang Hung-hsu	王鴻緒
Hu An-kuo	胡安國	Wang Lun	王綸
Hui Tung	惠棟	Wang Ming-sheng	王鳴盛
Hung-wu	洪武	Wang Po-hou (Ying-lin)	王伯厚（應麟）
jen-hsin Tao-hsin	人心道心	Wang Yin-chih	王引之
K'ang-hsi	康熙	Wu Ch'in	吾謹
Kao Yao	皋陶	Wu-ti	武帝
k'ao-cheng	考證	Yao	堯
k'e	克	Yen Jo-chü	閻若璩
Ku Hsien-ch'eng	顧憲成	Yen Yuan	顏淵
K'ung An-kuo	孔安國	Yü	禹
K'ung Ying-ta	孔穎達	Yung-cheng	雍正
li	理	Yung-lo	永樂

FIVE

Fang Pao and the *Ch'in-ting Ssu-shu-wen*

R. Kent Guy

Language has been the handmaiden of politics in all societies. Ch'ing China was hardly unique in measuring its political leaders by their ability to express classical ideals. China may have been unique, however, and particularly in the late imperial period, in the degree to which it institutionalized and formalized this measurement. The political competition for control of language was thus more visible in China than elsewhere: it took place in a more openly political arena, centered around assumptions which were expressed and reinforced in political institutions and was ritualized to an extraordinary degree. This competition was interesting not only in itself but also because its characteristics — the nature of the arena of literary competition, the assumptions that guided it, and the rituals that constrained it — constituted the parameters of pedagogy in late imperial China.

These parameters were illustrated in the *Ch'in-ting Ssu-shu-wen* (Manual of examination essays on the Four Books), prepared by imperial command and edited by Fang Pao in 1737. Fang Pao (1668–1749) was of an official type often encountered in late imperial Chinese educational circles: a court literatus whose authority rested less on his scholarly achievements than on his ability to serve as a bridge between the worlds of scholarship and political power. By the early Ch'ien-lung reign Fang might well have commented on the role with some asperity, for he had endured a death sentence, the vagaries of changing imperial favor, and the coalescing and dispersion of many factional allegiances to reach his position. But reach it he had, and although he was probably more inclined to regard his success as the product of timeless truth rather than timely factional victory, he was anxious to exercise the full measure of authority he had acquired and did so in ways reflective of the political dynamics of the time and the nature of the role.

Inevitably, others followed in Fang's footsteps, and as they did the importance of his manual as a "must-read" for examination candidates declined.

The manual was not privately reprinted, at least to present knowledge, and today it exists only in a reprint from the *Ssu-k'u ch'üan-shu* (Complete library of the Four Treasuries). Nonetheless, insofar as it suggested the nature of examination competition, the manual has a value for historians quite apart from its impact on examination practice. As Benjamin Elman argues in chapter 4 of this volume, one function of the examinations was certainly to assure the cultural loyalty of Chinese intellectuals to the dynasty. But a second function was to determine which, among those of a generation whose loyalty had been assured, might actually be permitted to serve the dynasty. The *Ch'in-ting Ssu-shu-wen* argued that such judgments of talent could be made on an objective basis, one that entailed both understanding of the orthodox tradition and clarity and vitality of moral reasoning. The essays the manual reprinted demonstrated how this standard could be applied and showed the range of variation that was possible within the framework of an established tradition. This chapter will first examine Fang Pao's life, then treat his manual, and finally explicate in some depth two of the examination essays it reprinted.

FANG PAO: LESSONS FROM A LIFE AT THREE COURTS

Fang Pao's fortunes waxed and waned to an extraordinary degree during his service under three Ch'ing emperors, and much of the color, conflict and pathos of Fang's life, and its interest as a study in the politics of literary authority in late imperial China, derived from the contrasts in his experiences of life in three different courts. The high points of his career were the years between 1690 and 1702 and between 1736 and 1740. Both were times of considerable literati influence in the Ch'ing court and of a rather elitist attitude on the part of the dominant literati. But the monarchs who reigned during the periods of Fang Pao's prominence had rather different attitudes toward the institutions of Chinese government. The K'ang-hsi emperor (r. 1663–1723) was far more experimental in his style of rule, tailoring institutions to suit his own perception of needs and the capacities of the individuals who served him, while the Ch'ien-lung emperor (r. 1736–96) was concerned with precedent, bureaucracy, and institution-building. Between these two periods, during the late K'ang-hsi (1710–23) and Yung-cheng years (1723–36), a different concern — with administrative ability and political accomplishment — came to prevail in imperial assessments of intellectuals. Fang Pao himself was profoundly affected by these changes in imperial attitudes toward scholars and scholarship. But he was not only an observer but also an activist who sought to institutionalize what he saw as the proper role of the educator at the Chinese court.

Patronage and Prosperity in the Late K'ang-hsi Years
The 1690s, when Fang Pao first arrived at the Ch'ing court, were an extraordinary decade in the history of the relationship of the dynasty with

intellectuals. Through his careful attention to scholarly mores and his assiduous cultivation of scholarly talent, the K'ang-hsi emperor had in the middle years of his reign lured many Chinese scholars from their reluctance to serve a foreign dynasty. Those who came to court found that they not only could enjoy a fairly lavish patronage of their scholarly projects but also had access to and influence over the emperor. By the beginning of the eighteenth century, three works of imperially commissioned scholarship had been published and more were on their way, while four of the emperor's seven grand secretaries were Chinese of scholarly background. One such scholar, Li Kuang-ti, became one of the K'ang-hsi emperor's closest councillors.[1]

Fang Pao had three entrées to the high society of his day. The first was his family, one of the most distinguished political and scholarly lineages of the empire. Although Fang's own father had dissipated his talents "in poetry and wine," the Fangs of T'ung-ch'eng county in Anhwei enjoyed a record of examination success dating back to 1399. During their years in the political limelight, the Fangs had acquired sufficient wealth and marital connections to be counted one of the most prominent families of southern Anhwei.[2] A second entry to the literary life of the capital was provided for Fang Pao by his elder brother Fang Chou (1661–1701), who had preceded Fang Pao at the capital by about ten years and earned a reputation as one of the best writers of examination essays in the empire.[3] Soon, however, Fang Pao's own prose earned him the respect of the Peking elite. Li Kuang-ti remarked of Fang Pao that his equal had not been seen "since the time of Han Yü and Ou-yang Hsiu." Another accomplished figure in Peking literary life, Han T'an, a *chuang-yuan* (optimus) of 1673 and member of the Hanlin Academy, was said with perhaps some exaggeration to have been so impressed on reading Fang Pao's writing that he destroyed his own drafts. The literati of T'ung-ch'eng were not yet the self-conscious literary force that, as Kai-wing Chow has demonstrated in chapter 6 of this volume, they would become in the later eighteenth century, nonetheless they were clearly stylists to be reckoned with.[4]

Fang shared with the members of the late K'ang-hsi elite another characteristic—a firm belief, indeed almost a sense of mission, in restoring the Neo-Confucian foundations of Chinese society and governance.[5] In Fang's case, this belief was expressed as a defense of Ch'eng-Chu Neo-Confucianism against the attacks both of late Ming followers of Wang Yang-ming (1472–1529), who had argued against the moral severity implicit in so much of Neo-Confucian writings, and against those of thinkers like Li Kung (1659–1733) who argued that Chu Hsi was not so much wrong as useless. To both Fang Pao answered that Chu Hsi had achieved such a thorough understanding of the nature of the human condition that he deserved to be the foundation for future political and intellectual activity. Fang Pao's belief in Neo-Confucianism was evidently quite literal: when Li Kung's son died, Fang was said to have written him a note blaming Kung's misfortune on his doubts about Chu Hsi.

Fang's own intellectual interests were in the ritual texts, on which Chu Hsi was said to have been working when he died. Although Fang's political involvement left him little time to devote to a full commentary on them, his *Wen-chi* (Collected writings) is full of short essays on various aspects of the ritual texts, and he must be seen as responsible for much of the work of the *San-li* editorial commission founded in 1736.[6]

For all of these reasons, Fang found himself warmly welcomed in Peking when he arrived there in 1691. As Fang Pao's student later recalled: "At that time all the best scholars of the empire were gathered in Peking. Between making and returning calls, there was not a day of leisure, and they all vied with each other to invite the master."[7] Having achieved a kind of informal acceptance, he gradually worked his way up the formal hierarchy: he was a stipend student at the Tai-hsueh until 1701, supplementing his income with private tutoring and an occasional trip home to T'ung-ch'eng. He received his *chü-jen* degree in 1699, and in 1706 passed the Board of Rites examination for the *chin-shih*. However, just as he was about to take the palace examination, in effect a placement test for those who had qualified for the highest degree, he received word that his mother had died and so returned home to T'ung-ch'eng to observe the rituals of mourning. As a result, he was not ranked among the *chin-shih* class of 1706; ironically, the man who compiled model examination essays for two hundred years of Ch'ing examination takers was not himself listed on the stone stelae that recorded, in order, those who completed the palace examinations and received the *chin-shih*.[8]

When Fang returned to Peking after mourning, however, he found a scholarly community in the midst of change. In the early days of his reign, the K'ang-hsi emperor had needed the public allegiance of some of the most famous scholars of the realm to establish the legitimacy of his reign and his dynasty. He was successful in his attempts to woo intellectuals, but the balance between Manchu rulers and Chinese scholars at his court was always tenuous. It was nearly upset by conflict that developed in the first years of the eighteenth century over which of the emperor's sons should succeed him.[9] The conflict deepened, and by about 1710 an aging emperor found himself increasingly frustrated both with Manchu partiality to an heir apparent whose moral failings were increasingly clear to Chinese scholars and with those scholars' tendency to form factions around other candidates for the succession. Imperial pronouncements to and about Chinese officials began to focus not on their moral educations but on their limited practical contribution to the management of the empire.[10] In 1708, for instance, the emperor wrote of the Chinese scholars who served him at court:

> When they are in subordinate positions, they seem promotable, but when they are given high office, they merely plot to protect themselves and preserve their reputations intact. Hsiung Tzu-li has often lectured about Neo-Confucianism,

but when he became a grand councillor, he too sealed himself off and was prevented by his followers' needs from accomplishing anything [for the dynasty].

What seems even stranger is when Chinese officials discuss political affairs; if a proposal has been made earlier, subsequent officials offer the same proposal, not even considering the rights and wrongs of the matter. They say only, 'There is a discussion on record.'[11]

The changing attitude of the emperor toward scholars was most apparent in 1713, when a censor accused Hanlin academician Tai Ming-shih (1653–1713) of publishing a collection of seditious works entitled *Nan-shan-chi* (Collection from the southern mountain). Tai was not particularly personable — he was in at least one view a "sour and withdrawn self-declared misfit." Nonetheless, as a member of the Hanlin Academy who had published a work of Neo-Confucian philosophy, he was clearly a member of the K'ang-hsi literary elite. That the emperor would even entertain a case against him had ominous implications. But Tai was not only condemned, he was found guilty and executed, an action that signaled for many then and later the end of the era of expansive and accommodating semiofficial patronage.[12]

The Tai case certainly signaled the end of an era for Fang Pao, who found himself implicated in the matter in two ways. A friend and probably distant relative of Tai's and the brother-in-law of Tai's publisher, Fang had written an apparently unobjectionable preface to the volume. Fang Pao was also a distant relative of one of the most obviously seditious of the contributors in the collection, one Fang Hsiao-piao. Hsiao-piao had earned his *chin-shih* degree and been appointed to the Hanlin Academy in 1649. Shortly thereafter, he was banished from court and exiled to Kwangsi where he became involved in the rebellion of Wu San-kuei. He wrote a reminiscence of this period, *Tien-ch'ien chi-wen* (Notes from Kwangsi and Kweichow), to which Tai referred in the *Nan-shan-chi*. Fang Hsiao-piao had long since died and the rebellion been put down, but the reference to the rebellion afforded the emperor an opportunity to make a point about the importance of scholarly loyalties and the strength of the political apparatus; scholarly distinction, however broadly recognized, no longer exempted the courtier from political attack. As a result of the episode the entire Fang lineage, one of the most distinguished in the empire, was sentenced to death. When Li Kuang-ti pled for mercy on Fang Pao's behalf, citing Fang's literary accomplishments, the sentence was commuted to hereditary enslavement and Fang Pao was instructed to serve in the emperor's study instructing the children of the royal family. Fang Pao may have escaped harm, but he could hardly have escaped a sense of loss — loss not only of freedom but of the power and prestige that had been so preeminently the prerogative of scholars in the late K'ang-hsi period.

Fang Pao and Yung-cheng Pragmatism

Initially at least, the subsequent reign of the Yung-cheng emperor (r. 1723–36) brought some relief to the Fangs. The new emperor freed the Fangs from hereditary enslavement, a reprieve which was said to have made Fang Pao weep for joy. Few other aspects of the new reign could have brought joy to Fang and his friends, however, for the Yung-cheng emperor was the Ch'ing monarch who appeared most to value practical accomplishment over scholarly distinction. Like many who had served during the K'ang-hsi period, Fang Pao held few offices during the Yung-cheng years. In the third year of the reign, Fang Pao requested a year's leave to return to T'ung-ch'eng to bury his mother, who had died nineteen years earlier. On his return to court, Fang was appointed to the Supervisorate of Imperial Instruction, and was eventually made lecturer in the Hanlin Academy. In this capacity, Fang proposed that the Yung-cheng emperor follow his father's footsteps and hold a second *Po-hsueh hung-ju* examination (Examination for scholars of broad learning and wide literacy), a suggestion that was adopted six years later during the first year of the Ch'ien-lung reign, and joined with contemporaries from T'ung-ch'eng to oppose the drain that wars against the Mongols imposed on the central government.[13] But on the whole, Fang remained uncharacteristically quiet about his political views in these years. Once, he was offered a position as grand secretary but declined it because of an ailment of his foot. There certainly was something wrong with Fang's foot: the emperor sent two of his household servants to conduct Fang to court, subsequently expressing his sympathy and permitting Fang to walk with a cane. However, it was also fairly common for Chinese officials to use the pretext of a physical ailment to avoid a position in which they chose not to serve.[14]

The indignities suffered by Fang's friend and future patron Wei T'ing-chen (1668–1756) suggested why men of more scholarly bent might choose not to serve the new monarch. Like Fang, Wei had been a member of the late K'ang-hsi literary elite: he had received his *chü-jen* degree on the recommendation of Li Kuang-ti, passed third (*t'an-hua*) on the *chin-shih* examinations of 1712, and been employed on many of the literary compilation projects at the K'ang-hsi court.[15] In the first year of the Yung-cheng reign, however, Wei's largely literary career came to an end when he was appointed governor of Hunan (then called P'ien-yuan). The emperor commented on the occasion of Wei's first memorial, a report of the rice harvest which the emperor judged to be insufficiently precise:

> In the past your conduct has been correct and balanced. But you have sought only to avoid disgrace and distance yourself from difficulty, and you've been unwilling to work hard or to commit yourself. The position to which you are presently

appointed cannot be compared to the loose and leisurely posts you have held in
the past. In the management of affairs, you must value sternness and constancy.
It will not do to retreat compliantly. Action must be taken in the matter of local
corruption to dismiss [the wrongdoers] and insure the success of the [incorrupt-
ible]. Worthy subordinates must be promoted and the incompetent ones charged
with error. You must act with energy; only then will you achieve results."[16]

The Yung-cheng emperor appeared as dissatisfied with the scholarly community as his father had been and for much the same reasons; unlike
K'ang-hsi, however, he was not content merely to fulminate and sought actively to change scholarly habits.

The results of Yung-cheng's experiment in molding scholarly behavior, if
such it was, were unsatisfactory; within eighteen months Wei T'ing-chen was
dismissed from office. Wei's ostensible mistake was the mismanagement of a
local legal case; in fact, as the emperor made clear, the problem lay deeper: "I
know you are an honest and accomplished scholar and for this reason
appointed you to a governorship. But since you took office, you have shown no
talent whatsoever for organization or management. All of your legal judgments
and financial accounts, if they are not actually in error, are at least incompetent. In all matters you are weak and confused." Wei was transferred to a
post in the Board of Works at the Manchus' shadow government in Sheng-
ching.

The virtues that Wei T'ing-chen embodied were so much a part of the
Ch'ing political landscape that the Yung-cheng emperor was evidently moved
to attempt a subsequent appointment of Wei as governor of Anhwei. This
time, Wei's term lasted longer—from 1725 to 1729—but proved no more satisfactory. When Wei failed to investigate adequately a tax corruption case in
1726, the emperor wrote: "When Wei T'ing-chen was governor of Hunan, he
proved too soft to exercise control over local affairs. So I had him returned to
the capital. But last year when there was a vacancy in Anhwei, I thought that I
might have misjudged him on the earlier occasion and so I reappointed him.
On the day I did so, I instructed him severely, and he swore before me that he
would change his bad habits. I see now that in his management of affairs, he is
as timid and indulgent as ever." After a similarly blistering reprimand two
years later, Wei petitioned the emperor to relieve him of his post in the
provinces and return him to his editorial labors in the capital. The emperor
responded: "Since you were appointed, you have sought only your own benefit
and done nothing to improve the life of the people or the good of the state....
How can you possibly want a transfer?" Two years later, Wei was in fact
dismissed from office, and after performing several temporary commissions for
the emperor transferred to the presidency of the Board of Rites, a post that
was evidently more to his liking.[17]

In the Yung-cheng emperor's criticism of Wei and of many of the literary
officials of his day, the issue was not so much degrees of competence as types of

competence. The emperor recognized that Wei had many of the skills that a good Chinese classical education was meant to inculcate. He was honest, morally upright, and a talented student of the Classics. But the emperor expected that classical education would also result in other types of ability, talents not so much in classical commentary, but in reporting, budgeting, accounting, and legal judgment. For officials like Wei and Fang Pao, who not only patterned themselves on classical models but were adept at classical scholarship, these represented new emphases that had major implications for the nature of education. The brevity of the Yung-cheng reign, however, prevented a full working out of these implications; instead, scholars like Wei and Fang found themselves confronted in the autumn of 1735 with a new imperial vision.

The Ascension of the Ch'ien-lung Emperor

The Yung-cheng emperor's son and successor seemed a man after the hearts of good Confucian scholars: the favorite grandson of the K'ang-hsi emperor, the Ch'ien-lung emperor had been raised in the K'ang-hsi court and received a good classical education at the hands of many of the patrons of Wei and Fang. The new emperor began his reign on a note that good Confucian scholars must have found promising, requesting advice on how to follow most exactly the ancient mourning rites in the burial of his father. The request was directed to the Board of Rites where Wei T'ing-chen found himself once again the focus of imperial attention. He turned to Fang Pao, whose interest in the ancient rites texts was well known, and Fang produced a brief treatise on mourning rites quoting from the *Chou-li*, *Li-chi*, and *Ch'un-ch'iu*, dealing with such subjects as the appropriate colors and styles of court costume and the proper ways to conduct official sacrifices during the period of mourning.[18] When Wei submitted the proposal on Fang's behalf to the emperor, the reaction at court was mixed. The concern of courtiers was apparently not so much Fang's interpretation of the texts as the practical difficulties involved in the literal enactment of ancient rituals. Moreover, Fang's main supporter failed him at a critical moment: at the first sign of resistance, the now perhaps justifiably timorous Wei T'ing-chen resigned his post. Fang was offered a post at the Board of Rites but declined it, once again citing the ailment of his foot. Finally, the rituals were not reenacted as Fang had proposed.[19]

Undaunted and perhaps even emboldened by the imperial interest in his proposal on mourning, Fang went on to submit proposals on a wide range of political and scholarly topics. In a memorial that must have been directed at the palace memorial system of secret communications monitored by a very few grand councillors, which had been developed in the Yung-cheng period, Fang argued that the emperor needed to seek advice more widely among all senior courtiers (lit., *chiu-ch'ing* or "nine senior ministers") on major policy decisions.[20] Fang also participated in the fairly general attack on the political legacy of one of the Yung-cheng emperor's favorite governors, T'ien Wen-ching (1662–

1732).[21] In three other memorials he argued, in the face of apparently unanimous opposition in the court, that the new emperor should prohibit the production of fermented liquors and the raising of tobacco in order to force the peasantry back to their more fundamental occupation, the production of cereal crops.[22] Other proposals by Fang dealt with scholarly projects. He urged the court, both by memorial and by an informal letter to Oerht'ai (1680–1745) to sponsor a new annotated edition of the three rites texts. Finally, he recommended that Hsiung Tsu-li, the intellectual whom the K'ang-hsi emperor had singled out in 1708 as representative of the faults of the scholarly class, and T'ang Pin (1627–87), a K'ang-hsi writer and teacher, be admitted to the Temple of Eminent Statesmen.[23]

If Fang, in offering these proposals, was expecting that his connections and scholarly reputation would translate immediately into political influence on the new emperor he was to be disappointed, for none of his political proposals was adopted. Contemporaries attributed this generally to Fang's acerbic personal manner and specifically to the enmity of Kao Pin (1683–1755), a senior Manchu official then serving as governor-general of river conservancy.[24] In the few extant court reactions to Fang's political proposals, however, the difficulty of implementation was stressed more than any specific political opposition. At any event, many of his political proposals were as much attacks on the style of the previous reign as they were practical suggestions for improvement of government. On the other hand, virtually all his scholarly proposals were adopted: Hsiung Tzu-li and T'ang Pin were admitted to the Temple of Eminent Statesmen, canonized as Wen-cheng and Wen-tuan respectively. Fang was himself appointed director of commissions to reprint the Classics and standard histories, and to prepare an annotated edition of the three ritual texts. The influence that Fang was denied in the political sphere he appeared to have won in the scholastic sphere.[25]

Yet on closer examination, Fang Pao and the Ch'ien-lung emperor seem to have had subtly different motivations in the literary projects of the late 1730s. In his memorial, Fang offered two rationales for the project of editing the ritual texts. It would represent a continuation, indeed a culmination, of the scholarly legacy of the K'ang-hsi emperor and would meet a need felt particularly acutely by the leading intellectuals of the day, of whom Fang fancied himself the representative, for an authoritative version of the *Li* texts.[26] The memorial began with a reference to the K'ang-hsi literary projects. During the course of his reign the K'ang-hsi emperor had authorized four collections of classical commentary of the sort Fang Pao was proposing, one each on the *Ch'un-ch'iu*, *I-ching*, *Shang-shu*, and *Shih-ching*. The ritual texts were the only works of the traditional Five Classics that had not received a commentary in the K'ang-hsi reign, and thus commissioning a work of commentary on them would constitute an act of filial piety on the part of K'ang-hsi's grandson. But this may not have been all that Fang Pao had in mind in his reference,

for he drew the emperor's particular attention to one of the K'ang-hsi
commentaries, the *Chou-i che-chung* (Assessment of commentaries on the
I-ching),[27] which he felt embodied a special cooperation between the emperor
and scholars. As he noted, it was the only one of the four editions to be labeled
an "assessment" (*che-chung*), rather than a mere "compilation" (*tsuan-yen*). It
was also the only one of the K'ang-hsi commentaries to be completed in the
emperor's lifetime. But perhaps as important for Fang Pao, it was also the only
one of the four commentary projects whose director was openly acknowledged,
and that director was none other than Fang Pao's former patron and savior, Li
Kuang-ti. Reminding the Ch'ien-lung emperor of the close intellectual and political relationship that had existed between Li and the K'ang-hsi emperor
served also to remind the young monarch that this relationship had been the
foundation of much of the patronage and political life of the late K'ang-hsi
years.

   In addition to his implicitly political justification, Fang also offered a scholarly rationale for his project. A commentary on the *Li* texts would also constitute a particularly worthwhile project for the new emperor, in Fang's view,
because of the importance and complexity of the work. While foundations for
the other editorial work had been laid by the Sung Neo-Confucians, much less
preliminary work had been done on ritual texts. As a result, it would not be
possible simply to assemble previous commentaries; it would be necessary to
do a fair amount of sorting and editing. As he would imply in a later letter to
imperial regent Oerht'ai, Fang envisioned the work to be of such complexity
that it could be entrusted only to a few carefully chosen specialists. Only then
could an authoritative edition be established that would meet the needs of an
increasingly educated and skeptical scholarly community. [28]

   The evocation of earlier scholarly patronage and the call for an elite and
specialized corps of editors no doubt reflected Fang Pao's view of the work to
be undertaken. The Ch'ien-lung emperor authorized the project and put Fang
Pao in charge of it, but his edict had rather different emphases than Fang's
memorial. The reference to the K'ang-hsi emperor's scholarly legacy no doubt
pleased the new monarch: K'ang-hsi had been one of the most successful and
long-lived monarchs in Chinese history, and Ch'ien-lung was no doubt flattered
by the idea that he could follow in K'ang-hsi's footsteps. However, the emperor
probably also knew of the factionalism of the late K'ang-hsi years and wanted
to avoid it in his own reign. Whereas Fang Pao called attention to the personal
relationship that had existed between K'ang-hsi and Li Kuang-ti, the
Ch'ien-lung emperor merely noted that his grandfather had summoned
scholars, ordered them to collect commentaries, and then pronounced
judgment on them. What had been valuable about the previous project had
been its results, not the close cooperation on which it was based. Moreover the
emperor, himself apparently more a consumer than a scholar of ritual, found
the project worthwhile not because of the difficulties it would entail or the long

history of scholarly neglect it would remedy but because the ritual texts were of such day-to-day importance to society they needed to be clarified.[29]

On the same day he was appointed to edit the ritual texts, 24 July 1736, Fang was authorized to prepare a volume of model examination essays. The fact that the orders for the edition of ritual texts and a volume of examination essays were issued on the same day strongly suggested a connection between the two endeavors, although there was no documentary evidence of the connection. Nonetheless, two versions of the edict ordering the compilation suggested that there were at the Ch'ien-lung court different views of the work that would be involved in compiling the manual, views parallel in a broad sense to the two rationales for the ritual commentary project. The earlier version of the edict, a draft prepared at court for imperial review and preserved in the edict record books (*Shang-yü-tang*), represented the work to be accomplished in rather grand terms. The goal of the manual was to provide a standard for examination takers and especially for those "deluded scholars who can only follow rustic ways, plagiarizing predecessors, so that essays resemble each other as one clap of thunder does the next." Fang Pao was represented in the draft as an especially worthy director for the project because he was a scholar "immersed in the structure and meaning of the Classics" who could "make clear the implications of the topics and carefully annotate them.[30]

The final version of the edict, edited by the emperor and published in the *Shih-lu* (veritable records) as well as the first *chüan* of the manual, took a more functional view of the process. More important than directing the deluded, and hence placed before it by the emperor in his list of goals of the manual, was the task of making available to candidates the essays of those previously successful that could serve as "luminous and elegant models" to their successors. From the emperor's point of view, the task was more one of compilation than of reformulation of scholarly morals. Moreover, Fang Pao's qualification to edit the manual was not, in the final version, his classical education but the fact that he was adept at examination essays (*kung yü shih-wen*). Ultimately, the *Ch'in-ting Ssu-shu-wen* was to be a useful manual by a competent stylist rather than an attempt to reform scholarly morals.

At one level, of course, these changes may not have mattered; the ritual text was directed by Fang Pao, while the *Chin-ting Ssu-shu-wen* ultimately contained the essays Fang chose and was organized as he decided. The significance of the difference in rationales for the ritual texts and the different versions of the edict ordering the manual was in the sort of mandate the emperor appeared to be giving Fang Pao. The Ch'ien-lung emperor did not regard Fang Pao as a classically educated confidant as, to a degree at least, the K'ang-hsi emperor had regarded the scholars who served at his court. Rather, he appears to have seen Fang as a convenient and appropriate representative of the scholarly community whose allegiance and orderliness was vital to the empire.

One rather pathetic footnote to Fang's political career remained to be written—an episode that, if anything, illustrated the limits of Fang's role as the Ch'ien-lung emperor's representative to the scholarly community. During the early Ch'ien-lung years, Fang became known for his strong opinions of candidates for political office and for his sharp interrogations of *chin-shih* degree-holders. In the course of his editorial labors, Fang apparently had several opportunities to meet the emperor and didn't hesitate to share his opinions of people at court. The emperor tolerated this to a degree, but imperial patience grew thin when in the summer of 1739 it was discovered that Fang had received a bribe from one of the people he recommended. Not only had he taken a bribe, the emperor said in an edict of condemnation, but Fang had had the temerity to recommend Wei T'ing-chen and criticize his successor at the Board of Rites at the very time when Fang was enjoying Wei's hospitality— it seemed that while in the capital Fang lived in Wei's house. The edict was perhaps more a fit of imperial pique than anything else, for the punishment was made to fit the crime: Fang was ordered to "work off" his guilt by continuing in his editorial capacities without salary.[31] Fang didn't lose his opportunity to speak in the emperor's name on matters of recruitment and ritual; he simply was not paid for it. This edict represented an embarrassing end to Fang's political career, but for a man of Fang's wealth and connections this was surely not fatal. As the edict itself pointed out, Fang didn't have to pay rent.

Fang thus ended his political career a court scholar of rather circumscribed authority, a man whose career illustrated both the possibilities and the limits of the role. Clearly the political environment—the monarch's vision of the sort of people he wanted as servitors—conditioned the role. In the middle of the seventeenth century, literati had been among the most influential advisors of the monarch, for in a sense the court had needed them for legitimacy and luster more than they had needed the court. During the Yung-cheng reign, however, the Ch'ing government had developed more streamlined mechanisms of rule. Classical scholars, with their commitment to ancient precedents and their paramount concern for integrity, seemed out of place. In the Ch'ien-lung reign, the classical scholars' education, experience, social prominence, and influence over the Ch'ien-lung emperor permitted them to mount a strong resistance to the trend of Yung-cheng government. On the other hand, respectful as he was of the importance of scholars in the order of the Chinese state, the new emperor wanted to put the relations between scholars and the state on a new footing.

One lesson of Fang's career was thus that the scholar's role in the Ch'ing state was constrained by political circumstances; perhaps as important, however, was the fact that it could not be eliminated altogether. Fang and his colleagues were a proud group, many of them men of wealth, who saw themselves quite consciously as the guardians of China's classical heritage and were the figurative and in some case literal teachers of the Manchu rulers. However, the Chinese political and social order was symbiotically enmeshed to such a degree with the world of education and classical scholarship that the claims to political influence of Fang Pao and his peers were not easily dismissed. In a practical sense, the literati who served in the Chinese bureaucracy and who in their capacities as landowners and taxpayers often paid for it also had to participate in the selection of those who would succeed them. The role of the literary authority and the assumptions rulers and literati made about the goals of the examination system therefore constituted a constant parameter of Chinese education.

THE *CH'IN-TING SSU-SHU-WEN*: ORGANIZATION AND ASSUMPTIONS

The writings and biographies of Fang Pao and his associates recorded how they acted and to a degree what they thought about the political conflicts of their day. These thoughts — or more specifically, the categories they used to view and evaluate their examination careers and the essays entailed — were not so evident in formal writings. Yet of course such habits of thought and unspoken assumptions were probably at least as important to the examination life of classical scholars of the eighteenth century as any narrow political goals they attained. In this regard, the *Ch'in-ting Ssu-shu-wen* was particularly significant both because of its explicit assertions and because of what it could take for granted. The manual's explicit argument, one certainly explicable in terms of Fang Pao's own mixed experience at the Ch'ing court, was that despite changing styles of essay writing there were relatively objective standards for judging essays that transcended time and political factions. Implicitly, the contents and organization of the manual describe perhaps as clearly as any commentator the intellectual regimen of the examination candidate and the skills it emphasized.

The manual clearly identified one part of the examinations, and perhaps also of the classical canon, as more important than the others. In the course of acquiring a degree, the examination taker had to write essays of several sorts. While the precise nature and order of questions changed during the course of the dynasty, there were three basic types of questions in Fang Pao's day corresponding to the three sessions of the tests. In the first session, the candidates were confronted with passages from two to about ten characters in length chosen from the Five Classics (the *Book of Documents*, the *Book of Poetry*, the *Spring and Autumn Annals*, the *Record of Rituals*, and the *Book of Changes*), and the Four Books (the *Analects*, the *Mencius*, the *Great Learning*, and the *Doctrine of the Mean*) and asked to elaborate on their significance. In the second session, the required questions included a "discourse" (*lun*) based on the *Classic of Filial Piety* and questions that tested the candidates' mastery of documentary style and juridical terms. The third session was composed exclusively of policy questions (ts'e) in which candidates were asked to comment on a brief essay prepared by examiners on the evolution of a given government policy.[32]

The interpretive tasks involved in answering these three sorts of questions were quite different. The "policy questions," as Benjamin Elman's work has shown, exacted an oath of political allegiance from candidates by requiring them to offer their comments on contemporary policy. These questions were, of course, vital for the successful candidate and very revealing of the evolving political claims and concerns of the dynasty. But they were not viewed as the most difficult part of the exam; in fact, in the view of a contemporary of Fang Pao's who was critical of the examinations, most candidates were able to ascertain the correct answer from the form of the question.[33] The tests of documentary style were, like the policy questions, essential to the basic functions of the examination process: the fact that all who passed the examinations wrote a common language was surely a major force for unity in a large and diverse empire. But for students who had prepared as long and carefully as had most eighteenth-century candidates, these questions probably did not pose major intellectual difficulties; they represented stylistic exercises rather than tests of political capacity or will.

The real challenge, it seemed—the one which separated the few who passed from the many who prepared—occurred in the first session. The sources of the questions in this session were the Four Books and Five Classics: every examination contained at least some questions from each type of text. The metropolitan examination for the chin-shih degree, for instance, required three essays on the Four Books and five essays on the Five Classics.[34] But even here different questions required different skills. The Five Classics were, in theory at least, collections of ancient poetry, historical documents, ritual records, and techniques of prognostication edited by Confucius as examples of the regulations of government and society in a golden age. In fact they were complex collections of material of varied provenance and date that, by the seventeenth and eighteenth centuries, had become not only difficult to read and interpret but often textually corrupt. The skills involved in understanding them were largely philological and the meaning of many passages was very much a matter of controversy. Candidates' answers here reflected very clearly the evolution of scholarly opinion on such controversial issues (see Elman, chap. 4 of this volume).

Essays on the Four Books posed issues of a rather different character. The Analects and the Mencius purported to record the actual words of the sages as they responded to questions from students and commented on critical political events of their day. The Great Learning and the Doctrine of the Mean were somewhat shorter philosophical disquisitions on man's moral, social, and political obligations. The meanings of these texts had been fairly well established: in their answers candidates were required to build on the understanding of the Four Books developed by Chu Hsi and published in commentaries in the thirteenth century.[35] In the cases of the *Great Learning* and *Doctrine of the Mean* questions were actually posed on Chu Hsi's commentaries; in the cases of the *Analects* and the *Mencius*, as the sample essays discussed below will demonstrate, answers were judged on the basis of their fealty to the Chu Hsi commentary. The essay questions on the Four Books tested the candidates' reasoning ability, memory, and mastery of the core values of the Neo-Confucian tradition; they constituted the competitive heart of the examination system.

Within these boundaries, however, there was room for evolution of style and differences of argumentation, and it was the purpose of the manual to highlight these. The *Ch'in-t'ing Ssu-shu-wen* was divided into five collections (*chi*), each containing essays written during one time period. The periods were defined by political events with each of the first four periods encompassing the reigns of two Ming emperors and the fifth period constituting the entire Ch'ing dynasty. The first collection included 57 essays written during the Ch'eng-hua and Hung-chih reigns (1465–88, 1488–1506); the second, 112 essays from the Cheng-te and Chia-ching reigns (1506–22, 1522–67); the third, 106 essays from the Lung-ch'ing and Wan-li reigns (1567–1573, 1573–1620); the fourth, 211 essays from the T'ien-ch'i and Ch'ung-chen reigns (1621–28, 1628–44); and the fifth, 296 essays written between 1644 and 1728. Within each collection, essays were divided into *chüan* according to the text with which they dealt. Thus, in the first collection the first *chüan* contained essays on the *Great Learning* only; the second and third, essays on the *Analects*; the fourth, essays on the *Doctrine of the Mean*; and the fifth and sixth, essays on the *Mencius*. Within each *chüan*, essays were grouped according to location within the Classic of the passages with which they dealt.

The *Ch'in-ting Ssu-shu-wen* was thus meant more as an anthology than as a commentary or catechism. In fact, no effort was made to include essays on all or even the most important passages that might be assigned from a given text. Even in the case of the *Great Learning*, shortest of the Four Books, coverage of the original text is far from complete. No essay was included, for instance, on the line "the extension of knowledge lies in the apprehension of things" over which Chu Hsi had labored so long or on chapter 5 of the commentary, in which the Master addressed this line. The problem was not lack of space, for there were a number of duplications among the essays in the volume, including five essays on the rather un-Confucian line "there is a great course to be followed in the production of wealth."[36] Duplication among topics was permissible, even desirable, since exposing the reader to different examples of successful essays was more important than presenting answers to all possible questions.

The preface to *Ch'in-ting Ssu-shu-wen* explained why this emphasis on the evolution of examination writing was necessary. Each of the first four eras delineated in the volume had its own characteristics. In the first period, 1465–

1506, essay writers stuck close to the original text and its commentaries, and their language was constrained by the rules of the form. The second age, 1506 –67, produced some of the best examination essays of the Ming dynasty, in which authors were able to penetrate to the heart of their assigned topics (lit., "melt them down") and make the themes coherent and meanings explicit. In the third age, 1567–1620, writing became overly clever as candidates sought to advance themselves solely through their verbal acuity rather than mastery of substance. Inevitably, some essayists of this third period stretched the language too far, and as a result the essays grew thin. The essays of the fourth period, 1621–44, were the most intellectually creative, written by candidates who were comfortable enough with the form that they could express "all that their hearts desired" within the rules of the examination essay. On the other hand, some essayists of the fourth period were more concerned with expressing their own views than with addressing the assigned topic, and so produced essays of less value.

There were thus models to be found and dangers to be avoided in each era. Among the essays of the first period, one studied those that truly had some vitality (ch'i) and ignored those that merely mimicked the Classics and their commentaries. From the second age, one read the essays that offered new insight. Among essays of the third period, one studied those that were solidly based in the Classics and forgot those that were merely clever, however interesting they might be. Finally in the fourth age, one looked to the essays that were genuinely creative and ignored those that misappropriated classical texts.[37]

Fang's admiration for the essays of the fourth period was rather thinly concealed. He included more essays from this twenty-four-year period than from any other era of comparable length and only eighty-six fewer essays than from the entire Ch'ing dynasty. Part of what Fang admired in this period — the shift of emphasis away from verbal acuity and toward an understanding of the original texts — had been one of the tenets of the Restoration Society, a group of late Ming intellectuals organized to influence the examination process. The Ch'ing dynasty had banned such societies and the collections of examination essays they produced. Nonetheless, Fang's emphasis on consistent standards of evaluation and attention to the philosophical import of the text echoed the concerns of his Ming predecessors.[38]

When it came to Ch'ing authors, Fang faced a much more difficult task and one that had to be performed much more discreetly. Literary style and political efficacy were closely linked in the traditional Chinese political and literary imaginations, and any comment on Fang's part about the style of the Ch'ing dynasty would almost certainly have been read as a comment on the history of Ch'ing rule. Also, as Fang Pao's organization suggested and his preface made clear, essayists in the Ch'ing period had many more positive and negative models to follow; Ch'ing examination style was meant to be a synthesis of what preceded it. The limits of the genre having been explored in the previous reign, finer and finer distinctions came to separate the candidates' examinations. Probably, therefore, no simple characterization of the reasons for candidates' success could be given.

Yet there were judgments being made among candidates in the Ch'ing examination system and implied in Fang's selection of Ch'ing authors. Altogether, the Ch'ing essays in the volume were written by 122 authors. The dates of the *chin-shih* degrees of 98 of these can be established and can be grouped into five periods:

1. Shun-chih (1644–61) — twenty-four authors
2. Early K'ang-hsi (1661–84) — nineteen authors
3. Middle K'ang-hsi (1684–1709) — forty-five authors
4. Late K'ang-hsi (1709–1723) — seven authors
5. Yung-cheng (1723–1736) — two authors

Nearly half of the *chin-shih* degree-holders represented in the collection thus received their degrees during the middle K'ang-hsi period; most of these had passed very high on the examinations and were therefore probably well known to Fang Pao himself. By contrast, Fang included essays by only seven people who received their degrees after the devastating effects of the Tai Ming-shih case and only three who received degrees during the Yung-cheng reign.

The influence of Fang's own associates on the collection was also apparent in the selection of authors whose work appeared most frequently in the collection. Most authors in the Ch'ing section of *Ch'in-ting Ssu-shu-wen* were represented by one to three essays. Eight authors, however, were represented by nine essays or more. Two of these, Liu Tzu-chuang (nine essays) and Hsiung Po-ling (twenty essays), both of whom received their *chin-shih* degrees in 1649, were mentioned as models to be emulated in the imperial edict commissioning the *Ch'in-ting Ssu-shu-wen*. Of the other six, three figured prominently in the literary and political career of Fang Pao: Li Kuang-ti (sixteen essays), the patron whose intervention had saved Fang Pao's life after the Tai Ming-shih case; Han T'an (twenty-two essays), Fang's friend and admirer; and Fang Chou (eleven essays), Fang Pao's older brother.[39] Fang may have been highlighting the work of his own friends and associates. But perhaps as important, the men whose work was represented in the manual were the most successful examples of the examination process in the Ch'ing, men whose philosophical mastery and literary ability made them fit models for examination takers.

It would not have seemed necessary, in Fang Pao's day, to defend the objectivity of the accepted understanding of the Classics. It was perhaps a mark of the importance of the issue at stake that Fang nonetheless concluded his review of the styles of examination essays included in the manual by quoting the Sung official Tseng Kung (1019–1083), who said that "although there have been many poets, separated by as much as a thousand years they have merely reinforced each other. Each expresses himself, but the truth is one."[40] Although there had been many authors, there could only be one truth; examination writers might express themselves differently but they all began from the same basic understanding.

Of more importance, at least in terms of the amount of time Fang devoted to it, was the issue of the objectivity of judgments based on style. Defending his contention in this regard, Fang articulated a definition of style that drew on the work of the founder of the *ku-wen* movement, Han Yü. In the passage of Han Yü with which Fang opened his argument, Han Yü responded to a prospective student who asked which models a student should follow in learning how to write: "And if someone asked, 'Should literature be easy or difficult?' I would answer respectfully, 'Neither difficult nor easy, but appropriate.'"[41] One need not labor over style, Han Yü argued, for only when writing style is appropriate to the substance it conveys will it be correct. As Han Yü's disciple Li Ao phrased the matter, "Neither creating ideas nor expressing in words should dominate." The writer who had a correct vision of truth and did not seek to be artificial would naturally write well. Ultimately, good writing consisted of the use of appropriate language rather than any kind of artful craftsmanship. Thus, judgments of style were also judgments of substance, and both could be equally objective, for quality of writing was related to the depth of understanding. Like Han Yü, Fang sought a directness and sincerity, even a kind of integrity in writing; he therefore urged his students not to labor over an artificial style. If one wanted to make the *li* clear, one had to draw on the language of the Classics as interpreted by the Sung Neo-Confucians. If one wanted verbal richness, one used the language of the three dynasties and of the Former and Later Han dynasty. If one wanted vitality of language, one drew on the *ku-wen* masters of all dynasties. The successful essay would combine all three types of language and achieve elegance in so doing.[42]

Because of the pedagogical purposes of the manual, Fang Pao reserved for himself certain prerogatives not ordinarily accorded anthologists. His main criterion for including an essay was its pedagogical value: he reserved the right to exclude older essays that though correct in form, were shallow and essays of recent vintage that, though popular, seemed to him unenlightening. Essays in the manual were drawn from all sources, including individual authors' printed collections and the handwritten and recopied scripts produced in the actual examinations.[43] Even essays by authors who did not reach the ultimate pinnacle of exam success, the *chin-shih* degree, could be included in the anthology if they had pedagogical value, although no essays produced at a level lower than the provincial examinations were to be included.[44] When only a portion of an essay was valuable, the manual reproduced only that portion, and when an author had seen fit to revise his writing after the examination, the manual reprinted the revised version.[45] When Fang himself felt it necessary to revise an essay for pedagogical purposes, he reserved the right to do so without notifying his readers. Finally, Fang and the other manual editors proposed to make a brief comment (in practice between twenty and a hundred characters, though sometimes longer) making clear the merit of a given essay, except in cases in which the merit of the work was obvious.

Fang Pao's goal was thus not so much to record literary history as to provide models for examination writers to follow. Although the essays in the *Ch'in-ting Ssu-shu-wen* inevitably reflected changing literary and political fashions, the standards of evaluation, Fang's manual implied, were relatively constant. Correct understanding of the Classics and clarity of writing were the goals; success in the examinations rested on knowledge of the Four Books (as Neo-Confucians understood them), knowledge of literary models from the early imperial era, and facility in the *ku-wen* writing style.

EXAMINATION ESSAYS

Examination essays have been treated in Chinese history primarily as a literary genre, and with good reason, for their authors were very much concerned with style and clarity of expression. But as the above discussion suggests, the stylistic devices of examination essays were not merely literary artifices. On the contrary, they were meant primarily as demonstrations of their authors' abilities to express with force and flexibility different dimensions of China's heritage of political wisdom. The organization of Fang's manual and its emphasis on internal comparison made it an especially valuable index of the variations that could occur within the framework of examination rules and the choices examiners made between essays. Close comparison of essays on similar topics was what the book was meant to foster. In the eighteenth century, such comparison served pedagogical purposes; today it can serve the historian's purpose of reconstructing the mentalities of the examination process and the criteria used for differentiating between essays. Two essays written in Ch'ing dynasty examinations on the passage "to get up with the crowing of the cock" (*chi-ming erh ch'i*) from the *Mencius*, Book 7A, illustrate the shared assumptions of examination writers, the points on which essays differed, and the effect in practice of Fang Pao's standards. Both authors were recipients of the *chin-shih* degree, and both understood the passage from Mencius and the task of examination essay writing similarly. The essays differed, however, in several respects: one was discursive and relativistic, the other taut and cerebral; one advanced a melancholy view of man's political and social potential, the other celebrated man's critical faculties of judgment.

Both writers certainly knew and drew upon the context in which the passage appeared and the standard interpretation of it. The crowing of the cock, as Mencius had it, was the moment at which man's propensity toward benevolence or selfishness was revealed: "He who gets up with the crowing of the cock and never tires of doing good is the same kind of man as Shun; he who gets up with the crowing of the cock and never tires of working for profit is the same kind of man as Chih. If you want to understand the difference between Shun and Chih, you need look no further than the gap separating the good and the profitable."[46]

In this passage, Mencius used two figures of Chinese myth as representatives of different human potentials. Shun, the legendary second emperor of China, typified man's potential for social benevolence, harmony, and self-government. Chih, a rather shadowy robber baron from the Ch'un-ch'iu period, represented the potential for self-aggrandizement. Both rose with the crowing of the cock but they almost immediately set about the pursuit of different aims, and the passage is concerned with expressing, metaphorically at least, the differences between the two aims.

Commentaries on the passage had formulated the nature of these differences. Chao Ch'i, the earliest commentator on the *Mencius*, had taken the passage as a definition of the nature of the *chün-tzu*, the man whose vocation it was to serve the ruler. For Chao the person who got up with the crowing of the cock and immediately busied himself with the pursuit of the beneficial was the natural ruler, whereas the person who only pursued profit was inevitably a *hsiao-jen*, or subject.[47] Sung Neo-Confucian commentators quoted by Chu Hsi in *Meng-tzu chi-chu* focused on the metaphysical implications of the passage. If the course of a life, whether in pursuit of profit or more benevolent aims, was determined in the brief moment of dawning, then surely everyone — not only the *chün-tzu* — must have the potential to pursue either kind of life. The moral tasks, then, were to understand how some came to pursue profit while others pursued the good and to strengthen the foundations of benevolence that existed within everyone. Chu Hsi's commentary quoted Ch'eng I as remarking that at the moment of dawning, when the choice between the ways of Shun and Chih was made, the paths were separated "but not by far." However, Ch'eng continued, "The way of Shun is that of public-spiritedness while the way of Chih is that of private interest. If the urge to good is not cultivated, the urge to profit will necessarily prevail." A student of Ch'eng I's added that, when fully realized, "the paths of Shun and Chih are indeed quite far apart. Therefore the moment of choice between good and evil has to be approached with caution. The difference between the two paths is not always clear, and it is easy to err, so the learned man could not but examine the moment carefully." When asked how to separate the two inclinations in actual affairs, Ch'eng I responded, "Only through reverence (*ching*) can one make the right choice."[48]

Just as context and commentary defined the nature of the interpretive task examination writers faced, so the rules of the examination essays provided the framework within which this task was to be accomplished. The form of examination essays was known throughout the Ming and Ch'ing dynasties as the "eight-legged essay" (*pa-ku-wen*). As Ching-i Tu has pointed out, drawing on Ku Yen-wu, the name was somewhat deceptive since there really weren't eight identifiable parts to the essay.[49] Rather, the form imposed on authors a logical structure of argumentation not unlike that imposed in, say, American collegiate debate format. The essayist was to begin with a brief statement of the proposition the essay itself was illustrating (known as *po-t'i*, "breaking of the title"); he was then to elaborate this proposition in four or five phrases (*ch'eng-t'i*, "receiving the title"); and finally to suggest the broad dimensions of the argument to be pursued (*ch'i-chiang*, or "preliminary discourse"). The meat of the essay was to be found in three passages known as comparisons (*pi*), written in roughly parallel form, that expressed the moral reasoning of the argument. As the burden of proof in an essay in the Western tradition would be borne by evidence, in Chinese examination essays it was borne by elegantly stated perception. Finally, a grand conclusion (*ta-chieh*) summarized the argument and stated its moral implications.

Chao Ping and Moralism

The first essay printed in *Ch'in-ting Ssu-shu-wen* on the subject of "getting up with the cock," by Chao Ping (*chin-shih* 1622), is one of the longer essays in the manual, 622 characters in length.[50] It explores one of the more pessimistic implications of the passage, at least as Neo-Confucian scholars understood it; namely, the question of why, if everyone had the potential (at least before the cock crowed) to follow either the way of Shun or the way of Chih, so many chose the path of Chih. Chao's opening proposition is that "human beings could be divided according to [whether they pursued] profit or the good, but the pursuit of profit is closer to man's natural inclination."

The reason, Chao argues, lies in human nature. People are inclined by nature to "love Shun but be unable to love the good, to hate Chih but be unable to hate the bad." Even though everyone knows that the difference between Shun and Chih is that between good and evil and tries to cultivate the good, the circumstances of life inevitably frustrate the fulfillment of good intentions. To explain this unfortunate fact, Chao proposes to argue throughout the essay that mankind has a dual nature: "Heaven has endowed me with a moral nature (*hsing*) to cultivate my mind, but it has also created things (*wu*) with which to nourish the body. That which cultivates the mind may not necessarily delight the body, and that which delights the body may well divide the mind." In any given circumstance, therefore, a person finds himself torn. Essentially, Chao is explaining the Mencian passage in terms of Neo-Confucian ontology, which sees humankind as composed of a heavenly endowment (*li*) that yearns for transcendence and a psycho-physical nature (*ch'i*) that unites it with the other things of the world.

In the comparisons that form the body of the essay, Chao explains how it is that human beings endowed with such a nature choose to pursue either benevolence or profit. In his first comparison, Chao examines the respective attractions of the two paths. Shun and Chih, he argues, are not so much human possibilities as "ideal types" that represent the two sides of the human personality. The inclinations toward benevolence and self-aggrandizement cannot be represented very effectively in the abstract, so they must be personified. The two figures, however, act somewhat differently in shaping human motivations: the image of Shun serves to motivate, while that of Chih serves all too often as a mirror of human aspirations. Nonetheless, in the moment of choosing, the two courses appear to be similar: "When a matter comes before me, the Shun (within me) seeks the good and the Chih (within me) seeks good as well. Shun's good is here, Chih's good is there. I cannot avoid the choice."

The second comparison is essentially of the way in which the decision is made: "My sacred intelligence (*shen-chih*) assists Shun in attracting me; my emotions (*ch'ing-hao*) assist Chih in attracting me. If Shun is victorious, I gain control over myself; if Chih is victorious, I lose myself. I cannot with one mind harmonize two paths." Alluding to the commentaries quoted by Chu Hsi in the *Meng-tzu chi-chu*, Chao continues: "There must be one path that is far, and having recognized it as far, I no longer pursue it. Who can but recognize what is near and incline in that direction?"

The choice is made in a flash, as Chao suggests in this third comparison. In the motionless silence before dawn "both Shun and Chih exist in the mind of the sage. But if you delay an instant there is danger. In those who incline toward benevolence [at that moment], the pursuit of profit can make no progress. In those who incline toward the pursuit of profit [at that moment], benevolence can make no progress. The myriad things of the world are as one, and with the crowing of the cock they are dispersed." Such is the moment in which man's moral fate is decided.

Given the rather asymmetric attractions of good and evil, the urge to profit triumphs all too easily over the urge to become good. Examples of Chih-like behavior exist all around us, but there has only been one Shun:

> Since time began there has only been one Shun. But what limit can there be to the Chihs of this world? Only one person has the name of Chih. But the number of those who have Chih in their hearts is limitless.... "Shun" and "Chih" are only words. Among those who consciously emulate Shun, if we carefully examine [the matter] everyone is a follower of Chih. Those who consciously emulate Chih are in fact followers of Chih, although since in their hearts they have an image of Shun, they call themselves Shun. Those who follow Shun also have Chih in their hearts, but are afraid of Chih, and so are Shuns. Therefore, I must take care about the difference. For if I don't perceive it early, I will surely pursue profit. Alas that there are so many Chihs.

No person can rise with the cock and automatically become a Shun, because much within inclines one to be a Chih. Nonetheless, the images of Shun and Chih are useful as they direct attention to the task of becoming good. Chao approaches the images of Shun and Chih not as a cynic, surely, but at least as a realist who recognized the awesome difficulties of morality.

Fang Pao appreciated Chao's essay in part because its language was well suited to the nature of the argument it made. As he commented: "We may be aware that the pursuit of profit and of benevolent aims represent two paths, but Mencius especially held up the images of Shun and Chih in order to differentiate between the two impulses. Recognizing that the passage establishes a norm represents one level of understanding, perceiving the fear and anxiety [associated with fulfilling the norm] represents another level. It takes a supple stylist to express these two levels."

But, Fang Pao continued, there were some flaws (lit., "slippery spots") in the essay, passages in which Chao's pen seemed too quick, too glib. From a Neo-Confucian point of view, Chao made the mistake of granting, or appearing to grant, equal ontological status to good and evil. Chao seemed inclined toward a kind of moral relativism that recognized the roots of Chih even in Shun. It was easy for those who exalt profit to slide down the slippery slope of relativism, Fang concluded: "The scholar cannot but be cautious." Thus, although the writing in the essay was skillful, its argument diverged from Neo-Confucian orthodoxy, and for this reason it seemed to Fang less successful than the effort of Lü Ch'ien-heng.

Lü Ch'ien-heng and Judgment

Lü Ch'ien-heng's essay on "getting up with the crowing of the cock" was shorter than Chao's (452 characters as opposed to 622) and had a different focus: on the critical faculties of judgment that enabled human beings to choose between courses of action. The comparative portions of the two essays most clearly illustrated the differences between them. Chao was at some pains to construct comparisons that conveyed many nuances of meaning and used 303 characters in doing so. Lü Ch'ien-heng's comparisons were much shorter, 192 in all, and much sharper. Lü also made more — and more precise — allusions to classical commentary on the Mencian passage. In almost every respect, Lü's was the more cerebral essay, tightly structured as if to demonstrate the very powers of judgment it sought to celebrate.

In a sense, Lü Ch'ien-heng's essay began where Chao Ping's left off, with an assertion of the importance of caution in moral behavior. However, Lü urged such caution not on the basis of an analysis of the human moral condition but as the advice of the sages: "The sages wished man to take care about his behavior and so regarded it as essential to establish the differences" between types of action. Mencius's essential message in the passage, according to Lü, was the importance of moral judgment. "If in pursuing good or profit," Lü continued in developing his opening proposition, "one goes as far as Shun or Chih, the differences are great indeed." However, for most people the choice is not so stark. Subtle differences of direction divide those who rise early in the morning to pursue their own interests from those who rise early to pursue more benevolent aims. "Human natures are not originally that far apart, but once they divide pursuing different courses, the consequences are innumerable." In the last sentence of this development, Lü alluded to the commentary of Chu Hsi. It was a mark of the difference between the two essayists that Lü's commentary was both somewhat more precise and served a different end. In the original commentary, Ch'eng I had observed that the thrust of Mencius's passage was that human natures were "separated but not by far." Chao Ping had used similar language but had given it a verbal thrust when he wrote that "there must be one path that is far, and having recognized it as far, I no longer pursue it." Lü's reference to human natures originally "not being that far apart" was somewhat more faithful to Cheng I and pointed to the critical distinction between courses that were similar rather than the fact that one road inevitably seemed farther than another.

In the body of Lü's essay, he examines the act of moral judgment and its consequences in behavior from a number of different points of view. As he writes in his preliminary discourse, rehearsing the basic directions of his argument:

> The sagely nature [present in each of us] is essentially without purposeful action; in a moment good and evil appear. They manifest themselves first in inclination and are fully realized in habits. If we are to distinguish between them, we must do so early. What is implicit in *ch'i* at night moves us in the morning, and if we are to think about it at all, we must do so quickly. When the cock crows and the [paths to] good and profit become visible, we may choose the kingdom of Shun or Chih. By what means can we distinguish them? [We do so] precisely in our choice of behavior.

The first sentence of this passage (*ch'eng-pen wu-wei erh yu shan-e*) was a direct quotation from the *T'ung-shu* (Essay on discernment) of the Neo-Confucian scholar Chou Tun-i in which he had sought to articulate those qualities of mind that enabled the sage to determine the correct behavior.[51] Lü's reference turns the reader's attention to the faculty of judgment with which his essay is concerned. The essay makes three points about correct judgment: first, that the perceptions involved are subtle; second, that the moment of perception is not necessarily apparent to the actor; and third, that with the help of the sages such judgments not only can but must be made.

Each of these points is illustrated by a comparison. The first illustrates the subtlety of the judgments required: "When the cock crows, the man who is inclined toward benevolence already busies himself with the good. Although he is not yet Shun, he is a follower of Shun. When the cock crows the man who is inclined toward self-aggrandizement already busies himself with profit. Although he is not yet Chih, he is a follower of Chih. Such is the distinction [between benevolence and profit]." That such a choice has been made might be apparent only in retrospect, Lü suggests in his second comparison: "If we consider the matter from the perspective of hindsight, Shun seems always to have been Shun, and Chih seems always to have been Chih"—two courses as different as

the speech of a madman and the speech of a sage, which cannot be uttered on
the same day by the same person. On the other hand, if the choice is examined
before it is made, it seems more like a sudden swerve, an inexplicable bend in
the moral road. "In an instant the one who pursues profit and the one who
pursues benevolence [go] this way and that" without apparent reason. The
critical element in choosing a course of action, Lü suggests in his third comparison, is knowing precisely what the passage from Mencius imparts: "What
are separated are the roads to benevolence and self-aggrandizement. What
separates them is the distance between the two" — that is to say, the difference
between Shun and Chih, with which Mencius was concerned. "If we are not
aware of the distance, then as large as the universe is" we may still go astray.
"There is one point to enter if we wish to exit at a set place. Heaven and earth
have no path that is not either Shun's or Chih's, at least no path that man can
follow." Lü's essay thus transforms Mencius's text from a metaphor into a
standard, a rule for moral choice.

For the ordinary person to make such a choice, however, he or she must
have access to the moral insight of the sage. The statement of that crucial
premise comes at the very beginning of the conclusion, when Lü argues that
"the mind of man and the moral mind can come together in thought." This
line is given special force by the fact that it embodies an allusion to a famous
line from the *Shang-shu*: "The human mind is precarious, the moral mind is
subtle. Have absolute refinement and singleness of purpose. Hold fast the
mean."[52]

Lü continues by celebrating the act of judgment informed by classical wisdom that enables the wise person to choose the correct course: "If in fact we
know the difference between the two paths, then fortunately we can make a
choice when [the options] first sprout before us." Armed with Mencius's words,
we must "look up and measure [the choices], thoughtfully consider them, and
without becoming anxious perceive the subtle differences between profit and
benevolence.... Focusing on one inch within a thousand *li*, concentrating all our
force in one breath, we can set to rest our anxieties and perceive the narrow
difference between courses of action." The fact that the ordinary person can
accomplish this task after study depends on the fact that the sage can accomplish it naturally. At base, he says, "only the sage can know inclinations
[naturally] and only the *chün-tzu* is [naturally] cautious about behavior.
Scholars admire the sage in order to recover his original nature and recognize
the good at the crowing of the cock."

In so concluding his essay, Lü refers once again to Chou Tun-i and through
him to one of the oldest texts of Confucian thought, the *I-ching*. In the
T'ung-shu, Chou continued the argument about the nature of the sage with a
quotation from the Great Appendix of the *I-ching*: "Does not he who knows the
inclinations of things possess spirit-like wisdom?" Chu Hsi in turn annotated
Chou's quotation with the comment, "Such a one is the sage."[53] Lü echoes

both remarks in his closing assertion that "only the sage can know inclinations," thus framing his own argument rather elegantly within the context of Neo-Confucian thought.

So at least it appeared to Fang Pao, who remarked that the language of the essay was "limpid and appropriate" and that it contained nothing superfluous. Fang continued that the use of the language from Chou Tun-i in the preliminary discourse and the conclusion was "excellently suited to the task of filling in the gaps in the *Mencius*. Whenever one uses language from the five masters of the Sung in an essay," Fang continued, "it must be so suited or one runs the risk of superfluous copying." Fang in fact had no fault at all to find with Lü's essay and offered it as a model of elegant and appropriate writing.

Fang thus found Lü's essay superior to Chao Ping's largely because it made better use of the Neo-Confucian tradition that constituted the foundation of the examination process. His judgment seems to have been shared by the examiners who evaluated the essays. For while both men were ranked similarly in the overall competition — Chao Ping as fifty-seventh in 1666 and Lü Ch'ien-heng was fifty-first in 1709 — Lü was singled out for membership in the Hanlin Academy, an honor normally reserved only for those who were ranked at the top of the list. Lü's literary abilities carried him through the Hanlin Academy to a position in the capital and finally to posts as chief examiner in the provincial examinations and examiner in the metropolitan examinations.[54]

CONCLUSION: THE BOUNDARIES OF PEDAGOGY IN LATE IMPERIAL CHINA

In history writing as in many pursuits, it is the squeaky hinge that gets the oil: in both Chinese and Western treatments, the examination system has often been characterized on the basis of the testimony of dissidents, those who either failed or, having passed, came to reject the principles on which the system was based. Fang Pao's life, his manual, and the essays it reprinted are valuable precisely because they provide the testimony of insiders. As such, they suggest not only the strategies of success but also the parameters within which successful teaching and learning took place in late imperial China. One of these parameters was certainly defined by the role of the scholar in Chinese government. As Fang Pao's rather checkered experience indicated, while scholars were ubiquitous at Chinese courts, their role was not unchanging. The Yung-cheng emperor's quest for different skills among those who served him and the young Ch'ien-lung emperor's interest in ritual texts inevitably had ramifications for scholarly life. The evolution of examination style that Fang traced in the preface to *Ch'in-ting Ssu-shu-wen* probably reflected political changes, although Fang himself was perhaps constrained from drawing the parallels. Certainly, the desire of Fang and his friends to institutionalize literati control of Ch'ing policy toward intellectuals was ample testimony to the importance they themselves attributed to that policy. Control, however, worked both ways: the symbiotic relationship of knowledge and power in China meant that rulers were constrained by the ideological foundations of their own thrones. So long as political legitimacy rested on fealty to Confucian principles, rulers would need Confucian doyens like Fang Pao, if only to certify the correctness of their choice of servants. As treacherous as the position of any individual scholar could be, the class as a whole was indispensable to Chinese government, and this fact was essential to their view of learning and education.

The close connection of knowledge and power meant that to a certain degree in all ages, and to a great degree in some, the examinations served as a political litmus test of those who would be willing to serve the established authority. But in an age like Fang Pao's an equally important role of the examinations was to determine who, among a cohort of willing servitors, might actually be privileged to hold political office. An institutionalized—and as the century progressed, increasingly strenuous—competition constituted a second parameter of scholarly life in the late eighteenth century, and it was to some of the issues raised by this competition that Fang's manual was at least implicitly addressed. Significantly, the manual ignored those parts of the examinations in which political loyalty was established and focused exclusively on those points in which intellectual virtuosity was demonstrated. Both Fang's emphasis on models and standards and the terms in which they were justified were important. By the beginning of the eighteenth century, as Fang Pao's preface so vividly demonstrated, there were many models, both positive and negative, for examination candidates to follow. There were so many, in fact, that judgment of examination essays could readily be perceived as subjective rather than objective in character. Moreover, many more candidates were taking the examinations than ever before. If the examinations were to remain the principle mechanism of political recruitment, some definition of standards was necessary. This may well have been an important reason why the young Ch'ien-lung emperor commissioned the manual. While Fang's specific recommendations were ultimately superseded, the principle of his manual—that in a highly competitive era differences in the quality of expression and mastery of the Neo-Confucian tradition should differentiate candidates—endured.

The perennial humanistic concerns of Chinese philosophy constituted a third parameter of pedagogy in late imperial China. The Confucian tradition, which was the foundation of both education and the examination system, shaped not only the content of the examinations but also the very sorts of intellectual activity that were required in both essay writing and evaluations. Fundamentally, it was not a tradition of truth testing, although certainly concern for scholarly accuracy was a feature of Confucian scholarship, particularly in the late imperial period. Nor was it a tradition that took techniques of logical argument as a core. Rather, Confucianism was a tradition concerned above all with the organization of human life and society and how such organization was grounded in human nature. There was room within this great tradition not only for scholarly claims and concerns but also for the articulation of assumptions about the nature and proper basis of human society. The examination essays tested, in some sense, candidates' capacities to articulate these assumptions and the conclusions that had been drawn from them through the history of Chinese philosophy. The essays by Lü Ch'ien-heng and Chao Ping discussed here thus differed primarily not in their literary quality but in the basic attitude toward human nature from which they approached the assigned task. Formal as it was in many other respects, the Chinese civil service examination system allowed for such fundamental variation among candidates; one could argue in fact that one purpose of the system was to measure such variation among potential civil servants, together with candidates' capacity to express this variation (see also Elman, chap. 4 of this volume). This is not to say that the range of permissible assumptions about the range of human nature was great; nor was the task of expressing one's values within the constraints of examination essays an easy one. The testimony of the many who failed amply demonstrates the difficulties examinations entailed. But the contents of the examinations demonstrate the degree to which education in China was fundamentally concerned with the manifestation of moral musculature.

NOTES

I am grateful to the participants in the Conference on Education and Society in Late Imperial China, and particularly to Peter Bol, Benjamin Elman, Frederic Wakeman, and Alexander Woodside, for their comments on this chapter, as well as for the suggestions of anonymous reviewers.

1. Lynn Struve has vividly portrayed the history of this period in two articles. See "Ambivalence and Action: Some Frustrated Scholars of the Late K'ang-hsi Period," in *From Ming to Ch'ing*, ed. Jonathan D. Spence and John E. Wills, Jr., (New Haven: Yale University Press, 1979); "The Hsu Brothers and Semi-Official Patronage in the K'ang-hsi Period," *Harvard Journal of Asiatic Studies* 42 (1982): 231–66. On Li Kuang-ti, see esp. Pierre-Henri Durand, "Manchous et Chinois: Kangxi et le Process du *Nanshan Ji*", *Études Chinois* 7 (Printemps 1988): 78–81, 89–91 as well as Arthur Hummel, ed. *Eminent Chinese of the Ch'ing Period* (hereafter *ECCP*) (reprint, Taipei: Literature House, 1964) 473–75.

2. Hilary J. Beattie, *Land and Lineage in China; A Study of T'ung-ch'eng County, Anhui, in the Ming and Ch'ing Dynasties* (Cambridge: Cambridge University Press, 1979), 31–32; Su Tun-yuan 蘇惇元, "Fang Pao nien-p'u" 方苞年譜 (Chronological biography of Fang Pao), in *Fang Pao chi* (hereafter *FBC*) (reprint, Shanghai: Ku-chieh Publishing Co., 1983), 1:856.

3. Fang Pao, "Hsiung Pai-ch'uan mu-chih-ming" 兄百川墓誌銘 (Epitaph for Hsiung Pai-ch'uan [Tzu-lü]), *FBC* 2:495–97. See also Chen P'eng-nien 陳鵬年,

"Mu-chieh" 墓碣 (Epitaph), in the note on Fang Pao in Li Yuan 李垣, ed. *Kuo-ch'ao chi-hsien lei-cheng ch'u-pien* 國朝耆獻類徵初編 (Classified collection of biographies of famous men of our dynasty; hereafter *KCCHLC*), Li Family (Hsiang-yin, 1884–90), 430: 15a–16a.

4. On Han T'an's admiration for Fang, see "Nien-pu," 1:869, and Shen Ting-fang 沈廷芳, "Fang Pao chuan" 方苞傳 (Biography of Fang Pao), *KCCHLC*, 66:11a. Several letters in Fang Pao's collected writings testify to his continuing friendship with Han T'an. See also Chow Kai-wing's chapter in this volume.

5. Chow Kai-wing has explored the evolution of this view very effectively in "Ritual and Ethics: Chinese Scholarship and Lineage Institutions in Late Imperial China" (Ph. D. diss., University of California Davis, 1987), 158–248. See also Wing-tsit Chan, "The *Hsing-li ching-i* and the Ch'eng-Chu School of the Seventeenth Century" in *The Unfolding of Neo-Confucianism*, Wm. Theodore de Bary, ed., (New York: Columbia University Press, 1979), 543–79.

6. On Fang Pao's views of Chu Hsi, see "Hsueh-an hsu" 學案序 (Preface to notes on [Chu Hsi's] scholarship), *FBC*, 1:89–90. The story about Fang's note to Li Kung is included in Fang's biography in *ECCP*, 235; the identification of Fang with the ritual texts is made most forcefully in the entry on Fang in *Ch'ing-hsueh-an hsiao-chih* 清學案小識 (Supplementary notes on the history of Ch'ing scholarship) (reprint, Taipei: Commercial Press, 1969), 334.

7. Shen Ting-fang, "Fang Pao chuan," *KCCHLC*, 69:11a.

8. In his index of Ch'ing dynasty examination takers, William Hung listed Fang in a special appendix.

9. The details of the succession crisis lie rather outside the scope of the present work. See Silas H.L. Wu, *Passage to Power* (Cambridge, Mass: Harvard University Press, 1979), *passim*; Jonathan Spence, *Emperor of China* (New York: Random House, 1975), 119–39.

10. Durand, "Manchous et Chinois," 89-91.

11. *Ta Ch'ing Sheng-tsu Jen huang-ti shih-lu* 大清聖祖仁皇帝實錄 (Veritable records of successive reigns of the Ch'ing dynasty; hereafter *SL*) (Tokyo: Okura, 1936–37), K'ang-hsi, 236:14a. Hsiung Tzu-li was at that point retired from his position as grand secretary but remained at the capital to give occasional advice on political matters.

12. Lynn A. Struve, "The Uses of History in Traditional Chinese Society: The Southern Ming in Ch'ing Historiography" (Ph.D. diss., University of Michigan, 1974) 354; See also the entry on Tai in *ECCP*, 701, and Durand, "Manchous et Chinois," 67–69.

13. See *"Nien-p'u," FBC*, 2:880–81

14. "Kuo-shih-kuan pen-chuan" 國史館本傳 (Biography from the state historical commission), *KCCHLC*, 69:1b.

15. Yu Chi, "Chi" 記 (Note), *KCCHLC* 71:56b. "Kuo-shih-kuan pen-chuan," *KCCHLC*, 71:53a.

16. *Yung-cheng chu-p'i yü-chih* 雍正硃批諭旨 (Vermilion endorsements of the Yung-cheng emperor) (reprint, Taipei: Wenhai, 1975), 3898–99.

17. "Kuo-shih-kuan pen-chuan" *KCCHLC*, 71:53b.

18. Ch'üan Tsu-wang 全祖望, "Shen-tao-pei" 神道碑 (Epitaph), *KCCHLC*, 69:7b–8a; *FBC*, 2:583–86.

19. Ch'üan Tsu-wang, "Shen-tao-pei", *KCCHLC*, 69:7b–8a; FBC, 2:577–78.

20. *FBC*, 2:574–76; see also "Kuo-shih-kuan pen-chuan," *KCCHLC* 69:4a-b, for the imperial reaction. See also Beatrice S. Bartlett, *Monarchs and Ministers* (Berkeley: University of California Press, 1991), 164–66.

21. *FBC*, 2:540–42. I have treated the early Ch'ien-lung reaction to T'ien Wen-ching briefly in "Zhang Tingyu and Reconciliation," *Late Imperial China* 7 no. 1 (Dec. 1986): 50–62.

22. *FBC*, 2:542–55. I am grateful to members of the University of Washington research seminar in Chinese history in 1987 for their thoughtful and stimulating reading of these documents.

23. On Fang's nominations for the Temple of Eminent Statesmen, see *Ch'ing-shih kao* 清史稿 (Draft history of the Ch'ing), (Taipei: National Defense Research Institute 1961), 4046. Fang's memorials are reprinted in his collected works, *FBC*, 2:564–68. See also his letter to Oerht'ai in *FBC*, 1:154–55.

24. Ch'üan Tsu-wang, "Shen-tao-pei," *KCCHLC*; 71: 7b–8a. There is some evidence at least of Fang's involvement in matters of river conservancy in his *Wen-chi*, which contains what appear to be an extraordinary number of proposals in this area, particularly from an official who never left the capital. On Kao Pin, see *ECCP*, 412–13.

25. Such is the interpretation presented in *Ch'ing-shih kao*, 4046.

26. *FBC*, 2:564–65.

27. *Ssu-k'u ch'üan-shu tsung-mu t'i-yao* 四庫全書總目提要 (Annotated catalog of the complete library of the Four Treasuries), (reprint, Taipei: Commercial Press, 1971) 1: 83–84.

28. *FBC*, 1:154–55.

29. *SL*, Ch'ien-lung, 21:1a–2a.

30. *Shang-yü-tang* (Edict record books) 1:1736, entry for 1/6/1. I am grateful to the First Historical Archives for allowing me to see this document during my visit there in 1984, and for the financial support of the Committee on Scholarly Communications with the People's Republic of China, which made possible my visit. Although there is no evidence on the point, it is hard to believe that this early version of the edict was not drafted by Fang or by hands close to his.

31. *SL*, Ch'ien-lung, 92:14a–16b. For Fang's interrogation of *chin-shih* candidates, see Ch'üan Tsu-wang, "Shen-tao-pei" *KCCHLC*, 69:9a–b.

32. The evolution of the form of the examinations is traced in the *Ch'ing-shih kao*, *chüan* 109.

33. On the significance of policy questions, see Elman, chap. 4 of this volume. For the criticism of policy questions, see the imperial response to Shu-ho-te's 舒赫德 fairly famous 1741 memorial criticizing the examinations. The response is reprinted in *Hsüeh-cheng ch'üan-shu* 學政全書 (Complete manual for education commissioners) (reprint, Taipei: Wenhai, 1968) 1:147–55, and summarized in *Ch'ing-shih kao, chüan* 109.

34. Miyazaki Ichisada, *China's Examination Hell* (New York: Weatherhill, 1976), 67.

35. *Ssu-k'u ch'üan-shu tsung-mu t'i-yao*, 1:72–73.

36. Daniel Gardner relates Chu Hsi's understanding of this passage as "when rulers treasure wealth, it is invariably because petty men guide them." *Chu Hsi and the Ta-hsüeh* (Cambridge, Mass.: Harvard University Press, 1986) 123–24. Essays on this topic can be found in Fang Pao, ed., *Ch'in-ting Ssu-shu-wen* 欽定四書文 (hereafter

CTSSW) (1738; reprint, Taipei, Commercial Press, 1979), vol. 2, *chüan* 1:13a–14a, 15a–16b, vol. 3, *chüan* 1:11a–12b, 13a–14a, vol. 5, *chüan* 1:64a–65b.

37. *CTSSW*, preface, 1a–3a.

38. On the Restoration Society, see William S. Atwell, "From Education to Politics: The *Fu She*," in *Unfolding of Neo-Confucianism*, ed. de Bary, 333-65.

39. The others were Chang Yü-shu 張玉書, Chang Chiang 張江, and Ch'u Ta-wen 儲大文.

40. Tseng was a Sung dynasty poet and anthologist. Two of his books were included in the *Ssu-k'u ch'üan-shu tsung-mu t'i-yao*: *Lung-p'ing chi* 隆平集 (2:1092), and *Yuan-feng lei-kao* 元豐類稿 (4:4317).

41. Han Yü's letter to Liu Cheng-fu 劉正夫, as translated in Charles Hartmann, *Han Yü and the T'ang Search for Unity* (Princeton: Princeton University Press, 1986), 254.

42. *CTSSW*, 3a–4a.

43. On the differences between the original and recopied versions of examination essays, see Ku Yen-wu 顧炎武, "Ch'eng wen" 程文 (Examination essays), *Yuan ch'ao-pen jih-chih-lu* 原抄本日知碌 (Original hand-copied edition of record of knowledge accumulated day by day), ed. Hsu Wen-san 徐文珊 (reprint, Taipei: Ming-lun, 1958), 481.

44. Ninety-eight of the 122 authors from the Ch'ing dynasty held *chin-shih* degrees.

45. Fang signified that he had abbreviated an essay by printing the number of *chang* 章 (portions) or *chieh* 節 (sentences) reprinted in the table of contents. The only clue that an author had revised his own essay occurred in cases in which the author's own comment on the essay (*tzu-p'ing* 自評, self-criticism) were included in *CTSSW*, which happened relatively rarely.

46. D.C. Lau, trans., *Mencius* (London: Penguin, 1970), 187.

47. Chao Ch'i, *Meng-tzu chu-shu* 孟子注疏 (Commentary on the *Mencius*), *Ssu-pu pei-yao* ed. (Shanghai, 1936), 13b:2a.

48. *Meng-tzu chi-chu*, 孟子集注 (Collected commentaries on the *Mencius*), (Tokyo: Meitoku Publishing, 1974) 399, 542. Legge's translation perhaps reflects the Ch'eng commentary when he articulates the difference between the two paths as a matter of time rather than space. Whereas Lau writes, "If you want to know the difference between Shun and Chih, look no further than the gap separating the good and the profitable," Legge writes, "If you want to know what separates Shun from Chih, it is simply this—the interval between the *thought of gain* and the *thought of virtue*" (Legge's emphasis). See James Legge, trans., *Mencius* (Oxford: Oxford University Press, 1892), 464.

49. Ching-i Tu, "The Chinese Examination Essay: Some Literary Considerations," *Monumenta Serica* 31 (1974–75): 397.

50. All passages from Chao's and Lü's essays are from *CTSSW*, vol. 5, *chüan* 14:4b–7a.

51. Chou Tun-i 周敦頤, "T'ung-shu" 通書 (On comprehension), in *Chou-tzu ch'üan-shu* 周子全書 (Collected works of Mr. Chou), (Taipei: Jen-jen wen-k'u, 1973), 126.

52. On the significance of this line in Neo-Confucian philosophy, see Benjamin A. Elman, "Philosophy (*I-li*) Versus Philology (*K'ao-cheng*): The *Jen-hsin Tao-hsin* Debate,"

T'oung Pao 69, nos. 4–5(1983):175–222; William Theodore de Bary, *Message of the Mind in Neo- Confucianism* (New York: Columbia University Press, 1989), 24–52.
    53. "T'ung-shu," 145. The *I-ching* passage is from the Great Appendix, sec. 2, ch. 5, as translated in Z.D. Sung, *The Text of the Yi-King* (Shanghai, 1935; reprint, Taipei: Ch'eng-wen Publishing Co., 1971), 321.
    54. Not surprisingly, Lü was a friend of Fang Pao's. See Fang's epitaph for Lü, "Kuang-lu ch'ing Lü-kung mu-chih-ming" 光祿卿呂公墓誌銘 (Epitaph for the honorable Mr. Lu), *FBC* 1:282.

GLOSSARY

Chao Ch'i	趙歧	Han Yü	韓愈
Chao Ping	趙炳	Hanlin	翰林
che-chung	折中	*hsing*	性
Cheng-te	正德	Hsiung Po-lung	熊佰龍
Ch'eng-Chu	程朱	Hsiung Tzu-lü	熊賜履
Ch'eng-hua	成化	Hung-chih	弘治
Ch'eng I	程頤	*I-ching*	易經
ch'eng-pen wu-wei	誠本無為	*I-li*	義禮
er chi yu shan-e	而幾有善惡	K'ang-hsi	康熙
ch'eng-t'i	承題	Kao Pin	高斌
chi	集	*k'ao-cheng*	考證
chi-ming erh ch'i	鷄鳴而起	*ku-wen*	古文
ch'i	氣	Ku Yen-wu	顧炎武
ch'i-chiang	起講	*kung yü shih-wen*	工於時文
Chia-ching	嘉靖	*li*	理
Ch'ien-lung	乾隆	*li*	里
Chih	躓	Li Ao	李翺
chin-shih	進士	*Li-chi*	禮記
Ch'in-ting Ssu-shu-wen	欽定四書文	Li Kuang-ti	李光地
ching	敬	Li Kung	李恭
ch'ing-hao	情好	*liu-ch'ing*	六卿
Chou-i che-chung	周易折中	Liu Tzu-chuang	劉子壯
Chou-li	周禮	Lü Ch'ien-heng	呂謙恒
Chou Tun-i	周敦頤	*lun*	論
Chu Hsi	朱熹	Lung-ch'ing	隆慶
chü-jen	舉人	*Meng-tzu chi-chu*	孟子集注
chuang-yuan	狀元	*Nan-shan-chi*	南山集
chün-tzu	君子	Oerht'ai	鄂爾泰
Ch'un-ch'iu	春秋	Ou-yang Hsiu	歐陽修
Ch'ung-chen	崇禎	*pa-ku-wen*	八股文
Fang Chou	方舟	*pi*	比
Fang Hsiao-piao	方孝標	P'ien-yuan	偏元
Fang Pao	方苞	*Po-hsueh hung-ju*	博學鴻儒
Han T'an	韓菼	*po-t'i*	破題

San-li	三禮	T'ien-ch'i	天啟
Shang-shu	尚書	T'ien Wen-ching	田文鏡
Shang-yü-tang	上諭檔	*ts'e*	冊
shen-chih	神智	*ts'e*	策
Sheng-ching	盛京	Tseng Kung	曾鞏
Shih-ching	詩經	*tsuan-yen*	纂言
Shih-lu	實錄	T'ung-ch'eng	桐城
Shun	舜	*T'ung-shu*	通書
Shun-chih	順治	Wan-li	萬曆
Ssu-k'u ch'üan-shu	四庫全書	Wang Yang-ming	王陽明
ta-chieh	大結	Wei T'ing-chen	魏廷珍
Tai Ming-shih	戴明世	Wen-cheng	文正
T'ai-hsueh	太學	*Wen-chi*	文集
t'an-hua	探花	Wen-tuan	文端
T'ang Pin	湯斌	*wu*	物
Tien-ch'ien chi-wen	滇黔紀文	Wu San-kuei	吳三桂

SIX

Discourse, Examination, and Local Elite
The Invention of the T'ung-ch'eng School in Ch'ing China

Kai-wing Chow

In 1765 Lu Wen-ch'ao (1717–95), a devoted student of textual scholarship, was appointed the examiner of the Kwangtung provincial examination. In addition to the required questions on the Four Books and the teachings of Sung Neo-Confucians, he asked the candidates questions on classical rituals and the textual problem regarding the authenticity of the *Ku-wen shang-shu* (Old Text Book of Documents).[1] Three years later, Yao Nai (1731–1815), an associate examiner for the provincial examination of Shantung, posed the following question to the candidates: "It is said that those who study principles (*li-hsueh*) revere Ch'eng I and Chu Hsi, while those who undertake evidential study of the Classics (*k'ao-cheng ching-i*) venerate scholars of the Han dynasty. Although [the record] of the conduct and activities of Han scholars is extant, would you revere them for making contributions to the Classics or for their devotion to moral practice, living like Confucians without shame?"[2]

Lu's question evidences a growing emphasis on textual and philological aspects of classical study in academic circles and an increasing concern with testing candidates on their knowledge of this new scholarship. By contrast, Yao's question betrays not only the mounting pressure to study Han exegeses for philological information but also a major concern among adherents of Sung Neo-Confucianism who feared that textualism would result in the neglect of moral teachings. Both questions, however, clearly demonstrate that changes in discourse on Confucian doctrine affected the content of civil service examinations in the mid-eighteenth century (see also Elman, chap. 4 of this volume).

Discourse, however, did not evolve independently of nondiscursive domains such as economic, social, and political institutions and processes.[3] In Ch'ing China, the civil service examination system was one of the public arenas in which various social groups strove to control the production and dissemination of discourses, and hence knowledge and texts, for the maintenance and promotion of their interests. The curriculum of the examinations and the criteria of success significantly determined who would succeed in the examinations and consequently who would have access to political power. The contests between individual candidates were therefore predetermined in great measure by the battle over the control of the curriculum and its criteria for success. In turn, the degree of influence any local elite group brought to bear on the civil service examination was determined by its relationship with the imperial regime.

Rather than investigate education of the Ch'ing period from an institutional perspective, this chapter treats education as a process that evolved as political, intellectual, and social conditions changed. Through this broader vista of education, this chapter attempts to chart the shifting contours of the complex relationships between the Manchu state, local elites, Confucian discourse, and the civil service examination by focusing on the genesis of an imaginary intellectual lineage — the T'ung-ch'eng school. What follows is an attempt at a deconstructive analysis of the T'ung-ch'eng school that breaks up the lineage and restores the individual members and their ideas to their specific contexts. This analysis is accompanied by a reconstructive narrative of how the fortunes of the elite families of T'ung-ch'eng rose and fell as political change and shifts in discourse affected their success rate in the civil service examination from the late seventeenth through the early nineteenth centuries.

This study will focus on Fang Pao (1668–1749) and Yao Nai, who are considered to be the leading exponents of the T'ung-ch'eng school. The choice of these two figures is not so much a result of accepting the conventional view as it is an attempt to see them as members of elite families from T'ung-ch'eng county. In addition, Tai Ming-shih (1653–1713), also a native of T'ung-ch'eng, will be included even though he was not given a place in Yao's lineage. Tai is regarded as a pioneer of the school in the Ch'ing period, and as it will become clear, he is entitled to a place even by Yao's own criteria for inclusion.[4]

The T'ung-ch'eng school was invented by Yao Nai in the 1770s. After Yao's declaration of its birth, the school acquired "historical reality" and came to represent a major approach to Confucian learning and education. Central to its thought were three elements — a faith in the Ch'eng-Chu ideology, a strong interest in *ku-wen* (ancient prose) style, and a didactic view of writing.[5] The T'ung-ch'eng school was further distinguished by its full accommodation of the "eight-legged" (*pa-ku*) essay, the highly structured style of writing that candidates taking the civil service examination had to observe. The T'ung-ch'eng school therefore had a strong tie with the Manchu government, Ch'eng-Chu orthodoxy, and the civil service examination. As we shall see, none of these characteristics had any special ties to the T'ung-ch'eng elite. Although the line of succession of the school was created by Yao Nai, the central teachings that Yao appropriated for the putative school had been rigorously championed since the early Ch'ing by such adherents of Ch'eng-Chu learning as Lü Liu-liang (1629–83), Lü Lung-ch'i (1630–93), and Li Kuang-ti (1642–1718).

The experience of the T'ung-ch'eng elite and the invention of the school cannot be adequately understood without considering their involvement in the civil service examination. In order to gain a better understanding of how these intellectual strains came to be associated with the T'ung-ch'eng school, it is necessary to investigate the political and intellectual milieus in which the Ch'eng-Chu school had reemerged strongly since the K'ang-hsi (1662–1722) period.

POLITICS AND THE CIVIL SERVICE EXAMINATION

In the early years of the K'ang-hsi emperor's reign, scholarship, education, and the civil service examination continued to be highly politicized. Early Ch'ing scholars came to Ch'eng-Chu learning for intellectual and political reasons. Ch'eng-Chu learning first revived in the K'ang-hsi period as an intellectual movement and later entrenched itself as an official orthodoxy. Evident in the writings of the exponents of Ch'eng-Chu learning was a strong objection to subjectivism and a categorical censure of the more radical developments of the Wang Yang-ming school.[6] There were those like Ku Yen-wu (1613–82), Chang Lü-hsiang (1611–74), and Lü Liu-liang who criticized the subjectivism and syncretism of the scholars of the left-wing Wang Yang-ming school. They were particularly strident in condemning Li Chih (1527–1602) and the proponents of the union of the Three Teachings. Many held subjectivism and syncretism responsible for the corruption of Confucian education, resulting in intellectual vacuity and moral anarchy.

Many of these Ch'eng-Chu scholars considered the moral degeneration of the scholar-officials in the late Ming to be a result of the eclipse of the Ch'eng-Chu teachings.[7] Lü Liu-liang, an outspoken critic of Wang Yang-ming and a Ming loyalist, came to see the promotion of Ch'eng-Chu learning as the basis for keeping Ming loyalism alive. Lü began to use critiques of model examination essays as an instrument for the advocacy of the Ch'eng-Chu doctrine and the dissemination of his anti-Manchu ideas.[8]

Like the examination practice of the Ming period, the Manchu state had adopted Chu Hsi's commentaries on the Four Books as official texts for the civil service examination. But in the early Ch'ing the Manchus did not have full control over the examination answers, which were determined to a significant extent by both the examiners and the professional writers who prepared study aids (chiang-chang) for the Four Books.[9] Despite the official requirement, examination answers since the Lung-ch'ing (1567–72) and Wan-li (1573–1619) periods not only departed from Chu Hsi's commentaries but also took pains to criticize them. Students included in their answers Wang Yang-ming's teachings and heterodox ideas.[10] These trends continued into the early Ch'ing.

Adherents of the Ch'eng-Chu orthodoxy such as Lü Liu-liang justified their profession as critics of examination essays in terms of the need to cleanse heterodox ideas and reestablish the authority of Chu Hsi's scholarship in the examination practice. Lü, however, was not the only one who sought to manipulate the civil service examination to serve his personal purposes. His strategy caught the eye of Tai Ming-shih.

Although born under the Manchu dynasty, Tai, a native of T'ung-ch'eng county, grew up in a world of literati still enchanted by anecdotes of the heroism and extraordinary demonstrations of moral courage of the late Ming. He lived in the same social environment as many of his generation such as Liu Hsien-t'ing (1648–95) and Wang Yuan (1648–1710). For this generation, however, the line between sympathy with the Ming and resentment toward the Manchus was not drawn as clearly as it had been for their fathers' generation.[11] They nonetheless felt an obligation toward their fathers' generation and sought to commit to writing the memories of highly regarded exemplars of moral courage (ch'i-chieh) who suffered and were martyred during attacks by peasant rebels and the Manchus. Tai Ming-shih was concerned with preserving fast-disappearing memories of the late Ming resistance saga.[12] He hoped to write a history of the Ming, a work to be remembered along the order of Ssu-ma Ch'ien's *Records of a Historian* and Ou-yang Hsiu's *History of the Five Dynasties*.[13]

KU-WEN AND THE CIVIL SERVICE EXAMINATION

Of the common genres of literary writing, prose is the most suitable style for historical narrative. Tai Ming-shih had been devoted to practicing *ku-wen* (ancient prose) as a child.[14] The term *ku-wen*, however, is very confusing in its connotations. For Tai, the models of *ku-wen* included the Six Classics, *Mencius*, *Hsun-tzu*, the *Tso-chuan* (Tso Commentary) on the *Ch'un-ch'iu*, *Chuang-tzu*, *Kuo-yü*, Ssu-ma Ch'ien's *Shih-chi*, Pan Ku's *Han-shu*, the writings of the T'ang-Sung Eight Masters and the Sung Neo-Confucians.[15] *Ku-wen* therefore denotes more than a style of writing. It is a prose ideologically grounded in the Confucian Classics and the Ch'eng-Chu doctrine and methodically steeped in the unadorned and versatile style of historians and T'ang-Sung writers.[16] It is anything but literature in the modern sense. It is no accident that Tai criticized writings that were embellished in style, heterodox in content, and unimaginative in articulation.[17] For him mechanical emulation of phrase and style of the ancients was by no means what he regarded as *ku-wen*.[18]

It is important to remember that "ancient prose" does not necessarily mean ancient language and style. In fact, the appeal of the prose of T'ang-Sung writers was that their language and usage were closer to those used in Ming-Ch'ing times.[19] It was this present-oriented prose of the *ku-wen* that made it possible for the students to apply its method to the writing of eight-legged essays, which was also called *shih-wen* ("present style of writing").

Tai Ming-shih's view of *ku-wen* was hardly original. Since its use by the great T'ang prose writer Han Yü, the term "ancient prose" had come to denote a didactic genre of writing.[20] On the grounds that the ancients always wrote with an edifying purpose, the practitioner of ancient prose did not recognize the intrinsic value of writing. Sung Neo-Confucians held Han Yü in great esteem for his literary theory. In their remarks about writing, they in general put it at the service of their moral philosophy (*i-li*). The well-known phrase *wen i tsai tao* (writing as a vehicle of the way) is the epitome of their view.

Interest in *ku-wen*, especially those by the T'ang-Sung Eight Masters, was widespread in Tai Ming-shih's time.[21] Ming writers such as Kuei Yu-kuang (1506–17) and T'ang Shun-chih (1507–60) were lauded as great writers in that tradition.[22] This style was especially promoted by writers such as Chiang Ch'en-ying (1628–99) and the Wei brothers, Hsi (1624–80), Chi-jui (1620–77), and Li (1628–93).[23] Many of those who were chosen to work on the Ming history project were accomplished writers in T'ang-Sung "ancient prose."[24] Chu I-tsun (1629–1709) and Wang Wan (1624–91) were especially distinguished for their literary skills in ancient prose.[25]

During the first half of the eighteenth century, T'ang-Sung ancient prose continued to be a major literary tradition. The period from 1704 to 1750 saw the publication of at least six anthologies of T'ang-Sung prose.[26] The popularity of ancient prose in the early Ch'ing owed much to the strong revival of Ch'eng-Chu orthodoxy, which had long been associated with the *ku-wen* tradition.[27] In fact, the late Ming popular critic of examination essays, Ai Nan-ying (1583–1646), had already promoted the idea of using the ancient prose of the T'ang-Sung masters as a vehicle for propagating Ch'eng-Chu orthodoxy.[28] It should be noted that there is no logical connection between the moral content of the *ku-wen* and Ch'eng-Chu orthodoxy. But for adherents in the early Ch'ing, to promote morality through writing was to promote conventional Confucian virtues, which they felt the followers of Wang Yang-ming in the late Ming had abandoned.

As the Ch'eng-chu school was invigorated in the early Ch'ing, the moral teachings that ancient prose writers came to promote were defined in terms of that tradition. In the K'ang-hsi period, many writers of ancient prose were also exponents of Ch'eng-Chu orthodoxy. Lü Liu-liang had published comments on an edition of T'ang-Sung prose.[29] And Wang Wan, a renowned writer, accused scholars of separating the T'ang-Sung ancient prose from the teachings of the Sung Neo-Confucians.[30]

In 1709 Chang Po-hsing (1651–1725), a staunch exponent of Ch'eng-Chu Confucianism and a friend of Tai Ming-shih's and Fang Pao's, reprinted a collection of T'ang-Sung prose originally edited by Mao K'un (1512–1601). He took particular note of the lack of consistency in the quality of the essays. He appended comments to the writings to warn against faults and shortcomings in the ideas and implications with respect to moral teachings.[31]

Like many of his contemporaries, Tai Ming-shih regarded the mastery of ancient prose style as essential not only to the writing of history but also to the revival of the Ch'eng-Chu doctrine.[32] His commitment to writing ancient prose and a history of the Ming notwithstanding, he was forced to learn and teach eight-legged essays, the highly structured style of writing required of all examination candidates. During his youth, he felt deep disdain for the civil service examination and entertained the hope of living as a hermit.[33] But the need to support his parents forced him to take up tutoring. To his displeasure, his students were willing to learn nothing but eight-legged essays.[34]

Later, Tai discovered a way to accommodate the formalistic requirement of the examination system. Between 1694 and 1702, Tai embarked upon a career as editor, writing critiques of examination essays in Nanking, the city where Lü Liu-liang had opened a bookshop.[35] As mentioned earlier, Lü had sought to spread anti-Manchu feelings and to promote the Ch'eng-Chu school as the Confucian orthodoxy by criticizing eight-legged essays.[36] Tai had taken note of the fact that Lü's critiques circulated widely and was convinced of the effectiveness of Lü's strategy.[37] As Tai came to appreciate the use to which eight-legged essays could be put, he began to promote the idea that there was no distinction between the method of ancient prose and that of eight-legged essays. Tai explicitly taught students "to write examination essays with the method of ancient prose" (*i ku-wen wei shih-wen*).[38] Like Lü Liu-liang, Tai sought to restore the authority of Chu Hsi's commentaries on the Four Books through the teaching of ancient prose.

Therefore, for Tai Ming-shih ancient prose was essential both to writing good history and to the correction of the inanity of the eight-legged essays. Furthermore, it was a vehicle for propagating Ch'eng-Chu Neo-Confucianism. He heralded the efforts of Lu Lung-ch'i and Wang Wan, who undertook to defend and clarify the commentaries written by Chu Hsi.[39] But by the 1690s and early 1700s, the concern to reestablish the Ch'eng-Chu tradition as Confucian orthodoxy among the Chinese literati no longer claimed urgency as the Manchu government came to endorse Sung Neo-Confucianism more vigorously.[40]

FANG PAO, ANCIENT PROSE, AND CH'ENG-CHU ORTHODOXY

The dissipation of the lingering tension between Chinese scholars and the Manchu state is further revealed in the case of Tai Ming-shih's good friend Fang Pao (on Fang, see also Guy, chap. 5 of this volume). While preparing for the civil service examination in Peking, Fang befriended a group of literati devoted to writing ancient prose.[41] Like Tai, Fang was repelled by the trivializing effects of the examination system but succumbed nonetheless to the demands of students who would learn nothing but eight-legged essays.[42] With Tai and some friends, Fang Pao came to promote the idea that there was no distinction between the method of eight-legged essays and that of the ancient prose.[43]

What Fang and Tai were advocating was not unique. It is ironic that, however different their motivations might be, both Ming loyalists such as Lü Liu-liang and those serving the Manchus like Li Kuang-ti and Lü's admirer, Lu Lung-ch'i, were striving to promote Ch'eng-Chu learning through the medium of eight-legged essays. Despite his admiration for Lü's loyalism, Lu Lung-ch'i found no contradiction in serving the Manchus and promoting the Ch'eng-Chu school. He believed that studying ancient prose would help candidates to improve their skills in writing eight-legged essays.[44] Wang Mou-hung (1668–1741), an admirer of Chu Hsi, wrote a preface to a collection of examination essays in which he essentially argued that writing skills acquired through learning T'ang-Sung ancient prose were essential to the elucidation of the Ch'eng-Chu expositions on the Classics and to the rectification of the examination essays that failed to stress didactic function.[45]

Fang Pao has been credited with the T'ung-ch'eng teaching of "moralizing method" (*i-fa*), which in essence means "writing with a moral purpose" (*yen yu-wu*), and "writing with an order" (*yen yu hsu*). Fang Pao's literary motto was by no means an original idea.[46] Although Tai Ming-shih did not use the term *i-fa*, he had very similar ideas.[47] It is in Fang's writing that the term figures prominently. According to Fang, that the *Spring and Autumn Annals* had *i-fa* was first pointed out by Ssu-ma Ch'ien.[48] Fang repeatedly spoke of *i-fa* as an important craft of the historian.[49] He did not stop aspiring to be a historian until 1711, when his interest in *i-fa* as a genre of historical writing declined after his implication in the literary inquisition of Tai Ming-shih.[50]

Tai had earned his *chin-shih* degree in 1708 and was serving in the Hanlin Academy. But in 1711 he was accused of using imperial titles of the southern Ming regimes in the biographical essays he wrote to commemorate martyrs and the courageous victims of violence. He was convicted of disloyalty and executed.[51] More than three hundred persons were ordered to be either executed or punished by exile for alleged involvement in the writing and printing of the work or for being Tai's relatives. Fang Pao was implicated because a preface in Tai's writing was attributed to him, and his kinsmen were consequently punished by incarceration and exile. Although the death punishments for Fang Pao and his lineage were commuted to hereditary enslavement, the extensive sufferings inflicted on Fang's family left an indelible imprint on him.[52] He cautioned himself against imprudence in the future.[53] It is no coincidence that in 1742 Fang Pao named his newly established ancestral hall "The Hall of Teaching Loyalty." Fang opened the preface to the clan rules with reference to his implication in Tai's case.[54] The traumatic experience greatly discouraged Fang from pursuing the goal of writing a history of the Ming and further strengthened his commitment to the defense of Ch'eng-Chu orthodoxy and the study of the classic *I-li*, which came to engross him thereafter.[55]

If the prosecution of Tai Ming-shih did not frighten those Ch'eng-Chu scholars who still harbored hostility toward the Manchus, they found it more difficult to argue for rejection of the Manchus on cultural and intellectual grounds as the Manchu regime came to embrace Ch'eng-Chu orthodoxy with greater vigor.[56] In 1712, one year before the Board of Punishment reached the final verdict in Tai's case, the K'ang-hsi emperor conferred on Chu Hsi the great honor of having his tablet installed in the Confucian temple. In 1714, *Chu-tzu ch'üan-shu* (Complete works of Chu Hsi) was printed under imperial auspices. With the blessing of the K'ang-hsi emperor, *Hsing-li ching-i* (Essential ideas of nature and principle) was printed in the following year.[57] When K'ang-hsi ordered the installation of Chu Hsi in the Confucian temple in 1712, the emperor also attempted to court the favor of the Chinese elite by freezing the head tax at the 1711 level. These imperial acts made it clear to the Chinese elite that the Manchus were responsive to their demand for making the Ch'eng-Chu school the official orthodoxy and, more importantly, were committed to the protection of the elite's interests.[58]

CONFUCIAN RITUALISM AND PURISM

As the Manchu regime succeeded in wooing those Chinese intellectuals who might still harbor suspicion and animosity, an emerging tension within the discourse of the Confucian canon of the late seventeenth and early eighteenth centuries was to claim the attention of fervent exponents of Ch'eng-Chu orthodoxy. This tension was to cause change after the mid-eighteenth century in the content of education, affecting some parts of the civil service examination and its criteria for success.

As the Ch'eng-Chu school gradually rose to prominence at the turn of the eighteenth century as both a state ideology and a powerful intellectual trend, an undercurrent was beginning to erode the credibility of Sung scholarship in general and the Ch'eng-Chu exegetical tradition in particular. It was in fact the continuation of the currents of Confucian ritualism and purism that had evolved since the mid-seventeenth century. These intellectual strains joined forces in shaping Confucian discourse in the Ch'ing. Central to this new intellectual movement were two components: a ritualist approach to morality and a consistent effort to employ evidential methods (*k'ao-cheng*) to expunge heterodox elements from the classical literature and to restore the textual integrity of the Classics.[59] By 1700, the "Diagrams of the Great Ultimate," which had been proved evidentially to be of Taoist origin in Hu Wei's *I-t'u ming-pien* (Clarifying critique of the diagrams associated with the *Book of Changes*), were extricated from the *Book of Changes*. Yen Jo-chü (1636–1704) had conclusively shown that the *Old Text Book of History* was a forgery.[60] While these scholars were concerned with restoring the original textual integrity of the Classics, most of them did not intend impiety toward Ch'eng-Chu learning.[61] But the effect of such philological research proved to be detrimental to its credibility.

An even more alarming threat came from two camps: the defenders of Wang Yang-ming's teachings and the disciples of Yen Yuan (1635–1704). Mao Ch'i-ling (1623–1716), an avowed student of the Wang Yang-ming school, was especially relentless in his diatribe against Chu Hsi.[62] The scourging criticism from Yen Yuan and his student Li Kung (1659–1733) was directed against all variations of Neo-Confucianism. Mao and Li aimed at nothing less than a total dismantling of the Ch'eng-Chu exegetical tradition by proving unreliable the scholarship of the Sung Neo-Confucians through rigorous philological research on the Classics.[63]

As early as 1702, Fang Pao was drawn into a battle against detractors of Ch'eng-Chu learning. Through his acquaintance with Li Kung and Wang Yuan, he came to know the teachings of a group of scholars who rejected categorically the value of Sung scholarship. Of them P'an P'ing-ko (1610–77) and Yen Yuan were the foremost critics, who in their own ways accused the Sung Neo-Confucians of insinuating Buddhist and Taoist ideas into Confucian exegeses.[64]

In 1703, Fang had a vigorous debate with Li Kung over the meaning of "investigation of things" (*ko-wu*).[65] What alarmed Fang was not so much their disagreement as Li Kung's categorical dismissal of the Ch'eng-Chu exegetical tradition as having been adulterated by heterodox teachings. In an epistle he wrote to Li Kung in 1721, Fang argued that Yen Yuan and Chu Hsi might differ in their renderings of the classical texts and in their approaches to education but they were nonetheless in accord with respect to fundamental teachings about the absolute principles of social ethics (*lun-ch'ang*).[66]

Fang Pao felt obligated to take up the gauntlet for the classical scholarship of Chu Hsi.[67] Fang's attempt, however, was part of the larger movement among followers of the Ch'eng-Chu school that aimed at putting Chu Hsi's scholarship on a more solid ground by eliminating minor mistakes and acquitting their master of errors of others' making. Wang Mou-hung was an outstanding example in this connection and so, to a certain extent, was Yen Jo-chü.[68]

During the second half of the seventeenth century, the purists employing philology as a method of restoring the textual integrity of the Classics still served the purpose of Ch'eng-Chu orthodoxy, and imperial backing in the early eighteenth century helped to keep the potential threat within bounds. Evidential scholarship did not pose a serious threat to Ch'eng-Chu orthodoxy until the mid-eighteenth century.

FANG PAO AND THE *CH'IN-TING SSU-SHU-WEN*

In light of the above discussion, the specific discursive elements of Yao Nai's T'ung-ch'eng school—an exclusive faith in the Ch'eng-Chu tradition, along with a deep interest in the literary method of ancient prose and its application to writing examination essays—were intellectual traits shared by many scholars of the early Ch'ing. These discursive elements were by no means unique to his fellow natives even though both Tai Ming-shih and Fang Pao were prominent writers of the T'ung-ch'eng county. What is interesting is that Yao did not include Tai in his lineage. The explanation is obvious enough; he did not want to affiliate with a "rebel." Fang Pao's reputation as a *ku-wen* writer probably would not have earned him a place in Yao's school had he not been involved in the compilation of an imperial collection of examination essays.

Control of the process by which the candidates were prepared for the civil service examination was as important as issuing standard texts. The Ming practice of publishing essays of successful candidates at higher levels of examination was revived with new vigor as soon as the Manchu government resumed holding examinations. Since its conquest of China, the Manchu government had been concerned about the circulation of examination aids published by private bookshops. As early as 1670, when Lü Liu-liang was printing his comments on eight-legged essays, the Manchus banned the printing of any such works by private bookshops and ordered the Board of Rites to publish an official selection for the candidates.[69] These early efforts did not seem to produce good results. In 1694, the K'ang-hsi emperor ordered that the essays of successful candidates at the metropolitan level be submitted for approval for publication as models to be distributed to provincial schools.[70] But the Board of Rites ceased to print official selections in 1704.[71]

Perhaps no Manchu ruler was more sensitive than the Yung-cheng emperor (1723–35) to the need for ideological control of Chinese subjects, especially the literati (cf. Guy, chap. 5 of this volume). In 1723, he ordered the Board of Rites and the Hanlin Academy to select the best examination essays to be issued to private printing shops for publication.[72] The notorious literary inquisition involving Lü Liu-liang apparently made the Yung-cheng emperor even more apprehensive of the privately authored and published critiques of examination essays.[73] In the fifth month of 1729, the emperor learned of the effect of Lü Liu-liang's anti-Manchu messages that had been subtly interweaved into his comments on examination essays. Lü's works had been in wide circulation among examination candidates. Tseng Ching (1679–1736), a candidate using Lü's essays as models in preparing for the examination, was so moved by Lü's essays that he tried to persuade Yueh Chung-ch'i (1686–1746), then governor-general of Shensi, to rebel against the Manchus.[74] Yueh reported the case to the emperor, and Tseng was arrested and put on trial by the emperor himself. In addition to issuing a personal rebuttal of Tseng Ching's accusations of the Manchus, Yung-cheng ordered Chu Shih (1665–1736) to write a detailed critique of Lü's ideas in the examination aid *Po Ssu-shu chiang-i yü-lu* (Refutation of the *Record of Remarks Regarding the Lectures on the Four Books*), which was to be copied and delivered to all government schools.[75] Yung-cheng was obviously convinced that greater control should be applied to privately published materials.

The selection of successful examination essays by the Board of Rites and the Hanlin Academy was again abandoned in 1736. But when the Ch'ien-lung emperor ascended the throne the same year, there was a new effort to provide a standard for evaluating examination essays. Of the several tutors of the Ch'ien-lung emperor, Chu Shih and Ts'ai Shih-yuan were Fang Pao's good friends.[76] The ascension of the new emperor created some hope for regaining the political influence that the scholars had enjoyed under the K'ang-hsi reign (see also Guy, chap. 5 of this volume). Both Chu and Ts'ai were leading exponents of Ch'eng-Chu Neo-Confucianism.

Fang Pao submitted to the emperor several proposals on the need to compile and publish an official edition of the Thirteen Classics and Twenty-one Histories. He also recommended a project on an annotated edition of the three classics on rituals. The Ch'ien-lung emperor, perhaps at the insistence of Chu Shih, made Fang Pao take charge of the compilation of an official anthology of model examination essays.[77] For his reputation as an renowned writer in ancient prose and as an expert in writing critiques of examination essays, Fang Pao was designated the chief editor of an anthology of eight-legged essays that would be published as the standard reference against which subsequent examination essays would be evaluated.[78]

The final product was the *Ch'in-ting Ssu-shu-wen* (Imperial edition of essays on the Four Books) completed in 1739 and printed in the following year.[79] It includes essays from both the Ming and Ch'ing periods arranged by reigns (see also Guy, chap. 5 of this volume).[80] Among the Ch'ing writers included, many were Fang's friends like Li Kuang-ti and Han T'an (1637–1704); Fang also took care to include the writings of his brother, Fang Chou. As blatantly partial as Fang's selection was, he did not include writings by Tai Ming-shih, nor did he suggest that the secret of writing skills had been transmitted along a lineage of ancient prose writers. No claim, implicit or explicit, was made about the superiority of the writing skills of literati from T'ung-ch'eng.

The selection of essays was clearly guided by an attempt to reinforce the Ch'eng-Chu classical tradition as Confucian orthodoxy, an aspiration common to Fang Pao and associates like Chu Shih, Li Kuang-ti and Ts'ai Shih-yuan.[81] It was clearly stated in the editorial rules that essays included would have to be in accord with the Classics and the Sung-Yuan Neo-Confucians' exegeses, which primarily meant Chu Hsi's expository works. Ch'eng-Chu orthodoxy therefore formed the ideological underpinning of the collection. Although a few essays by

Wang Yang-ming were included, the comment on one of Wang's essays took pains to point out that even Wang in his examination followed Chu Hsi's commentary.[82]

Some of the major concepts of Fang Pao's literary thought were clearly articulated in the text. His criteria for *cheng* (correct) writing, and in this connection eight-legged essays, were that it be *ch'ing-chen ku-ya* (pure and authentic, ancient and elegant).[83] By *ch'ing-chen* Fang meant "correctness of principle," which was to be measured against Ch'eng-Chu learning. The quality of "ancientness and elegance" was what Fang called "correctness of words," which in his understanding required the avoidance of "vulgarity," "colloquialism, " and heterodox language such as Buddhist terms. Even conversational expressions were to be avoided.[84]

These principles of writing constituted what Fang called *i-fa* (moralizing methods). His preference for the term *i-fa* now came to represent the correct way of writing prose as well as the eight-legged essays. He upheld the method of applying the rules of ancient prose to writing examination essays.[85]

From its publication in 1740, the *Ch'in-ting Ssu-shu-wen* became the standard for the civil service examination at both the prefectural and metropolitan levels. The Manchu court had repeatedly demanded observance of the criteria set forth in the imperial anthology.[86] The reiteration of the imperial plea, however, suggests the wide existence of deviation from this standard.[87] Be that as it may, after its issuance, the anthology became the official reference for examiners and the Manchu government was committed to upholding it.[88]

Ch'eng-Chu orthodoxy continued to receive imperial support in the early years of the Ch'ien-lung emperor, who revived many literary projects initiated under the K'ang-hsi reign, reassuring the elite of his commitment to Confucian rule.[89] But the tension within the Confucian discourse on the Classics began to polarize the Confucians into two camps. The harmonious relationship between the state and Ch'eng-Chu orthodoxy was not to remain long as scholars engrossed in evidential scholarship came to hold Sung and Yuan exegetical traditions in disrepute. This was to a considerable degree the consequence of the purist movement aimed at purging all heterodox elements from the Classics. Since the early eighteenth century, the credibility of Sung scholarship had been undermined in academic circles as evidential scholarship came to reveal that Sung scholars were responsible for tampering with the classical texts.[90]

By the late 1740s, the purist quest for authentic Confucian teachings led some evidential scholars to reach a radical decision regarding Sung scholarship.[91] The founder of Han Learning (*Han-hsueh*), Hui Tung, told his students to avoid Sung sources as a matter of principle for fear that their works, so corrupted by Taoist and Buddhist interpretations, would prevent the pristine meanings of the Classics from being revealed.[92] The influence of Hui Tung (1697–1758) began to grow in Soochow in the mid-eighteenth century. Despite his growing appeal, classical scholars underscoring the primacy of Han exegeses had as yet to gain state patronage. But the seething tension between evidential scholarship and Ch'eng-Chu orthodoxy was brought into the open by the *Ssu-k'u ch'üan-shu* (Complete library of the four treasuries) project mandated by the Ch'ien-lung emperor in 1772.

YAO NAI AND THE INVENTION OF THE T'UNG-CH'ENG SCHOOL

Yao Nai was made a compiler at the Ssu-k'u Commission in 1773. The chief editor Chi Yun, however, took a strong dislike to the exegetical scholarship of Sung and Yuan Confucians. A year later Yao found it difficult to continue his work there because most of the compilers were contemptuous of Sung and Yuan scholarship.[93] Most of the reviews he wrote were rejected.[94] The advantage that adherents of Ch'eng-Chu classical scholarship had enjoyed since the K'ang-hsi and the early Ch'ien-lung reigns began to disappear.

The Ssu-k'u project helped to bring honor and official appointments to scholars working in the bureau.[95] Tai Chen (1724–77) was not a *chin-shih* degree-holder but his reputation as a towering scholar in philological studies earned him a position on the imperial project. Despite his failure in the metropolitan examination in 1775, he was granted *chin-shih* status and appointed a bachelor in the Hanlin Academy by a special decree of the Ch'ien-lung emperor.[96] By contrast, Yao Nai had every reason to feel offended because back in 1766 he failed to retain his bachelor position in the Hanlin Academy.[97] Yao must have been in deep anguish when he learned that six of the eight non-Hanlin scholars, who took part in the Ssu-k'u project, were made bachelors of the Hanlin Academy after they completed their assignments. Yao and Jen Ta-ch'un (1738–89) were the only participants who did not receive imperial grace.[98] The famed historian Chang Hsueh-ch'eng (1738–1801) had noted, perhaps with similar discontent, that "many literary officials were rapidly promoted as compilers, and poor scholars, offering proposals through others, could easily get excellent secretarial jobs if they were good at bibliographical research."[99]

The invention of the T'ung-ch'eng school by Yao Nai must be understood against the background of the growing tension that evidential scholarship had created at the level of state ideology, within Confucian discourse, and in the civil service examination system (see also Elman, chap. 4 of this volume). In 1776, Yao first alluded to the existence of a lineage of writers of ancient prose. The three members of the lineage in the Ch'ing were all natives of T'ung-ch'eng — Fang Pao, Liu Ta-k'uei (1698–1779), and Yao himself. Yao had studied ancient prose with Liu.[100] In 1779, Yao completed an anthology of prose *Ku-wen-tz'u lei-tsuan* (Classified anthology of ancient prose) in seventy-five *chüan*.[101] But the work was not printed until 1820 for lack of resources on Yao's part. In this collection, Yao further strove to substantiate his idea of a T'ung-ch'eng school by including only the writings of Fang Pao and Liu Ta-k'uei for the Ch'ing period. The fact that Fang Pao was the chief compiler of the *Ch'in-ting Ssu-shu-wen* lent strength to Yao Nai's claim that writers from T'ung-ch'eng county had mastered the secret of prose writing. It should be noted that although Yao Nai did not include Tai Ming-shih as a member of the T'ung-ch'eng school for the obvious reason that Tai was executed because of his alleged disloyalty, Yao's literary views owed perhaps as much, if not more, to Tai than to Fang Pao.

Yao's attempt to credit only the T'ung-ch'eng writers with the highest achievement in ancient prose provoked objections from his contemporaries.[102] Yao's appropriation of the *ku-wen* style as a unique product of T'ung-ch'eng literati drew criticism from some of his contemporaries. A critic pointed out that Yao Nai deliberately placed himself at the end of a putative line of writers beginning with the eight eminent prose writers of the T'ang-Sung period, continuing through Kuei Yu-kuang in the Ming, and positing Fang Pao and Liu-Ta-k'uei as the immediate heirs to the methods of writing ancient prose in the Ch'ing.[103]

It should be noted that the T'ung-ch'eng school did not represent an intellectual tradition commonly shared by the scholars from T'ung-ch'eng county. Scholars from T'ung-ch'eng did not uniformly espouse the ancient prose of the T'ang-Sung masters. Nor did the three prominent families, the Changs, the Yaos, and the Fangs, which intermarried, form a common scholarly tradition — although they did share intellectual resources. The Fangs and the Yaos produced several eminent scholars whose learning was rooted in a combination of ancient prose and Ch'eng-Chu learning, but the illustrious official from T'ung-ch'eng, Chang Ying (1638–1708), excelled in parallel prose *p'ien-wen* rather than ancient prose.[104] Ma Ch'i-ch'ang (1855–1929), a native of T'ung-ch'eng, noted that it was not until Yao Nai that T'ung-ch'eng began to take pride in the literary tradition of T'ang-Sung ancient prose.[105] To state it differently, Yao Nai was the first to promote the idea that T'ung-ch'eng produced the best writers in ancient prose. But even as late as the early nineteenth century, scholars from T'ung-ch'eng did not regard ancient prose as a unique literary tradition of their own.[106]

The growing pressure of the emerging Han Learning helps to explain the timing of the invention of the T'ung-ch'eng school in the 1770s.[107] This decade saw a sharper split among scholars over the validity of the Han and Sung traditions of classical scholarship. The Ssu-k'u project brought scholars of opposite camps into direct confrontation, resulting in the defeat of adherents of Sung scholarship as evidenced by Yao Nai's voluntary withdrawal from the project. More significant for Yao Nai is that the waning influence of Sung scholarship came at a time when the luster of the early success of T'ung-ch'eng literati began to fade.

LOCAL ELITE STRATEGIES, CULTURAL RESOURCES, AND EXAMINATION SUCCESS

The heroic success and traumatic failure of examination candidates registered more than a contest of intelligence and memory among individuals: it masked the intensity of competition among local elites for access to imperial privileges and political power. The success of candidates from local elite families depended to a considerable degree on the resources of their local communities, and the strategies they adopted regarding government service, learning, and investment patterns. These factors significantly determined how well they were able to adjust to new circumstances.

From the early Ch'ing on, literati from T'ung-ch'eng fared extremely well in the civil service examination. This was to a significant degree the result of efforts of the local elite to minimize the damage caused by peasant rebellions and the Manchu conquest during the Ming-Ch'ing transition. Unequivocal acts of loyalty to the Ming were exceptional in T'ung-ch'eng. While the local elite in the Yangtze Delta was putting up resistance to the Manchus, members of many T'ung-ch'eng elite families began to render service to the Manchus.[108] For example, Yao Nai's great-grandfather, Yao Wen-jan (1621–78), who had served as a Hanlin bachelor under the Ming, took up office as supervising secretary in the Ministry of Rites in the early Shun-chih reign. He was appointed president of the Ministry of Punishment in 1676.[109]

The willingness of the local elite to collaborate with the Manchus to some degree accounts for the early success of T'ung-ch'eng literati in the civil service examinations. During the first half of the eighteenth century, T'ung-ch'eng county produced an average of five to six *chü-jen* per examination; in 1736 there were thirteen.[110] It was a time when T'ung-ch'eng county was at the pinnacle of success. During that time period, it produced a grand secretary, a minister, a governor general, a governor, a nationally acclaimed scholar, and many minor officials.[111] Successful candidates came from prominent families like the Fangs, the Yaos, the Changs, the Tsos, the Mas, and the Tais. More significantly, most of these T'ung-ch'eng officials were related through marriage.[112]

Of the local elite families from T'ung-ch'eng, the Changs had been the most successful at the Manchu court since the K'ang-hsi and Yung-cheng periods. Both Chang Ying (1638–1708) and his son Chang T'ing-yü (1672–1755) rose to the post of grand secretary. The remarkable success of the Chang lineage at the Manchu court is evidenced by its members' exceptionally high rate of success in the civil service examinations. It produced twelve *chin-shih*, half of whom received the privileged appointment in the Hanlin Academy.[113]

The remarkable achievement of the Chang lineage also helped the Yaos. There is no doubt that it was through collusion with other high officials that the Changs and Yaos were able to promote their kinsmen in the examinations and the bureaucracy. Control over the appointment of examiners was crucial to maintaining a high rate of success in the examinations, as the elite families knew very well. In 1744, a censor accused high officials of collusion for recommending only their friends as examiners for provincial examinations.[114]

The Manchus were not insensitive to the large number of successful candidates from official families. As early as 1700, the Manchu government did try to undermine the advantages of the descendants and kinsmen of officials by setting up special quotas for official families.[115] But official families were able to bring their personal influence to bear on examiners. Members of the Chang and Yao lineages were so successful in the examinations that in 1742 Liu T'ung-hsuan (1700–73), then a censor, made the hyperbolic statement that the Changs and Yaos from T'ung-ch'eng filled up half of the register of officials.[116]

But the fortune of the T'ung-ch'eng scholars was on the wane in the latter half of the eighteenth century. Yao Nai earned his *chin-shih* degree in 1763. T'ung-ch'eng was not to see another *chin-shih* until 1772. By the time Yao Nai left the Ssu-k'u Commission in 1774, there was no one from T'ung-ch'eng occupying a high position at court or in the academic circles.[117] Yao Nai was very much concerned about the poor performance of natives of his county, and in particular of members of his lineage, in competition against scholars from Chekiang and Kiangsu. The heightened expectations of the T'ung-ch'eng literati during the first half of the eighteenth century was constantly met with frustrating results in the third quarter of the eighteenth century.[118] Yao also noted in a letter that his county no longer produced writers of eminence.[119] No one was more honored than Fang Pao when he was given the privileged assignment of editing the imperial anthology of examination essays. But Yao did not even succeed in retaining his position in the Hanlin Academy.

The decline of the T'ung-ch'eng men in the examinations, and hence national politics, was in some degree the result of the growing impact of evidential scholarship from the mid-eighteenth century on. At that time, questions on philological and textual problems began to appear in provincial examinations (cf. Elman, chap. 4 of this volume). Questions requiring knowledge of etymology and recent scholarship appeared with growing frequency in the third session on policy at both the provincial and metropolitan levels. Although the third section was less important than the first and second, it provided examiners with some advantages. By putting questions about philology in the third section, examiners were able to identify candidates conversant with evidential learning. Whereas essays on the Four Books did not require erudition, candidates writing on questions about philological and textual problems could easily distinguish themselves by virtue of the breadth of their knowledge.

High officials such as Chi Yun (1724–1805) and Chu Yun, (1729–81), in their capacities as director of education and examiner respectively, fervently promoted evidential scholarship. There were also officials like Pi Yuan

(1730–97), who assembled a coterie of scholars to work on literary projects.[120] Not only did evidential scholarship receive support from high officials such as Chi Yun and Juan Yuan (1764–1849) but also it had the support of private patrons.[121]

Evidential scholarship could only flourish in a social environment in which a wide range of institutions supported the increasing professionalization of scholarship. To do textual criticism, to compare different editions, and to collect bibliographical information required easy access to large collections of books.[122] It was difficult for those from culturally less advanced regions to achieve excellence when many of the texts required for textual examination were rare items. Yao's own experience in the Ssu-k'u Commission testified to his fear that his native county could not compete with the scholars from Chekiang and Kiangsu. It is perhaps a testimony to bitter defeat that Yao spoke of the *k'ao-cheng* skills and bibliographical knowledge as a method "most suitable for crushing [one's] enemy."[123]

Scholars in Chekiang and Kiangsu did enjoy various kinds of support. It is well known that the salt merchants of Yangchow were generous patrons of *k'ao-cheng* scholars. The associations between rich merchants and scholars such as Hui Tung, Tai Chen, Ch'ien Ta-hsin (1728–1804), and Wang Ming-sheng (1722–97) were motivated to a significant degree by the scholars' need to gain access to the rich collection of books that the merchants possessed.[124]

Most of those engaged to work on large philological projects were natives and residents of Chekiang and Kiangsu. Of the forty-two scholars who helped Juan Yuan to compile the *Ching-chi tsuan-ku* (Collected glosses on the Classics), thirty-seven were from Chekiang, four from Kiangsu, and one from She county of Hui-chou.[125] In 1829, Juan Yuan published the momentous compendium of the best classical scholarship of the Ch'ing period, the *Huang Ch'ing ching-chieh* (Ch'ing Commentaries on the Classics). A look at the geographical origins of the scholars whose works are included further attests to the disproportion among regional contributions to evidential scholarship. Of the sixty-eight classical scholars whose native place can be determined, fifty were literati of Kiangsu and Chekiang; only one came from T'ung-ch'eng county.[126]

The large number of evidential scholars from Kiangsu and Chekiang points to the deeper divergence of local regions in terms of their economic structure and social and cultural conditions. Despite its exceptional performance in producing degree-holders in the late seventeenth and eighteenth centuries, T'ung-ch'eng county was no match for the culturally and economically more advanced areas such as Hangchow, Soochow, Yangchow and Changchow.[127] The production of scholars who participated in shaping the Confucian discursive practices depended to a considerable extent on nondiscursive practices and, in this case, the investment strategies of local elites and regional resources.

During the Ming-Ch'ing period the elite of T'ung-ch'eng county showed little interest in commerce.[128] The lack of commercial wealth naturally explains the absence of large private libraries and of support for professional connoisseurs and bibliophiles. While in Ch'ing times Chekiang and Kiangsu produced the largest number of private book collectors worthy of note, Anhwei had none.[129] When the Ch'ien-lung emperor launched the mass project for collecting books in 1772, Chekiang and Kiangsu contributed the largest numbers.[130] Anhwei, however, as a whole contributed less than 1 percent.[131] But these statistics are misleading. Although three of the four families that submitted more than five hundred items were residing in Hangchow and Yangchow, they were originally Anhwei salt merchants from Hui-chou prefecture, which was made up of six counties—Hsiu-ning, Hsi, She, Ch'i-meng, Chi-hsi, and Mou-yuan. The three families orginally from Hui-chou, each contributing more than five hundred items, were the Paos, the Wangs, and the Mas. Both the families of Pao T'ing-po (1728–1814) and Wang Ch'i-shu (1728 –99?) resided in Hangchow, and Ma Yü's family lived in Yangchow. The total number of books submitted by these families (1,855) exceeds 40 percent of all the books sent by the provinces.[132]

Hui-chou merchants had a long history of emigrating to big cities in the Lower Yangtze region. At least eighty merchants from Hui-chou prefecture had moved to Yangchow since the Ming; others moved to Soochow and Nanking.[133] But these Hui-chou emigrants did not cut off their ties with their native place. Therefore, elite families in Hui-chou had a close connection with the cultural centers in the Lower Yangtze areas through commercial and kinship ties. Hui-chou merchants were great patrons of scholars and private academies.[134] They turned their enormous wealth to support scholarly and educational activities, which strengthened considerably their competitiveness against elite families from other regions.

While scholars from most counties of Anhwei suffered from the changing discourse at higher levels of examinations, scholars from Hui-chou prefecture were in the forefront of the emerging *k'ao-cheng* scholarship. The leading exponent of evidential scholarship, Tai Chen, came from Hsiu-ning county in Hui-chou prefecture.

However, it should be noted that scholars from Hui-chou prefecture had a competitive edge even before the triumph of *k'ao-cheng* scholarship. They had been active participants in the reorientation of Ch'eng-Chu learning since the early Ch'ing. Despite the strong hold of Ch'eng-Chu Neo-Confucianism on Hui-chou, many scholars who professed faith in Chu Hsi's scholarship contributed considerably to the growth of philological and textual studies. Among Hui-chou scholars, Chiang Yung (1681–1762), Tai Chen's mentor, and Wang Fu (1692–1759) were prominent representatives of this trend.[135]

In the same light, Chiang Fan's *Kuo-ch'ao Han-hsueh shih-ch'eng chi* (Record of the succession of Han Learning masters) is more than a partisan record of *k'ao-cheng* scholarship. It reveals the disproportionate distribution of cultural resources among regions and the differences in local elites' survival strategies. Thirty-five of the fifty-four scholars included in Chiang's register were natives of Kiangsu. There were six scholars from Anhwei, all of whom without exception came from Hui-chou. They were Chiang Yung, Tai Chen, Chin Pang (1735–1801), Hung Pang (1745–79), Ch'eng Chin-fang (1718–84), and Ling T'ing-k'an (1757–1809).[136] These scholars had been called the Anhwei (Wan) School. In fact, it is more accurate to call them the Hui-chou School.

The frustration of Yao Nai in his encounter with Han Learning scholars can be viewed as typical of the disappointment felt by scholars from culturally less advanced areas who were less equipped to compete with scholars from Hui-chou, Kiangsu, and Chekiang. But it is a mistake to believe that only scholars from areas with limited cultural resources felt the threat of *k'ao-cheng* scholarship. Yao Nai's invention of the T'ung-ch'eng school was by no means an exceptional response to the *k'ao-cheng* challenge.

Chang Hsueh-ch'eng, the renowned expert in historical scholarship, had similar misgivings about his contemporaries' obsession with philological and textual research. Chang opposed it on the ground that not all scholars would be interested in and good at doing bibliographical and philological studies. Chang himself justified his devotion to methods of historical writing in terms of his particular intellectual capabilities.[137] He too declared himself an adherent of an imaginary school — the Eastern Chekiang school of historical writing, which included Wang Yang-ming, Liu Tsung-chou, and Huang Tsung-hsi. Chang argued that this school represented the proper approach to Confucian learning for it did not seek to understand human nature in abstract terms. While Yao Nai upheld T'ung-ch'eng scholarship as a combination of moral teachings (*tao*) and writing (*wen*), namely, Ch'eng-Chu Neo-Confucianism and ancient prose, Chang Hsueh-ch'eng prided himself on the use of "writing and history" (*wen-shih*) to explore human nature and destiny (*hsing-ming*).[138] But as Ying-shih Yü has aptly pointed out, Chang's historical scholarship owed little to other scholars from eastern Chekiang, nor did they form a distinct school of historical scholarship.[139]

To take exception to the intellectual lineages that Yao Nai and Chang Hsueh-ch'eng created, however, is not to deny the important role of kinship ties in the perpetuation of scholarly traditions. We have seen how the lineages of the Changs, the Fangs, and the Yaos through marriage and regional ties shared political influence.[140] The Fangs and Yaos also made available to each other their intellectual resources. It is no accident that scholars from these lineages all excelled in ancient prose. Yao Nai studied ancient prose with Fang Tse, who was a good friend of Yao's uncle, Yao Fan.[141] And Fang Tung-shu (1772–1851), the great-grandson of Fang Tse (1697–1767), was one of Yao Nai's best students.[142] But for members of these lineages, to share scholarly traditions was to a certain extent to share the consequences of any shifts in discourses.

DIVERGENT APPROACHES TO EDUCATION

Evidential scholarship rose at the expense of Sung classical traditions. The knowledge that the Sung-Yuan Neo-Confucians had produced regarding the Classics not only had become problematic but was rejected as an obstacle to understanding the authentic teachings of the Classics. Students seriously engaged in textual scholarship took as their point of departure Tai Chen's belief that the principles of propriety can only be comprehended after the literal meanings of the Classics are illuminated.[143] This premise redefined the immediate goals of classical study as textual and philological research. Knowledge of the Classics could only be obtained by meticulous study of the exegeses of Han scholars and reconstruction of the lexical meanings of the ancient language in which the Classics were written. It is natural that candidates were expected to be trained in these new disciplines.

This new structure of the goals of learning challenged Ch'eng-Chu orthodoxy on several fronts: the reliability of Sung scholarship, the curriculum of the educational system, and the raison d'état for supporting it. These areas were closely related. A threat to any one would upset the entire system.

The ascendancy of *k'ao-cheng* scholarship hence created new objects of discourse and a demand on examination candidates to acquire new knowledge. Since students' immediate concerns lay in the mastery of basic skills in linguistic and textual studies and the new knowledge of the classical language, there was a continual decline of interest in the writings of Sung Neo-Confucians and ancient prose.

Han Learning scholars insisted that classical research could only regain validity by jettisoning Sung-Yuan exegeses, which, they believed, had been pervasively contaminated by heterodox ideas.[144] The commentaries that Chu Hsi wrote for the Four Books were therefore to be abandoned for the pernicious effects they had on examination candidates. This intellectual position was at odds with the practice of the civil service examination, which was still designed primarily to test students' knowledge of Chu Hsi's commentaries. Small wonder that the leading evidential scholars took a strong dislike to the eight-legged essay, which continued to test candidates' writing skills in reproducing Neo-Confucian discourse on the Four Books.[145] The renowned philologist Tuan Yü-ts'ai (1735–1815), after reading the essays of Chang Hsueh-ch'eng, expressed his disapproval of the similarities between Chang's writings and eight-legged essays.[146]

The general importance of the theory and practice of writing skills was marginalized as evidential scholars reduced literary expression to a secondary endeavor to be attended to, if at all, only after philological research.[147] Ch'ien Ta-hsin, whose breadth of classical knowledge was unparalleled, scoffed at Fang Pao's promotion of the T'ang-Sung ancient prose.[148]

Evidential scholars also opposed T'ang-Sung ancient prose on purist grounds. Juan Yuan in his "Wen-yen shuo" (On writing and speech) argued against exalting T'ang-Sung prose as "ancient." For him, the correct style of ancient prose was the writings of Confucius as preserved in the commentary on the *Book of Changes*. The sage's writing style was not prose but parallel and rhythmic lyric.[149] He found *fu* (parallel poetry), the structured and rhythmic style of the Six Dynasties, to be closer to this ancient model.[150] In fact, *fu* was widely practiced by evidential scholars such as Wang Chung, Sun Hsing-yen, and Ling T'ing-k'an.[151]

The evidential scholars' onslaught threatened to destroy the relatively harmonious relationship between the state ideology, the discourse on the Confucian canon, and the educational system that had come into existence since the early eighteenth century. The greater specialization in scholarship not only had resulted in the growth of auxiliary disciplines such as epigraphy, bibliography, and collation but also had prompted further growth of interest in astronomy and mathematics.[152] These new ancillary disciplines threatened to establish themselves as autonomous areas of inquiry, leaving Confucian concern about the existing socio-moral order in the penumbra.[153]

These educational trends were clearly revealed in Yao Nai's teaching experience at the Chung-shan Academy in Nanking where he taught from 1790 to 1801 and from 1805 until his death in 1815. There were very few students interested in learning ancient prose and Ch'eng-Chu teachings. Even when he had found an avid student who would pursue the learning of Chu Hsi, Yao was disappointed to find that hardly any booksellers carried those texts. Publishers were reluctant to print them and booksellers found no reason to stock them for there was simply no demand.[154]

For Yao Nai, the increase in specialization in classical scholarship was as disquieting as it was threatening to the dominance of classical Sung learning. He attempted to contain the *k'ao-cheng* within a scheme of discourses that divided learning into three branches: *i-li* (moral principles), *k'ao-cheng*, and *tz'u-chang* (literary writing). Yao Nai's threefold scheme of learning can be seen as an attempt to provide an alternative structure reinstating the larger goal of Confucian education in its place.[155] The scheme served two purposes. First, by dividing the realm of learning into three domains, Yao hoped to accommodate the emerging *k'ao-cheng* scholarship. Second, by making *k'ao-cheng* one of the three branches of learning, Yao could subsume it under "moral principles" and hence the Ch'eng-Chu interpretation. In fact, Yao was holding fast to the philological and textual scholarship that had been at the service of Ch'eng-Chu orthodoxy before the 1750s.[156] Yao's hierarchical scheme represents a symbolic attempt to subordinate the growing power of the practitioners of philological studies under the classical tradition in which he excelled.

In response to the Han Learning scholars' accusation that Sung scholarship was unreliable, Yao insisted that it was not until the Sung that the Classics were clearly explained. If Sung scholars made some minor errors in the rendering of the Classics, this fact did not warrant an excessive emphasis on meticulous—and in Yao's view often misguided and fragmented—research on the classical language.[157] Since Confucian teachings had been clearly explained by Sung scholars, Confucians of later generations were to concern themselves primarily with how to convey the moral truths more effectively. Writing skills were therefore essential to the achievement of this goal. Impregnated with moralism as it was, Yao's theory of prose writing nonetheless enriched the concept of *ku-wen* to include "a broad range of aesthetic considerations."[158]

Learning how to write good ancient prose not only increased scholars' ability to articulate the moral teachings expounded by Sung Neo-Confucians but also improved the technical skills required of them by the eight-legged essay. Like Fang Pao, Yao Nai opposed using "vulgar," "colloquial," and conversational expressions. The stress that *ku-wen* put on contemporary style (*chin chih wen-t'i*) enabled the literati to understand the ancient sages' teachings, resulting in the upholding of the Confucian moral order.[159]

Although the evidential scholars' ultimate goal was to reconstruct the social order of high antiquity, their methodical concerns with philological and textual issues tended to claim their immediate attention. In contrast, Yao Nai and his followers insisted on making writing directly relevant to Confucian morality and allowing "every educated person access to participation in cultural discourse."[160] This was one of the important reasons why writing reemerged in late Ch'ing intellectual discourse.

The tension between Sung scholarship and Han Learning notwithstanding, one can by no means consider these two classical traditions mutually exclusive and completely irreconcilable. In terms of commitment to the "moral orthodoxy" of Confucianism—the basic social ethics of filial piety, loyalty, and the hierarchical structure of society—Sung and Han Learning remained solidly in accord.[161] They may have disagreed on how these values should be expressed and on the concrete details of the classical language and ancient history, but their disputation never made Confucian social ethics the object of contention. Confucianism proved to be a belief system flexible enough to accommodate tensions between discursive traditions on the one hand and between the state ideology and intellectual developments on the other.

A note should be made of the question about the extent of the influence of Yao Nai's T'ung-ch'eng school. Students of literature and intellectual history offer a wide range of opinions on this issue. No claim is more farfetched than the one Liu Sheng-mu made in *T'ung-ch'eng wen-hsueh yuan-yuan k'ao* (Study of the lineage of the T'ung-ch'eng literary tradition). This work lists a total of 641 adherents of the T'ung-ch'eng school, including two women and two Japanese! Liu has included practically everyone who professed to practice the T'ang-Sung ancient prose since Kuei Yu-kuang.[162] Many take Yao's own words literally and suggest that the T'ung-ch'eng school lasted about two hundred years, from Fang Pao to the early twentieth century.[163] Some pushed its beginning back to

Tai Ming-shih.[164] But as Theodore Huters has aptly pointed out, the T'ung-ch'eng school in the last years of the eighteenth and early years of the nineteenth centuries "essentially consisted of one person, Yao Nai." Even when Yao's *Ku-wen-tz'u lei-tsuan* was printed in 1820, the T'ung-ch'eng school did not attract a large following in literary circles.[165]

Yao's "four great disciples"—Fang Tung-shu, Liu K'ai, Kuan T'ung (1780–1831), and Mei Tseng-liang (1786–1856)—did not achieve prominence in the government.[166] Only Mei succeeded in obtaining a *chin-shih* degree in 1823. They were influential in neither literary circles nor classical scholarship during their times. According to Yao Ying, it was Mei who, having a long career in the Board of Finance, helped spread the influence of Yao.[167] It was Fang Tung-shu who continued to promote enthusiastically the idea that the T'ung-ch'eng school possessed knowledge of the skills of writing ancient prose.[168] Fang, however, contributed to the reputation of the T'ung-ch'eng school more by virtue of his powerful critique of the assumptions and methodological fallacies of the Han Learning school.[169] But the T'ung-ch'eng school continued to be the esoteric belief of an extremely small group of writers and scholars, mostly from T'ung-ch'eng. The poor success rate of his students in gaining higher degrees perhaps explains why Yao Nai regarded Ch'en Yung-kuang (1768–1835) as the disciple who would transmit his *tao*, because Ch'en was the only student of his who succeeded in obtaining the *chin-shih* degree before Yao's death.[170]

In turning the T'ung-ch'eng school into a popular tradition, no person was more instrumental than Tseng Kuo-fan (1811–72).[171] Tseng's admiration for Yao Nai and his promotion of ancient prose and the Ch'eng-Chu school (see also K.C. Liu, chap. 3 of this volume) did not help the local elite in T'ung-ch'eng to regain its power in politics and scholarship. The popularity of the T'ung-ch'eng school came to enhance the political clout that the Hunan elite had gained during the suppression of the Taipings. The myth of the longevity of the T'ung-ch'eng school was given its finishing touches by the literary reformers of the the New Culture Movement who applauded the T'ung-ch'eng school's rejection of parallelism and rhythmic requirements. Hu Shih (1891–1962) credited the T'ung-ch'eng school with clearing the way for the literary revolution whose goal was to teach the Chinese to write simple and unadorned prose.[172]

CONCLUSION

In the life and thought of Tai Ming-shih, Fang Pao and Yao Nai, we see how local elites from T'ung-ch'eng county responded differently to political and intellectual change during the K'ang-hsi and Ch'ien-lung periods. To maintain their success locally and nationally, they had to participate in the civil service examination—the major avenue to political power and social privilege. Their intellectual endeavors, literary activities, and relationships with the Manchu government were to a considerable extent shaped by their attempt to strive for success in the civil service examination. Their ability to outcompete literati from other localities in turn depended on the human, cultural, and economic resources made available by the local society of T'ung-ch'eng county.

The elite families of T'ung-ch'eng had been among the beneficiaries of the revival of Ch'eng-Chu orthodoxy and the political power of the Changs in the early Ch'ing. But the gradual triumph of *k'ao-cheng* scholarship after the mid-eighteenth century greatly increased the competitive edge of literati from economically superior areas where vast cultural resources allowed the new scholarship and educational programs to flourish. The invention of the T'ung-ch'eng school by Yao Nai can be seen as an ideological attempt by scholars from areas with less resources to regain hegemony over the discursive domain as well as the civil service examination.

NOTES

I would like to thank the participants of the conference from which this volume resulted; my colleagues at the University of Illinois, Urbana-Champaign, Lloyd Eastman and Patricia Ebrey; and Lynn Struve of Indiana University for their suggestions and comments on earlier drafts.

1. Lu Wen-ch'ao 盧文弨, *Pao-ching t'ang wen-chi* 抱經堂文集 (Collected writings from the Studio of Embracing the Classics) (Shanghai: Commercial Press, 1935), 23: 321–23.

2. Yao Nai, *Hsi-pao hsuan ch'üan-chi* 惜抱軒全集 (Complete works of Pavilion of Hsi-pao; hereafter *HPHCC*) (Hong Kong: Kuang-chih shu-chü, n.d.), 99.

3. I follow Michel Foucault in the use of the term "nondiscursive practices." *The Archaelogy of Knowledge* (New York: Harper & Row, 1971), 162. Foucault in this and other early works stressed the regulating function of discourse in organizing nondiscursive relationships. In his later works, however, he placed a premium on relationships of domination in the shaping of discourse. For a discussion of the change in Foucault's emphasis from earlier to later works, see Hurbert L. Drefus and Paul Rabinow, *Michel Foucault: Beyond Structuralism and Hermeneutics* (Chicago: University of Chicago Press, 1983).

4. Wei Chi-ch'ang 魏際昌, *T'ung-ch'eng ku-wen hsueh-p'ai hsiao-shih* 桐城古文學派小史 (Brief history of the T'ung-ch'eng school of ancient prose) (Hopeh, Shih-chia-chuang: Chiao-yü ch'u-pan-she, 1988), 1–19.

5. I am using the term "ideology" in the sense analyzed by Paul Ricoeur, who argues that the functions of ideology, in addition to distortion, include integration by giving legitimacy to a system of authority. "Ideology occurs in the gap between a system of authority's claim to legitimacy and our response in terms of belief." Ricoeur, *Lectures on Ideology and Utopia*, ed. George H. Taylor (New York: Columbia University Press, 1986), 183. For a brief discussion of the history of the meaning of "ideology," see his "Introductory Lecture."

6. Wing-tsit Chan, "The *Hsing-li ching-i* and the Ch'eng-Chu School of the Seventeenth Century," in *Unfolding of Neo-Confucianism*, ed. Wm. Theodore de Bary (New York: Columbia University Press, 1975), 551–55.

7. For Ku Yen-wu 顧炎武, see *Jih-chih lu chi-shih* 日知錄集釋 (Collective annotations to records of daily-acquired knowledge) (Taipei: Chung-hua shu-chü, 1965), 18:19a–b, 21a–23a. See also Mou Jun-sun 牟潤孫, "Ku Ning-jen ti hsueh-shu yuan-yuan" 顧寧人的學術淵源 (Origins of Ku Yen-yu's scholarship), *Chu-shih chai ts'ung-kao* 注史齋叢稿 (Draft of collected essays from the Study of Historical Exegesis) (Hong Kong: New Asia Institute of Advanced Chinese Studies, 1959), 166–70. For Lü Liu-Liang 呂留良, see *Lü Wan-ts'un hsien-sheng wen-chi* 呂晚村先生文集 (Collected writings of Lü Liu-liang; hereafter *LWTWC*) (Taipei: Chung-ting wen-hua ch'u-pan-she, 1967), 73–77, 82, 402–3. See also Jung Chao-tsu 容肇祖, *Lü Liu-liang chi ch'i ssu-hsiang* 呂留良及其思想 (Lü Liu-liang and his thought) (Hong Kong: Ch'ung-wen shu-chü, 1974), 58–62, 75–76. For Lu Lung-ch'i 陸隴其, see *Lu Chia-shu hsien-sheng wen-chi* 陸稼書先生文集 (Collected writings of Lu Lung-ch'i) (Shanghai: Commercial Press, 1936), 50–52.

8. Lü Liu-liang, *LWTWC*, 1:9a–11a, 22a–24b; Pao Lai 包賚 *Lü Liu-liang nien-p'u* 呂留良年譜 (Chronological biography of Lü Liu-liang) (Shanghai: Commercial Press, n.d.), 101–18.

9. For testimony to the great influence of examination aids, see Lü Liu-liang, 401–2; Tai Ming-shih 戴名世, *Tai Ming-shih chi* 戴名世集 (Collected writings of Tai Ming-shih) (Peking: Chung-hua shu-chü, 1986; hereafter *TMSC*), 138.

10. Ai Nan-ying 艾南英, *T'ien-yung tzu chi* 天傭子集 (Collected writings of Heaven's servant) (preface 1699), 1:28b–29a; Lü Liu-liang, 402–3.

11. Lynn Struve, "Ambivalence and Action: Some Frustrated Scholars of the K'ang-hsi Period," in *From Ming to Ch'ing: Conquest, Region, and Continuity in Seventeenth-Century China*, ed. Jonathan D. Spence and John E. Wills, Jr. (New Haven: Yale University Press, 1979), 323–56. See also Satō Ichirō 佐藤一郎, "Tai Meisei Hō Hō no kōyū yori mitaru Tōjōha kobun no seiritsu" 戴名世 · 方苞の交遊より見る桐城派古文の成立 (Founding of the T'ung-ch'eng school viewed through the relationship between Tai Ming-shih and Fang Pao), *Geibun kenkyū* 16, no. 47 (October 1963).

12. *TMSC*, 11, 30. For a discussion of the activities of Wan Ssu-t'ung 萬斯同 and Liu Hsien-t'ing 劉獻庭, see Lynn Struve, "Ambivalence." Others such as Ch'ien Ch'ien-i 錢謙益 also had written a private history of the Ming in one hundred *chüan*. Arthur W. Hummel, ed., *Eminent Chinese of the Ch'ing Period* (hereafter *ECCP*) (reprint, Taipei: 1970), 149. As early as 1646, he was appointed editor-in-chief of the official *Ming History*. Frederic Wakeman, "Romantics, Stoics, and Martyrs in Seventeenth-Century China," *Journal of Asian Studies* 43, no. 4 (Aug. 1984):637.

13. *TMSC*, 2–3, 11, 16, 30, 59, 454; Wang Yüan, *Chü-yeh t'ang chi* 居業堂集 (Shanghai: Commercial Press, 1936), 7:102. See also Sutō Yōichi 須藤洋一, "Tai Meisei—kō shi no mujun to sono tenkai" 戴名世—公私の矛盾とその展開 (Tai Ming-shih—Development of the contradiction between *Kung* and *Ssu*), *Nippon-Chūgoku gakkai hō*, 28 (1976): 202–3. Tai had written many biographical essays in honor of those who died in resisting peasant rebels. For these biographies, see *TMSC*, 159–60, 163–65, 166–67; for biographies of Ming loyalists, see 160–61, 162–63, 168–70, 207–9.

14. *TMSC*, 21.

15. *TMSC*, 64, 89, 99, 109.

16. *TMSC*, 93.

17. *TMSC*, 20–21, 104. For Tai's anti-Buddhist attitude, see 51, 399–400.

18. *TMSC*, 20.

19. *TMSC*, 88, 90–91, 100. Fang Pao explained that the prose by Ou-yang Hsiu, Su Shih, Tseng Kung, and Wang An-shih was "ancient" (*ku*) because their writings were free from difficult and abstruse phrases and sentences. Fang Pao, *Fang Pao chi* 方苞集 (Collected writings of Fang Pao) (hereafter *FPC*) (Shanghai: Ku-chi ch'u-pan-she, 1983), 775.

20. For Han Yü's theory of the unity of literature (*wen*) and morality (*tao*), see Charles Hartman, *Han Yü and the T'ang Search for Unity* (Princeton: Princeton University Press, 1986), 212–27.

21. *TMSC*, 64. See Aoki Masaru 青木正兒 *Shindai bungaku hyōronshi* 清代文學評論史 (History of Chinese literary criticism), trans. Yang T'ieh-ying 楊鐵嬰 (Peking: Chung-kuo k'o-hsueh ch'u-pan-she, 1988), ch. 4.

22. Wang Wan 汪琬, *Yao-feng wen-ch'ao* 堯峰文鈔 (Hand-copied writings of Wang Wan), in *Wen-yuan ko Ssu-k'u ch'üan-shu* 文淵閣四庫全書 (Complete library of the four treasuries in the Chamber of Deep Spring of Literature; hereafter *SKCS*) (Taipei: Commercial Press, 1986), 1315: 491; Lü Liu-liang, *LWTWC*, 85.

23. Aoki, *Shindai bungaku*, ch. 4

24. For a list of the scholars chosen from successful candidates from the *Po-hsüeh hung-tz'u* 博學宏詞 examination to work on the Ming history project, see Li Chin-hua 李晉華, "Ming-shih tsuan-hsiu k'ao" 明史纂修考 (Writing and compilation of the Ming History), in *Ming-shih pien-tsuan k'ao* 明史編纂考 (Study of the compilation of the Ming history) (Taipei: Hsueh-sheng shu-chü, 1968), 56.

25. Aoki, ch. 4; Yu Hsin-hsiung, 尤信雄 *T'ung-ch'eng wen-p'ai hsueh shu* 桐城文派學述 (Account of the literary school of T'ung-ch'eng) (Taipei: Wen-chin ch'u-pan-she, 1975), 47–52. For a list of the major scholars working on the Ming history project, see Huang Yun-mei 黃雲眉, "Ming-shih pien-tsuan k'ao-lueh" 明史編纂考略, in *Ming-shih pien-tsuan k'ao*, 12.

26. Aoki, 70–71; Chiang Shu-ko 姜書閣, *T'ung-ch'eng wen-p'ai p'ing-shu* 桐城文派評述 (Evaluative study of the T'ung-ch'eng school) (Taipei: Commercial Press, 1966), 11–13; Yu Hsin-hsiung, *T'ung-ch'eng wen-p'ai*, 2–3; Sakuma Mayumi 佐久間まゆみ, "Min Shin kobunka ni yoru danraku hyōji no seiritsu katei" 明清古文家による段落表示の成立過程 (Development of paragraph marking by literary scholars of the ancient style in the Ming-Ch'ing periods. *Tōhōgaku* 61 (Jan. 1981): 4.

27. Theodore Huters, "From Writing to Literature: The Development of Late Qing Theories of Prose," *Harvard Journal of Asiatic Studies* 47, no.1 (June 1987): 65. For a detailed discussion of the revival of Ch'eng-Chu learning in the early Ch'ing, see William Theodore de Bary, *The Message of the Mind in Neo-Confucianism* (New York: Columbia University Press, 1990), chs. 4, 5.

28. Hsieh Kuo-chen 謝國楨, *Ming-Ch'ing chih chi tang-she yun-tung k'ao* 明清之際黨社運動考 (Study of the movements of political cliques and associations) (Peking: Chung-hua shu-chü, 1982), 129–31.

29. Pao Lai, *Nien-p'u*, 121.

30. Wang Wan, *Yao-feng wen-ch'ao*, 29:2a. Wang Mou-hung held a similar view. Wang Mou-hung 王懋竑, *Pai-t'ien ts'ao-t'ang ts'un-kao* 白田草堂存稿 (Preserved draft of writings from the study of White Field) (Taipei: Han-hua wen-hua shih-yeh, 1972), 623 –24.

31. Charles Price Ridley, "Educational Theory and Practice in Late Imperial China: The Teaching of Writing as a Specific Case" (Ph.D. diss., Stanford University, 1973), 417–19; Chang Po-hsing, 張伯行, *T'ang-Sung pa-ta-chia wen-ch'ao* 唐宋八大家文鈔 (Selection of the writings of the eight great masters of T'ang-Sung times) (Taipei: Commercial Press, 1936), preface; Wu Yuan-ping 吳元炳, *Chang Ch'ing-lo kung nien-p'u* 張圌恪公年譜 (Chronological biography of Chang Po-hsing), in *San-hsien cheng-shu* 三賢 正書, 4, *shang chüan* (Taipei: Hsueh-sheng shu-chü, 1976), 1785–86.

32. *TMSC*, 94–95, 101, 137–38.

33. *TMSC*, 35, 54, 136–37. For a discussion of widespread discontent with the civil service examination in the early Ch'ing, see Alan Barr, "Pu Songling and the Qing Examination System," *Late Imperial China* 7, no. 1 (June 1986) : 87–109.

34. *TMSC*, 123.

35. *TMSC*, 507–11.

36. Lü Liu-liang, *LWTWC*, 61-67. Tai Ming-shih suggested that Lü's comments on examination essays did help the renewal of faith in Ch'eng-Chu learning in the late seventeenth century. *TMSC*, 101–2. Tai's remarks were further substantiated by Ch'eng Chin-fang (1718–84). See Ch'ien Mu 錢穆, *Chung-kuo chin san-pai-nien hsueh-shu shih* 中 國近三百年學術史 (History of scholarship in the last three hundred years; hereafter *HSS*) (Taipei: Commercial Press, 1957), 264.

37. *TMSC*, 101–2. Pao Lai, *Nien-pu*, 116–18.

38. *TMSC*, 88–89, 90, 92, 96, 100–2.

39. *TMSC*, 75–77, 94–96.

40. Wing-tsit Chan, "*Hsing-li ching-i*," 555–56. For a discussion of the cultural symbolism associated with rituals of the Ming and the Ch'eng-Chu tradition and its disappearance as a result of the Manchu adoption of Chinese rituals, see Kai-wing Chow, "Ritual and Ethics: Classical Scholarship and Lineage Institutions in Late Imperial China, 1600–1830" (Ph.D. diss., University of California, Davis, 1988), 484–90.

41. Liu Yen-chieh 劉言潔, Liu Ta-shan 劉大山, Ho Ch'o 何焯, and Wang Wu-ts'ao 汪武曹. *TMSC*, 5–6, 10–12, 18–20, 100; *FPC*, 120–122, 335, 346–47, 617, 666, 678, 769.

42. *FPC*, 609, 621, 659.

43. *TMSC*, 88–89, 91, 101, 105; *FPC*, 621, 776.

44. Lu Lung-ch'i, *Lu chia-shu*, 1:24.

45. Wang Mou-hung, *Pai-t'ien ts'ao-t'ang*, 14:10a–b.

46. The accomplished writer Ch'ien Ch'ien-i already regarded *yen yu-wu* as the purpose of writing. Lynn Struve, "Huang Zongxi in Context: A Reappraisal of His Major Writings," *Journal of Asian Studies* 47, no. 3 (Aug. 1988): 488.

47. *TMSC*, 6. Satō Ichirō, looking at the close relationship between Fang Pao and Tai Ming-shih and their backgrounds, points out that both Tai Ming-shih and Fang Pao were instrumental in laying the foundation of the theory of ancient prose of the T'ung-ch'eng school. Satō, "Tai Meisei," 41–57.

48. *FPC*, 49, 58–64. Chang Hsueh-ch'eng also entertained such a notion. David Nivison suggests that Chang was influenced by the T'ung-ch'eng school. *The Life and Thought of Chang Hsüeh-ch'eng* (Stanford: Stanford University Press, 1966), 111-14.

49. *FPC*, 58–59, 62–64, 111, 165, 613, 615.

50. In the epitaph Fang wrote for Wan Ssu-t'ung, the eminent historian, Fang claimed that Wan encouraged him to complete Wan's unfinished project of the Ming history by writing in ancient prose with *i-fa*. *FPC*, 333–34.

51. For an excellent discussion of Tai Ming-shih's anti-Manchu expressions, see Ho Kuan-piao 何冠彪, *Tai Ming-shih yen-chiu* 戴名世研究 (A study of Tai Ming-shih) (Taipei: Tao-hsiang ch'u-pan-she, 1988), 259–75. See also "Chi T'ung-ch'eng Fang Tai liang-chia shu an" 記桐城方戴兩家書案 (Notes on the literary inquisitions of Fang and Tai of T'ung-ch'eng), in *Ku-hsueh hui-k'an* 古學彙刊 (Collection of ancient learning) (Taipei: Li-hsing shu-chü, 1964), 1305–18; Wang Shu-min 王樹民, "Nan-shan chi an ti t'ou-shih" 南山集案的透視 (Unraveling of the literary inquisition of the writings of Nan-shan); *Ch'ing-shih yen-chiu t'ung-hsun* 2(1985): 54–57, 59.

52. For the pardoning of Fang and his lineage by the Yung-cheng emperor, see Ho Kuan-piao, *Tai Ming-shih*, 295–96. See also Guy, chap. 5 of this volume.

53. His allusion to the painful experience of the exile of his family was vividly revealed in a letter to Li Kuang-ti. *FPC*, 142–43, 139.

54. *FPC*, 91–93, 886.

55. *FPC*, 874–75.

56. Wing-tsit Chan, 543–47; Kent Guy, *The Emperor's Four Treasuries: Scholars and the State in the Late Ch'ien-lung Era* (Cambridge, Mass.: Harvard University Press, 1987), 20–21.

57. *ECCP*, 701; Wing-tsit Chan, 555–56.

58. Ch'üan Han-sheng 全漢昇, *Ming-Ch'ing ching-chi shih yen-chiu* 明清經濟史研究 (Studies of the economic history of the Ming-Ch'ing period) (Taipei: Lien-ching ch'u-pan-she, 1987), 51–52.

59. For a discussion of ritualism and purism in relation to the rise of the Ch'eng-Chu school, see Chow, "Ritual and Ethics," ch. 6.

60. Benjamin A. Elman, *From Philosophy to Philology: Intellectual and Social Aspects of Change in Late Imperial China* (Cambridge, Mass.: Harvard University Press, 1984), 30–31.

61. *HSS*, 232–33.

62. *HSS*, 229–32.

63. Benjamin A. Elman, "The Unravelling of Neo-Confucianism: From Philosophy to Philology in Late Imperial China," *Tsing-hua hsueh-pao* 15, no. 1–2 (Dec. 1983): 67–88.

64. *HSS*, 51–55, 66, 69. Ch'en Ch'ueh 陳確 was one these critics of Neo-Confucianism of any variety. *Ch'en Ch'ueh chi* 陳確集 (Collected writings of Ch'en Ch'ueh) (Peking: Chung-hua shu-chü, 1979), 442. See Chow, "Ritual and Ethics," ch. 6. If Fang Pao knew nothing of the teachings of Ch'en and P'an Ping-ko, he had no escape from the growing influence of the teachings of Yen Yuan through his disciple, Li Kung. In fact, P'an's teachings were known to Wan Ssu-t'ung and Li Kung, with both of whom Fang Pao was acquainted. *FPC*, 869, 872–73. Li Kung, *Shu-ku hou-chi* 恕谷後集 (Later collected writings of Shu-ku) (Shanghai: Commercial Press, 1936), 13:162; *HSS*, 67. Lü Liu-liang had defended Chu Hsi against P'an's attack. *LWTWC*, 43–46.

65. *FPC*, 872.

66. *FPC*, 139–40.

67. *FPC*, 135–36, 659–60.

68. *HSS*, 232–33, Liang Ch'i-ch'ao 梁啟超, *Chung-kuo chin san-pai-nien hsueh-shu shih* 中國近三百年學術史 (History of Chinese thought during the last three centuries), (Shanghai: Commercial Press, 1937), 100–102.

69. *Ch'in-ting ta-Ch'ing hui-tien shih-li* 欽定大清會典事例 (Collected statutes and precedents of the Ch'ing dynasty; hereafter *TCHTSL*) (Taipei: Chung-wen shu-chü, 1963), 332:lb–2a.

70. *Ch'in-ting hsueh-cheng ch'üan-shu* 欽定學政全書 (Complete guide to educational commissioners; hereafter *CTHCCS*) (Taipei: Wen-hai ch'u-pan-she, 1973), 6:2b.

71. *TCHTSL*, 332:2b.

72. *TCHTSL*, 332:2b–3a. For a discussion of Yung-cheng's various attempts to control ideas, see Pei Huang, *Autocracy at Work: A Study of the Yung-cheng Period, 1723–35* (Bloomington: Indiana University Press, 1974), ch. 8.

73. Wang Hsien-ch'ien 王先謙, comp., *Shih-erh-ch'ao tung-hua lu* 十二朝東華錄 (Tung-hua records of twelve reigns; hereafter *THL*) (Taipei: Wen-hai ch'u-pan-she, 1963), under *"Yung-cheng reign"* 雍正朝, vol. 2, 7:19a.

74. Pei Huang, *Autocracy at Work*: 215 — 20.

75. Pao Lai, *Nien-pu*, 181–82.

76. *FPC*, 259–62; 688–90.

77. *THL*, under *"Ch'ien-lung reign"* 乾隆朝, vol. 1, 1:45–46a.

78. *TCHTSL*, 332:6a–b, *Ch'in-ting Ssu-shu-wen* (*Imperial edition of essays on the Four Books; hereafter CTSSW*), in *SKCS*, 1451, 1–2.

79. *FPC*, 885. *CTSSW*, 6.

80. There are 486 essays from the Ming and 297 from the Ch'ing. The smaller number for the Ch'ing period is the result of excluding the essays of living persons. *CT SSW*, 4.

81. For a discussion of the political group to which Fang Pao belonged, see Guy, chap. 5 of this volume.

82. *CTSSW*, 39.

83. *FPC*, 581.

84. *FPC*, 166, 581.

85. For reference to ancient prose see *CTSSW* 3, 88, 99–100, 220. For the need to observe the commentary of Chu Hsi and the teachings of Sung Neo-Confucians, see 36, 38, 135.

86. A 1744 edict reiterated the imperial order that the work be the yardstick of examination essays. *TCHTSL*, 332:6b–7a. In 1745, there was an imperial edict calling for observing the guidelines of *ch'ing-chen ya-cheng* 清真雅正 (pure, authentic, elegant, and correct). CTHCCS, 6:14b–15a.

87. Li Pei-en 李培恩, educational commissioner of Chekiang in 1759, reported to the Ch'ien-lung emperor that candidates in that province wrote in flowery language, deviating from the *ch'ing-chen ya-cheng* ideal. *Huang-Ch'ing tsou-i* 皇清奏議 (Memorials of the Ch'ing dynasty) (Taipei: Wen-hai ch'u-pan-she, 1967), 51:17a–19a. Ch'ien Shih-fu, 錢實甫, *Ch'ing-tai chih-kuan nien-piao* 清代職官年表 (Chronological chart of Ch'ing officials) (Peking: Chung-hua shu-chü, 1980), 4: 2663.

88. There were imperial orders demanding observance in 1744, 1754, 1758, 1760, 1765, 1778, 1779. *TCHTSL*, 332:6b–7a, 8b, 10a, 358:13b, 17a, 23b.

89. Kent Guy, "Zang Tingyu and Reconciliation," *Late Imperial China*: 7, no. 1 (June 1986): 52–53. See also his *Four Treasuries*, 30–31.

90. For a detailed discussion of fundamentalist attacks first on spurious texts and later on the entire exegetical tradition since the Sung, see Chow, "Ritual and Ethics," chs. 6, 7.

91. For a discussion of the growth of interest in Cheng Hsuan's scholia and the rising reputation of Han exegeses during the 1730s and 1740s, see Chow, "Ritual and Ethics," 409–21.

92. Benjamin A. Elman, "Philosophy (*I-li*) Versus Philology (*K'ao-cheng*): The *Jen-hsin Tao-hsin* Debate," *T'oung Pao* 69, nos. 4–5 (1983): 212–13. For Hui Tung's students and academic fashion in the mid-eighteenth century, see Elman, *From Philosophy to Philology*, 122.

93. Yao Ying 姚瑩, *Tung-ming wen-chi* 東溟文集 (Collected works of Tung-ming), in *Chung-fu t'ang ch'üan-chi* 中復堂全集 (Complete works of the Studio of Restoration; hereafter *CFTCC*) (Taipei: Wen-hai ch'u-pan-she, 1983), 6:6b–7a.

94. Yeh Ch'ang-chih 葉昌熾, *Yuan-tu lu jih-chi* 緣督廬日記 (Diary of the Cottage of Yuan-tu), *chüan* 4, cited in Ch'en Lien-hsing 陳聯星, "T'ung-ch'eng san ta-chia shih-tai hsueh-shu wen-hua chih heng-kuan" 桐城三大家時代學術文化之橫觀 (Synchronic view of the intellectual and cultural conditions of the three writers of the T'ung-ch'eng school), in *T'ung-ch'eng p'ai yen-chiu lun-wen hsuan* 桐城派研究論文選 (Selected essays on the study of the T'ung-ch'eng school) (Anhwei, Hofei: Huang-shan shu-she, 1986), 79–80. For a discussion of the differences of concerns and style between Yao Nai and other evidential scholars in the Ssu-k'u Commission, see Guy, *Four Treasuries*, 145–54.

95. Yao mentioned in particular that at the completion of the Ssu-k'u project, six of the eight scholars who began without an appointment in the Hanlin Academy were granted such an honor. *HPHCC*, 146.

96. *ECCP*, 695–99.

97. *HPHCC*, 65; *ECCP*, 695–97, 900.

98. Ch'en Yuan 陳垣, "Pien-tsuan Ssu-k'u ch'üan-shu shih-mo" 編纂四庫全書始末 (Account of the compilation of the Complete Library of Four Treasuries), in *Ch'en Yuan hsueh-shu lun-wen chi* 陳垣學術論文集 (Collection of research papers of Ch'en Yuan) (Peking: Chung-hua shu-chü, 1982), 2:5.

99. Chang Hsueh-ch'eng 章學誠, *Chang Hsueh-ch'eng i-shu* 章學誠遺書 (Bequeathed writings of Chang Hsueh-ch'eng) (Peking: Wen-wu ch'u-pan-she, 1985), 85.

100. As some scholars have pointed out, it was Yao Nai who first promoted the idea of a T'ung-ch'eng school in the 1760s. *ECCP*, 900–901. The first reference to the idea of a lineage of T'ung-ch'eng scholars practicing a distinct method of writing appears in an essay Yao wrote to celebrate the eightieth birthday of Liu Ta-k'uei (1698–1779). It was written several years after Yao Nai left the bureau for compiling the *Ssu-k'u ch'üan shu*. *HPHCC*, 87.

101. *ECCP*, 900.

102. Yeh Lung 葉龍, *T'ung-ch'eng p'ai wen-hsueh shih* 桐城派文學史 (Literary history of the T'ung-ch'eng school) (Taipei: Wen-chin ch'u-pan-she, 1975), 154; Chiang Shu-ko, *T'ung-ch'eng wen-p'ai*, 15.

103. Chiang Shu-ko, *T'ung-ch'eng wen-p'ai*, 15.

104. Chang T'ing-yü 張廷玉, *Ch'eng-huai yuan wen-ts'un* 澄懷園文存 (Preserved writings from the garden of *Ch'eng-huai*) (Taipei: Wen-hai ch'u-pan-she, 1973), 15:3a.

105. Ma Ch'i-ch'ang 馬其昶, *T'ung-ch'eng ch'i-chiu chuan* 桐城耆舊傳 (Records of the elders of T'ung-ch'eng) (Taipei: Wen-hai ch'u-pan-she, 1973), 6.

106. Yao Ying's friend, Chang Juan-lin 張阮林, a great grandson of Chang Ying, attained a reputation in symmetric and rhythmic writing (*p'ien-t'i*). Yao Ying, *Tung-ming wen wai-chi* 東溟文外集 (Outer collection of writings of Tung-ming), *CFTCC*, 6:3b–4a.

107. Kent Guy has already suggested that the Ssu-k'u project was the catalyst for the development of Sung Learning. *Four Treasuries*, 140–45. For the psychological impact of the rise of *k'ao-cheng* scholarship on the development of the historical thought of Chang Hsueh-ch'eng, see Yü Ying-shih 余英時, *Lun Tai Chen yü Chang Hsueh-ch'eng: Ch'ing-tai chung-ch'i hsueh-shu ssu-hsiang shih yen-chiu* 論戴震與章學誠：清代中期學術思想史研究 (On Tai Chen and Chang Hsueh-ch'eng: a study of intellectual history in the mid-Ch'ing) (Taipei: Hua-shih ch'u-pan-she, 1980), 5–13, 31–75.

108. For a discussion of the general attitude of cooperation among the local elite families in T'ung-ch'eng, see Hilary Beattie, "The Alternative to Resistance: The Case of T'ung-ch'eng, Anhwei," in *From Ming to Ch'ing: Conquest, Region, and Continuity in Seventeenth-Century China*, ed. Jonathan D. Spence and John W. Wills, Jr. (New Haven: Yale University Press, 1979), 256–60. For a detailed narrative of the Kiangnan resistance movement, see Frederic Wakeman, Jr., *The Great Enterprise: The Manchu Reconstruction of Imperial Order in Seventeenth-Century China* (Berkeley: University of California Press, 1985), ch. 8.

109. Wakeman, *The Great Enterprise*, 864; Ch'ien Shih-fu, *CTCKP*, 1, 179.

110. The examination success of the T'ung-ch'eng elite is discussed in Hilary Beattie, *Land and Lineage in China: A Study of T'ung-ch'eng County, Anhwei, in the Ming and Ch'ing Dynasties* (New York: Cambridge University Press, 1979), 50–51.

111. Yao Fen (1726–1801) was a scholar and governor of Hunan and Fukien. Fang Kuan-ch'eng (1698–1768) rose to the position of governor general of Chihli and was appointed senior guardian of the heir-apparent. *ECCP*, 233–35. Fang Pao had attained a great reputation as a scholar and prose writer. Chang T'ing-yü (1672–1755) was a trusted confidant of the K'ang-hsi emperor and continued to be influential during the Yung-cheng and Ch'ien-lung reigns. *ECCP*, 54–56. See Kent Guy, "Zhang Tingyu and Reconstruction," 57–59.

112. Beattie, *Land and Lineage*, 51–52, 92–93, 104–5.

113. Ch'en K'ang-ch'i 陳康祺, *Lang-ch'ien chi-wen ch'u-chi* 郎潛紀聞初集 (Hearsay recorded by Lang-ch'ien) (Peking: Chung-hua shu-chü, 1984), 5:93; Chu Pei-lian 朱沛蓮, *Ch'ing-tai ting-chia lu* 清代鼎甲錄 (Registers of successful candidates at the [metropolitan] examinations) (Taipei: Chung-hua shu-chü, 1968), 100–101. During the K'ang-hsi reign, two sons of Chang Ying earned *chin-shih* degrees. In the Yung-cheng period two more sons and one grandson obtained the *chin-shih* degree. Three more grandsons received the *chin-shih* degree in the Ch'ien-lung period. All of them, like Chang Ying himself, were honored to receive appointment in the Hanlin Academy. See Fang Chao-ying, *Ch'ing-tai chin-shih t'i-ming pei-lu* 清代進士題名碑錄 (*Chin-shih* roll of the Ch'ing dynasty) (reprint, Taipei: Harvard-Yenching Institute Sinological Index Series, supp. no. 19, 1966), 29–90.

114. *TCHTSL*, 345:3b, 333:8a–b. During the Ch'ing period, there were several major incidents concerning corruption of examiners and educational officials. Before the Tao-kuang period, the most notorious ones had happened in 1657, 1711, 1733, 1750, and 1752. Huang Kuang-liang 黄亮光, *Ch'ing-tai k'o-chü chih-tu chih yen-chiu* 清代科舉制度之研究 (Study of the civil service examination system of the Ch'ing dynasty) (Taipei: Chia-hsin shui-ni kung-ssu wen-hua chi-chin-hui, 1976), 258–75.

115. *TCHTSL*, 345:1a–2a.

116. Ch'en K'ang-ch'i, *Lang-ch'ien chi-wen* 2:352. See also *ECCP*, 533. For an analysis of the success of the Chang lineage in the examinations, see Ping-ti Ho, *The Ladder of Success in Imperial China* (New York: John Wiley & Sons, 1962), 137–41.

117. See Fang Chao-ying, *Ch'ing-tai*, 109–115. For Yai's expression of anxiety, see *HPHCC*, 64–65.

118. On many occasions, Yao gave vent to his frustration about the declining fortune of his county in the political arena and the unsatisfactory performance of the T'ung-ch'eng candidates in the examinations. *HPHCC*, 65, 130; *Yao Chi-ch'uan ch'ih-tu* 姚姬傳尺牘 (Letters of Yao Nai) in *Ching-hsuan chin-tai ming-jen ch'ih-tu* 精選近代名人尺牘 (Best selection of letters by renowned scholars) (Taipei: Hsin wen-feng ch'u-pan-she, 1974), 156, 160, 162–65.

119. Yao Nai, *Ch'ih-tu*, 28.

120. *ECCP*, 399; Elman, *From Philosophy to Philology*, 105–8.

121. Benjamin Elman has convincingly demonstrated that corresponding developments in institutions such as private and imperial libraries and patronage networks contributed to the rise and spread of *k'ao-cheng* scholarship in Chekiang and Kiangsu. *From Philosophy to Philology*, 96–169.

122. Elman, *From Philosophy to Philology*, chs. 3, 4.

123. Quoted by Wei Yuan 魏源, *Wei Yuan chi* 魏源集 (Peking: Chung-hua shu-chü, 1976), 510.

124. Ping-ti Ho, "The Salt Merchants of Yang-chou: A Study of Commercial Capitalism in Eighteenth-Century China," *Harvard Journal of Asiatic Studies* 17 (1954):156–57.

125. Juan Yuan 阮元, *Ching-chi tsuan-ku* 經籍纂詁 (Collected glosses on the Classics) (Taipei: Shih-chieh shu-chü, 1969).

126. *Huang Ch'ing ching-chieh pien-mu* 皇清經解編目 (Classified table of contents of the Ch'ing exegeses of the Classics) (Taipei: Tai-lien Kui-feng ch'u-pan-she et al., 1974). The only scholar was Ma Tsung-lien, who earned the *chin-shih* degree in 1824 and had studied with Yao Nai. They were also related through marriage. Ma Ch'i-ch'ang, *Ch'i-chiu lu*, 10:7b–8a. Cf. Elman, *From Philosophy*, 91–92.

127. In the Ming, Anhwei ranked ninth in the country in producing *chin-shih*. Of the 1,036 *chin-shih* from Anhwei, 8.2 percent came from T'ung-ch'eng. Beattie, *Land and Lineage*, 39, 50–51. The provinces with the largest numbers of *chin-shih* degree-holders were Chekiang and Kiangsu. Ho, *The Ladder of Social Success*, 227.

128. Beattie, *Land and Lineage*, 35.

129. Of the fifty-three collectors of the Ch'ing period, Kiangsu had twenty-eight and Chekiang fifteen, together constituting 81 percent. There is only one collector from Hsi County of Anhwei. Hung Yu-feng 洪有豐, *Ch'ing-tai ts'ang-shu chia k'ao* 清代藏書家考 (Study of the bibliophiles of the Ch'ing dynasty) (Hong Kong: Chung-shan t'u-shu, 1972), 1–70.

130. Of all the books submitted by provincial governors, 4,831 were eventually included in the imperial library. Hangchow in particular was a major source of books for the Ssu-k'u project. See Guy, *Four Treasuries*, 47. One merchant from Chekiang alone submitted 685 texts in three accruements. See Kuo Po-kung 郭伯恭, *Ssu-k'u ch'üan-shu tsuan-hsiu k'ao* 四庫全書纂修考 (Shanghai: Commercial Press, 1937), 81.

131. Anhwei had only 532 titles to offer, of which only 327 were accepted by the editors of the Ssu-k'u Commission. In contrast, Kiangsu submitted 1,726. Wu Wei-tsu 吳慰祖, *Ssu-k'u ts'ai-chin shu-mu* 四庫採進書目 (Catalog of books collected for the Ssu-k'u project) (Peking: Commercial Press, 1960), 5, 29; Guy, *Four Treasuries*, 90.

132. Kuo Po-kung, *Tsuan-hsiu k'ao*, 79–80. Both Pao T'ing-po and Wang Ch'i-shu were from She-hsien, and Ma Yü from Ch'i-meng. *ECCP*, 559–60, 612–13, 810–11. Cf. Elman, *From Philosophy*, 148–49.

133. Yeh Hsien-en 葉顯恩, *Ming-Ch'ing Hui-chou nung-ts'un she-hui yü t'ien-p'u chih* 明清徽州農村社會與佃僕制 (Bond servant system and rural society of Hui-chou in the Ming-Ch'ing periods) (Anhwei: Jen-min ch'u-pan-she, 1983), 135.

134. See Ho, "Salt Merchants," 156–158; Chang Hai-p'eng 張海鵬 et al., *Ming-Ch'ing Hui-chou tzu-liao hsuan-pien* 明清徽州資料選編 (Selected documents on Hui-chou in Ming-Ch'ing times) (Hofei, Anhwei: Huang-shan shu-she, 1985), 479–80.

135. See *HSS*, 307–10.

136. Of the fifty-four scholars to whom Chiang Fan devoted individual biographies in this work, thirty-five (64 percent) came from Kiangsu and four (7 percent) from Chekiang. While there were six scholars from Anhwei, none were natives of T'ung-ch'eng. All but one of these Anhwei scholars came from Hsi County. The exception was Tai Chen, who was a native of Hsiu-ning. *Kuo-ch'ao Han-hsueh shih-ch'eng chi* 國朝漢學師承記 (Lineage of Han Learning in the Ch'ing Dynasty) (Taipei: Chung-hua shu-chü, 1962).

137. Chang Hsueh-ch'eng, 14, 84–86.

138. Chang Hsueh-ch'eng, 2:14–15.

139. Ying-shih Yü has documented the psychological response of Chang Hsueh-ch'eng to Tai Chen's overemphasis on classical studies. The historian Chin Yü-fu 金毓黻 had long maintained that Chang's claim about the existence of a school of historians from Eastern Chekiang was dubious at best. See Ying-shih Yü, *Lun Tai Chen*, 53–62.

140. Beattie, *Land and Lineage*, 51–52. To be sure, the relationship between these families did not remain constant in terms of their political and intellectual affinities. For discussion of the connection between scholarly traditions and lineages in Changchow, see Benjamin A. Elman, *Classicism, Politics, and Kinship: The Ch'ang-chou School of New Text Confucianism in Late Imperial China* (Berkeley: University of California Press, 1990).

141. Yao Nai, *HPHCC*, 13:157–58.

142. *ECCP*, 238. Another prominent example of the role family and lineage played in the perpetuation of scholarly traditions can be found in the Chuangs and the Lius of the Changchow prefecture. They were to lead the movement of Confucian discourse in the direction of statecraft and New Text tradition from the 1820s on. See Benjamin A. Elman, "Scholarship and Politics: Chuang Ts'un-yü and the Rise of the Ch'ang-chou

New Text School in Late Imperial China," *Late Imperial China* 7, no. 1 (June 1986): 63–80.

143. Tai Chen, *Tai Chen chi* 戴震集 (Collected writings of Tai Chen) (Shanghai: Shanghai ku-chi ch'u-pan-she, 1980), 191–92, 214. For a discussion of Tai Chen's educational thought, see Brokaw, chap. 8 of this volume.

144. For a detailed discussion of the relationship between antiheterodoxy and evidential scholars, see Chow, "Ritual and Ethics," 532–36.

145. According to Ch'ien Mu, the aversion toward eight-legged essays was one factor in the rise of evidential scholarship. *HSS*, 139–42.

146. Nivison, *Chang Hsüeh-ch'eng*, 107.

147. Huters, "Late Qing Theories of Prose," 59.

148. Ch'ien Ta-hsin, *Ch'ien-yen t'ang wen-chi* 潛研堂文集 (Collected writings of the Studio of Ch'ien-yen) (Taipei: Commercial Press, 1968), 17:249–51; Ho Ch'ang-ling 賀長齡, *Huang-ch'ao ching-shih wen-pien* 皇朝經世文編 (Anthology of essays on statecraft of the Ch'ing dynasty) (Taipei: Wen-hai ch'u-pan-she, 1973), 5:15a–b.

149. Ho Ch'ang-ling, *Ching-shih wen-pien*, 5:17b–18a. The purist Li Kung had already argued in 1732 that the literary style of the T'ang-Sung writers was not the authentic *ku-wen* — that of the Classics was. See Li's preface to *P'ing-i ku-wen* 評乙古文 (Critique of ancient prose), in *Ts'ung-shu chi-ch'eng ch'u-pien* 叢書集成初編 (Shanghai: Commercial Press, 1960).

150. Aoki, *Shindai bungaku*, 171–77.

151. For Ling T'ing-k'an 淩廷勘, see Chiang Fan, 7:10a; For Hung Liang-chi 洪亮吉, see Chang Shun-hui 張舜徽, *Ch'ing-jen wen-chi pieh-lu* 清人文集別録 (Reviews of collected writings of Ch'ing literati) (Taipei, Ming-wen shu-chü, 1982), 258. See also Huters, "Late Qing Theories of Prose," 84.

152. Elman, *From Philosophy to Philology*, 45–55, 67–85.

153. Kent Guy has argued that the Sung Learning school represented by Yao Nai arose as a response to the "overspecialization" of the Han Learning school. *Four Treasuries*, 140, 144–45.

154. Yao Nai, *Ch'ih-tu*, 27, 62, 70, 155.

155. In fact, this threefold division was not Yao's idea. Both Tai Chen and Weng Fang-kang 翁方綱 had spoken of such a division. As early as 1755, Tai Chen already entertained the idea that learning could be divided into *i-li*, *k'ao-cheng* and *tz'u-chang*. See Ying-shih Yü, *Lun Tai Chen*, 110–12. For Weng's statement, see *Fu-ch'u chai wen-chi* 復初齋文集 (Collected writings from Studio of Returning to the Beginning) (Taipei: Wen-hai ch'u-pan-she, 1973), 4:20a–b.

156. For a discussion of the revival of Sung and Yuan classical studies in the K'ang-hsi period, see Chow, "Ritual and Ethics," 356–60, 397–409.

157. Yao Nai, *HPHCC*, 227, 308.

158. Huters, "Late Qing Theories of Prose," 72.

159. Yao Nai, *HPHCC*, 40, 46, 67–68.

160. Huters, "Late Qing Theories of Prose," 91.

161. For a discussion of social ethics as the "moral orthodoxy" of Confucianism, see Kwang-Ching Liu, "Socioethics as Orthodoxy: A Perspective," in Liu, ed., *Orthodoxy in Late Imperial China* (Berkeley: University of California Press, 1990), 53–100. When Tseng Kuo-fan promoted the idea that Han Learning and Sung Learning could be

reconciled by ritual, he was pointing to their common bond in Confucian social ethics. *HSS*, 585–87.

162. Liu argues that the T'ung-ch'eng school had no exclusive claim to this method of prose writing. If the ancient prose method had been used by writers other than those from T'ung-ch'eng, then it is a methodological fallacy to use the school's name as a comprehensive label for the T'ang-Sung ancient prose. See his *T'ung-ch'eng wen-hsueh chuan-shu k'ao* 桐城文學撰述考 (Study of the works of scholars of the T'ung-ch'eng school), in *T'ung-ch'eng wen-hsueh yuan-yuan k'ao* 桐城文學淵源考 (Study of the lineage of the T'ung-ch'eng literary tradition) (Taipei: Shih-chieh shu-chü, 1974), preface, 1a. For the list, see Yu Hsin-hsiung, "*T'ung-ch'eng wen-p'ai,*" ch. 2, app. 70–75.

163. Yeh Lung, *T'ung-ch'eng wen-hsueh*, 1–2.

164. Wei Chi-ch'ang, *T'ung-ch'eng ku-wen*, ch. 1; Hsu Shou-k'ai 徐 壽 凱, "T'ung-ch'eng p'ai yen-mien chiu-yuan ti yuan-yin" 桐城派延綿久遠的原因 (Speculative account for the longevity of the T'ung-ch'eng school), in *T'ung-ch'eng p'ai yen-chiu lun-wen hsuan*, 86.

165. Following T'ang Chi-ch'uan, Theodore Huters overstates his case that with the printing of Yao's *Ku-wen-tz'u lei-tsuan* in 1820 the T'ung-ch'eng school began to emerge as a popular literary school. See Huters, "Late Qing Theories of Prose," 70–80.

166. See Huters, "Late Qing Theories of Prose," 77–78.

167. Yao Ying, *Tung-ming wen hou-chi* 東溟文後集 (Appending essays to the works of Tung-ming), in *CFTCC*, 10:13b.

168. Kuo Shao-yü 郭紹虞, *Chung-kuo wen-hsueh p'i-p'ing shih* 中國文學批評史 (History of Chinese literary criticism) (Hong Kong: Hung-chih shu-tien, n.d.), 546–48.

169. Fang Tung-shu, *Han-hsueh shang-tui* 漢學商兌 (Polemic against Han Learning) (Taipei: Commercial Press, 1978). Fang criticized the Han Learning scholars for taking Han exegeses for granted and for their intellectual bias against Sung scholarship, a view shared by Chang Hsueh-ch'eng. For Chang's view, see Ying-shih Yü, *Lun Tai Chen*, 57–59. See also *HSS*, 517–21, ch. 13. Cf. Elman, *From Philosophy*, 242–48.

170. Yao Nai, *Ch'ih-tu*, 28. Ch'en Yung-kuang 陳用光 became a *chin-shih* in 1801. But Ch'en received training in ancient prose from his father-in-law who was a student of Chu Shih-hsiu 朱士琇, a noted writer of ancient prose in his own right. Chang Shun-hui, *Ch'ing-jen wen-chi*. 336–37. Mei Tseng-liang 梅曾亮 did not become a *chin-shih* until 1822.

171. *ECCP*, 901.

172. Chiang Shu-ko, *T'ung-ch'eng wen-p'ai*, 93.

GLOSSARY

Ai Nan-ying	艾南英	Ch'eng Chin-fang	程晉方
Chang Hsueh-ch'eng	章學誠	Ch'eng-Chu	程朱
Chang Lü-hsiang	張履祥	Chi Yun	紀昀
Chang Po-hsing	張伯行	*ch'i-chieh*	氣節
Chang T'ing-yü	張廷玉	Ch'i-men	祁門
Chang Ying	張英	Chiang Ch'en-ying	姜宸英
Changchow	常州	Chiang Fan	江藩
Ch'en Yung-kuang	陳用光	Chiang Yung	江永

Ch'ien Ch'ien-i	錢謙益	*ko-wu*	格物
Ch'ien Ta-hsin	錢大昕	*ku-wen*	古文
chin chih wen-ti	今之文體	*Ku-wen shang-shu*	古文尚書
Chin Pang	金榜	*Ku-wen-tz'u lei-tsuan*	古文辭類纂
Ch'in-ting Ssu-shu-wen	欽定四書文	Ku Yen-wu	顧炎武
Ching-chi tsuan-ku	經籍纂詁	Kuan T'ung	管同
ching-hsueh	經學	Kuei Yu-kuang	歸有光
ch'ing-chen ku-ya	清真古雅	*Kuo-yü*	國語
Chu I-tsun	朱彝尊	Li Chih	李贄
Chu Shih	朱軾	*li chih shih*	理之是
Chu-tzu ch'üan-shu	朱子全書	*li-hsueh*	理學
chü-jen	舉人	Li Kuang-ti	李光地
Chu Yun	朱筠	Li Kung	李塨
Ch'un-ch'iu	春秋	Ling T'ing-k'an	淩廷堪
Chuang-tzu	莊子	Liu Hsien-t'ing	劉獻庭
Fang Chao-ying	房兆楹	Liu K'ai	劉開
Fang Chou	方舟	Liu Ta-k'uei	劉大櫆
Fang Kuan-ch'eng	方觀承	Liu Tsung-chou	劉宗周
Fang Pao	方苞	Liu T'ung-hsuan	劉統勳
Fang Tse	方澤	Lu Lung-ch'i	陸隴其
Fang Tung-shu	方東樹	Lu Wen-ch'ao	盧文弨
fu	賦	Lü Liu-liang	呂留良
Han-hsueh	漢學	*lun-ch'ang*	倫常
Han-shu	漢書	Ma Ch'i-ch'ang	馬其昶
Han T'an	韓菼	Ma Yü	馬裕
Han Yü	韓愈	Mao Ch'i-ling	毛奇齡
Hou Fang-yü	侯方域	Mao K'un	茅坤
hsing-ming	性命	Mei Tseng-liang	梅曾亮
Hsiu-ning	休寧	Mencius	孟子
Hsuan-te	宣德	Ou-yang Hsiu	歐陽修
Hsun-tzu	荀子	*pa-ku*	八股
Hu Shih	胡適	P'an P'ing-ko	潘平格
Hu Wei	胡渭	Pao T'ing-po	鮑廷博
Huang-Ch'ing ching-chieh	皇清經解	Pi Yuan	畢沅
Huang Tsung-hsi	黃宗羲	*p'ien-wen*	駢文
Hui Tung	惠棟	*Po-hsüeh hung-ju*	博學鴻儒
Hung Pang	洪榜	*Po Ssu-shu chiang-i yü-lu*	駁四書講義語錄
i-fa	義法	*shih-chi*	史記
i ku-wen wei shih-wen	以古文為時文	*shih-hsueh*	史學
i-li	義理	*shih-wen*	時文
I-t'u ming-pien	易圖明辨	*Ssu-k'u ch'üan-shu*	四庫全書
Jen Ta-ch'un	任大椿	Ssu-ma Ch'ien	司馬遷
Juan Yuan	阮元	Su Shih	蘇軾
k'ao-cheng	考證	Sun Ch'i-feng	孫奇逢
k'ao-cheng ching-i	考證經義	Sun Hsing-yen	孫星衍

Tai Chen 戴震

Tai Ming-shih 戴名世

T'ang Shun-chih 唐順之

tao 道

Ts'ai Shih-yuan 蔡世遠

Tseng Ching 曾靜

Tseng Kung 曾鞏

Tseng Kuo-fan 曾國藩

Tso-chuan 左傳

Tuan Yü-ts'ai 段玉裁

T'ung-ch'eng 桐城

tz'u-chang 詞章

Wan Ssu-t'ung 萬斯同

Wang An-shih 王安石

Wang Ch'i-shu 汪啟淑

Wang Chung 汪中

Wang Fu 汪紱

Wang Mou-hung 王懋竑

Wang Wan 汪琬

Wang Yang-ming 王陽明

Wang Yuan 王源

Wei Chi-jui 魏際瑞

Wei Hsi 魏禧

Wei Li 魏禮

wen 文

wen i tsai-tao 文以載道

wen-shih 文史

"Wen-yen shuo" 文言說

Yao Fan 姚範

Yao Fen 姚鼐

Yao Wen-jan 姚文然

Yen Yuan 顏元

Yueh Chung-ch'i 岳鍾琪

PART THREE

Technical Learning and Intellectual Challenge in Ch'ing Educational Life

SEVEN

Learning Mathematical Sciences during the Early and Mid-Ch'ing

Catherine Jami

The study of the role of scientific knowledge in learning and education in Ch'ing China can be linked to the concerns of comparative history, exemplified by what is known as "the Needham problem:" "Why did modern science, the mathematization of hypotheses about Nature, with all its implications for advanced technology, take its meteoric rise *only* in the West, at the time of Galileo?" which is translated in *Science and Civilisation in China* into attempts to explain "why modern science had not developed in Chinese civilization?"[1] This question, which stems from concerns typical of the European view of China, was already raised in the eighteenth century by Voltaire.[2] It also fits in with the idea that science stagnated or had a slow development in late imperial China. Until recently, this approach has dominated literature on the history of Chinese science.[3]

In contrast, this chapter discusses some aspects of scientific knowledge in learning and education in late imperial China in an effort to contribute to a better understanding of the role of science in the intellectual life of the period. From the seventeenth century on, there occurred a significant change in the status of mathematical sciences and a radical renewal of their content: large numbers of scholars became interested in mathematical sciences whose revival was stimulated by the introduction of some elements of Western scientific knowledge.[4]

It is necessary to comment briefly on the terms used here to discuss scientific knowledge. As Nathan Sivin has argued, in China "there was no tradition in philosophy or elsewhere of comprehensive discourse on the sciences considered as a single enterprise." He distinguishes between "quantitative sciences, concerned mainly with number and its application to physical reality," which consisted of mathematics, mathematical harmonics, and mathematical astronomy, and "qualitative sciences, application of Five Phases (*wu-hsing*) and other verbal concepts to different realms of human experience," which included medicine, materia medica, alchemy, astrology, geomancy, and physical studies.[5] This chapter focuses on the former category, and especially on mathematics, which will be used to illustrate the discussion of the internal organization of knowledge and modes of study. The terms "science" and "scientific" used here refer not to the concept familiar in the Western context, but to this category of quantitative sciences.

This category can be contrasted to "natural philosophy," which was the framework of the elements of European scientific knowledge introduced into China by the first Jesuits. Natural philosophy refers to a unitary concept of "knowledge about the entire physical universe" that was essential in the European Renaissance worldview.[6] This was not adopted by the Chinese scholars interested in "Western studies" (hsi-hsueh). The classification of knowledge does not seem to have been significantly altered by the inclusion of the new elements coming from outside. Much greater impact was felt on the content of scientific knowledge. Thus, the introduction of Euclidian geometry at the beginning of the seventeenth century provided mathematics and astronomy with new methods, so that quantity (i.e., numbers, as opposed to geometrical objects) became only one aspect of the tools used in these disciplines: this is why I use the term "mathematical" rather than "quantitative." Remarkably, this category is not so different from that covered by the term "mathematics" in eighteenth century Europe: not only astronomy but also mechanics (both theoretical and practical), optics, and navigation (including the construction of boats and marine chronometers) were considered as belonging to the mathematical sciences.[7]

Skill in mathematics and astronomy was not required of scholars in the Chinese tradition. The fact that a significant number of scholars became interested in these subjects is a remarkable feature of intellectual life from the late Ming on. This fact raises such questions as: Why did scholars set out to study mathematical sciences? How much did they actually learn? How did they learn? Did they conceive this study as an aim in itself or merely as a tool for dealing with other issues? What did they apply their knowledge to? These questions are also relevant from the viewpoint of the history of science: in order to assess a particular mathematical or astronomical work, it is obviously necessary to have some understanding of its author's scientific education.

The year 1644 is by no means significant in the history of mathematical sciences from an internalist point of view; the most common periodization considers the Jesuits' arrival in China as the major turning point.[8] However, the dynastic change certainly had some impact on scientific development: the scholars' emphasis on statecraft, which has been analyzed as a response to the fall of the Ming, clearly implied a growing concern for fields such as astronomy and cartography.[9] Moreover, the Ch'ing emperors set up new institutions for the study of mathematics and astronomy. We shall see that a specific imperial policy was adopted in this field by the K'ang-hsi emperor.

During the seventeenth and eighteenth centuries, the study of mathematical sciences took place in two different settings, namely, the imperial court in Peking and the network of academies in the Lower Yangtze region. The existence of two centers of scholarly activity was by no means specific to mathematical sciences but simply reflected the split between scholars and officials that was one of the characteristics of the period. In some respects they were in opposition, but they also interacted constantly through collaboration.[10] Several aspects of this opposition between the imperial court and the academic milieu will appear in this chapter.

One of our major sources is the *Ch'ou-jen chuan* (Notices on mathematicians and astronomers) compiled at the end of the eighteenth century by several scholars under Juan Yuan's patronage. In the following century the book was extended three times.[11] The notices contain some biographical data (when they were available) and brief discussions of the works of the *ch'ou-jen* since antiquity.[12] There are more than two hundred names mentioned for the Ch'ing dynasty alone.[13] *Ch'ou-jen* also include Western authors whose names were known in China. Here, the *Ch'ou-jen chuan* will be used not only as a source of information but also as an indicator of who was recognized as a specialist at the time.

REHABILITATION OF MATHEMATICAL SCIENCES

According to the *Li-chi*, mathematics was one of the Six Arts (together with rites, music, archery, charioteering, and calligraphy) in which a gentleman should be accomplished. As Libbrecht has argued, "Although mathematics was not considered a suitable livelihood for a gentleman, it was among the foremost of the arts of which he was encouraged to become an amateur."[14] Knowledge of mathematics was hardly ever mentioned among prestigious scholars' accomplishments before the late Ming.[15] During the Sui and T'ang dynasties, a small number of officials were trained in mathematics. The textbooks then in use were the *Suan-ching shih-shu* (Ten Mathematical Classics).[16] These officials were minor clerks in charge of solving problems related to taxes and civil engineering. They had to pass special examinations. A scholar preparing for the "standard" examinations had no reason to acquire any knowledge of the *Mathematical Classics*, whereas the career of official mathematicians remained on a much lower level and the study of mathematics did not interact with the main examination system.

Astronomy was heavily loaded with political implications. On the one hand, it was one of the emperor's duties and monopolies to provide the calendar, thus regulating life and harmonizing the rhythm of human activities with that of the Heavens' cycles. On the other hand, it was crucial to predict irregular celestial phenomena and to interpret them in political terms. Astronomical knowledge was by and large restricted to imperial institutions. Since the Han dynasty, there had been official astronomers, who usually received special training rather than being selected from those who succeeded in the general examinations; they worked at the Imperial Board of Astronomy (*Ch'in-t'ien-chien*).[17] Even though there were cases of scholars setting out to study astronomy "privately," such as Chu Tsai-yü in the late Ming, on the whole astronomy was considered an affair of state.[18]

Whereas mathematics and astronomy did not have equal political and ritual significance, they were always closely connected as far as content was concerned: "Mathematics was the servant of the more important sciences of the heaven."[19] Specialists in both disciplines enjoyed little social prestige: they were minor officials in charge of technical aspects of the regulation of Heaven and Earth. During the Sung and Yuan, major developments took place in mathematics, mainly in the field of algebra.[20] In contrast to previous developments, they were brought about outside the imperial institutions by "independent mathematicians," that is, scholars who were not employed as officials in that field. Little is known about this tradition, which seems to have developed during the tenth to the thirteenth centuries.[21] It seems that at the time mathematical knowledge was transmitted from teacher to disciple. By the late Ming, the best part of this tradition, and especially the *t'ien-yuan* algebra, had fallen into oblivion. Similarly, it is often said that there was a decline in astronomy.[22] However, the two disciplines were maintained and some interest in mathematics still existed independently of imperial institutions.

The unprecedented interest in mathematical sciences among scholars during the seventeenth and eighteenth centuries was one aspect of the development of "concrete studies" (*shih-hsueh*); it was linked to the criticism of Neo-Confucianism — more specifically, of cosmology — and to the development of textual studies.[23] Other fields of study included in *shih-hsueh* were more or less correlated with mathematical sciences. Chronology, for instance, played a major role in historical studies, and there were also important developments in geography, both involving the use of mathematical and astronomical knowledge.[24] In this context, the argument usually put forward to justify the study of mathematics was the social usefulness of the mathematical sciences and of their applications, an argument supported by the precedent of Confucian scholars of antiquity. In his preface to Mei Wen-ting's (1633–1721) work on linear algebra *Fang-ch'eng lun* (1690), P'an Lei (1646–1708), Ku Yen-wu's nephew and disciple, states: "The gentlemen of antiquity did not devote themselves to useless studies. The Six Arts that follow the Six Virtues and the Six Behaviors are all concrete studies and suffice to manage the world. Although mathematics is the last of the Arts, it has wide applications. Without mathematics, it is impossible to understand the measurement of Heaven and the survey of Earth; it is impossible to regulate taxes and to manage finances; it is impossible to raise armies and dispose troops; it is impossible to administer civil engineering."[25]

P'an Lei then laments the failure of later generations to follow the example of their forebears so that officials became incompetent in their task of management. P'an Lei himself is said to have had a superficial knowledge of astronomy.[26] His view is not that of a "specialist" defending his own field of study; it is on the contrary representative of the opinion many men of breeding professed at the time.

The argument of social usefulness was by no means a new one: the study of mathematical sciences was part of the return to the essentials of "genuine Confucianism." The meaning of ancient mathematical and astronomical texts was essential in that respect; moreover, the scientific content of all ancient texts was considered as relevant to a thorough understanding of their meaning. Contemporary mathematics and astronomy (including elements of Western origin) were necessary tools for the restoration of this original meaning, and as such they were considered one of the bases of the methodology of documentary studies.[27] On the whole, it can be stated that there was consistency between the discourse and the actual practice.

However, there were limits to the "concreteness" of the scholars' concerns. The scholars were in general more interested in understanding ancient scientific texts—for example, in using mathematics and astronomy for purposes of chronology or cosmological commentaries—than in applying their knowledge to practical concerns. Concrete studies and concern for the public good did not mean going so far as to deal directly with civil engineering. These tasks fell to the lot of officials. The state, rather than scholars, was directly interested in using mathematical sciences for public management. This is one of the above-mentioned oppositions between scholars and the state concerning the relevance of the study of mathematical sciences.

New developments in astronomy stimulated the criticism of traditional cosmology. John B. Henderson noted that the two most famous astronomers of the early Ch'ing, Mei Wen-ting and Wang Hsi-shan (1628–82), were among the leading cosmological critics.[28] One of the arguments put forward by Mei was that astronomical constants should be derived from observations and calculations, not from numerology, if accuracy of the calendar was to be the aim of calendar-makers.[29] Questioning the validity of cosmology as the foundation of astronomy was indeed a blow to the status of cosmology. Although this was not stated explicitly, the interest of many scholars in astronomy was probably linked to their view of it as a tool for criticizing cosmology. This throws a new light on the fact that, whereas astronomy had by and large been a monopoly of imperial institutions until the late Ming, since the early Ch'ing most of the contributors to this field were scholars independent from court patronage: cosmological criticism was an aspect of the contestation of Neo-Confucian state orthodoxy.[30] On the other hand, the calendar established at the Imperial Board of Astronomy following "Western methods" met Mei Wen-ting's demands for accuracy and observational bases, so that one cannot simply contrast a "scientific attitude" among academics to the state orthodoxy.

It seems that the main motivations of scholars' interest in mathematics and astronomy evolved during the seventeenth and eighteenth centuries. The three aspects mentioned above, namely, concern for the social implications of learning underlying "concrete studies," evidential scholarship, and cosmological criticism, were not independent from each other. However, they may have been dominant in turns. Yabuuti has identified the central and most influential figures of Chinese science during that period as being successively Hsu Kuang-ch'i (1562–1633), Mei Wen-ting, and Tai Chen (1724–77); according to Porter, one may add Juan Yuan (1764–1849) to this list.[31] Considering these scholars' approaches to mathematics and astronomy, one could attempt to interpret this list in terms of motivations. In the late Ming the social usefulness of concrete studies seems to have been dominant: Hsu Kuang-ch'i was not only the translator of Western scientific books and the promoter of calendar reform but also the author of a treatise on agriculture administration, the *Nung-cheng ch'üan-shu* (Complete Treatise on Agricultural Administration), which emphasized the role of administration in agricultural development not only by insisting on it as a principle but also by proposing a consistent and applicable agricultural policy (which was never put in practice).[32] Mei Wen-ting owed his influence on early Ch'ing intellectual life to his writings on cosmology as much as to his skill in mathematics and astronomy.[33] Tai Chen's main direct contribution to these fields was his edition of the *Ten Mathematical Classics* as part of the *Ssu-k'u ch'üan-shu* project.[34] Juan Yuan acted as a patron and was the editor of the *Ch'ou-jen chuan*.[35] Tai and Juan are figures of major importance in evidential scholarship, so that their centrality in the mathematical sciences of the eighteenth century can be taken to reflect the correlation between science and *k'ao-cheng* scholarship.[36] Neither is considered a "mathematician" or "astronomer" by today's historians of science, who sometimes deplore the subordination of science to evidential scholarship as a major hindrance to scientific development.[37] This view takes the European pattern of scientific development as the implicit reference. Indeed, the status of the mathematical sciences in Chinese learning determined their style and content, which were not surprisingly quite different from those of the same fields of study in post-Renaissance Europe. This periodization is only tentative: scholars of the same generation approached mathematics and astronomy from different perspectives. Mei Wen-ting himself can be regarded as the initiator of the interest in the history of these disciplines in China. There was also a remarkable evolution in attitudes toward Western learning.

THE RENEWAL OF SCIENTIFIC KNOWLEDGE

After the turn of the seventeenth century, there was a drastic change in the knowledge available in China in the fields of mathematics and astronomy brought about by the introduction of Western science. The first Jesuit missionaries had arrived in China at the end of the sixteenth century; in order to arouse scholars' interest in Christianity, they introduced some elements of European scientific knowledge, mainly in mathematics and astronomy.[38] These elements did not reflect the development of European science at the time; nevertheless, the revival of mathematics and astronomy in China was strongly marked by the missionaries' works.[39]

In the 1630s the Tychonic model was adopted at the Imperial Board of Astronomy and the calendar was reformed accordingly; some of the Jesuits worked as official astronomers.[40] The European scientific knowledge made available to Chinese scholars at that time essentially corresponded to the mathematics and astronomy necessary to work out this calendar reform. The works on astronomy written at the time of the calendar reform gave descriptions and directions for use of some observation instruments of European origin; the theories of the motions of the Sun, Moon, and five planets according to Tycho's system; and the astronomical tables based on these theories together with their mode of construction.[41] The works on mathematics gave the prerequisites for the geometrical model used in astronomy: Euclidian geometry, as well as plane and spherical trigonometry.[42] Also introduced were written arithmetic as a method of calculation and certain instruments of calculation, mainly Napier's bones and Galilean proportional dividers. All these innovations were explained in Chinese works written by the Jesuits, some of which were put together as the Ch'ung-chen li-shu (Astronomical treatises of the Ch'ung-chen reign), comprising 137 chüan, and presented to the emperor in five sets between 1631 and 1635.[43] Other "concrete" subjects such as geography and hydraulics were also represented in books published by the Jesuits.[44] They presented a slightly revised version of the Ch'ung-chen li-shu to the new dynasty as early as 1645 under the title Hsi-yang hsin-fa li-shu (Astronomical treatises according to the new methods of the West). One hundred of the 103 chüan of this collection were published for the first time under the title Hsin-fa suan-shu (Mathematical treatises according to the new methods). This third version, published in 1669, was a major source for academics interested in mathematical sciences.[45]

The introduction of this scientific knowledge provided methods to deal with existing preoccupations; the need for calendar revision had been felt before the arrival of the Jesuits, and some attempts to reform astronomy had already been made.[46] In this context, what the Jesuits provided was a system allowing more accuracy in the calendar and in the prediction of astronomical phenomena. Employing "foreigners" and methods perceived as foreign was not a novelty: since the Yuan there had been Muslim astronomers in Peking. At the beginning of the Ch'ing dynasty, the Board of Astronomy had a Muslim section (*Hui-hui k'e*).[47]

Prior to the Jesuits' arrival in China, mathematics was a rather lively discipline in which the instrument of calculation was the abacus.[48] The Chinese mathematics of that time is sometimes characterized as based on merchant arithmetic. We know of a few treatises on that subject written in the late Ming before the introduction of Western mathematics.[49] This mathematical tradition seems to have flourished in the Lower Yangtze area: the author of the most remarkable of these treatises, Ch'eng Ta-wei, was a merchant and native of Anhwei. His 1592 book the *Suan-fa t'ung-tsung* (Systematic treatise on arithmetic) contained not only the abacus arithmetic necessary for trade but also problems stemming from a tradition that went back to the *Nine Chapters on the Mathematical Art (Chiu-chang suan-shu)* of the first century A.D., even as it ignored thirteenth century algebra.[50]

Western mathematics was based on written arithmetic (*pi-suan*). Its adoption by the Chinese scholars resulted in a major gap between "popular arithmetic" practiced on the abacus (*chu-suan*) and the arithmetic used by scholars versed in mathematical sciences, since the two calculation methods were based on the memorization of different tables.[51] These scholars can be regarded as the continuators of Ch'eng Ta-wei: one may speak of continuity in interests and radical changes in content and methods of mathematical sciences.[52] The fact that abacus arithmetic was not an object of scholarly study and that written arithmetic remained unknown outside scholarly circles until the end of the dynasty reveals the social limits of the spread of the Western methods.[53] The abacus seems to have been used as well by the accountants of the Ch'ing bureaucracy. Western knowledge did not reach account keepers, whether merchants or bureaucrats.

The main interlocutors of the Jesuits changed during the two centuries of their presence in China. Their first disciples in science were scholars as private persons; but after the most famous of these, Hsu Kuang-ch'i, introduced them to the Board of Astronomy to implement the calendar reform, they addressed the official astronomers (their role in teaching in imperial institutions will be discussed below). During the Shun-chih and K'ang-hsi reigns, some Jesuits were at court and had direct contacts with the emperor. This was in accordance with their evangelization policy, since they thought that converting the emperor was the way to christianize China and that science would promote religion. But their influence on scholars interested in mathematics and astronomy declined in the process. At the same time, the attitudes of Chinese scholars toward Western knowledge evolved: they became more critical, while their approach became more syncretic. This attitude reflects the acceptance of

Western science simply as a part of learning and, as such, open to criticism and acceptable in a common corpus with Chinese learning.

Acceptance of the "foreign knowledge" was facilitated by putting forward the idea that Western science had a Chinese origin (*hsi-hsueh chung-yuan*). Mei Wen-ting seems to have been the first to express this idea, which was adopted by the K'ang-hsi emperor—whose promotion of it was an aspect of the imperial approval of Western science—and became generally accepted among eighteenth century scholars. There was more to this idea than mere chauvinism: it was a way of legitimizing the fact that imported knowledge could have the same status as knowledge found in the Chinese tradition. The K'ang-hsi emperor's political motivations can be seen clearly: having understood the usefulness of Western science to government, he who sought reconciliation with the Chinese elite was eager to claim that he was not bringing in anything foreign but rather restoring the most authentic Chinese tradition. Besides that, this idea sometimes had an heuristic value: it helped the interpretation of rediscovered Chinese texts in the light of what had been taught by the Jesuits. Mei Wen-ting himself devoted an important part of his work to the interpretation of Euclidian geometry in terms of *kou-ku*.[54] The idea that Western science originated in China also reveals the value attached to the Jesuits' scientific writings (as opposed to their religious writings) in that the knowledge contained in these writings was considered "civilized"; they were given epistemological status. Juan Yuan also defended this idea in the *Ch'ou-jen chuan*, which Nathan Sivin described as "a programmatic synthesis of traditional and Western astronomy designed to encourage the study of the latter in order to improve the former."[55] In all these cases, the thesis of *hsi-hsueh chung-yuan* was linked to advocating the study of mathematical sciences.[56]

CONTENT AND STRUCTURE

Although there is no account, to my knowledge, of the process of learning mathematical sciences in China, it is possible to describe the content and organization of the knowledge that was studied: the *Lü-li yuan-yuan* (Origins of mathematical harmonics and astronomy), published in 1723, can be taken as representative of the curriculum in the imperial institutions of the eighteenth century. In 1818, the study of mathematics and astronomy at the Academy of Mathematics (*Suan-hsueh kuan*), then a subsection of the Imperial College, took five years, with three years devoted to mathematics followed by two years devoted to astronomy: "Lines, surfaces, and volumes should each be studied for one year. The Sun, Moon, and planets should be studied for two years."[57]

This organization of the studies followed the structure of a part of the *Lü-li yuan-yuan*, which is composed of three parts: the *Li-hsiang k'ao-ch'eng* (Compendium of observational and computational astronomy) with forty-two chapters, the *Shu-li ching-yun* (Collected basic principles of mathematics) with fifty-three chapters, and the *Lü-lü cheng-i* (Exact meaning of the pitch-pipes). The three disciplines dealt with in the encyclopedia constitute the "quantitative sciences" as defined by Nathan Sivin. The *Lü-li yuan-yuan* remained a "classic" for these disciplines well into the nineteenth century; the parts on astronomy and harmonics were revised in the 1740s. Although the encyclopedia contained a lot of knowledge of Western origin, all its compilers were Chinese.

The *Lü-lü cheng-i* consists of five *chüan*: the first two discuss acoustics and harmonics, the next two describe Chinese musical instruments, and the last *chüan* introduces some Western notions on the subject. In 1741, the Ch'ien-lung emperor commissioned his uncle, Prince Yin-lu, and Chang Chao to revise the *Lü-lü cheng-i*. The new work, *Lü-lü cheng-i hou-pien* (Sequel to the exact meaning of the pitch-pipes), was completed in 1746; it consisted of 120 chapters.[58] The sheer size of this revision indicates that much more importance was then attached to the subject than at the time of the publication of the *Lü-li yuan-yuan*.

The *Li-hsiang k'ao-ch'eng* consists of forty-two *chüan* altogether and is divided in three parts. The first part (16 *chüan*) discusses the astronomical notions that were the basis of the calendar. The first *chüan* is a general introduction; *chüan* 2 and 3 are devoted to spherical trigonometry; the movements of the Sun and the Moon are explained in *chüan* 4 and 5, respectively; the next three *chüan* discuss eclipses; *chüan* 9 through 15 deal with the movements of the five planets; *chüan* 16 is devoted to the positions of the fixed stars. The second part (10 *chüan*) introduces the astronomical constants used in the tables; a physical explanation for them is given in the cases of the Sun, Moon, and the five planets as well as the fixed stars. The third part (16 *chüan*) gives the tables of position for the stars and planets; the two last *chüan* give the conversions between ecliptic and equatorial coordinates.

The *Li-hsiang k'ao-ch'eng* relies on the same theoretical basis as the *Ch'ung-chen li-shu*, but all the numerical values given in the tables are different, since the constants used for their computation were corrected according to observations made at the *Ch'ang Ch'un Yuan* after 1714. Some of the technical differences between the two works are taken from the works of Flemish Jesuit Ferdinand Verbiest. Mei Wen-ting's influence is also perceptible in the more critical attitude toward Western science displayed in the *Li-hsiang k'ao-ch'eng*. Thus, the coordinates used are equatorial in accordance with Chinese astronomical tradition and in contrast to the Jesuits' works in which ecliptic coordinates were always used.[59]

Less than twenty years after its publication, the *Li-hsiang k'ao-ch'eng* was revised under the supervision of the Jesuit director of the Board of Astronomy, Ignatius Kögler. The *Li-hsiang k'ao-ch'eng hou-pien* (Sequel to the compendium of observational and computational astronomy) was printed in 1742. While still based on the geocentric system, it introduced the Keplerian elliptic orbits.[60]

I will give a more detailed analysis of the structure of the mathematical part of the encyclopedia, the *Shu-li ching-yun*. Interestingly, this work contained only that mathematical knowledge considered "valid," that is, belonging to a corpus of knowledge in which the elements were related to the whole system by some process (e.g., proof, algorithm). For instance, Jartoux's formulae, which were certainly known to Mei Chueh-ch'eng before 1720, are not mentioned: they were only proved half a century later by Ming An-t'u.[61]

The *Shu-li ching-yun* is not limited to the traditional problem-and-solution form: it also includes definitions, proved statements, geometric constructions, and so on.[62] This is one aspect of the synthesis of Chinese and Western mathematics that characterizes the book. Some parts of the *Shu-li ching-yun* were adapted from lecture notes that the Jesuits had written for the emperor when they taught him mathematics. Thus, the *Chi-he yuan-pen* is a translation of Pardies's *Elémens de Géométrie*, a textbook of Euclidian geometry used in the French Jesuit colleges by the end of the seventeenth century.[63] In other cases, such as linear equations, Chinese traditional methods are explained rather than those taught by the Jesuits.[64] Objects or methods belonging to both traditions are not classified according to a unique hierarchy. For example, in the study of triangles, the Chinese right-angled triangle (*kou-ku*), often regarded as the basis of Chinese geometry, is discussed first.[65] The "general" triangle (*san-chiao-hsing*) is introduced in the next *chüan*, the first paragraph of which shows how the study of any triangle can be reduced to that of a *kou-ku*. But in the rest of the *chüan* the triangle is studied in the context of Euclidian geometry. *Kou-ku* is the traditional Chinese term for right-angled triangle: *kou* and *ku* are respectively the smaller and greater sides of the right angle. This distinction between the two sides was very fruitful in the Chinese mathematical tradition and does not belong to the Euclidian vocabulary.[66] On the other hand, the *kou-ku* is not a subcategory of the category of triangles, as opposed to the Euclidian term *chih-chiao san-chiao-hsing* (lit., triangle with a right angle) elaborated by Ricci and Hsu Kuang-ch'i at the beginning of the seventeenth century.[67] The *Shu-li ching-yun*'s approach to triangles exemplifies the synthesis between Western and traditional Chinese knowledge: here, as in several other parts of the book, Mei Wen-ting's influence is obvious. Chinese mathematicians of the time were able to reason in one or the other system. In the particular case of right-angled triangles, both were described since both were regarded as having a specific mathematical value: the choice of the methods given in the book depended on criteria internal to mathematics, not on their origin.

The *Shu-li ching-yun* is divided in two parts, the first (five *chüan*) containing the "foundations" and the second (thirty-five *chüan* and eight *chüan* of numerical tables) the methods and results derived from these foundations. The first part consists of: "Foundations of Mathematics" (*Shu-li pen-yuan*) (*chüan* 1), "Elements of Geometry" (*Chi-he yuan-pen*) (*chüan* 2 through 4), and "Elements of Arithmetic" (*Suan-fa yuan-pen*) (*chüan* 5). These contents refer to a "dualistic" conception of mathematics considered to be based on geometry and arithmetic. Here again the authors of the *Shu-li ching-yun* were influenced by Mei Wen-ting's ideas.[68] Such a conception was clearly derived from Western ideas: the opposition between discrete and continuous objects (or between number and magnitude) does not appear in the previous Chinese mathematical tradition. It is used to interpret the origin of mathematics according to Chinese tradition. This origin is related in the first *chüan*, which quotes the famous passage of the *Chou-pi suan-ching* (Chou mathematical classic of the Gnomon) from the first century B.C.:

> Of old, Chou Kung addressed Shang Kao, saying: "I have heard that you are versed in the art of numbering. May I ask you how Fu Hsi anciently established the degrees of the celestial sphere? There are no steps by which one may ascend the heavens, and the earth is not measurable with a foot-rule. I would like to ask you, what was the origin of these numbers?"

> Shang Kao replied: "The art of numbering proceeds from the circle and the square. The circle is derived from the square and the square from the rectangle. The rectangle originates from nine-times-nine-is-eighty-one."[69]

In this quotation, mathematics appears once more as a tool used to organize the world through its survey, a task that is part of the imperial function. This dialog refers to the handing over of power from the Shang to the Chou, a transfer of legitimacy that the Manchus put forward as a precedent for their conquest. Heaven and Earth are the two domains in which this science applies and traditionally corresponded to offices for which mathematical skills were needed. This reflects the legitimation of the study of mathematical sciences as a part of Confucian statecraft discussed above.

The term used in the *Chou-pi suan-ching* that is here translated as "rectangle" is *chü* (the carpenter's square); "nine-times-nine-is-eighty-one" is the first sentence of the Chinese multiplication table. The authors of the *Shu-li ching-yun* interpreted this symbolic duality between numbers and figures as a mathematical duality between arithmetic and geometry. They read the last sentence of the quotation as a statement of the equivalence between multiplication and the construction of a rectangle from its sides. Taking this into account, the content of the *Lü-li yuan-yuan* coincides with the scholastic *quadrivium* discussed in Ricci's preface to the *Chi-he yuan-pen*, in which arithmetic is characterized as dealing with the numbering of objects and geometry as dealing with their measurement. Harmonics is then an application of the former while astronomy is an application of the latter.[70] The authors of the *Lü-li yuan-yuan* were certainly acquainted with this text. They interpreted Chinese tradition according to Western notions which allowed them to legitimize this particular Western notion (namely, the duality between arithmetic and geometry) by rooting it in the Chinese tradition; the coincidence between the two classifications of disciplines gives consistency to this 'internalist' argument in favor of the *hsi-hsueh chung-yuan* thesis.

It should be mentioned that the first chapter of the *Shu-li ching yun* also contains discussions of the *Ho-t'u* and the *Lo-shu*. Relying partly on quotations from the *I-ching* as well as from Chu Hsi and Shao Yung, the *Ho-t'u* is taken to be the source of numbers whereas the *Lo-shu* is regarded as the origin of multiplication and division. This idea, which gives mathematics a different source of legitimacy, linking it to Neo-Confucian cosmology and more specifically to its numerological concerns, could be regarded as a tribute to state orthodoxy. However, it does not seem to have any bearing on the mathematical content of the rest of the *Shu-li ching-yun*.

The second part of the *Shu-li ching-yun* is divided into five sections: "Initial Section" (elementary *written* arithmetic), "Section of Lines" (dealing with one-dimensional objects), "Section of Areas" (dealing with two-dimensional objects), "Section of Solids" (dealing with three-dimensional objects), and "Final Section" (dealing mainly with equations in one unknown).[71] Although the names of the three middle sections are taken from Euclidian geometry, the corresponding contents also include numerical objects; when geometrical objects are involved in a question, the criterion of dimension that is applied concerns the method used for solving it (e.g., the degree of the equation involved) rather than the geometrical dimensions of the objects involved. The second part of the *Shu-li ching-yun* is organized according to progressive degrees of difficulty, rather than to subjects. Thus, square root extraction and second-degree equations are explained in the "Section of Areas," while cubic root extraction and third-degree equations are explained in the "Section of Solids." They are found again in the "Final Section," almost word for word. After having dealt with problems of increasing difficulty—a progression that corresponds to the three years mentioned in the syllabus of 1818—the book gives a recapitulation according not to the objects treated but to the general method that actually underlies the different algorithms given in the three former sections. The structure of the book reveals both a reflection on the organization of mathematical knowledge and a didactic concern.

The content of the *Shu-li ching-yun* corresponds to the mathematical knowledge available to scholars at the time; even if they studied in different books, the above description gives an idea of what they had access to when they learned mathematics. The same holds true for the *Li-hsiang k'ao-ch'eng* in astronomy. Both works are the result of elaborations worked out by Chinese scholars after Western and traditional Chinese science had been known to them for more than a century.

THE SETTINGS OF STUDIES

As mentioned before, studies of the mathematical sciences, as of most branches of scholarship, took place both under imperial sponsorship and among scholars working in the milieu of academies. It seems that there was no basic difference in the knowledge that was the object of study in these two backgrounds. However, the purposes of the studies were different: imperial institutions aimed at training competent officials, whereas "independent scholars" who studied mathematical sciences did so because they had come to consider these fields as part of general education.

Imperial Institutions

To some extent Western scientific knowledge had already been adopted at the Imperial Board of Astronomy under the Ming dynasty when the Jesuits had been commissioned to reform the calendar according to the Western method. But the teaching of science was reorganized, taking these new elements into account, as part of the establishment of imperial institutions by the new dynasty. In this context, the compilation of the *Lü-li yuan-yuan* at the end of the K'ang-hsi reign represented the ordering of the corpus of mathematical and astronomical knowledge that was to set the imperial standards in those fields. This is the "internal" aspect of the integration of Western science during the K'ang-hsi reign. The emperor's policy discussed below was crucial for the institutional aspect of this integration.

The calendar based on the Western Method was adopted immediately by the new dynasty because of the need for a reliable calendar as a symbol of legitimacy. This meant that officials had to be trained to maintain it over the years. The teaching of science was mainly connected with two institutions (as it had been during previous dynasties): the Imperial Board of Astronomy and the Imperial College (*Kuo-tzu chien*).[72] Although there is no complete account of the organization of scientific education in these institutions, it is possible to gather a few data on the subject.

In 1644, there were sixty-six Chinese students at the Imperial Board of Astronomy. In 1666, their number increased to ninety-four. They were studying at the Astronomical College (*T'ien-wen suan-hsueh*), the teaching department of the board. In 1668, the K'ang-hsi emperor became interested in the calendar controversy, in which for almost ten years Yang Kuang-hsien and other Chinese officials of the Board of Astronomy had opposed the Jesuits. Yang attacked Western methods of astronomy mainly for the alleged seditious implications of the Jesuits' activities, but also on scientific grounds.[73] The K'ang-hsi emperor managed to have the difference settled by applying what we would call a scientific criterion, giving preference to the method that proved more accurate in prediction. This was a significant step in the young emperor's assertion of personal rule against the Oboi regency. On the other hand, given the imperial monopoly of the calendar and the interpretation of coincidence between predictions and astronomical events as a symbol of a dynasty's legitimacy, the political implications of K'ang-hsi's choice were obvious: it was part of his efforts to establish Ch'ing authority. This episode seems to be the origin of both his personal interest in Western learning and his awareness of the need for some officials competent in technical matters. The training of mathematicians, which he then started to organize, also aimed at the appropriation of Western scientific knowledge by the Chinese.[74] In 1668, an imperial edict was issued: "Celestial phenomena are of great concern. It is necessary that there be men thoroughly versed in them. Make known to the governors and governors general of the metropolitan area and all provinces that they are to proclaim in all the districts they administer that all those well versed in astronomy are to proceed to the capital in order to be examined. They are to serve at the Office of the Board of Astronomy. They shall be promoted in rank according to the same rule as in other ministries."[75]

In 1670, another edict was issued: "From each banner, six Manchu official students are to be selected, and from each Chinese banner four official students. They are to be detached to the sections [of the Board] to study [astronomy]. The accomplished ones are to serve as Erudites. Students of astronomy from Manchu and Chinese banners should send essays to the Imperial College so that some of them may be chosen to fill the vacancies. Han students from the board can also be chosen."[76] The bannermen thus selected studied astronomy alongside the ninety-four Chinese students who were there already. Unfortunately, there is no information available concerning the content of the essays that were the basis for selection of students for the study of mathematical sciences.

It seems that Manchu education put a rather strong emphasis on technical subjects (see also Crossley, chap. 10 of this volume), especially considering their absence in the general examination system. The will to train bannermen in these fields is probably only one aspect of the question of the balance between bannermen and Chinese in the bureaucracy, an important issue at the beginning of the dynasty.[77] However, very few bannermen are known to us among the mathematicians of the Ch'ing dynasty.[78] The reduction of the quota of bannermen among students that took place only a few years after these decrees suggests that there might not have been enough people "well versed in astronomy" in the banners for the initial quota to be respected. According to Verbiest, "for scientific matters the Tartars trust the Chinese more than they trust themselves."[79] The gap between the initial plan and the results in terms of numbers of bannermen competent in the field may simply reflect the fact that the impetus for the study of mathematical sciences derived from preoccupations more familiar to Chinese scholars than to bannermen.

As for the total number of students, Verbiest mentions that at the Board of Astronomy he had from 160 to 200 disciples who sometimes came to listen to his lectures in astronomy. The number of students one can obtain by adding up those in the different edicts mentioned above is about the same. The disciples attended lectures and made astronomical observations in turns. Verbiest does not distinguish between students and more senior officials among those he lectured; he mentions only that they were "of various ranks and grades."[80]

There does not seem to be much information concerning education in mathematical sciences at the Imperial College during that period. It is likely that some students of the Imperial College actually studied at the Board of Astronomy. Before 1662, the students of the Imperial College whose mastery of the Classics was considered unsatisfactory were sent to government departments.[81] In the nineteenth century the science examinations of the Imperial College were common with those of the Board of Astronomy.[82] This practice was very likely maintained during the interval between these two dates. This selection of students reveals a strong hierarchy of disciplines: the study of the mathematical sciences, as a technical subject, was much less prestigious than classical education.

Towards the end of his reign, the K'ang-hsi emperor took a further step to institutionalize the study of mathematics. An academy connected to the Imperial College was created in 1713. A report of 1734 mentions it:

> In the fifty-second year of the K'ang-hsi reign, an Academy of Mathematics was established in the Studio for the Cultivation of the Youth (*Meng-yang-chai*) located in the Ch'ang Ch'un Yuan.[83] A grand minister well versed in mathematics was put in charge of its affairs. The emperor's third son was specially designated to supervise it. Young men from the honorable families of the eight banners were chosen to study mathematics there. In addition, grand ministers and Hanlin academicians, both Manchus and Hans, were appointed to compile the *Shu-li ching-yun* and the *Lü-lü cheng-i*, which were completed, prefaced, and printed in the first year of Yung-cheng's reign [1723]. At the end of the previous dynasty, those who were in charge of astronomy had failed in their task. They had made hardly any verifications, and there were so many mistakes that calculations and measurements went wrong and did not coincide with observations. While regulating these numbers and putting them in order, the teaching should go back to the origins, so that they can be handed down for innumerable years. In the banner schools it is necessary to add sixteen instructors in mathematics. They should teach the students mathematics; from each banner more than thirty gifted students should be put to study mathematics from 1 to 5 p.m.[84]

Jean-François Foucquet, a French Jesuit who was one of the K'ang-hsi emperor's teachers in mathematics and astronomy at that time, also mentions the creation of this academy:

> A kind of school had been established. A select audience would come before [the emperor] every day and he would explain to them himself some proposition from Euclid, enjoying the pleasure of appearing to be skilled in those abstract sciences and delighting in the praise that his new disciples, often without understanding,

would not fail to give him. But this school did not last and was only the beginning of a kind of academy that the emperor then created. He had sought everyone skilled in the different fields of mathematics among Chinese and Tartars, in Peking and in the provinces. The viceroys and great mandarins, in order to pay court to him, introduced the elite of great minds, and the most suitable for sciences. They were brought to him from all directions, mainly young men, in order to constitute the academy we are talking about. He chose more than a hundred of them: learned officials who are in charge of it, calculators, geometers, musicians, astronomers, chosen for all these abilities, to say nothing about a great number of workers who make the instruments. For this troupe [*Ch'ang Chun Yuan*] he set a vast area with many buildings of the *Tchang Tchun Yuen* and established his third son as the head of this new academy.[85]

This guardedly ironical account reveals the K'ang-hsi emperor's personal involvement in the creation of the academy. There are a few scholars whose biographies mention that they learned mathematics from the emperor.[86] In all likeliness, this expression refers to the episode described by Foucquet. Though the emperor's teaching was largely symbolic, it certainly had more significance than a mere court ceremony; it was part of his "self-display" as a scholar. It also meant imperial approval and legitimation of Western mathematics. But it seems that the function of the Academy of Mathematics was similar to that of the *Nan-shu-fang* created in 1677 in that it was a place where the emperor could meet informally with scholars versed in the mathematical sciences and discuss with them.[87]

The evidence we have shows that there was indeed not only study but also systematic *teaching* of mathematics and astronomy in the imperial institutions: the students got their knowledge not merely from books or practice but also from teachers. The Academy of Mathematics had two functions that were closely linked: the training of mathematicians and astronomers (the name of the institution puts an emphasis on mathematics) and the compilation of the *Lü-li yuan-yuan*. This compilation represented not only an unprecedented enterprise of gathering and structuring all scientific knowledge, but also the elaboration of a "classic," intended to become a textbook used in the same way as the *Ten Mathematical Classics* at the Imperial College during the T'ang dynasty.[88]

The role of Jesuits in the teaching of science is difficult to assess. At the Board of Astronomy, supervising the students' training was one of Verbiest's functions. At court, he and his successors became the K'ang-hsi emperor's teachers. Their model for teaching was clearly that of the Jesuit colleges in Europe, where several of them had taught before joining the China mission. Thus, the French Jesuits had established a plan for the study of philosophy by the emperor, including logic, physics (in the Aristotelian sense), and other subjects, and they wrote treatises in Manchu on some of these subjects.[89] The "lecture notes" they wrote for him (in Manchu or in Chinese), some of which were used as a basis for some parts of the *Shu-li ching-yun*, were adapted from textbooks used in Jesuit colleges. Elements of Jesuit scientific education were thus taken up in the imperial institutions.

But on the whole this influence remained secondary. One of the original plans of the French Jesuits was to create in China an academy comparable to the French Académie Royale des Sciences that would provide the latter with scientific data and observations (mainly in astronomy and geography) concerning China.[90] In fact, although they did send reports of their observations to the Académie, the French Jesuits, sent by Louis XIV to the K'ang-hsi emperor with the title of "the King's mathematicians," simply became court savants. Instead of founding new institutions, they became integrated in the preexisting framework.[91] The K'ang-hsi emperor used them in the same way he did Chinese officials, commissioning them to work on specific projects: their most famous achievement certainly was the great map of China.[92] They did supervise the work, but the cartographical techniques they used were never taught to the Chinese.

What the Jesuits actually taught the emperor depended more on his curiosity than on any internal logic. Only that which he approved of was to be adopted by the Chinese working in imperial institutions. His insistence on acting as supreme arbiter of scientific matters was sometimes a hindrance to the transmission of Western learning; this was the other side of the coin. The consequence of his not understanding symbolic algebra when Foucquet tried to teach it to him was that symbolic algebra was never taught at the Academy of Mathematics.[93] It seems that the Jesuits' relationship with the emperor rather limited their influence on the teaching of science at the Academy of Mathematics as far as the choice of subjects and the organization of scientific knowledge were concerned. On the other hand, there are cases of transmission of information from Jesuits to Chinese scholars or of direct collaboration in the eighteenth century, such as the transmission of Jartoux's formulae to Mei Chueh-ch'eng, and the revision of the *Li-hsiang k'ao-ch'eng*.[94]

For the emperor, the use of mathematical sciences in statecraft was not a mere discourse. The making of the map of China is a typical example of what it actually meant to him. The K'ang-hsi emperor studied mathematics and astronomy from the Jesuits during most of his reign and personally saw to it that his sons studied mathematical sciences. He regarded these disciplines not only as a tool for statecraft but also as a part of Confucian education. Prince Yin-chih, the emperor's third son, seems to have been especially versed in them. This is probably why he was designated to supervise the Academy of Mathematics and the *Lü-li yuan-yuan* project in 1713. It was a sign of favor bestowed on him by the emperor and a significant one. A few years later, the Yung-cheng emperor put his brother Yin-lu (the K'ang-hsi emperor's sixteenth son) in charge of the reedition of the *Lü-li yuan-yuan*, which was also a sign of favor (Yin-lu was said to be the emperor's favorite brother).[95] This shows that a lot of prestige was attached to these subjects as well as to more traditional aspects of scholarship that were sponsored at the Ch'ing court.

The creation of the Academy of Mathematics in 1713 seems to have been part of a policy of appropriation of Western knowledge, or in other words an attempt to end dependence on the Jesuits for scientific matters.[96] The fact that there were no Jesuits among the compilers of the *Lü-li yuan-yuan* should also be interpreted in that light.

The students trained in imperial institutions were to become officials. To what extent did specialization in mathematical sciences determine their careers? It is difficult to answer this question, but let us give brief accounts of the careers of four of the compilers of the *Lü-li yuan-yuan*; this will provide some idea of the situation for the generation of those selected to work at the Academy of Mathematics when it was created in 1713. Among the charges held by these four officials, only those requiring technical skills will be mentioned here. The main sources used here are Hummel's *Eminent Chinese of the Ch'ing Period (ECCP)* and the *Ch'ou-jen chuan*, as the space devoted to a scholar in both works reflects the importance he was given in contemporary sources.

Ho Kuo-tsung (?–1766) was a native of Ta-hsing in Shun-t'ien prefecture. "Because the Ho family were astronomers by profession, Kuo-tsung received teaching in mathematics from the emperor. By imperial decision he was given the title of *chin-shih* and was made a Hanlin bachelor [in 1712]."[97] The next year he was appointed editor of the *Lü-li yuan-yuan*. After the project was completed, he held several offices; in particular he was in charge of inspecting water conservancy works. In 1730, he was removed from all offices on the grounds that he had committed errors that resulted in floods.[98] After memorializing to the throne in 1737 on the necessity of revising the *Li-hsiang kao-ch'eng*, he was put in charge of this work, and in 1741 he was put in charge of the revision of the *Lü-lü cheng-i*. After the completion of these revisions he held different offices again, mainly at the Board of Works (*Kung-pu*). In 1755, he was sent to supervise the surveying of the territories newly conquered by the Ch'ien-lung emperor. In 1757, he was ordered to teach, most probably mathematics, at the Palace School for Princes (*Shang-shu-fang*).[99]

Mei Chueh-ch'eng (1681–1763) was a native of Hsuan-ch'eng (Anhwei) and the grandson of Mei Wen-ting. He was recommended to the emperor and given the rank of student of the Imperial College in 1712. He was given the degree of *chü-jen* and then was allowed to take the palace examination without passing the metropolitan examination; he became a *chin-shih* and a Hanlin bachelor in 1715. All these favors were granted to him as a reward for his grandfather Mei Wen-ting's achievements. From 1712 until the K'ang-hsi emperor's death, he worked on the *Lü-li yuan-yuan* at the Studio for the Cultivation of the Youth. Thereafter, he held several offices, none of which seems directly connected with his scientific skills; however, it is worth noting that in 1729 he was sent to supervise the transport of the grain tribute.[100] He participated, together with Ho Kuo-tsung, in the revisions of the *Li-hsiang k'ao-ch'eng* and the *Lü-lü cheng-i*. He also contributed to the *Ming-shih* (Ming dynastic history) by editing the section on astronomy that is attributed to his grandfather.[101]

Ku Tsung (1685–1755) was a Manchu of the Bordered Yellow Banner, the grandson of Gubadai. In 1713, he was selected to study mathematics and to work on the *Lü-li yuan-yuan*. Because of this contribution he was appointed an official in 1722. Among the various charges he held was that of director general for the conservancy of waterways in two different provinces.[102]

Ming An-t'u (?–1765?) was a Mongol of the Plain White Banner. He studied at the Imperial Board of Astronomy, where he seems to have worked for most of his life. He too "received the emperor's teaching in mathematics" and worked on the *Lü-li yuan-yuan* from 1713 to 1723. In the 1740s he was among those who revised the *Li-hsiang k'ao-ch'eng*; according to Ku Tsung, he was the only person at the time (apart from the Jesuits of the Board of Astronomy) who understood the new astronomical tables.[103] In 1751, he was awarded the title of *chin-shih*. In 1755, he was sent to Sungaria to supervise the survey together with Ho Kuo-ts'ung. In 1759, he was appointed director (*chien-cheng*) of the Board of Astronomy.[104] The range of Ming's activities is reminiscent of the definition of "mathematics" at that time in Europe;[105] there, mathematics and not astronomy was considered more important. The Jesuits' reference to the Board of Astronomy as the "Tribunal of Mathematics" reflects this difference in hierarchy.[106]

These four savants all held offices in the Chinese administration without having passed the examinations. Their titles were bestowed on them (three of them were made *chin-shih* by imperial decision) as rewards for scientific work, even though they were not always appointed to posts for which technical skills were required. Being in charge of water conservancy works, land surveying, or grain transport at least involved supervising officials who were using mathematical skills; this implied responsibility, among other things, for mistakes in calculations, as the career of Ho Kuo-tsung reveals. Ming An-t'u, who remained an official astronomer, had the least prestigious position of the four. There is no biographical notice of Ming An-t'u either in *ECCP* or in the first edition of the *Ch'ou-jen chuan*. Fifty years of service in imperial institutions and his participation in the imperially commissioned works did not entitle him to be considered a *ch'ou-jen*. Even though it was not taken into account in the examination system, competence in the mathematical sciences could open the way to an official career; but there was little advantage attached to a career exclusively limited to using this competence. It was not an attractive alternative to a more "standard" career. Dominique Parrenin, a French Jesuit who was in China between 1698 and 1740 and worked at the imperial court summarized this situation nicely: "Those who might distinguish themselves [by their scientific skills] have no reward to expect. One sees in history mathematicians' negligence severely punished; but one sees none whose work has been rewarded or who freed himself from financial worries by his application in observing the heavens. All that those who spend their lives at the Tribunal of Mathematics can hope for is to obtain the best positions at that Board; but the income of these positions hardly provides means for support.... In a word, as the astronomer has nothing to see on earth, he has almost nothing to claim there."[107]

It seems that Ming An-t'u, who in contrast to the three others owed nothing to his family connections, was in the situation described by Parrenin. In the cases of Ho and Mei, their family connections meant that they had already some knowledge of mathematics and astronomy when they entered the imperial institutions (it is mentioned in Mei Chueh-ch'eng's biography that he studied at home as a child).[108] As for Ming and Ku, it is likely that they had studied these subjects as part of their education in bannermen schools (see also Crossley, chap. 10 of this volume). The edicts quoted above mention that "talented men" should be selected. But except for bannermen there were no official or unofficial institutions providing elementary education where such talents could be developed. The study of mathematical sciences outside imperial institutions was pursued in very different conditions.

The Academic Milieu

Among the scholars interested in mathematical sciences that we know of, the majority never studied in the imperial institutions. How widespread were the knowledge and practice of mathematical sciences? Concerning the elementary calculations involved in keeping accounts, Evelyn S. Rawski concludes "the likelihood that the simple rhymed methods presented in arithmetic books, and perhaps some familiarity with the abacus, were fairly widespread even among ordinary citizens who lacked the specialized training given to apprentices in large commercial establishments."[109] This knowledge was, *a fortiori*, available to the literati; it was not, however, a direct first step in learning formal mathematical sciences since these were based on written arithmetic. It seems that mathematical study by scholars often depended on personal initiative. The study of mathematics was usually undertaken by adults who got their knowledge from books and from "masters." This seems to have been the case already in the sixteenth century in the Lower Yangtze region: Ch'eng Ta-wei (who may be taken as representative of the Ming mathematical tradition) mentions that in his youth he had "sought out expert teachers" (we don't know who they were) and then "retired and studied very hard for twenty years." We also know that he collected mathematical books.[110] A few years later, Hsu Kuang-ch'i, Li Chih-tsao (1565–1630), Hsueh Feng-tso (?–1680), and Fang Chung-t'ung (1633–98) also studied privately with Jesuit teachers, the first two with Ricci, the two others with the Polish Jesuit Smogulenski.[111] Apparently, many scholars studied from books because teachers were not easy to find; this was the case for Wang Hsi-shan and also two centuries later for Ting Ch'ü-chung, who complained that he could not find a master.[112]

In China, there is a long tradition of hereditary astronomical charges.[113] In the Ch'ing, family connections were important not only in an official context but also in the academic milieu. From Mei Wen-ting's biography, we know that he used to observe the stars as a child with his father and the teacher of the family school; however, he did not start studying calendrical astronomy and mathematics before the age of twenty-seven; he then learned mainly from books.[114] We know that he studied together with his two brothers. Both of them, as well as his son, his grandson Mei Chueh-ch'eng, and two of his great-grandsons, are mentioned in the *Ch'ou-jen chuan*. The Meis were the most outstanding lineage of *ch'ou-jen*, but there were others: we have seen that Ho Kuo-tsung came from a family of astronomers and Ming An-t'u's son, Ming Hsin, seems to have continued his father's mathematical work.[115] Li Kuang-ti had two brothers and a son mentioned in the *Ch'ou-jen chuan* together with him. However, associations between scholars versed in science were not usually based on family connection.[116]

More than two thirds of the Ch'ing scholars mentioned in the *Ch'ou-jen chuan* were natives of Kiangnan.[117] The specific interest in mathematics that existed there already in the Ming dynasty has been analyzed in light of the economic development of that area as a consequence of the prosperity of merchants. In this respect, there seems to be no reason for dissociating mathematics from other aspects of scholarly activities, especially in a period when it was considered as a part of scholarship. The geographic repartition of *ch'ou-jen* simply reflects that of the academic community.

The Mei lineage seems to have played a crucial role in the transmission of knowledge and in the orientation of the studies. Several scholars of the province of Anhwei learned the mathematical sciences from Mei Wen-ting either directly or indirectly.[118] Thus, Tai Chen probably learned the mathematical sciences from Chiang Yung who had read Mei Wen-ting's works and written a commentary.[119] But Mei's influence was not limited to Anhwei province or even to the Lower Yangtze region. Li Kuang-ti and his brother and son studied with him.[120] *Chüan* 40 of the *Ch'ou-jen chuan* mentions ten scholars (including a woman) who studied either with Mei Wen-ting or from his works; two of them are said to have traveled more than one thousand *li* to become his disciples.[121] It is not clear whether mathematical sciences were a "speciality" of Anhwei, but there is no doubt that the Mei clan, and later Tai Chen, all natives of Anhwei, had an overshadowing influence on that particular field of studies all over the country and were associated with the Wan-nan school to which a significant number of scholars interested in mathematics and astronomy were linked.[122]

The way in which Mei Wen-ting influenced his contemporaries and later generations illustrates the process of transmission of scientific knowledge among academics at the time: they learned from books and could sometimes discuss with a "master," but there were no specific institutions for the study of mathematical sciences; they were part of the scholarship circulated among academics. In some cases the subject was taught in academies: Ch'ien Ta-hsin (1728–1804) taught mathematics when he was director of the Tzu-yang Academy in Soochow.[123] But the existence of such courses seems to have depended on the interests and competence of the teachers, and there was no systematic course on the subject. It is not surprising then that, contrary to the situation in the imperial institutions, there was no such thing as a standard curriculum in mathematics and astronomy; nor is there known to be any description of the method and progression of the study for any of the scholars who studied outside imperial institutions.

However, one suggestion can be made concerning the style of mathematical books: in their analysis, one should consider the way in which they were used, especially as textbooks, and the way in which teachers and students worked with them. The fact that the traditional concision of algorithmic texts gave way to a more explanatory style (most mathematical texts contained justifications and explanations) in the seventeenth and eighteenth centuries is usually interpreted as an influence of the Euclidian style in mathematics. But other factors could also have contributed to this change of style, among them particularly the development of evidential scholarship. Commentaries of previous works on mathematics and astronomy were the most common form of writing among scholars interested in these fields, which is in keeping with the general trend of scholarship of the time. Besides, the production of self-contained books may be related to the fact that, in the absence of teachers, they represented the only source of knowledge and understanding available to students. Ch'eng Ta-wei's *Suan-fa t'ung-tsung* (1592), written in a context in which the study of mathematics had to be pursued essentially from books, already contained definitions as well as descriptions of the setting out of operations on the abacus. The change of style is already perceptible in this book. The Euclidian proofs in the Jesuits' books may not have been the most decisive factor in the evolution of the scientific writings.

From what has been said before, it is clear that the two environments in which study of mathematical sciences took place were continuously connected. In the late Ming, Hsu Kuang-ch'i, who had learned Western science from the Jesuits, introduced them to the court, and Western astronomy became institutionalized as the basis for the new calendar. During the early Ch'ing and especially during the K'ang-hsi reign, mathematicians and astronomers were recommended to the court. Thus, Mei Wen-ting was given audience several times by the emperor; the *Lü-li yuan-yuan* is marked by his influence. He had been recommended by Li Kuang-ti, who acted as his patron. Conversely, no scholar gained reputation as an expert in mathematical sciences among Lower Yangtze scholars by studying or working in the imperial institutions. Competent scholars were attracted toward the court because no collective projects were sponsored elsewhere.

THE STATUS OF MATHEMATICAL SCIENCES
AND OF THE *CH'OU-JEN*

The word *ch'ou-jen* is found in the *Shih-chi*, where it refers to the hereditary officials in charge of calendar making.[124] The use of the term by Juan Yuan seems to emphasize the idea of transmission of knowledge from generation to generation; those he considers as *ch'ou-jen* were not all officials, and being an official astronomer did not necessarily entitle one to be regarded as a *ch'ou-jen*.[125] On the contrary, the *ch'ou-jen* of the Ch'ing dynasty formed a group that can be opposed to official astronomers: whereas they belonged to the literati milieu, less than half of them ever held an official position.[126] Some historians of science contrast *ch'ou-jen* to officials concerning skill in mathematical sciences: considering as "astronomers" only those who contributed to "scientific progress," they conclude that only one fifth of them were officials, while those "whose achievements were the most outstanding" were not.[127] The comparison of the *Ch'ou-jen chuan* with today's historiography of Chinese science shows how strongly the modern notion of scientific progress determines the assessments of past scientific works. Whatever may be the case, the criteria for considering a scholar as a *ch'ou-jen* are not very clear: one extreme case is that of P'an Lei, who is mentioned in an appendix to the notice on his elder brother P'an Cheng-chang only to inform readers that due to the casualness of his study he did not master the calendar thoroughly.[128] Yet we have seen that in the preface he wrote to one of Mei Wen-ting's works P'an Lei strongly advocated the study of mathematics: his attitude towards mathematical sciences cannot be judged only from his personal achievements.

There is a detailed notice on Juan Yuan in the third edition of the *Ch'ou-jen chuan*.[129] Although he has left no mathematical or astronomical writings strictly speaking, as a patron he played a central role among the *ch'ou-jen* of his time. His attitude toward mathematics and astronomy had a decisive influence: "His efforts marked the culmination of an ongoing process whereby the value of mathematics and astronomy was reaffirmed as part of a Confucian education."[130] This affirmation, rather than scientific progress, was the major stake of the period. But this does not mean that there was no idea of progress in scientific knowledge. In astronomy, the conception of progress was not limited to acquiring more precise numerical data but included a theoretical evolution.[131] When Ming An-t'u's mathematical work was published in 1839, it was praised as unprecedented, as contributing something new to the field; this entitled Ming An-t'u to be eventually mentioned in the second edition of the

Ch'ou-jen chuan. There is still no mention of Ming An-t'u's contribution in astronomy, which was part of his official duties, as opposed to his mathematical work, which represented "private research." The notice mentions only that he was director of the Board of Astronomy.[132] The fact that his mathematical work was prior to that of Tung Yu-ch'eng on the same subject (1819) was considered as important at the time: innovation in mathematics and in astronomy was highly regarded and priority was significant.[133] This notion of progress was not limited to mathematical sciences: the cumulative aspect of evidential research was clearly perceived.[134] But while the restoration of the Chinese scientific tradition was regarded as of utmost importance, innovation was not explicitly pointed out as an aim of the study of mathematics and astronomy.[135] Neither was the scientific education in the imperial institutions meant to produce innovative scholars in the field; the aim was simply to fulfill the need for officials competent in technical matters.

Did *ch'ou-jen* have a special status among scholars? Jonathan Porter has used the term "scientific community," arguing that *ch'ou-jen* had "a distinct self-image as scientific specialists and a sense of identity with an intellectual community."[136] But it is questionable whether they actually perceived themselves as forming a specific group within the academic community. They were simply a part of it, and regarded by other scholars as especially well versed in a particular branch of learning. Mathematics and astronomy were indeed specific branches of knowledge and were regarded as such, but they were not opposed to other branches of scholarship as in the European conception of scientific versus humanistic knowledge.[137] They had become elements in a whole that included phonology, epigraphy, archeology—all fields with "a shared epistemological perspective.[138] A methodology based on "independent and objective criteria" was not the prerogative of mathematical sciences, but rather characterized all the disciplines included in evidential scholarship.[139] In other words, the integration of the mathematical sciences in scholarly studies in late imperial China is more a matter of redefinition of learning than a new conception of "science" as distinguished from other types of learning. Despite an unprecedented revaluation of their status, mathematical sciences did not stand as an alternative, much less a rival, to classical learning.

NOTES

I wish to thank Gregory Blue, Elisabeth Hsü, and Nathan Sivin for their helpful comments and criticism on an earlier version of this chapter.

1. Joseph Needham, *The Grand Titration: Science and Society in East and West* (Toronto: University of Toronto Press, 1969), 16; Joseph Needham, *Science and Civilisation in China* (hereafter *SCC*) (Cambridge: Cambridge University Press, 1954).

2. "It is surprising that this ingenious nation never went beyond the elements of geometry, that they were ignorant of semitones in music, that their astronomy and all

their sciences were at the same time so ancient and so limited. It seems as if nature had given to this species of men, so different from ours, organs formed for discovering all at once whatever was necessary for them, and incapable of going any further. We on the contrary have made our discoveries very late; but we have been quick in bringing things to perfection." Voltaire, *Essai sur les moeurs et l'espirit des nations et sur les principaux faits de l'histoire depuis Charlemagne jusqu'à Louis XIII* (Paris 1756; trans., Edimburgh, 1782), 1:16.

3. For a critical discussion of this approach, see Nathan Sivin, "Why the Scientific Revolution Did Not Take Place in China—Or Didn't It?," *Chinese Science* 5 (1982): 45–66.

4. For a brief description of Chinese science in that period, see Kiyosi Yabuuti, "The Main Current of Chinese Science in the 17th and 18th Centuries," in *Prismata: Naturwissenschaftsgeschichtliche Studien*, ed. Y. Maeyama and W.G. Saltzer (Wiesbaden: Franz Steiner Verlag GmbH, 1977) 449–56.

5. Nathan Sivin, "Introduction," in *Science and Technology in East Asia*, ed. Nathan Sivin (New York: Science History Publications, 1977), xii–xiii.

6. Willard J. Peterson, "Western Natural Philosophy Published in Late Ming China," *Proceedings of the American Philosophical Association* 117, no. 4 (1973): 295–322. Ideas of science changed rapidly in Europe, so that the Jesuit missionaries who were in China during the early and middle Ch'ing sometimes had quite different visions.

7. This is taken from the table of contents of Etienne Montucla, *Histoire des mathématiques*, 4 vols. (Paris, 1797–1800).

8. According to Needham, "The year 1600 is the turning point, after which time there ceases to be any essential distinction between world science and specifically Chinese science," *SCC* 3:437. Although not all historians agree on such a strong statement, they all consider the coming of the Jesuits as a break in the history of the mathematical sciences. See Shigeru Nakayama, "Periodization of the East Asian History of Science," *Revue de Synthèse* 4, no. 3–4 (1988): 375–79.

9. See Benjamin A. Elman, *From Philosophy to Philology: Intellectual and Social Aspects of Change in Late Imperial China* (Cambridge, Mass.: Harvard University Press, 1984), 53–54.

10. On imperial sponsorship and the relationship between scholars and the state in the early Ch'ing, see Kent Guy, *The Emperor's Four Treasuries: Scholars and the State in the Late Ch'ien-lung Era* (Cambridge, Mass.: Harvard University Press, 1987), 16–25.

11. Juan Yuan 阮元, *Ch'ou-jen chuan* 疇人傳 (hereafter *CJC*) 8 vols. (Shanghai: 1935). The successive versions were completed in 1799, 1840, 1886, and 1898. Li Yan and Du Shiran, *Chinese Mathematics: A Concise History*, trans. J.N. Crossley and A.W.C. Lun (Oxford: Clarendon Press, 1987), 232–33. See Wang P'ing 王萍, "Juan Yuan yü Ch'ou-jen chuan" 阮元與疇人傳 (Juan Yuan and the *Ch'ou-jen chuan*), *Chung-yang yun-chiu-yuan chin-tai-shih yen-chiu-so chi-kan* 4: 601–11 (1974).

12. In the present study the term *ch'ou-jen* refers to scholars whose competence in the mathematical sciences was acknowledged by their contemporaries. With a few exceptions, these scholars are mentioned in one of the editions of the *Ch'ou-jen chuan*.

13. Jonathan Porter, "The Scientific Community in Early Modern China," *Isis* 73 (1982): 529–44, esp. 530.

14. Ulrich Libbrecht, *Chinese Mathematics in the Thirteenth Century: The Shu-shu chiu-chang of Ch'in Chiu-shao* (Cambridge, Mass.: MIT Press, 1973), 4.

15. There were remarkable exceptions such as Shen Kua (1031–95) and Chu Tsai-yü (1531–1610?). Nathan Sivin, "Shen Kua," in *Dictionary of Scientific Biography*, ed. Charles Gillispie, 16 vols. (New York: Charles Scribner's Sons, 1970–80); "Chu Tsai-yü," in *Dictionary of Ming Biographies*, ed. L. Carrington Goodrich, 2 vols. (New York: Columbia University Press, 1976).

16. Robert Des Rotours, *Traité des fonctionnaires et de l'armée, traduit de la nouvelle histoire des Tang*, 2 vols. (Leiden: Bibliothèque de l'Institut des Hautes Études Chinoises, 1932), 456–58; Li Yen 李儼, "T'ang Sung Yuan Ming shu-hsueh chiao-yü chih-tu" 唐宋元明數學教育制度, in *Chung-suan-shih lun-ts'ung* 中算史論叢 (Peking: Chung-kuo k'e-hsueh yuan, 1955) 4: 253–85.

17. There had been an office of astronomy and astrology since the Han dynasty; *SCC*, 3:186–94. In the late Ming and Ch'ing, it was called *Ch'in-t'ien-chien*. On its organization, see Porter, "Bureaucracy and Science in Early Modern China: The Imperial Astronomical Bureau in the Ch'ing Period," *Journal of Oriental Studies* 18 (1980): 64–65.

18. Willard Peterson, "Calendar Reform Prior to the Arrival of Missionaries at the Ming Court," *Ming Studies* 21 (1986): 49—54.

19. Libbrecht, *Chinese Mathematics*, 4. The "Chinese remainder theorem" (Ch'in Chiu-shao's *ta-yen* rule, thirteenth century) is a striking example of a significant development of mathematics stemming from the concerns of astronomy. Libbrecht, *Chinese Mathematics*, 367–69.

20. Ch'ien Pao-ts'ung 錢寶琮, ed., *Sung-Yuan shu-hsueh shih lun-wen chi* 宋元數學史論文集 (Collected papers on the history of mathematics in the Sung and Yuan (Peking: K'e-hsüeh ch'u-pan-she, 1966).

21. Only the work of four mathematicians of the thirteenth century are extant.

22. *SCC*, 3:206.

23. As for the meaning of "concrete studies," let us give an example. In the academy directed by Yen Yuan (1635–1704) at the end of the seventeenth century, military training, strategy, archery, boxing, mechanics, mathematics, astronomy, and history were among the disciplines taught; Jacques Gernet, *Le monde chinois* (Paris: Armand Colin, 1972), 439. On the criticism of cosmology, see Elman, *From Philosophy to Philology*, 53–56, John B. Henderson, *The Development and Decline of Chinese Cosmology* (New York: Columbia University Press, 1984), 150–55.

24. Benjamin A. Elman, "Geographical Research in the Ming-Ch'ing Period," *Monumenta Serica* 35 (1981–83): 1–18.

25. Jean-Claude Martzloff, *Recherches sur l'oeuvre mathématique de Mei Wending (1633–1721)* (Paris: Collège de France, Institut des Hautes Études Chinoises, 1981), 19–20.

26. Arthur Hummel, ed. *Eminent Chinese of the Ch'ing Period* (hereafter *ECCP*) 2 vols. (Washington: United States Government Printing Office, 1943–44); *CJC*, 448.

27. Elman, *From Philosophy to Philology*, 180–84.

28. Nathan Sivin, "Wang Hsi-shan," in *Dictionary of Scientific Biography*.

29. Henderson, *Chinese Cosmology*, 144–45, 166–67.

30. Chiang Hsiao-yuan 江曉原, "Shih-ch'i shih-pa shih-chi Chung-kuo t'ien-wen-hsueh ti san-ke hsin t'e-tien" 十七十八世紀中國天文學的三個新特點 (Three new characteristics of the seventeenth to eighteenth century Chinese astronomy), *Tzu-jan pien-cheng-fa t'ung-hsun* 10, no. 3 (1988): 53–54.

31. Yabuuti, "Main Current"; Porter, "Scientific Community," 541. Analyzing the network of relationships between *ch'ou-jen*, Porter takes Ch'ien Ta-hsin, not Tai Chen, to be the central figure of his time.

32. Francesca Bray, "Agriculture," pt. 2 of *Biology and Biological Technology*, vol. 6 of *Science and Civilization in China*, ed. Needham, 70.

33. Henderson, *Chinese Cosmology*, 144.

34. Li and Du, *Chinese Mathematics*, 226–30.

35. Elman, *From Philosophy to Philology*, 108–11.

36. Elman, *From Philosophy to Philology*, 83–85.

37. Chiang, "San-k'e hsin t'e-tien, 55–56. Yabuuchi Kiyoshi 藪內清, *Chūgoku no kagaku to Nihon* 中國の科學と日本 (Chinese science and Japan) (Tokyo: Asahi Shinbunsha, 1978), 162–63.

38. Catherine Jami, *Les Méthodes Rapides pour la Trigonométrie et le Rapport Précis du Cercle (1774): Tradition chinoise et apport occidental en mathématiques* (Paris: Collège de France, Institut des Hautes Études Chinoises, 1990), 23–25.

39. They gave a rather outdated and in some respects quite distorted image of European science. This was especially true in astronomy, due to the religious implications of the heliocentric theory, which was not introduced in China before the second half of the eighteenth century. Nathan Sivin "Copernicus in China," *Studia Copernica* (Warsaw) 6 (1973): 76–82, 89–92.

40. Keizo Hashimoto, *Hsü Kuang-ch'i and Astronomical Reform: The Process of the Chinese Acceptance of Western Astronomy 1629–1635* (Osaka: Kansai University Press, 1988), 77–103.

41. The difference between the Tychonic system and the Aristotelian worldview first introduced by Ricci was not stated very clearly in the Jesuits' writings. Sivin, "Copernicus in China," 78.

42. The first six books of Euclid's *Elements of Geometry* had been translated into Chinese from Clavius's Latin version (Rome: Vincentius Accoltus, 1574) by Matteo Ricci and Hsu Kuang-ch'i in 1607. Other geometrical treatises were included in the *Ch'ung-chen li shu*. See Pasquale D'Elia, "Presentazione della prima traduzione cinese di Euclide," *Monumenta Serica* 15, no. 1 (1956):161–202. Li and Du, *Chinese Mathematics*, 204.

43. Henri Bernard-Maître, "L'encyclopédie astronomique du Père Schall," *Monumenta Serica* 3 (1938): 35–77, 441–527; Hsu Tsung-tse 徐宗澤, *Ming-Ch'ing Yeh-su hui-shih i-chu t'i-yao* 明清耶穌會士譯著提要 (Bibliography of the Jesuits' writings in the Ming and Ch'ing) (Taipei: Chung-hua shu-chü, 1958), 239–56, gives an annotated list of the works included in the *Ch'ung-chen li-shu*.

44. Henri Bernard-Maître, "Les adaptations chinoises d'ouvrages européens: bibliographie chronologique," *Monumenta Serica* 3 (1938): 35–77, 441–527; Hsü Tsung-tse, *Ye-su hui-shih t'i-yao*, 289–326.

45. Chiang, "Shih-ch'i shih-pa shih-chi Chung-kuo t'ien-wen-hsueh te san-ke hsin t'e-tien," 52–53.

46. Peterson, "Calendar Reform."

47. Porter, "Bureaucracy and Science," 66–67.

48. In contrast to earlier periods, when counting rods were used. Li and Du, *Chinese Mathematics*, 6–19.

49. On the *Nine Chapters on the Mathematical Art*, the most important of the *Ten Mathematical Classics*, see Li and Du, *Chinese Mathematics*, 33–56. For a description of abacus arithmetic and a bibliography of Ming treatises on the subject, see Li Yen 李儼 , *Chung-kuo shu-hsueh shih ta-kang* 中國數學史大綱 (General outline of Chinese mathematics) 2 vols. (Peking: K'e-hsueh ch'u-pan-she, 1958), 315–74.

50. Li and Du, *Chinese Mathematics*, 185–89.

51. Evelyn S. Rawski, *Education and Popular Literacy in Ch'ing China* (Ann Arbor: University of Michigan Press, 1979), 125–28; Catherine Jami, "Rencontre entre arithmétiques chinoise et européenne aux XVIIe et XVIIIe siècles," in *Histoire de Fractions, Fractions d'Histoire*, ed. P. Benoit, K. Chemla, and J. Ritter (Basel: Birkhäuser, forthcoming).

52. Chang Ping-lun 張秉倫 , "Ming-Ch'ing shih-ch'i An-hui ti k'e-hsueh fa-chan chi ch'i t'ung-yin ch'u-hsi" 明清時期安徽的科學發展及其動因初析 (Scientific development of Anhwei in the Ming and Ch'ing and its causes), *Tzu-jan pien-cheng-fa tung-hsun* 7, no. 2 (1985): 39–48.

53. Rawski, *Education and Popular Literacy*, 52–53. Today both methods are taught in Chinese schools, and the most efficient use of the abacus involves combining both types of tables.

54. Martzloff, *Mei Wending*, 246–49. Mei Chueh-ch'eng reconstructed the *t'ien-yuan* algebra as an equivalent to the *chieh-ken-fang* algebra: there were several Chinese transcriptions of the Latin word "algebra" (derived from the Arabic "al-jabr") such as *a-er-je-pa-la* and *a-er-je-pa-ta*. The Jesuits told the K'ang-hsi emperor that this word was of oriental origin, so Mei Chueh-ch'eng concluded that it was Chinese. Rita H. Peng, "The Kangxi Emperor's Absorption in Western Mathematics and Astronomy and His Extensive Application of Scientific Knowledge," *Li-shih hsueh-pao* 3 (1975): 382–84.

55. Sivin, "Copernicus in China," 99–100.

56. Chiang Hsiao-yuan 江曉原 , "Shih-lun Ch'ing-tai 'Hsi-hsueh Chung-yuan' shuo" 試論清代西學中源說 (Thesis of the "Chinese origin of Western science" in the Ch'ing period), *Tzu-jan k'e-hsueh shih yen-chiu* 7, no. 2 (1988):101–8.

57. *Ch'in-ting Ta-Ch'ing hui-tien* 欽定大清會典 (1899), 76:15b.

58. *ECCP*, under "Yin-lu" and "Chang Chao."

59. At that time in Europe, ecliptic coordinates were gradually replaced by equatorial coordinates. *SCC*, 3:438. Other astronomical works written by Jesuits after the *Ch'ung-chen li-shu* were also taken into account in the *Li-hsiang k'ao-ch'eng*. For a more detailed analysis of this work, see Hashimoto Keizō 橋本敬造, "Rekishō kōsei no seiritsu" 曆象考成の成立 (Origin of the *Compendium of Observational and Computational Astronomy*), in *Min-Shin jidai no kagaku gijutsu shi* 明清時代の科學技術史 (History of science and technology in the Ming and Ch'ing periods), ed. Yabuuchi Kiyoshi 藪內清 and Yoshida Mitsukuni 吉田光邦 (Kyoto: Institute for Humanistic Studies, 1970), 49–92.

60. Sivin, "Copernicus in China," 90–91. On Ignatius Kögler (1680–1746), see the biographical notice in Louis Pfister, *Notices biographiquse et bibiliographiques sur les jésuites de l'ancienne mission de Chine 1552–1773*, 2 vols. (Shanghai, 1934), 643–51.

61. Jami, *Les Méthodes Rapides*, 42–45.

62. Most of the *Ten Mathematical Classics* are divided into chapters, each chapter consisting of a few groups of problems, each group of problems corresponding to an algorithm usually given at the end of the list of problems and solutions for which it is to

be used. Karine Chemla, "La pertinence du concept de classification pour l'analyse des textes mathématiques chinois," *Extrême-Orient Extrême-Occident* 10 (1988): 61–87, gives an interesting interpretation in mathematical terms of the way in which problems and algorithms are grouped. The same form was used in mathematical books until the translation of Euclid's *Elements* into Chinese in 1607.

63. *Chüan* 2 through 4 of the first part of the *Shu-li ching-yun* have the same title as the translation of Euclid's *Elements*. The French Jesuits used Pardies's textbook to teach the K'ang-hsi emperor geometry. I.G. Pardies, *Elémens de Géométrie où par une méthode courte et aisée l'on peut apprendre ce qu'il faut savoir d'Euclide, d'Archimède, d'Apollonius et les plus belles inventions des anciens et nouveaux géomètres* (Paris, 1671). Peng, "The Kangxi Emperor's Absorption," 370, gives a list of the sources of the *Shu-li ching-yun*.

64. *Shu-li ching-yun*, 2:10.

65. *Shu-li ching-yun*, 2:12–14.

66. Karine Chemla, "Du parallélisme entre énoncés mathématiques: Analyse d'un formulaire rédigé en Chine au XIIIe siècle," *Revue d'Histoire des Sciences* 43(1990): 57–80.

67. Catherine Jami, "Classification en mathématiques: la structure de l'encyclopédie *Yu Zhi Shu Li Jing Yun* (1723)," *Revue d'Histoire des Sciences*, 42(1989): 391–406, 397.

68. Hashimoto Keizō, "Mei Wending and His Dualistic Idea in Mathematics," in *Proceedings no. 3: XIVth International Congress of the History of Science* (Tokyo: Science Council of Japan, 1974), 288–90.

69. *SCC*, 3:22. See Li and Du, *Chinese Mathematics*, 25–32.

70. Jami, "Classification en mathématiques," 399.

71. The algebra used there is nonsymbolic. Symbolic algebra was not known to Chinese mathematicians until the second half of the nineteenth century. Li and Du, *Chinese Mathematics*, 257.

72. Adam Y. Lui, "The Imperial College (*Kuo-tzu-chien*) in the Early Ch'ing (1644–1795)," *Papers on Far Eastern History* 10 (1974): 147–66; Porter, "Bureaucracy and Science."

73. Jacques Gernet, "Visions chrétienne et chinoise du monde au XVIIe siècle," *Diogène* 105(1979): 93–115, 105–7; Lawrence Kessler, *K'ang-hsi and the Consolidation of Ch'ing Rule 1661–84* (Chicago: University of Chicago Press, 1976), 59–60.

74. Kessler, *K'ang-hsi*, 58–64.

75. *Ch'in-ting Ta-Ch'ing hui-tien shih-li* (1899), 1103:2a.

76. *Ch'in-ting Ta-Ch'ing hui-tien shih-li*, 1103:2a.

77. Kessler, *K'ang-hsi*, 112–24.

78. In that respect, the Mongol astronomer Ming An-t'u, whose career is discussed below, was quite exceptional.

79. Ferdinand Verbiest (1623–88) was the main defender of the Western methods during the calendar controversy. After that he served at the Board of Astronomy until his death and was one of the K'ang-hsi emperor's teachers. Noël Golvers and Ulrich Libbrecht, *Astronoom van de keizer: Ferdinand Verbiest en zijn Europese Sterrenkunde* (Leuven: Davidsfonds, 1988), 146.

80. Golvers and Libbrecht, *Astronoomv van de keizer*, 146, 181.

81. Lui, "Imperial College," 159–60.

82. *Ch'in-ting Ta-Ch'ing hui-tien*, 76:4b; the edict was issued in 1818.

83. At the *Meng-yang-chai*, books were compiled and edited under imperial supervision; Porter, "Bureaucracy and Science," 63. The astronomical observations on which the *Li-hsiang k'ao-ch'eng* was based were made there.

84. *Chin-ting Ta-Ching hui-tien shih-li*, 1102:10b–11a.

85. Jean-François Foucquet, *Relation exacte de ce qui s'est passé à Péking par raport à l'astronomie européane depuis le mois de juin 1711 jusqu'au commencement de décembre 1716*. Manuscript (Archivum Romanum Societatis Iesu, Jap. Sin. II 154), 3.

86. It is the case for Mei Chueh-ch'eng, Ho Kuo-tsung, and Ming An-t'u, whose careers are discussed below. *CJC*, 486, 518, 623.

87. Guy, *Four Treasuries*, 20. Foucquet, *Relation exacte*.

88. Li and Du, *Chinese Mathematics*, 92.

89. Joachim Bouvet, *Histoire de l'empereur de la Chine* (The Hague: Meyndert Uytwerf, 1699; reprint, Tientsin, 1940), 99–107.

90. Pfister, *Notices biographiquse*, 420–23.

91. The manuscript Jap. Sin. 165 ff. 100-2, Archivum Romanum Societatis Iesu, contains one of these reports. Some of them were published in the *Lettres édifiantes et curieuses de Chine par des missionnaires jésuites*, 34 vols. (Paris, 1702–73).

92. Theodore N. Foss, "A Western Interpretation of China: Jesuit Cartography," in *East Meets West: The Jesuits in China, 1582–1773*, ed. C.E. Ronan and B.B.C. Oh (Chicago: Loyola University Press, 1988), 209–51.

93. This is one of the events related in Foucquet, *Relation exacte*.

94. Jami, *Les Méthodes Rapides*, 40–41; Sivin, "Copernicus in China," 91.

95. According to *ECCP* (under "Yin-chih" and "Yin-lu"), it seems that Yung-cheng tried to transfer to Yin-lu the credit of supervising scientific activities, partly to revenge Yin-chih's antagonism in the fight for succession.

96. This is reflected in Foucquet's account by the way he describes the third prince as "the enemy of European astronomy."

97. *CJC*, 518.

98. Water conservancy was a typical example of civil engineering to which mathematics were traditionally applied in China; chapters of several of the *Ten Mathematical Classics* are devoted to calculations for construction. Li and Du, *Chinese Mathematics*, 34, 101–2.

99. *ECCP*.

100. As water conservancy, this was a charge involving the application of mathematics. The *Ten Mathematical Classics* contain problems dealing with grain tributes. Li and Du, *Chinese Mathematics*, 34.

101. See Mei Ku-ch'eng's notices in *ECCP* and *CJC*.

102. *ECCP*, 271.

103. Sivin, "Copernicus in China," 91.

104. Li Ti 李迪, *Meng-ku-tsu k'e-hsueh-chia Ming An-t'u* 蒙古族科學家明安圖 (The Mongol scientist Ming An-t'u) (Huhehot, 1978).

105. Montucla, *Histoire des mathématiques*.

106. See e.g., letter from Fr. Dominique Parrenin to the director of the French Académie des Sciences, Peking, 11 August 1730, in I. and J.L. Vissière, eds., *Lettres édifiantes et curieuses de Chine par des missionnaires jésuites: 1702–1776* (Paris: Garnier-Flammarion, 1979), 360. Voltaire knew of this letter when he wrote the passage quoted in n.3.

107. Vissière, *Lettres édifiantes*.

108. *CJC*, 485.

109. Rawski, *Education and Popular Literacy*, 127.

110. Li and Du, *Chinese Mathematics*, 186; Jean-Claude Martzloff, *Histoire des mathématiques chinoises* (Paris: Masson, 1988), 156.

111. Li and Du, *Chinese Mathematics*, 193, 196, 204. Fang Chung-t'ung was the son of Fang I-chih.

112. On Wang, see Sivin, "Copernicus in China," 73; on Ting, see Martzloff, *Histoire des mathématiques chinoises*, 79.

113. Astronomy already appears as a familial charge in the myth of Emperor Yao commanding the Hsi and Ho families—each composed of three brothers—to observe the stars and make the calendar, which is found in the *Shu-ching*. See *SCC*, 3:186–88.

114. *CJC*, 459.

115. *CJC*, 626–27, compares them to their famous predecessors Tsu Ch'ung-chih and his son Tsu Keng (fifth century A.D.); cf. Li and Du, *Chinese Mathematics*, 80–87.

116. According to Porter's analysis of the Ch'ing scholars mentioned in the *Ch'ou-jen chuan*. Porter, "Scientific Community," 539–40.

117. Porter, "Scientific Community," 540.

118. Chang Ping-lun, "An-hui ti k'e-hsueh fa-chan," 39.

119. Benjamin A. Elman, "Ch'ing Dynasty 'Schools' of Scholarship," *Ch'ing-shih wen-t'i* 4, no. 6(1981): 16; Elman, *From Philosophy to Philology*, 205.

120. Kuo Chin-pin 郭金彬, "Ch'ing-tai Pa-min shu-hsueh lueh-lun" 清代八閩數學略論 (Outline of Fukien mathematics during the Ch'ing), *Tzu-jan pien-cheng-fa t'ung-hsun* 6, no.2 (1984): 66.

121. Chiang Hsiao-yuan, "Shih-ch'i shih-pa shih-chi Chung-kuo t'ien-wen-hsueh ti san-ke hsin t'e-tien," 51.

122. Elman, "Ch'ing Dynasty 'Schools' of Scholarship," 16.

123. *ECCP*, 152.

124. Li and Du, *Chinese Mathematics*, 232.

125. On Ming An-t'u's case, see Li and Du, *Chinese Mathematics*, 28. His disciple Ch'en Chi-hsin, who completed his mathematical work and was one of the editors of the mathematical parts of the *Ssu-k'u ch'üan-shu*, is not mentioned in the first edition of the *Ch'ou-jen chuan* either. His name appears together with that of his master in the second edition. Since Ming's name is mentioned among those of the compilers of the *Lü-li yuan-yuan*, and Ch'en's name is mentioned in the *Ssu-k'u ch'üan-shu*, it is very unlikely that the compilers of the *Ch'ou-jen chuan* did not know of them.

126. Porter, "Scientific Community," 539–40. Unfortunately, Porter does not distinguish between the different positions held concerning the scientific and technical competence that they required.

127. Chang Pin-lun "An-hui ti k'e-hsueh fa-chan," 53; Sivin, "Copernicus in China," 100.

128. *CJC*, 448.

129. *CJC*, 749–54. The third edition of the *Ch'ou-jen chuan* was published in 1868 by Chu K'e-pao.

130. Elman, *From Philosophy to Philology*, 63.

131. Henderson, *Chinese Cosmology*, 165–68; Hashimoto, *Hsü Kuang-ch'i and*

Astronomical Reform, 34–36.

132. *CJC*, 623–27.

133. Jami, *Les Méthodes Rapides*, 178–80. See the preface to the *Ch'ou-jen chuan*. Elman, *From Philosophy to Philology*, 221–22.

134. Elman, *From Philosophy to Philology*, 204–7.

135. See, e.g., Juan Yuan's preface to Ming An-t'u's work. Jami, *Les Méthodes Rapides*, 17.

136. Porter, "Scientific Community," 539.

137. In the philosophy section of the *Ssu-k'u ch'üan-shu*, one subsection is devoted to astronomy and another to mathematics.

138. Elman, *From Philosophy to Philology*, 38–39.

139. Porter, "Scientific Community," 542. Many of the specificities considered by Porter as attached to the sciences are actually also found in evidential scholarship at large.

GLOSSARY

a-er-je-pa-la	阿爾熱巴拉	Fu Hsi	伏羲
a-er-je-pa-ta	阿爾熱八達	Hashimoto Keizō	橋本敬造
Anhwei	安徽	Ho	何
Chang Chao	張照	Ho Kuo-tsung	何國宗
Ch'ang Ch'un Yuan	暢春園	*Ho-t'u*	河圖
Ch'en Chi-hsin	陳際新	Hsi	羲
Ch'eng Ta-wei	程大位	*hsi-hsueh*	西學
Chi-he yuan-pen	幾何原本	*hsi-hsueh chung-yuan*	西學中源
Chiang Yung	江永	*Hsi-yang hsin-fa li-shu*	西洋新法曆書
chieh-ken-fang	借根方	*Hsin-fa suan-shu*	新法算書
chien-cheng	監正	Hsu Kuang-ch'i	徐光啟
Ch'ien-lung	乾隆	Hsuan-ch'eng	宣城
Ch'ien Ta-hsin	錢大昕	Hsueh Feng-tso	薛鳳祚
chih-chiao san-chiao-hsing	直角三角形	*Hui-hui k'e*	回回科
Ch'in Chiu-shao	秦九韶	*I-ching*	易經
Ch'in-t'ien-chien	欽天監	Juan Yuan	阮元
Chiu-chang suan-shu	九章算術	K'ang-hsi	康熙
Chou Kung	周公	*k'ao-cheng*	考證
Chou-pi suan-ching	周髀算經	*kou*	句
ch'ou-jen	疇人	*kou-ku*	句股
Ch'ou-jen chuan	疇人傳	*ku*	股
Chu Hsi	朱熹	Ku Tsung	顧琮
Chu K'e-pao	諸可寶	Ku Yen-wu	顧炎武
Chu Tsai-yü	朱載堉	*Kung-pu*	工部
chu-suan	珠算	*Kuo-tzu-chien*	國子監
Ch'ung-chen li-shu	崇禎曆書	*Li-chi*	禮記
chü	矩	Li Chih-tsao	李之藻
Fang-ch'eng lun	方程論	*Li-hsiang k'ao-ch'eng*	曆象考成
Fang Chung-t'ung	方中通	*Li-hsiang k'ao-ch'eng*	曆象考成
Fang I-chih	方以智	*hou-pien*	後編

Li Kuang-ti	李光地	Shun-chih	順治
Lo-shu	洛書	*Shun-t'ien*	順天
Lü-li yuan-yuan	律曆淵源	*Suan-ching shih-shu*	算經十書
Lü-lü cheng-i	律呂正義	*Suan-fa t'ung-tsung*	算法通宗
Lü-lü cheng-i hou-pien	律呂正義後編	*Suan-fa yuan-pen*	算法原本
Mei Chueh-ch'eng	梅瑴成	*Suan-hsueh kuan*	算學館
Mei Wen-ting	梅文鼎	*Ssu-k'u ch'üan-shu*	四庫全書
Meng-yang-chai	蒙養齋	Ta-hsing	大興
Ming An-t'u	明安圖	*ta-yen*	大衍
Ming Hsin	明新	Tai Chen	戴震
Ming-shih	明史	*T'ien-wen suan-hsueh*	天文算學
Nan-shu-fang	南書房	*t'ien-yuan*	天元
Nung-cheng ch'üan-shu	農政全書	Ting Ch'ü-chung	丁取忠
P'an Cheng-chang	潘檉章	Tsu Ch'ung-chih	祖沖之
P'an Lei	潘耒	Tsu Keng	祖恒
pi-suan	筆算	Tung Yu-ch'eng	董祐誠
san-chiao-hsing	三角形	Tzu-yang	紫陽
Shang Kao	商高	Wan-nan	皖南
Shang-shu-fang	上書房	Wang Hsi-shan	王錫闡
Shen Kua	沈括	*wu-hsing*	五行
Shao Yung	邵雍	Yang Kuang-hsien	楊光先
Shih-chi	史記	Yao	堯
shih-hsueh	實學	Yen Yuan	顏元
Shu-ching	書經	Yin-chih	胤祉
Shu-li ching-yun	數理精蘊	Yin-lu	胤祿
Shu-li pen-yuan	數理本原	Yung-cheng	雍正
Shu-shu chiu-chang	數術九章		

EIGHT

Tai Chen and Learning in the Confucian Tradition

Cynthia J. Brokaw

Scholars are generally agreed that the eighteenth century was not one of the more fertile periods in the history of Chinese philosophy. By mid-century, "evidential research" (*k'ao-cheng*) was on its way to becoming the dominant trend within the highest intellectual circles. The great scholars of the day devoted themselves to exacting philological study of the Classics and other ancient texts, consciously and often self-righteously eschewing consideration of the philosophical questions—about the nature of man and the universe, the source of good and evil, and the process of self-cultivation—that had guided the great thinkers of the Confucian tradition in their interpretations of the Classics. Tai Chen (1724–77) was one of the rare exceptions to this trend: among the great *k'ao-cheng* advocates of the eighteenth century, he stands out as perhaps the only scholar to develop an original moral philosophy (*i-li*). In the face of the skepticism and outright criticism of his fellow *k'ao-cheng* researchers, he propounded from a fresh reading of the Classics, particularly *Mencius*, a new view of the structure of the universe and the path to perfect knowledge and virtue.

As was the case with most previous Confucian and Neo-Confucian thinkers, learning was the central issue in Tai's new philosophy. Of course, Tai's principles of education derived from his metaphysics and to some degree can be explained only in terms of his metaphysical views. But the primary goal of his writing was the explication of the way to sagehood, the route the student aspiring to perfect wisdom and perfect goodness had to take. What are the proper objects of learning? What are the correct methods of study? What is the relationship between knowledge and goodness? What is the final purpose of study? These are the questions that shaped Tai's philosophy.

Tai developed his program of learning to a considerable degree in resistance to two competing views of education: the program of learning associated with the Ch'eng-Chu school of Neo-Confucianism and the view of true learning upheld by scholars of the *k'ao-cheng* movement. Well before Tai's birth, the curriculum of the Ch'eng-Chu school had achieved the status of state orthodoxy when it became, in 1313, the foundation of the civil service examination system. Despite attacks by many prominent eighteenth-century thinkers, the philosophy of the Ch'eng-Chu school remained very influential simply because it dominated the conventional educational system: anyone who aspired to pass the examinations had to be familiar with Ch'eng-Chu teachings. On the other hand, the *k'ao-cheng* movement, whose adherents were devoted to the rescue of the true meaning of the Classics from what was perceived as centuries of careless interpretation by Neo-Confucian scholars, attracted the major intellectuals of the day. Tai, refusing to rely exclusively on either, drew on both of these main educational trends of the mid-Ch'ing, the orthodox learning long associated with the Ch'eng-Chu school and the new, supposedly more accurate and concrete, scholarship advanced by leading contemporary thinkers.

Tai Chen, like most scholars of the eighteenth century, received his first education in orthodox Neo-Confucianism. Tai studied with a follower of the Ch'eng-Chu school, Chiang Yung (1681–1762), and his early letters and writings express some admiration for Sung Neo-Confucianism. (The fact that Tai was from Hui-chou, Anhwei, Chu Hsi's [1130–1200] native prefecture, might also have strengthened his ties to this brand of Confucianism.)[1] But as early as 1755, in a letter to Fang Hsi-yuan (n.d.), Tai was beginning to voice criticisms of Ch'eng-Chu scholars. Foreshadowing his later, more open attacks, he complained that in their classical scholarship they had neglected the study of institutions and regulations for the sake of moral philosophy.[2] Thereafter, his criticism of Ch'eng-Chu Learning, at least as it was expressed in the Ch'ing educational system, gradually increased in intensity. His first full work of moral philosophy, *Yuan shan* (On the Good, 1766), expounded ideas inconsistent with Neo-Confucian orthodoxy, though it did not openly challenge the views of the Ch'eng-Chu thinkers. Tai then explicitly announced his differences with the orthodox school in all of his other philosophical works: his two preliminary studies of the *Mencius*, the *Hsu-yen* (Clues to the Way, 1769) and the *Meng-tzu ssu-shu-lu* (Account of indirect learning from *Mencius*, 1772); and his final masterpiece, the *Meng-tzu tzu-i shu-cheng* (Elucidation of the meaning of words in *Mencius*), completed just months before his death in 1777.[3] In these, he held the Ch'eng-Chu school and its continuing impact on education responsible for the failure of contemporary scholar-officials to fulfill their Confucian task of "bringing peace to the world." According to Tai, the Sung Neo-Confucians' sloppy readings of classical texts and their tendency to speculate wildly on these readings led them to propound a highly distorted moral vision, one that not only betrayed the message of the sages, but also encouraged the creation of a scholarly elite skilled at the manipulation of Neo-Confucian ideas to suit their own selfish interests, almost always at the expense of the common people. It is fair to say that Tai formulated his own view of what learning was in part to counter the damaging influence of the "empty speculations" of the Sung Neo-Confucians on the Classics and to develop a new system that might succeed, in their place, in creating a ruling elite of sages—or, at least, a sage —genuinely committed to the welfare of the people.

In the accomplishment of the first of these goals—the perfectly accurate understanding of the Classics—Tai had the wholehearted support of the *k'ao-cheng* movement. Indeed, he was considered one of the leading practitioners of *k'ao-cheng* scholarship in his own day, celebrated by Ch'ien Ta-hsin (1728–1804), Chu Yun (1729–81), Chi Yun (1724–1805), and Wang Mingsheng (1722–98) for his studies of the *Chou-li* (Rites of Chou), mathematics, phonology, dialects, and the *Shui-ching chu* (Annotated classic of waterways), among others.[4] Tai's program of learning was to a degree an exaltation of the value of *k'ao-cheng* scholarship; as we shall see, he made it the way to the attainment of sagehood. How then can it be said that he was resisting the *k'ao-cheng* movement in the formulation of his program of learning?

The problem lies in the fact that Tai put *k'ao-cheng* practice to a use not approved by his colleagues—namely, the creation of a moral philosophy. Tai's first considerable attempt to derive morally significant philosophical interpretations from *k'ao-cheng* study of the Classics, two essays on the concept of human nature in the *I-ching* (Book of changes) and *Mencius*, were dismissed as "empty talk of moral philosophy, better not done at all" by Ch'ien Ta-hsin and Chu Yun.[5] Indeed, Tai's philosophical writings were generally seen by his contemporaries as awkward reversions to the mistaken concerns of the Sung Neo-Confucians. But for Tai, the distinction, even opposition, that his colleagues drew between philology and philosophy was false. It was not simply that he believed (along with the forerunners of the *k'ao-cheng* movement) the goal of philology to be philosophy; Tai's stand was more radical than that. For him, philology, properly practiced, was philosophy: as we shall see, he believed that exact knowledge of the meaning of the Classics automatically revealed moral truth.

This unusual view helps us to make sense of the course of Tai's work, of his persistent efforts, despite criticism, to define a program of moral learning at the same time that he was pursuing philological research. He had certainly begun his first philosophical work, *Yuan shan*, by 1757, the year he first met Hui Tung (1697–1758) and became an enthusiastic admirer of this leader of the school of Han Learning. He continued to write philosophy through the 1760s until 1777, the year of his death; yet for much of this period he was also producing works of *k'ao-cheng* scholarship. What most contemporaries saw as vacillation between "good," solid *k'ao-cheng* scholarship and "empty" philosophizing becomes, once we understand Tai's views, evidence of a coherent intellectual program merging the practice of philology and the attainment of sagehood.

The purpose of this chapter is to reconstruct that program from the comments on learning in Tai's mature philosophical work, the *Meng-tzu tzu-i shu-cheng*, occasionally drawing as well on earlier writings and letters, but only when these works illuminate points made in his final work. The *Meng-tzu tzu-i shu-cheng* is organized as a series of discursive examinations of philosophical terms—*li, t'ien-tao, hsing, ts'ai,* and so forth. Tai demonstrates, in each entry, what he believed the true meaning of the term in question to be — that is, what its meaning was for Mencius and Confucius — and how the Sung Neo-Confucians distorted the sense of the term. The text does not present a coherent "system" of philosophy, nor does it explicitly outline a neat program of learning. To understand Tai's views on learning, then, it is necessary to piece together comments made in the *Meng-tzu tzu-i shu-cheng* and other writings, to reconstruct the assumptions about the goals and methods of education that underlie Tai's efforts to rectify Confucian philosophical terminology.

In taking the reconstruction of Tai's program of learning as a goal here, I have not attempted to provide an explanation of his philosophy as a whole, but rather, have simply summarized those aspects of his philosophy that are essential to an understanding of this program. Nor have I attempted to provide an extensive critique either of his general philosophy or of his program of learning. There is, admittedly, much to question in Tai's thought — his attacks on the Sung Neo-Confucians are sometimes unfounded, his own definitions of terms (most notably of *li*) are sometimes inconsistent, and his interpretation of *Mencius* is no more accurate than the one he criticizes. I have, to be sure, raised a number of problematic points in the notes; in the body of this chapter, however, I have chosen to concentrate on explicating Tai's views on learning and their place in contemporary scholarly discourse.

Tai's views on learning have little representative value — apparently very few contemporaries either sympathized with or understood his philosophy.[6] Rather, his views are significant because they reflect the efforts of one of the great minds of the Ch'ing to reformulate a Neo-Confucian program of learning (or, as Tai would have insisted, to return to a Confucian program) that would lead the serious student to an understanding of the truths of the Classics and hence to reform of social and political institutions. Tai is interesting and important for the history of Chinese educational ideas because he attempted to follow through on the broad claims of the *k'ao-cheng* movement, to apply the techniques of learning embedded in evidential research to the education of a new Confucian sage.

TAI CHEN'S PROGRAM OF LEARNING

The basic goal of Tai Chen's program of learning is the fulfillment of the potential goodness that lies in man's nature: the tranformation, to put it in Tai's own words, of "what is naturally so in man" (*tzu-jan*) to "what is necessarily so" (*pi-jan*) — that is, to moral perfection. What is naturally so in man is given him as his nature through the ceaseless transformations of *ch'i* (cosmic pneuma, material force), through the constant process of producing and reproducing that is the Way.[7] Tai, like most late Ming and Ch'ing thinkers, identifies *ch'i* as the primary stuff of the universe, the source of all things, and ultimately, through its transformations in the Way, the source of all goodness.[8] For there is no doubt that for Tai, as for most Confucians, the process of creation is in substance good: "the process of producing and reproducing is humaneness (*jen*)," he affirmed.[9]

This means of course that man's nature — what is naturally so in him — has potential goodness in it.[10] It also has its own principle or pattern, its own *li* (or its "principle of differentiation," *fen-li*), the unchangeable rule that it follows when it realizes its potential for goodness and becomes "what is necessarily so." This principle, existing in each man and thing, derives from the pattern (*t'iao-li*) that governs the ceaseless production and reproduction of the Way, and brings order to what would otherwise be an entirely random and arbitrary process:

> As for heaven and earth, people and creatures, events and actions, I have never heard of any that can be said to be lacking principle. The *Shih-ching* (Book of odes) says, "If there are things, there are standards (*tse*)." "Things" refers to actual objects and actual events; "standards" refers to their purity and rectitude. Actual objects and actual events are what is naturally so. When they tend toward what is necessarily so, then they acquire the principles of heaven and earth, people and creatures, events and actions. No matter how vast heaven and earth are, how numerous people and creatures are, or how varied and complex events and actions are, if each acquires its principle — as something straight might accord with the plumb line, as something round with the compass, as something square with the measuring square — then forever after it remains standard for them, even if applied to everything under heaven for thousands of generations.[11]

The principle of each thing is what it follows when it fulfills its own nature most completely and properly, when it transforms what is naturally so into what is necessarily so.[12]

Tai claims that what is naturally so in man and what is necessarily so are simply different aspects of man's nature: "What is necessarily so and what is naturally so are not two separate matters. What is necessarily so is just man's exhaustive and utterly flawless understanding of what is naturally so. In this state, he has no regrets and is at peace — this, then, is what the worthies and sages call what is naturally so."[13] The purpose of education, generally stated, is to lead man to this "thorough and flawless understanding" of the Way so that he can realize fully the potential goodness in him. It is learning that enables man to realize the goodness ("what is necessarily so") of his nature ("what is naturally so").

For Tai Chen, this realization is not so easy a task as it might at first seem: if man is born with the potential for perfect goodness and his own principle for realizing that potential, education might appear to be a natural process of increasing self-knowledge. But Tai argues that barriers to this process arise quite commonly through errors in the functioning of human nature in the world. Human nature "unfolds" or manifests itself differently in each man through his physical substance or body (*hsueh-ch'i*), reflecting the solid "fact" (*shih*) of his existence and distinctness from other things, and his mental faculty (*hsin-chih*), representing his individual ability or talent (*neng*).[14] These two components are in turn the source of man's functions: desire (*yü*), feeling (*ch'ing*), and perception (*chih*). The physical being produces desire (which distinguishes sounds, colors, smells, and tastes) and feeling (which distinguishes joy, anger, sorrow, and pleasure). The mental faculty produces perception, which distinguishes beauty from ugliness and truth from falsity, and if cultivated properly, yields knowledge or wisdom (*chih*). Desire, feeling, and perception are all seen as potentially good, for they are the channels through which men have contacts with the things of the world. Tai explains:

> Man is born with desire, feeling, and perception; these three are what is naturally so of the physical being and the mental faculty. Desire allows the recognition of sounds, colors, smells and tastes; it is through these that a man develops love and fear. Feeling allows expression of joy, anger, sorrow, and happiness; it is through these that a man develops anxiety or a sense of ease. Perception distinguishes ugliness, truth, and falsity; it is through these that a man develops likes and dislikes. The desire for sound, color, smell, and taste aid in the nourishment of life; the feelings of joy, anger, sorrow, and happiness move man into contact with other things; the perception of beauty and ugliness, truth and falsity, when completely fulfilled, enables a man to comprehend heaven and earth and the spirits.[15]

For Tai Chen, then, a man's desire, feeling, and perception are all equally functions of his nature, his endowment of *ch'i*; and all are equally essential to his functioning in the world.

Tai goes even further — he insists that these functions of the nature are the means through which goodness is realized in man. Arguing against what he perceives to be the orthodox Neo-Confucian devaluation of desire in particular, he claims that desire (and, for that matter, feeling and perception) is a source of moral principle. He explains: "The world survives only because the Way of production and nourishment has not been abandoned. All activity comes from desire; if there is no desire, there is no activity. Only when there is desire is there activity; and activity that conforms to what is most proper and unchanging is known as principle. Where would principle be if there were no desire or activity?"[16] The same holds true for feeling; *li* or principle exists in feeling when it is perfectly measured:

Principle is feelings that are not mistaken; it is impossible to fulfill principle if feelings are not fulfilled. Whenever you do something to other people, you should reflect seriously on your action: "Would I be able to accept this if someone did it to me?" Whenever you give someone a responsibility to fulfill, reflect seriously on your action: "Would I be able to fulfill this responsibility if someone asked it of me?" Principle is manifested when you use the measure of the self in dealing with others. Those who speak of heavenly principle speak of it as the principle of differentiation of what is naturally so.... [This principle operates] when you use your own feelings to measure the feelings of others and there are none that are not equitably balanced.[17]

Thus for Tai, desire and feeling, if expressed in accord with a common standard of reasonableness, are both the manifestations of virtue in man, the means through which he develops what is naturally so within him to what is necessarily so.

The problem—and the need for education—arises because of the disjuncture that may exist between what is naturally so and what is necessarily so. The very functions that express the potential goodness of man are also the potential source of his wrongdoing and evil. If desire, feeling, or perception suffer any kind of imbalance—that is, if they are either overindulged or repressed—then they may lead man astray. A failure to regulate one's desires, to make them correspond to the reasonable desires common to all people, results in selfishness (*ssu*).[18] It is clear that, for Tai, denial of desires, for the reasons summarized above, will result in selfishness just as surely as overindulgence of desires will. Overindulgence of desires means that a man has lost sight of the common human ground of desires—those "reasonable" desires shared by all people—and thus has violated what is natural within him. But denial of desires is equally dangerous, for it renders one insensitive to the "natural" and "reasonable" needs of others. Here Tai sets himself in opposition to the orthodox Neo-Confucian view presented in Chu Hsi's suggestion that the aspiring sage "follow the principle of heaven and expel human desires."[19] This advice is folly for Tai Chen, for it would result in the production of a sage uncomprehending of basic human needs, and thus incapable of fulfilling these needs. Claiming support from Mencius, Tai argues:

When Mencius says, "Nothing is better for nourishing the mind than reducing desire," it is clear that one cannot be completely without desires, but that one should simply reduce them. In human life, there is nothing worse than lacking the means to live. Desiring to live in such a way that one allows others to live as well is humaneness. Desiring to live, but to the point that you ignore the harm you do to others' lives, is evil. This evil certainly arises from the desire for life; if there were no longer this desire, then there would no longer be this evil. But if there were no longer this desire, then all people in the world would view unmoved the extinction of life. There is no feeling that enables one to allow others to live without necessarily wanting to live oneself.[20]

Thus the denial of desires would produce, not men with greater compassion for the people, but, rather, men incapable of imagining the value of life itself, both for themselves and others.

The feelings, too, require the same kind of attention as desires: both natural and potentially good, their appropriate expression is necessary to the attainment of genuine goodness. And, as with desires, the denial of feelings is just as dangerous as overindulgence of feelings: it is, Tai points out, the feeling of compassion for others (the ability to empathize with another's desire for life and fear of death) that moves a man to rescue the child from the well in Mencius's famous story. Without such a feeling, goodness becomes impossible. Failure to regulate one's feelings so that they are neither repressed nor overindulged causes partiality or one-sidedness (p'ien).[21]

Finally, there is the danger of failure in perception. Failure in perception results in the beclouding or obstruction (pi) of goodness and inevitably leads to errors in judgment and, ultimately, in action. Tai summarizes these three different "failures":

> The failure of the function of desire causes selfishness, and selfishness then leads to greed and depravity. The failure of the function of feeling causes prejudice, and prejudice leads to perversity and unreasonableness. The failure of the function of knowledge causes obstruction, and obstruction leads to error and mistakenness. If there is no selfishness, then the desires are all in accord with humanity, propriety, and righteousness; if there is no prejudice, then the feelings will necessarily be harmonious and easy, equable and altruistic; if there is no obstruction, then perception will achieve what is known as intelligence and sagely wisdom.[22]

The functions of man's nature thus take a key place in Tai's views on education. Education is necessary as a means of guiding these functions to full goodness; thus they serve as the objects of education in Tai's philosophy.

How is man able to avoid the "failures" of selfishness, partiality, and obstruction? The quality of man's nature that makes it possible for him to avoid or correct these failures is his mental faculty or hsin-chih, which governs the function of perception, the ability to acquire and apply knowledge and to make distinctions and judgments. By extension, this faculty rules the other functions of desire and feeling as well, for it is the function of perception that enables a man to regulate his desires and feelings properly: "Only when the desires and feelings are supplemented by perception do these desires gain fulfillment and these feelings gain expression."[23] Here Tai seems to be very close to both Sung and Ming Neo-Confucians (not to mention Hsun-tzu), in insisting on the power of the mind, and in particular its capacity for knowledge, to lead man to a knowledge of what is right. Indeed, Tai attributes an almost magical power of illumination and enlightenment to the mental faculty, suggesting that knowledge automatically reveals the right as a light illuminates form:

All things that have physical form have spiritual qualities. The spiritual qualities of the mind vary in degree. It is like a fire whose light shines on things: if the light is small, and it illuminates only what is close by, it will not mistake what it illuminates; what it does not illuminate is what it will perceive incorrectly.... Not perceiving incorrectly is called fulfilling principle. If the light of the fire is great, it will illuminate what is far away, and will usually fully realize principle, only rarely mistaking it. But it is not only a question of close by or far away; even when light reaches its object, there is the difference of clarity or obscurity. For this reason, there is the choice of investigating things or not investigating them. Those who investigate things exhaust the truth of things, while not investigating leads to mistaken perceptions of them. Mistaken perception is called "losing principle." Those who have lost principle are limited by the cloudiness of their substance, what is called stupidity. Only through study can you correct your inadequacies and advance toward wisdom, improving continuously until you reach your maximum. Then your brightness will equal that of the sun and moon and your light will necessarily extend everywhere — then you will have become a sage.... Therefore principle and righteousness are nothing other than what is illuminated and investigated without error.... How can principle and righteousness be divided as if they formed one separate thing sought outside of what is illuminated and investigated?[24]

Just as a light illuminates forms, so does knowledge — almost automatically, it appears — "light up" moral principle, clearly pointing the path that man must follow. Tai argues elsewhere that a man who simply tries to be good will fail without the necessary amount of knowledge: "It is true that when the sages and worthies discussed conduct, they strongly emphasized the virtues of loyalty, faithfulness, and reciprocity. But when we consider a man's quality and management of affairs, we find that if his learning is inadequate, then this inadequacy in knowledge will cause errors in conduct. Even though there is nothing disloyal, unfaithful, and lacking in reciprocity in his intention, he has nonetheless severely harmed the Way."[25]

It is man's mental faculty, this ability to learn, that sets the human species off from all others: "[Other] creatures are incapable of comprehending the correct standards of heaven and earth; therefore, they lack internal restraints and each simply follows what is natural to it. Man has knowledge of the heavenly virtues and is able to follow these correct standards."[26] Only man is able to distinguish what is naturally so from what is necessarily so — that is, necessary to the fulfillment of human nature through the actualization of its potential goodness. It is study that makes a man good: as the student accumulates factual knowledge (particularly of the Classics), he is also accumulating his knowledge of moral principles.[27]

Tai develops, then, a very intellectual and scholastic solution to man's moral dilemma: knowledge truly maketh the man. (This scholastic solution contrasts fascinatingly with the more simple optimism about universal innate moral sense that characterized the thought of less scholastic mass educators like

Ch'en Hung-mou in the 1700s; see also Rowe, chap. 12 of this volume). What, though, of people whose misfortune it is to be born with limited mental faculties? According to Tai, differentiation is part of the process of production; by fate, each being is endowed with a different quality of physical substance and mental faculty. As a result, some people are simply born less intelligent or less perceptive than others. Are these stupid men barred from the necessity and even the possibility of education? If use of the mental faculty leads to knowledge and ultimately to goodness, does stupidity doom man to evil?

Tai denies that this could be the case. While he admits that intelligent people have an advantage — their mental faculties are sharper and therefore it is easier for them to see goodness — it is by no means impossible for those with more limited abilities to improve and eventually achieve the knowledge necessary for sagehood.[28]"Stupidity is not evil," Tai asserts. For knowledge of the appropriate sort is not acquired simply through possession of a keen mind: as Confucius himself argued, it requires both study (*hsueh*) and reflection (*ssu*). A man who neglects study and reflection will lapse into evil no matter how intelligent he is. So, too, a man endowed by fate with limited mental faculties can, through hard study and careful reflection, achieve goodness.[29] Man, unlike other creatures, is capable of change: "Even though the world has never lacked extremely stupid men, whose abilities approximate those of creatures, in the end they are nonetheless different from creatures in that there are none who cannot change."[30] Thus, education is essential for the realization of moral necessity in man: men endowed with high intelligence must keep up the habit of study and reflection or they will lapse into evil; men not so endowed must work hard to expand their talents, studying to become good.

What kind of knowledge enables men to realize the moral necessity of their natures? For Tai, students have to learn the principles of the natures of various things so that they suffer from no obstruction in their conduct of affairs. The investigation of things is "knowing a thing's nature correctly without error and thinking thoroughly about it without neglecting the minutest point." The "extension of knowledge" (*chih-chih*) results from this process: free of delusion himself, "a man can manage the affairs of his household, his country, and the whole empire without regret."[31] Since man's own nature is potentially good, he alone has the ability to understand moral principle from his study of the principles of things: "The mind is capable of understanding principle and righteousness. Heaven's transformation of *ch'i* is the ordered process of producing and reproducing. Man and things are differentiated in the process of the transformations of *ch'i* and each entity develops its own nature. If the nature is pure, then the man is enlightened and can know a thing's nature and [even] heaven. If he then practices what he knows thoroughly and faultlessly, then he is achieving nothing less than accord with the virtues of heaven and earth."[32] Thus, for Tai, as for the Neo-Confucians of the Ch'eng-Chu school, principle is the proper object of study.

But Tai insists that the orthodox Neo-Confucian understanding of principle was wrong, and thus, of course, that the approach to learning founded on it was equally wrong. The Sung Neo-Confucians, in defining *li* as that which is "received from heaven and embodied in the heart," were in essence making *li* into a separate thing, an entity in itself, or so Tai claims. If *li*, as the Ch'eng brothers and Chu Hsi asserted, is "above form," it becomes then an abstract, transcendent, unitary principle, some "thing" that exists above and separate from real things in the world. Indeed, it is above even *ch'i* itself, the very stuff of the universe, and thus distinct from identifiable and knowable things.[33]

Tai argues vehemently that *li* is *not* a transcendent principle distinct from things but rather the multiple, discrete principles existing in things and giving order to them. The *li* of things, their distinct "principles of differentiation," never exist in a single principle separate from the real, concrete things they define: "it is not the case that principle and righteousness exist outside of matters and things."[34] Thus, the study of principle becomes, not a process of induction leading to comprehension of one transcendent principle (as Tai believes the Sung Neo-Confucians would have it), but the study of the principles or patterns underlying things and facts. He explains:

> When we speak of Heaven and Earth and talk subtly about their principles, it is like speaking of the sage and saying that he can be emulated. To exalt principle and say that heaven and earth and *yin* and *yang* are not equal to it is to deny that there can be a principle for heaven and earth and *yin* and *yang*. The principles of heaven and earth and *yin* and *yang* are like the sageliness of the sages–how can you exalt sageliness and say that the sages are not equal to it? The sages are also people; because they have fulfilled the principle of people, everyone praises them as sagely and wise. Fulfilling the principle of people is nothing more than fulfilling what is necessarily so in human relationships in daily life…. If we seek what is unchangeably necessarily so in heaven and earth, people and creatures, events and actions, then principle becomes clear. But there are those who go further, speaking of not only the principle of heaven and earth, people and creatures, events and actions, but also claiming that there is nowhere without principle, seeing it as if it were a thing. Even if scholars searched for such a thing until they were white-haired and befuddled, they still would not find it.[35]

As something existing outside of identifiable things, principle becomes an entity beyond objective verification, beyond common agreement, Tai warns; each man is, in a sense, free to define it as he wishes. Then it is possible — indeed almost necessary — for students of principle to make up their own interpretations of what principle is. The definition of principle becomes, inevitably and dangerously, a matter of personal opinion (*i-chien*).[36]

For Tai this mistaken understanding of principle is a philosophical error that has tragic social and political repercussions. In an oft-quoted passage, Tai explains what he believes to be the insidious practical effects of Chu Hsi's definition of principle, the definition that by Tai's own day had long been accepted as orthodox:

> The honored use principle to blame the dishonored, elders use principle to blame the young, those of high status use *li* to blame the lowly. Even when they have lost principle, they call what they do in accord with right. When the dishonored, the young, and the lowly use *li* to fight back, even if they have attained principle, they are called rebellious. Consequently, people of lowly status cannot make the feelings and desires they share with all the world understood by those of high status. Those of high status use principle to blame them for their lowly status, but there are countless numbers of people who have committed the "crime" of lowly status. When someone dies under the law, there are still people to pity him; who pities the man who dies under principle?[37]

Thus Chu Hsi, in making principle an abstraction existing outside of things, unknowable by any generally agreed upon, objective, standards, made it also, Tai claims, a weapon of the powerful and corrupt. In the hands of unscrupulous men, principle (or the claim to true knowledge of principle) becomes a tool for oppression rather than good government.

To counter this tendency, Tai insists on a careful, unbiased, "objective" search for the principles in discrete things. But he warns that two common tendencies inhibit the scholar's attainment of this goal: obstruction by received opinions (*jen-pi*) and obstruction by one's own opinions or prejudices (*tzu-pi*). In a letter to Cheng Mu (n.d.), Tai explains:

> To be successful at study, do not allow either received opinions or your own to obstruct you. Do not seek temporary fame nor expect lasting fame. There are two ways in which well-known opinions are obstructive: people attack the views of men of earlier ages in order to show off, or they use the ideas of former Confucians to get ahead in the world, as a fly clings to a horse's tail. The two are not the same, but the baseness of mind involved in each case is. Therefore, the superior man concentrates on hearing the Way without obstruction.[38]

Tai is critical even of some of the most distinguished contemporary *k'ao-cheng* scholars, who, he feels, invest too great a stock in the interpretations of earlier Han Confucians: "Today's men of broad learning can write essays and are good at investigating facts, but none has yet devoted himself to hearing the Way — they simply draw on earlier Confucians and trust in their reliability. So too men of the Northern and Southern Dynasties said, 'Better to say the Duke of Chou and Confucius were mistaken, than to pronounce Cheng [Hsuan] or Fu [Ch'ien] wrong.'"[39] Thus Tai, despite his sympathy for Han Learning, in his day the dominant school within the *k'ao-cheng* movement, recognizes the danger of too great a faith in the infallibility of Han commentaries: a scholar should never allow the opinions of others — including his Han predecessors — to obstruct his understanding of the true meaning of the Classics.

But Tai is even more disturbed by the kind of error made by the Sung Neo-Confucians. They are guilty of "self-obstruction" (*tzu-pi*), of depending on their own unsubstantiated opinions and even their "gut feelings" to interpret the classical texts. They read what they want into the canon, inventing meanings to suit their own philosophical concerns and predilections: "Ever since the Sung, Confucians have obstinately taken their own opinions as the ideas established in the speech of the ancient worthies and sages, but these scholars really have no knowledge of the language and words of the ancients. In carrying out the affairs of the world, they impose their own judgments, acting on the basis of what they themselves call principle. As a result, affairs are utterly confused and never really capable of successful completion. The great Way is thereby lost and the management of affairs declines."[40]

Abandoning careful examination of the Classics and the commentaries on them, the Sung scholars have nothing but their own imaginings on which to base their ideas. They are thus all too easily "self-obstructed," and their speculations have to be dismissed as unsubstantiated personal opinion.

Tai argues, then, that the best strategy for the student of the Way is to approach the text with a mind free of preconceptions, received opinions, and personal biases; he must rely on a clear and "objective" reading of the words of the text to learn its meaning. Tai explains his own success with this approach, admitting too his occasional failures:

> I investigate the Classics because I am afraid that the subtle words left by the sages have been obscured in their transmission to later generations. But in my researches I have sometimes achieved complete understanding and sometimes only incomplete understanding. What I mean by complete understanding is that when I verified my findings with the ancients, none did not match; they accorded with the Way, leaving me with no doubts. The great and small points were completely exhausted, the fundamental and secondary points all investigated. But as for relying on hearsay to arrive at an answer, choosing the best from among a variety of theories, reaching a decision from empty words, or basing understanding on inadequate evidence — although one can, by tracing the flow, know the source of a stream, when I employ these methods, I have not seen for myself the source; although one can, by following up from the root, reach the tip of a branch, when I employ these methods, I have not felt for myself the twigs that fork off. All are cases of incomplete understanding.[41]

To avoid the failings of previous scholars, Tai warns, one should empty one's mind of previous opinions and carefully study the ancient texts until one achieves a complete understanding of them.

No personal authority — not even that of a respected Han commentator — is to come between the scholar and his careful study of the Classics, then. Tai's insistence on this point perhaps helps to explain his reluctance to accept the bonds of the traditional teacher-student relationship in his own life. He never acknowledged any contemporary scholar, not even his teacher Chiang Yung, as his "master"; so too, he was extremely reluctant to accept disciples, writing to one eager applicant, "It would be much better if we became each other's teacher, consulting one another in order to seek a complete view of things."[42]

For Tai, the burden of complete and accurate understanding of the Classics rests largely on the individual scholar. Over and over Tai emphasizes the importance of exact and objective study of these texts: "It is best to understand the classical texts with an objective mind (*p'ing-hsin*); if there is a single unexplained character, then there will certainly be an error in your explanation of the meaning and the Way will thus be lost."[43] Thus, for Tai Chen true knowledge is the result of exhaustive investigation, free of both slavish reliance on ancient or contemporary authorities, no matter how famous, and personal prejudices that might seduce one into misinterpretation.

The object of this exhaustive investigation, as is obvious from the passages above, must be the classical canon. The Classics, though written two millennia before, remain for Tai the essential guides to sagely knowledge. Tai passionately asserted the absolute necessity of the classical texts to the study of *li*; he agreed with Ku Yen-wu (1613–82) that the study of the Classics was simply the study of principle.[44] Principle and righteousness exist quite literally in the texts of the Classics; exact understanding of the texts becomes the path to truth.

This means that language is of paramount importance to Tai; it is through study of each character, through careful verification of its true meaning, that one gradually builds up to an understanding of a whole text and, eventually, of moral principle itself. One builds first from a knowledge of individual characters, to understanding of phrases, then to comprehension of the Way. It is a gradual and slow process: "The essence of the Classics is the Way; the means by which one understands the Way is through their phrases, and the means by which one understands their phrases is through their characters. From the characters one comprehends the phrases, and from the phrases one comprehends the Way—it must be a gradual process."[45] And failure to understand even just one character prevents perfect understanding of the Way: "If there is one character that is not precisely understood, then understanding the meaning of what is said necessarily falls short and the Way is lost thereby."[46]

Indeed, it is difficult to exaggerate the degree to which Tai stresses the need for complete and perfect understanding of the language of the Classics. In a letter to Shih Ching (1693–1769), usually dated to 1753, he explains:

> If a man were reciting a few lines from the *Yao tien* ["The Canon of Yao," a section of the *Shu-ching* (Book of documents)], and came to the phrase *nai ming Hsi-Ho* [which opens the chapter describing how Yao ordered Hsi and Ho to develop the calendar on the basis of their study of heavenly phenomena], he would not be able to finish his reading if he did not know the movement of the stars and planets. If a man were reciting the *Chou nan* ["The Songs of Chou and the South"] and the *Shao nan* ["The Songs of Shao and the South"] sections [of the

Shih-ching], beginning with the [first song], "Kuan chü," without knowing the ancient pronunciations, so that he forced the rhymes, he would stumble and fail in his reading. If a man were reciting from the ancient *I-li* (Ceremonial), starting from the "Shih-kuan li" ["Ritual for capping an official's son," the first section of the *I-li*], if he did not know the rules for palace attire, he would confuse them and be unable to distinguish their proper usage. If a man did not know the changes in place names over time, then the sources of tribute in the *Yü kung* ["The Tribute of Yü," in the *Shu-ching*] would be lost to him. If a man were unfamiliar with the mathematical terms of *shao-kuang* [the extraction of roots, one of the nine methods of mathematical calculation mentioned in the *Chou-li*] and *p'ang-yao* [trigonometry, another of the nine methods], then he would not be able to figure out the rules for making instruments from the statements in the *K'ao-kung* (Records of technology) [section of the *Chou-li*]. If a man were unfamiliar with the forms and names of birds, animals, insects, fishes, grasses, and trees, he would miss the point [when the poets of the *Shih-ching*] use metaphor and simile. In the study of characters, there is a close connection between the explanation of the meaning and the sound and pronunciation of the character; the sound and pronunciation must both be exactly and correctly distinguished.[47]

Thus, for Tai "understanding" means not just a grasp of the dictionary definition of the characters and phrases but an accurate knowledge of their ancient pronunciation and a full comprehension of the context in which they are used. Moreover, Tai insists that consistent readings be established for characters and phrases in all their appearances in the canon. Describing his own early study of the Classics, he explains, "The meaning of each character had to be consistent throughout the canon and the six categories of writing before I could agree to it."[48] As utterances of the sages, each word has here a sacred importance; to misunderstand one is to lose the intentions of the sages.

Exact knowledge of each character and phrase of the Classics gives the student a profound comprehension of the historical and moral reality each designated. The regulations and institutions (*tien-chang chih-tu*) described in the Classics and the terminology (*ming-wu*, lit., "names and their referents") and concepts employed by the sages—all become clear at this stage.[49] Through this knowledge, the student shares the sages' insights into common human needs and feelings and their understanding of the measures required for the fulfillment of these needs and feelings. Tai himself apparently felt that he had earned this kind of knowledge; in the last year of his life, in a letter to his disciple Tuan Yü-ts'ai (1735–1815), he summarizes his approach to learning and the progress he felt he had made since first beginning his search for the Way: "Since the age of 17 *sui*, I set my mind on hearing the Way, and I believed that if I didn't seek the Way in the Six Classics, Confucius, and Mencius, I would not find it; if I did not set myself to the task of learning the meaning of the characters, institutions, and terms in the Classics, then I would have no basis from which to understand their language. I have worked at this goal for over thirty years and thus know the source of order and disorder throughout all time."[50]

Although Tai never completed a formal curriculum to guide students, his constant references to certain of the Classics and his own focus on these texts allow us to reconstruct what he thought students of the Way should read. He identifies the Six Classics—the *Shih-ching*, *Shu-ching*, *I-ching*, the three ritual texts (the *Chou-li*, *I-li*, and *Li-chi* [Record of rites]), the no-longer-extant *Yueh-ching* (Book of Music), and the *Ch'un-ch'iu* (Spring and Autumn Annals; with its three commentaries, the *Tso-chuan* [Tso Commentary], the *Kung-yang chuan* [Kung-yang Commentary], and the *Ku-liang chuan* [Ku-liang Commentary])—as the foundation for study: "The Way of the sages rests in the Six Classics."[51] These texts should be read with the aid of Hsu Shen's (58–147) *Shuo-wen chieh-tzu*, a reference Tai himself found very useful, and the ancient Han dynasty dictionary the *Erh-ya*, which "penetrates and opens up the Six Classics."[52] Here again we see the importance of an "unblocked" understanding of language to Tai's study of the Classics—ancient dictionaries provide the best guide to the texts.

Tai also frequently alludes to a group of texts he called the Seven Classics —he simply dropped the *Yueh-ching* and added the *Lun-yü* (Analects) and *Mencius* to the five original core texts of the Six Classics.[53] These seven texts probably represent Tai's most serious effort to define a curriculum; he even planned to write a comprehensive guide to them called the *Ch'i-ching hsiao-chi* (Notes on the Seven Classics). Tuan Yü-ts'ai, Tai's most prominent disciple, explains that this text was one of his teacher's central concerns: "The master spoke day and night of the *Ch'i-ching hsiao-chi*—for he wanted it as a guide to the mastery of the Classics."[54] Since Tai never completed the text, Tuan's comments on the projected contents of this collection are the closest thing we have to an outline of Tai Chen's ideal curriculum. Tai had decided to deal with the seven texts topically, for the *Hsiao-chi* was to consist of sections on textual analysis, mathematics, cosmological phenomena, ritual, geography, and ontology:

> Mastery of the Classics requires division into topics and general principles and the comprehension of the origins of each of these. It begins with philology [study of the six categories of characters] and mathematics; therefore, there is [in the *Ch'i-ching- hsiao-chi*] "Ku-hsun p'ien" ["On explaining ancient meanings," on textual analysis] and "Yuan hsiang p'ien" ["On heavenly bodies," on cosmology]. These are followed by "Hsueh li p'ien" ["On learning ritual"] and "Shui ti p'ien" ["On waterways and geography"]. All these chapters are summarized in "Yuan shan p'ien" ["On the Good"]. The study of the sages is this program and nothing more.[55]

Sections of this textbook were finished; "Yuan hsiang p'ien" and "Yuan shan p'ien" were written, and Tuan notes that although the other sections were never given final form, what were to be parts of "Ku-hsun p'ien," "Hsueh li p'ien," and "Shui ti p'ien" can be found in Tai's collected works.[56]

In advocating the study of the Six or Seven Classics as the source of principle, Tai opened out the curriculum for students, at the same time emphasizing the difficulty of the search for moral truth. But while Tai may have opened out the curriculum, he was not necessarily an advocate of "broad learning" (po-ya), if it came at the expense of exacting investigation (ching-shen) of narrower fields of learning. Despite Tai's own reputation for extensive learning, he valued penetrating analysis and thorough examination over a superficial breadth of knowledge. "It is better to know one thing well than ten things not very well," he advises a friend.[57] Of course, the truly dedicated student is to acquire this profound knowledge of a broad range of topics. He is to combine the specialist's passion for detail and precision with the generalist's comprehensive interests so that, as an aspiring sage, he can understand thoroughly the li of all discrete "things" in the entire Confucian canon.

For Tai, then, the search for sagehood begins with close empirical study of the language of the basic Classics. With the aid of ancient dictionaries and many of Tai's own writings, the student gradually and slowly learns to understand the characters and phrases of these texts and the larger concepts—the regulations, institutions, and terminology—these designate. In short, the student finally discovers the li in the Classics.

Having discovered or "discriminated" the li in the words of the sages, the student then must apply or "extend and fulfill" (k'uo-ch'ung) his knowledge in practice. The knowledge he has acquired in his study of the Classics makes this task possible for it naturally clarifies or enlightens the mind much as food and drink nourish the body:

> It is like the way the body relies on food and drink for nourishment. With their assimilation, the food and drink become part of the body; they do not revert to their original state. The mental faculty relies on study; it grasps things for itself in the same way that the body is nourished by food and drink. With regards to the body, it is amply nourished when one grows from weakness to strength. With regard to the mental faculty, it is amply nourished when one's mind grows from narrowness to breadth, from obscurity to discerning intelligence.[58]

The mind, then, is enlightened through study; the wisdom acquired through study automatically "leads to understanding of propriety and righteousness. One thereby satisfies human feelings and completes the virtues of human relationships."[59] Aware of the dangers of selfishness and partiality, the scholar is able to practice reciprocity or altruism (shu), the virtue of considering the desires or feelings of others before acting on one's own.[60] At this point he is ready to realize the goal of the sage: "Having followed his own desires, he can, by extension, follow human desires. Having expressed fully his own feelings, he can, by extension, fully express human feelings. The highest morality consists simply of ensuring that human desires are fully followed and that human feelings are fully expressed."[61]

Wisdom cultivated through learning also gives the sage the power to judge right from wrong and what is important from what is not. Judgment (lit., "weighing," *ch'üan*) reveals the constant, age-old rules that should guide behavior: "Judgment is the means by which the importance of things is determined. Whenever the judgment that 'this is important and that not' has remained unchanged for a thousand ages, it is a constant. A constant then is a judgment of importance that has been, by general consensus, clearly evident for thousands of ages without change."[62] More subtly, judgment also enables the sage to interpret changes in values, to investigate these changes, and to derive the standard that rules them. Thus, the scholar who succeeds in Tai's rigorous program of study emerges with a comprehensive vision not only of the obvious unchanging principles of the universe but also of those constant principles that lie behind change — in short, he "fully realizes the whole scope of right and wrong."[63]

But these principles, Tai repeatedly stresses, are not the abstract, transcendent, and essentially impenetrable principle he associates with learning in the Ch'eng-Chu school. Rather, they are the principles of the Way of men (*jen-tao*), those manifested concretely in daily human relationships (*jen-lun jih-yung*). The Way of men is simply the expression of the Way of heaven in practical, everyday human terms. "What the ancient worthies and sages called the Way," Tai notes, "is simply daily human relationships."[64] Thus, "for men, fully realizing principle is nothing other than fully realizing moral necessity in daily human relationships."[65] Again, Tai emphasizes that study is the means to success here: "Study in order to understand human relationships in daily life, devote yourself to the search for the full realization of humaneness, and the full realization of propriety and righteousness, and then you will improve daily until you achieve the full flowering of the virtues of the sages."[66] According to Tai, then, humaneness, righteousness, and propriety, the virtues of "daily human relationships," are the fruits of intellectual effort. They are naturally expressed when the intellect is fully developed; indeed, they are "nothing other than the resting point of the mind's brilliance, the extreme limit of the intelligence."[67]

Of course not everyone is intellectually capable of reaching the state of wisdom and goodness described here. But, Tai notes, 'being incapable of change' is not the same as 'being incapable of being changed.'"[68] Thus, very stupid people can be forced to change under the direction of the sage. Indeed, most men, Tai suggests, even moderately intelligent ones, have to rely on the instruction of the sages to understand the rules of good conduct. Indeed, this instruction is the great task of the sage: "The superior man causes all men to know and follow the constant standards of heaven and earth."[69] Just as the sage Yü directed the flow of the floodwaters, so too the modern-day sage knows how to direct the flow of human desires and needs in accord with the Way:

When Yü was ordering the floodwaters, he directed the water flow through the fields. The superior man, in ordering the desires, makes them adhere to the Way and righteousness. If, in controlling the waters, one simply tries to prevent the flow, then if it were blocked in the east, it would simply flow to the west. Even worse, it might break the embankment and flow in all directions, in an unmanageable flood. In governing yourself and others, if you simply try to prevent the fulfillment of desires, it will be just like this situation. And even if one could seek quiet in this way, by cutting off all natural desires, it would not be the choice of the superior man. The superior man adheres to the Way and righteousness and prevents others from opposing the Way and righteousness....[70]

The sage is one who, through the exercise of his mental faculty, has "learned" human desires and feelings from study of the *li* in the Classics, and then is able to regulate the needs of others in accord with these desires and feelings. Through this means he creates harmony and order, the full realization in the world of "what is necessarily so."

TAI CHEN AND THE NEO-CONFUCIAN TRADITION OF EDUCATION

One of the clearest developments over time in Tai's philosophical works is the escalation of his attacks on the Sung Neo-Confucians. Although he had made minor criticisms of their reading of the Classics earlier, his attacks began to take coherent form in the *Hsu-yen*, the first draft of the *Meng-tzu tzu-i shu-cheng*, completed in 1769.[71] By the time he finished the *Meng-tzu tzu-i shu-cheng* itself, repudiation of the orthodox school had become one of his primary goals; the work is very much an attempt to interpret Mencius *against* the Ch'eng-Chu school. Certainly by then Tai saw himself as an opponent of orthodox Neo-Confucianism and its understanding of learning and the process of self-cultivation.

Yet many of Tai's prescriptions for education appear to be rather similar to Chu Hsi's.[72] Tai sides with Chu Hsi, against Wang Yang-ming (1472–1529), in emphasizing that knowledge has to precede action: "In no way does sage learning ever consist in ... stressing action without first stressing knowledge."[73] For both men knowledge essentially means knowledge of the Classics; for both, learning the meaning of the sacred texts is the way to understand principle. And both recognize that philological study is the key that unlocks the exact meaning of the texts.[74]

Most striking, however, is the close resemblance between Chu's and Tai's injunctions about how to read the Classics. Each stresses the necessity for an objective reading of the Classics. Chu Hsi's program of study was founded on this method: over and over he urged that the student approach the texts with an open or unprejudiced mind—that is, one free of preconceived ideas or accepted opinions about what the text might reveal. In a passage that might well be read as a warning against what Tai Chen called "self-obstruction," Chu explained the proper approach to classical study: "In reading don't force your ideas on the text. You must get rid of your own ideas and read for the meaning of the ancients."[75] And like Tai, Chu Hsi also cautioned against too heavy a reliance on commentaries in the interpretation of a text, against what Tai later calls "obstruction by others": "The classical texts of the sages are like the master, the commentaries like the slave. Nowadays people are unacquainted with the master and turn to the slave for an introduction to him. Only thus do they become acquainted with the master. In the end it's not as good as [turning to] the classical texts themselves."[76] Chu urged his students to avoid reliance on commentaries whenever possible; it was best for the student to work out the meaning of the text with his own "open" mind.

Furthermore, Chu Hsi shared Tai's preference for narrow but profound knowledge over broad but shallow learning: he advised his students to read less, in order to understand more, for clear and perfect understanding of one text was more illuminating than a vague and superficial reading of many texts.[77] Both thinkers, then, emphasize the value of scholasticism on the road to sagehood, a scholasticism dependent on classical learning, which had, in turn, to be based on an unobstructed and precise reading of the Classics. Both sought an "objective" understanding of the words of the sages.

To be sure, Tai himself did not acknowledge any of these similarities; indeed, he would have been quite horrified at the idea that he and Chu Hsi shared a common approach to the reading of the Classics. For in Tai's mind Chu's great failure as a philosopher lay in his sloppy and biased approach to these texts; he and the other Sung Neo-Confucians, in Tai's words, "slighted textual analysis and thought lightly of language and characters. This is wanting to ford a river after throwing away the boat and oars; it is wanting to climb high without the use of stairs."[78]

If Tai, in his vehement attacks on Chu Hsi, overlooked the striking resemblance between his and Chu's hermeneutics, he was much more accurate in his claim that the content of his reading, his actual interpretation of the canon, was quite different. For in his understanding of the Classics, Tai differs from Chu Hsi on at least one point, a point so crucial that it leads him to the formulation of a very different program of learning: the understanding of *li* and its relationship to *ch'i*. Tai Chen insists that *ch'i* is prior to *li*, that *li* is only immanent in things, not also transcendent over them. This understanding, common to several other leading eighteenth-century philosophers,[79] leads to a very different understanding of moral knowledge. To know *li* now means no more than knowing the many different patterns underlying the "things" contained in the Classics. To be sure, for Chu Hsi as well, *li* was best revealed in the "things" in the Classics; but for Chu Hsi the student, in reading the Classics with an open mind, was ultimately interested in abstracting *li* from the texts, understanding it as the transcendental moral principle of the universe. Here, the process of the "investigation of the principles of things and the extension of knowledge" was essentially a process of radical induction: the student examined *li* most efficiently as it was expressed in the Classics, and then generalized from particular cases to a whole, coherent comprehension of principle, the transcendent moral standard existing in a sense outside the material world. At that point, he could even leave the Classics behind, having understood principle.[80]

For Tai Chen, since one all-encompassing, transcendent principle cannot be abstracted out of things, such a process is essentially meaningless. Each thing has its *li*, its own unchanging principle, but this principle does not partake of some abstract, transcendent principle, nor can it be merged or generalized into such a principle. Since principles are only immanent in things, they can be known only through the study of individual things, most profitably the "individual things" in the Classics. The scholar carefully accumulates knowledge of the characters and phrases of the Classics, building on this a knowledge of institutions and terms; this knowledge then gives him knowledge of principles. "The principles of the worthies and sages... are nothing other than what can be found in the regulations and institutions [of the Classics]."[81]

If we apply the logic of Tai's understanding of principle to learning, we can characterize his view of education as a painstaking, cumulative, scholastic process utterly and eternally dependent on the Classics. The scholar must master the principles of all things in these texts, gradually building up this comprehensive knowledge through a precise study of words and phrases. Such an approach makes the study of principle, for Tai, a much more solid, more soundly verifiable enterprise, for the scholar could always return to the specific institution or "thing" in the text to check his understanding of principle. His plan for a guide to the Seven Classics, although it contained works on cosmology and ontology, consisted largely of a series of essays explaining the institutions, rituals, mathematical methods, and geographical allusions appearing in the Classics, suggesting that these concrete "facts" were necessary to an understanding of the messages of the sages. In Tai's program, there is no inductive leap, as there was in Chu Hsi's program, from the texts to an abstract understanding of one universal, unchanging, transcendent moral Principle, no point at which the scholar, even as a sage, can leave the Classics behind. Intellectual understanding of the Classics thus *is* moral knowledge; the latter advances incrementally with the former. It is hard to imagine Tai Chen suggesting that a student could ever forget the Classics. Quite literally the repositories of the unchanging rules of things, they take on a radically sacred nature that makes them indispensible to knowledge of principle. To lose the Classics would be to lose principle.

Perhaps the clearest indicator of the difference in attitudes toward learning and the classical canon lies in the different basic curricula developed by Tai Chen and Chu Hsi. Chu Hsi selected out of the canon of Thirteen Classics the

four texts he felt most clearly and completely embodied the message of the
sages: the *Ta-hsueh* (Greater learning), the *Chung-yung* (Doctrine of the Mean)
(both chapters of the *Li-chi*), the *Lun-yü*, and the *Mencius*. The Four Books, as
they came to be called, were (with the *I-ching*) placed by Chu before the Five
Classics as the primary textbooks of Neo-Confucian education. The nature of
man and the universe, the process of self-cultivation, the powers of sagehood—
all the topics dear to Sung Neo-Confucian thinkers—were addressed directly
in these texts. As concise guides to the essence of the sages' teachings, the
Four Books, Chu believed, would lead students to a comprehension of *li* as
transcendent moral principle. This principle is of course revealed in other
Classics in the canon and in the histories—and indeed, it was clear that Chu
Hsi eventually expected his students to master these other texts as well—but
he believed that it was most efficiently manifested in the Four Books.[82]

For Tai (and indeed for most other *k'ao-cheng* scholars), the Four Books were
not really the most effective introduction to principle in the Classics. Tai certainly never repudiated the Four Books—indeed he quoted freely from them
all—but he clearly believed that other, more institutionally oriented Classics
should be the focus of the curriculum. Since *li* is to be found in the specific
institutions, terms, and historical cases in the Classics, then those Classics that
emphasize institutions, terms, and cases are likely to be most useful to the
student. Thus, the Seven Classics, which describe ancient institutions, laws,
and rituals and recount the specific events and powerful personalities of
Chinese history, replace the more metaphysically oriented Four Books as the
central objects of study. Certainly, another reason for this shift is a desire to
return attention to the older of the canonical texts—the *Shih-ching*, *Shu-ching*,
I-ching, and *Ch'un-ch'iu*. But these texts are valuable—indeed necessary—because they (the *Shu-ching* and *Li-chi* in particular) describe the specific institutions, rituals, and terms that form the richest source for *li* in the canon. Tai
feared that Chu Hsi's program of learning made sagehood appear too easy,
while at the same time encouraging scholars to confuse their search for the
universal, transcendent principle with the development of their own personal
opinions. By changing the identification of the essential Confucian textbooks
and by insisting that *li* could be understood only in context—that is, in the
different contexts of the institutions and regulations within the Classics—Tai
was emphasizing both the difficulty of moral learning and the necessity of textual verification. The rules or principles of things could only be grasped
through painstaking and arduous textual analysis and an accumulation of
text-based truths and needed to be constantly verified against the evidence of
the sacred texts.

TAI CHEN AND THE K'AO-CHENG MOVEMENT

In his opposition to the orthodox Neo-Confucian understanding of principle,
Tai Chen outlined a program of learning at first glance perfectly supportive of

the *k'ao-cheng* movement. Tai's understanding of knowledge seems to coincide perfectly with the *k'ao-cheng* view of knowledge as the accumulation of facts drawn from careful philological analysis of the Classics. Moreover, though his efforts were not appreciated by *k'ao-cheng* scholars themselves, Tai developed what amounts to a Confucian glorification of their approach with his claim that study and intellectual knowledge, particularly knowledge of the Classics, automatically results in moral knowledge. Knowledge of moral principle is knowledge of the institutions and terms in the Seven Classics: since principle is immanent in the texts themselves, unobstructed knowledge of the texts cannot but yield knowledge of *li* and thus knowledge of the shared needs of all people. Perfection of *k'ao-cheng* skills becomes, in Tai's hands then, the road to sagehood.

Most *k'ao-cheng* scholars, however, repudiated this equation. For them, philology was not the training of a sage but simply an end in itself. Understanding of the true meaning of the characters and phrases of the Classics bore no relationship to the study of moral philosophy; indeed, it was a waste of time for the scholar to concern himself with abstruse questions about human nature and heaven, questions that *the* sage, Confucius himself, had declined to discuss. Chu Yun, urging Tai's biographer to exclude mention of Tai's philosophical writings, explains, "We cannot hear anything of human nature and the heavenly Way from Confucius—why should there be further discussions of them after those of the Ch'eng brothers and Chu Hsi?"[83] Thus, for most *k'ao-cheng* practitioners, the nature of the knowledge to be gleaned from study of the Classics was far more limited than Tai was willing to concede. The philologist could hope to learn the true meaning of the language of the Classics, but this knowledge would not reveal the Way of heaven or the responsibilities of sagehood.

Tai himself seemed to recognize the difference here, that what was for him the way to attain moral perfection was for other scholars the goal of study. He is said to have remarked on his reputation among *k'ao-cheng* scholars, "Mastering the six categories of characters and mathematical techniques is like the work of a sedan-chair carrier—to lift the passenger in the chair. If I am acclaimed for my mastery of such matters, [those who praise me] are making the mistake of confusing the sedan-chair passenger with the sedan-chair carrier."[84] For Tai, then, *k'ao-cheng* was the way to sagehood; for his contemporaries it had become an end in itself.

THE GOAL OF LEARNING FOR TAI CHEN

Nothing separates Tai Chen more clearly from the *k'ao-cheng* devotees than his faith in the possibility of sagehood. The purpose of learning for Tai is not simply an accurate reading of the Classics and a thorough understanding of the words of the ancient sages but the creation of a modern sage. He justifies his emphasis on study with just this goal in mind: "The purpose of study is to nourish a man's innate goodness (*liang*), to make him develop into a worthy or a sage."[85] Elsewhere he assures the student:

> Only through study can you correct your inadequacies, advance toward wisdom, improving continously until you reach your maximum. Then your brightness will equal that of the sun and moon, your light will necessarily extend everywhere, and then you will be a sage. Thus, the *Chung-yung* says, "Though stupid you will surely become brilliant," and Mencius says, "A sage is he who extends and develops [the four sprouts]." With your spiritual illumination (*shen-ming*) at its height, you will grasp the *li* of all facts, and your humanity, righteousness, propriety, and wisdom will be complete.[86]

One of Tai Chen's most pointed criticisms of Hsun-tzu is simply that Hsun-tzu assumed that there was a crucial difference between the nature of the sage and that of the ordinary man. Tai vigorously denies that it is man's nature that prevents him from becoming a sage; rather, it is his refusal to cultivate his nature through study that prevents a man from attaining sagehood.[87]

Sagehood, then, remains the final goal of Tai's program of learning; and the student achieves this goal through a kind of self-cultivation.[88] Certainly, however, this sagehood and this process of self-cultivation are very different from those defined by Neo-Confucians of either the Sung or the Ming. For Tai, self-cultivation consists essentially of study; it is through study that man "nourishes" (*yang*) his nature and realizes "what is morally necessary" in "what is natural" in him. Study of the discrete *li* in the Classics is enough to bring about this realization because there is no necessary disjuncture for Tai between what is natural and what is morally necessary—the latter is simply the highest expression of the former. Or, to put it another way, there is no epistemological barrier between physical substance or body and mental faculty or spirit; the nourishment and illumination of one naturally entails the nourishment and "enlightenment" of the other. Since principle is perfect desire and feeling, and since there is no opposition between mind, which knows principle, and physical substance, which expresses desire and feeling, intellectual knowledge results naturally in the appropriate expression of desires and feelings.

Thus, there is no need for the kind of discipline or mental attentiveness (*ching*) Chu Hsi prescribed as a means to separate cultivation of the moral nature.[89] Such a practice, Tai argues, unnecessarily creates a false division within the process of self-cultivation: the student must study and then, in a separate step, cultivate his moral nature. And this duality in the self-cultivation process encourages students to think of spirit and body as two distinct things, one of which, the body, is inferior to and subject to restraint by the other, the spirit. In fact, Tai asserts, such a dichotomy and hierarchy are false: "Heaven produces things in such a way that they have one source. But if nature is ascribed solely to the spirit (*shen*), then the body (*hsing-t'i*) is seen as something provisionally joined to it; if nature is ascribed solely to principle, then, unless one is a sage with innate knowledge, one cannot but censure one's physical substance (*ch'i-chih*). In both cases the problem is that there are two sources."[90]

Study of discrete principles, then, nourishes all of a man—because his mental faculty and physical substance are of the same source, are ontologically linked, the action of one automatically transforms the other, without the need for any intervening force or discipline. Thus, as a man's knowledge of the *li* in the Classics increases, so too, naturally and inevitably, does his ability to regulate his feelings and desires in accord with the rationally moderate feelings and desires of all men. For Tai, there is really no need to separate "inquiry and study" (*tao wen-hsueh*) and "honoring the moral nature" (*tsun te-hsing*), for "inquiry and study" subsumes "honoring the moral nature." Inquiry and study, by the very nature of Tai's ontology, inevitably result in the nourishment of man's nature, the realization of what is morally necessary in him.[91]

There is, too, a difference in the effects of self-cultivation for Tai Chen and the Sung Neo-Confucians. Tai's study of discrete *li* as a method of self-cultivation produces a gradual "enlightenment" or "spiritual illumination," what Tai calls "*shen-ming.*" There is no mention here of sudden enlightenment of the sort claimed by many Ming Neo-Confucians; nor is there any ecstatic celebration of the unity of all things in the cosmos found even in Sung Neo-Confucian writings.[92] Indeed, Tai questions the Sung Neo-Confucian search for unity or oneness, a search doomed to failure because it rests on a false understanding of principle. Since the Sung Neo-Confucians saw principle as an entity existing outside things, Tai argues, then any attempt to achieve "oneness" with it would take them outside the concrete world of facts and things, away from reality into delusion and emptiness. Confucius and Mencius, Tai points out, "never emptily point to some 'oneness' that they tell people to know and seek. If someone extends his mind's illumination, he can naturally evaluate and measure facts and situations without making the slightest mistake. What need is there then to know 'oneness,' to seek 'oneness'?"[93] Rather, Tai focuses on the completion of wisdom and the profound and thorough perspicacity that comes with sagehood ("Your brightness will equal that of the sun and the moon, and your light will extend everywhere"). At this stage, one understands the essence of the Way.[94]

For Tai, then, sagehood is an achievement quite different from that of the traditional Neo-Confucian sage. For Chu Hsi (and perhaps even more for some Ming Neo-Confucians) sagehood entailed a transformation of the mind that resulted in a full comprehension of the self and its interconnectedness and resonance with all creatures and things. Proper study of the Classics led to an almost mystical sense of the unity of all things and the individual's participation in the great transcendent principle of the universe.[95] Sagehood for Tai is a more down-to-earth affair. To be sure, proper study of the Classics does have a transforming power in his system—as we have seen, such study automatically "activates" a man's moral nature. But Tai, in denying the existence of a transcendent, unitary principle, denies too the mystical element of Chu Hsi's sagehood. Tai's sage has perfect knowledge of the discrete principles in the Classics and he is able, as a result, to comprehend and empathize with the proper common feelings and desires of all people. But he never achieves the religious consciousness of his unity with all things celebrated by Sung and Ming Neo-Confucians. His is a sage who knows all there is to know not to become one with universal principle but to fulfill the needs of the people and restore social harmony.

Few of Tai's ideas were completely new in the eighteenth century. His definition of *li* as principles immanent in things and his identification of *li* with "appropriate" human desires and feelings were foreshadowed in the writings of several Ming and early Ch'ing thinkers. The curriculum he outlined, in its focus on the Classics as the sources of truth, was very much in the Confucian tradition; and in its emphasis on exacting philological study of the texts, it was very much in accord with both the Ch'eng-Chu school and the *k'ao-cheng* movement of his own day.[96]

But Tai worked these components into an educational program, one that offered a comprehensive challenge to the assumptions underlying the prevailing educational orthodoxy. In the end, then, his understanding of the educational process—of what happens as a man learns—and of the goal of learning was quite original. Certainly, his new understanding of *li* transformed the nature of learning: instead of reasoning inductively from the Classics to a knowledge of a transcendent principle, a mystical enlightment that reveals the unity of all things, the student seeks knowledge of all the many separate principles in the Classics, a cumulative illumination that yields perfect wisdom and humanity. The goal of this process is comprehension of the desires and feelings shared by all people—desires and feelings that must be fulfilled, not regulated or restrained, if the world is to be brought to order.

Most striking in Tai's system is his affirmation of a causal link between intellectual knowledge (that is, classical book learning) and the realization of appropriate desires and feelings: for him, unobstructed mental perception, applied to the Classics, naturally and automatically ensures "good" desires and feelings. The sage is the consummate researcher, the scholar willing to devote himself to the painstaking study necessary for genuine comprehension of the regulations, institutions, and terminology of the Classics, and thus of the way to fulfill shared human needs, to "bring peace to the world."

Ironically, then, at the very time when *k'ao-cheng* research—some of it done by Tai himself—was calling into question the authenticity of the Classics, Tai was developing a program of learning that made the student utterly dependent on an exact and complete understanding of those texts. His program reaffirmed the original rationale of the *k'ao-cheng* movement and, if anything, increased the pressure on classical scholars to identify and study exhaustively the real, true texts of the ancient sages, the only acceptable guides to sagehood.

NOTES

Research for this chapter was funded in part by grants-in-aid from the American Council of Learned Societies and the Oregon Committee for the Humanities. I would like to thank John Ewell, Tetsuo Najita, Yü Ying-shih, and the other participants in the Conference on Education and Society in Late Imperial China for their comments and suggestions. I am particularly grateful to Philip Ivanhoe for his very helpful suggestions and to Daniel Gardner for his searching criticism of the various drafts of this chapter.

1. For Tai's early career, see Ch'ien Mu 錢穆, *Chung-kuo chin-san-pai-nien hsueh-shu-shih* 中國近三百年學術史 (History of scholarship in China over the past three hundred years; hereafter *Hsueh-shu-shih*) (Taipei: Shang-wu yin-shu-kuan, 1936), 1:307–18; Yü Ying-shih 余英時, *Lun Tai Chen yü Chang Hsueh-ch'eng—Ch'ing-tai chung-ch'i hsueh-shu ssu-hsiang-shih yen-chiu* 論戴震與章學誠—清代中期學術思想史研究 (On Tai Chen and Chang Hsueh-ch'eng—research on the history of scholarship of the mid-Ch'ing period; hereafter *Lun Tai Chen*) (Hong Kong: Lung-men shu-tien, 1976), 151–78.

2. "Yü Fang Hsi-yuan shu" 與方希原書 (Letter to Fang Hsi-yuan), in *Tai Chen chi* 戴震集 (Collected writings of Tai Chen; hereafter *TCC*), ed. T'ang Chih-chün 湯志鈞 (Shanghai: Shanghai ku-chi ch'u-pan-she, 1980).

3. For the dating of Tai's philosophical works and letters, see Ch'ien Mu, *Hsueh-shu-shih*, 1:327, and his *Chung-kuo hsueh-shu ssu-hsiang-shih lun-ts'ung* 中國學術思想史論叢 (Collected essays on the history of scholarship and thought in China) (Taipei: Tung-ta t'u-shu yu-hsien kung-ssu, 1970), 8:206–12; Yamanoi Yū 山井湧, *Min Shin shisōshi no kenkyū* 明清思想史の研究 (Research on the history of thought in the Ming and Ch'ing) (Tokyo: Tōkyō Daigaku shuppansha, 1980), 414–21; and Yü, *Lun Tai Chen*, 21, 251–89.

4. For the titles of these studies, see Arthur W. Hummel, ed., *Eminent Chinese of the Ch'ing Period (1644–1912)* (Washington D.C.: United States Government Printing Office, 1943), 2:695–97.

5. Yü, *Lun Tai Chen*, 96–99.

6. Although Tai's evidential research techniques had a considerable impact on Ch'ing scholarship, his philosophy had little influence on either his contemporaries or the next generation of scholars. As mentioned, his *k'ao-cheng* colleagues were generally uninterested in philosophical speculation, and those scholars who placed themselves outside the *k'ao-cheng* movement tended to be staunch supporters of Sung Neo-Confucianism and thus not sympathetic to Tai's views. Tai's reluctance to take disciples may also have restricted the influence of his philosophy. See Hu Shih 胡適, *Tai Tung-yuan ti che-hsueh* 戴東原的哲學 (Tai Tung-yuan's philosophy) (Taipei: Shang-wu yin-shu-kuan, 1966), 90–196; Ch'ien, *Hsueh-shu-shih*, 1:364–79; Ann-ping Chin and Mansfield Freeman, *Tai Chen on Mencius: Explorations in Words and Meanings: A Translation*

of the Meng Tzu tzu-i shu-cheng (New Haven: Yale University Press, 1990), 14; Benjamin A. Elman, *From Philology to Philosophy: Intellectual and Social Aspects of Change in Late Imperial China* (Cambridge, Mass.: Council on East Asian Studies, Harvard University, 1984), 20–22; Liu Chao-jen 劉昭仁, *Tai Tung-yuan ssu-hsiang yen-chiu* 戴東原思想研究 (Research on Tai Tung-yuan's thought) (Taipei: Kuo-li T'ai-wan shih-fan ta-hsueh kuo-wen yen-chiu-so, 1973), 208–15.

7. See "T'ien tao," *Meng-tzu tzu-i shu-cheng (hereafter MTTISC)*, in *TCC*, 287–88.

8. See Yamanoi, *Min Shin shisōshi no kenkyū*, 361–64.

9. *Yuan shan*, in *TCC*, 332.

10. Tai explains in *Yuan shan*, *TCC*, 332: "By implication, goodness is the common share of all things and all men under heaven; nature is the function and capability by which all men accomplish that goal. Nature is the origin of the acts of men and the movement of things. This so-called goodness is just this. We can recognize the presence of goodness by observing the process of the formation and transformation of heaven and earth and the function and capability of the natures of men and things." See also Chung-ying Cheng, trans., *Tai Chen's Inquiry into Goodness* (Honolulu: East-West Center Press, 1970), 71, 73.

11. "Li," *MTTISC*, *TCC*, 278; *Shih-ching*, Ode 260. See also 265, and Anda Jirō 安田 二郎 and Kondō Mitsuo 近藤光男, *Tai Shin shū* 戴震集 (Collected writings of Tai Chen), vol. 8 of *Chūgoku bunmei sen* 中國文明獻 (Offerings from Chinese culture) (Tokyo: Asahi shinbunsha, 1971), 41–42.

12. Tai explained in *Hsu-yen*, in *TCC*, 371: "What is naturally so can be seen in a man's specific daily activities; what is necessarily so harmonizes each of these activities to the mean and restrains the man [to do what is right]. Knowing what is naturally so, he can comprehend the transformations of heaven and earth; knowing what is necessarily so, he can comprehend the virtue of heaven and earth. Thus Mencius says, 'To know one's nature is to know heaven....'" See *Meng-tzu yin-te* 孟子引得 (Index to *Mencius*), Harvard-Yenching Institute Sinological Index Series Supplement 17 (Peking: Harvard-Yenching Institute, 1941), 50 (7a.1).

13. *Hsu-yen*, in *TCC*, 367; Ch'ien, *Hsueh-shu-shih*, 1:341.

14. To explain Tai's view of this process of differentiation in a little more detail: The process of production inevitably involves differentiation, and differentiation inevitably entails inequality. Heaven ordains the allotment that each creature gets in this process; the individual nature is the result of this allotment. Tai did acknowledge some order in the ordainment process: things receive different allotments, though some groups of things, or species (*lei*), receive roughly similar allotments. But even within a species all things are given different allotments. Since the transformations of the *yin*, *yang* and Five Agents in the process of creation consists of "countless scattered changes," when these actually produce forms the result is not only differences among things but also differences even among things of the same species.

Once endowed with its nature, a thing then unfolds in accordance with its special allotment, and its difference from other things becomes obvious through the operation of its capacity (*ts'ai*). Just as the full flower exists potentially in the seed, so too man's complete growth and character exist potentially in his nature at birth; his endowed capacity ensures their development. It is, then, the heavenly endowed capacity in each man that makes his particular nature visible or manifest.

What in fact precisely unfolds or manifests itself in man is his physical substance and his mental faculty. The physical body is the concrete reality of the nature, its "fact" (*shih*); the mental faculty is the nature's ability (*neng*) or talent, which enables man to cultivate himself intellectually and morally. This is what man receives from the *yin, yang* and Five Agents through the transformations of *ch'i*. These are the qualities man is endowed with at birth; they are simply what is naturally so in man. See "Hsing," "Li," and "Ts'ai," *MTTISC*, in *TCC*, 271, 291–94, 305, 307–8; Ch'ien, *Hsueh-shu-shih*, 1:342; Fung Yu-lan, *A History of Chinese Philosophy* (Princeton: Princeton University Press, 1952), 2:658.

15. "Ts'ai," *MTTISC*, in *TCC*, 308–9.

16. "Ch'üan," *MTTISC*, in *TCC*, 328; see also "Li," *MTTISC*, in *TCC*, 273; Ch'ien, *Hsueh-shu-shih*, 1:347–48.

17. "Li," *MTTISC*, in *TCC*, 265–66. See also Ch'ien, *Hsueh-shu-shih*, 1:347.

18. "Ts'ai," *MTTISC*, in *TCC*, 309.

19. Here Tai, as in many of his attacks on Chu Hsi, was not doing full justice to the complexity of Chu's philosophy; Tai is perhaps confusing what had become the generally accepted interpretation of Sung Neo-Confucianism with Chu's own ideas. To be sure, Chu Hsi's understanding of the role of desire in self-cultivation is not entirely clear. Chu certainly sees desire as a *potential* evil. As he remarks in his commentary to the *Ta-hsueh*: "'Inborn luminous virtue' (*ming-te*) is what man acquires from Heaven; it is unprejudiced, spiritual, and completely unmuddled and thereby embodies the multitudinous manifestations of principle and responds to the myriad affairs. But it may be restrained by the endowment of *ch'i* or concealed by human desire, so at times it will become obscured. Never, however, does its original luminosity cease. Therefore, the student should look to the light that emanates from it and seek to keep it unobscured, thereby restoring its original condition." This passage suggests that desire threatens man's knowledge of the principle in his nature. Elsewhere, Chu Hsi condemns "selfish desires" as impediments to sagehood. But this of course does not necessarily mean that he thought *all* desires were evil and should be consistently repressed. Yet Tai certainly thought that this was what Chu thought — it is the complete denial of desires, a stand he associated with Taoism and Buddhism, that he was attacking in Chu Hsi. Daniel K. Gardner, *Chu Hsi and the Ta-hsueh: Neo-Confucian Reflection on the Confucian Canon* (Cambridge, Mass.: Council on East Asian Studies, Harvard University, 1986), 89; "Li," "T'ien-tao," "Hsing," "Ch'üan," *MTTISC*, in *TCC*, 273–74, 279–81, 285–86, 290–94, 297, 302, 326–27; Chin and Freeman, *Tai Chen on Mencius*, 43; Mizoguchi Yūzō 溝口雄三, *Chūgoku zenkindai shisō no kussetsu to tenkai* 中國前近代思想の屈折と展開 (The refraction and unfolding of thought in pre-modern China) (Tokyo: Tōkyō Daigaku shuppansha, 1980), 300–313; Benjamin A. Elman, "Criticism as Philosophy: Conceptual Change in Ch'ing Dynasty Evidential Research," *Tsing Hua Journal of Chinese Studies*, n.s. 17, nos. 1, 2 (Dec. 1985): 172–74.

20. "Li," *MTTISC*, in *TCC*, 273; *Meng-tzu yin-te*, 58 (7b. 35).

21. "Hsing," "Ts'ai," *MTTISC*, in *TCC*, 295–96, 309.

22. "Ts'ai," *MTTISC*, in *TCC*, 309.

23. Ibid., 309. See Fung, *History*, 2:660.

24. "Li," *MTTISC*, in *TCC*, 270.

25. *Hsu-yen*, in *TCC*, 385; Ch'ien, *Hsueh-shu-shih*, 1:343.

26. "Tu *Meng-tzu* lun hsing" 讀孟子論性 (Reading *Mencius* on human nature), *TCC*, 164. See Fung, *History*, 2:661. See also "Li," *MTTISC*, in *TCC*, 270, 281–83.

27. Fung, *History*, 2:662; Yü Ying-shih, "Tai Chen and the Chu Hsi Tradition," *Essays in Commemoration of the Golden Jubilee of the Fung Ping Shan Library (1932–1982)* (Hong Kong: Fung Ping Shan Library of the University of Hong Kong, 1982), 392.

28. "Hsing," *MTTISC*, in *TCC*, 315. See also Mao Li-jui 毛禮銳, Ch'ü Chu-nung 瞿菊農, and Shao He-t'ing 邵鶴亭 eds., *Chung-kuo ku-tai chiao-yü-shih* 中國古代教育史 (History of education in pre-modern China) (Peking: Jen-min chiao-yü ch'u-pan-she, 1979), 520–22.

29. "Hsing," *MTTISC*, in *TCC*, 298. *Lun-yü yin-te* 論語引得 (Index to the Analects), Harvard-Yenching Sinological Index Series Supplement 16 (Peking: Harvard-Yenching Institute, 1940), 3(2.15).

30. "Hsing," *MTTISC*, in *TCC*, 297. Tai believed, however, that most men of limited mental faculty could most efficiently be *taught* by a sage to do right. The process of change is presumably too long and arduous to expect men with severely limited talents to accomplish it; their greatest hope was the paternalistic instruction of men who had grasped moral principle. Chang Kuang-fu 張光甫, *Tai Tung-yuan chiao-yü ssu-hsiang chih yen-chiu* 戴東原教育思想之研究 (Research on the educational thought of Tai Tung-yuan) (M. A. thesis, Kuo-li Cheng-chih Ta-hsueh, 1968); *Chia-hsin shui-ni kung-ssu wen-hua chi-chin hui yen-chiu lun-wen* 嘉新水泥公司文化基金會研究論文 (Research essays from the Chia-hsin shui-ni Company Cultural Foundation), no. 116.

31. *Yuan shan*, in *TCC*, 347.

32. *Hsu-yen*, in *TCC*, 359; Ch'ien, *Hsueh-shu-shih*, 1:341.

33. "Li," *MTTISC* in *TCC*, 277. Tai Chen is not, strictly speaking, representing Chu Hsi's ideas accurately here, for Chu did repeatedly say that *li* never existed outside of *ch'i*, or material things. But it is nonetheless easy to see how Tai might have interpreted Chu as he did, for Chu Hsi does concede, when pressed by his disciples, a logical priority to *li*. See Daniel K. Gardner, *Learning to Be a Sage: Selections from the Conversations of Master Chu, Arranged Topically* (Berkeley: University of California Press, 1990), 90–92. It can also be argued that, by suggesting that principle is one and that *ch'i* is dependent on it for its operation, Chu Hsi does make *li* into a separate thing, one that is immanent in other things perhaps but also transcendent over them.

34. "Li," *MTTISC*, in *TCC*, 272, 277–78. For a critique of Tai's definition of *li*, see Fung, *History*, 2:655–57, 671–72.

35. "Li," *MTTISC*, in *TCC*, 278.

36. "Li," *MTTISC*, in *TCC*, 274; see also 267–69.

37. "Li," *MTTISC*, in *TCC*, 275; see also 280. See Benjamin A. Elman, "Philosophy (*I-li*) Versus Philology (*K'ao-cheng*): The *Jen-hsin Tao-hsin* Debate," *T'oung Pao*, 69, nos. 4–5 (1983): 216–17.

38. "Ta Cheng Chang-yung Mu shu" 答鄭丈用牧書 (Reply to Cheng Mu), in *TCC*, 186. See also Chang, *Tai Tung-yuan chiao-yü ssu-hsiang*, 68–70.

39. "Ta Cheng Chang-yung Mu shu," *TCC*. See also 186. See also 185; "T'ien-tao," *MTTISC*, in *TCC*, 290. It is this criticism that sets Tai and his followers, the Wan school of Anhwei, apart from the school of Han learning (centered in Soochow). Although Tai was heavily influenced by the research techniques developed by such Han Learning leaders as Hui Tung, he insisted that all sources, whether from the Han or the Sung,

had to be subjected to critical examination. See Elman, *From Philosophy to Philology*, 59–60.

40. "Yü mou shu" 與某書 (Letters to Someone) (1777?), *TCC*, 187. See also Chang, *Tai Tung-yuan chiao-yü ssu-hsiang*, 68–69.

41. "Yü Yao Hsiao-lien Chi-chuan shu" 與姚孝廉姬傳書 (Letter to Yao Chi-chuan) (1755), *TCC*, 184–85.

42. Tuan Yü-ts'ai 段玉裁, *Tai Tung-yuan hsien-sheng nien-p'u* 戴東原先生年譜 (Chronological biography of Master Tai Tung-yuan; hereafter *Nien-p'u*); *TCC*, 466; Chin and Freeman, *Tai Chen on Mencius*, 14, 180, n. 50.

43. "Yü mou shu," *TCC*, 187.

44. Liang Ch'i-ch'ao, *Intellectual Trends in the Ch'ing Period*, trans. Immanuel Hsü (Cambridge, Mass.: Harvard University Press, 1959), 30.

45. "Yü Shih Chung-ming lun hsueh shu" 與是仲明論學書 (Letter to Shih Chung-ming on learning) (1753), *TCC*, 183. Sixteen years later he repeated much the same admonition in his preface to the *Ku-ching chieh kou-ch'en* 古經解鉤沈序 (Preface to *Clarification of obscurities in ancient explanations of the Classics*); see *TCC*, 192.

46. "Yü mou shu," *TCC*, 187. See also Chang, *Tai Tung-yuan chiao-yü ssu-hsiang*, 69–70; Elman, *From Philosophy to Philology*, 28–29.

47. "Yü Shih Chung-ming lun hsueh shu," *TCC*, 183. See Ch'ien, *Hsueh-shu-shih*, 1: 313–14.

48. "Yü Shih Chung-ming lun hsueh shu," *TCC*, 183.

49. "T'i Hui Ting-yü hsien-sheng shou-ching t'u" 題惠定宇先生授經圖 (Colophon on the painting of Master Hui Ting-yü teaching the Classics, 1765), *TCC*, 214; Tuan, *Nien-p'u*, in *TCC*, 455, 480. See also Elman, From *Philosophy to Philology*, 45; Tu Wei-ming, "Perceptions of Learning (*Hsueh*) in Early Ch'ing Thought," in Feng Ai-ch'ün 馮愛羣, ed., *T'ang Chün-i hsien-sheng chi-nien lun-wen chi* 唐君毅先生紀念論文集 (Collection of essays on the anniversary of Master T'ang Chün-i) (Taipei: Hsueh-sheng shu-chü, 1979), 29–30.

50. Tuan, *Nien-p'u*, in *TCC*, 480.

51. "Yü Fang Hsi-yüan shu," *TCC*, 189; see also "Feng-i shu-yuan pei" 鳳儀書院碑 (Tablet for the Feng-i Academy), in *TCC*, 221–22. On Tai's curriculum, see Chang, *Tai Tung-yuan chiao-yü ssu-hsiang*, 65–67.

52. "Yü Shih Chung-ming lun hsueh shu," *TCC*, 183; "Erh-ya chu-shu chien-pu hsu" 爾雅注疏箋補序 (Preface to *Supplement to Commentaries on the Erh-ya*), *TCC*, 52; Chang, *Tai Tung-yuan chiao-yü ssu-hsiang*, 65–66.

53. Tuan, *Nien-p'u*, in *TCC*, 482. See also Chang, *Tai Tung-yuan chiao-yü ssu-hsiang*, 65–66.

54. Tuan, *Nien-p'u*, in *TCC*, 483.

55. Ibid., 483; Ch'ien, *Hsueh-shu-shih*, 1:315–16.

56. Tuan, *Nien-p'u*, in *TCC*, 481–83; see also Ch'ien, *Hsueh-shu-shih* 1:315-16.

57. Tuan, *Nien-p'u*, in *TCC*, 489. See Chang, *Tai Tung-yüan chiao-yü ssu-hsiang*, 70–72; Yü, *Lun Tai Chen*, 83–85.

58. "Li," *MTTISC*, in *TCC*, 272–73. The idea of the mind "grasping something for itself" (*tzu-te*) — that is, to gain a personal understanding of something — is from *Mencius* (see *Meng-tzu yin-te*, 31 [4b.14]); I am grateful to Philip Ivanhoe for this reference and advice on the translation.

59. *Yuan shan*, in *TCC*, 331. See Cheng, *Tai Chen's Inquiry into Goodness*, 70.

60. "Li," "Ch'üan," in *MTTISC*, in *TCC*, 284–85, 324–25 respectively.

61. "Ts'ai," *MTTISC*, in *TCC*, 309; Yü, *Lun Tai Chen*, 20. Presumably (though Tai never makes the point), the process of reasoning or "extension" that takes the scholar from understanding of the Classics and rectification of his own desires and feelings to comprehension of the "common desires and feelings of all people" is possible because all men are of the same species. When things are produced, though each is given a different allotment, a different nature, some groups of things are more alike than certain other things. Thus, though each individual person is different from another, he nonetheless shares certain characteristics that make him identifiable as a member of the human species. The existence of these species-shared characteristics makes it possible for the sage to identify, with his perfect knowledge, the common, "reasonable" desires and feelings of all men. See "Li," "Hsing," *MTTISC*, in *TCC*, 269–72, 298–306 respectively; and Hou Wai-lu 侯外廬, *Chung-kuo ssu-hsiang t'ung-shih* 中國思想通史, (General history of Chinese thought), vol. 5: *Chung-kuo tsao-ch'i ch'i-meng ssu-hsiang-shih* 中國早期啟蒙思想史 (History of Chinese thought in the early enlightenment period) (Peking: Jen-min ch'u-pan-she, 1956), 450–51.

62. "Ch'üan," *MTTISC*, in *TCC*, 321–22.

63. "Ts'ai," *MTTISC*, in *TCC*, 309.

64. "Tao," *MTTISC*, in *TCC*, 314.

65. "Li," *MTTISC*, in *TCC*, 278. See also Tu, "Perceptions of Learning (*Hsueh*) in Early Ch'ing Thought," 30.

66. "Jen I Li Chih," *MTTISC*, in *TCC*, 320.

67. "Hsing," *MTTISC*, in *TCC*, 298–99.

68. *Yuan shan*, in *TCC*, 344. See also Cheng, *Tai Chen's Inquiry into Goodness*, 103.

69. *Yuan shan*, in *TCC*, 332. See also Cheng, *Tai Chen's Inquiry into Goodness*, 73.

70. *Yuan shan*, in *TCC*, 342. Here Tai is playing off Mencius's frequent references to Yü; see, for example, *Meng-tzu yin-te*, 24 (3b.9) and 32 (4b.26).

71. Ch'ien, *Hsueh-shu-shih*, 1:339–40.

72. The fullest treatment of this issue — Tai Chen's place in the Neo-Confucian tradition — is Yü Ying-shih's *Lun Tai Chen*, esp. 83–147. See also Yü's "Tai Chen's Choice between Philosophy and Philology," *Asia Major*, 3rd ser., 2, pt. 1 (1989): 79–108; "Tai Chen and the Chu Hsi Tradition," 376–92; and "Some Preliminary Observations on the Rise of Ch'ing Intellectualism," *The Tsing Hua Journal of Chinese Studies*, n.s. 11, nos. 1, 2 (Dec. 1975), 105–36.

73. Yü, "Tai Chen and the Chu Hsi Tradition," 282–83; and "Ch'üan," *MTTISC*, in *TCC*, 326.

74. Gardner, *Chu Hsi and the Ta-hsueh*, 44.

75. Daniel K. Gardner, "Transmitting the Way: Chu Hsi and His Program of Learning," *Harvard Journal of Asiatic Studies*, 49, no. 1 (June 1989):159.

76. Gardner, "Transmitting the Way," 160.

77. Gardner, "Transmitting the Way," 157.

78. Tuan, *Nien-p'u*, in *TCC*, 455.

79. See Yamanoi, *Min Shin shisōshi no kenkyū*, 149–71.

80. Gardner, "Transmitting the Way," 151.

81. "T'i Hui Ting-yü hsien-sheng shou-ching t'u," *TCC*, 214. See also Yü, *Lun Tai*

Chen, 23–24, for another argument about the difference between Chu's and Tai's views of *li*.

82. Daniel K. Gardner, "Principle and Pedagogy: Chu Hsi and the Four Books," *Harvard Journal of Asiatic Studies*, 44, no. 1 (June 1984), 57–82.

83. Chiang Fan 江藩, *Kuo-ch'ao Han-hsueh shih-ch'eng chi* 國朝漢學師承記 (Record of Han Learning masters of the Ch'ing dynasty) (Taipei: Kuang-wen shu-chü, 1966), 6.5b. This is a reference to a statement in the *Lun-yü* that Confucius never spoke of topics like human nature and heaven. See *Lun-yü yin-te*, 8 (5.13); Yü, *Lun Tai Chen*, 99, 127 n. 41.

84. Tuan Yü-ts'ai, "*Tai Tung-yüan chi* hsu," *TCC*, 452; Ch'ien, *Hsüeh-shu-shih*, 1:332–33.

85. "Ts'ai," *MTTISC*, in *TCC*, 311.

86. "Li," *MTTISC*, in *TCC*, 270. For the reference to *Chung-yung*, see James Legge, trans., *The Chinese Classics* (Hong Kong: Hong Kong University Press, 1960), 1:414; for the reference to *Mencius*, see *Meng-tzu yin-te*, 13 (2a.6). I consulted the translation of Torbjörn Lodén, "Dai Zhen's Evidential Commentary on the Meaning of the Words of Mencius," in *The Museum of Far Eastern Antiquities*, no. 60 (1988), 184.

87. For Tai's view of Hsun-tzu, see "Hsing," *MTTISC*, in *TCC*, 298–99; Fung, *History*, 2:669–72.

88. For a conflicting view, see Yamanoi, *Min Shin shisōshi kenkyū*, 407–9. Yamanoi argues that Tai is not interested in self-cultivation or government, traditionally the two concerns of Confucian scholars; nor, he claims, was Tai interested in sagehood. His works, particularly the *Meng-tzu tzu-i shu-cheng*, reveal Tai's interest rather in pure theory, in philosophical issues beyond the more practical concerns of most Confucian thinkers.

89. Yü, "Tai Chen and the Chu Hsi Tradition," 384, 387; "Li," *MTTISC*, in *TCC*, 280–81.

90. "Li," *MTTISC*, in *TCC*, 284; cf. Lodén, "Dai Zhen's Evidential Commentary," 212. The opening line of this passage is from *Mencius*; see *Meng-tzu yin-te*, 21 (3a.5). The mention of a sage with innate knowledge is an allusion to the *Lun-yü*; see *Lun-yü yin-te*, 34 (16.9). I am grateful to Philip Ivanhoe for these references and for assistance with the translation.

91. Tai attacked the emphasis placed on "honoring the moral nature" by the Lu-Wang school, asserting that this process could never be separated from "inquiry and study": "How can anyone apply the name 'honoring the moral nature' to one's learning when it is divorced from 'following the path of inquiry and study'?" "Yü Shih Chung-ming lun hsüeh shu," *TCC*, 184; see Yü, "Tai Chen and the Chu Hsi Tradition," 378–79.

92. Yü, "Tai Chen and the Chu Hsi Tradition," 390. See, for examples of earlier Neo-Confucian experiences of enlightenment, Wing-tsit Chan, *A Source Book in Chinese Philosophy* (Princeton: Princeton University Press, 1963), 497–98, 593–95, 659–66, and Tu Wei-ming, *Neo-Confucian Thought in Action: Wang Yang-ming's Youth (1472–1509)* (Berkeley: University of California Press, 1976), 118–21.

93. "Ch'üan," *MTTISC*, in *TCC*, 325–26; I consulted Lodén, "Dai Zhen's Evidential Commentary," 288, for the translation.

94. "Ch'üan," *MTTISC*, in *TCC*, 325.

95. Chu Hsi describes his understanding of the process of enlightenment in his commentary to the *Ta-hsueh*: "The first step of instruction in greater learning is to teach the student, whenever he encounters anything at all in the world, to build upon what is already known to him of principle and to probe still further, so that he seeks to reach the limit. After exerting himself in this way for a long time, he will one day become enlightened and thoroughly understand [principle]; then, the manifest and the hidden, the subtle and the obvious qualities of all things will be completely illuminated." See Gardner, *Chu Hsi and the Ta-hsueh*, 105.

96. Ming thinkers had already begun to repudiate the dualism of *li* and *ch'i* found in the Ch'eng-Chu school, arguing rather for a monism of *ch'i*. Hsueh Hsuan (1389–1464) and Lo Ch'in-shun (1465–1547) also insisted that principle must be studied in concrete things and objects. And Lo, like Tai, attacked Sung Neo-Confucians (and Wang Yang-ming) for denigrating desires—desires are not evil, he claimed. These ideas, particularly the belief in the monism of *ch'i*, influenced late Ming thinkers like Kao P'an-lung (1562–1626) and Liu Tsung-chou (1578–1645) and early Ch'ing scholars such as Huang Tsung-hsi. Yen Yuan (1635–1704) and Li Kung (1659–1746), though their connection to these earlier thinkers is not clear, develop very similar views. Thus, by Tai Chen's time, the monism of *ch'i* and the positive value of the physical desires had become more widely accepted concepts. Furthermore, the philological concerns of the eighteenth-century *k'ao-cheng* scholars can be traced back beyond Ku Yen-wu to such late Ming figures as Ch'en Ti (1541–1617) and Chiao Hung (1541–1620). See Fung, *History*, 2:636–50; William Theodore de Bary, "Neo-Confucian Cultivation and the Seventeenth-Century 'Enlightenment'," in *The Unfolding of Neo-Confucianism*, ed. de Bary (New York: Columbia University Press, 1975), 200–203.

GLOSSARY

Ch'en Ti	陳第	Chu Hsi	朱熹
Cheng Hsuan	鄭玄	Chu Yun	朱筠
Cheng Mu	鄭牧	*ch'üan*	權
Chi Yun	紀昀	*Ch'un-ch'iu*	春秋
ch'i	氣	*Chung-yung*	中庸
ch'i-chih	氣質	*Erh-ya*	爾雅
Ch'i-ching hsiao-chi	七經小記	Fang Hsi-yuan	方希原
Chiang Yung	江永	*fen*	分
Chiao Hung	焦竑	*fen-li*	分理
Ch'ien Ta-hsin	錢大昕	Fu Ch'ien	服虔
chih	智	*hsin-chih*	心知
chih	知	*hsing*	性
chih-chih	致知	*hsing-t'i*	形體
chih-tu	制度	Hsu Shen	許慎
Chin	晉	*Hsu-yen*	緒言
ching	敬	*hsueh*	學
ching-shen	精神	*hsueh-ch'i*	血氣
ch'ing	情	Hsueh Hsuan	薛王宣
Chou-li	周禮	"Hsueh li p'ien"	學禮篇
Chou nan	周南	Hsun-tzu	荀子

Huang Tsung-hsi	黃宗羲	*shen-ming*	神明
Hui Tung	惠棟	*sheng-chih*	生知
i-chien	意見	*shih*	事
I-ching	易經	Shih Ching	是鏡
i-li	義理	*Shih-ching*	詩經
I-li	儀禮	"Shih-kuan li"	士冠禮
jen	仁	*shu*	恕
jen-lun jih-yung	人倫日用	*Shu-ching*	書經
jen-pi	人蔽	*Shui-ching chu*	水經注
jen-tao	人道	"Shui ti p'ien"	水地篇
Kao P'an-lung	高攀龍	*Shuo-wen chieh-tzu*	說文解字
k'ao-cheng	考證	*ssu*	私
K'ao-kung	考工	*ssu*	思
"Ku-hsun p'ien"	詁訓篇	*Ta-hsueh*	大學
Ku-liang chuan	穀梁傳	Tai Chen	戴震
Ku Yen-wu	顧炎武	*tao wen-hsueh*	道問學
"Kuan chü"	關雎	*t'iao-li*	條理
Kung-yang chuan	公羊傳	*tien-chang chih-tu*	典章制度
k'uo-ch'ung	擴充	*t'ien-tao*	天道
lei	類	*ts'ai*	才
li	理	*ts'ai-chih*	材質
Li-chi	禮記	*tse*	則
Li Kung	李塨	*Tso-chuan*	左傳
liang	良	*tsun te-hsing*	尊德性
Liu Tsung-chou	劉宗周	Tuan Yü-ts'ai	段玉裁
Lo Ch'in-shun	羅欽順	*tzu-jan*	自然
Lun-yü	論語	*tzu-pi*	自蔽
Meng-tzu ssu-shu lu	孟子私淑錄	Wang Ming-sheng	王鳴盛
Meng-tzu tzu-i shu-cheng	孟子字義疏證	Wang Yang-ming	王陽明
ming-te	明德	*wen-li*	文理
ming-wu	名物	*wu-hsing*	五行
nai ming Hsi Ho	乃命羲和	*yang*	陽
neng	能	*yang*	養
p'ang-yao	旁要	Yao tien	堯典
pi	蔽	Yen Yuan	顏元
pi-jan	必然	*yin*	陰
p'ien	偏	*yü*	欲
p'ien	篇	*Yü kung*	禹貢
p'ing-hsin	平心	"Yuan hsiang p'ien"	原象篇
po-ya	博雅	*Yuan shan*	原善
shao-kuang	少廣	"Yuan shan p'ien"	原善篇
Shao nan	召南	*Yueh-ching*	樂經
shen	神		

NINE

Legal Education in Ch'ing China

Wejen Chang

Every society has its norms and its ways to teach them. In traditional China there were large numbers of norms, which in people's minds formed a hierarchy, with *t'ien-li* (heavenly reason) or *tao* (the Way) as the broadest, most rational, and hence most important of principles at the top; *te* (morality), *li* (rules of propriety), and *hsi-shu* (customary rules) as widely accepted standards in the middle; and *fa* (positive laws), as the narrowest, most arbitrary, and hence least important rules at the bottom—together forming a sort of upside-down pyramid.[1] Therefore, traditional Chinese society developed an elaborate program of teaching people the higher norms. Did it also have a program to teach people its positive laws? We would think that it had to, because it had an elaborate legal system; there had to be ways to train legal specialists to make, interpret, and enforce laws and to prepare the people to obey laws.

The case of Ch'ing China makes this point quite clear. By present standards the Ch'ing legal system was grossly understaffed, yet because of the country's vast territory and population, a large number of people were involved in the system. For instance, although in each district there was only one magistrate, who was the district judge, the chief executive officer, and the maker of local ordinances, there were over a thousand districts—hence over a thousand magistrates.[2]

In addition to magistrates, there were higher officials to review decisions of their subordinates, hear appeals, and make regulations and laws; law enforcement officials and officers; government clerks and runners; private legal secretaries of officials and some high ranking officers; personnel of local security systems; scriveners who helped people draft legal documents; and litigation masters who provided people with legal counsel for a fee.[3] The total number of these people must have been in the tens of thousands. More or less they all needed knowledge of law. Furthermore, for the system to function properly, the general public had to have some legal knowledge as well.

The question is, how did all these people learn law? More specifically, where did they learn it? Who were their teachers? What were the curricula, the teaching materials, and the teaching methods? Are these questions relevant to legal education in Ch'ing China? Are there materials that can provide answers?

Generally, source materials for Ch'ing studies are abundant, but unfortunately, materials that directly answer these questions are not. Therefore, the research for this chapter has been very broad. Naturally, we shall first look into regular school education for the general public. Because this education was closely connected with the civil examination system, we must briefly study that as well. Whether or not the examinations tested law and regular schools taught it, we shall explore the reasons. Then we shall investigate the background of various types of persons involved in the Ch'ing legal system, hoping to find out how they acquired their legal knowledge.

Fortunately, there is a wealth of materials that can help us study this education indirectly. Many law books of the Ch'ing period clearly meant to be teaching materials have survived. We also have some detailed studies of the judicial system and the responsibilities of those deeply involved in it. From these materials we can infer what kind of intellectual, ethical, and practical training such people had.

Thus, we shall be led by our materials. Since they are far from sufficient, we shall not be able to describe how every type of person who needed to know the law learned it. At best, we hope to find out roughly how some people did it. We hope to show a broad outline and some detailed aspects of the Ch'ing legal education. Many areas, unfortunately, will remain unclear.

Whatever we learn from the materials, we shall try to answer the question why. We shall search for the social, political, economic, and ideological reasons. Finally, we shall try to evaluate Ch'ing legal education as we know it against some generally accepted standards and what the present-day Chinese law schools offer.

LEGAL EDUCATION FOR THE COMMON PEOPLE IN THE CH'ING

People must have some knowledge of the legal system under which they live. The questions are where do they get this knowledge? And how accurate is it? Ordinarily, people learn in schools. Were there schools in Ch'ing China that taught law? If not, where else could the common people learn law? How accurate would the knowledge they acquired be?

School Education

In traditional Chinese schools, youngsters studied mainly the Confucian Classics, some history, and a bit of literature.[4] During the first half of the

Ch'ing, more materials were added to the reading list, including the Yung-cheng emperor's *Sheng-yü kuang-hsun* (Commentary on the sagacious teachings of the K'ang-hsi emperor), Yang Shih-ch'i's *Li-tai ming-ch'en tsou-i* (Memorials of prominent officials of previous dynasties), and several works on *hsin-li* (human nature and reason) by Sung scholars.[5] Most of these reading materials are about social norms; some specifically discuss law. In 1729, an imperial edict ordered students in government-sponsored schools to study *Ta-Ch'ing lü-li* (Ch'ing code), so that they might some day use it properly in government.[6]

This education was designed to prepare a student for civil examinations. For the two most important ones — the provincial and the metropolitan — a mid-Ch'ing student was required (1) to write several *wen* (essays), one *shih* (poem), one *lun* (comment), and five *ts'e* (proposals); (2) to draft one *piao* (petition to the throne) or one *chao* (imperial edict) or one *kao* (government proclamation); and (3) to render five *p'an* (hypothetical judicial decisions).[7]

Obviously, to ask a student to draft a judicial decision was to appraise his knowledge of law. The remaining tests were to assess his other talents, but one may think that they too could and probably should have been designed to help determine his legal knowledge because the whole examination system was, after all, to select candidates for government posts. For this purpose, the most appropriate questions would have been those about social problems, and most social problems involve law.

But unfortunately things did not turn out that way. The questions, whether given by the emperor or an examination commissioner, usually addressed only noncontroversial problems.[8] The reason was mainly political. The commissioners were frightened by a number of cruel campaigns in the early Ch'ing against persons who allegedly used examination questions to slander or denounce the Manchu regime.[9] The emperor, of course, did not have such fears, but even if he asked sensitive questions he would not receive straightforward, critical answers, because if examination commissioners were fearful, so were the students. In any event, the Manchu regime was not anxious to solicit criticism. That was why only a limited number of passages in the Confucian classics were safe to be quoted in essay questions and were therefore used repeatedly.[10] Apparently for the same reason, an imperial edict was issued in 1745 requiring students, in writing essays, "to speak for the sages," namely, to repeat or paraphrase the statements of ancient Confucian thinkers.[11] The purpose of this edict becomes even clearer when read together with an earlier one issued in 1654, which mandated that students, in exploring the meaning of the sages' statements, follow the interpretations of the Sung scholars.[12] The message was unmistakable: the government was not interested in the students' personal opinions of the Classics.

The same was true with most other tests. The examiners asked politically safe questions based on the Classics and phrased them in a way to invite flattery to the regime, and the students would give politically safe answers offering such flattery.[13] There was little chance to find out a student's view on serious social problems, and this was one of the reasons why the tests that required students to draft imperial edicts and government proclamations and write petitions to the throne were abolished one by one in 1681, 1756, and 1757.[14]

The *ts'e* test was meant to be different. Its questions were supposedly about concrete problems, such as famine relief, water conservation, grain transportation, frontier security, military provision, local order, economic development, crimes, the use of punishment, public education, and so on.[15] But as many of these issues were politically sensitive, all of them were closely scrutinized. Numerous imperial edicts were issued warning against improper questions and ordering disciplinary action against those who gave them.[16]

In response, the examiners resorted to two tactics: to repeat *shu-hsi t'i* (familiar questions) and to *tzu-wen tzu-ta* (to ask a question and answer it oneself.)[17] The former appealed to the authority of precedent, the latter precluded unintended interpretations and ensured correct answers.[18] The question concerning the use of punishment as a means of social control can be used as an example here. It was given many times in many examinations. Invariably, it stated the unfortunate need of punishment, spelled out the danger of its abuse, and suggested some measures of precaution and safeguard—although all these were phrased as questions. It often was so lengthy and comprehensive that little was left for a student to do except to paraphrase, converting the question into his answer.[19]

Both tactics were condemned by the Ch'ing regime, and *tzu-wen tzu-ta* was impeded by an edict of 1771 limiting the question to within three hundred words.[20] However, judging by the archival materials, familiar questions apparently continued to be asked throughout the Ch'ing.[21] This caused enterprising scholars to write model answers and sell them to students who would memorize them before taking their examinations.[22] Consequently, the *ts'e* questions, though practical, were not always useful in eliciting original responses from students.

Finally, let us look at the law test. To design a hypothetical case and ask for a reasoned decision is a common method of testing a student's knowledge of law. If this method were used in the Ch'ing examinations we would have reason to believe that it helped promote legal education. But again, unfortunately, this was not the case, and again the trouble started with the questions. Those we find in *Ch'ing-tai nei-ko ta-k'u tang-an* (Ch'ing dynasty Grand Secretariat archive) were not about hypothetical cases.[23] Instead, a "question" was often just a quotation of the title of a section in the Ch'ing Code. For instance, the second *p'an* "question" for the 1661 metropolitan examination was "Ch'i-yin t'ien-liang" (Evasion of land tax)[24] That is the title of the first article of Chapter 3, Section 2 of the Code.[25] The article has four statutes and five substatutes, proscribing various offenses by taxpayers and collectors. What was the examiner asking? How was a student supposed to reply? A survey of the answers of those who had passed that examination indicates that they merely guessed the meaning of the "question" and made some commonsense comments, which invariably consisted of only a few lines in moralistic language with no citation of any specific statute or substatute. For instance, the answer of Lo Jen-chung, who ranked ninth among those who passed the examination, had one hundred and one words. It said in effect that land tax was of importance to the state; if someone cheated the system he must be punished.[26] To answer such a "question" in such a manner a student obviously needed no legal knowledge at all. In 1756, this test was abolished by an imperial edict.[27]

It was a sensible policy to require students who aspired to be officials to take the law test. But why was the policy not properly implemented? One of the possible reasons is that those who administered the examination system were Confucians, who generally had a low regard for positive law.[28] But the Manchus did not have a Confucian tradition; why did the Ch'ing regime let the Confucians sabotage its policy? One suspects that it did not really care much for the examination system. The Manchus, after all, had different channels to get into government service;[29] the examinations were designed mainly for restricting Han Chinese aspirants.

Whatever the reason, the Ch'ing government measures—initially giving a law test that did not really evaluate the students' legal knowledge and eventually abolishing it—certainly did not encourage people to study law. As a result, in spite of the 1729 imperial edict, law did not become a serious subject in regular school education.

Public Education

During the Ming, a chapter entitled "Chiang-tu lü-ling" (Teaching and learning laws and orders) was added to the traditional criminal code. One of the statutes in this new chapter provided that if, due to mistake or negligence, an ordinary person with good knowledge of law and no previous criminal record committed an offense less serious than treason or was implicated in the crime of another person, he was for one time only to be exempted from punishment.[30] This was a rather strange statute, but its purpose is clear—it was to encourage the common people to know law.[41] The Ch'ing inherited this provision, and the Ch'ing *Li-pu tse-li* (Regulations of the Board of Rites) ordered that in every village or town a *chiang-yueh-ch'u* (lecture hall) was to be built and residents of the community were to be called to the hall on the first and the fifteenth days of every month to listen to lectures on law and *Sheng-yü kuang-hsun* by elders selected by local officials.[31] Many officials emphasized the importance of such lectures, but no one explained how the elders learned law.[32] More significantly, one of the officials who carried out this order wrote that no one in his district had ever heard about such lectures before.[33] He was, of course, boasting about his good deed of sponsoring such lectures, but it was probably true that most local officials simply ignored this order and he was an exception. Here again a good government policy was thwarted by those who were supposed to implement it. As a result, the general public did not get the legal education the government prescribed.

Informal Education

Although regular schools did not provide legal education and government orders to teach law to the general public were largely ignored, there were conceivably many other ways in which people could learn law. To begin with, there was no shortage of relevant materials for those who could read. Most of the Classics discuss norms, including law. Law codes and their commentaries were generally available.[34] Many who administered or practiced law left writings about cases they had decided or learned about.[35] Case reports were also compiled and published by scholars, obviously for educational and reference purposes.[36] Most clan rules included some statutory and customary law provisions.[37] Moreover, law was a popular theme of novels, plays, and other forms of literature.[38] For the illiterate, there was a rich oral tradition — many operas and folklore dramatized the judicial process.[39] Above all, whenever a person was involved in litigation or other judicial and law enforcement processes, his story spread among his relatives, friends, and neighbors, teaching them something about law. With so much material and information around, one may argue that in spite of the lack of formal legal education the Chinese probably knew a lot about law.

Is this argument valid? Let us first consider the Classics. It is true that most of them are about norms — particularly, moral principles and *li* (rules of propriety). Since these principles and *li* are considered higher and more comprehensive than positive law, one may argue that by learning and obeying them the Chinese would have indirectly learned and obeyed law. But *li* were mostly about refined attitudes and stylized behavior and presupposed a generally stable and prosperous social order. To those who lived in poverty and social turbulence, *li* in this sense meant very little. Refined attitudes and stylized behavior were luxuries that these miserable souls could hardly afford.

It is also true that traditional Chinese laws were greatly influenced by moral principles and, in many instances, complemented *li*.[40] But law never completely embodied all moral principles and, while both were norms, law and *li* were in many ways different. Moreover, as pointed out by Han Fei, and tacitly admitted by the Confucians, moral principles and *li* often conflicted with one another and with law.[41] Therefore, ordinary people did not necessarily know law even if they had learned all the *li* and the moral principles.

Though readily available, the Ch'ing Code and its commentaries were highly technical and very difficult to understand. It is doubtful that many of the common people bothered to read them. The statutory provisions quoted in clan rules were easy to comprehend, but they were only a small fragment of the Code and were often greatly simplified.[42] Even complete familiarization with them would not enable a person to know much about the Ch'ing legal system.

Case reports could be interesting, but most of them were very brief.[43] Unless a person was familiar with the statutes and substatutes he was unlikely to learn much from these reports.

Writings of judicial officials about their personal experiences could be fascinating. Unfortunately, the authors were often self-righteous and self-serving. As a result, the accuracy of their stories is questionable.[44]

Even more popular and less accurate were novels, plays, and operas. To begin with, it was always the more sensational and scandalous cases that were turned into novels and other forms of literature and performing art, but such cases were often handled according to extraordinary rules. Secondly, in order to attract attention, the novels and other works often overdramatized. For instance, one particular genre, a combination of detective story and courtroom drama known as *kung-an hsiao-shuo*, was devoted to depicting judicial and law enforcement processes.[45] But compared to what we learn from the law codes, the commentaries, case reports, and writings of law officials, the picture of the legal system shown in such novels is always vague, exaggerated, or distorted.[46]

Finally, one could have learned about law from those who had been involved in litigation or other judicial and law enforcement processes; but here too accuracy is a problem. First of all, these processes often aroused strong emotions, and people with strong emotions toward something are often unable to relate it objectively. Second, these processes were complicated. Thus, even if not emotionally involved, a lay person would find it difficult to grasp their details and understand their significance. Third, personal experiences were subjective; any broad generalizations can be risky.

Thus, people could conceivably learn about law from many sources and in many ways outside regular schools, but the lessons they learned were often fragmented and usually imprecise. Their understanding of law could only be characterized as popular impressions, images, or beliefs of law rather than accurate knowledge of law. This fact is brought to light not to dismiss such understanding as irrelevant. The popular image of law is very much a part of a legal system, powerfully affecting its operation and effectiveness. The point is to make clear that such understanding is not what a serious legal education wants to install.

LEGAL EDUCATION FOR PERSONS WHO WORKED IN THE CH'ING LEGAL SYSTEM

So the question remains, where and how did the Ch'ing people, particularly those who worked in the legal system, get their precise knowledge of law?

Legal Education for Officials, Clerks, Scriveners, and Litigation Masters

Officials. Let us start with the officials. According to the Ch'ing Code, all officials were to study law, take annual examinations, and suffer disciplinary sanctions if they failed.[47] But as we have seen, they could not get much legal education at regular schools, and we know of no special legal training program for them after they took office. In fact, there is no evidence that the said annual examinations took place regularly. Nevertheless, we know some high judicial officials were well versed in law. Where and how did they get their legal education? A survey of their writings and biographies failed to produce a clear answer.[48] As to lower officials, it is reasonable to assume that they had to know enough law to function in office. And we know that some of them proudly published their judicial opinions.[49] But reading these opinions with care, one finds that most of them were based not on law but on customary rules and higher norms. Precedents might have been followed but they were almost never cited. It is thus difficult to say what these opinions prove about the authors' legal knowledge. And, of course, there is the possibility that the opinions were actually written by legal secretaries. In any case, neither in these opinions nor in other writings of or about these lower officials is there much material about their legal education. They probably obtained it the same way as did the high judicial officials, but in their case the details are even less clear.

Clerks. In theory, clerks, particularly those in provincial and local governments, were merely to record, copy, store, and retrieve documents. But in fact they were regularly consulted by officials while handling government affairs. Several factors caused this result. First, clerkship in most government offices during the Ch'ing was practically hereditary. A clerk remained in a post for life and left it to his heir. The long tenure and inheritance enabled clerks to learn a great deal of law and precedents. Second, in provincial and lower government offices most clerks were local people. They knew the place and its customs. Third, Ch'ing government archives were generally poorly kept. Few people other than the clerk filing the documents could find them.[50] In contrast, the Ch'ing officials as a rule were quickly transferred from post to post, prohibited from serving in their native provinces, and had no easy access to the archive.[51]

Thus, clerks acquired considerable knowledge of law; but it is difficult to determine how much, because when a clerk, particularly one in the lower governments, was consulted, he usually gave an oral opinion or produced some materials in the archive for reference. He might also be asked to draft some simple documents according to strictly established formats. We can find no evidence of his legal training in them. Few of them left much writing of other kinds.

In any case, we do not know exactly how the clerks acquired their legal knowledge. They could of course learn from their job, and because their posts were practically hereditary, we speculate that they also learned a lot from their family seniors. But we do not have records showing how this was done.[52] The problem is in the fact that clerking was generally considered a low job. Few self-respecting intellectuals were willing to take it, and those who did were not proud. That is why they left no description of their education and work. Some officials and scholars did write about clerks, but few probed their legal education.

Scriveners. Scriveners wrote complaints and other legal documents for people. Naturally, we think they had to know law, customary rules, and precedents. But according to the Ch'ing Code, the only qualifications for a scrivener were being honest and literate. A person with these qualifications was selected by the magistrate and granted a license to write down exactly what his clients told him. If he added or detracted any important part, he was to be punished.[53] Thus, he was not required to know law.

The complaints collected in *Tan-hsin tang-an* (Archive of Tan-shui sub-prefecture and Hsin-chu district of Taiwan) seem to confirm that scriveners did not need much knowledge of law—or if they did, they did not demonstrate it in the complaints they wrote. A complaint had to be written on a form that had only some three hundred squares, each for one character. There was barely enough space to state the facts. To make legal arguments and cite laws or precedents in a complaint were physically impossible.[54] One may argue that to use this limited space to present the facts of a case in a favorable light required true mastery of law. But judging by the fact that many complaints were promptly rejected because of inconsistencies or unreasonable allega-tions,[55] this argument seems to be an exaggeration.

Although scriveners did not have to have much legal knowledge, they could have acquired some if they studied the outcomes of the lawsuits for which they wrote the complaints. But there is no evidence of such study. Probably because scribing was also considered a lowly job, few scriveners were proud enough of the profession to write about how one prepared for it.

Runners. One would think runners in local governments also had some legal knowledge because they had law enforcement responsibilities. But again, there were no such requirements because their assignments were supposed to be very simple, namely, to serve summonses and to make arrests. Another reason is that they were mostly illiterate, this because their job was considered so demeaning—being ordered around by a magistrate to do both his official and his personal chores—that nobody who had any education or skill would want it. Only those who could not otherwise make a decent and honest living became runners. Such people could not be expected to learn much about law, and cer-tainly none of them has left any writing about their legal education.

Litigation masters. On the fringe of the Ch'ing legal system were the practicing lawyers. They, like the scriveners, wrote complaints for litigants. In addition, they probably also advised clients on litigation strategies. The Ch'ing Code did not prohibit such activities, provided that the person engaging in them did not thereby instigate litigation or falsely accuse someone of a crime.[56] However, if he did it professionally for a fee, he was called a *sung-shih* (litigation master) or, more derogatorily, a *sung-kun* (litigation trickster) and could be exiled to the remotest, malaria-infested frontier.[57]

Therefore, it was unlikely that anyone would publicly practice this trade or openly teach it. If it was taught secretly, no record of this education was left behind. More probably, an aspiring litigation master had to educate himself; there were books specifically written for this purpose, but they were condemned as *kou-sung chih-shu* (books that help instigate litigation), placed in the same category as pornography, and ordered to be burned. Anyone who wrote or printed them was to be sentenced to one hundred blows of the heavy bamboo and exiled to a place three thousand *li* (Chinese miles) from home; anyone who reprinted or distributed them was to receive one hundred blows of the heavy bamboo and to do three years of penal servitude.[58] Nevertheless, such books did not cease to exist; we can find some copies even today.[59] In any case, the Ch'ing Code, its commentaries, case reports, and many other relevant materials were readily available. An aspiring litigation master could study them by himself.

How much law did a litigation master have to know? Let us see what kind of work he actually did. The Ch'ing Code listed writing complaints and instigating litigation; some writers mentioned many other misdeeds, including coaching false testimony, advising manipulation of evidence, and arranging collaboration with runners and clerks in obstructing the judicial process.[60] For these undertakings, litigation masters might have needed knowledge of law, but it is difficult to tell how much, for besides the complaints they left few records. Some complaints by supposedly notorious litigation masters have survived.[61] They are mostly simple statements of fact, often distorted or fabricated. One may or may not need knowledge of law to tell a smart lie or to play with words in presenting a fact in a favorable light. As far as these complaints are concerned, there was little evidence to prove one way or the other, because they were neither accompanied by legal arguments nor followed by citation of law. The limited space on complaint forms simply did not allow elaboration.

If a litigation master were allowed to represent his client in court, his legal arguments would have been kept in court records. But he was not allowed to do so unless he and his client happened to be members of the same household.[62] Conceivably, he could coach his client to make the arguments himself, but it would be risky if the client was intellectually not up to the task. In fact, few such arguments were ever recorded. Hundreds of court proceeding documents in *Tan-hsin tang-an* contain no legal arguments of the parties. If some litigation masters were behind those proceedings, they did not demonstrate their legal knowledge.

Thus, although the Ch'ing officials, clerks, scriveners, runners, and litigation masters all needed knowledge of law, they did not have formal, institutionalized legal education. Many may have gained the knowledge by studying the

Ch'ing Code and other materials on their own and through on-the-job training, but few of them wrote much about their experiences and, in any case, such experiences were too subjective to produce general rules.

The Education of Legal Secretaries

The legal secretaries played a significant role in the Ch'ing legal system. In previous dynasties, many officials had also hired private assistants for legal work, but the dependence on legal secretaries became universal among provincial and local officials during the Ch'ing. Two institutional changes were primarily responsible for this development. First, in the late Ming and early Ch'ing, high officials of the central government were sent as governors and governors general to coordinate the work of provincial authorities (the administrative, judicial, and military commissioners) and, similarly, officials of provincial governments were sent as circuit intendants to supervise the operation of the prefectural and district governments. As troubleshooters on temporary assignments, these emissaries did not have regular staffs.[63] Second, in 1667, the post of *t'ui-kuan* (prefectural judge), who helped the prefect hear appeals and supervise judicial work of the magistrates in the prefecture, was eliminated, depriving the prefect and the magistrates of professional legal assistance and guidance.[64] For these reasons, the governors, governors general, circuit intendants, prefects, and magistrates all found it necessary to hire private assistants, especially legal secretaries. Soon after, other officials and some high-ranking military officers in the provinces also adopted the practice, as they all realized that legal secretaries were better educated than the regular staff, provided superior service, and as private helpers were more loyal and easier to control.

The practice was tolerated by the Ch'ing regime because, first of all, it did not increase the size of the government bureaucracy and budget. Second, legal secretaries were supposed to help the government, not challenge it. Individually, they may have, because of personal principles, disagreed with their employers and, in small numbers, engaged in questionable activities to advance their private interests.[65] But as a profession they never posed a threat to the regime because they worked for the officials, and most harbored hopes of becoming officials themselves. Thus, though not a formal part of the government,[66] they were its loyal servants.

The importance of the legal secretaries' service cannot be exaggerated. They prepared all the legal work in provincial and local governments and were thus an essential element in the Ch'ing legal system. As such, they needed legal knowledge more than any other group of government personnel except the small band of officials and clerks in the Board of Punishments. Therefore, their legal education was of great importance.

To study their legal education is not easy because directly relevant materials are meager. The two works that are well known are Wang Hui-tsu's

Wang Lung-chuang i-shu (Collected works of Wang Hui-tsu) and Ch'en T'ien-hsi's *Ch'ih-chuang hui-i-lu* (Chen T'ien-hsi's memoirs).[67] Both were Ch'ing legal secretaries: Wang (1730–1807) served for thirty-four years (1752–85), Ch'en (1885–1980?) for fourteen (1891–1904). One would hope to learn some details of their education from these two works, but they said very little, and an interview with Ch'en T'ien-hsi did not add much.[68] However, a careful study of their works reveals one interesting point: Although the authors were more than a century apart, the little bits and pieces of information about their legal education they provided were remarkably similar. This is important. We can therefore reasonably assume that no drastic changes were introduced to legal education through these years, and hence we do not have to look for small possible differences in the various periods; we can talk generally about legal education of at least the mid- to late Ch'ing.

Indirect materials are abundant. First, there is a handful of books by Ch'ing legal secretaries discussing their work experiences.[69] Second, there is a great wealth of information on the Ch'ing legal system — laws, case records, writings of officials, and so on. We shall use these materials together with writings of Wang Hui-tsu and Ch'en T'ien-hsi to try to find out who aspired to become legal secretaries, who their teachers were, what their education was, and what kind of product it yielded.

Who Aspired to Become Legal Secretaries? During the Ch'ing, most students whose families could afford the expense continued to study the regular subjects and take civil examinations; only poor but talented students chose to study law and become legal secretaries. Usually, they made this decision when they were about twenty years of age (a few years after finishing their basic education) and began to feel the pressure of providing for their families–this was the case with both Wang Hui-tsu and Ch'en T'ien-hsi.[70] It was not an easy decision because, first of all, the profession was considered less worthy than government service and, secondly, it was believed to be dangerous; a legal secretary had the potential to do great harm to others and eventually, by retribution, to himself and his family. Wang had to swear that he would abide by the highest moral rules in conducting himself as a legal secretary before his mother reluctantly allowed him to pursue legal study.[71]

Who Was the Teacher and How Was the Relationship Established? When a young man was ready to study law, he usually found a teacher through family connections. Wang Hui-tsu first studied with the legal secretary of a friend of his father-in-law;[72] Ch'en T'ien-hsi learned his initial lessons from his elder brother, also a legal secretary.[73] The teacher had to be a person who could provide practical training; therefore, he had to be a practicing legal secretary. In retirement, Wang Hui-tsu offered advice to many who aspired to do legal work,[74] but he was unable to take on any formally as a student.

While legal secretaries were hired by many officials, those who worked for district magistrates were the most active; their work was the most complex and heavy. Therefore, Ch'en T'ien-hsi said, it was best for a person who wanted to study law to start under a magistrate's legal secretary. After finishing his training in about three to four years, he could pursue further study under a legal secretary of a higher official for a year or two, but that was not necessary.[75] For this reason, the following discussion focuses mainly on the legal education of students under magistrates' legal secretaries.

When a legal secretary accepted someone formally as a student, he took the person to live in his quarters in the yamen, educated him and provided him with a stipend; the student, in return, helped the teacher with his work. Thus, they formed a master-apprentice relationship that was, according to Ch'en T'ien-hsi, very close.[76]

A Legal Secretary's Work and an Apprentice's Practical Training. Ch'en T'ien-hsi reported that the education of a law apprentice consisted of two parts: book learning (reading books relevant to the work of a legal secretary) and practical training (assisting the teacher in handling actual legal work). Reading started first and was soon followed by practical training. Several reading lists have survived and, while some books are clearly relevant, others are less so. Why were certain books included? This question is better answered if one has some knowledge of a legal secretary's job.

Concerning practical training, Ch'en T'ien-hsi stated that after studying the Ch'ing Code for a few months, an apprentice was taught to read case records, review the paperwork of the clerks, and draft various documents, including responses to complaints, judicial decisions, and various types of official communication.[77] This brief statement is the only direct description we can find in Ch'en's book; Wang Hui-tsu was silent on this matter. But a legal secretary's job was very complex, having many other aspects in which an apprentice needed to be practically trained.

Thus, in order to understand the law apprentice's reading list and know more about his practical training, we should study the legal secretary's job. Because it is more closely connected with practical training, we shall investigate that first, and then look into the reading list.

Let us start with the first item Ch'en T'ien-hsi mentioned—reading case records. A case record consisted of many types of documents. In a robbery case, for instance, there were the original complaint, numerous petitions for speedy action by the local government to apprehend the suspects, the magistrate's initial reports to his superiors, his instructions to the runners, his request for assistance from the local *Lü-ying* (Green Standard) officer, instructions from higher officials to the magistrate, arrest warrants, summonses, a coroner's report on the wound(s) (if any) inflicted by the robbers on the victim(s), a list of stolen goods, statements of the victim(s) and captured robber(s) (if any), the magistrate's follow-up reports to his superiors, his decision, his final report, and so on.[78] In other criminal and civil cases there were similar and different types of documents. Each type had its own format, language, and technicalities. Reading these documents enabled an apprentice to see the various types of work he was going to do and the important points in each of them.

Having read enough case records, an apprentice then learned how to draft the magistrate's initial response to a complaint. This response, known as a *p'i* (rescript), was a statement to be attached at the end of the complaint. It indicated the magistrate's acceptance or rejection of the complaint. In the latter case, it was in fact a summary decision denying a hearing. To draft such responses taught an apprentice how to analyze the issues and find the applicable laws.[79]

Probably at a very early stage, a law apprentice was trained to review the work of the clerks. Magistrates normally assigned routine matters to the clerks to be processed according to established rules and precedents. For instance, after a complaint was accepted, the clerk assigned the case suggested that a warrant or a summons be issued and prepared such a document. It was then reviewed by the legal secretary, who presented to the magistrate his own suggestion.[80] This work required an apprentice to learn many details of government affairs and relevant rules and precedents.

A magistrate was constantly in communication with other officials and the local populace. Documents sent to officials and officers of equal or lower rank and instructions to clerks, runners, and the people of his district included memoranda, notices, orders, proclamations, warrants, and summonses. Each type was addressed to a person or persons of a specific status for a specific purpose and each used a specific format and a particular style of language.[81] In drafting them an apprentice learned many technicalities.

After a trial, when the legal secretary was to write a decision, he might tell an apprentice to do a first draft. The apprentice would have to analyze the facts and apply a law or, in many civil cases, a customary rule or, in some difficult cases where there was no applicable law or customary rule, a principle of equity or ethics based on Confucian classics.[82] This job had to be done with great care because a wrong decision could subject the magistrate to administrative sanction or criminal punishment.[83]

As the Ch'ing regime practiced extreme centralization of power, the magistrate was required to report to his superiors practically everything that had any effect on the government. In a robbery case, for instance, he had to report the occurrence of the offense, his investigation, his effort to search and capture the suspects, and, if applicable, the actual arrest, the recovery of the loot, the abuse of a captured suspect by the runners or the jailer, the death of a suspect in custody, the trial, the decision, the transportation of the convict and the records to higher offices for review, the carrying out of the sentence, and, at the end of certain period, the impeachment of officials and officers who had failed to prevent the offense.[84] Different reports used different formats and styles of language. A final report of a criminal case, for instance, had to include three parts: a statement of the facts and procedure, an analysis of the facts, and the decision. In each part certain specific issues had to be addressed and clarified.[85] Thus, for a report, both its content and its presentation were important; they reflected the ability of an official. Drafting reports was not easy even for an experienced legal secretary; an apprentice had to have close supervision and much practice to learn this work.

Apparently, the six items listed above were mentioned by Ch'en T'ien-hsi because of their obvious importance. The list could easily include many more. For instance, there were many steps in the judicial process leading to a decision and at each step a legal secretary could be requested to provide assistance — a law apprentice could learn a lot if he was allowed to help or observe. For example, after a crime was reported to the magistrate, he had to investigate the site of the crime and examine physical injuries (if any) on the victim's person. If it was a dispute over land, the magistrate had to inspect the property.[86] Normally, a legal secretary need not accompany the magistrate on such trips, but he had to study the case with care and point out the important aspects for the magistrate to look into.

After the investigation or survey, a date was set for the trial. Before making a suggestion, the legal secretary had to consider the facts of the case, the time it would take to have the parties and witnesses brought to court, and the magistrate's schedule. According to Wang Hui-tsu, he also kept in mind the ability of the magistrate so that he would not be overbooked, and so that the parties and witnesses would not waste time waiting.[87]

Then the legal secretary had to prepare the magistrate for the trial. He analyzed the issues and advised the magistrate on techniques and tactics for finding the truth, including what questions to ask and what signs to observe, what issues to pursue and what pitfalls to avoid, what attitude he was to take and what responses he was to expect, and so on.[88]

When the magistrate conducted the trial, the legal secretary could sit behind a curtain and listen. Wang Hui-tsu used to do this. When he noticed that the magistrate missed a point or asked a wrong question he handed him a note to suggest some remedy.[89]

If the first hearing was not conclusive, the legal secretary, according to Wang Hui-tsu, had to discuss the case with the magistrate and devise new techniques and tactics for a second hearing.[90]

In addition to these steps leading to a decision in a criminal case, there were many things in civil proceedings and law enforcement work for a law apprentice to learn. And there were more if he got further training under the legal secretary of a higher official, for instance the judicial commissioner. The commissioner had to coordinate law enforcement efforts throughout the entire province, review cases decided by lower officials, hear appeals, order retrials or corrections, conduct autumn assizes, file impeachments of incompetent officials, and recommend new provincial regulations and even new national laws.[91] These responsibilities were very different from a magistrate's and to get to know them was an additional dimension of a law apprentice's education.

A Law Apprentice's Reading. While practical training was important, a law apprentice had to have some basic knowledge of law and government affairs before he could try his hand on actual work. He had to read law and other materials. Now that we know what kind of work he was going to do, we can look at his reading list with a better understanding.

Wang Hui-tsu repeatedly said in his works that a legal secretary should "read books" and "read history" in his spare time and, of course, "study the Code, especially the chapter on terms and principles."[92] But he did not provide a reading list, nor did he say much about how to pursue these studies. Ch'en T'ien-hsi listed in his memoir eight titles: (1) *Ta-Ch'ing lü-li* (Ch'ing code), (2) *Hsing-an hui-lan* (Conspectus of penal cases), (3) *Hsi-yuan lu* (Coroner's handbook), (4) *Ta-Ch'ing hui-tien* and *Ta-Ch'ing hui-tien shih-li* (Compendium of Ch'ing laws), (5) *Liu-pu tse-li* (Regulations of the Six Boards), (6) *Liu-pu ch'u-fen tse-li* (Disciplinary regulations of the Six Boards), (7) *Tso-chih yao-yen* (Advice to private secretaries), and (8) *Fu-hui ch'üan-shu* (Complete book on good government).[93] He also explained why and how these works should be studied.[94] In *Ch'ing-tai mu-fu jen-shih chih-tu* (Private secretaries of Ch'ing officials), Professor Miao Ch'üan-chi listed thirty works that the legal secretary was required to read.[95] It is not clear whether he got this list from Ch'en T'ien-hsi, whom he interviewed in 1966, or elsewhere.

The eight titles mentioned by Ch'en were, of course, only the basics. Even Miao's list was not comprehensive. Today we still have hundreds of Ch'ing works that were clearly relevant to a legal secretary's job and therefore were probably studied by apprentices of law. An analysis of six types of such works is made below. This will help us understand Ch'ing legal education a little better.

Laws. The Ch'ing Code was a collection of *lü* (statutes) and *li* (substatutes) partly inherited from the Ming and partly enacted during the Ch'ing. In the early Ch'ing there were 436 statutes and 321 substatutes. Later, 30 statutes and 1,572 substatutes were added.[96] They were divided into six categories corresponding to the responsibilities of the Six Boards. But the categories were not entirely logical, the articles were not numbered, and there was no index. It was thus very difficult to study. Ch'en T'ien-hsi suggested that it was important to memorize the table of contents.[97] Wang Hui-tsu went further, insisting that the whole code should be memorized.[98]

Both Wang and Ch'en emphasized the importance of the chapter on "Ming li lü" (Terms and principles).[99] In addition, Wang said one should know not just the provisions but more importantly "the spirit" of them.[100] According to him, once "the spirit" was understood "the ramifications could easily be grasped and contradictions harmonized."[101] Ch'en was familiar with this teaching and gave some examples to illustrate it.[102]

The *Ta-Ch'ing hui-tien* and its supplement, *Ta-Ch'ing hui-tien shih-li*, are compilations of laws enforced by the various branches of the Ch'ing central government. (The Ch'ing Code, enforced mainly by the Board of Punishments, is therefore also included.) Being so voluminous — the 1899 edition of both works, for instance, has 1,320 *chüan* (chapters) and over 38,300 *yeh* (leaves) — they were overwhelming and difficult. Ch'en T'ien-hsi suggested that an apprentice could only select a few important parts to read.[103]

In addition to national laws, there were many provincial regulations and local ordinances.[104] An apprentice would not have time to study them but should know where to find and how to use them when needed.

It is worth noting that "customary law" was not included in a law apprentice's curriculum although many civil matters now regulated by law were then left to customary rules. Some such rules were recorded in local gazetteers, clan rule books, community covenants, and guild charters. But few efforts were made to collect, compare, and analyze them.[105] This fact must have made teaching and learning them difficult. But excluding them did not seem to bother the legal secretary and his apprentice, probably for two reasons: first, conceptually, these rules were not recognized as law but as another set of norms; second, practically, as these rules varied geographically and temporally, it must have been considered unprofitable for a law apprentice to study them before knowing where he was to practice.

Excluding customary rules from a law apprentice's curriculum did not mean that a Ch'ing legal secretary did not have to know them. He had to study them as customs, not as laws, and was to begin after arriving at his post. Wang Hui-tsu suggested that the newly arrived legal secretary establish contacts with the elders of the local community and ask about the customs.[106] As a magistrate, Wang often stopped the hearing at a trial and talked to elders in the audience to find out relevant customs.[107] Kang I, a magistrate of the late Ch'ing, suggested similar measures.[108]

Works that comment on or reorganize the Ch'ing code. Because the Code was so difficult to study, many Ch'ing legal scholars offered help. Some wrote commentaries to explain obscure points and reconcile contradictions; others reorganized the Code in more logical ways by grouping related statutes and substatutes together or adding cross references.[109] Still others analyzed important provisions and restated them in charts or lyrics to help people memorize them. [110] Most likely such works were done with law apprentices in mind.

Precedents. In making decisions, particularly decisions for serious criminal cases, the Ch'ing judges had to apply enacted laws. A precedent was occasionally used to illustrate how an obscure law had been interpreted by the Board of Punishments — provided such interpretation was officially promulgated by the board in the form of a *t'ung-hsing* (general notice).[111] Such a notice was binding for future cases, and it might later be formally made a substatute. Apart from such specially sanctioned precedents, ordinary cases decided by Ch'ing tribunals, including the Board of Punishments, were not regularly published, studied, and cited as sources of law. However, law officials, legal secretaries, and apprentices of law found cases decided by the Board of Punishments useful as teaching and reference materials. Therefore, a number of compilations of such cases were published, some by the Board itself.[112] Ch'en T'ien-hsi mentioned *Hsing-an hui-lan* as an example and said that careful study of this work was necessary for an apprentice of law to understand how law should actually be applied.[113]

In addition to compilations of cases decided by the Board of Punishments, there were a number of works of prefects and magistrates reporting the cases they decided.[114] Such cases did not become binding precedents, but because they were often reported in greater detail, they could be of considerable educational value to law apprentices.

If a law apprentice was especially studious, he could find many case reports and works of officials of past dynasties.[115] They were relevant because the Ch'ing inherited practically all the basic features of the traditional Chinese legal system.

Books relevant to local government. As the majority of legal secretaries worked for local officials, they had to know the operational rules of local government. Many such rules could be found in the Code, the provincial regulations, and local ordinances. Other relevant materials were in local gazetteers and works by former local officials. Ch'en T'ien-hsi mentioned *Fu-hui ch'üan-shu*, but there were many more — some discussing local government in general, others describing the authors' own experiences as local officials.[116] Moreover, there were works on local officials' specific responsibilities — for instance, *Hsi-yuan lu* on Chen's list. In the same category were works on trial techniques, famine relief, local security, grain transport, and so on.[117] A law apprentice did not have to study them all but needed to know how to use them.

Works by legal secretaries about their experiences. A small number of Ch'ing legal secretaries reported their experiences. The most famous work was Wang Hui-tsu's *Tso-chih yao-yen* and his autobiographical works *Ping-t'a meng-heng-lu* and *Meng-heng lu-yü*. Other well-known writings include *Hsing-ch'ien pi-lan* (Necessary reading for legal and financial secretaries) and *Pan-an yao-lueh* (Essential rules for handling legal cases) by Wang Yu-huai, a contemporary of Wang Hui-tsu, who also served as a legal secretary for over thirty years, *Mu-hsueh chü-yao* (Basics of a secretary's training) by Wang Wei-han, a legal secretary of the early Ch'ien-lung period (1736–95), and *Hsing-mu yao-lueh* (Basics of a legal secretary's work) by an anonymous author who, according to Chang T'ing-hsiang, must also have been a successful legal secretary, as was Chang himself, who served a number of local and provincial officials in the late Ch'ing.[118] He compiled the works of these four persons into a volume entitled

Ju-mu hsu-chih (Instructions to aspiring legal secretaries).[119] It was the most useful collection of materials for Ch'ing legal secretaries and law apprentices.

There was a belief that legal secretaries had some secret manuals that they passed on to their favorite apprentices. Ch'en T'ien-hsi denied this.[120] Indeed, there was no need for a secret manual because a law apprentice had so much to read, and many of their reading materials were written by great legal secretaries.

General books on government and culture. A legal secretary's work touched on many subjects. He needed more than mere knowledge of law and government institutions. This is why Wang Hui-tsu insisted that, beside law, legal secretaries had to "read books." By "books," he apparently meant general works on government and culture. So it was reported that when he was a legal secretary the walls of his study were lined with Confucian Classics and history books; law books, in comparison, were negligible in number.[121] Confucian Classics and history were, of course, required reading for those (like Wang) who still hoped to pass the civil examinations. But they were also needed in deciding difficult cases. Wang often resorted to them when he found existing law inapplicable.[122]

Thus we see law apprentices had many things to read, ranging from law to philosophy, from the practical to the theoretical, and from the very specific to the very general. No one could possibly read so much within a few years. The concentration was naturally on the laws. But, as Wang Hui-tsu and Ch'en T'ien-hsi both stressed, law apprentices had to read broadly all along.

Ethical Education for a Law Apprentice. Traditional Chinese education emphasized making a student a moral person; Ch'ing legal education was no exception. That was another reason why the Confucian Classics were kept on the reading list. In addition, many of the early legal secretaries' writings offered specific advice on how to be a morally good legal secretary. The most comprehensive among them were the works of Wang Hui-tsu. Indeed, all his works were of this nature and, as we shall see, they covered practically every aspect of a legal secretary's life. His works were highly regarded by his contemporaries, especially officials and legal secretaries.[123] They were repeatedly reprinted in large numbers during his lifetime and remained on Ch'en T'ien-hsi's required reading list.[124] Therefore, we can assume that they were widely read by law apprentices from the mid-eighteenth century to the late nineteenth century and had considerable influence on their moral outlook. The following is an analysis of his teachings regarding what mentality and life-style a legal secretary should have; what goals he should pursue; what relationship he should have with his employer, his colleagues, and the local populace; what his attitude should be toward authority and law; what role he should play in the legal system; what interests he should protect; what evils he should fight; what responsibilities he should take; what pitfalls he should avoid; what principles he should uphold; what concessions he could make; and, above all, in what way these moral decisions were to be carried out.

To cultivate a mind that is fair and to make the pursuit of justice a personal goal. Wang Hui-tsu pointed out that because a legal secretary's work could affect people's life and property, he was often subjected to undue influence. Wang himself had many such experiences.[125] Therefore, he had to be a fair-minded person to begin with, and he had to constantly resist temptations and intimidations and persistently seek justice.[126]

To live a clean and meaningful life and to preserve personal integrity. A legal secretary's salary, according to Wang Hui-tsu, was just about enough to support a small family in plain living. To avoid hardship every member had to be frugal. The legal secretary himself had especially to refrain from extravagance, lest he be caught in debt and fall under his creditor's control. He also could not indulge in drinking wine, playing chess, reading novels, or any other bad habits, or associate with evil friends. All these could place him in a compromising position. He was to spend his spare time in "reading useful books", namely, laws, Classics, and history.[127]

To be careful in seeking employment and follow certain principles in service. Because a legal secretary had to work closely with his employer he had to be very careful in selecting a person to serve. He was to seek someone who shared his ideas and ideals and was temperamentally compatible. Once employed, he was to do his best to serve his employer and to be responsible, diligent, and loyal. He was not to be fussy about small things like food (which was, as a rule, provided by his employer) and etiquette (particularly, the way his employer treated him); but on important matters—matters of principle and law, matters that affected the interests of the people—he was to make his view clear. If his employer's position was seriously wrong and he was unable to change it, he was to resign. In order to be effective in arguing his points, he was to keep himself respectable and never become too familiar with his employer. And he should never owe him money.[128]

To be strict but reasonable with clerks and runners. The trouble with the clerks and runners was that they were all inclined to "squeeze" the people. It was an important part of a legal secretary's work to prevent them from this wrongdoing. He could uncover their misdeeds, or he could reduce their opportunities. For instance, if he did not unnecessarily require people to appear in court, the runners and clerks would have fewer chances to extort them.[129] But he also needed to realize that a runner's stipend was meager and that clerks did not have regular salaries; they had to rely on various fees paid by persons who came to ask for their services. Therefore, he had to be strict but reasonable. As long as their demands were not excessive, he was not to stop them. But if they cheated the people and abused the law, he was to promptly report their offenses and subject them to severe punishment.[130]

To be dedicated to his work and to care for the people. It is always unfortunate that people get involved in lawsuits. When they came to the magistrate for adjudication they placed their vital interests in his hands. A legal secretary, in handling a lawsuit on behalf of a magistrate, was to have compassion for them and not betray their trust. He was to have no bias but to seek only truth and justice; he was not to be lax but work on the case with complete dedication.[131]

Here is some of Wang's more specific advice. First, a person who filed a lawsuit often tended to exaggerate the seriousness of his case. A legal secretary needed to read the complaint with care. If he discovered that it was a dispute between relatives and neighbors, he was to recommend that the case be dismissed with an instruction for the parties to settle out of court. Even after formal hearings had started, the plaintiff in a civil suit or minor criminal case was to be allowed to withdraw his complaint if he and the defendant had agreed to mediation or arbitration. The purpose for these measures was to ensure family and community harmony and reduce the chances of the parties being exploited by runners, clerks, and litigation tricksters. If in fact some such evil persons were involved in instigation or extortion, they were to be promptly brought to trial and severely punished; there was to be no mercy for them.[132]

Second, if a trial was necessary, a legal secretary was to carefully study the records and decide who was to be brought to court and how many runners were to serve the summonses or carry out searches and arrests. This decision was to be made especially carefully if it was in relation to a criminal case uncovered by the private attendants of an official, because it might involve various forms of corruption and evil designs. In any event, the number of persons to be summoned or arrested was to be kept as small as possible. Women, except those directly involved in murder or adultery, were not to be casually brought to court. Witnesses were not to be arrested and placed in custody. All these and many more details were to be spelled out in the summonses and arrest warrants drafted by a legal secretary. Any inappropriate decision on his part could have caused unnecessary hardship to those concerned and was to be avoided.[133]

Third, when a legal secretary was going to advise the magistrate before and during the trial, he was to keep his equanimity and consciously avoid prejudice. The purpose of the trial was to seek truth. Questions were to be properly designed and skillfully presented. If one hearing was not enough, more were to be scheduled. The magistrate was advised to be patient and compassionate. He should not casually order torture. Although as a means to extract confession torture was permissible, it was to be avoided as much as possible, because it could result in serious injustice. Another result was that the victim could recant when his case was appealed or reviewed, causing delay and complication to the judicial process.[134]

Fourth, after the trial, a legal secretary was to investigate every piece of evidence, study every argument, and take into consideration all circumstances surrounding the case before arriving at a decision. Again, he had to make a conscientious effort to free himself from bias and preconception and to be very careful in his search for an applicable law. The latter task was always difficult because, while laws were usually rather simple and rigid, facts were often complicated and changed from case to case. Thus, even if there were basically applicable laws, they always needed to be interpreted and adjusted to fit the facts of an actual case. For this reason a legal secretary had to know not just the letter of a law but more importantly its spirit. Moreover, inevitably there were cases for which there was no existing law, or where the application of an existing law would have resulted in injustice. In such cases a legal secretary was to look to the Confucian Classics for a higher norm as the basis of his decision.[135]

The objective of the search for a proper law or higher norm was to achieve the most appropriate result for the case at hand. The result was of course to be just. Moreover, it was to be conducive to lasting peace between the parties and educational for the people in the same community. Therefore, while compensation for the injured was to be adequate, the punishment for the wrongdoer was to be just enough; excessive penalties were to be avoided.[136]

Finally, if after a legal secretary's decision was approved by his employer and reported to the superiors it was refuted by them, he was to study their opinion with care and make the proper corrections. But if he found their opinion groundless, he was to draft a reply for his employer to defend the original decision. He was never simply to obey instructions and sacrifice justice.[137]

The above is a summary of some of Wang Hui-tsu's ethical teachings for legal secretaries. His bottom line was that if one could not follow these fundamental moral rules he should not be a legal secretary, and if the circumstances would not allow a legal secretary to follow these rules he should resign and find a more suitable employer. That was exactly what he did seven times during his own career as a legal secretary.[138]

A GOOD PRODUCT OF CH'ING LEGAL EDUCATION

Due to lack of materials we have no way to tell what an "average" product of the Ch'ing legal education was like. But we have enough materials about one of its products—Wang Hui-tsu. While he was a filial son, a loving father, and many other things, he was above all a lawyer, a good legal secretary, and a good judicial official. As an example of what the Ch'ing legal education could hope to yield, he deserves a more thorough study.[139] But for this chapter, a brief assessment of him is sufficient.

Wang studied law with a legal secretary and apparently learned well. He was therefore able to apply law when it could achieve justice but adjust or even avoid law when the result of its application would be inequitable. He knew the spirit of law, and he was versed in Confucian Classics; thus, he always had the higher norms in mind and was never a petty legal technician. His objective was not merely justice for the cases at hand but peace for the community in which the parties lived. He was strict with himself but compassionate with the common people. He was dedicated to his work and to his principles. He generally sided with the weak and oppressed and stood up against the strong and over-bearing. (In many cases he defended criminal suspects and saved them from false charges; in numerous others he utilized law and higher norms to protect the interests of widows and orphans.) As a poor legal secretary he seven times gave up his job (and the much needed income) in order to preserve his integrity and uphold his principles. As a magistrate he refused to be a crony of a provincial judicial commissioner and to decide cases as instructed. He even defied the orders of a governor so that the people of his district could have access to inexpensive salt. In the end, his fierce loyalty to his principles did him in; the judicial commissioner impeached him for disobedience. But he kept his pride and retired. He was indeed one of the great lawyers of all times, and the Ch'ing legal education that produced him deserves to be commended.

REASONS BEHIND THE INSTITUTIONS AND PRACTICES

We have seen that in Ch'ing China legal education was not widespread. But many China specialists today are not convinced. They insist on asking, How could a complex society lack widespread knowledge of law? How could it function without large numbers of lawyers assisting not only the government but also the people in handling legal problems? They argue that these questions are not yet answerable because not enough research has been done. Some point out that Ch'ing society was no less litigious than most others, and there-fore knowledge of law had to be popular; that many *sheng-yuan* (students who had passed the local government examination and were qualified for admission into local government schools) were experts in law who formed a nascent law-yer class; that the scriveners surely knew a great deal of law and precedents, for they were to help decide whether or not to initiate lawsuits; and that as there were twenty-four categories of murder, the ordinary person had to know about this.[140]

These are statements of belief. The burden of proof is on the believers, and it is a heavy burden. To prove that Ch'ing society was litigious, for instance, they need statistics, interviews, and surveys for qualitative and quantitative analysis. Whether in the future any such materials can be found is difficult to predict.

The existing evidence presently points to the opposite. First, let us consider litigiousness. The China specialists probably got this idea from the writings of some Ch'ing officials who give the impression that litigation in Ch'ing China could last years, even generations, and that repeated appeals were common, some of which were directly presented to the throne.[141] Indeed, there were such cases, and each one attracted an inordinate amount of attention. But there were no statistics. We do not know the number of such cases and the percentage they represent in the total number of cases of any given period and area. Considering the cost and hazards of bringing appeals to provincial or imperial capitals, it is unimaginable that such cases were numerous. Anyhow, they reflect more on the legal system than on the people's disposition. Traditional Chinese judicial procedure set no limit on appeals, and presenting serious grievances to the emperor was allowed as a last resort.[142] These features indicate that the judicial system was not sure of itself. In fact, the Chinese did not even regard the emperor as the highest judicial authority. That is why some who perceived themselves as victims of gross injustice did not wait for the judicial process to complete its course before committing suicide in order to seek a fair trial by spirits and deities.[143] This is not litigiousness. On the contrary, it shows that the people had little faith in the judicial system.

The China specialists may have been led to think of Ch'ing society as litigious by another fact: Ch'ing people brought to court many seemingly trivial matters, such as a verbal assault or a dispute over something of small value.[144] Is this evidence of litigiousness? We should realize that in closely knit communities the use of slanderous language could cause serious damage and that, due to widespread poverty, something of small value to us meant a great deal to many people then. Moreover, we should know that many of the lawsuits were brought with an intent not to seek a decision but to cause trouble for the defendant or to induce him to a settlement—that was why after filing the complaint the plaintiff often ignored repeated summonses and refused to appear in court. The reason why filing a complaint could produce the effect desired by the plaintiff was that judicial process was costly and hazardous. It was partly because of this reason that elaborate mechanisms and procedures of mediation and arbitration were developed in Ch'ing China, applying customary rules rather than law.[145]

Another reason for this development was the inefficiency of the judicial system. For a district of several tens of thousands of people there was only one magistrate with a very small staff.[146] He was not only the trial judge but also the chief administrator, responsible for tax collection, local security, education, public works, and many other things. How many lawsuits could he handle? As an extremely diligent magistrate, Wang Hui-tsu reported that he needed an average of three days for each case left to him by his predecessor.[147] He also recorded that many of the cases he handled as a legal secretary had been in court for several years previously.[148] If there were not enough judges to adjudicate, how litigious could Ch'ing society be?

Were there actually many practicing lawyers who assisted the common people in solving their legal problems? We know there were scriveners and litigation masters, but how many? Huang Liu-hung said in *Fu-hui ch'üan-shu* that as a magistrate he appointed only a few scriveners for each of the two districts he served.[149] Liu Heng, a magistrate during the Chia-ch'ing reign (1796–1820), suggested that each district could license two to three scriveners.[150] A survey of *Tan-hsin tang-an* shows that at any given time the Hsin-chu district had no more than two scriveners.

Litigation masters are difficult to count. Because many Ch'ing officials lambasted these troublemakers, one gets the impression that they were numerous.[151] But what corroborating evidence do we have? Wang Hui-tsu was very efficient in detecting litigation masters but only identified two during his four years as a magistrate in two districts.[152] Lan Ting-yuan, another able magistrate who served in several districts during the Yung-cheng reign (1723–35), mentioned in his *Lu-chou kung-an* (Cases decided by Lan Ting-yuan) only three litigation masters.[153] Toward the end of the Ch'ing, social order deteriorated badly. Wu Kuang-yao, an acting magistrate of Hsiu-shan in 1901–02, recorded in his *Hsiu-shan kung-tu* (Official records of Hsiu-shan district) five cases in which litigation masters were involved.[154]

The few numbers mentioned above are, of course, not sufficient statistics, but they demonstrate that the impression of numerous scriveners and litigation masters involving themselves in other people's litigations was overstated. Rather, given the high cost of litigation and inadequate number of judges, it was normal that each district had only a few of these people—otherwise there would not be enough work for them to do.

Of course, lawyers do more than litigate. Ch'ing lawyers probably also drafted contracts and other legal documents for their clients. But a survey of a collection of such documents from Taiwan reveals two facts.[155] First, the language was plain vernacular, the contents commonsensical, and no law, statutory or customary, was cited. Thus, the need for a lawyer's assistance in preparing these documents seems to have been small. Second, the majority of the documents were for sales of land and division of family property. Even if they were drafted and written by lawyers, there was not enough business for them, because such transactions did not take place frequently. It is thus difficult to imagine that many *sheng-yuan* or, for that matter, anyone who was literate, could make a living out of this practice and join a "nascent lawyer class." Besides, there were imperial edicts and a substatute specifically proscribing *sheng-yuan* involvement in other people's litigations.[156] Some violations were unavoidable, but not by a whole "class."

If a person could not get a legal education from regular schools, was prohibited from representing a client in court or otherwise being involved in other people's litigations, and did not have much nonlitigation work to do, how could he become an expert of law? How could a large number of people survive as lawyers?

Yet, if lawyers were few in number, why did many Ch'ing writers also accuse the people of being *hao-sung* (litigious)?[157] Why did practically all officials talk about litigation masters as serious troublemakers? Why were campaigns launched against them? More fundamentally, what are the reasons behind the institutions and practices that prevented private lawyers as a class from emerging in traditional China? How could a complex society function without widespread knowledge of law?

To answer the first set of questions we need to understand the traditional Chinese attitude toward litigation. Litigation was never considered as a normal part of social interaction. It was perceived as a disturbance to social order, a social illness. More importantly, it was considered the result of an official's failure to teach the people to live in harmony, an indication of his inability to govern by example, and an unfavorable reflection on his moral character. A magistrate whose district had many lawsuits earned low grades at periodic official evaluations. If he was unable to solve them satisfactorily he was to be disciplined or punished. Is it any wonder that he would frown upon litigation and hate anyone who caused it, particularly one who was not personally involved in a dispute but instigated lawsuits or helped complicate the judicial process? The fact that he normally did not have much legal knowledge further aggravated his feelings.

For these reasons, many magistrates exaggerated the litigiousness of the common people and the number of litigation masters. They not only complained about this "fact" publicly but also reported it to their superiors. After repeating it often, they and their superiors began to believe it and repeatedly ordered that the troublemakers be rounded up and punished. But the campaigns were all perfunctory exercises with little results. The reason is that there were not many professional litigation masters around. The "fact" was a myth created by frustrated officials to cover up their incompetence.

In contrast, a magistrate who was familiar with law and efficient in handling litigation often boasted how wicked people would bring outlandish lawsuits to him and be moved by his moral teachings and repent, dropping not only their charges but also their animosity against each other.[158] Such stories and the inflated accounts of litigiousness and litigation masters were two sides of the same ideological and political reality, and both were self-serving for the magistrate and his superiors.

To answer the fundamental question about the reasons behind the institutions and practices that prevented an emerging class of lawyers in Ch'ing China, we need to look further into traditional Chinese thought and behavior. As pointed out at the beginning of this chapter, traditional China had many norms, and in people's mind they formed a hierarchy. Positive law was at the bottom because it was perceived as more removed from reason, human feelings, and a natural sense of justice. Such laws were manmade, not necessarily by the wisest of men; therefore, they were often arbitrary and usually ad hoc. Their arbitrariness made the application of laws difficult, as strict construction could lead to injustice and absurdity, while liberal interpretation invited abuse. On the other hand, their ad hoc nature made the positive laws full of loopholes and thus inadequate as a comprehensive social norm. The Ch'ing Code, for instance, was basically criminal, while the laws applied by other government agencies were preponderantly administrative. Civil matters, with which the ordinary people were naturally most concerned, were largely ignored by positive law and left to customs. It is no wonder the majority of the ordinary people living nonviolent, private lives considered positive law as a low norm, unworthy of much attention.

Moreover, in traditional China, law was made solely by the power elite. The common people, excluded from the legislative process, generally perceived law as a tool to oppress and exploit them, and they were resentful. We may wonder why they did not seek the assistance of legal experts to challenge and change the law. The answer is that, first of all, they were unable, because the government employed all the "lawful" lawyers and suppressed others as litigation tricksters. Second, the common people did not think law could be perfected. They apparently pessimistically believed, "The more law, the less justice."[159] Considering their total lack of political power, this belief was not entirely groundless. So they developed instead other responses. First, they tried to avoid the law and the judicial system and seek justice elsewhere. Thus, they widely resorted to mediation and arbitration and, in extreme cases, suicide — in order to present their case to the gods and spirits in the netherworld. Second, some of them abused the judicial system by misrepresentations and false accusations; that is why they needed litigation tricksters. Finally, as a last resort, they revolted against the law and the entire power structure — hence China's many popular uprisings.

Ironically, the power elites practically encouraged these responses, for they too ostentatiously exalted the higher norms over positive law, and they indeed used law and the judicial system to their own advantage as instruments of control. The most frequently heard maxim for the supreme power holder, the emperor, was that he should *i-hsiao chih-t'ien-hsia* (use filial piety as the principle for governing the country). The emphasis on higher norms freed the power elite from the rigidity of law and enabled it to manipulate or disregard its own rules. And because it saw law as a powerful tool, the elite did not want others to touch it. That is why it neglected legal education and launched campaigns against litigation masters, even though these people did not pose a real threat.[160] Thus, the power elite helped to make the people ignorant of law and encouraged them to despise it.

Another strategy the power elite used was the creation and dissemination of the myth that rulers in general were *min-chih fu-mu* (parents of the people), that the magistrates, in particular, were *fu-mu kuan* (parent officials), and that in relation to them, the common people were *tzu-min* (children-subjects).[161] In short, the myth was used to make the state analogous to a family. In a traditional family, there were two basic assumptions — that the father knew best and that he naturally loved his children. These assumptions gave great power to the father in making rules and solving disputes. Because he supposedly loved his children, they could have no doubt about his intentions; because he

supposedly had superior knowledge, they needed complete trust in his
decisions. If a dispute occurred between two children, they only had to present
the facts: there was no need for them to argue about right and wrong or invoke
any rule. The father would find out the truth one way or another—therefore,
procedural safeguards were unnecessary; physical chastisement for the purpose of finding the truth was permissible.[162] And he could apply whichever
rules he saw fit. In this process, it was obviously improper for a third person to
represent or advise either of the parties. Such intervention was an intolerable
challenge to the paternal authority and was angrily rejected—that is why litigation masters were punished. But if the father needed some assistance, it was
all right for him to hire helpers—hence legal secretaries were employed.

Long oppressed and exploited, the common people welcomed this myth and
wished that it were true. This is why when an official showed some sign of care
for the people, they responded with great affection.[163] It also explains why
many people, after failing to obtain justice in lower courts, took tremendous
trouble and risk to present their appeals to the emperor. Unfortunately, many
officials were not caring and they often decided lawsuits according to the
amount of bribe or pressure they received. Even emperors were not necessarily
reliable. In many cases, it was apparent that political expediency, not justice,
guided imperial decisions. To the people who had been taught the paternal
myth, this fact was especially hard to accept. It made them extremely resentful
and cynical. They were convinced that the power elite was full of liars and that
the law and the judicial system were tools of oppression and exploitation. This
conviction also relieved the people from any sense of compunction when they
avoided or violated the law and abused the judicial system—they felt they
were fighting an evil institution and its corrupt beneficiaries.

Thus, there were conceptual and political reasons behind the traditional
Chinese low regard for positive law and the judicial system. With this attitude
prevailing, there was no chance for a lawyer class to emerge. Nor was there a
clear need for knowledge of law. Did these facts create problems in traditional
Chinese society, causing it to malfunction or breakdown? Apparently not, because above law there were higher norms, and while there were not many
lawyers, there were numerous experts on the higher norms. Traditionally, the
Chinese people might not have been law-abiding, but they obeyed *t'ien-li
jen-ch'ing* (heavenly reasons and human feelings). They were concerned with
what was right, though not necessarily with what was lawful.

CONCLUSION AND EVALUATION

The conventional view is that in traditional China legal education was not
widespread. Today's China specialists challenge this view but have not
produced enough evidence to prove otherwise. This chapter has shown that the
legal education of the Ch'ing was largely limited to legal secretaries and that

there were many social, political, and philosophical reasons why Ch'ing China could afford to have this limitation. Conditioned by our own experiences, we modern people cannot imagine a society without private lawyers and widespread knowledge of law—although we cannot say with much confidence that knowledge of law is really widespread in modern society. How many people know, for instance, the difference between the first and the second degrees of murder in American law?

Concerning the education of Ch'ing legal secretaries, this chapter was able to describe their intellectual, practical, and ethical training and to study, thanks to Wang Hui-tsu, a fine example of what such training could produce. But he was probably far above the average, and few materials of other legal secretaries are available. Therefore, a final question remains: How is one to evaluate this education? It cannot simply be compared with the law education of today because their backgrounds are different. However, for an education to be effective it has to comply with certain generally accepted principles. Also, comparing modern law education to the Ch'ing program can make even clearer its advantages and shortcomings.

As a principle, an educational system should open its door to as many qualified students as possible. On this point, the Ch'ing legal education failed; it had no program for educating officials, clerks, defense lawyers, law enforcement officers, or the general public. It was designed for training law apprentices, but even for them it offered very limited opportunities. Not all legal secretaries took apprentices; those who did, usually took only a few junior relatives or family friends. It is no wonder that when the need for lawyers and knowledge of law increased as traditional Chinese society changed, new law schools with the capacity to educate thousands had to be created to replace the Ch'ing system.

If courses are numerous, it is accepted that they are best taught by different specialists. A Ch'ing apprentice of law studied with only one teacher and the education could be quite inadequate. Quite often, the apprentice was the only student, without much opportunity of being with and learning from people of the same status. As fellowship is generally recognized as important to a young person's intellectual and emotional growth, a Ch'ing law apprentice's loneliness was unfortunate. With scores of teachers and hundreds of students, modern Chinese law schools, of course, do not have this problem.

Law is a complicated subject, touching on many aspects of social life. Therefore, legal studies demand knowledge in many fields as prerequisites. The Ch'ing legal education was quite strict on this point. A young man had to have sufficient training in the Classics and history before starting legal study. Thus, it is safe to assume that before becoming a law apprentice he was already familiar with his cultural tradition. More significantly, the Ch'ing system designed a very broad curriculum—while learning law, an apprentice was required to acquaint himself with a wide range of other subjects and continue his classical and historical studies. This broad education improved his understanding of the traditional values and enabled him to see more clearly the road his society had traveled and the direction in which it was heading. As a result, he learned not only law but also its spirit based on those values; not only how to apply law but also how to follow its spirit in keeping or correcting the direction of his society. Unfortunately, most Chinese law students today are not properly prepared for such tasks.

Like medicine, law is both theoretical and practical, and a good legal education provides both types of training. In modern law schools, however, book learning predominates; most students do not get to know legal practice until after graduation. In this respect, the Ch'ing system was better. A law apprentice learned law from both books and the actual cases he assisted in handling. Because theory and practice were checked against each other constantly in his mind, he learned both more effectively.

In its application, law is like a tool. To use it one needs not only skill but also a proper state of mind. But modern Chinese law schools concentrate on teaching legal skill, paying little attention to legal ethics. Consequently, they produce, at best, narrow-minded legal technicians who know only the mechanics of law and are oblivious to the higher priniciples governing the law itself, the lawyers, their clients, and society as a whole. In contrast, the Ch'ing legal education prepared a law apprentice to apply law according to some higher norms, and legal ethics was a major part of the curriculum. Among other materials, a law apprentice was required to study works of upright and virtuous lawyers such as Wang Hui-tsu and Chang T'ing-hsiang. These works not only discussed basic principles but also provided practical suggestions. They could not solve all ethical problems that a law apprentice would encounter later as a legal secretary, but they certainly helped him to see many of them more clearly and to better prepare for searching his own solutions.

Thus, checked against some commonly accepted standards for good legal education, the Ch'ing training of law apprentices is found to have some defects but surprisingly many commendable features. Modern Chinese legal education, in contrast, has more shortcomings. Due to major changes in society—increasing urbanization, industrialization, integration of national and world economies, popularization of Western ideas and practices, and so on—China cannot return to the Ch'ing system; it needs more lawyers and knowledge of law: good lawyers with knowledge of not only the rules but also the spirit of law. To achieve these purposes, the modern Chinese law schools are not quite ready; they need many improvements. It will be a good start if they learn a few things from the Ch'ing education of the law apprentices.

NOTES

1. *Fa* 法 in traditional China always meant positive law. It was often used together with the word *shu* 術 (tactics) to indicate a means to control and govern.

In Western jurisprudence, some moral principles are called "natural law" and some more established rules of custom are called "customary law." These terms were introduced to China in the late nineteenth century and are now widely used in legal discourse. But to the traditional Chinese legal mind, *tzu-jan fa* 自然法 (natural law) and *hsi-kuan fa* 習慣法 (customary law) are misnomers. They are self-contradictory because law is by definition manmade, particularly by the power elite.

Because of the broad use of the word "law" in the West, legal knowledge means knowledge of natural and customary laws as well as positive law. In traditional China, however, the term referred only to knowledge of positive law. People were, of course, fully aware that there were other norms and that knowledge of them was of great importance. In fact, most civil matters were regulated not by positive law but by customary rules and moral principles, and traditional China's elaborate ways of teaching these rules and principles are famous. But they were not taught as "laws;" they were taught as norms higher than or parallel to law.

As this chapter discusses legal education of the Ch'ing, "law" will be understood in the traditional sense. The chapter will not address the teaching and learning of "customary law" and "natural law" because they were considered as different disciplines.

For an analysis of the pyramid concept, see Chang Wei-jen 張偉仁, "Ch'uan-t'ung kuan-nien yü hsien-hsing fa-chih" 傳統觀念與現行法制 (Traditional concepts and the present legal system), *Kuo-li Tai-wan ta-hsueh fa-hsueh lun-ts'ung* 17, no. 1 (1987):1–64.

2. During the Ch'ing, the number of districts varied between twelve hundred and over thirteen hundred. For an analysis, see Chang Wei-jen (Wejen), *Ch'ing-tai fa-chih yen-chiu* 清代法制研究 (Study of the Ch'ing legal system) (Chung-yang yen-chiu-yuan, Li-shih yü-yen yen-chiu-so, Taipei, 1983), 1:163, 236.

3. The higher officials included prefects, circuit intendants, commissioners, governors, governors general, and officials in the Board of Punishments and other central government offices that had judicial responsibilities. For descriptions, see ibid., 169–79, 249–62.

The law enforcement personnel included, on the civil side, deputies to magistrates and prefects and, on the military side, lieutenants, majors, and colonels. For a description, see ibid., 165–72, 241–42.

For a description of various types of clerks and runners and their responsibilities, see ibid., 160–63, 227–36.

For a description of private legal secretaries and their duties, see ibid., 158–160.

Security personnel included heads of *pao-chia* 保甲, *li-chia* 里甲, *t'uan-lien* 團練, and *ti-fang* 地方. For descriptions, see ibid., 152–55, 216–22.

For description of scriveners and their functions, see ibid., 156–57, 223–24.

The last category of persons who played a role in the Ch'ing legal system was known as *sung-shih* 訟師 (litigation master) or *sung-kun* 訟棍 (litigation trickster). For a brief study, see ibid., 157–58, 224–25.

4. For a description of these subjects see, Chang Wei-jen, "Ch'ing-tai ti fa-hsueh chiao-yü (shang)" 清代的法學教育(上) (Ch'ing legal education part 1), *Kuo-li T'ai-wan ta-hsueh fa-hsueh lun-ts'ung*, 18, no.1 (1988): 7.

5. *Sheng-yü Kuang-hsun* 聖諭廣訓 was added to the reading list in 1734. See Chi Huang 嵇璜, et al., eds. *Huang-ch'ao wen-hsien t'ung-k'ao* 皇朝文獻通考 (Ch'ing historical records) (1761; reprint, Taipei, 1962) 1:5498. The teachings were mainly to urge people

to live morally and avoid trouble (like litigation). For a description of this book and its various editions, see Chang Wei-jen, *Chung-kuo fa-chih-shih shu-mu* 中國法制史書目 (Bibliography of Chinese legal history), Chung-yang yen-chiu-yuan, Li-shih yü-yen yen-chiu-so, (Taipei 1976) 1:172.

Li-tai ming-ch'en tsou-i 歷代名臣奏議 was added to the reading list in 1652. See K'un Kang 崑岡, et al., eds., *Ta-Ch'ing hui-tien shih-li* 大清會典事例 (Compendium of Ch'ing laws), (1899; reprint, C'hi-wen, Taipei, 1963) 13:10215. For a description of this work, see Chang Wei-jen, *Chung-kuo fa-chih-shih shu-mu*, 3:1147.

The works on *hsing-li* 性理 included mainly Chou Tun-i 周敦頤, *T'ai-chi-t'u shuo* 太極 圖説, (Comments on the T'ai-chi diagram); Chou Tun-i, *T'ung shu* 通書 (General treatise); Chang Tsai 張載, *Hsi ming* 西銘 (Western inscriptions); Chang Tsai, *Cheng meng* 正蒙 (Primary reader). These works were added in 1700. See K'un Kang, *Ta-Ch'ing hui-tien shih-li*, 12:9505. They were mainly moral teachings. For a brief description of these works, see Chang Wei-jen, "Ch'ing-tai ti fa-hsueh chiao-yü (shang)," 17, n. 47.

6. K'un Kang, *Ta-Ch'ing hui-tien shih-li*, 13:10127–28.

7. Ibid., 12:9504–5. Many of these tests were started during the T'ang dynasty (619 –907). At that time, different sets of tests were given to different categories of students. A person who specialized in law could take just the *ming-fa* 明法 (Knowledge of Law) test, which asked mainly questions about law, and become qualified for government service. During and after the T'ang, new tests were often added and old ones dropped; this also happened during the Ch'ing. For instance, the *chao* 詔 and *kao* 誥 tests were dropped in 1681 but were reinstated in 1702 for students who took the *wu-ching* 五經 (Five Classics) test. See ibid., 12:9505. But since few took the *wu-ching* test, *chao* and *kao* tests were thus in fact abolished. In 1756, the *lun* 論; *piao* 表, and *p'an* 判 tests were eliminated from provincial examinations. But in the metropolitan examination, the *piao* test remained. Ibid., 9508. In the next year, the *shih* 詩 test was first introduced, replacing the *piao* test. Ibid., 9508–9.

8. Initially, all questions were given by examination commissioners. After 1676, metropolitan examination questions based on *Ssu-shu* 四書 (the Four Books) were given by the emperor. After 1685, such questions for the Shun-t'ien provincial examination were also given by the emperor. See K'un Kang, *Ta-Ch'ing hui-tien shih-li*, 12:9504–6; Shang Yen-liu 商衍鎏, *Ch'ing-tai k'o-chü k'ao-shih shu-lueh* 清代科舉考試述略 (Brief study of Ch'ing examination system), (Wen-hai, Taipei, 1956), 65.

9. For instance, in 1726 Cha Ssu-t'ing 查嗣庭, an examination commissioner for Kiangsi province, chose as examination questions two sentences from the Four Books: one from the *Confucian Analects*, which says, "A noble person will not recommend someone merely because of his words, nor will he dismiss an idea because its author is a bad character;" the other from *Mencius*, which says, "If a small path in the mountain is often used by the public, it becomes a road; if it is not often used, it will be blocked by weeds. Now your heart is blocked by weeds." The Yung-cheng emperor thought Cha was maliciously criticizing a policy of his that requested local officials to recommend talents to the government. Cha was sentenced to death and his brothers to internal exile, and students from Chekiang, Cha's native province, were barred from taking the next national examination. See Shang Yen-liu, *Ch'ing-tai k'o-chu k'ao-shih shu-lueh*, 327–28; Hsiao I-shan 蕭一山, *Ch'ing-tai t'ung-shih* 清代通史 (General history of the Ch'ing), (Shang-wu, Taipei, 1963) 1:878; Fa Shih-shan 法式善, *Huai-t'ing tsai-pi* 槐廳載筆

(Notes taken in the imperial academy) (1799; reprint, Wen-hai, Taipei, 1963), 13:7; *Ch'ing-tai wen-tzu-yü tang* 清代文字獄檔 (Ch'ing censorship archives), (1934; reprint, Hua-wen shu-chü, Taipei, 1969).

10. This fact was pointed out by several imperial edicts issued in 1713, 1715, 1735, 1764, 1775, 1796. See K'un Kang, *Ta-Ch'ing hui-tien shih-li* 12:9505, 9506, 9507, 9509, 9511.

11. This order of *tai sheng-jen li-yen* 代聖人立言 was repeated in imperial decrees of 1745, 1759, and 1814. See K'un Kang, *Ta-Ch'ing hui-tien shih-li*, 12:9517–21. Since according to Confucian orthodoxy all basic truth is already in the Classics, anyone who writes on a subject that has been addressed by the early Confucian sages can only expound their themes. Thus, the practice of *tai sheng-jen li-yen* was not a Ch'ing invention; it had a long tradition.

12. Ibid., 13:10213.

13. For an example, see Chang Wei-jen, "Ch'ing-tai ti fa-hsueh chiao-yü (shang)," 20–21 n. 63.

14. See n. 7.

15. These are recurring topics found in examination papers kept at the Institute of History and Philology, Academia Sinica. Over 310,000 Ming and Ch'ing government documents, as a part of *Ch'ing-tai nei-ko ta-k'u tang-an* 清代內閣大庫檔案 (Ch'ing dynasty Grand Secretariat archive), are now in the possession of the institute and are preserved, edited, and published under the title *Ming-Ch'ing tang-an* 明清檔案 (Ming-Ch'ing archives) since 1988. Many are examination papers.

16. Such edicts were issued in 1697, 1730, 1732, 1811, 1882, 1883, and 1886. See K'un Kang, *Ta-Ch'ing hui-tien shih-li*, 12:9505, 9506, 9512, 9513, 9514.

17. As noted in n.10, giving familiar questions was a serious problem for the essay test. The *ts'e* 策 test had the same problem. It was pointed out in an edict of 1745. Ibid., 12:9508. And that is why a 1788 edict prohibited scholars from publishing model answers to likely *ts'e* questions. Ibid., 9511.

As *tzu-wen tzu-ta* 自問自答 would make a question lengthy, the practice was not popular in the early Ch'ing when questions were usually rather brief—within two to three hundred words. During the K'ang-hsi reign (1662–1722), questions were often several times as long and practically all of them were *tzu-wen tzu-ta*.

18. An imperial edict of 1754 suspected another motive—the examiner wanted to influence the students' thinking on the subject matter in question. Ibid., 12:9508. That may have been true. But as an examiner's question could be misinterpreted not only by the students but also by his political enemies and cause serious problems for him, it is more likely that he wanted to define his question in a way that was politically safe.

19. Such a question given for the 1685 metropolitan examination and the answer of a successful student, Lu K'en-t'ang 陸肯堂, who later passed the palace examination with the highest honor, are quoted in full in Chang Wei-jen, "Ch'ing-tai ti fa-hsueh chiao-yü (shang)," 22–23. The question was over seven hundred words. It raised many points and suggested many responses. Lu's answer was about the same length and said very little beyond repeating the suggestions. According to Fu Ko 福格, a magistrate of the mid-Ch'ing, to answer such a question was easy: all a student had to do was to change a few words in the question itself. See Fu Ko, *T'ing-yü ts'ung-t'an* 聽雨叢談 (Discourse on miscellaneous topics while listening to rain) (reprint, Taipei, n.d.).

20. The practice of giving familiar questions was condemned in a 1745 edict. K'un Kang, *Ta-Ch'ing hui-tien shih-li* (1856 [?]; reprint, Taipei:Wen-hai ch'u-pan-she, n.d.), 12: 9508. In 1788, another edict prohibited scholars from distributing model answers to likely *ts'e* questions. Apparently, familiar questions were still given. The practice of *tzu-wen tzu-ta* was prohibited by a Board of Rites regulation of 1736. Ibid., 9507. The purpose of the 1771 edict was not clear, but it certainly would have impeded the practice of *tzu-wen tzu-ta*. Ibid., 9509.

21. In addition to questions concerning the perennial problems mentioned above, several new ones became popular and were repeated in late Ch'ing examinations, including how to suppress rebellions and restore social order and how to bring about various reforms.

22. This practice was prohibited in 1788. See n. 20.

23. About the archive see n. 15.

24. *Ch'ing-tai nei-ko ta-k'u tang-an*, Document no. 65830.

25. Li Han-chang 李翰章, ed., *Ta-Ch'ing lü-li hui-chi pien-lan* 大清律例彙輯便覽 (Ch'ing code with commentaries and other materials) (reprint, Wen hai, Taipei, 1975) 4:1509–17.

26. This answer is quoted in full in Chang Wei-jen, "Ch'ing-tai te fa-hsüeh chiao-yü (shang)," 22, n. 64. The other four questions for the same test were also titles of Ch'ing Code articles. Lo Jen-chung's 羅仁琮 answers to these questions were, like his answer to the second question, commonsense remarks in stylized language with no specific reference to the relevant statutes and substatutes. A survey of many other examination papers in the Ch'ing Grand Secretariat archive proves that Lo's case was typical.

It is interesting to note that this rhetorical tradition apparently started in the T'ang dynasty (619–907). A person named Chang Tsu 張鷟 was extraordinarily successful in civil examinations partly because he wrote good *p'an*. He then chose some actual cases of his time involving serious official misconduct and wrote hypothetical decisions. Because these decisions were written in the elaborate flowery style in which all sentences ran in pairs, when they were later collected and published the book was given the title *Lung-chin feng-sui p'an* 龍筋鳳髓判 (Decisions [so well written and therefore so precious that they are] like dragon's sinew and phoenix's marrow) (T'ang publication; reprint, Hu-hai-lou, 1811). But they also were moral judgments based more on principles in the Classics than on law. Another example of this tradition was Chiao Hung's 焦竑 *Piao-lü p'an-hsüeh* 標律判學 (Study of law and hypothetical decisions) (Ch'iao-shan-t'ang, 1596). It was a collection of *p'an* answers to questions based on Ming Code provisions. The answers were also moral comments and also in the elaborate flowery style.

With some rare exceptions, this rhetorical tradition was not followed by officials in writing actual decisions. Most decisions were written in plain classical style. Thus, the *p'an* test did not serve a useful purpose in preparing officials for writing decisions. However, the traditional *p'an* answers had one thing in common with most decisions of civil and minor criminal cases by trial officials. In such decisions Code provisions were not regularly cited and applied. Instead, reason, common sense, and local customs were used as the basis of judgment. Most decisions in *Tan-hsin tang-an* 淡新檔案 (Archives of Tan-shui subprefecture and Hsin-chu district [of Taiwan prefecture under the Ch'ing]) are in this manner; so are those collected in such works as Chu Hsi 朱熹, et al., *Ming-kung shu-p'an ch'ing-ming-chi* 明公書判清明集 (Collection of just decisions by famous officials) (Chung-hua, Peking, 1987). For more examples of such collections, see Chang Wei-jen, *Chung-kuo fa-chih-shih shu-mu*, 2:804–13.

27. K'un Kang, *Ta-Ch'ing hui-tien shih-li*, 12:9508. The edict that abolished the *p'an* test together with the *lun* and the *piao* tests gave three reasons. First, most students' answers to these tests were *lei-t'ung chiao-shuo* 雷同勦說 (random talks echoing one another). Second, the examiners paid little attention to the results of these tests; their focus was on the essay test, particularly on answers to questions based on the Four Books. Third, a student's answers to the essay and the *ts'e* questions were enough to demonstrate his knowledge, moral character, and aspirations. There was no need for him to elaborate the same in other answers. Ch'ing Kui 慶桂 et al., eds., *Ta-Ch'ing kao-tsung ch'un-huang-ti shih-lu* 大清高宗純皇帝實錄 (Veritable records of the Ch'ien-lung reign) (Peking, 1807; reprint, Hua-Lian, Taipei, 1964), 2:7631.

How could the students' answers echo one another? Because, as pointed out by an edict of 1745, examiners often asked familiar, predictable questions. K'un Kang, *Ta-Ch'ing hui-tien shih-li*, 12:9508–9. Such questions induced model answers, which students emulated. Why did the examiners not pay much attention to answers to the *p'an*, *piao*, and *lun* questions? Because they considered the essay and the *ts'e* questions to be more important. Why were a student's knowledge of the Confucian Classics, his moral character, and his aspirations the most important things for the government to test? There are many reasons, among which the most crucial is probably the traditional Chinese preference of *t'ung-ts'ai* 通才 (generalists) over *chuan-ts'ai* 專才 (specialists) for the government service. But it is not necessary to discuss them here. The important point is that this 1756 edict clearly indicates that the Ch'ing regime, in administering the civil examinations, did not really care how much law a student knew.

Here is an inevitable question: If the law test did not really measure a student's legal knowledge and received low regard from the ruling class, why did it continue to be given since T'ang times? Probably, this was due to inertia on the part of the traditional Confucian intellectuals. Most of the examiners and students were accustomed to the test. It took a Manchu emperor (an outsider to the Confucian tradition) to see its futility. But even Manchu emperors could not make drastic changes that affected the vested interests of the intellectuals. For instance, in 1663 the Manchu regime dropped the *pa-ku wen* 八股文 (eight-legged essay) test. See K'un Kang, *Ta-Ch'ing hui-tien shih-li*, 12:9505. This caused an uproar among intellectuals both in and out of government. After only two examinations (1663–64, 1666–67) the old test was reinstated in 1668. Ibid.

28. See Chang Wei-jen, "Ch'uan-t'ung kuan-nien yü hsien-hsing fa-chih," 1–64.

29. See sections on "Man-chou ch'üan-hsuan" 滿洲銓選 (Selection of Manchu officials), "Man-chou k'ai-lieh" 滿洲開列 (Selection of high Manchu officials), "Man-chou lin-hsuan" 滿洲遴選 (Selection of low Manchu officials), and "Man-chou sheng-pu" 滿洲陞補 (Promotion of Manchu officials), in K'un Kang, *Ta-Ch'ing hui-tien shih-li*, 6:5481–5602, 5683–5722, 5735–92, 5957–70.

30. *Ta-Ming Lü chi-chieh fu-li* 大明律集解附例 (Ming statutes, substatutes, and annotations) (1610; reprint, Ch'eng-wen, Taipei, 1969), 2:469–73.

31. For the same statute in the Ch'ing code, see Li Han-chang, *Ta-Ch'ing lü-li hui-chi pien-lan*, 4:1240. For *Chiang-yueh-ch'u* 講約處, see K'un Kang, *Ta-Ch'ing hui-tien shih-li*, 13:10332–3.

32. See, for instance, Hsu Wen-pi 徐文弼, *Li-chih hsuan-ching* 吏治懸鏡 (Mirror for the officials) (Ch'ing publication; reprint, Kuang-wen, Tai 1976) 1:189; Ch'eng Yen 程 炎, ed., *Chou-hsien hsu-chih* 州縣須知 (Magistrate's handbook) (Pao-jen-t'ang, 1862) 1:7– 9b; Ho Ken-shen 何耿繩, *Hsueh-chih i-te pien* 學治一得編 (Lessons a magistrate learned) (Pao-jen-t'ang, 1841) 34–34b; T'ien Wen-ching 田文鏡, *Ch'in-ting chou-hsien shih-i* 欽定州縣事宜 (Magistrate's responsibilities) (Pao-jen-t'ang, 1871) 6–7b.

33. Wang Hui-tsu 汪輝祖, *Ping-t'a meng-heng-lu* 病榻夢痕錄 (Sickbed reminiscence) (Chiang-su shu-chü, Kiangsu, 1862) 2:16.

34. Official editions of the Ch'ing Code were distributed to government-sponsored schools and government offices. See K'un Kang, *Ta-Ch'ing hui-tien shih-li*, 13:10215–27. Commercial editions of the Code, e.g., Li Han-chang, *Ta-Ch'ing lü-li hui-chi pien-lan*, and its commentaries, e.g., Hsueh Yun-sheng 薛允升, *Tu-li ts'un-i* 讀例存疑 (Doubts arising from reading the substatutes) (Han-mao-chai, Peking, 1905), were readily available.

35. For instance, Li Chih-fang 李之芳, *Chi-t'ing ts'ao* 棘聽草 (Draft decisions) (published by the author, 1654); Lan Ting-yuan 藍鼎元, *Lu-chou kung-an* 鹿洲公案 (Decisions by Lan Ting-yuan) (published by the author, 1732); Hsu Shih-lin 徐士林, *Hsü Yü-feng chung-ch'eng k'an-yü* 徐雨峰中丞勘語, (Governor Hsu Yü-feng's decisions) (Sheng-i-lou, 1898); K'uai Te-mo 蒯德模, *Wu-chung p'an-tu* 吳中判牘 (Decisions made while in Soochow) (published by the author, 1874); Wang Hui-tsu, *Ping-t'a meng-heng-lu*; Li Chun 李鈞, *P'an-yü lu-ts'un* 判語錄存 (Selected decisions) (published by the author, 1833); Ch'iu Huang 邱煌, *Fu-p'an lu-ts'un* 府判錄存 (Decisions of a prefect) (published by the author, 1840). For more examples, see Chang Wei-jen, *Chung-kuo fa-chih-shih shu-mu*, 2:807–13.

36. The popular ones included: Ch'üan Shih-ch'ao 全士潮, ed., *Po-an hsin-pien* 駁案 新編 (New collection of cases corrected by high judicial authorities) (reprint, Ch'eng-wen, Taipei, 1968); Chu Ch'in-g-ch'i 祝慶祺 and Pao Shu-yun 鮑書芸, eds., *Hsing-an hui-lan* 刑案滙覽 (Conspectus of criminal cases) (preface dated 1834; reprint, Ch'eng-wen, Taipei, 1968); Chu Ch'ing-ch'i and Pao Shu-yun, eds. *Hsu-tseng hsing-an hui-lan* 續增刑案滙覽 (Supplement to conspectus of criminal cases); P'an Wen-fang 潘 文舫 and Hsü Chien-ch'uan 徐諫荃, eds., *Hsin-tseng hsing-an hui-lan* 新增刑案滙覽 (New supplement to conspectus of criminal cases) (preface dated 1886; reprint, Ch'eng-wen, Taipei, 1968); Ho Hsi-yen 吳錫儼 et al. eds., *Hsing-an hui-lan hsu-pien* 刑案 滙覽續編 (Conspectus of criminal cases, second series) (preface dated 1884; reprint, Chungking, 1900). For more examples, see Chang Wei-jen, *Chung-kuo fa-chih-shih shu-mu*, 1:306–13.

37. See Liu, Wang Hui-chen, *The traditional Chinese Clan Rules* (J. J. Augusrin, New York, 1959); Taga Akigoro 多賀秋五郎, ed., *Sō-fu no kenkyū (shiryo hen)* 宗譜の研究（資 料篇）(Analytic study of Chinese genealogical books [materials]) (The Tōyō Bunkō, Tokyo, 1960).

38. For an analysis of some of the most famous novels and plays, see Yu Kuo-en 游 國恩, ed., *Chung-kuo wen-hsueh-shih* 中國文學史 (History of Chinese literature) (Peking; reprint, Taiwan, 1982).

39. For brief descriptions of some of the most popular Peking operas of the Ch'ing and early Republican periods, see T'ao Chun-ch'i 陶君起, *P'ing-chü chü-mu ch'u-t'an* 平劇 劇目初探 (Preliminary study of Peking opera stories) (Ming-wen, Taipei, 1982); Hu Chü-jen 胡菊人, ed., *Hsi-k'ao ta-ch'üan* 戲考大全 (Complete Peking operas) (Hung-yeh,

Taipei, 1986). For famous operas of earlier periods, see Lo Chin-t'ang 羅錦堂, *Yuan tsa-chü pen-shih k'ao* 元雜劇本事考 (Stories of Yuan operas) (Shun-hsien, Taipei, 1976); Mei Ch'u 梅初, *Ming-jen tsa-chü hsuan* 明人雜劇選 (Selected Ming operas) (Shun-hsien, Taipei, 1979); Ko Yün-lung 郭雲龍, *Chung-kuo li-tai hsi-ch'ü hsuan* 中國歷代戲曲選 (Selected Chinese operas of various periods) (Hung-yeh, Taipei, 1990). For famous folklore, see Pi-chi hsiao-shuo ta-kuan 筆記小說大觀 (Collected folklore notes) (Hsin-hsing, Taipei, 1973).

40. In most societies, the ruling class tries to make its positive laws conform to the moral principles it endorses. In traditional China, this effort was made by the Confucians, who had been in influential positions since the Han dynasty (204 B.C. to A.D. 220). The result is known as the Confucianization of law. See T'ung-tsu Ch'ü, *Law and Society in Traditional China* (Mouton, Paris and The Hague, 1961).

41. See sections "Kui-shih" 詭使 (False pretense) and "Liu-fan" 六反 (Six perversities) in *Han Fei-tzu* 韓非子. Mencius clearly recognized these conflicts. That is why he spent a lot of space in his book trying to help people find solutions to these conflicts. See sections "Li Lou," 離婁, "Kung-sun Ch'ou," 公孫丑 "Kao Tzu," 告子, "Wan Chang," 萬章 "Chin-hsin," 盡心 and "Teng Wen-kung" 滕文公 in *Mencius*.

42. Many examples can be found in the works of Liu, Wang Hui-chen, and Akigoro. See n. 37.

43. *Hsing-an hui-lan*, for instance, reduces the facts of most cases to a few lines. Nor is the legal reasoning elaborate. Most other case reports are similar in style and substance.

44. This is true with most works listed in n. 35. Even Wang Hui-tsu's work clearly boasts his ability as a judge.

45. For instance, *Lung-t'u kung-an* 龍圖公案 (Cases decided by Pao Ch'eng 包拯) (Wen-ten-t'ang, n.d.); *Hai-kung ch'i-an ch'üan-chuan* 海公奇案全傳 (Cases decided by Hai Jui 海瑞) (Tzu-yun-hsien, Shanghai, 1893); *Shih-kung-an chuan* 施公案傳 (Cases decided by Shih Shih-lun 施世綸) (preface dated 1839 n.p.) *Liu-kung-an* 劉公案 (Cases decided by Liu Yung 劉墉 (Ch'ing publication by Hsieh-yu-t'ang, n.d.). For more examples, see Chang Wei-jen, *Chung-kuo fa-chih-shih shu-mu*, 2:816–21.

46. Practically all *kung-an* 公案 novels were badly researched and poorly written. This is why no one claimed authorship. They seem to be transcripts of what was being told by storytellers. Certainly, they were not meant to be accurate accounts of the traditional Chinese legal system.

47. Li Han-chang, *Ta-Ch'ing lü-li hui-chi pien-lan*, 2:2139–40.

48. The two most famous high legal officials of the Ch'ing were Hsueh Yun-sheng 薛允升 and Shen Chia-pen 沈家本, Hsueh was copresident of the Board of Punishments for seven years (1893–97, 1900–1901) and wrote two great legal works: *T'ang-Ming-lü ho-pien* 唐明律合編 (A comparison between the T'ang and the Ming codes) and *Tu-li ts'un-i* 讀例存疑 (Doubts arising from reading the substatutes) (T'ai-ken-t'ang, 1922). Shen spent nearly thirty years with the Board of Punishments (renamed the Ministry of Law in 1906). From 1901 to 1911, he was first a vice-president and then president of this office. He was responsible for the late Ch'ing law reform and wrote many legal articles, some of which were collected in *Shen Chi-i hsien-sheng i-shu* 沈寄簃先生遺書 (Posthumously published works of Mr. Shen Chia-pen) (Ch'ing publication; reprint, Wen-hai, Taipei, 1964). Neither their biographies nor their own works

tell us much about legal education of Hsueh and Chen. Another example was Hu Chi-t'ang 胡季堂. He served on the Board of Punishments longer than anyone else during the Ch'ing (as a vice-president from 1774 to 1779, as a copresident from 1779 to 1798). But it seems none of his legal writings survived, and his biography says nothing about his legal education.

49. See n. 35.

50. See Miao Ch'üan-chi 繆全吉, *Ming-tai hsu-li* 明代胥吏 (Clerks of the Ming dynasty) (Chung-kuo jen-shih hsing-cheng yueh-k'an-she, Taipei, 1969); Miao Ch'üan-chi, *Ch'ing-tai hsü-li* (Clerks of the Ch'ing dynasty) (Taipei, unpublished manuscript).

51. As a rule, a Ch'ing official was assigned to a post for three years. After this period he could be promoted, demoted, dismissed, or transferred to a post of the same rank but of more or less importance. See K'un Kang, *Ta-Ch'ing hui-tien shih-li*, 7:5793, 5849, 5980, 6095–6106, 6123–41. But because there were more candidates than posts, a candidate was often appointed as a *shu-li kuan* 署理官 (temporary substitute or acting official). As such he could be more frequently transferred from post to post or removed from a post and returned to the status of a candidate again.

Regarding the prohibition against serving in one's native province, see sections on *pen-chi hui-pi* 本籍迴避 (officials avoiding their native places), ibid., 7:5663–66.

Officials did not file documents themselves; they relied on clerks. But clerks did not really keep archives in good order for easy retrieval, or they had a system not known to others. Given the fact that tradition meant so much in pre-modern China, this sounds incredible but was true. Ch'en T'ien-hsi 陳天錫 said he, as a legal secretary, was unable to find documents filed only a few years earlier. Ch'en T'ien-hsi, *Ch'ih-chuang hui-i-lu* 遲莊回憶錄 (Ch'en T'ien-hsi's memoirs) (published by the author, Taipei, 1970) 75. Wang Hui-tsu related that the documents of a case he decided were kept by a clerk at home. Wang Hui-tsu, *Meng-heng-lu-yü* 夢痕錄餘 (Sickbed reminiscence, supplement) (Chiang-su shu-chü, Kiangsu, 1864) 76b.

52. Miao Ch'üan-chi's *Ming-tai hsu-li* and his manuscript on Ch'ing clerks are the most comprehensive studies of the clerks to date. But his description of their legal education is sketchy. A few other works have promising titles but their contents are mostly ethical admonitions to clerks or technical knowledge about government work rather than description or analysis of a clerk's legal education. For instance, Hsu Yuan-jui's 徐元瑞 *Hsi-li yu-hsueh chih-nan* 習吏幼學指南 (Guide to youngsters wishing to learn to be clerks) (Soochow, 1301) was a collection of technical terms and brief explanations; Ch'en Hung-mou's 陳宏謀 *Wu-chung i-kuei* 五種遺規 (Five sets of rules bequeathed by prominent officials and scholars of the past) (Ch'ing publication; reprint, Taipei, 1970) has one chapter entitled "Tsai-kuan fa-chieh-lu" 在官法戒錄 (Advice to officials) that mentions that clerks learned their trade from the seniors in their families. But that was the only sentence about a clerk's education. The rest of the chapter listed 308 examples of things that a clerk should or should not do.

53. The substatute was enacted according to imperial decrees of 1729 and 1735. See Li Han-chang, *Ta-Ch'ing lü-li hui-chi pien-lan*, 11:4354–57; K'un Kang, *Ta-Ch'ing hui-tien shih-li*, 20:15363.

54. *Tan-hsin tang-an* has hundreds of such complaints. For an example, see Chang Wei-jen, *Ch'ing-tai fa-chih yen-chiu*, 2:14–15.

55. Many of the complaints in the *Tan-hsin tang-an* were followed by rescripts spelling out the reasons why they were rejected. For an example, see Chang Wei-jen, *Ch'ing-tai fa-chih yen-chiu*, 2:15.

56. Li Han-chang, *Ta-Ch'ing lü-li hui-chi pien-lan*, 11:4347; K'un Kang, *Ta-Ch'ing hui-tien shih-li*, 20:15362.

57. Li Han-chang, *Ta-Ch'ing lü-li hui-chi pien-lan*, 11:4352–53; K'un Kang, *Ta-Ch'ing hui-tien shih-li*, 20:15364.

58. Li Han-chang, *Ta-Ch'ing lü-li hui-chi pien-lan*, 11:4351–52; K'un Kang, *Ta-Ch'ing hui-tien shih-li*, 20:15363–64.

59. For instance, a copy of *Ching-t'ien-lei* 驚天雷 (Sky-shaking thunder) (Ch'ing publication; anon.; n.p., n.d.), which was mentioned in the substatute that banned such books, is now kept in Harvard-Yenching Library, Harvard University. That library also has *Hsin-k'o fa-chia Hsiao Ts'ao liang-tsao hsueh-an ming-yuan-lu*, 新刻法家蕭曹兩造雪案鳴冤錄 (New printing of lawyers arguments for both parties) (Ch'ing publication, author, publisher, date unknown); Chin-hsia-ko chu 襟霞閣主, *Tao-pi ching-hua* 刀筆菁華 (Selected works of litigation lawyers) (Tung-ya shu-chü, Shanghai, 1923); Chin-ya-ko chu 襟亞閣主 *Chung-kuo ta-chuang-shih* 中國大狀師 (Great Chinese litigation masters) (Chung-kuo fa-hsueh-she, Canton, 1927). The last two books reported many of Ch'ing litigation masters' deeds and works, which must have been preserved in folklore before Chin-hsia-ko chu and Ching-ya-ko chu (probably the same person) put them in writing.

60. See, for instance, Pai Ju-chen 白汝珍, "Lun-p'i ch'eng–t'zu" 論批呈詞 (On writing rescripts), and Wang Yuan-hsi 王元曦, "Chin lan-chun tz'u-sung" 禁濫准詞訟 (Prohibition against indiscriminatingly granting trial), in Hsu Tung 徐棟, *Mu-ling shu* 牧令書 (Textbook for the magistrate) (publisher unknown, 1838) 18:2b, 3; Wang Hui-tsu, "Ti-kun sung-shih tang chih ch'i ken-pen" 地棍訟師當治其根本 (It is necessary to treat the roots of hoodlums and litigation masters), "Chih ti-kun sung-shih chih-fa" 治地棍訟師之法 (Methods of treating hoodlums and litigation masters), "Chin shih-tzu kan-sung chih-fa" 禁士子干訟之法 (Methods of prohibiting licentiates from intervening in litigation), in *Hsueh-chih i-shuo* 學治臆説 (Lessons learned from administering local governments) (Chiang-su shu-chü, Kiangsu, 1862) 2:4–5b.

61. For examples, see Lan Ting-yuan, *Lu-chou kung-an*, 45b, 59, 68b; Chin-hsia ko chu, *Tao-pi ching-hua*; Ching-ya-ko-chu, *Chung-kuo ta-chuang-shih*.

62. Li Han-chang, *Ta-Ch'ing lü-li hui-chi pien-lan*, 11:4180–81, 4345–46; K'un Kang, *Ta-Ch'ing hui-tien shih-li*, 19:15322, 15362.

63. For an analysis of the origin of the posts of governor and governor general and their responsibilities and assistants, see Chang Wei-jen, *Ch'ing-tai fa-chih yen-chiu*, 1:259–62.

64. See K'un Kang, *Ta-Ch'ing hui-tien shih-li*, 1:173–74, 175–76, 178.

65. Wang Hui-tsu was an example of such a principled secretary. He resigned seven times because of disagreements with his employers. Wang Hui-tsu, *Ping-t'a meng-heng-lu*, 1:14–14b, 17b, 25b, 27, 33b, 2:49, 53. Ch'en T'ien-hsi offered to resign once for the same reason. Ch'en T'ien-hsi, *Ch'ih-chuang hui-i-lu*, 75. For analysis of these two legal secretaries' careers, see Chang Wei-jen, "Ch'ing-chi ti-fang ssu-fa: Ch'en T'ien-hsi hsien-sheng fang-wen-chi" 清季地方司法:陳天錫先生訪問記 (Late Ch'ing local judicial system: an interview with Mr. Ch'en T'ien-hsi), in *Shih-huo yueh-k'an*, 1, no. 6 (Sept. 1971): 319–39, 1, no. 7 (Dec. 1971): 388–97; Chang Wei-jen, "Liang-mu hsun-li

Wang Hui-tsu 良幕循史汪輝祖 (Wang Hui-tsu, a model secretary and magistrate) in *Kuo-li T'ai-wan ta-hsueh fa-hsueh lun-ts'ung*, 19, no. 1 (Jan. 1990): 1–49, 19, no. 2 (June 1990): 19–50.

A profession that transmits its knowledge and skill only to relatives and friends naturally tends to draw its members from a small community. The legal secretaries were mostly from Shao-hsing prefecture, Chekiang province. Having family connections or teacher-student relations, they naturally extended to one another some assistance. See James H. Cole, *Shaohsing: Competition and Cooperation in Nineteenth-Century China* (University of Arizona Press, 1986) 118–29; G. William Skinner, "Mobility Strategies in Late Imperial China: A Regional Systems Analysis," in Carol Smith, ed., *Regional Analysis*, vol. 1 of *Economic Systems* (New York, 1976). Some of them, inevitably, became involved in questionable activities. For an example, see K'un Kang, *Ta-Ch'ing hui-tien shih-li* 8:6360–61.

66. As private assistants to officials, legal secretaries were not government employees. They received no government remuneration. Although their actions could seriously affect the government and the people, they were not legally responsible for the consequences unless they personally violated law. Therefore, the many rules adopted by the government to regulate their behavior actually applied only to their employers. See K'un Kang, *Ta-Ch'ing hui-tien shih-li*, 8:6358–63.

67. *Wang Lung-chuang i-shu* 汪龍莊遺書 is a collection of Wang Hui-tsu's works, including *Tso-chih yao-yen* 佐治藥言 (Advice to secretaries), preface dated 1785; *Hsu tso-chih yao-yen* 續佐治藥言 (Supplement to *Tso-chih yao-yen*), preface, dated 1785; *Hsueh-chih i-shuo* 學治臆説 Lessons learned from administering local governments), preface dated 1793; *Hsueh-chih hsu-shuo* 學治續説 (Supplement to Hsueh-chih i-shuo), (postscript dated 1794); *Hsueh-chih shuo-tsui* 學治説贅 (Second supplement to *Hsueh-chih yao-yen*), preface dated 1800; *Ping-t'a meng-heng lu* 病榻夢痕錄 (Sickbed reminiscence), preface dated 1796; *Meng-heng lu-yü* 夢痕錄餘 (Supplement to *Ping-t'a meng-heng lu*), preface dated 1798; and *Shuang-chieh-t'ang yung-hsun* 雙節堂庸訓 (Plain teachings for the Wang family), preface dated 1794. The collection had been published and reissued many times. The edition referred to here was published in 1862 by Chiang-su shu-chü, Kiangsu. For Ch'en T'ien-hsi's *Ch'ih-chuang hui-i-lu*, see n. 51.

68. The interview took place in 1970–71. For the published result, see n. 65.

69. They include Wang Hui-tsu's *Tso-chih yao-yen*, *Hsu tso-chih yao-yen*, *Ping-t'a meng-heng lu*, and Meng-heng lu-yu; Chang T'ing-hsiang 張庭驤, ed., *Ju-mu hsu-chih* 入幕須知 (Instructions to aspiring secretaries) (Che-chiang shu-chü, Chekiang, 1892) (Wang Hui-tsu's *Tso-chih yao-yen* and *Hsu tso-chih yao-yen* are also included in this work); Wang Yu-huai 王又槐, *Hsing-ch'ien pi-lan* 刑錢必覽. (Recommended reading for legal and financial secretaries) (publisher unknown 1793); Wang Yu-huai, *Ch'ien-ku pei-yao* 錢穀備要 (Essentials for financial matters) (publisher unknown, 1793); Wang Yu-huai, *Pan-an yao-lueh* 辦案要略 (Essential rules for handling legal cases), in Chang T'ing-hsiang, *Ju-mu hsu-chih*, 429–533.

70. See Wang Hui-tsu, *Ping-t'a meng-heng-lu*, 1:10; Ch'en T'ien-hsi, *Ch'ih chuang hui-i-lu*, 33.

71. See Wang's preface to *Tso-chih yao-yen*, 1:1–1b.

72. See Wang Hui-tsu, *Ping-t'a meng-heng-lu*, 1:10.

73. See Ch'en T'ien-hsi, *Ch'ih-chuang hui-i-lu*, 34.

74. See Wang Hui-tsu, *Meng-heng lu-yu*, 61–63.

75. Ch'en T'ien-hsi, "Ch'ing-tai mu-ping chung hsing-ming ch'ien-liang yü pen-jen yeh-ch'ih ching-kuo" 清代幕賓中刑名錢糧與本人業此經過 (Ch'ing legal and financial secretaries and my own experience as a secretary), in Miao Ch'üan-chi, *Ch'ing-tai mu-fu jen-shih chih-tu* 清代幕府人事制度 (Private secretaries of Ch'ing officials) (published by the author, Taipei, 1971), 288.

76. See ibid., 145–47.

77. Ibid., 228.

78. In *Tan-hsin tang-an* there are many such documents. See Chang Wei-jen, *Ch'ing-tai fa-chih yen-chiu* 2:11–12, 16–21, 33, 98, 122, 225, 354, 481 for descriptions of the various types of documents.

79. For important points to which a person drafting a *p'i* was to pay attention, see Wang Hui-tsu, *Tso-chi yao-yen*, 6, 7; Wang Yu-huai, *Pan-an yao-lueh* in Chang T'ing-hsiang *Ju-mu hsü-chih*, 483–85; Ho Shih-ch'i 何士祁. "Tz'u sung" 詞訟 (Litigation), in Hsu Tung, *Mu-ling shu* 18:11b–12.

80. Because a warrant or summons could be used as an instrument of extortion, the legal secretary had to be careful to see that only the persons who really needed to appear in court were arrested or summoned. See Wang Hui-tsu, *Tso-chih yao-yen*, 11–12; Hsu Tung, *Mu-ling shu*, 18:26–26b.

81. There are samples of various documents in *Tan-hsin tang-an*. Miao Ch'üan-chi listed some of the technical terms in *Ch'ing-tai mu-fu jen-shih chih-tu*, 150. Although there were books that discussed the use of such terms and the various formats, e.g., T'ung Pao-lien 同寶廉, *Kung-wen shih* 公文式 (Formats of public documents) (n.p., n.d.), an apprentice certainly could do better if he had a teacher to help him in learning the fine points.

82. In many cases the use of Confucian Classics was necessary; Wang Hui-tsu did this quite often. See *Ping-t'a meng-heng-lu*, 35, 44, 68, 92, 110; *Meng-heng lu-yü*, 12, 48, 59.

83. See K'un Kang, *Ta-Ch'ing hui-tien shih-li*, 20:15576–79.

84. For the reports and the impeachment procedure, see Chang Wei-jen, *Ch'ing-tai fa-chih yen-chiu*, 1:319–321, 329, 330–363, 2:20–21.

85. See Wang Yu-huai, "Lun hsiang-an" 論詳案 (On reporting cases), "Hsü-kung" 敍供 (Restating testimonies), "Tso-k'an 作看 (Making analysis of facts and preliminary decisions), in Chang T'ing-hsiang, ed., *Ju-mu hsü-chih*, 491–514.

86. For a description of this investigation and examination, see Chang Wei-jen, *Ch'ing-tai fa-chih yen-chiu*,1:311–14, 2:18, 48, 49, 74, 83, 368, 3:251; K'un Kang, *Ta-Ch'ing hui-tien shih-li*, 8:6779, 20:15662. For inspection of property, see Wang Hui-tsu, *Hsueh-chih i-shuo*, 21–21b.

87. Wang Hui-tsu, *Tso-chih yao-yen*, 6b–7.

88. Such advice was seen in writings of famous legal secretaries. See for instance Wang Yu-huai, *Pan-an yao-lueh*; Wang Wei-han 王維翰, *Mu-hsueh chü-yao* 幕學舉要 (Basics of a secretary's training), preface dated 1770, in Chang T'ing-hsiang, ed., *Ju-mu hsü-chih*, 11–105.

89. Wang Hui-tsu, *Tso-chih yao-yen*, 4b; *Ping-t'a meng-heng-lu*, 25; *Meng-heng lu-yu*, 13.

90. Wang Hui-tsu, *Meng-heng lu-yu*, 74.

91. For a description of the judicial commissioner's responsibilities, see Chang Wei-jen, *Ch'ing-tai fa-chih yen-chiu*, 1:175, 258–59.

92. Wang Hui-tsu, *Tso-chih yao-yen*, 12–14b.

93. Ch'en T'ien-hsi, *Ch'ih-chuang hui-i-lu*, 34–35. *Hsi-yuan lu* 洗冤錄 was by Sang Tz'u 宋慈 of the Sung dynasty. In later dynasties, the book was revised and annotated many times. For some surviving editions, see Chang Wei-jen, *Chung-kuo fa-chih-shih shu-mu*, 1:314–18. *Liu-pu tse-li* 六部則例 and *Liu-pu ch'u-feng tse-li* 六部處分則例 also had many editions. See ibid., 1:67–69. *Fu-hui ch'üan-shu* 福惠全書 was by Huang Liu-hung 黃六鴻, first published in 1694.

94. Ch'en T'ien-hsi, *Ch'ih-chuang hui-i-lu*, 34–35.

95. Miao Ch'üan-chi, *Ch'ing-tai mu-fu jen-shih chih-tu*, 154–56.

96. See Hsu Shuo-heng 許受衡, et al., eds., "Hsing-fa chih" 刑法志 (Treatise on the legal system), in Chao Erh-sun 趙爾巽, et al., eds., *Ch'ing-shih kao* 清史稿 (Draft history of the Ch'ing) (preface dated 1927; reprint, Taipei, 1977), 1:1294.

97. Ch'en T'ien-hsi, *Ch'ih-chuang hui-i-lu*, 34.

98. Wang Hui-tsu, *Hsueh-chih shuo-tsui*, 8–8b.

99. Ibid., 9b–11; Ch'en T'ien-hsi, *Ch'ih-chuang hui-i-lu*, 34.

100. The terms Wang Hui-tsu used were *fa-chih shen-ming* 法之神明, and *fa-wai-i* 法外意. See his *Meng-heng lu-yu*, 29, and his *Tso-chih yao-yen*, 10–10b, and also Shao Chin-han 邵晉涵, et al., *Wang Hui-tsu hsing-shu* 汪輝祖行述 (Anecdotes of Wang Hui-tsu) (a Ch'ing publication, reprint, Kuang-wen, Taipei, 1977) 38.

101. Wang Hui-tsu, *Meng-heng lu-yü*, 29. For similar ideas see ibid., 86b; Wang Hui-tsu, *Tso-chih yao-yen*, 10–10b; Wang Hui-tsu, *Hsueh-chih hsu-shuo*, 7b; Shao Chin-han, *Wang Hui-tsu hsing-shu*, 37.

102. Ch'en T'ien-hsi, *Ch'ih-chuang hui-i-lu*, 34–35.

103. Ibid., 35.

104. See Chang Wei-jen, *Chung-kuo fa-chih-shih shu-mu*, 1:94–100.

105. The first such effort was made by the Ministry of Justice of the Republic of China in the 1930s. The result was a three-volume *Chung-kuo ming-shang-shih hsi-kuan tiao-ch'a pao-kao-lu* 中國民商事習慣調查報告錄 (Survey of Chinese civil and commercial customs) (reprint, Ku-t'ing, Taiwan, 1969).

106. See Wang Hui-tsu, *Tso-chih yao-yen*, 18–18b; Wang Hui-tsu, *Hsueh-chih i-shuo*, 1:13–13b.

107. See Wang Hui-tsu, *Ping-t'a meng-heng lu*, 2:46b–47.

108. See Kang I 剛毅, *Mu-ling hsu-chih* 牧令須知 (What a magistrate ought to know) (Chiang-su shu-chü, Kiangsu, 1889) 1:6b–7.

109. See Chang Wei-jen, *Chung-kuo fa-chih-shih shu-mu*, 1:30–32, 34, 36–39, 40; 3:1232–33.

110. Ibid., 1:38, 39.

111. For some general notices, see ibid., 1:307, 309, 310, 313.

112. Ibid., 1:307, 309, 313.

113. Ch'en T'ien-hsi, *Ch'ih-chuang hui-i-lu*, 35.

114. See Chang Wei-jen, *Chung-kuo fa-chih-shih shu mu*, 2:807–12.

115. Ibid., 1:302–6, 318–21, 804–6.

116. Ibid., 1:146–55.

117. Ibid., 1:314–18, 1:320–22, 1:454–59, 1:514–15.

118. See n. 69, 88. See Chang T'ing-hsiang, *Ju-mu hsu-chih*, 533–631, for the text of *Hsing-mu yao-lueh* 刑幕要略 (Basics of legal secretary's work).

119. See n. 69.

120. See Miao Ch'üan-chi, *Ch'ing-tai mu-fu jen-shih chih-tu*, 157.

121. See Chang T'ing-hsiang's epilogue to Wang Hui-tsu's *Tso-chih yao-yen* in Chang T'ing-hsiang, *Ju-mu hsu-chih*, 178.

122. Such instances were analyzed in Chang Wei-jen, "Liang-mu hsun-li Wang Hui-tsu," 21–26.

123. See Chang T'ing-hsiang, *Ju-mu hsu-chih*, 107–10, 177–80; Ch'en T'ien-hsi, *Ch'ih-chuang hui-i-lu*, 35.

124. See Wang Hui-tsu, *Ping-t'a meng-heng-lu*, 2:59–59b, 65b–66, and *Meng-heng lu-yü*, 92–93b; Ch'en T'ien-hsi, *Ch'ih-chuang hui-i-lu*, 35.

125. On many occasions Wang was asked by his colleagues, his employers, and the superiors of his employers to change his judicial opinions. See Wang Hui-Tsu, *Ping-t'a meng-heng-lu*, 1:25b, 27, 29, 49.

126. See Wang Hui-tsu, *Tso-chih yao-yen*, 3b, 19–19b.

127. Ibid., 4–5, 10b–11b.

128. Ibid., 1–2b, 3–3b, 19–20b; Wang Hui-tsu, *Hsu tso-chih yao-yen*, 6b–8b.

129. See Wang Hui-tsu, *Tso-chih yao-yen*, 6–6b, 11b–13; Wang Hui-tsu, *Hsu tso-chih yao-yen* 1, 2–2b, 3b–4.

130. Wang Hui-tsu, *Tso-chih yao-yen*, 5–5b, 6–6b.

131. Ibid., 7–7b, 13–13b, 14b–15b.

132. Ibid., 7–7b, 9b–10; Wang Hui-tsu, *Hsueh-chih i-shuo*, 19b, 21b–22b, 23–23b.

133. Wang Hui-tsu, *Tso-chih yao-yen*, 11b–12b, 14–14b; Wang Hui-tsu, *Hsü tso-chih yao-yen* 1, 2–2b, 3b–4; Wang Hui-tsu, *Hsueh-chih i-shuo*, 21b–22.

134. Wang Hui-tsu, *Tso-chih yao-yen*, 6b–7, 18b–19; Wang Hui-tsu, *Hsueh-chih i-shuo*, 14–19.

135. Wang Hui-tsu, *Ping-t'a meng-heng-lu*, 1:11b–12b, 14b–15, 17b–19, 20, 20b–21b, 23–24, 24b–25b, 26, 26b–28, 28b–30b, 31–32, 32b–33, 36b–37, 37b–38, 46b, 47b–48b, 49–51, 2:23b–24b. For an analysis, see Chang Wei-jen, "Liang-mu hsun-li Wang Hui-tsu," 16–26.

136. Wang Hui-tsu was a Confucian, but he also believed in ghosts, deities, the afterlife, and retribution. One of his favorite books was Ko Hung's 葛洪 *T'ai-shang kan-ying p'ien* 太上感應篇 (Supernatural interactions), a Han dynasty Taoist book about retribution. When he drafted a decision, he always thought about retribution and tried hard to achieve justice. See his *Shuang-chieh-t'ang yung-hsun.* 2:6–6b, 7–7b, 4:13–14, 5:1–1b, 22–22b. For an analysis of the many instances of retribution he recorded, see Chang Wei-jen, "Liang-mu hsun-li Wang Hui-tsu", 68–69. Similar to *T'ai-shang kan-ying p'ien* were many works known as *shan-shu* 善書 (books of good deeds). They usually consisted of two parts: first, a set of moral principles and rules applicable to daily behavior; second, stories about people who followed or violated these principles and rules. The theme was always that the good are rewarded and the evil punished—if not presently, then in their afterlives. The purpose was to urge people to do good and avoid evil. And it was believed that making such books available was itself a good deed. Therefore, during the Ming and Ch'ing many well-to-do people financially supported the writing and printing of such books. As a result such books became very popular. The high intellectuals, however, did not pay much attention to them, probably because they considered the moral principles too rudimentary and the stories not entirely credible. Hui

Tung was probably the only famous Ch'ing scholar who annotated such a book— *T'ai-shang kan-ying p'ien.* See Hui Tung 惠棟, *T'ai-shang kan-ying p'ien ch'ien-chu* 太上感應 篇箋注 (Annotations to *T'ai-shang ken-ying p'ien*), (Wan-ch'eng fan-shu, Anhwei, 1798). But recently some Western and Japanese scholars have used such books for various studies. See, for instance, Wolfram Eberhard, *Guilt and Sin in Traditional China* (California, 1967); Tadao Sakai, "Confucianism and Popular Educational Works," in Wm. Theodore de Bary, ed., *Self and Society in Ming Thought* (New York: Columbia University Press, 1970).

137. Wang Hui-tsu often wrote communications for his employers arguing with their superiors and was therefore known as "Wang Ch'i-po" 汪七駁 (the seven-times refuted Wang). See Shao Chin-han, et al., eds., *Wang Hui-tsu hsing-shu*, 131. For an analysis of the cases in which he argued against his employers' superiors, see Chang Wei-jen, "Liang-mu hsun-li Wang Hui-tsu," 44–45.

138. Wang resigned eight times as a legal secretary. Once he did so for financial reasons; the other seven instances were the result of disagreeing with his employers on some principle. For an analysis of the circumstances of these seven resignations, see Chang Wei-jen, "Liang-mu hsun-li Wang Hui-tsu," 39.

139. See ibid.

140. These opinions were expressed at the Conference on Education and Society in Late Imperial China.

141. For examples of prolonged litigations and repeated appeals, see Wang Hui-tsu, *Ping-t'a meng-heng-lu*, 1:14b–15, 17b–19, 23–23b, 2:21–22b; William P. Alford, "Of Arsenic and Old Laws: Looking Anew at Criminal Justice in Late Imperial China," *California Law Review* 72 (1984): 6. For Ch'ing laws that allowed appeals to the throne, see Li Han-chang, *Ta-Ch'ing lü-li hui-chi pien-lan*, 11:4171–79, 4185–87, 4188–89, 4193–4200, 4201–5, 4349.

142. Ch'ing law required only that appeals be brought first to the immediate superior of the trial judge and then go up the judicial hierarchy level by level. It prohibited an appellant from presenting his case to a higher authority and bypassing a lower one. See Li Han-chang, *Ta-Ch'ing lü-li hui-chi pien-lan*, 11:4171, 4173–74, 4179–80, 4182–83, 4184–87, 4188.

143. *Hsing-an hui-lan* reports 569 suicide cases, out of which 62 were caused by fear of litigation. The idea that one who failed to receive a fair trial could commit suicide and seek justice in the world of deities and spirits was traditional. The *Tso-chuan* 左傳 (Tso's commentary on the *Spring and Autumn Annals*) recorded several such instances. Wang Hui-tsu also related quite a few cases; he himself was involved in one. In 1761, he made a legally correct but morally imperfect decision that caused the plaintiff, a woman, to commit suicide and bring her case to deities. He was summoned in a dream to face her charges. See Wang Hui-tsu, *Tso-chih yao-yen*, 12–12b; Wang Hui-tsu, *Ping-t'a meng-heng-lu*, 1:21b, 2:75; Wang Hui-tsu, *Meng-heng lu-yu*, 64, 76.

144. For instance, in the 1761 case mentioned in the previous note, the woman committed suicide because the defendant had made in public a veiled proposal to have sexual relations. *Tan-hsin tang-an* has many cases involving relatively small amounts of money.

145. This practice, known as *t'u-chun pu-t'u-shen* 圖准不圖審 (seeking to have a complaint accepted by the authorities without intending to go to a trial), was apparently

widespread. It was condemned as one of the reasons for the proliferation of litigation. See Hsu Tung, ed., *Mu-ling shu*, 18:1b; K'ui Lien 魁聯, *Hou shou pao-lu* 後守寶錄 (Treasured lessons learned by a prefect serving his second term) (preface dated 1853; published 1874, publisher unknown) 1:18b. There are numerous examples of this practice in *Tan-hsin tang-an*. The Ch'ing judicial process was very costly and hazardous. Litigants and witnesses could be "squeezed," tortured, and kept lawfully or unlawfully in custody for long periods while awaiting trial or review, resulting in financial ruin, serious physical injury, or death. This is why most clan rules condemned litigation among family members and warned them against lawsuits with outsiders. The same admonition was repeated by many officials. See, for instance, proclamations, announcements, and orders issued by governors, censors, and magistrates of the early Ch'ing in Li Yü 李漁, ed., *Hsin-tseng tzu-chih hsin-shu* 新增資治新書 (New collection of works useful for government) (preface dated 1663, Tai-yueh-lou), vol. 2, no. 9:16–27b; Ho Ken-shen, *Hsueh-chih i-te pien*, 37b–38b, 43; Hu Yen-yü 胡衍虞, ed., *Chü-kuan kua-kuo lu*, 居官寡過錄 (Advice for officials to avoid mistakes) (Ch'ing-chao t'ang, 1775), 1:7, 13b, 3:20–20b; Yuan Shou-ting, *T'u-min lu*, 圖民錄 (Notes on government for the people) (preface dated 1756, n.p.), 2:5–5b, 6–7, 13b, 17b–18b; Pao Shih-ch'en 包世臣, *Ch'i-min ssu-shu*, 齊民四術 (Four methods for governing the people) (1851, n.p.), 8:7–8b; Liu Heng, *Yung-li yung-yen*, 1:30b, 37–37b, 2:1; Yü Ch'ien 裕謙, "Chieh-sung shuo" 戒訟說 (Warning against litigation) in Hsu Tung, ed., *Mu-ling shu*, 17:46–48.

146. Most Ch'ing magistrates had about two to four subordinate officials, one or two secretaries, ten to twenty clerks, and several tens of runners. For an analysis of the magistrate's staff and its responsibilities, see T'ung-tsu Ch'ü, *Local Government in China under the Ch'ing* (Cambridge, Mass., 1962), 1–13; Chang Wei-jen, *Ch'ing-tai fa-chih yen-chiu*, 1:163–66.

147. See the recollection of Wang Chi-fang 汪繼坊, Hui-tsu's eldest son, in Shao Chin-han, et al., eds., *Wang Hui-tsu hsing-shu*, 135.

148. For instance, in 1758 Wang Hui-tsu decided a dispute over a grave site that had been litigated more than ten years. In 1760, he decided an adoption case that had been in court for eighteen years. See Wang Hui-tsu, *Ping-t'a meng-heng-lu*, 1:14b–15, 17b –19.

149. Huang Liu-hung, *Fu-hui ch'üan-shu*, 3:21b.

150. Liu Heng 劉衡, "Li-sung shih-t'iao" 理訟十條 (Ten rules for handling litigation), in Hsu Tung, *Mu-ling shu*, 17:34b.

151. See for instance, Huang Liu-hung, *Fu-hui ch'üan-shu*, 11:14b–16; Wang Hui-tsu, *Tso-chih yao-yen*, 7–7b; Wang Hui-tsu, *Hsu tso-chih yao-yen* 1, 1b–2, Wang Hui-tsu, *Hsueh-chih i-shuo*, 2:4–4b; Kang I, *Mu-ling hsu-chih* 1:14b–15; Tseng Kuo-fan 曾國藩, "Chih-li ch'ing-sung shih-i shih-t'iao" 直隸清訟事宜十條 (Ten rules for clearing the judicial process), in Sheng K'ang 盛康, *Huang-ch'ao ching-shih-wen hsu-pien* 皇朝經世文續 編 (Collection of treatises on Ch'ing government, a supplement) (reprint, Taipei, Ssu-pu-lou, Kiangsu, 1897; reprint, Wen-hai, Taipei, 1972), 19:4726–28; K'ui Lien, *Ch'ien-shou pao-lu* 前守寶錄 (Treasured lessons learned by a prefect serving his first term) (preface dated 1853, published 1874, publisher unknown) 1:10b, 17b–18; Liu Heng, "I-fu li-sung chang-ch'eng shu" 議覆理訟章程書 (Response to the regulations for clearing the judicial process), in Sheng K'ang, *Huang-ch'ao ching-shih-wen hsu-pien*, 19: 4749–51; Wu Kuang-yao 吳光耀, *Hsiu-shan kung-tu* 秀山公牘 (Official records of

Hsiu-shan district) (preface dated 1903) 1:27, 35, 45, 48, 54. Many more such attacks are recorded in Hsu Tung, *Mu-ling shu*, 1:27, 35, 45, 48, 54, 17:26b–27, 40b–42, 46–46b, 18:1–4b.

152. See Wang Hui-tsu, *Ping-t'a meng-heng-lu*, 2:7, 28, 45b.

153. Lan Ting-yuan, *Lu-chou kung-an*, 2:45–50b, 59–64, 68–73b.

154. Wu Kuang-yao, *Hsiu-shan kung-tu* 1:35b, 38b, 45b, 48b, 54b.

155. Over six thousand documents were collected and cataloged by Wang Shih-ch'ing 王世慶 during 1974–84. Photocopies of these documents, known as *T'ai-wan kung-ssu ts'ang ku-wen-shu ying-pen* 台灣公私藏古文書影本, are now kept in the Harvard-Yenching, Hoover, and Fu Ssu-nien libraries.

156. An imperial edict of 1652 not only condemned *sheng-yuan* 生員 for involvement in other people's litigation, including giving testimony, but also prohibited them from appearing in judicial proceedings in which their personal interests were affected, ordering that such cases be brought to court by a non-*sheng-yuan* member of the household. See K'un Kang, *Ta-Ch'ing hui-tien shih-li* 13:10228. These rules were emphasized repeatedly by later edicts. Ibid., 10228–29, 10379. In 1771, a substatute was adopted prescribing punishments for the prohibited behavior. Li Han-chang, *Ta-Ch'ing lü-li hui-chi pien-lan*, 11:4281–82.

157. See for instance, Wang Hui-tsu, *Ping-t'a meng-heng-lu*, 2:2b; Lan Ting-yuan, *Lu-chou kung-an*, 1:5b; Hsia Sun-tung 夏聲桐, et al., eds., "Hsun-li chuan" 循史傳 (Biographies of meritorious lower officials), in Chao Erh-sun, et al., eds., *Ch'ing-shih kao*, 3:3497, 3498, 3503, 3507, 3513, 3520, 3525, 3530.

158. For examples, see Yuan Shou-ting 袁守定, "T'ing-sung" 聽訟 (Hearing lawsuits), in Hsu Tung, *Mu-ling shu*, 17:25–26; Lan Ting-yuan, *Lu-chou kung-an*, 1:51–53b; Shao Chin-han, *Wang Hui-tsu hsing-shu*, 140–41.

159. This perception was succinctly articulated by Lao-tzu. There was an interesting parallel in late nineteenth-century France; see "From Justice, Lord, Deliver Us!" in Eugen Weber, *Peasants into Frenchmen: The Modernization of Rural France 1870–1914* (Stanford, 1976), 50–66.

160. Imperial edicts were issued and Board of Civil Appointments regulations enacted in 1725, 1736, 1815, 1825, and 1850 to demand that provincial and local officials and officers launch campaigns against litigation masters. Provincial authorities and magistrates in turn issued orders to arrest or expel litigation masters. For an analysis of these edicts, regulations, and orders, see Chang Wei-jen, *Ch'ing-tai fa-chih yen-chiu*, 1:383–84, n. 27.

161. This myth was probably first recorded in *Shih-ching* 詩經 (Book of odes). See James Legge, *The Chinese Classics IV: The She King* (reprint, Hong Hong, 1949), 273, 489. It is not clear when the terms *fu-mu kuan* 父母官 and *tzu-ming* 子民 were first used, but during the Ch'ing they were certainly popular.

162. Most of the modern procedural safeguards against the abuse of judicial power were unknown in Ch'ing China. The judges were largely free to devise their own methods for finding the truth. For instance, some magistrates conducted hearings in temples of local deities. See Lan Ting-yuan, *Lu-chou kung-an*, 1:18; Wang Hui-tsu, *Ping-t'a meng-heng-lu*, 2:23b. Other questionable methods, such as leading questions, harsh scolding, and threats of diabolic consequences, were regularly used. In most criminal cases, torture was permitted by law. See Li Han-chang, *Ta-Ch'ing lü-li hui-chi*

pien-lan, 12:4954–55, 4957–60, 4961–67. For exceptions, see ibid., 5035–37, 13:5261–63, 5305–06.

163. Wang Hui-tsu related that the people of his district (Ning-yuan, Hunan) responded enthusiastically to many of his programs. Because he had the reputation of being a good judge, people of other districts brought their lawsuits to him. After he was dismissed from office, the local gentry wrote a long poem commemorating many of his worthy deeds. Several persons from the district continued to visit him in Hsiao-shan, Chekiang, long after his retirement. See Wang Hui-tsu, *Ping-t'a meng-heng-lu*, 2:13, 14, 16, 17, 23, 27b, 48; *Meng-heng lu-yü*, 8b. Similar responses were recorded in *Hsun-li chuan* (biographies of good local officials) in every official dynastic history.

GLOSSARY

Chang T'ing-hsiang	張廷驤	Ch'ü T'ung-tsu	瞿同祖
Chang Tsai	張載	*chüan*	卷
Chang Wei-jen	張偉仁	Chung-yang yen-	中央研
Chao	詔	chiu-yüan	究院
Ch'en-pi-lou ts'ung-shu	枕碧樓叢書	*fa*	法
Ch'en T'ien-hsi	陳天錫	Fa Shih-shan	法式善
cheng-fa hsueh-t'ang	政法學堂	*Fu-hui ch'üan-shu*	福惠全書
Cheng meng	正蒙	*fu-mu kuan*	父母官
Chi Huang	秸璜	Han Fei	韓非
"Ch'i-yin t'ien-liang"	欺隱田糧	*hao-sung*	好訟
"Chiang-tu lü-ling"	講讀律令	*Hou shou pao-lu*	後守寶錄
chiang-yueh-ch'u	講約處	*Hsi ming*	西銘
Ch'ien-lung	乾隆	*hsi-su*	習俗
Chih-chuang hui-i-lu	遲莊回憶錄	*Hsi-yüan lu*	洗冤錄
"chih shih-tzu kan-	治士子干	*Hsiao-ching*	孝經
sung chih-fa"	訟之法	Hsiao I-shan	蕭一山
"chih ti-kun sung-	治地棍訟	*Hsing-an hui-lan*	刑案滙覽
shih chih-fa"	師之法	*Hsing-ch'ien pi-lan*	刑錢必覽
Chin-ya-ko chu	襟亞閣主	*hsing-li*	性理
ching-ch'a	京察	*Hsing-mu yao-lüeh*	刑幕要略
Ch'ing Kuei	慶桂	*hsiu-li ts'ang-k'u*	修理倉庫
Ch'ing-tai hsü-li	清代胥吏	*Hsüan-tai kuan-fang*	懸帶關防
Ch'ing-tai k'o-chü	清代科舉	*p'ai-mien*	牌面
k'ao-shih shu-lüeh	考試述略	Hu Yen-yü	胡衍虞
Ch'ing-tai mu-fu	清代幕府	*Huai-t'ing tsai-pi*	槐庭載筆
jen-shih chih-tu	人事制度	Huang En-t'ung	黃思彤
Ch'ing-tai nei-ko	清代內閣	Huang Liu-hung	黃六鴻
ta-k'u tang-an	大庫檔案	*i-hsiao chih-t'ien-hsia*	以孝治天下
Ch'ing-tai t'ung-shih	清代通史	*I-te ou-t'an*	一得偶談
Ch'ing-tai wen-tzu-yü tang	清代文字獄檔	*Ju-mu hsü-chih*	入幕須知
Ch'in-ting chou-hsien shih-i	欽定州縣事宜	Kao	誥
Chou Tun-i	周敦頤	*kou-sung chih-shu*	構訟之書
Chung-kuo li-tai	中國歷代	*kuan-yüan hsi-yin*	官員襲蔭
hsi-ch'ü hsüan	戲曲選	*Kung-an hsiao-shuo*	公案小說

Lan Ting-yüan	藍鼎元	*Ta-Ch'ing hui-tien*	大清會典
li	禮	*shih-li*	事例
li	里	*Ta-Ch'ing kao-tsung*	大清高
li	例	*ch'un-huang-ti shih-lu*	宗皇帝實錄
Li-pu tse-li	吏部則例	*Ta-Ch'ing lü-li*	大清律例
Li-tai ming-ch'en tsou-i	歷代名臣奏議	*Ta-Ming-lü chi-chieh*	大明律集解
Liu Heng	劉衡	*fu-li*	附例
Liu-pu ch'u-fen tse-li	六部處分則例	*T'ai-chi-t'u shuo*	太極圖説
Liu-pu tse-li	六部則例	*Tan-hsin tang-an*	淡新檔案
Lu-chou kung-an	鹿洲公案	*tao*	道
lü	律	*te*	德
Lü-ying	綠營	*t'ien-li*	天理
lun	論	*t'ien-li jen-ch'ing*	天理人情
"Lun hsiang-an"	論詳案	T'ien Wen-ching	田文鏡
Mao Yung-hsieh	毛永燮	*T'ing-yü ts'ung-t'an*	聽雨叢談
Miao Ch'üan-chi	繆全吉	*ts'e*	策
min-chih fu-mu	民之父母	*Tso-chih yao-yen*	佐治藥言
"Ming li lü"	名例律	*Tso-chuan*	左傳
Mu-hsüeh chü-yao	幕學舉要	*t'ui-kuan*	推官
Pan-an yao-lüeh	辦案要略	*t'ung-hsing*	通行
p'an	判	*T'ung shu*	通書
p'i	批	*tzu-jan fa*	自然法
piao	表	*tzu-min*	子民
ping-t'a meng-heng-lu	病榻夢痕錄	*tzu-wen tzu-ta*	自問自答
shang-shu ch'en-yen	上書陳言	"Wan Chang"	萬章
Shang Yen-liu	商衍鎏	Wang Hui-tsu	汪輝祖
Shao-hsing	紹興	*Wang Lung-chuang i-shu*	汪龍莊遺書
sheng-pu	升補	Wang Wei-han	王維翰
Sheng-yü kuang-hsün	聖諭廣訓	Wang Yu-fu	王有孚
Sheng-yüan	生員	Wang Yu-huai	王又槐
shih	詩	*wen*	文
shu-hsi t'i	熟習題	Wu Kuang-yao	吳光耀
sung-kun	訟棍	Yang Shih-ch'i	楊士奇
sung-shih	訟師	*yeh*	葉
Ssu shu	四書	Yu kuo-en	游國恩
ta-chi	大計	*yu-hsü chün-shu*	優恤軍屬
Ta-Ch'ing hui-tien	大清會典	Yü Ch'ien	裕謙

TEN

Manchu Education

Pamela Kyle Crossley

The title of this chapter contains an intended confusion, indicating both education of unspecified persons in the Manchu language and education of Manchus in unspecified languages.[1] These are separate issues, but they are linked in ways that reveal distinctive aspects of the institutional and ideological lives of the Ch'ing dynasty. To a degree, both the Manchu language and the Manchu people were inventions of the state, which attempted to control their development to serve its inner priorities. These priorities mandated a transformation of Manchu culture from an orally transmitted to a classicized heritage, a program to prepare bannermen generally to serve as the foundation of state administration, and finally a hope on the part of the court to specialize, redefine, and reacculturate the Manchus. The alterations in state outlook that prompted these changes, as well as some of the reasons for the overall failure of these policies, are examined in this chapter.

LANGUAGE AND AUTHORITY UNDER THE CH'ING

The late eighteenth century was a watershed in the development of the programs applied to banner education and the role of the Manchu language in it. The fundamental cause of the changes overseen by Hung-li, the Ch'ien-lung emperor (r. 1736–95), in his very old age may have been an earlier but ongoing movement toward ideological absolutes.[2] Many of these developments fall outside the scope of this chapter, but it is important to understand the two roles that the Manchu language played in the historical and cultural reconstructions of the Ch'ien-lung court. The first role was symbolic. Like the Mongolian great-khans, Hung-li considered himself as ruling a universal realm that had no external boundaries but was internally marked by distinctions of history, culture, and status. A monumental expression of the universal integration of historical particulars—the role of the emperor, or the *čakravartin*, as Hung-li characterized himself—was found in polylingualism. Architecture and literature could equally be put to monumental uses. Like the Mongolian khans before him who had expressed their universalism in displays such as that which survives at Chü-yung Kuan, Hung-li used both. His state was, indeed, heavily dependent on Mongolian, which since Yüan times had remained intimately connected with expressions of imperial universalism in China. Manchu, as the orthographic expression of the origins and nature of the Manchu people, was also a necessary visual component in such displays. One result was a visual ubiquity of Manchu and Mongolian, which is still evident in the architectural relics of Peking and Shenyang. Another result was the symbolic use of literature, publishing, and curatorship.

Manchu was a problematic element in bureaucratic and intellectual life in Ch'ing China. The perception of the late seventeenth- and eighteenth-century emperors was that Manchu noblemen were deficient in the language and Manchu bannermen were becoming all but ignorant of it, while the emperors themselves bore the burden of personally perusing edicts translated into and out of Manchu (and Mongolian) in order to minimize errors resulting from carelessness or incompetence. It is somewhat ironic that this language, which the Manchus themselves wrote with such difficulty and such (for the emperors) traumatizing results, was the descendant of one of the earliest and best-attested languages of the Tungusic branch of the hypothesized Altaic language family.[3] Jurchen was relatively closely related to Evenk, Gold, Orochon, Nanai, and other languages of the tribal peoples of northeastern China and the Soviet Maritime Province and is evidently much more remotely connected to Korean, Japanese, and Okinawan. In Ch'ing and modern times, Manchu has had, apart from the standard language, one important dialect in Sibo, which is recognized by the government of the People's Republic of China as a distinct language.[4] Manchu proper has had many subdialects, from the earliest times to the present day, though the eighteenth-century Ch'ing court did all it could to minimize dialects and all other forms of cultural informality.

Like their Jurchen predecessors, Manchu speakers in areas affected by Chinese commerce or settlement have freely adopted Chinese loanwords, which in a majority of cases have been assimilated—verbs being declined according to Manchu rules, nouns being pluralized according to Manchu rules. The result was an enlargement of the Manchu vocabulary, though the Ch'ien-lung emperor, in particular, lamented the apparent mongrelization of the tongue. Moreover, anyone working with Manchu documents soon comes to realize that many dialectal and colloquial usages were incorporated into certain Manchu writings, and few of these were ever recognized by the compilers of Ch'ing period dictionaries or their derivatives. Such "errors" were likely to be committed by writers who understood the phonetic principles of Manchu and were able to record their own speech. Examination candidates — whether banner or civilian — who took up the practice of memorizing Manchu writings from memorials and copybooks with little or no understanding of the phonetics were likely to pass as competent until their memories failed.[5] It should be stressed that imperial concern for the decline of Manchu was strictly limited to standard Manchu speech (*Ch'ing-yü*, or *kuo-yü*) and writing (*Ch'ing-wen* or *kuo-wen*) — both creations of the court and extensions of its authority — and not to the popular forms of Manchu, Sibo, and the Manchu-Chinese (or Chinese-Manchu) dialects that are known to have survived in Manchu communities into the twentieth century.[6]

The history of the orthographic representation of Jurchen/Manchu has been rather unusual and took its toll on attempts by the Ch'ing state to make Manchus universally literate in Manchu. In the twelfth century, the Jurchens of the northeast created the Chin dynasty and for a time (1121–1234) controlled a portion of northern China. Their language, which was ancestral to Manchu, was written in a script adopted virtually without alteration from the Kitans, whose Liao dynasty the Jurchens had destroyed in 1121. The Kitans had spoken a language more closely related to Mongolian, probably, than to any other surviving language. As such it was not identical to Jurchen. But as an Altaic language, Kitan was what is often called "agglutinative," meaning that case and tense were established by particle endings on words (as well as by other devices), and thus in its basic grammatical structure resembled Jurchen. By contrast, medieval Chinese was monosyllabic and without case particles. The Kitans had devised a so-called "large-character" script, which used ideographs derived from Chinese but unintelligible to the Chinese. They also created a "small-character" script that contained phonetic elements compounded in a schematic form conceptually resembling the *han'gul* script of Korea, with particle markers.[7] This small-character script was adopted by the Jurchens, who over the course of time made small alterations to bring it into greater agreement with the special characteristics of Jurchen itself. During the course of the Jurchen Chin dynasty, it appears that Jurchen translations of the Chinese works *I-ching, Shu-ching, Shih-ching, Lun-yü, Li Chi, Meng-tzu, Lao-tzu, Yang-tzu, Wen-chung-tzu, Ch'un-ch'iu, Liu-tzu, Hsin T'ang-shu, Shih-chi, Han-shu,* and *Chen-kuan cheng-yao* (see also Elman, chap. 4 of this volume) were completed. Some material from these works was the foundation for the Jurchen-language *chin-shih* examinations, under which Jurchens competed for appointment to bureaucratic office.[8]

The Jurchen script survived the downfall of the Chin dynasty (which was destroyed by the Mongols in 1234) and had at least some official recognition under the Yüan, who carved *dhārani* in the language on major gateways and other monumental displays. In Ming times, it was the official mode of communication between the Jurchen functionaries of the *wei-so* system in the northeast and the Chinese court; the Yung-ning Ssu, at the military settlement in present-day Heilungkiang province, was inscribed in Chinese, Mongolian, and the Jurchen script.[9]

In later times, however, Jurchens protested against the use of the medieval script in official communications. The Chien-chou Jurchens from whom the early Ch'ing state arose, for instance, were part of the eastern Jurchens — those who were in much closer contact with the Yi Korean court than with the Chinese — who had lost this script. The point at which they ceased to use it is unclear, but the "translators' bureaus" (*ssu-i kuan*) received a communication from the western Jurchens in 1444 that stated, "Nobody out here in the forty garrisons (*wei*) understands Jurchen script, so please write to us in Mongolian (*ta-ta*) from now on."[10] Korean emissaries to the headquarters of the Chien-chou chieftains in the late sixteenth century had noted repeatedly that the headmen demanded communications not in Jurchen but in Uigur-script Mongolian. It is evident that the Jurchens actually spoke Jurchen but for purposes of written communication translated their tongue into and out of written Mongolian.

Cultural legend attributes the great change in this policy to Nurgaci. It is reported that one day in 1599 he had the idea of using the phonetic Mongolian script to write not Mongolian but Jurchen and instructed two of his *baksi*, or literate men (from Mongolian *bagshi* and ultimately from Chinese *po-shih*), Gagai and Erdeni, to devise a suitable system. The two men demurred at first, protesting that the present method of using Mongolian was ancient and seemed in no need of alteration, which caused Nurgaci to thunder, "The Chinese write their own speech, the Mongols write their own speech. Are you telling me that it is better for us all to continue learning and writing a foreign language than for you to find a way for us to write our own?" The two learneds, according to tradition, withdrew and devised a new Jurchen script.[11] Thus, the construction of Nurgaci's role as cultural interventionist provides both a chronological horizon for Manchu civilization and a model for the Ch'ing ruler. The creation of a new script for Manchu was the historical marker for the end of the Jurchen language and the beginning of Manchu. And the regional particularism in Nurgaci's expression would remain, to the end of the dynasty and beyond, a well from which Ch'ing authority would continue to be drawn.

The shift to the new script was troublesome, and there is no evidence that an upsurge in literacy among Jurchens ensued. The Koreans, who knew both old Jurchen and Mongolian, did not know this new thing, and for a considerable time foreign communications were handled just as they had been before; Mongolian remained the *lingua franca*.[12] Moreover, the new device, which like all of its Syriac-derived ancestors up to Mongolian was unvocalized, confused many readers who could not easily associate the written word with the spoken, partly due to the impracticability of using Mongolian vowel harmony in deciphering Jurchen words. Not until 1632 did [Giolca] Dagai, with license from the next khan, Hung Taiji, begin to invent a means of vocalizing the script by the addition of circles and dots, which was thereafter called the "circled and dotted script" (*tongki fuka i hergen*).[13] This allowed the state, for the first time, to represent the sounds of the language that would soon come to be known as "Manchu."

The design of the state under Nurgaci's successor Hung Taiji made possible the survival of the recently formalized Manchu orthography, and by extension the Manchu language. It was unavoidable that in its early stages the state would be partially dependent on a class of Chinese and Korean scribes who were competent in Chinese, Mongolian, the new Manchu script, or all three. There seems, however, to have been a strong desire to bring an increasing number of state functions into the hands of Jurchen/Manchus. Together with the apparent nationalism voiced by Nurgaci, this political concern may have been the impetus behind the creation of a formal Manchu literature, education and examination programs in Manchu and for Manchus, the elaboration of state organs accommodating selected political traditions of the northeast, the primary military role of the bannermen, and the strategic advantages and increasing symbolic significance of Manchu as a medium of official communication. Translations from Chinese into Manchu proceeded apace with the development under Hung Taiji of a bilingual bureaucracy, which was completed as the "civil departments" (*wen-kuan*) in 1636. The first Board of Appointments (*li-pu*) was headed by [Suwan Gūwalgiya] Garin (Kang-lin), who was granted a *chü-jen* degree in 1634. Together with two other Manchus and three Oirat Mongols who had learned Mongolian script, all *chü-jen*, he continued to draw up the plans for elaboration of the civil government. For the state to grow, examinations had to be established, and it appears that the first examination of Manchus, Mongols, and Chinese martial bannermen was held at Mukden in 1638.[14] The content of subsequent examinations, in both Manchu and Chinese, was established by Cabuhai and Giyanghedei in 1639.[15]

The continuing functions of Manchu in the Ch'ing state and in eighteenth- and nineteenth-century Chinese society were sufficient to continue the need for at least limited education in Manchu. Indeed, as the state bureaucracy, and particularly its interior communication channels (and the system of "secret memorials" refined by the K'ang-hsi emperor) became more elaborate in the very late seventeenth and earlier eighteenth centuries, Manchu began to take on a greater documentary role than ever before. State organs such as the Court of Colonial Affairs (*tulergi golo be dasara jurgan*, *li-fan yüan*) and the Grand Council (*cooha-i nashūn i ba*, *chün-chi-ch'u*), both of which represented Ch'ing innovations in the imperial bureaucratic structure, continued in the use of documentary Manchu and Mongol for reasons of both strategy and protocol.[16]

There are other aspects to the role of Manchu in the middle Ch'ing period that deserve mention.[17] It was preferred that ritual communications (for example, *ch'ing-an che*) from garrison officers to the court be accomplished in Manchu, and most administrative matters for the Eight Banners were handled in the language. It was also the normal medium of diplomatic exchange between Russians and Chinese officials before the Treaty of Aigun in 1727 and was used by tributary states in their communications to the Ch'ing court.[18] The role of the language in governance made it necessary that a certain number of civilian bureaucrats be educated in Manchu, and selected recipients of the *chin-shih* degree were normally sent to the Hanlin Academy for instruction. It has not been sufficiently noted in previous scholarship that it was usual for high-ranking civilian administrators to have had some training in Manchu and that evidence of such preparation can be found in the backgrounds of virtually all the outstanding bureaucrats of the seventeenth and eighteenth centuries. A formal application of Manchu and Mongolian skills was demanded by the Ch'ien-lung court in the Four Treasuries (*Ssu-k'u ch'üan-shu*) program of the later eighteenth century. Related to this, extant materials also suggest that Manchu readers—whether banner or civilian—exerted themselves to create and maintain a field of recreational literature that went far beyond what the state was requiring. In the eighteenth and nineteenth centuries, a private scholarship of Manchu and Mongolian emerged, clearly prompted by interests in geographical questions—as when Kung Kung-hsiang took up the study of the two languages in order to augment the strategic geographical treatises of his father Kung Tzu-chen—and comparative linguistics, as was the case with Liang Chi (father of Liang Shou-ming) and Wang Kuo-wei. Finally, there was during the eighteenth and nineteenth centuries in particular an intense foreign interest in Manchu, which was often used as a bridge for the study of classical Chinese texts. Trafficking in Manchu materials contributed to the establishment of the great "oriental" collections of Europe, which still contain vast reserves of unexploited materials for the study of Ch'ing culture.[19]

From the earliest times, Manchu education was guided by state priorities. The Ch'ing attempted to provide the pedagogical materials necessary to import Chinese historical, legal, and ethical materials into Manchu and—later—to allow Chinese speakers to manage communications in written Manchu. Following the creation of the Manchu script, there was still no Manchu literary corpus. Hung Taiji commissioned "Confucian officials" (*ju-ch'en*)—who were not "Chinese" exclusively, but included Garin, Cabuhai, and others registered as Manchus—to translate selected works into Manchu "in order to instruct the national population (*kuo-jen*, i.e., bannermen)."[20] Though the original texts are not extant, there are indications that during Hung Taiji's regime the *Hsing-pu hui-tien, Ssu-shu, San-lüeh, Meng-tzu, San-kuo chih, T'ung-chien kang-mu, Hsing-li,* and *Ta ch'eng-ching* were all translated, while the translation of the histories of the Liao, Chin, and Yüan dynasties (from all of which Hung Taiji claimed legitimacy) was ordered.[21] The flagship of Hung Taiji's translation project was the *Chin-shih*, of which Hung Taiji proclaimed himself an avid reader and from which he learned both the necessity and the dangers of bicultural education for the Manchus.[22] Among Hung Taiji's intentions in sponsoring these translations was very obviously a program for the importation and legitimation of terms and concepts, primarily emperorship and its corollaries, that were not well established within the later Chin khanate.

The postconquest state continued to facilitate the creation of pedagogical aids for the study of Manchu. The K'ang-hsi emperor had authorized the compilation of a glossary, published in 1708 as *Han i araha manju gisun i buleku bithe* (*Yü-chih Ch'ing-wen chien*). One of the most commonly used works was the *Ch'ing-wen ch'i-meng* of 1729. The *Ch'ing-wen hui-shu* (*Manju isabuha bithe*) was authored in 1750 by Li Yen-chi. The earlier K'ang-hsi text was revised and much elaborated in *Han i araha nonggime toktobuha manju gisun i buleku bithe* (*Yü-chih tseng-ting ch'ing-wen chien*), 1772, and [Aisin Gioro] I-hsing's *Manju gisun be niyeceme isabuha bithe* (*Ch'ing-wen pu-hui*) was first published in 1786, then revised and reissued by his son-in-law Fakjingge in 1802.[23]

By virtue of its state-within-a-state structure, the Ch'ing regime preserved the history of and, in some form, the institutions (the Translators' bureaus, the *T'ai-ch'ang ssu*, the *Hung-lu ssu*) that in earlier ages had managed written intercourse with non-Chinese speaking regions. At the interface of the remnant state and the novel state was the role of translators. The Ch'ing had a choice of dependency on Chinese—which in the eyes of the emperors would mean overwhelming historical, ideological, strategic and personal sacrifices—or dependency on translators. This meant systematic cultivation of skills in translation, which was always a problematic proposition. Whether from the vantage of northeastern culture or of Chinese classicism, a translator's status was inferior. In the early Ch'ing, state translators were normally captured (and often enslaved) Chinese, Koreans, or Mongols who worked as high-level factotums for the princes and khans. The unrealistic and unrealized hope of the early emperors was that bannermen would be adept at all imperial languages and so would be spared the degradation of either serving as translators or needing the services of translators. For Chinese officialdom the question of translators was equally distasteful, not in the least because of its obvious association with conquest regimes. China had long had translators, and though they had never been a caste, as they were for a time in Korea, they remained condemned by, and in the shadows of, the examination elite.[24]

The early history of interpreting and translating in China can be only partially reconstructed, but it appears to have been recognized as a profession only in the T'ang period. Translation and management of tributary ritual were amalgamated through similar departments during the Sung era, until the destruction of the institutions of translation and ritual subordination under the Yüan. The Ming claimed to restore the ritual congruence of sovereignty over foreign peoples and the translation of foreign scripts, but there is reason to believe that, contrary to the ideology of the Hung-wu court in particular, Mongolian remained a significant consideration. Certainly, in their communication institutions the Ming were quick to adapt to the strategic importance of competence in Mongolian. A preliminary measure was continuation of the Mongolian Hanlin Academy, chartered at Nanking in 1376, which remained distinct from the translators' bureaus that were revived in 1407. Though attached to the regular Hanlin, the translators' bureaus themselves enjoyed no improvement in their reputation.[25] Their task was not regarded as important, and the faculty and students were so irresponsible that in 1580 they were denounced by their own director, Li K'ai-hsien.[26]

Though their pre-conquest experience with the translators' bureaus engendered a certain contempt for the institution in the Manchus, the Ch'ing decided, for reasons that may have been more ideological than anything else, to retain them. The purpose of the translators' bureaus under previous dynasties, after all, had been to isolate and thus denigrate visual representations of foreign cultures, and the Ch'ing had uses for such an institution. Indeed, Tso Mou-ti, when he arrived at Peking in 1645 on a mission from the Ming remnant court in the south, was directed straight to the translators' bureaus.[27] They were, however, a tiny and hollow appendage within the imperial bureaucracy. Certain languages—Mongolian, Manchu, and Tibetan for the early dynasty, these three plus Uigur for the later dynasty—were taken extremely seriously by the Ch'ing, and the embarrassing history of the translators' bureaus was not permitted to encumber communications in the these languages. In the period of their early state formation, the Ch'ing had developed their own Mongolian Bureau (*monggo yamun* [*monggo i jurgan*], *Meng-ku ya-men*), which after 1638 became the Court of Colonial Affairs (*tulergi golo be dasara jurgan, li-fan yüan*) and expanded its jurisdiction to Turkic, Tibetan, and in some cases Russian affairs. Thus, in the Ch'ing period the translators' bureaus retained a symbolic and curatorial role, but all bureaucratic functions that they occasionally had been intended to fulfill were superseded by new forms, many of which had evolved in the predynastic period.

Whether in domestic, tributary, or diplomatic matters, the Ch'ing court was scrupulous in denying the historical claim of Chinese as the sole vehicle of imperial expression. It was an ancient and constituent role of the Ch'ing khanship that the Manchu language should be actively nurtured, but Mongolian (for its historical link to the great khans and to the contemporary Mongol nobility), Tibetan (for its access to the spiritual legitimacy of the Ch'ing), and Uigur (as the expression of Ch'ing sovereignty over Central Asia) all became profoundly valued, while Chinese (as a vehicle of ethical self-validation of the Chinese bureaucracy) was certainly indispensable. Indeed, in the eighteenth century, as the court became more explicit in its formal claims to universalism, the emperorship's "simultaneous" (*kamciha, ho-pi*) expression in two or more languages took on a fundamental symbolic role in the imperial culture. But the court was not precise or consistent in its ascription of language use to sectors of society. Until the middle eighteenth century, languages in the imperial scheme were linked to function and, to a certain extent, to taste—not to identity. The reformism of the Ch'ien-lung era was too late and, in terms of social impact, too superficial to alter the evolution of cultural identities that had taken on vitality and momentum in the century and a half since the conquest.

"The Eight Banners take *ch'i-she* as their root, to their left is *wu*, to their right is *wen*."[28] This retrospective and not altogether graceful formulation from "Draft History of the Ch'ing" (*Ch'ing-shih kao*) attempts to summarize the very contradictory state objectives in education of the bannermen. The educational policies laid out by the Ch'ing court for the banner populations in the early postconquest period were a weathervane of the uncertain direction of the early regime in China. What is obvious is that the state did not envision a career for the bannermen in China proper that in any important way resembled that of the Mongols under the Yüan dynasty. The nobility was not enfeoffed in China proper, the military population was not given direct land rights, and the economic life of the Manchus underwent a profound and irremediable transformation after the immurement of the population in the Chinese provinces. The common ranks of the soldiery were in permanent occupation of the country and made none of the economic contributions that had been part of their role in the northeast. And the elite of the military sector were subjected to a series of educational policies whose purposes can be misunderstood if they are removed from the general context of Manchu social development in the late seventeenth and eighteenth centuries.

BANNER EDUCATION AND THE CONQUEST STATE

In the early postconquest period, the court hoped that the bannermen would learn to serve as an omnifunctional governing class. Banner officers were instructed to learn Chinese, the better to manage state affairs. The K'ang-hsi emperor, whose official profile was that of an exemplar in combining both military and civil brilliance, was uncompromising in his demand that the bannermen should follow his model. "The Manchus take riding and archery as the root (*pen*), and this was originally no impediment to book learning. Those bannermen examined as *hsiang* and *hui* candidates should also be required to show proficiency in riding and archery."[29] The book learning in question was Chinese classical studies. Though there were deviations from the policy during the K'ang-hsi and Yung-cheng reigns, as late as the 1750s the Ch'ien-lung emperor was still assuming that Manchu was the first language of most Manchus and that the only advances to be wrought through education were improvements in the bannermen's grasp of Chinese. Several misapprehensions underlay this program, but there is little evidence that they were explicitly recognized. Rather, they were merely superseded by new state ambitions of an even more unattainable nature.

Whatever functions the examinations for bannermen may have served in terms of identifying and cultivating talent, their administration was also affected by social and political developments. The court never stated an intention of supporting a growing banner population forever. On the contrary it seems to have utilized the examinations as a means of attracting a certain proportion of men (and their families) out of the garrisons and out of the military altogether, to become self-supporting in the world of civilian officialdom. In accord with this aim, incentives were often applied, though the examinations never became as attractive for the bannermen as the court hoped. Preferential routes for Manchus into the bureaucracy were a reflection of the early state strategy to gradually diminish the dependent banner population. A more acute example of the social and political significance of the examinations was the changing design of quotas in such a way as to sharply restrict the access of Chinese martial bannermen, a policy that was consonant with a host of social and ideological developments of the early and middle Ch'ing periods. The result was the progressive elimination of a significant portion of the Chinese martial population from the banner rolls by the late eighteenth century. Vacant places went, in a majority of cases, to Manchus. The very large advantage given to Manchus in the examinations becomes quite distinct when illuminated by figures recently published suggesting that in the immediate postconquest period the Chinese martial bannermen may have represented as much as 40 percent of the military population; in the decades immediately following the conquest of northern China, their numbers may have ballooned to as large a proportion as 70 percent.[30] Manchu bannermen were enticed to use the quotas and—when they were available—the special banner examinations to transfer themselves to the bureaucracy, while Chinese martial bannermen (who were given a large role in the first decade of governing because of their expertise in the use of Chinese) were gradually deterred from use of the banner quotas and examinations.

As early as the reign of Hung Taiji, maturation of the civil bureaucratic institutions had established an examination for the selection of prospective banner officers. The role of examinations remained small in the ensuing years, however, as clan affiliation, hereditary status, and merit gained in the ongoing campaigns of conquest continued to be the more powerful determinants of elevation within the banners. Two major factors enlarged the role of examinations after 1644. The first was the consolidation of the conquest in northern and inland regions, narrowing the theater of battle merit and making systematic selection by examination necessary. Second, the establishment of the garrisons both at the capital and in the provinces created an unprecedented demand for new officers to administer the stations.

In 1643, Hung Taiji had decreed that literate bannermen should be sent to the academy (*shu-yüan*) in Shun-t'ien (Abkai Imiyangga) prefecture, which remained the center for all banner examinations until 1814. They were permitted to take the *hsiang-shih* there, and those who succeeded in the examinations eventually became officials; this remained the policy until 1657. For a brief period, a special examination was devised for bannermen featuring the option to do all work in Manchu. In fact, the bannermen were poorly prepared for the special examinations, and between 1659 and 1675 the banner examinations were sometimes held, sometimes not, depending on whether a minimum of candidates could be collected. From 1663 to 1685, the bannermen were again allowed to participate in the Shun-t'ien *hsiang-shih*.[31] Absolute quotas for the banner *hsiang* examination were established in 1653 at fifty Manchus, fifty Chinese martials, and twenty Mongols, which was afterward altered to a proportional quota of one in five for Manchus and Chinese martial, and one in four for Mongols. After readmission of bannermen to the civil *hsiang-shih* at Shun-t'ien, absolute quotas were reestablished for bannermen in 1671, when they were fixed at fifty each for Manchus and Chinese martial, and twenty for Mongols.[32]

In 1669, a primary distinction was made for the first time between Manchus and Mongols on the one hand and Chinese martial on the other: the *man-tze hao* was thereafter to apply to Manchus and Mongols and the *ho-tze hao* to Chinese martial, each of which comprised ten places. In comparison to the evident population of the Chinese martial, this ratio was a distinct disadvantage to them and adumbrated the gradual narrowing of their opportunities (often through reversal of Mongol and Chinese martial ratios) through the eighteenth century. A very small number of bannermen generally went on to the *hui-shih*, and in 1662 the Board of Appointments (*li-pu*) attempted to make the *chin-shih* more attractive by stipulating that *baksi* (erudites) and *bithesi* (lit., "scribes," but trained to serve as clerks and translators as well) who participated in the examinations would automatically become sixth and seventh *pin* officials and would concomitantly be released from military service. Three years later, the lineage leaders (*mukūnda, tsu-chang*), under the jurisdiction of the garrison yamens, were instructed to act as leaders in preparing bannermen for the new *hui* and *hsiang* examinations.[33] All preliminary examinations for bannermen were also to be held within the Shun-t'ien jurisdiction, and for the *sui* and *k'o* held before 1661, the following absolute quotas pertained: Manchus, and Chinese martials 120 each, Mongols sixty. During the K'ang-hsi period, this was altered—and, importantly, the ratios of the Mongols and Chinese martial were reversed—to Manchus and Mongols forty each, Chinese martial twenty.[34]

In 1687 the Board of Appointments (*li-pu*) drew up a new plan for banner participation in the examinations, and under the terms of this new design bannermen took the examinations of 1688. The effect of the *man-tze hao* was to cause Manchu and Mongol candidates to be graded in one group (*pang*) rather than separately as they had been before.[35] It was also stipulated that Manchus and Mongols could take the Chinese or the Manchu examinations, and absolute quotas for the *hui-shih* at Mukden (after which candidates could join the *tien-shih* at Peking) were fixed at twenty each for Manchus and Chinese martial, ten for Mongols. At the same time, it was ordered that the banner *hsiang-shih* be reinstituted, and *baksi* and *bithesi* serving in a yamen were required to prepare for the Mukden *hui-shih*.[36]

The plan of 1687 seems to have been the court's nearest approach to actually being rooted in *ch'i-she* yet balanced between *wen* and *wu*. It allowed garrison and provincial officials to ascertain that candidates were to some degree proficient in horsemanship and archery, since they were examined separately on these skills before being admitted to the *k'o*, *sui*, or *hsiang* examinations. At this time, bannermen participating in the *man-tze hao* were required at both the *hsiang* and *hui* levels to prepare an examination essay in either Manchu or Mongolian. Chinese martial candidates had to prepare one essay each on calligraphy and the arts as well as one on the Classics. In fact, it appears that the introduction of a Manchu or Mongolian essay presented an option to Chinese martial as well as civilian candidates to demonstrate their skills in these languages, an opportunity that was in at least a few instances exploited. The open *hsiang* and *hui* examinations, to which bannermen could be admitted after satisfactory demonstration of martial skills and to which they had to contribute an essay in either Manchu or Mongolian if they were participating in the *man-tze hao*, remained the general pattern through the late eighteenth century, though it was suspended for short periods of experimentation. A proportional quota for the *hui-shih* was introduced in 1744 that limited Manchus and Mongols to one successful candidate per ten aspirants, with absolute totals of no more than twenty-seven, while Chinese martial successes could number no more than twelve.

An additional route to the *chü-jen* and *chin-shih* degrees was offered by the gradual refinement of the "translators" or *fan-i* examinations. In 1653, when the first bannerman's *hsiang-shih* was held, those who did not know Chinese wrote an essay in Manchu and then progressed to preparation for the special *hui-shih*. The *fan-i* examination was first introduced in 1661; students translated either from Manchu into Chinese or from Chinese into Manchu. In 1722, *fan-i* degrees were introduced at *sheng-yuan*, *chü-jen*, and *chin-shih* levels. There seems to have been a fear that devoting a certain portion of the examination to translation, which was after all a technical skill like mathematics or astronomy, would lower the intellectual cachet of the test. In 1738, the provision was therefore added that besides the translations there must be an original composition, limited to three hundred words, in Manchu. In 1742, it was ordered that each first sitting of the *hui-shih* also require a Manchu essay on the Four Books (Ssu-shu), the Filial Classic (*Hsiao-ching*), and the "Principles of Nature" (*Hsing-li*); the second sitting concentrated on translation skills. All banner *kung-sheng*, *chien-sheng*, and *bithesi*, whether Manchu or Chinese martial, were required to participate in the *hsiang-shih*. Both those prepared for the

regular examinations and those who had prepared for the military examinations but could also translate were eligible for the *hui-shih*, so long as all had
passed their tests in riding and archery, as the regulations required.

A Mongolian option was added to the *fan-i* track in 1730.[37] Thereafter in
hsiang-shih and *hui-shih*, Mongols could translate selections from the Four Books
from Manchu into Mongolian. This was slightly altered in 1735, when it was
decreed that Mongols would sit for the translation examination on the
"Principles of Nature" (*Hsing-li*) and "Lesser Learning" (*Hsiao-hsueh*) together
with the Manchus but would be graded as a separate group. Whatever the motive for the comparative leniency in examining Mongols, it was also reflected in
the contemporary quotas, which stood at 33 out of 500 or 600 for Manchus in
the *hsiang-shih* and 6 out of 50 or 60 for Mongols. In reality, there were never
enough participants from either group, and as further incentive it was
stipulated that those who participated in the *hui-shih* examinations would automatically become secretaries (*chu-shih*) in one of the Six Boards. From 1757 to
1778, the *fan-i* examinations were suspended because of lack of interest among
the bannermen and poor performance by those who participated. After 1778
they were reestablished with some minor modifications and continued as an institution to the end of the nineteenth century.[38]

A factor in the disappointing performance by bannermen in the examinations was the failure of the state to devise a universal, effective means of elementary education for the banner populations—a failure that is possibly akin
to the absence of state-sponsored elementary educational institutions in the
civil sector but also is characteristic of many aspects of garrison financing. Instead of creating a school system, the state created and supervised the examination system on the apparent principle that control of standards through the
medium of the examinations obviated control of the institutions of education
(and responsibility for their maintenance).

The system of schools authorized by the Ch'ing for the education of imperials,
nobles, and bannermen might best be conceived of as a set of concentric circles,
which from the center out represent decreasing degrees of prestige, state aid,
and political demands. The model for most of the education programs was the
National Academy (*kuo-hsueh*), an adjunct institution of the National University
(*kuo-tzu chien*).[39] It was originally chartered for the education of those who had
been ennobled by the court, a status that in the aftermath of the conquest
encompassed a great many people within the loose confines of the banner
world. In spirit and design, it was the direct descendant of the Mongolian
National University (*Meng-ku kuo-tzu chien*) under the Yuan, to which the old
Mongolian Hanlin Academy had been attached and where Mongolian nobles
were educated. It should be emphasized that a characteristic of Ch'ing relations with the bannermen generally also marked the policies of the National
Academy with regard to banner enrollment: attendance at the school was largely
voluntary, and those who were "of a mind to study" were invited to enroll.[40]

In time, Manchu students' and instructors' statuses were defined within the Academy. The curriculum, derived from that devised by Cabuhai and Giyanghedei in the preconquest period and adjusted to encompass the territory of the civilian examinations, comprised the Four Books, Five Classics (*Wu ching*), *Principles of Nature* (*Hsing-li*) *Comprehensive Mirror* ([*Tzu-chih*] *T'ung-chien*), Thirteen Classics (*Shih-san ching*), and Twenty-one Histories (*Erh-shih-i shih*), all of which could be studied in either Manchu or Chinese. The bannermen chosen for study at the National Academy were all officers, and their number was extremely small. At the entry level, then, the National Academy worked to parallel and reinforce the profound stratification that characterized the structure of both the banners and the garrisons. After completing the primary course, students concentrated successively in the National Academy's two subdivisions of astronomy (*t'ien-wen*) and mathematics (*suan-hsueh*).[41] In 1739, the mathematics division, to which students went last, is reported to have enrolled fifty-two students, along these quota lines: twenty Manchus, twenty civilians, six Mongols, and six Chinese martial bannermen. The study text was the "Imperially Commissioned Selection of Standard Writings on Numerical Principles." Banner students who completed the mathematics section were to be replaced with students from their own banners.[42]

The next circle in this schematic conception of elite schools would represent the Imperial Clan Academies (*tsung-hsueh*), which were, in form if not in name, an innovation required by the inner constitution of the Ch'ing state.[43] Here, the sons of men who satisfied the formal requirements for being members of the Imperial Clan were educated according to the strictest cultural requirements of the court. The Imperial Clan Academies remained the last bastion of high standards of *ch'i-she* and when, under Hung-li, cultural formalism struck, it struck the Imperial Clan Academies first and hardest. Members of the imperial clan were liable to be punished if they were found lacking in military skills. Given the high priority placed on the education of Aisin Gioro clansmen, it is yet characteristic of the Ch'ing that the Imperial Clan Academies—though under the jurisdiction of the Imperial Clan Court (*tsung-jen fu*)—were not supported by the state but by the Eight Banners. Each banner was commissioned to establish its own Imperial Clan Academy in 1654, and Manchus who had already qualified as *sheng-yuan* were chosen as instructors.

All *tzu-ti* of the imperial clan who had not been ennobled and who were older than ten *sui* were to enter the school to study literary Manchu.[44] In 1724, the system was established in which the left and right divisions at Peking supported both a Manchu and a Chinese school, each to be overseen by an Aisin Gioro nobleman. These new schools received the *tzu-ti* of the princes (*wang*), nobles (*kung*), garrison generals-in-chief (*chiang-chün*), and unemployed (*hsien-san*) Aisin Gioro who were younger than eighteen *sui* and instructed them in Manchu, Chinese, and *ch'i-she*. The overseer and his assistants were to be chosen from the imperial clan on the basis of seniority. Two Manchu instructors were to be chosen from unemployed banner officers or from among *chin-shih, chü-jen, kung-sheng,* or *chien-sheng* holders who were adept at translation. Two *ch'i-she* instructors were also to be appointed, chosen from among unemployed banner officers or from the ranks of active Imperial Guard (*hu-chün*) officers who were excellent in archery. Each school had ten students with one instructor of Chinese (appointed for three years) chosen by the *li-pu* by examination of *chü-jen* or *kung-sheng*. In 1734, the two schools were assigned two Hanlin scholars each to oversee the curriculum, and on alternate days they lectured first on interpretation of the Classics and then on composition.

The problem of finding suitable employment for the lowlier members of the enormous imperial clan made the examinations administered to the students of the Imperial Clan Academies a priority. In 1736, the Left and Right schools were each assigned a permanent principal and there were monthly examinations on interpretation of the Classics, translation, and archery. It was determined in 1745 that every five years an official of the Imperial Clan Court (*tsung-jen fu*) was to be appointed to examine the two schools together, and the ranks were to be registered as *hui-shih* and *chung-shih*. In each year that the *hui-shih* was administered, the students of the schools were to be examined together with the *fan-i kung-sheng* of the banners, and those chosen as *chin-shih* could be employed in any branch of government. Those who studied Chinese were examined together with all other scholars in the palace examination, and those taking first class honors (*chia-ti*) were appointed to the Hanlin Academy.

In 1746, the court noted that those studying Chinese and translation in the Imperial Clan Academy had inelegant composition in Manchu. Adumbrating future changes, Hung-li said:

> Our dynasty esteems martiality as its primary occupation. *Tzu-ti* of the imperial clan must be thoroughly versed in literary Manchu, and they must be experts at *ch'i-she*. I am frankly concerned that those who study Chinese will gradually become lost in Chinese ways. The Shun-chih emperor once ordered us to stop studying Chinese, the better to serve our primary interests, rather than decline to a state of dissolution (*fou-hua*). From now on, *tzu-ti* of the imperial clan may not study Chinese. They are strictly required to study the military arts in order to preserve themselves as tools for the use of the state.[45]

Enrollment for the Imperial Clan Academies at Peking was fixed in 1747 at sixty students for the Left Wing and sixty students for the Right. By 1756, the prohibition on the teaching of Chinese changed the status of the nine Chinese instructors to instructors of translation, and *ch'i-she* instructors were increased to one per banner.

A similar philosophy of Ch'ing elite banner education dominated the next ranked school, the Gioro Academy (Chueh-lo *hsueh*), where the descendants of the paternal uncles of Nurgaci were educated. Instruction was patterned after that in the Imperial Clan Academy and Gioro bannermen were subjected to fines if they were found incompetent in *ch'i-she*. The academy, established in 1729 adjacent to the garrison offices in the inner city of Peking, had both a Manchu and a Chinese school. Gioro *tzu-ti* ages eight to eighteen *sui* could enter to study reading, writing, and archery. The overseer was a prince or nobleman and examinations were held in the spring and fall. Every three years, the Gioro students were subjected to examination along with the imperial clan students and divided between the advanced and the deficient. When their studies were completed, they were to participate together with the bannermen in the *sui* and *hsiang* examinations and to compete together for employment as bureaucratic secretaries (*chung-shu*) or banner clerks (*bithesi*). The quotas seem to have reflected proportional Gioro representation within the respective Manchu banners.[46]

Another circle out from the center of the concentric model would represent the academies of the Imperial Household Department (*nei-wu fu*), which governed the bondservant (*boo-i, pao-i*) companies of the Three Superior Banners (*san shang ch'i*). It ran its own officer schools at Prospect Hill (*Ching-shan*) and the Hsien-an Palace (*Hsien-an-kung*).[47] The Prospect Hill Officers' School was established 1685, in two buildings at Pei-shang Gate in the north wall of the imperial city (*huang-ch'eng*). Youths selected from the companies of the Imperial Household Department were eligible to attend, to a total enrollment of 360. Three of the rooms of the school were devoted to instruction in Manchu, with three instructors. Three were devoted to instruction in Chinese, with three instructors. At first, retired officials from the Imperial Household Department were chosen as Manchu instructors, and as Chinese instructors the Board of Appointments (*li-pu*) chose by examination those who were proficient in literary composition. This was later changed so that those secretaries from the Privy Council (*nei-ko*) who were expert in both calligraphy and archery were chosen as Manchu instructors, while Chinese instructors were chosen either from new *chin-shih* or from retired secretaries of the Privy Council. After the Yung-cheng period, Chinese instructors were chosen by examination from the ranks of *chü-jen* and *kung-sheng* for a tenure of three years to be followed by transfer to another department. Students studied for three years. Those who passed in the first class in examinations were employed as clerks (*bithesi*), those who passed in the second class as inspectors (*k'u-shih* or *k'u-shou*). In 1779, Muslim banner companies were permitted to select four expectant students.

The Hsien-an Palace Officers' School (*Hsien-an-kung kuan-hsueh*) was established in 1728 for children from the Imperial Household Department companies and outstanding families of the Eight Banners, and a Mongolian section was added in 1747. The school was located in the vicinity of the Wu-ying Palace inside the Hsi-hua Gate. There were ninety students all together, who were instructed by Hanlin officials living in the Hsien-an Palace.

Twelve classrooms were devoted to instruction in spoken Chinese and three to Manchu, each with one instructor in Classics, archery, and literary Manchu. The students were examined by an Imperial Household Department official for employment as banner clerks (*bithesi*, seventh or eighth *pin*) on the same schedule as—but possibly not together with—the Prospect Hill Officers' School. In 1735, it was decreed that Chinese instructors should be recruited from among new *chin-shih*, though not much hope seems to have been held out that aspirants with such lofty credentials would flock to the opportunity.[48] Incentives to attract better instructors were added. Should they complete a three-year tenure at the school, instructors were assured of employment as board secretaries (*chu-shih*) or as magistrates (*chih-hsien*), *chü-jen* as magistrates (*chih-hsien*) or instructors in the civil academies. After 1758, regardless of seniority, students were to take the *fan-i* examinations, then to serve as clerks or assistant inspectors. The number of Chinese instructors was at that time fixed at nine, Manchu at six.[49]

The next circle out encompasses the banner commoners of Peking. They could attend the Eight Banners officers' schools (*pa-ch'i kuan-hsueh*), which were independent of the National Academy, though modeled on it in basic ways. In 1644, it was stipulated that each banner would build a college (*hsueh-she*) and that each company (*niru, tso-ling*) of each banner in Peking would send one student to the college. Of the total number of students (which would have been something over seventy in the seventeenth century), ten were to be tutored in Chinese and the rest in Manchu (the latter category includes those attempting to master classical Chinese for the examinations). The next year the size and scope of the school were reduced; it was ordered that two banners would combine to form one school—that is, there would be four schools all together—and that each school would accept ten students, all preparing to qualify as *sheng-yüan*, in exact parallel to the National Academy program.

In contrast to the larger schools established for Gioro and bondservants, these smaller schools established for commoners actually had fewer places than applicants. Competition for the berths was so intense that students who would previously have qualified on the basis of *en, po, fu*, or *sui* privileges were no longer accepted. When vacancies occurred, only students who were already regular *chien-sheng* were permitted to take the entrance examination. In 1723, the officers' schools added a Mongolian section, selecting sixteen tutors from among the *hu-chün, ling-ts'ui*, and *hsiao-ch'i-hsiao* ranks of the Mongolian banners, and students were chosen by banner to compete in the entrance examination.

By 1728, the Eight Banners Officers' Schools at Peking were reaching their maturity in terms of organization, enrollment, and prestige. The student body had now increased to about eight hundred students, on a quota of one hundred students from each of the Eight Banners. Of these, a strict quota gave a substantial advantage to Manchu students, stipulating that 60 percent of all matriculants be Manchu, 20 percent Mongol, 20 percent Chinese martial. Of the Manchu students, half were to be educated in Chinese and half in Manchu, with the division to follow lines of age; the youngest among the students were to study Manchu and the more experienced were to study Chinese.[50] For support of the schools, thirty Manchu, ten Mongol, and ten Chinese martial cadetships (*yang-yü*) within the banners were abolished and the money was given to students in the officers' schools — a small component in the general banner distribution patterns sharply privileging the elite at the expense of the humbler population. Five instructors of Chinese were assigned to each banner classroom. Interestingly, the matching of ages to languages was reversed. In 1735, it was ordered that younger, more accomplished men join the Chinese division and that men willing to concentrate on translation join the Manchu division. In 1743, the period of study was fixed at three years, after which students were examined and either kept on to study or appointed to bureaucratic rank.

As early as the immediate aftermath of the conquest of Peking, officials of the Manchu garrisons at the capital began to complain that it was inconvenient for bannermen of the various and far-flung installations of the capital garrisons (*ching-shih chi-fu*) to travel to the single, small academy that had been established for education of banner officers in the northeast corner of the inner city. Permission was thereafter given for each of the Eight Banners at Peking to create a conveniently located school (*shu-yuan*) for the education of their own personnel. State plans for a centralized, standardized system of banner education at this time may have been rather grand. Each company was supposed to send a student to its respective school, which, taking into account modern revisions of the probable enrollment in banner companies, would mean that the plan projected education for one out of every two hundred or three hundred actively enrolled bannermen, with a total enrollment of something under six hundred. Of these, half were to be educated in Chinese and half in Manchu. Before this plan could be implemented, however, the state planners quickly replaced it with a much more modest design. The new plan called for one school to be shared by two banners, with only ten students in each school, for a total of forty students.[51]. The intention seems to have been to shift the financial burden to the banners themselves instead of the state (a policy characteristic of the banner and garrison support systems generally, which were evolving in tandem with the educational system) and to modify the scale of the enterprise accordingly.[52] We know, too, that the court felt confident at this time that education in Manchu was unnecessary for Manchus and that the primary purpose of these schools was to provide a minimal number of bannermen competent in Chinese, the better to oversee the management of the Chinese-based bureaucracy.

The outermost circle finally touches the banner population of the provinces. Garrison (*chu-fang*) examinations were established in 1645, when all literate

bannermen and *tzu-ti* were permitted to go to Shun-t'ien to take the examination. During the Ch'ien-lung period, this was changed to allow provincial
generals-in-chief (*chiang-chün*) to first examine the students (on a *sui*, *k'o* schedule) in *ch'i-she*, after which they were sent to the capital for further examination.
The patterns and the objectives of garrison education were controlled by the
changes in examination and education policy in Peking, since at the provincial
and capital levels (which, geographically, were the same for all bannermen) garrison aspirants were expected to compete with graduates of the schools discussed above. How they prepared themselves for the challenge was their own
business, and it is probable that many provincial garrisons very rarely if ever
furnished candidates to the Shun-t'ien examination halls since, unlike civilians,
the bannermen enjoyed no leverage through geographical quotas before 1814.
Anecdotal evidence suggests that in many garrisons education took place either
in private academies (*shu-yuan*) within the garrisons, many of which were modeled
on traditional Chinese academies and many of which employed Chinese scholars
as tutors, or in charitable schools run by the banners and by some clans.

Peking bannermen, too, turned to private academies and charitable schools
when they were ineligible for or unsuccessful in gaining admission to the state
officers' schools.[53] Standards for *ch'i-she* were enforced by the requirement that
provincial generals-in-chief regularly examine their bannermen in martial
skills and take personal responsibility for preparing them for the examinations
at Peking. This may have put a burden on provincial generals-in-chief that actually militated against the cultivation in the garrisons of candidates for examination and service in Peking. There is ample evidence that garrison officers
were punished when their bannermen appeared at the capital deficient in
speaking Manchu or shooting from moving horses; there is, by contrast, no evidence that they were punished if no bannermen at all from their garrisons
presented themselves for examination. Whether or not bannermen intended
to proceed for examination to the Shun-t'ien jurisdiction, there was a need for
literacy in both Chinese and Manchu for the conduct of business at all levels of
the garrisons, and a requirement for the rank of "corporal" (*bosokū, ling-ts'ui*)
was literacy in Manchu. This was normally attained through elementary education within the garrison academies or charity schools.

Students were expected to underwrite a great portion of the cost of their
education, particularly at the most introductory levels. This was sometimes direct, as when students were required to pay in cash or supplies — grain, wood,
coal, or peat, for instance — for their lessons, but was more often indirect, as
garrison and banner administrations were required to found and maintain
state-controlled schools. A small number of student stipends were supplied by
the state. Stipends and annual rates of increase were established for the
Chinese martials in 1643 (very soon after the Chinese martial banners were
created) and for the Manchus and Mongols in 1671. Chinese martial stipends
were normally awarded at a ratio of half the number awarded to Manchus or

Mongols in any given year—again, grossly out of relationship to the proportion of the banner population they represented. For Chihli province—where the capital garrisons were located—the stipends and additional quotas were set at forty per *fu*, thirty per *chou*, twenty per *hsien*, ten per *wei*. [54] Students of high standing who had been in residence six years or less were eligible to receive stipends. This meant, in practice, that two failures—in some cases, one—in the examinations while matriculating would result in a loss of support. Students placing first or second class in the *k'o* examinations were given a raise in stipend and sent on to the *hsiang* examination. Those bannermen who placed in the third class or below in the *k'o* examination could stay at the school if they paid their own fees; those placing in the fourth class had to leave.

The structural defects of the system described above were evident well before the Ch'ien-lung period. Attempts to enforce systematic education were made only at the capital and affected a tiny portion of the adult males of the banner population. Banner males of eligible age must, at any one of these times, have numbered in the hundreds of thousands, of whom not more than a thousand were being educated in the Peking higher schools. Moreover, the proportional emphasis put on educating Aisin Gioro, Gioro, and bondservants was overwhelming; it appears that in the middle eighteenth century this group represented half of all bannermen attending the higher schools in Peking. More compromising, perhaps, was the profound ambiguity in the design of bannermen education in the earlier dynastic era. As Hung-li in his later reign would articulate many times, it was not really possible for the bannermen or anybody else to be rooted in *ch'i-she* and balanced between *wu* and *wen*. The role of governors once envisioned for the bannermen had faded very early in the Ch'ing period under insurmountable pressures to meet continuing military challenges and to give way in civil affairs to the well-entrenched Chinese bureaucratic class. But the curriculum still demanded not only competence in the Four Books and other foundational works of the civil examinations but also technical competence in military skills, translation, mathematics, and astronomy. Small wonder that few bannermen were attracted by either the challenges or the rewards of the banner educational institutions.

BANNER IDENTITY AND THE CH'IEN-LUNG AND CHIA-CH'ING REFORMS

The centralization and reform of banner education came, technically, after the end of the Ch'ien-lung reign but was in fact overseen by Hung-li and was very clearly imprinted with the new attitudes toward Manchu identity and Manchu culture that he had attempted to inculcate during his period as emperor. Specifically, the early, rather vague notion that bannermen should be adept at all governing skills, whether military or civil, was discarded. The idea of the bannermen as a liberally educated governing class was rejected in the same stroke and replaced by an increasingly specialized understanding of who Manchus were and what they were expected to do. The new reforms prescribed rigorous study of the Manchu language, both written and spoken, and of military skills. The educational programs were very deliberately designed to include *tzu-ti* as well as active or prospective bannermen and, by virtue of this design, claimed jurisdiction over a much broader portion of the Manchu population than could ever possibly have exercised their new skills in service of the state. Unlike his father and grandfather, Hung-li was not primarily interested in improving governance by elevating the competence of the bannermen. He was instead bent on refining the cultural character of the Manchus, who were now in his eyes representative not only of the cultural origins of the Ch'ing but of a dedicated component in his universal realm.

From an early period, the Ch'ing court was wary about allowing inadequately educated bannermen to pervade the court and central bureaucracy. Court distrust of Manchu preparation probably led for a time to favorable employment opportunities for middle-level Chinese martial bannermen in the early Ch'ing period and may have been reflected in the restoration of Chinese martial quotas in 1687.[55] In his turn, Hung-li also denounced bannermen whose accomplishments in Manchu and in Chinese were thin, accusing them of averting the challenges of truly mastering either the Manchu language or military skills or the Chinese Classics by always shifting their specialty.[56] They were not only useless but also, he may have suspected, becoming dangerous; there is a strong continuity with the emperor's suspicions of "rough" literacy, whose effects at the popular level have been vividly explored by Alexander Woodside. Indeed, a large number of mid-eighteenth-century bannermen would have resembled those Miao tribesmen Hung-li denounced in 1751; their education was inadequate for the subtleties of the Four Books but made it "'very easy' to read Chinese novels and heterodox tracts."[57]

At first, like his father and grandfather, Hung-li had been inclined to encourage more effective study of Chinese and continued his ancestors' practice of rewarding development of Chinese erudition among the bannermen.[58] Later, on the basis of better information about garrison conditions and Manchu performance, Hung-li reconsidered the policies he had inherited and in his own right encouraged.[59] After 1765, he advised bannermen that they need no longer disturb him with notifications of their households' success in the examinations unless the candidates had also distinguished themselves at *ch'i-she*.[60] And again he stressed the primary importance of the Manchu language. "Speaking Manchu is the Old Way (*chiu-tao, fe doro*) of the Manchus," Hung-li admonished four Manchu officials of the *li-fan yüan* who had been unable to keep up their end of an audience in the winter of 1762. Though the K'ang-hsi emperor had established himself as a grand exemplar to the bannermen and frequently demonstrated his literary and military skills before them for their improvement, Hung-li had a very different concept of his relationship to the bannermen. He was a paragon of multiliteracy, the esthete of all cultures, and the universal emperor. They were not. The emperor generalized to them the prohibition on Chinese studies that he had earlier applied to the Imperial Clan Academy. They were to apply themselves to their language, their religion, and to *ch'i-she*. "Whether you have studied classical literature is a matter of no concern to me."[61]

In reemphasizing the Manchu military arts in his reform campaigns, the Ch'ien-lung emperor was to a certain extent building on precedents. The earlier postconquest emperors, concerned about the effect of urbanization upon the bannermen, had made riding and archery part of the formal instruction for all bannermen. Hung-li retained these regulations and further stipulated that they should apply to *tzu-ti* as well as to actively serving bannermen. "We fear," the editors of "Researches on Manchu Origins" (*Man-chou yuan-liu k'ao*) said on his behalf, "that in later days the banner descendants will forget the old order and do away with riding and archery, taking up Han customs."[62] A passing mark in riding and archery was made a prerequisite to admission to the examination halls; imperial clansmen and Gioro Manchus were rewarded for their achievement in riding and archery or punished for inadequacy.

Apart from an increasingly abstract emphasis on physical training, Hung-li had also expressed some real concerns about the impact on the bureaucracies of declining command of Manchu speech. Despite an insistence that bannermen preparing for service in the civil or military bureaucracies learn Manchu orthography, unfamiliarity with the spoken language still wreaked havoc with communications in Manchu and Mongolian. In 1779, Hung-li in exasperation ordered that translations of edicts issued in Mongolian be submitted to him for grammatical review, as was already the practice for Manchu; the emperor proposed to augment his normal duties of edict review by becoming a Manchu and Mongolian language tutor as well.[63]

By the latter part of his reign, Hung-li was well on his way to formalization of what he called the Old Way (*fe doro*) of the Manchus. This, as has been suggested, was an ideological construct, a code of life for the banner population that prescribed immersion in the military arts, the speaking and writing of Manchu, shamanism, and reverence for the clans as the basic elements in the correct life of those who the state identified as Manchus.[64] The educational policies were quickly reformed to promote both the speaking and writing of Manchu as primary objectives. In 1791, Hung-li outlined his plan for the establishment of standard banner officer schools in all garrisons. However, it was not until after his abdication of the emperorship (but during a time in which he still controlled fundamental state affairs) in 1796 that he devoted himself to implementing plans for a centralized, standardized educational system for the garrisons; for the ensuing twenty years, additions to the basic program augmented reform of banner education throughout China.

The reforms began at the higher schools in Peking. At the National Academy (*kuo-hsueh*), where enrollment pressures had continued steadily, crowding within the Inner Department had become a serious problem. In 1796, bannermen and students of families residing in the general neighborhood of the National Academy (that is, within Ta and Yüan *hsien*, which encompassed most of the inner city) were ejected from the Inner Department and told they could thereafter enter only by examination (*k'ao-tao*). Those testing in the first and second ranks could take the second round of tests. First- and second-rank *kung-sheng* as well as first-class *chien-sheng* could also enroll in the Inner Department. This meant that bannermen who had received the *chien-sheng* by imperial favor (*en*) or privilege (*yin*), or who were doing the translation curriculum or equine arts (*ch'i-she*), were excluded even from testing for the Inner Department. Moreover, their tenure in the Outer Department was not assured; three unexcused absences from the compound resulted in expulsion.[65]

Special pressure was put on the elite to respond to the court's new educational imperatives. The Imperial Clan Academy (*tsung-hsueh*), whose enrollments had declined rather dramatically in the later eighteenth century (despite a steady population increase for the imperial clan itself), had ten students (to be attracted by handsome stipends) added to each wing in 1795. Three additional Manchus and four Chinese were assigned as instructors to each school. In 1808, enrollment in each wing was raised by another addition of thirty students so that there were one hundred students all together, a number that remained fixed.[66] The conditions under which imperial clan students participated in the examinations were also changed. Before 1801, students of the Imperial Clan Academy were not obliged to participate in the *hsiang* or *hui* examinations but were examined independently by the Imperial Clan Court (*tsung-jen fu*) on *ch'i-she*, arts, and poetry. Now, all imperial clansmen were required to take the *fan-i* examination unless they petitioned to participate in the regular *hsiang* and *hui* tests.[67] Their proportional quota for the Shun-t'ien *hsiang-shih* was one in nine, probably a tight quota in view of the long-term over-proportionate representation of imperial clansmen in the higher school system. In the *hui-shih* their numbers were separated from the general *man-tze hao*, but for the *tien-shih* and *ch'ao-shih* they were forced to compete without quotas and those who were successful were rewarded with high bureaucratic appointments.

The greatest change was in the provincial garrisons, where for the first time officer schools under the jurisdiction of the Board of Appointments (*li-pu*) were established and all bannermen became eligible to compete for admission. The curriculum, which was not intended to be distinguished for innovation, was based on the program of the National Academy and the Eight Banners Officers' Schools in Peking: Manchu, Chinese, astronomy (*t'ien-wen*), and mathematics (*suan-hsueh*), with frequent and rigorous testing in riding and shooting. The charters were imbedded in Hung-li's continuing demands that written

Manchu be revived among the bannermen. "Every single man has a responsibility to study written Manchu," the emperor had continued his endless and largely unheeded sermon. "This is the root of his mission!" Instructors' salaries in the schools as well as student expenses were covered partly by government grants, partly by banner and clan charities, and when possible were drawn from personal expenditures.[68] It is difficult to know how quickly the various garrisons did in fact manage to find buildings, instructors, and students for their schools, but by 1800 most garrisons were choosing their officers from the new schools established within their own garrisons.[69]

The reform of higher education within the garrisons was, however, quickly seen to be useless without a corresponding emphasis on the cultivation of boys. The perceived cultural and social condition of the garrison populations is revealed in the edict of 1800 (after Hung-li's death) demanding that garrison officers identify talented boys, on the order of about one out of every five or six, to receive intensive instruction from their company corporals in Manchu, *ch'i-she*, and a small number of administrative arts. At the same time, the state affirmed its intentions never to return to the unfocused, comprehensive education policies of earlier times. "Of the Manchus' roots, *ch'i-she* is the first. If the Eight Banner *tzu-ti* concentrate on and are allowed to be successfully examined on [the Four Books], they will despise the bow and the horse, and that will not enhance our military preparedness; on the contrary, they will contravene the very purpose for which the nation established the garrisons. Hereafter, the officers of each provincial garrison will select *tzu-ti* who will be dedicated to the task of preparing for the examinations, and they will thus advance our fundamental interests."[70]

In the same way that the state now recognized that only a minority of the garrison population would represent suitable ground for the cultivation of military dedication, it gradually resigned itself to the fact that the *shu-yuan* traditions within the garrisons had produced a class of Manchu literati who identified themselves with their localities and intended to pursue civil careers.[71] The requirement that all bannermen take the *hsiang-shih* at Shun-t'ien was abolished in 1814, and provincial bannermen were permitted to participate in the regions where they resided. This was a profound symbolic acknowledgment on the part of the court that the bannermen were no longer native "residents" of the imperial core at Shun-t'ien, that they had on the contrary made the provinces their habitats. Proportional quotas were established for the open *hsiang-shih*, with one bannermen in ten being permitted to pass, though an absolute total of three successful bannermen was imposed.[72]

The abandonment of the Shun-chih-K'ang-hsi idea of bannermen as universal functionaries who were as well adapted to the Hanlin Academy as to the command of an elite cavalry corps in favor of a rigid regime of cultural purification, physical reinvigoration, and spiritual reintegration had implications far beyond what the Ch'ien-lung and Chia-ch'ing courts foresaw.

What later emperors were advocating, in essence, was a vocational, even professional, course of study for the bannermen in which adeptness in Manchu—
as the language of the military sector—was fundamental and in which the
more liberal, more obviously civil educational elements had little or no place.
There is evidence that the Chia-ch'ing court was far more interested in the
professionalizing aspects of the Ch'ien-lung reforms than in their ideology.[73]
The significance of this did not emerge until the military and educational
reforms of the period after the Opium War. Courses on armaments, both
Ch'ing and foreign, were added to the garrison officers' schools, and this inevitably led to limited technical studies—most related to the understanding and
manufacture of percussion caps—by mid-century.

Concurrently, the development of hybrid forms of military organization, beginning with the Grand Battalions formed in Kiangnan to attempt to repulse
the British invaders in 1841, created a new demand for the talents of
translators, as banner officers assigned to these composite armies were
required to maintain records in both Chinese and Manchu in order to keep the
court informed—in the security language, Manchu—of the movements and
internal power alignments within these forces. Indeed, the Tao-kuang emperor, foreseeing renewed need for banner expertise in Manchu as the
country's military organization became more complex, required all banner
officers to prepare and sit for the fan-i examinations from at least the
sheng-yuan level after 1843, a regulation the court kept until the general at-
tenuation of court administration of the garrisons in 1865.[74] It has, moreover,
been hypothesized on very good evidence that the Foreign Language Colleges
(t'ung-wen kuan) established under the Ministry of Foreign Affairs (tsung-li
ya-men) were actually patterned after the banner officers' schools, and it is certainly true that they were administered by garrison officials and attended
almost exclusively by Manchu bannermen.[75] By the end of the century, the
Foreign Language Colleges had added French, German, and Japanese—in addition to the original English course—and the old Russian school in the imperial city had been absorbed and reformed by the Foreign Language College
at Peking. An expanded curriculum ultimately included mathematics, astronomy, and chemistry (an outgrowth of the identification of banner officers with
percussion-cap manufacture), so that the Foreign Language College and its
provincial branches took on the appearance of the forerunners of the Imperial
University founded at Peking in 1896.[76]

If the banner officers' schools were, due to their vocational and later their
professional emphasis, the ancestors of the Foreign Language Colleges and the
Imperial University, they were nevertheless only ancestors. They did not in and
of themselves make the transition to modernity. Indeed, as late as the 1870s
I-huan (Prince Ch'un) was still calling for the bannermen to resist any modern
reforms that would override their commitment to the ancestral arts of ch'i-she.
Some of the banner forces were reformed into elite units under the leadership

of [Suwan Gūwalgiya] Wen-hsiang, [Suwan Gūwalgiya] Jung-lu, and others that became the foundation of the new armies who led the revolution of 1911– 12 and went on to form the vanguard of the forces of Yüan Shih-k'ai and many other warlords. Nevertheless, the Eight Banners themselves went the way of the banner officers' schools, becoming obsolete, decrepit, and overshadowed by the new forms to which they had given birth. And like the Eight Banners, the banner officers' schools endured a protracted senescence before finally being dispatched by the Ch'ing government. Not until 1902, when Hanlin scholar (and Manchu) Pao-hsi made the specific request, did the state allow the buildings of the Imperial Clan Academy, the Gioro Academy, and the officers' schools of Peking to be vacated, cleaned, fixed, and painted for use as elementary and middle school buildings under the jurisdiction of the new education ministry. [77]

The preconquest ideal of the Manchu language as a comprehensive state language and of the bannermen as comprehensive state functionaries appears to have continued to shape imperial educational policies after the conquest. Circumstances ultimately forced the abandonment of such a design, but the lingering three-point emphasis on the Manchu, Mongolian, and Chinese languages, as well as on both military and civil preparation for the bannermen, remained the hallmarks of the educational and administrative policies relating not only to the enrolled bannermen but also to the *tzu-ti* until the late eighteenth century. As the universalism of the Ch'ien-lung emperor's style began to change the shape of intellectual preparation and inquiry, the court directed greater attention to the status of Manchu among the Manchu population (still a difficult and in some ways contradictory idea at the time). Reports to the court that bannermen were neglecting both their education in Manchu language and their cultivation of military skills appear to have prompted the frequent admonitions from the emperor that bannermen remedy their defects and avoid become coming "lost" in Chinese culture. The resulting specialization of banner identity and banner education created the foundation for the reprofessionalized military of the late nineteenth century and the emergence of technical, vocational and professionalized education in the languages, sciences, and military arts.

EXAMINATIONS AND ALIEN REGIMES

Without a sensitivity to the ideological issues attached by the Ch'ien-lung court to the problems of language and orthography, it is difficult to reconstruct the impulses behind the Ch'ing preoccupation with Manchu education — and education in Manchu. From the modern perspective, it cannot be demonstrated that a sense of banner or Manchu identity was fundamentally dependent upon their speaking and writing a distinctive language. Like the Chinese Muslims (*hui*), the Manchus maintained and still maintain an ethnic identity in China despite the fact that they are urban and sinophone. For Hung-li, however, it was impossible to realize a universalist cultural mosaic within the empire without well-constructed archetypes of particular cultures, and the Manchus were intended to play this role. It is also clear that Hung-li remained profoundly attached to the notion of the northeast as a wellspring of Manchu history, culture, and legitimacy; the Manchus may, for him, have represented a sense of living legacy and strengthened his insistence on their cultural reconstruction and purification.

However important Manchu may have been to the eighteenth-century court, the policies and institutions created to revive Manchu outside state symbolism failed. As the language of a small minority settled in China, Manchu's decline and virtual disappearance perhaps need no explanation. But certain factors contributing to the state's inability to strengthen the language are worth noting. They are partly structural. Though it is too obvious a point to make much of, the fact was that until the late nineteenth century, educational programs in the garrisons, such as they were, were exclusively for men. The proposition of a garrison culture in which men learned to speak standard Manchu but women continued speaking Chinese dialects (or the hybrid Manchu-Chinese vernacular attested in many garrison communities) was obviously untenable. Moreover, the opportunities for the average bannermen to find advantageous employment for skills in Manchu were not extensive, and educational institutions for boys and young men were entirely neglected by the state until a late period. In the garrisons, the officers' schools remained small and exclusive attendance by the hereditary banner elite (sons of officers) may have been assumed. In Peking, the schools were dominated by a huge group of hereditary nobles and entrenched elites.

Beyond these factors, the history of Manchu and its relationship to Mongolian before and during the Ch'ing period must be recalled. There is first of all the failure of Manchu and Manchu script to gain much prestige before the conquest of China. From the thirteenth century on, Inner Asia had a great lingua franca in Mongolian, which the Jurchens themselves relied on and patterned their own literate culture after. Like the Ming before them, the Manchus had always to deal with the problems of Mongol power, even in a reduced or refracted form, and sustenance of literacy in Mongolian. The Ch'ing emperors were intimately tied to Mongolian through their historical connections to the Mongols (and, they liked to think, their own links to the great-khans) as well as through their own Mongolian empresses and bannermen. In their rhetoric, Manchu and Mongolian were always linked, whether as languages, as cultures, or as people. The emperors, in other words, never put all their weight on Manchu, and certainly Hung-li never believed that Manchu could in fact bear the weight of his universal rule. His policies worked, instead, to isolate, polish and display the language as one might a single stone in a collection of gems.

It is difficult to separate the weakness of Manchu as a cultural vehicle from the neglect of the Ch'ing emperors for the old corpus of works in the Jurchen script. From Nurgaci to Hung-li, the emperors had rejoiced for one reason or another in their ancestral connection to the imperial Jurchens. Yet no effort was ever made to reclaim the medieval "classical" literature in Jurchen either in the original or by means of transliteration into the new script. The reason lies perhaps in the ancient contempt—shared by the Ch'ing—for the translators' bureaus, in whose collections such fragments as survived of the old Jurchen texts and *lai-wen* were preserved. As determined by its function, which was to segregate and demean the ritual stature of non-Chinese cultures, the translators' bureaus and their collections offered nothing to the Ch'ing that seemed worth ruminating on. The institution of the translators' bureaus had stained the Jurchen literary past, and Manchu thus began the seventeenth century as a novel script with no literature.

This neglect is the more marked for the fact that Manchu as a written standard was a state invention to a degree unusual with living languages. At every point, its development was guided by the state and motived by state objectives: the nationalism of Nurgaci, who demanded a distinct mode of communication for his regime; the requirement of Hung Taiji that an easy script be devised to allow the translation into Manchu of important Chinese historical and political works; the desire of the Shun-chih, K'ang-hsi, and Yung-cheng emperors for a competent medium for the conduct of sensitive state business, including secret memorials, certain military communications, and exchanges with representatives of the Romanov rulers; and finally the search by Hung-li for a cultural taxonomy of the Manchus and ideological representation of his own universalism. State creation and control of the Manchu language parallels, not surprisingly, the shaping of the Manchus, who were organized and named by the state, were legally defined by it in ensuing centuries, and were the object of state cultural policy until the nineteenth century.

Quite apart from the special considerations behind Ch'ing treatment of the dynastic language and its constituency, the features of education and examination in Manchu—and of the education of the Manchus—lend themselves to broader comparisons serving the goals of this volume. The features of Manchu education may also be horizontally compared with other components of the Ch'ing education and examination systems. It had been a normal feature of the Ming and Ch'ing examinations to make space, both in terms of quotas and to a limited degree (particularly in the military examinations) in terms of content, for professional diversity. The segment of the examination system dedicated to the review of bannermen may be seen in this context. Indeed, from this perspective the creation of the banner and *fan-i* examinations during the Ch'ing may be seen as only minor alterations in the continuing Ming institutions.[78] (Such a view, however, must not only overlook the degree to which changes in banner education prepared the ground for the rise of technical studies in nineteenth-century China but also ignore the patterns through which the profound ideological ambitions of the eighteenth-century court were revealed.) The fundamental mores of the examination system did not alter greatly from the Ming to the Ch'ing. Nor was the basic intimacy between court ideology and the examinations as an institution attenuated. This final similarity is in fact the great point of divergence between the two last dynasties, for the explosion of imperial universalism under the Ch'ien-lung emperor changed profoundly the court's view of the substance and meaning of knowledge. The impact of those changes is vividly apparent in the microcosm of Manchu education.

Manchu education and examination may be perpendicularly compared to the cognate policies of earlier alien dynasties in China. The Kitans, the Jurchens, and the Mongols during their respective dynasties had faced the problems of formalizing folk cultures, authorizing and enforcing orthographic practices, and familiarizing some critical portion of their population with the Chinese knowledges necessary to stabilize their regimes. In each case, choices were made respecting not only the style of education to which nobles and elites were subjected but also whether the examinations were used to raise those perceived as "commoners" to the ruling class or to rationalize access to high office among the hereditary elites.

Not surprisingly, the Manchu approach to these questions most resembles that of the Jurchens before them. The Kitans and Mongols retained, at least in official policy, a strong attachment to the principles of nomadic life among their peoples and a toleration for traditional segmented political structures. They appear to have been disinclined to effect drastic changes in their economic and social lives by linking status or achievement to time-consuming attainments in civil or literary pursuits. Traditional markers of status, including birth affiliations, were not intruded on by state requirements for examination success. Indeed, Kitans were by edict barred from participating in the examinations held under the Liao, and the suspension of the examinations for the greater part of the Yüan dynasty left the question of Mongol achievement in the examinations moot.[79] It must be underscored that this observation is directed against the question of examination as a criterion for professional advancement and by extension a state tool for the shaping of the cultural life and political influence of its constituency; clearly, neither the absence of examinations nor the official state indifference to Mongolian classical education barred the emergence of Mongol scholars of the stature of Toghto or Qoninci.

In the cases of the Jurchens and the Manchus, however, the establishment of bilingual examinations and official attempts to encourage participation in the examinations by the peoples in question are evidence of a very different state posture. Unlike Mongols and Kitans, neither Jurchens nor Manchus were enfeoffed in China proper, nor were they committed to cultural precepts or political structures that were characteristic of nomadism. Attempts to use the examinations for promotion of commoners and to restrict high access to hereditary elites were characteristic, in the Chin and Ch'ing periods, of aggressive state programs to limit the privileges and influence of the nobility, to centralize the state, and to prepare the dynastic constituency for a broad role in the maintenance of a civil system.

NOTES

I am grateful to my two discussants at the conference from which this volume resulted, Cynthia Brokaw and William T. Rowe, for their extensive comments on the draft and to all the conference participants (foremost, Alexander Woodside and Frederic Wakeman) for their challenges and insights. Subsequent discussion of particulars relevant to the chapter has been provided by Yan Chongnian, Samuel Martin Grupper, and especially Evelyn Rawski, from whom I have learned much in our collaborative work on Manchu collections. The chapter has benefited in many ways from conversations at various times with Gertraude Roth Li. All stubbornly persisting errors of fact or interpretation are claimed by me. Further research and revisions of the chapter have taken place during a period when the author was supported by a Dartmouth College Junior Faculty Fellowship and a grant from the Marion and Jasper Whiting Foundation. I thank them.

1. "Manchus" is used throughout this chapter to identify those within the Eight Banners who were legally classified as Manchus from the ratification of the Manchu Banners in 1635 to the dissolution of the dynasty in 1912. As I have discussed elsewhere, registration within the banners was an administrative process and does not absolutely imply Jurchen/Manchu ancestry or Manchu cultural identity; conversely, there were from the beginning of the dynastic period persons of attestable Jurchen or Manchu ancestry who for various reasons were not registered as Manchus. Finally, the intertwining ambiguities, in both official and common language, between the terms "Manchu" (*manju, manju niyalma, man-jen, man-chou jen*) and "bannerman" (*gūsa i niyalma, ch'i-jen*) must be noted. With respect to the topics discussed here, all Manchus were bannermen, but some bannermen were Mongols or Chinese martial (*han-chün pa-ch'i*) or, in the late seventeenth century, Albazinians (*o-lo-ssu ch'i-jen*), and a very small number of bondservant bannermen were Muslim, which was regarded as a separate classification. On general background of the Eight Banners and the Manchus see these recent studies: Kaye Soon Im, *The Rise and Decline of the Eight-Banner Garrisons in the Ch'ing Period (1644–1911): A Study of the Kuang-chou, Hang-chou, and Ching-chou Garrisons* (Ann Arbor: University Microfilms, 1981); Pamela Kyle Crossley, *Orphan Warriors: Three Manchu Generations and the End of the Ch'ing World* (Princeton: Princeton University Press, 1990); Crossley, "The Qianlong Retrospect on the Chinese-martial (*hanjun*) Banners," *Late Imperial China* 10, no.1 (June 1989): 63–107.

2. For more extensive discussion, see P.K. Crossley, "*Manzhou yuanliu kao* and Formalization of the Manchu Heritage," *Journal of Asian Studies*, 46, no. 4 (Nov. 1987): 761–90; Crossley, "The Qianlong Retrospect on the Chinese-martial (*hanjun*) Banners"; Crossley, *Orphan Warriors*, esp. 20–30.

3. On Jurchen, See Wilhelm Grube, *Die Sprache und Schriften der Jucen* (Leipzig, 1896); Ishida Mikinosuke 石田幹之助, "Joshin-go kenkyū no shin shiryō" 女真語研究 の新資料 (New materials for researches on the Jurchen language) in *Tōa bunkashi sōkō* (1943; reprint, Tokyo, 1970); Daniel Kane, *The Sino-Jurchen Vocabulary of the Bureau of Interpreters*, (Bloomington: Indiana University Research Institute for Inner Asian Studies, 1989); Gisaburo Kiyose, *A Study of the Jurchen Language and Script: Reconstruction and Decipherment* (Kyoto, 1977); Chin Kuang-p'ing and Chin Ch'i-tsung, *Nü-chen yü-yen wen-tze yen-chiu* (Researches on Jurchen language and script) (Peking, 1980) Chin Ch'i-tsung, *Nü-chen wen tz'u-tien* (Jurchen language dictionary) (Peking, 1984).

4. Most of the ancestors of the people today recognized as Sibo had been incorporated into the Eight Banners as "New Manchus" (Ice Manju) in the middle and later seventeenth century. They are best known for having been settled in Sinkiang and having retained an unusual degree of traditional culture there. A history of the Sibos with the Chinese title *Hsi-po tsu chien shih* 稀伯族簡史 (Brief history of the Sibo people) but written in Sibo, was published in Peking in 1984 by Wu Yuan-feng 吳元豐 and Chao Chih-ch'iang 趙志強. The most important work on the Sibos, however, is Giovanni Stary, *Geschichte der Sibe-Mandschuren* (Wiesbaden: Otto Harrasowitz, 1985); the reader is also referred to Stary's extremely valuable study of the contemporary Sibo writer Kuo Chi-nan [Guo Jinan], "Note sulla vita e L'opera di G'ujinan, poeta e scrittore del popolo Sibe" in *Miszellen zur mandschurischen Sprache, Literatur und Geschichte im 17. und 20. Jahrhundert (Miscellanea di studi sulla lingua, letteratura e storia mancese del 17° e 20° secolo)* (Wiesbaden: Otto Harrasowitz, 1987).

5. There are many passing references to this practice, but see as an example *Ch'ing Kao-tsung shilu* 清高宗實錄, 1417:17a. This technique was also used by Chinese on the Manchu section of their *chin-shih* examinations; examples may be found among the Manchu materials of the Han Yushan Collection of the University Research Library at the University of California at Los Angeles. I am indebted to Benjamin A. Elman and James Cheng for inviting me to examine these materials.

6. Some of the best surviving evidence of this vernacular is contained in transcriptions of drum songs, particularly of the genre called "bannermen tales," *tzu-ti shu*. See Kuan Te-tung 關得棟 and Chou Chung-ming 周中明, *Tzu-ti shu ts'ung-ch'ao* 子弟書叢炒 (Collected bannerman tales), 2 vols. (Peking, 1984), esp. 1–18. See also Crossley, *Orphan Warriors*, 82–86, 251 nn. 18–21.

7. The comparison here with *han'gul* is meant to convey the visual organization of the characters; *han'gul* was created much later. It is possible that the phonetic script used by the Uigurs (and later adapted by the Mongols) was the inspiration for the use of phonetic principle in the Kitan small characters. Kitan large-character script is still largely undeciphered. On Kitan small-character script, which is partially deciphered but still cannot be phonetically reconstructed with complete confidence, see Cinggertai et al., *Ch'i-tan hsiao-tze yen-chiu* (Researches on the Kitan small script) (Peking: Chung-kuo she-hui k'o-hsueh, 1985).

8. The history and social aspects of the Jurchen examination during the Chin dynasty have been treated in Tao Jingshen, *The Jurchen in Twelfth-Century China: A Study of Sinicization* (Seattle: Publications on Asia of the Institute for Comparative and Area Studies, University of Washington, 1976), 57–61. Seee also Peter K. Bol, "Seeking Common Ground: Han Literati under Jurchen Rule," in *Harvard Journal of Asiatic Studies*

47, no. 2 (Dec. 1987): 477–78. On examinations during the Liao period, when only those recognized by the state as *han* were permitted to participate, see Chu Tzu-fang and Huang Feng-ch'i, "Liao tai k'o-chü chih-tu shu-lueh," in Ch'en Shu, ed., *Liao Chin shi lun-chi* no. 3 (Peking: Shu-mu wen-hsien, 1987).

9. The Yung-ning Ssu of the Nurgan territories, whose stelae bear Yung-le period and later inscriptions in Jurchen, Mongolian, and Tibetan, has been described in two published works. See Samuel M. Grupper, "The Manchu Imperial Cult of the Early Ch'ing Dynasty: Texts and Studies on the Tantric Sanctuary of Mahâkâla at Mukden" (Ph.D. diss., University of Indiana, 1980), 37 n.34, 39 n.40, 41; Yang Yang 楊楊 et al., *Ming-tai Nu-erh-kan t'u-ssu wei-so yen-chiu* 明代奴兒干都司及其衛所研究 (Henan: Chung-hua shu-chü, 1982), 52–68.

10. Though the *ssu-i kuan* were small and politically insignificant under the Ch'ing, they had a long and symbolically significant career during the entire later imperial period. There are many studies, but for unsurpassed primary information see Paul Pelliot, "Le Sseu-yi-kouan et le Houei-t'ong-kouan," in "Le Hoja et le Sayyid Husain de l'Histoire des Ming," in *T'oung Pao* 38 (1948): 2–5, app. 3: 207–90; for a more recent interpretation, see P.K. Crossley, "Structure and Symbol in the Ming-Ch'ing Translator's Bureaus (*ssu-i kuan*)," in *Central and Inner Asian Studies* 5 (1991): 38–70.

The quotation comes from Yen Ch'ung-nien, *Nu-erh-ha-ch'ih chuan* (Life of Nurgaci) (Peking: Pei-ching ch'u-pan-she, 1983), 134. The ascendancy of Mongolian as a written medium among the Chien-chou Jurchens was noted at length by Louis Ligeti in his 1958 article "Deux Tablettes de T'ai-tsong des Ts'ing,'" and Ligeti's discussion has been amplified by Cleaves in "A Mongolian Rescript of the Fifth Year of Degedü Erdem-tü (1640)," in *Harvard Journal of Asiatic Studies* 46, no. 1 (June 1986): 182–200, esp. 182–83. See also Crossley, "Structure and Symbol," 52–53.

11. *Man-chou shih-lu* 滿洲實錄 (Manchu annual) (reprint, Taipei, 1964), 109; *Huang Ch'ing k'ai-kuo fang-lüeh* 皇清開國方略 (Narrative of the founding of the imperial Ch'ing) (reprint, Taipei, 1966), 75–76. The text, as it was finalized in the eighteenth century, has Nurgaci instructing Erdeni and Gagai on how to accomplish their task.

12. Koreans retained materials and a curriculum for instruction in Jurchen as part of their court bureaucracy long after Jurchen communications had been overshadowed by a revival of communications in Mongolian. See also Hiu Lie, *Die Manschu-Sprachkunde in Korea* (Bloomington: Uralic and Altaic Studies Program, 1972), 14–17, and Song Ki-Joong, "The Study of Foreign Languages in the Yi Dynasty (1392–1910)," in *Bulletin of the Korean Research Center: Journal of the Social Sciences and Humanities* 54 (1981): 1–45.

13. See also J.R.P. King, "The Korean Elements in the Manchu Script Reform of 1632," in *Central Asiatic Journal* 31 nos. 3, 4 (1987) : 252–86.

14. Chang Chung-ju et al., *Ch'ing-tai k'ao-shih chih-tu tz'u-liao* (hereafter *CKCT*) (Documents on the examination system of the Ch'ing period) (n.d.; photoreprint, Taipei: Wenhai, 1968) 1:3a.

15. *CKCT*, 1:9a.

16. On the Grand Council, see Beatrice S. Bartlett, *Monarchs and Ministers: The Grand Council in Mid-Ch'ing China, 1723–1820* (Berkeley: University of California Press, 1991).

17. For more detailed discussion, see Pamela Kyle Crossley and Evelyn S. Rawski, "The Value of Manchu Documents for Ch'ing Research," in *Harvard Journal of Asiatic Studies* (forthcoming).

18. Russian was taught in China, with no detectable effectiveness, from the early eighteenth century, when a small language school (*o-lo-ssu-wen-kuan*) was established for the Albazinian bannermen at Peking, and it may have enrolled Manchus from the time, or nearly the time, of its founding. On its chronology and beginnings, see Eric Widmer, *The Russian Ecclesiastical Mission in Peking during the Eighteenth Century* (Cambridge, Mass.: Harvard East Asian Research Center, 1976), 109. The school stood outside the Tung-hua Men, very near the present-day office of the Kung-an-chü responsible for processing the affairs of foreigners in Peking, and was administered by the *nei-ko*. The grounds and the school were absorbed by the reformed translators' bureaus in the middle eighteenth century. See also, Crossley, "Symbol and Function of the Ming-Ch'ing Translators' Bureaus."

The extent of tributary communications in Manchu still surviving is unknown to the author, but for an example see the memorial (in very frail condition) from the Liu-ch'iu *wang* Shang-mu 流球王尚穆, dated Ch'ien-lung 21 (1756), retained among the documents once belonging to Joseph Fletcher and now in the possession of the Harvard-Yenching Library.

19. For further discussion, see Pamela Kyle Crossley, "The Inside Edge: Chinese Scholars and Ch'ing Knowledge" (Paper presented at the annual meeting of the New England Conference of the Association for Asian Studies, 1990); Crossley and Rawski, "Value of Manchu Documents".

20. [Aisin Gioro] Chao-lien 昭槤, *Hsiao-t'ing tsa-lu* 嘯亭雜錄 (hereafter *HTTL*), *chüan* 1:1b.

21. Sun Wen-liang and Li Chih-t'ing, *Ch'ing T'ai-tsung ch'üan-chuan* (Biography of Ch'ing T'ai-tsung) (Chi-lin: Chi-lin jen-min, 1983), 310.

22. *HTTL*, *chüan* 1:1b–2b.

23. This is a selection of the most frequently encountered and copied literature. For further discussion, see Crossley and Rawski, "Value of Manchu Documents."

24. In Korea, where under the earlier Yi dynasty castes had made a social phenomenon of technical knowledge, translators were part of the *chung'in*, the adept nonelites who acted as scribes, mechanics, translators, and so on. From Silla times, the *yangban*, the elite of the bone-ranks system, had maintained a monopoly on high administrative office, a situation that in its basic features pertained through the Koryo and early Yi periods. The *chung'in* of late Koryo and Yi times encompassed both commoners who had managed to qualify for technical administrative and artisanal tasks by means of the *chap op*, the lowest tier of the three-tiered examination system, or who were illegitimate sons of the *yangban* class who had received some technical education. Translating was one of the most fundamental and visible tasks of the *chung'in*, so important that in later Yi times, when trade with Japan, China, and the Jurchens flourished, some translators made fortunes large enough to disrupt the social restrictions by which they would have been hereditarily bound. See also Ki-Baik Lee, *A New History of Korea*, trans. E. Wagner (Cambridge, Mass.: Harvard University Press, 1984), 118–19, 174, 230; Edward Willett Wagner, *The Literati Purges: Political Conflict in Early Yi Korea* (Cambridge, Mass.: East Asian Research Center, 1974), 12.

25. The *ssu-i-kuan* at this time numbered eight: Mongol, Jurchen, Tibetan, Sanskrit, Persian (*hui-hui*), Shan (*pai-i*), Uigur (*kao-ch'ang*) and Burmese. In 1511, Pa-pai (a Yunnanese dialect) was added; Thai was added in 1579. Thirty-eight students from the

National University (*kuo-tze chien*) were assigned as translators (*i-shu*). These students, having passed the *hsiang-shih* but having failed the *hui-shih* were made eligible for a slightly modified *hui-shih* that included the writing of several passages in foreign scripts. Thereafter, they were presented to the Hanlin Academy, which might accept or reject them. *Dictionary of Ming Biography*, 362.

26. *DMB*, 1121. Li K'ai-hsien is famous apart from his connection with the *ssu-i kuan*, of course; he is considered among the possible authors of *Chin P'ing Mei*. See also Mary Elizabeth Scott, "Azure from Indigo: *Honglou meng's* debt to *Jin ping mei*" (Ph.D. diss., Princeton University, 1989).

27. See Arthur Hummel, ed., *Eminent Chinese of the Ch'ing Period* (Washington, D.C., 1943) (hereafter *ECCP*), 792; Crossley, "Structure and Symbol," 63 (in which, due to the author's carelessness, part of the line referring to this incident has been lost).

28. Chao Er-hsün et al., *Ch'ing shih kao* (Draft history of the Ch'ing; hereafter *CSK*) (1928; punctuated reprint, Peking: Chung-hua shu-chü, 1977), 108:3160.

Ch'i-she, literally "riding and shooting," is the Chinese attempt to convey what in all Inner and Central Asian languages is a single word (in the Manchu case, *niyamniyambi*) describing the distinctive Inner Asian skill of shooting from a moving horse. See also Crossley, *Orphan Warriors*, 15, 22–24.

29. Liu Shih-che, "Man-tsu 'ch'i-she' ch'ien-shu" (Brief overview of the "riding and shooting" of the Manchus), in *Min-tsu yen-chiu* 5(1982): 53.

30. See particularly Kuo Ch'eng-k'ang, "Ch'ing-ch'u niu-lu ti shu-mu" (Numbers of *niru* in the early Ch'ing) in *Ch'ing-shih yen-chiu t'ung-hsün* 1(1987): 31–35, in which he proposes that Chinese martial companies in the years just prior to 1644 may have numbered 100 out of 500, and increased during 1643-44 to more than 160 out of 500. See also Crossley, "Qianlong Retrospect," 13.

31. *CKCT*, 1:8b. The change in policy was at least in part prompted by a memorial from the *li-pu* recommending that bannermen be sent back to compete in the regular *hsiang-shih*: "Among the Eight Banners are some outstanding talents, who could prepare themselves for examination by enhancing their abilities, and then be sought out by means of *ke, sui, hsiang* and *hui* examinations. The best of them could then be appointed to office." *CSK*, 108:3160.

32. *CKCT*, 1:7a.

33. *CKCT*, 1:12b, 16b.

34. *CSK*, 106:3115. There was subsequent alteration to Manchus and Mongols sixty, Chinese martial thirty.

35. *CSK*, 108:3161.

36. *CKCT*, 1:7a.

37. A general history of Mongolian education is provided by Man-Kam Leung in "Mongolian Language Education and Examinations in Peking and Other Metropolitan Areas During the Manchu Dynasty in China (1644–1911)," *Canada Mongolia Review (Revue Canada-Mongolie)* 1, no.1 (1975): 29–44. In most respects, Mongolian education paralleled Manchu education rather exactly, with the exceptions noted in this chapter. It was often the case, however, that the Mongolian curriculum was introduced at a later date than the Manchu. For instance, it was introduced into the garrison schools in 1691, the Eight Banners Officers' Schools in 1723, and the Hsien-an Palace Officers' School in 1734.

38. It may have been, as Chao-lien has suggested (*HTTL*, 1:18b–19a), that [Janggiya] A-kuei and the officials of the Board of War requested the reinstatement of the *fan-i* degrees in order to attempt to inspire more bannermen to compete and succeed at the examinations, a goal that, while distasteful to the Ch'ien-lung emperor, was accepted.

39. On the *kuo-tzu chien*, see Adam Lui, "The Imperial College (*Kuo-tzu-chien*) in the Early Ch'ing (1644–1795)." in *Papers on Far Eastern History* 10 (1974): 147–66.

40. *CSK*, 106:3099. For a larger discussion of state-bannerman relations, see also Crossley, *Orphan Warriors*, ch. 13–30, 47–73.

41. Using the same source as myself (CSK), Adam Lui has come to the conclusion that *t'ien-wen suan-hsüeh* represented a single curriculum; see "Imperial College," 150. I read them as distinct and sequential, since the source provides not only an indication of the sequence (*t'ien-wen*, then *suan-hsüeh*) but also of the text for the *suan-hsüeh* course, which evidently did not encompass *t'ien-wen*. *T'ien-wen suan-fa* ("astronomical calculations") was not a curriculum but a discipline. For comments on the differences between Ming and Ch'ing *suan-fa*, see *HTTL*, 1:6b–7a.

42. *CSK*, 106:3110.

43. *CSK*, 106:3111, states that the name *tsung-hsüeh* is found in the T'ang and Sung records, but no details regarding its purposes or organization can be ascertained. The Jurchen Chin had established a *kuo-tsu hsüeh* (subordinate to the *kuo-tzu chien*) where instruction in Jurchen and Chinese was administered to Jurchen noblemen. *Chin-shih*, (Peking: Jen-min, 1974), 56:468. There is no direct Mongolian precedent; the Ch'ing *kuo-hsüeh* is the descendant of the Mongolian Imperial University (*kuo-tzu chien*) under the Yüan; provincial Mongols were educated at a *Meng-ku tzu-hsüeh* under the administration of the Central Secretariat. *Hsin Yüan-shih*, Peking: Jen-min, 1976), 64: 621–23. The grounds of the *tsung-hsüeh* were located on the site of the present Nationalities College (*min-tsu hsüeh-yuan*) on Pai-shih ch'iao Road. The education of the imperial clan in this setting should not be confused with the education of princes eligible for emperorship and their siblings, who were tutored in the palace and maintained both literacy and fluency in Manchu until the end of the dynasty and beyond.

44. Literally "sons and younger brothers," *tzu-ti* was used at the end of the Ch'ing period to indicate, loosely, all Manchus. However, prior to the nineteenth century the term was more definitive, and indicated (as it had for previous dynasties in China) the male dependents of an active serviceman. The significance in the pronouncements on educational policy was that not only active bannermen but also *tzu-ti* — any one of whom might become an active bannerman, and all of whom were included under the "Manchu" rubric — were eventually explicitly included in all banner education programs. See also Crossley, *Orphan Warriors* 17, 24.

45. *CSK*, 109, 3110.

46. They were reported as: Bordered Yellow Banner, sixty-one; Plain Yellow Banner, thirty-six; Plain White Banner, Plain Red Banner, forty each; Bordered White Banner, fifteen; Bordered Red Banner, sixty-four; Plain Blue Banner, thirty-nine; Bordered Red Banner, five. Two Manchu and two Chinese instructors were assigned for each banner, with the exception of the Bordered White Banner, which had only one for each language. I suspect that "five" with reference to the Bordered Red Banner is a mistake for "fifty" which would make the passage more reasonable. *CSK*, 106:3112–13.

47. *CSK*, 106:3113. The Plain Yellow, Bordered Yellow and Plain White banners were together known as the Three Superior Banners (*san shang ch'i*) and, being the property of the emperor, were exclusively administered by the Imperial Household Department, under whose auspices the Prospect Hill and Hsien-an Palace schools were administered. These were the two best known of the five schools operated by the Imperial Household Department, which included a facility for the teaching of Arabic and Burmese to bondservants. See Preston Torbert, *The Ch'ing Imperial Household Department: A Study of Its Organization and Principal Functions, 1662–1796*, (Cambridge, Mass.: Harvard University East Asian Monographs, 1977), 37–39, for descriptions of all the schools.

48. If there should not be enough *chin-shih* applicants, the new regulations declared, outstanding *chü-jen* could be considered. On the surface, this appears to be a compromise of the standards of the school but may in fact have represented an attempt to elevate them. Tai Ming-shih, for instance, had taught at the school in 1686–89, when still struggling to pass the *hui-shih*. After his service in the school, he was offered a magistracy, indicating that the regulation of 1735 may only have formalized long-standing custom. See *ECCP*, 701.

49. *CSK*, 106:3113.

50. *CSK*, 106:3110.

51. *CSK*, 106:3110.

52. For a larger perspective on this, see Crossley, *Orphan Warriors*, 47–55.

53. *CSK*, 106:3114. Charitable schools in Peking were located, among other places, in the outlying garrisons, the artillery garrisons, the *Yuan-ming yuan*, and the *hu-chün* garrisons.

54. Newly established schools were overseen by the nearest superior school in the hierarchy. That is, *fu* schools oversaw *chou* schools, *chou* schools oversaw *hsien* schools. If one school divided into two, they split quotas and resources. *CSK*, 106:3117.

55. Certainly, this was the case with high-level Chinese martial bureaucrats, who served disproportionately during the first twenty-five years after the conquest and whose percentages lowered gradually thereafter. See Lawrence Kessler, "Ethnic Composition of Provincial Leadership during the Ch'ing Dynasty," in *Journal of Asian Studies* 28, no. 3 (May 1969): 489–511.

56. For details and discussion, see Crossley, *Orphan Warriors*, 25–26, 136 nn. 40, 41.

57. "Some Mid-Ch'ing Theorists of Popular Schools: Their Innovations, Inhibitions, and Attitudes Toward the Poor," in *Modern China* 9, no.1 (1983): 23–24.

58. *CKCT*, 1:40a–b.

59. On language customs in the garrisons, see also Crossley, *Orphan Warriors*, 84, 250 –51 nn.15, 16.

60. *CKCT*, 1.41a, 1:50b–51a.

61. Raymond W. Chu and William G. Saywell, *Career Patterns in the Ch'ing Dynasty* (Ann Arbor: University of Michigan Center for Chinese Studies, 1984) 52.

62. Liu Shih-che, "Man-tsu 'ch'i-she' ch'ien-shu," 54 from *Man-chou yüan-liu k'ao*, 6: 13b.

63. *CKCT*, 1:60b–61a. A portion of this passage has been translated in Crossley, *Orphan Warriors*, 27, and a different portion has been translated by Man-Kam Leung, "Mongolian Language Education," 40, from a reprinted text in Hsi Yü-fu, *Huang-ch'ao cheng-tien lei-ts'üan* (Taipei, 1969).

64. See Crossley, "*Manzhou yuanliu kao*," 779-81; Crossley, *Orphan Warriors*, 19–30.

65. *CSK*, 106:3100.

66. *CSK*, 106:3111–12.

67. *CSK*, 108:3170.

68. Lei Fang-shen, "Ching-chou ch'i-hsüeh te shih-mo chi ch'i t'e-tien," in *Min-tsu yen-chiu* 3(1984): 57–59.

69. Crossley, *Orphan Warriors*, 87–88.

70. *CSK*, 106:3117.

71. Residence, property, and vocational regulations within the garrison administration had already been altered in recognition of these changes during the later eighteenth century. See also Crossley, *Orphan Warriors*, 56ff.

72. *CSK*, 108:3161.

73. For instance, though the commissioning of academies and reform of educational criteria continued, the massive generation and institutionalization of cultural literature did not. Sungyun's *Emu tanggū orin sakda-i gisun sarkiyan*, a didactic treatise in Manchu on social morality that was evidently written to appeal to the Ch'ien-lung court's program for Manchu improvement, was brought to Peking in manuscript in the last years of the eighteenth century but did not gain the patronage of the Chia-ch'ing court. It was later translated into Chinese and is now a curiosity. See also Crossley and Rawski "Value of Manchu Documents."

74. Thomas Taylor Meadows, *Translations from the Manchu with the Original Texts* (Canton: S. Wells Williams, 1849), 19.

75. Nancy Evans, "The Banner-School Background of the Canton T'ung-wen Kuan," in *Papers on China* 22A (May 1969): 89–103. See also Crossley, *Orphan Warriors*, 143–44.

76. T'an I, "Wan Ch'ing T'ung-wen kuan yu Chin-tai hsüeh-hsiao chiao-yu," in *Ch'ing-shih yen-chiu* 5 (1986): 349–50; Lei Fang-sheng, "Ching-chou ch'i-hsüeh te shih-mo," 57.

77. *CSK*, 106:3114.

78. I take this as the implication of the recent discussion of the Ch'ing examinations in Wang Te-chao, "Ch'ing-tai te k'o-chü ju jen yü cheng-fu," in *Hsiang Kang Chung-wen Ta-hsüeh Chung-kuo wen-hua yen-chiu-so hsüeh-pao* 12 (1981): 1–21, esp. 5.

79. It appears that the edict barring Kitans from the examinations was strictly enforced until the late Liao period, and Kitans could be punished even for requesting permission to participate in the examinations. This did not preclude the spread of literacy in both Kitan and Chinese among the Kitans, however, and by the end of the dynasty Yelu Dashi—the imperial scion who in 1121 fled to Central Asia to found the Western Liao (Karakitai) dynasty—was a *chin-shih* recipient of 1114 and a Hanlin appointee. The Ch'ing emperors would note with approval that he was also expert at Kitan writing and *ch'i-she*. See Chu and Huang, "Liao tai k'o-chü chih-tu shu-lüeh," 7.

GLOSSARY

A-kuei	阿桂	*ch'ao-shih*	朝試
Cabuhai	查布海	*chap op*	雜業
Chang Ta-ch'ang	張大昌	*chen-kuan cheng-yao*	貞觀政要
Chao-lien	昭槤	*cheng k'ao-kuan*	正考官

ch'i-she	騎射	ho-tzu hao	合子號
Chia-ch'ing	嘉慶	Hou Chin	後金
chia-ti	甲第	Hsi-hua	西華
chiang-chün	將軍	hsiang	鄉
Chien-chou	建州	hsiang-shih	鄉試
chien-sheng	監生	hsiao-ch'i-hsiao	驍騎校
Ch'ien-lung	乾隆	Hsiao-ching	孝經
chih-hsien	知縣	Hsiao-hsueh	小學
Chin	金	hsien	縣
Chin P'ing Mei	金瓶梅	Hsien-an-kung	咸安宮
chin-shih	進士	Hsien-an-kung kuan-hsueh	咸安宮官學
Ching-shan	景山	hsien-san	閑散
ching-shih chi-fu	京飾畿輔	Hsin T'angshu	新唐書
ch'ing-an che	情安摺	Hsing-li	性理
Ch'ing-shih kao	清史稿	Hsing-pu hui-tien	形部會典
Ch'ing-wen	清文	hsueh-she	學舍
Ch'ing-wen ch'i-meng	清文啟蒙	hu-chün	護軍
Ch'ing-wen hui-shu	清文彙書	huang-ch'eng	黃城
Ch'ing-wen pu-hui	清文補彙	hui	會
Ch'ing-yü	清語	hui	回
chiu-tao	舊道	hui-hui	回回
chou	州	hui-shih	會試
chu-fang	駐方	Hung-li	弘曆
chü-jen	舉人	Hung-lü ssu	鴻臚寺
Chü-yung kuan	居庸關	Hung Taiji	洪太亟
Chueh-lo hsueh	覺羅學	I-ching	易經
Ch'un-ch'iu	春秋	i-huan	奕環
chün-chi-ch'u	軍機處	ju-ch'en	儒臣
chung-shu	中書	Jung-lu	榮祿
chung'in	中人	Jurchen	女真
en	恩	K'ang-hsi	康熙
Erdeni	額爾德尼	Kao-ch'ang	高昌
Erh-shih-i-shih	二十一史	k'ao-tao	考到
fan-i	翻譯	Kiangnan	江南
fan-i kung-sheng	翻譯公生	Kitan	契丹
fou-hua	浮化	k'o	科
fu	府	Koryo	高麗
fu	副	k'u-shih	庫使
fu k'ao-kuan	副考官	k'u-shou	庫手
Gagai	噶蓋	kung	公
Garin	剛林	Kung Kung-hsiang	龔公襄
Giyanghedei	蔣赫德	kung-sheng	貢生
han-chün pa-ch'i	漢軍八旗	Kung Tzu-chen	龔自珍
Han shu	漢書	kuo-hsueh	國學
Hanlin	翰林	kuo-jen	國人
ho-pi	合璧	kuo-tsu hsueh	國族學

Kuo-tzu chien	國子監	*Ssu-shu*	四書
kuo-wen	國文	*suan-hsüeh*	算學
kuo-yü	國語	*sui*	歲
lai-wen	來文	Sun Wen-liang	孫文良
Lao-tzu	老子	Sung-yun	松運
Li-chi	禮記	Tai Ming-shih	戴名世
Li Chih-t'ing	李治亭	*T'ai-ch'ang ssu*	太常寺
li-fan yuan	理藩院	Tao-kuang	道光
Li K'ai-hsien	李開先	*tien-shih*	殿試
li-pu	吏部	*t'ien-wen*	天文
Liang Shu-ming	梁漱溟	*tso-ling*	佐領
ling-ts'ui	領催	Tso Mou-ti	左懋第
Liu-tzu	六子	*tsu-chang*	族張
Lun-yü	論語	*tsung-hsüeh*	宗學
Man-chou yuan-liu k'ao	滿洲源流考	*tsung-jen fu*	宗人府
man-jen, man-chou-jen	滿人，滿洲人	*tsung-li ya-men*	總理衙門
man-tzu hao	滿子號	*T'ung-chien kang-mu*	通鑑綱目
Meng-ku kuo-tzu chien	蒙古國子監	*T'ung-chien kuan*	通鑑館
Meng-ku ya-men	蒙古衙門	*t'ung-k'ao kuan*	同考官
Meng-tzu	孟子	*t'ung-wen kuan*	同文館
nei-ko	內閣	*(Tzu-chih) T'ung-chien*	(資治)通鑑
nei-pan	內班	*tzu-ti*	子弟
nei-wu fu	內務府	*wai-pan*	外班
o-lo-ssu-wen-kuan	俄羅斯文館	*wang*	王
pa-ch'i	八旗	Wang Kuo-wei	王國維
pa-ch'i kuan-hsüeh	八旗官學	*wei*	衛
pai-i	百夷	*wei-so*	衛所
Pao-hsi	保熙	*wen*	文
pao-i	包衣	Wen-hsiang	文襄
pen	本	*wen-kuan*	文官
p'in	品	*wu*	武
po	拔	*Wu-ching*	五經
San-kuo chih	三國誌	*Wu-ying*	武英
San-lüeh	三略	Yang-tzu	揚子
san shang ch'i	三上旗	*yang-yü*	養育
Shen-yang	瀋陽	*yangban*	兩班
Shih-chi	史記	Yi	李
Shih-ching	詩經	*yu chih hsiang hsüeh*	有志想學
Shih-san ching	十三經	*Yü-chih Ch'ing-wen chien*	御志清文鑑
Shu-ching	書經	*Yü-chih Shu-li ching-yun*	御志數理精蘊
shu-yuan	書院	*Yü-chih tseng-ting*	御志增定
Shun-t'ien	順天	*Ch'ing-wen chien*	清文鑑
Sibo	稀柏	*Yuan-ming yuan*	圓明園
ssu-i kuan	四夷官	Yuan Shih-k'ai	袁世凱
Ssu-k'u ch'üan-shu	四庫全書	*Yung-ning ssu*	永寧寺

PART FOUR

The Theory and Practice of Schools and Community Education

ELEVEN

Elementary Education in the Lower Yangtze Region in the Seventeenth and Eighteenth Centuries

Angela Ki Che Leung

Since the pioneering work of Evelyn Rawski on elementary education in Ch'ing China, which gives a most valuable overview of the problem, little has been done to further examine this important question.[1] Alexander Woodside's relative pessimism concerning popular literacy in relation to Rawski's obvious optimism is one of the few stimulating reactions to her work, though one must confess that it is yet too early to arrive at any final conclusion as to the difficult question of the rate of literacy.[2] Other aspects of elementary education on which Rawski has set the agenda in her book also remain to be dealt with — the content of education and the roles of the state, the community, and the family.[3]

What this chapter attempts to do is trace the relative importance of the state, the community, and the clan or family in the matter of elementary education in the late Ming and early Ch'ing periods. It also looks more closely at the form and content of school education for children from about six to about fifteen years of age in order to find out the respective aims of the state, the community, and the family in educating the child. This chapter limits its survey to the Lower Yangtze region, which was incontestably the richest and, culturally speaking, one of the most developed regions of China of the seventeenth and eighteenth centuries. It was not a "typical" region, but it should show us a version of elementary education closest to the Chinese ideal.

POLICIES OF THE STATE, THE COMMUNITY, AND THE CLAN

Elementary schools of premodern China were mainly creations of three institutions: the state, the community, and the clan or family. Each had its own priorities, which, however, sometimes overlapped. For example, passing the imperial examination was the ultimate goal of many children and their families. Indeed, though a child entering primary school had a long way to go before he would consider the possibility of sitting for the imperial examinations, this ultimate possibility did affect the curricula of elementary education. But the fact that the great majority of children would not sit for the examinations convinced many educators that the content of primary education should be independent of the requirements of the civil examination system and be focused essentially on moral training and social discipline. This profound ambiguity of elementary education in the whole process of cultural reproduction with the civil examination system at its center explains the very different aims, needs, and policies of the state, the community, and the family in the matter.[4]

The State and the She-hsueh System

The she-hsueh (community school) system, created in 1375 by the imperial order of the first Ming emperor, was an obvious effort to uphold orthodox Confucian values in the empire after the "barbarian" rule of the Mongols and their overthrow by popular movements of anti-elite doctrines.[5] There was no fixed format for the schools; an 1504 edict, which was possibly a statement of the existing conditions, decreed that children under fifteen sui be admitted to learn rites and rituals in the schools.[6] The schools were to be established especially in rural communities so that even children of country people could be baptized into Confucian culture.[7] This imperial order was reiterated several times by Emperor Hung-wu himself and his successors in 1375, 1436, 1465, 1504.[8] In local gazetteers, there are also records of local officials constantly restoring and financing local community schools all through the Ming period. This initiative, however, should not be seen as a state policy attempting to achieve mass literacy. It was more a symbolic gesture to celebrate the return of Confucian orthodoxy and the political order that was based on it. A few magistrates, however, did consider the schools to be preparatory institutions for children who aimed at sitting for the imperial examination.[9] No matter how the schools were perceived, the fact was that the she-hsueh system did not benefit from a persistent policy. This could be shown by two points: the state's inability and unwillingness to overcome the first difficulties of the system, and the apparently peripheral role and discontinuous existence of the schools in various localities.

The difficulties of the application of the she-hsueh system were known to the emperor soon after it was initiated. In the Imperial Announcements (Ta-kao) published in 1385, Emperor Hung-wu attributed the failure of the system to the incompetence and the corruption of local officials who "do not allow those who want to learn but are without money to enter the schools, while letting some three or four worthless persons continue to dwell in their stupidity (in the schools) after having received money (from them)...." His immediate reaction to the unmanageable behavior of the local officials was to call for a temporary suspension of the system.[10]

With such feeble support from the state, the community schools in the localities were totally dependent on the support of local officials for their stability. One typical example is Kao-yu, where 172 schools were set up in 1375 under the imperial order. By 1467, none of these existed and the prefect had to create five schools in the area that, by 1572, were again reported to be no longer in existence.[11] In Chu-jung, Ch'en Yü-wang (*chin-shih* 1606) — the father of the famous late Ming scholar from Chia-shan, Ch'en Lung-cheng (1585–1645) — was reported to have revived the five schools in the city while he was the magistrate there in 1597; these schools had been defunct since their reestablishment in 1570.[12] The same story can be told about Chin-t'an, where schools were set up in 1375 and had to be revived several times in 1462, 1466, the 1480s, and the last time in 1515. Each time, the magistrate found it necessary to rebuild the abandoned schools. By the early 1520s, the schools were again in a devastated state.[13] Despite the discontinuous existence of the schools, which showed the difficulties in their management, it is important to note that it was always the local officials who revived and financed them. They believed that it was their duty to uphold a state institution. In this sense, despite a lack of continuity in state support, the community schools were testimony to the state's presence and its concern with primary education as an instrument of cultural control.

By the end of the Ming, however, some officials began to adopt a new policy toward the schools that were then in the process of acquiring a different meaning. The new attitude was most explicit in a 1599 attempt of the Chekiang administration commissioner, Chang Ch'ao-jui, aided by two prefects, to integrate the schools into a larger local system that would also consist of the *hsiang-yueh* (village lecture system), the *pao-chia* (police security system), and the local granary. The attempt was to "simplify red tape and to concretize policies." In fact, this effort was nothing more than the reinvigoration of social control on the local level by reinforcing the police and ideological indoctrination system essentially run by local leaders.[14] Whether the attempt was a success is anybody's guess, but the end result was a new status for the school. Similarly, the magistrate of Hui-an (Fukien) from 1570 to 1574, Yeh Ch'un-chi (1552 *chü-jen*), in the famous gazetteer he compiled for the *hsien*, only mentioned four local institutions after detailed geographical descriptions of the place: *hsiang-yueh*, *pao-chia*, *li-she* (local sacrificial institution), and *she-hsueh*.[15] Apparently, the *she-hsueh* institution was now thought to be part of a local system that inevitably put community leaders in the responsible positions and that essentially aimed at the consolidation of the community.

The change was not an accident. There were already an increasing number of community schools that were used as sites for village lectures or as the community granary. For example, the Shang-yang community school in Shanghai was restored in the early 1520s by the prefect, who also used the school for village lectures, and schools at Ch'ing-p'u, established in the early 1590s, were transformed into granaries.[16] What is even more significant is that some community schools at the end of the Ming period were already performing a new function. In the earlier period, the schools were commonly said to train "talented children," and in 1465 there was even an edict forbidding the authorities to force children of poor families to attend classes.[17] From the late sixteenth century on, there were schools that claimed to train "poor children of the community." This was the case in the school in Ch'ang-shu, established in the Wan-li period, and the one in Changchow, which was already called *i-hsueh* (charity school) in 1530 when it was created by the prefect. The Ch'ang-shu school received important donations from the local people in 1586 and 1587. Some schools were taken over by local people, as the Ju-kao community school in 1617.[18] All these changes appeared sporadically in the late sixteenth and early seventeenth centuries, indicating at the same time the unstable situation of the state primary schools as well as the first timid efforts to absorb these schools into the community system.

The late Ming official and thinker Lü K'un (1536–1618) was probably one of the last to call for another state effort to restore the original community school system and to reinforce the state's authority. There were essentially two new ideas in his famous proposal to restore the *she-hsueh*: a systematic state financed teacher-training program and compulsory education for all children for three years.[19] Lü's contemporary, the above-mentioned Yeh Ch'un-chi, suggested reforming the *she-hsueh* by institutionally linking the system to the imperial examination (only pupils of the schools could sit for the primary examinations).[20] These changes would have necessitated tighter state control and the formulation of a more consistent central policy. But there was neither the social demand nor the imperial incentive for such a policy. Lü's and Yeh's renovative proposals were out of tune with the times and fell on deaf ears.

The Community and the i-hsueh System

Many Ch'ing documents took the *she-hsueh* and the *i-hsueh* systems to be different terms for the same thing, with the former denoting the system under the Ming and the latter under the Ch'ing.[21] This simplification masks the fundamental differences in nature between the two systems that are crucial to an understanding of the social development of the school: the *i-hsueh* was more genuinely a school of the community than the state *she-hsueh* and its charitable aspect was essential. (See Rowe, however, for the account of an exceptional state relationship to the *i-hsueh* of the southwest in the 1700s.) This was a natural outcome of the development of the *she-hsueh* during the late Ming period described above.

One of the first persons to understand the novel character of the *i-hsueh* was the early Ch'ing local official Huang Liu-hung (*chü-jen* 1651). In his famous manual for would-be local magistrates, *Fu-hui ch'üan-shu* (Complete book concerning happiness and benevolence, 1699), Huang applauded the replacement of the *she-hsueh* by the *i-hsueh*:

> At the present time youngsters of rich and powerful families are taught by private tutors who are engaged by these families. Those of poor and lowly families cannot study because they lack financial support. But local authorities look upon education as something nonessential and superfluous, not to be undertaken with limited resources, so the ancient community public school system (*she-hsueh*) cannot be revived....
>
> I think with the free contributions from the local gentry and the leadership of the authorities, an educational system with features similar to those of ancient public schools can be established. This is the system of free schools (*i-hsueh*). The free schools are established for the youngsters of poor families.... In the city and suburban areas, free schools should be established only if there are enough poor families to warrant their existence. In rural areas, each town, village or hamlet should have one to several depending on its size and need....[22]

Huang understood perfectly that the *she-hsueh* system, in form and in content, was by then moribund if not defunct and the only way to retain some indirect state influence over elementary education was to encourage the active support and participation of the resourceful local degree-holders.

Official records show that the imperial edict to establish charity schools came at about the same time as the publication of Huang's book—1702, to be precise—whereas all the preceding edicts were without exception for the setting up of *she-hsueh*. It was not until 1713 that an imperial order stated clearly that these charity schools were for poor children. It should be noted that as late as 1670 the K'ang-hsi emperor tried to revive the obsolete *she-hsueh* system in an edict that was no more than a repetition of the 1652 imperial order of the Shun-chih emperor who probably wanted the announcement to be a token of the continuity of Chinese culture under Manchu rule.[23] During the thirty years after 1670, Ch'ing authorities learned to understand the real condition of local schools and adopted a more appropriate cultural policy.

Meanwhile, schools continued to be restored or created in the localities during the first years of Manchu rule. In the absence of clear state directives, the schools increasingly took on a charitable nature and were often managed by the local elite. Table 11.1 shows a preliminary survey of early Ch'ing elementary schools established in the Lower Yangtze region before 1702.[24] It is obvious that most of the institutions were still at least nominally created by magistrates on behalf of the state (nine out of fifteen). But the growing number of schools officially established by commoners as compared to the few in the late sixteenth century is the striking phenomenon here. Moreover, the fact that most of the schools (thirteen out of fifteen) were now called "charity schools" clearly reveals an essential change in the function of these schools as perceived by their promoters. It is worth emphasizing again that these

TABLE 11.1 Early Ch'ing Elementary Schools in
the Lower Yangtze Region

County/ Prefecture	I-hsueh/ She-hseuh	Year	Establisher
Changchow	i-hsueh	1661	commoners
K'un-shan	she-hsueh	1673	commoners
Tan-yang	i-hsueh	1681	magistrate
Hangchow	i-hsueh	1681	magistrate
Hua-t'ing	i-hsueh	1682	magistrate
Hua-t'ing	i-hsueh	1682	magistrate
Kao-ch'un	i-hsueh	1682	magistrate
Yü-hang	she-hsueh	1683	magistrate
P'ing-hu	i-hsueh	1688	magistrate
P'ing-hu	i-hsueh	1692	commoners
Sung-chiang	i-hsueh	1699	magistrate
T'ai-hsing	i-hsueh	K'ang-hsi	commoners
Kan-t'ang	i-hsueh	K'ang-hsi	commoners
Kan-ch'üan	i-hsueh	K'ang-hsi	commoners
T'ai-ts'ang	i-hsueh	K'ang-hsi	magistrate

important developments in the early Ch'ing period were a continuation of social changes that were already occurring in the late sixteenth century.

The *i-hsueh* system flourished during the eighteenth century and all the changes that were emerging since the late Ming now came into full swing. Our preliminary survey of schools established in the eleven prefectures of the Lower Yangtze region, as recorded by gazetteers, shows that of all the eighty-three schools set up during the Ch'ing and before 1820, fifty were started by local leaders and thirty-three by magistrates (60 percent against 40 percent). These do not even include those schools that were incorporated into general charitable institutions essentially created and managed by local leaders.[25] The proportion may not seem impressive, but if we look at the survey done by Wang Lan-yin on Ming community schools, we will realize that the change in Ch'ing times was no trivial matter: of all the 1438 *she-hsueh* established under the Ming that record founders, more than 99 percent were set up

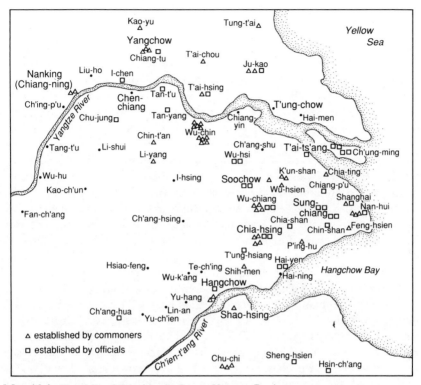

Map 11.1 *I-hsueh* Established in the Lower Yangtze Region

by officials of various ranks and less than 1 percent by commoners (map 11.1).[26] The ground gained by local leaders in the matter of popular education was indeed considerable. It had also become common knowledge that these *i-hsueh* were to provide elementary education to children of needy families and not to prepare "talented" youth for the imperial examination. The new conception of popular elementary schools had become so well accepted that society turned a deaf ear to the incomprehensible order of the Yung-cheng emperor in 1723 to go back to the *she-hsueh* system.[27] From 1743 onward, as the gazetteer of Chiang-yin county indicates, *i-hsueh* began to be widespread in cities and countryside alike.[28]

Just like the model described in Huang Liu-hung's manual, many of the charity schools were managed by community leaders with the sanction of the state. A memorial written by an official named Tai San-hsi (native of Tan-t'u, d. 1830, *chin-shih* 1793) to promote the creation of more charity schools suggested that "for [the expenses of] the building, the furniture, the teacher, and the meals, we should persuade the local people to donate and then choose an honest and reliable person among them to be the manager. He could either give the money to the merchants to earn interest or buy real estate." A certain Ch'en Wen-shu of the Ch'ien-t'ang area proposed the same idea in his "Regulations for Charity Schools" (*I-hsueh chang-ch'eng*): "In every city and in every rural district, [one should] create one or two schools through popular donation, and then ask philanthropists (*hao i shih min*) of the area to draft regulations [of the school] to be approved by the authorities."[29] Both the official, representing state power, and the local philanthropist saw it as appropriate to organize schools from the bottom up with official approval. Like other eighteenth-century charitable institutions in the Kiangnan region, more and more charity schools were locally initiated and managed with state permission. However, while local leaders were gaining importance, magistrates never ceased to promote, directly or indirectly, local elementary schools throughout the Ch'ing. In this sense, there was a real expansion in educational efforts and resources in the seventeenth and eighteenth centuries. This formed the basis for further education development in the nineteenth century.[30]

Despite all the obvious changes in the conception and administration of popular elementary education in the seventeenth and eighteenth centuries, one ambiguity remained: primary education was never considered entirely a matter of charitable relief, even though it had lost its earlier Ming status as being solely the privilege of the well-off or "talented." In local gazetteers, information on schools, including charitable elementary schools, was always recorded in those particular chapters devoted to schools and academies and to depictions of the cultural environment of the locality. By contrast, histories of other charitable institutions, some of which even financed charity schools inside them or in other parts of the county, were grouped either in the chapter on "establishments" or in the chapter on "charitable deeds." Moreover, until the end of the eighteenth century, there were still a significant minority of charity schools that were reported to be established by magistrates. This was in contrast to other charitable institutions which were, by then, almost exclusively created by local leaders.[31] In other words, although popular philanthropy was in practice incorporating primary schools into its program, elementary education and relief, conceptually speaking, still belonged to different categories of the eighteenth-century Chinese mind.[32] Educating the people was a task too important for the perpetuation of state ideology to be left entirely in the hands of communitarian leaders.

Education was, above all, an almost sacred tool for maintaining cultural stability. The nation was, indeed, essentially a cultural concept for the Chinese. The best model of proper education was always that which was provided by the basic unit of Chinese culture—the clan and the family. The importance of family education was an essential and unique feature in any Confucian culture. The Chinese had to wait for another century, when Western influence came marching in, to get a glimpse of what "state schools" were like.

Clan Schools and Family Education

There were of course types of private schools and tutorial classes that were not run by the clan or family, but as institutions these are of less interest than the clan or family school, which was more comparable to the public *i-hsueh* and more typical of the period under study.[33]

The form of the public *i-hsueh* was clearly an imitation of clan schools, which often provided a much coveted type of primary education. The best of them were tightly organized and amply financed from the clans' estates. Clan schools were normally highly exclusive, accepting only children of the main branches of the clan and a few close cousins.[34] Such restrictions limited classes to a very manageable size of around ten pupils. Many clans had two elementary classes of two levels, the *meng-kuan* (introductory section) and the *ching-kuan* (Classics section), the latter of which was essentially for pupils who wished to sit for the imperial examinations. Children who managed to get into a clan school were essentially free of material worries. Many schools had a boarding system through which furniture, stationery, meals, and sometimes clothes were provided free of charge. The luckier ones even had modest monthly stipends. The stricter boarding system only allowed the pupils to leave the school on special occasions; the looser one permitted them to go home once a month.[35] In the famous 18th-century novel *Story of the Stone*, the young boy of a poorer relative of the Chia family was sent to the clan charitable school not only because his parents could not afford a private tutor but also because the boy was given free meals in the school, thus saving considerable expense for the family.[36] In ideal form, clan school education tended to involve the entire daily life of the children. The progress of the pupils was regularly monitored by the teacher and, above all, by clan members who were responsible for the school. Tests might take place every fortnight (first and fifteenth days of the month) or during the first few days of each month. The examinations were supervised by the clan principal who would ask the children to recite texts, explain words or sentences, and write characters. The pupils' performance was usually ranked into three grades. Those with a good performance or who showed progress were awarded stationery or even money; those who did poorly were punished or made to feel ashamed of their unsatisfactory performance. Sometimes clan schools required pupils to carry diaries or handbooks in which the teacher recorded daily work done, progress made, and the time at which the children arrived and left school, as well as special leaves that they had taken. The diaries were to be shown to parents every day after school and to be kept by the clan principal at the end of the scholastic year.[37]

The considerable organizational and financial investment in elementary clan education is understandable: the prosperity and the stability of the clans could only be assured if some of these children one day became successful bureaucrats. (In fact, many clan schools were financed by bureaucratic members of the clan, as happens in the novel *Story of the Stone*, Chapter 9.) And their chance for eventual success in this enterprise depended heavily on the quality of their primary education. Most of the rules of the clan schools stated clearly that the aim of the institution was to train "talents" for the clan. "The greatness of the clan does not depend on the size of its population but on the number of its talents so that the world will look on it with admiration. How can one [cultivate such talents] if not by education?"[38] This ultimate aim of clan schools explains the importance of the daily homage paid to the ancestors by the pupils.[39] They were constantly reminded that they should work hard in school in order one day to glorify the clan. The significance of the ritual was better revealed in its absence. When the sole aim of the clan school was to provide basic education for fatherless orphans of the clan so that they could start to earn a living as early as possible, such a sense of mission was not inculcated in the pupils. The ritual was reduced to bowing to the teacher at the beginning and end of the day.[40] The motivation behind the latter kind of clan school was obviously less high-minded: it was more a relief measure for underprivileged members of the clan than the calculated policy to train "talents" who would enrich the clan's cultural capital.

The ultimate goal of the idealistic clan school was not always achieved, perhaps less for reasons of the quality of the education than for the structural problems of the clan and the ever changing socioeconomic environment.[41] The reason for the very small number of existing clan schools, wrote Chang Hsüeh-ch'eng (1738–1801) in 1796 in a discussion of the school of the Sun clan, "certainly lies in the fact that there are loopholes in the legislation that make it difficult for [the schools] to last."[42] We do not know how long an average clan school lasted in the seventeenth and eighteenth centuries, but judging by evidence from some of the records of nineteenth-century clan schools that we have consulted, most seem not to have had a very early origin. Of examples located to date, only the Sun clan school in Shao-hsing, which began in the early eighteenth century and which apparently was still functioning in the 1830s, had a long record of continuous operation.[43]

In many ways, clan and family schools provided a model for public charity schools. Like the clan charity schools, the public ones claimed to provide education for children of poor families. Some charity schools also had two teachers (teaching two classes of different levels), each responsible for a class of some dozen pupils.[44] Better financed ones also provided pupils with stationery and books that, with the teacher's salary, could come to a budget of two hundred taels a year.[45] Public charity schools rarely provided room and board for the pupils. The financial organization of the two types of schools was also very similar: their long-term funding was assured by donations of land, houses, and money. In the case of public charity schools, funding came from magistrates or local notables.[46] This similarity in financing as well as in organization also put charity schools in the same precarious situation as the clan schools: the average charity school, it seems, did not last very long, sometimes ending with the term of an enthusiastic magistrate, or when donations from a private individual stopped.[47]

In fact, most well-off families had their own private tutors and more modest ones either sent their children to private tutorial classes in the neighborhood or had them taught by members of the family. Ch'en Ch'ueh (1604–77), the important thinker from Chekiang province, recalled that his father taught his elder brother, who later taught him and his two younger brothers, while Ch'en Ch'ueh took responsibility for teaching his youngest brother. This family tradition was to him an appropriate alternative to sending the children to classes taught by respectable teachers in the community.[48] And if Chia Pao-yü, hero of *Story of the Stone*, went to the clan's charitable school, it was because his tutor was away for some time and Pao-yü's father wanted him to go to the school in order to revise texts that he had already learned while waiting for the return of his own teacher (Chapter 7).

Though the elementary school, be it private or public, was not an indispensable institution for the transmission of primary education in Ming-Ch'ing China, the school curriculum did reveal the set of values and the body of knowledge thought to be necessary to be transmitted to the child.

FORM AND CONTENT OF ELEMENTARY SCHOOL EDUCATION

One most interesting characteristic of elementary education in Ming-Ch'ing China is that, despite the lack of active state intervention in its form and content, there was a surprising agreement on what these should be. In this aspect, China was quite the opposite of eighteenth-century France, where the content of primary education was not specified but "the royal will was asserted" in the creation of the "petites écoles."[49]

"Regulations" of primary schools written by seventeenth- and eighteenth-century educators or thinkers, especially those of the Lower Yangtze region, not only reveal elementary education as it was practiced in school but also help us to reconstitute the common body of educational conceptions of the region at the time. It is important to note that these educators or scholars, while writing the regulations and recommendations, based their arguments mainly on their own experience or convictions; they did not in any way speak for the state.[50] Textbooks quoted by these regulations were most of the time the same. Even the school in a tiny village of thirty or so households, in a remote part of the Kwangtung province in the second half of the nineteenth century, used these standard texts.[51]

Form

The ideal school calendar corresponded to the natural year and began around the fifteenth of the first month and ended around the twenty-fifth of the twelfth month with a total of about ten days off for the celebration of various festivals. A complete school year consisted of eleven full months.[52] Not only was the year rather long but the school day also lasted practically from sunup to sundown. A typical schedule consisted of four parts: the early morning session held before breakfast, the morning session after breakfast, the afternoon session, and a brief evening session.[53] Clearly, the school calendar and the daily schedule reflected notions of time natural to an essentially agrarian society.

The schools accepted children between the ages of about eight to fifteen *sui*, even though it is likely that some younger children, who had been taught a number of characters at home, started school earlier at six or seven.[54] There was no yearly program governing the progress of learning of the children during the seven or so years they spent in the school. There seemed to be a tacit agreement among educators that children be taught according to their individual aptitudes: "Teaching should not be uniform for everybody."[55] One can thus imagine that children from six or seven to about fifteen were taught together in the same class while the teacher, if he was a responsible one, had to attend to each pupil's individual progress and give him suitable guidance. This explains the small number of pupils in an ideal typical primary school.

The teacher was either employed by the family or the management of the community school or was himself manager of the school. In either case, unless he was exceptionally famous, he was poorly paid.[56] Worse still, he did not enjoy much respect socially. Many educators warned that parents were wrong in not paying enough attention to the selection of a good primary teacher: "People only know respecting the teacher of the Classics section and do not know that the work of the teacher of the introductory section ... is several times more exhausting...."[57] The advice that once a teacher was chosen his authority inside the classroom should not be challenged also revealed his usual lowly status.[58] The great eighteenth-century artist from Hsing-hua, Cheng Pan-ch'iao (1693–1765), was once a miserable village schoolteacher before he passed the imperial examinations. He obviously did not have pleasant memories of those days:

> Teaching in a school is from the beginning a last resort;
> Spending years under the roof of others,
> Half full, half starving, one is an insignificant outsider;
> Without chains, without handcuffs, one is a voluntary prisoner;
> The parents would speak of laziness if too little work is given;
> The pupils would react with hatred if too much;
> Fortunately, one has climbed up the social ladder;
> The shame of those years could be wiped away in one brush.[59]

Indeed, Cheng was far from being an exception in taking the teaching job as merely transitional in his career. Of the twenty-four teachers who had taught in the Sun clan school in Shao-hsing from the early eighteenth century until 1789, fourteen later passed higher levels of the imperial examinations and became officials.[60] But the impatience of the more gifted or luckier scholars in teaching children should not conceal the devotion of other less ambitious ones who stuck to the profession for years. Ch'en Fang-sheng from the Hangchow area was such a teacher. He had been a primary teacher for over ten years before he wrote down his ideas on what made a good elementary school and a good teacher. He modestly admitted, "[If] the scholar ... does not necessarily become an official, then teaching is his inescapable responsibility".[61] This implies a considerable supply of teachers as again was the case of the Sun clan school, which had only two teachers (out of twenty-four) who were not natives of Shao-hsing. In a culturally rich area, one rarely had to go outside one's locality to look for a teacher. This constant supply might also explain the modest compensation offered primary school teachers.[62]

Acquisition of Knowledge

Contrary to what many may think, the first years of elementary education, at least in the seventeenth and eighteenth centuries, were not particularly trying: the child could apparently learn at his own pace. Except for those who entered school already knowing some characters, the first thing to be learned in school was to recognize characters and to review them regularly after they were taught. There seemed to be different methods of teaching characters to children. Besides the classical way (since Sung times) of recognizing and memorizing characters in the three major primers—the *Trimetrical Classic* (*San-tzu ching*), the *Thousand Character Classic* (*Ch'ien tzu wen*), and the *Hundred Surnames* (*Pai chia hsing*) —characters were also taught separately on paper or wooden squares.[63] One character was written on each square and a child was taught to recognize some ten characters a day; the memorized characters were tied with a string and these were reviewed constantly while new ones were being taught.[64] There was general agreement that a child should know between one and two thousand characters before he was taught to read a text. Thereafter, difficult new characters that appeared in texts were singled out and posted up by the teacher every day. The pupils learned to recognize these as they proceeded on to different texts.[65] Again, there was no precise rule on the time to be spent on this phase of preliminary learning: everything depended on the ability of the child.

Writing with the brush began slightly later than, or at the same time as this first phase. The teacher had to hold the hand of the pupil to show him the correct way to hold the brush and to draw a character before he was permitted to write on his own. These beginners were only allowed to write simple, big characters by imitating popular models of the standard script (*cheng-k'ai*). The first characters written were not exactly the same as the thousand or so characters in the primers that the child had now recognized. (Most of these were too complicated to be drawn at this early stage). Small characters could be practiced only after the child could handle the big ones with ease. Writing was practiced every day during the second morning session and the teacher marked each well- and badly written character in order to encourage or to correct the child.[66]

Besides the three classical primers that almost all children learned to recite during their first years in school, there were other textbooks that the child started to learn as soon as he had acquired a sufficient number of characters to read them. These texts contained knowledge of all kinds and were written in song or poetic form to make them more interesting and easier for the child to memorize. Some of the more popular texts included the late Ming history primer *Chien-lueh* (Brief history), which summarized the history of China from the mythical age to the late Ming in three short chapters of quinmetrical verses. Later editions added post-Ming historical events in the same spirit as the original.[67] Another widely used text was the *Ming-wu meng-ch'iu* or "Encyclopedic Primer," which explained astronomical, geographical, biological, social, and technological terms in four-character verses. A series of poems for children containing vulgarized Confucian values such as the "Shen t'ung shih" (Poem for the child) and its sequel and a collection of short historical and biographical stories in easy prose were also popular.[68]

At the same time, some children started to learn some of the standard texts. Almost every teacher found it necessary at one time or at another to teach the Four Books and some of the Five Classics, which were to be learned by heart by the children as soon as they could recognize some one thousand or so characters.[69] On methods of teaching this core material, however, there seemed to be slight differences among educators. For some, the child was receptive enough at eight or nine to understand the teaching of the Classics. Thus, the teacher had to explain the texts to the child before he could memorize them in order to "stimulate his intelligence." According to the late Ming scholar Liu Tsung-chou (1578–1645, native of Shan-yin, Chekiang), every text was to be explained word by word, phrase by phrase before the overall meaning was explicated. The moral content of the texts received particular emphasis.[70] In contrast, other authorities believed children of this age could not possibly understand the true meaning of the Classics: "Children only use their mouths and their ears, and not their hearts and their eyes...."; "children before they are fifteen can memorize better than they understand ... and they can understand better and memorize less after they are fifteen."[71] However, whatever the teachers' conceptions of a child's learning ability at this early stage, they all agreed on one essential aspect of the learning of the Classics, which is also the best-known characteristic of classical primary education: drilling and rote memory.

One of the typical ways of drilling a child was provided by the experienced primary teacher Ch'en Fang-sheng:

> Texts well-memorized during childhood will be remembered the whole life. For every new text one learns each day, one has to revise ten old texts. The new text

has to be read aloud one hundred times, after which one has to revise the old texts according to the order in which they have been learned. A fixed number of pages have to be revised every day. When they are finished, they have to be revised all over again. At the beginning page of the text, one has to mark the day when the text is first revised; at the end of the text, one has to mark the day when the study of the text is completed.... [The teacher] has to make a list of the texts that each pupil has learned and stick it on the right side of his seat; each time the pupil has finished revising a text, the teacher will mark a circle against the title of the text in red ink.[72]

Indeed, a child was considered intelligent only if he could quickly memorize a great quantity of texts. All educators recommended that all reading aloud and recitation of previously learned texts be done in the first morning session, probably because the children's minds were at their freshest then. The explanation and reading aloud of new texts, on the other hand, were done in the second morning session.

One of the disagreements of educators on texts was over the use of Chu Hsi's famous book (1130–1200) for primary education, *Hsiao-hsueh* (Little learning), and the *Classic on Filial Piety* (*Hsiao-ching*). Apparently, these two were considered to be standard textbooks in primary education by the Ch'ing authorities. Two important Ch'ing officials and educators, Ch'en Hung-mou (1696–1771) and T'ang Pin (1627–87, governor of Kiangsu in 1684), assigned the two books to be the first texts learned in state primary schools.[73] However, not every seventeenth- and eighteenth-century educator appreciated Chu Hsi's text. The late Ming scholar from T'ung-hsiang (Chekiang), Li Lo, in his 1632 collection of miscellaneous writings had told that he was taught the *Hsiao-ching* and *Hsiao-hsueh* in elementary school when he was a child, but "after I was forty, rare were those who studied them...."[74] His contemporary Lu Shih-i (1611 –72) tried to explain the reason for *Hsiao-hsueh*'s fall into disuse: "There are too many difficult characters [in *Hsiao-hsueh*] for today's usage, making it inconvenient for the children. That is why *Hsiao-hsueh* is often abandoned [by today's primary schools]."[75] Li Chao-lo (1769–1841), the famous scholar-official from Kiangsu, gave an opposite reason for the same phenomenon:

The [Hsiao-hsueh] is more than sufficient for its discussions but less than enough for the purpose of practical learning. Moreover, its language is too easy and simple, so that those who have finished their studies are annoyed by its superficiality and do not read it. [The adults do not know that] the original purpose of Master Chu was to enlighten the young and not to teach the adults. That is why [although] he had the deepest will to enlighten and to stimulate the kindness of the world, the effect of educating the people has not been realized.[76]

It looked as if this text, which explained the Five Relations and taught the first steps in self-cultivation, was too difficult for children who did not plan to sit for the imperial examination and useless for those who did. Whatever the true reason, the likelihood is that *Hsiao-hsueh*, and for the same reasons the *Hsiao-*

ching, seemed not to be as popular for use in primary schools from the late Ming onward as one might think.[77]

A comic eighteenth-century poem on a village elementary school best sums up the texts popularly used in an average elementary school in this time:

> "The night breeze is disturbed by the cries of the crows,
> those pupils altogether showing off the strength of their throats:
> Chao-Ch'ien-Sun-Li-Chou-Wu-Cheng, Heaven-Earth-Black-Yellow-Cosmos;
> after the *Thousand characters* it's *Chien lueh*,
> when the *Hundred Surnames* is revised it's *Poem for the Child*;
> that exceptional one amongst the class
> memorizes three lines a day the *Great Learning* and *Doctrine of the Mean*."[78]

Clearly, not everyone was ready for the more difficult Classics, and most spent their first school years on easier rhythmic primers.

After the pupils mastered the basics, they could go on to a more advanced level at which they learned phonology, which was necessary for poetry, couplet, and prose writing. Both were practiced every day during the second morning session.[79] This training was generally reserved for the upper level of the primary school, the "Classics section." Some warned that the two levels not be mixed because they demanded different teaching techniques from the teacher.[80]

Moralization and Discipline

For scholastic curricula of all kinds and all times, it is always difficult to distinguish between the practical knowledge they transmit and the set of values they try to convey.

All the texts mentioned above, even the more difficult Classics, had the practical function of teaching new characters to the pupils. Some of the primers taught them history, geography, important cultural references, names of tools and utensils, common plants and animals, social rules, and so on, all of which were useful knowledge for daily functioning in Ming-Ch'ing society: for reading notices and family handbooks (*lei-shu*), for writing official letters and other documents, for keeping accounts and recording simple business transactions, and for enjoying theatrical performances and popular novels.[81] But more was taught by these same texts during the same process: the worldview common to the average Chinese of the time, common notions of time and space, and a shared set of values. For many educators, this, more than the practical learning, was the main purpose of elementary education.

Indeed, as Ch'en Ch'üeh put it, the elementary education that one gave to a child of six or seven and above "should first teach him how to follow rites and manners, the most fundamental of which is to let him know what are filial piety and respect. Let him practice loyalty and honesty; reading and writing come only in second place."[82] Li Chao-lo reminded his contemporaries that in ancient times there had been no so-called "primary school." Small children had learned the rites from their fathers and seniors: they had first been taught filial piety, humility, self-discipline, and trustworthiness; the learning of texts came afterwards.[83] Lu Lung-ch'i (1630–93, native of P'ing-hu, Chekiang), the famous scholar-official, advised his son of the correct way to read the *Tso chuan* (Tso commentary on the *Spring and Autumn Annals*): "There are two kinds of characters (in the *Tso chuan*]: the good and the bad. When you read the book you have to distinguish between the two. When you come across a good character, a feeling of admiration should be roused inside you [and you say to yourself,] 'I must desire to imitate him'; when you come across a bad character, a feeling of hatred should be roused inside you [and you say to yourself,] 'I must not imitate him'."[84] For Liu Tsung-chou, the last session of the school day was to be consecrated to moral teaching: the teacher was to narrate and explain two stories that extolled loyalty, filial piety, and diligence. Pupils were to be constantly interrogated on the meaning of these stories so that they would not be lost from memory.[85] Lü Te-sheng (d.1568), the father of Lü K'un, wrote a primer in rhyme entitled *Hsiao-erh yü* (Words of the child) incorporating most of these values and conveying a popularized version of the Chinese philosophy of life. His book became one of most popular texts used in primary schools from the late Ming onward.[86]

On this delicate question of moral teaching, there indeed seemed to be a new development in elementary education beginning in the late Ming: the inclusion of the *shan-shu* (morality books) in the daily reading list. The same Li Lo who observed that Chu Hsi's *Hsiao-hsueh* was gradually falling into disuse also noticed that more and more elementary schools used the commentary texts of Yuan Huang (1533–1606), the famous syncretic thinker of the Soochow region who promoted the genre of the ledgers of merit and demerit.[87] The early Ch'ing educator Ts'ui Hsueh-ku recommended that morality books like the *Ti-chi lu* (Records of right behavior and good fortune) published by the late Ming scholar Yen Mao-yu in 1631, ledgers of merit and demerit and other books on retribution be read and explained to the pupils in their spare time.[88] From Li Chao-lo we know that many educators of his time replaced Chu Hsi's *Hsiao-hsueh* with the ledgers or with Lü Te-sheng's *Words of the Child* and also with Liu Tsung-chou's *Jen p'u* (Portraits of Man), which essentially recorded charitable deeds of people of Liu's time.[89] Some of the early Ch'ing elementary school rules simply imitated the form of the ledgers of merit and demerit.[90] In the later Ch'ing period, some charitable schools even put seven "morality books" including the *Trimetrical Classic, The T'ai-shang Tractate on Actions and Their Retribution (T'ai-shang kan-ying-p'ien), Words of the Child,* and four others into the regular syllabus, with the study of the Four Books coming only at a later stage.[91]

This new interest in training the child to do good deeds was accompanied by an accentuated obsession with forbidding children to read popular novels. The fact that children who knew a number of characters could read simple texts greatly worried scholars and educators of the time: "I have seen youth un-enthusiastic about their studies and vulgar people knowing a few words who are completely absorbed by [these licentious writings]"; "youngsters who can read a few characters could sing and narrate [these licentious writings].... Out of ten persons there are not one or two who understand the countless words of the sages, but there are eight or nine who know perfectly well these gross and licentious small books." Horror stories were circulated to warn against insufficient supervision over a child's reading habits: "A son of a big family in Nanking could memorize anything that came to his eyes. He was thirteen when he had learned all the Classics and dynastic histories; then one day he secretly read the opera *The West Chamber*, which made him lose all interest in eating and sleeping. In seven days, his vital energy was gone. The doctors said that his heart and his kidneys were exhausted and he died."[92] Indeed, a little learning was considered dangerous for such semiliterate but emotionally immature groups as children and women.[93] Some school rules thus explicitly forbade the reading of *yin-shu* (licentious books) or *hsien-shu* (unserious books), and families were strongly advised not to keep these kinds of books.[94]

While in the West, educators and church confessors believed that causes of the moral or sexual corruption of youth were innate and should be repressed by strict corporal discipline, the sources of temptation for the Chinese youth were believed to be mainly from the external world, including licentious litera-ture.[95] The rejection of bad external influences was thus considered as essen-tial for the first steps in self-cultivation. The purpose of discipline for the child was thus not so much the repression of undesirable instincts as preparation for self-cultivation.

One can in general divide discipline in Ming-Ch'ing elementary schools into three categories: physical, social, and intellectual. Physical discipline was mainly to train the child's sense of cleanliness and orderliness and to exercise his body. According to classical Confucian training, each pupil had to take a turn sweeping the floor, cleaning the desks and the chairs of the classroom, and putting everything in order. Each also had to see to it that his attire was clean and his hair properly done. Lu Shih-i tells us that by his time, that is the late seventeenth century, cleaning and sweeping of the home and of the class-room were almost exclusively done by servants. Very few stuck to the old train-ing.[96] For many educators, however, the daily cleaning of the classroom was in fact an excellent physical exercise for the pupils.[97] Cleaning and sweeping were likely practiced symbolically as a kind of physical training. Social discipline was one of the most important aspects of elementary school education. The child was taught how to address his teacher and his classmates who were older or younger than he was as well as how and when to bow, walk, stand, sit, and take a meal properly. In other words, such discipline was to give him an elementary

idea of his social position and the basic and formal rules of daily social intercourse with his superiors and inferiors.[98]

Intellectual discipline was not as harsh as one might think. There were certainly strict and horrifying elementary schoolteachers, but they were certainly
not the commonly accepted type of the time, at least not by the more
enlightened educators. These latter authorities never harshly punished a child
at the tender age of six or seven. Harsher punishments including standing,
kneeling, and beating could only be used on children above eight or nine when
words seemed to have no effect. Beating, which was divided into light and
heavier degrees, was rarely to be employed (once every two to six months) so
that children remained sensitive to it. Punishments were balanced against the
system of rewards: paper, brushes, paper fans, and so on were given to worthy
pupils.[99] Punishment and rewards were only small parts of the methods used to
discipline the child. For most educators, the essential thing was to keep the
pupils intellectually occupied all the time: "to tighten their loosened hearts,"
"to tame and moderate their energy, and to prevent leisure [from getting into]
their hearts."[100] This training was to be practiced incessantly day after day with
infinite patience by a teacher who was to display a serious expression at all
times. After all, it was emphasized, since the great majority of pupils in elementary school would not sit for the imperial examination, the goal of
elementary education was not to turn pupils into scholars within a short time
but to tame them gradually into obedient and disciplined social beings.[101]

On this last point, there was a new challenge during the late Ming and early
Ch'ing periods. Wang Yang-ming (1472–1527) was one of the first to criticize
this orthodox disciplining of young children: "The inclination of the child is to
like amusement and to dislike discipline ... today's elementary educators ...
emphasize the discipline [of the child] and neglect guidance through rites
(*li*).... [The child] is whipped and tied and treated like a prisoner, so that he
sees the school as a prison and refuses to enter, [and] he regards his teacher as
an enemy and refuses to see him...." What Wang Yang-ming recommended
was a curriculum of songs and poetry that would "free [the child's impulse] in
jumping and yelling out" and of rites consisting of bowing and other body
movements that would "shake up his blood and pulses [and]... strengthen his
muscles and bones...."[102] About a century later, Lu Shih-i echoed the same
recommendations and advocated the study of music and rites to satisfy the
child's natural penchant for songs and dances. He also drew the educators' attention to the ancient curriculum of the Six Arts (rites, music, archery, equi-
tation, calligraphy, mathematics), which had by then been largely forgotten.[103]

However, the challenge did not seem to have much influence on subsequent
elementary education. This recommendation in some way represented a "going back" to the more naturalistic form of aristocratic education of ancient
times, which was not in tune with the social needs of the Ming-Ch'ing period.
In this period, elementary education had to perform two functions: to prepare

the qualified ones for more advanced studies leading to a career in officialdom and to train the ordinary ones into disciplined subjects respectful of the existing social hierarchy. For these purposes, the "orthodox way" of discipline was clearly considered to be more efficient. Moreover, this new challenge did not bring anything new to the concept of the child as the subject of education. In fact, it conformed to the one already common in Ming-Ch'ing times: the child was intrinsically good; education was not to suppress what was evil or immoral in him but to prepare him against immoral influences that existed in the outside world. Wang Yang-ming's and Lu Shih-i's preference for a more "liberating" form of education and the other educators' conception of a more "restraining" form did not conflict in their basic assumptions.

CONCLUSION

Having briefly looked at the changes that took place in elementary education during the seventeenth and eighteenth centuries, we may now discuss in more detail the their significance. By looking at its content, one can divide the aims of elementary education into two main parts: transmission of knowledge and moralization. The state, the local community, and the family had different motivations behind achieving the two aims, which explains the evolution of their roles in this matter.

Theoretically speaking, both the state and the family had a strong interest in the schools as the main instrument in the transmission of knowledge. For the state, the elementary schools were essential in the basic training of future officials. For the family, schools were important in its struggle for upward mobility or for the maintenance of an already prominent social position. However, there was an important institutional link missing between the state elementary schools, the *she-hsueh*, and the imperial examination that carried out the selection of "talents" for the state. The common division of elementary schools, both public or private, into introductory and Classics sections and the constant remark by educators that most primary pupils would not pursue a career in officialdom show us that most of the elementary schools were not simple preparatory schools for the higher academies (thus, the curriculum was not to be overloaded with difficult Classics and too much prose writing). When Yeh Ch'un-chi suggested that only pupils of the *she-hsueh*, which emphasized teaching of the rites, could sit for the imperial examinations, he was trying to bridge this institutional gap between the two so as to improve the moral character of the candidates and revive the moribund *she-hsueh* system.[104] But this project was unrealizable and the state's interest remained all through the late imperial period more directly linked to the higher levels of education.[105]

The family, on the other hand, was more aggressive in providing a high-quality elementary education to its young members, on whom was placed the hope of the family's future. It understood perfectly that the competitiveness of the youth in the higher levels of education and in examinations greatly depended on his primary curriculum. As a result, the family or clan, by organizing clan schools, paying private tutors, or obliging learned older members as teachers, provided perhaps the most coveted primary education in this time. In fact, these elite families were conscious of the subtle link between the family and the state in elementary education. Lu Shih-i clearly stated: "The education of the family is also based on the education of the court. If the court teaches with morality [as paramount], then the family also teaches with morality [as paramount]. If the court teaches with material interests [in mind], then the family also teaches with material interests [in mind]."[106] This was an elegant way of acknowledging the concrete role of the family in the domain of primary education. The state was essentially a remote but ultimate model of behavior that did not have to play any concrete role. Since the clan and the family had strong interests in providing efficient elementary education for its members, the state did not have much to lose in downplaying its part in promoting primary schools as instruments of the transmission of knowledge.

Schools as machines for moralization were not unique to premodern China. In nineteenth-century France, elementary education "remained subordinate to the 'moralization' of the working people which was the fundamental aim. At no time during the nineteenth century ... did elementary education really bow to the demands of growth and the emergent industrial society...."[107] Neither were schools in seventeenth- and eighteenth-century China designed to satisfy practical socioeconomic needs. Values favorable for the maintaining of the status quo were of course taught in the Chinese schools of all times. But there seemed to be an even stronger emphasis on this during and after the late Ming, when the state *she-hsueh* system was inextricably linked to the village lecture system. This was also the moment when the local community began to play an important role in public schooling. Gradually, public elementary schools became part of the philanthropic movement led by local community leaders — a movement that had strong moralistic colors. The main cause for disorder in the changing society was believed to be moral degradation. Philanthropy and primary education were considered to be remedies to cure the increasing social malaise. In this sense, philanthropy and education as concepts were alienated from the idea of relief as a practical socioeconomic policy. The association of philanthropy and primary education was even reflected in the changes in textbooks in primary schools during and after the late Ming period, when morality books became more popular, and later when charitable schools became one of the main establishments to fight the "two big enemies of culture *(chiao-hua)*: licentious books and operas."[108]

In other words, the moral war against a "subversive" popular culture in which the charitable schools were believed to be an important instrument was largely left to be fought by community philanthropists who, later in the nineteenth century, organized regional "bureaus to burn and destroy licentious writings" as part of their charitable movement.[109] The aim was obviously to re-establish a certain lost social order. The state, which was in no direct control of the popular philanthropic movement becoming widespread in the Lower Yangtze region after the late sixteenth century, was content to watch this sacred war with condescending approval.[110] If the more difficult texts such as the *Hsiao-ching* and Chu Hsi's *Hsiao-hsueh* recommended by the state for primary schools were gradually substituted as textbooks by easier morality books, it was another indicator of the ever-increasing share of influence of the community, which was striving toward similar goals as the state in the matter of elementary education but with more practical considerations and probably greater efficiency. In fighting "immoral" elements of popular culture, elementary education itself became more vulgarized in its content, bringing itself closer to the culture it wanted to despise.[111]

The persistent concern of the family and the increasing interest of the local community were the main trends in the development of elementary education in seventeenth- and eighteenth-century China. The state was never absent from the scene and even played an active though indirect role in reforming public elementary schools in the seventeenth century and in encouraging their establishment subsequently. But its share of real responsibilities was reduced compared with the expanding influence of local societal leaders. These trends were further accentuated in the nineteenth century when the Ch'ing state was gradually losing control of local society.

There were, however, no major conflicts of interest among the state, the community, and the family in the matter of elementary education. The corpus of texts used, the general form and teaching method, and the concept of the child as an intrinsically good and malleable being were largely culturally determined and varied little among the three groups. Elementary education, for the Chinese of the seventeenth and eighteenth centuries, was above all a cultural matter and not a politico-economic one. The disciplining of the child at school was parallel to the purification of popular mores of the locality, just as the aim of charitable deeds was primarily to revive a moral social order.

The strength of the Ch'ing state during its heyday obviously had not led to any weakening of the community and the family. On the contrary, one sees the expansion of the sphere of influence of the community. Neither was the rather high literacy of the time, if we accept Evelyn Rawski's figures, related to any "new kind of relation between state and individual" as had happened in seventeenth-century England and eighteenth-century France.[112] It might even have had something to do with a new relationship the individual had with the community. The fact that the most ideal learning environment for children was considered to be inside the clan or family, and that community schools were in fact an imitation of clan schools, shows that learning was not as "decontextualized" (removing children from the family, placing them under special authorities) a process as in the West.[113] That direct link between the state and

the individual was never quite established. The reason behind all this, I believe, lies in radical differences between the natures of the Ch'ing and modern
Western states, and their relations with their respective societies, on which we
know still too little to venture any valid generalizations. China had to wait until
the twentieth century, when she began to imitate the Western state (a process
that some would term "modernization"), to start working consciously at "mass
literacy" through elementary schools with a westernized form and curriculum.
Even then, the program was essentially based on the already existing school
network created by traditional society. The share of the state remained relatively limited.[114]

APPENDIX: PUBLIC ELEMENTARY SCHOOLS ESTABLISHED
1644–1820 IN THE LOWER YANGTZE AREA

Prefecture/country	*no. of* i-hsueh (she-hsueh) *established by commoners*	*no. of* i-hsueh (she-hsueh) *established by officials*
Chiang-ning pref. 江寧	2	
Chu-jung 句容		1 (4)
Soochow pref. 蘇州		
Wu-hsien 吳縣	1	2
Wu-chiang 吳江	4	2
K'un-shan 崑山	2 (1)	
Ch'ang-chou 長州	1	
Sung-chiang pref. 松江		1
Ch'ing-p'u 青浦		1
Chin-shan 金山		1
Feng-hsien 奉賢	1	
Hua-t'ing 華亭		2
Shang-hai 上海	1	1
Nan-hui 南滙	3	1
Changchow pref. 常州		
Wu-chin 武進	10	
Chiang-yin 江陰	many (not specified)	
Wu-hsi 無錫		2
Chen-chiang pref. 鎮江		
Chin-t'an 金壇	1	
Tan-t'u 丹徒		1
Tan-yang 丹陽		1
Li-yang 溧陽	1	
Yangchow pref. 揚州	4 (5)	1 (3)
Tung-t'ai 東臺	1	

Prefecture/country	*no. of* i-hsueh (she-hsueh) *established by commoners*	*no. of* i-hsueh (she-hsueh) *established by officials*
T'ai-chou 泰州	1	
I-chen 儀真		1
Kao-yu 高郵	1	
T'ai-ts'ang pref. 太倉		1
Ch'ung-ming 崇明		4
Chia-ting 嘉定	1	
T'ung-chou pref. 通州		(1)
T'ai-hsing 泰興	1 (1)	1
Ju-kao 如皐	2	1
Hangchow pref. 杭洲	2	1
Yu-hang 餘杭		(1)
Ch'ang-hua 昌化		1
Chia-hsing pref. 嘉興	4	2 (1)
P'ing-hu 平湖	1	
Hai-yen 海鹽		2
Shih-men 石門	1	
T'ung-hsiang 桐鄉		1
Chia-shan 嘉善		1
Shao-hsing pref. 紹興	1	
Sheng-hsien 嵊縣		1 (1)
Hsin-ch'ang 新昌		1
Chu-chi 諸暨	3	

Gazetteers consulted: *Chiang-ning fc*, 1880; *Liu-ho hc*, 1883; *Kao-ch'un hc*, 1881; *Su-chou fc*, 1883; *Wu-chiang hc*, 1847; *Wu-chiang hc*, 1747; *Ch'ing-p'u hc*, 1879; *Chin-shan hc*, 1878; *Feng-hsien hc*, 1878; *Sung-chiang fc*, 1817; *Hua-t'ing hc*, 1878; *Shang-hai hc*, 1872; *Nan-hui hc*, 1927; *Wu-chin Yang-hu hsien ho-chih* 1886; *Wu-chin Yang-hu hc*, 1906; *Chiang-yin hc*, 1878; *Wu-hsi Chin-k'uei hc*, 1881; *Chin-t'an hc*, 1921; *Tan-t'u hc*, 1879; *Tan-yang hc*, 1885; *Li-yang hc*, 1813; *Yang-chou fc*, 1733; *Yang-chou hc*, 1810; *Yang-chou fc*, 1834; *Tung-t'ai hc*, 1817; *Chiang-tu hc*, 1881; *T'ai-ts'ang cc*, 1919; *Ch'ung-ming hc*, 1930; *Chia-ting hc*, 1881; *T'ung-chou chih-li cc*, 1875; *T'ai-hsing hc*, 1885; *Ju-kao hc*, 1808; *Hang-chou fc*, 1922; *Yu-hang hc*, 1899; *Chia-hsing fc*, 1879; *P'ing-hu hc*, 1886; *T'ung-hsiang hc*, 1887; *Shao-hsing fc*, 1792; *Shao-hsing fc*, 1922.

NOTES

Abbreviations

cc *chou-chih* (prefecture gazetteer)
cs *chin-shih*
fc *fu-chih* (prefecture gazetteer)
hc *hsien-chih* (county gazetteer)

I would like to express my gratitude to David Strand for his valuable comments on the first draft of this chapter. I am also grateful to the participants of the Montecito conference and the anonymous readers of ACLS whose criticism and comments were very helpful for subsequent revisions.

1. Evelyn S. Rawski, *Education and Popular Literacy in China* (Ann Arbor: University of Michigan Press, 1979).

2. Alexander Woodside, "Some Mid-Qing Theorists of Popular Schools: Their Innovations, Inhibitions, and Attitudes toward the Poor," *Modern China* 9, no.1 (Jan. 1983): 3–35.

3. With the exception of the interesting work of Sally Borthwick, *Education and Social Change in China: The Beginnings of the Modern Era* (Hoover Institute Press, 1983), which largely deals with the late Ch'ing and the early Republican period. For comparison with modern France, see Francois Furet and Jacques Ozouf, *Reading and Writing: Literacy in France from Calvin to Jules Ferry* (French original, 1977; Cambridge: Cambridge University Press, 1982).

4. For a thorough discussion of the process of cultural reproduction via the civil service examination system in the Ming-Ch'ing period, see Benjamin A. Elman, "Political, Social, and Cultural Reproduction via Civil Service Examinations in Late Imperial China," *Journal of Asian Studies*, 50, no. 1 (Feb. 1991): 7–28.

5. *She* is an ancient administrative unit that includes 25 families. In the Ming context, the number of families was no longer strictly respected. *She-hsueh* can thus be loosely translated as "community school."

The question of rebuilding social order after Ming power was established is dealt with at length by Edward L. Farmer, "Social Order in Early Ming China: Some Norms Codified in the Hung-wu Period," in B.E. Mcknight, ed., *Law and the State in Traditional East Asia* (Honolulu: University of Hawaii Press, 1987), 1–36.

6. *Ta Ming hui-tien* 大明會典 (Institutions of the Ming) (1587; Taipei: Hsing-wen-feng ch'u-pan kung-ssu, 1976), 78:23a.

7. *Ming shih-lu* 明實錄 (True Records of the Ming), first month of the eighth year of the Hung-wu reign, 96:4a.

8. For a description of the series of imperial orders on the matter, see Wang Lan-yin 玉蘭蔭, "Ming tai chih she-hsueh 明代之社學" (*She-hsueh* of the Ming dynasty), *Shih-ta yueh-k'an* 21 (1936): 49–52.

9. Wang Lan-yin, 53.

10. "She-hsueh," in *Ta Kao* 大誥 (Imperial Announcements) 1385, no. 44: 23b–24a. The call for the halt was in fact announced two years earlier, in 1383; see Wang Lan-yin, 50.

11. *Kao-yu cc*, 1572, 4:16b–17b.

12. Ch'en Lung-cheng, *Chi-t'ing wai shu* 幾亭外書 (Supplementary works of Ch'en Lung-cheng) in *Chi-t'ing ch'üan-shu* 幾亭全書 (Complete works of Ch'en Lung-cheng) (preface dated 1631; publisher unknown), Ch'ung-cheng ed., 3:18a; *Chiang-ning fc*, 1880 (1811), 16:15b. We are told by this gazetteer that there used to be sixteen schools in the area (including the countryside) during the late fourteenth and early fifteenth centuries.

13. *Chin-t'an hc*, 1921, 6:9b.

14. "Pao-yueh-ts'ang-shu" 保約倉塾 (On *pao-chia, hsiang-yueh*, granary, school), in *Huang Ming ching-shih shih-yung pien* 皇明經世實用編 (Works on practical matters of statecraft of the Ming) (Wan-li ed.; Taipei: Ch'eng-wen shu-chü, 1967), 26.

15. Yeh Ch'un-chi 葉春及, *Hui-an cheng-shu* 惠安政書 (Administrative book on Hui-an), preface dated 1573 (Foochow: Fu-chien jen-min ch'u-pan-she, 1987).

16. *Sung-chiang fc* 松江府志, 1815, 32:17a; *Ch'ing-p'u hc*, 1879, 9:29a.

17. *Su-chou fc* 蘇州府志, 1883, 26:25b–26a, on the 1447 and 1466 community schools in Wu-hsien; *Li-yang hc* 溧陽縣志, 1813, 7:7b, on the school established in the late fifteenth century; *Chiang-yin hc* 江陰縣志, T'ien-i-ke ed. (late Ming), 7:5a, on the school restored in 1497. For the 1465 edict, see Wang Lan-yin, 52.

18. *Su-chou fc*, 1883, 26:46b–47a, 27:36a; *Ju-kao hc*, 1808, 9:63b.

19. Lü proposed that each county select some twenty honest persons above forty years of age to be taught Chu Hsi's *Hsiao-hsueh*, the *Filial Piety Classic* (*Hsiao-ching*), and simple linguistics. They were to take an examination at the end of their one-year course and those who were good were to be assigned to local community schools. Lü also proposed that all children attend a minimum of three months of school every year after the harvest of the tenth month, and for three years. Those who were good would continue their study; those who were not good would then be allowed to leave school definitively. Lü K'un, "Fu-hsing she-hsueh" 復興社學 (To restore the community schools), in *Shih cheng lu* 實政錄 (On practical policies), *Lü-tzu ch'üan shu* 呂子全書 (Complete works of Lü K'un), Yunnan Library ed., early twentieth century, 3:7b–8a.

20. Yeh Ch'un-chi, *Hui-an cheng-shu*, 361.

21. Evelyn Rawski thinks they are the same; cf. Rawski 35, 35 n. 56. Benjamin Elman seems to put the *i-hsueh* on the same status of the academies; see Benjamin A. Elman, *From Philosophy to Philology* (Cambridge, Mass.: Harvard University Press, 1984), 119–120. But I think here he overestimates government control in this area, as well as the intellectual significance of these charitable schools in Ch'ing times.

Some contemporaries also thought that the *i-hsueh* and the *she-hsueh* were the same; see *I-hsing Ching-hsi hc* 宜興荊溪縣志, 1882, 4:15a. For detailed descriptions of the organizers, financing, and rules of various Ch'ing *i-hsueh*, cf. Ogawa Yoshiko 小川嘉子 "Shindai ni okeru gigaku setsuritsu no kiban" 清代に於ける義學設立の基盤 (Social basis of *i-hsueh* founding in the Ch'ing period), in Hayashi Tomoharu 林友春, ed., *Kinsei Chūgoku kyōiku shi kenkyū* 近世中國教育史研究 (Studies in the history of education in modern China) (Tokyo: Kokudosha, 1958), 273–308.

22. Translated by Djang Chu, *A Complete Book Concerning Happiness and Benevolence* (Tucson: University of Arizona Press, 1984), 536–37.

23. *Huang-ch'ao cheng-tien lei-tsuan* 皇朝政典類纂 (Compilation of imperial institutions) (1903; Taipei: Ch'eng-wen shu-chü, 1969), 231:1a. The compilation was a more complete version of the record in (*Ch'in-ting*) *hsüeh-cheng ch'üan-shu* 欽定學政全書 (Imperial complete book on educational policies) (1774; Taipei: Wen-hai ch'u-pan-she, 1967), 73:1a–b.

24. *Sung-chiang fc* 松江府志, 1817, 30:35a; *Hua-t'ing hc* 華亭縣志, 1878, 5:23a; *Su-chou fc*, 1883, 27:16a, 17b, 26:46b; *Tan-yang hc* 丹陽縣志, 1885, 10:10b; *T'ai-hsing cc* 泰興州志, 1885, 3:21b; *Yang-chou fc* 揚州府志, 1733; *Chiang-tu hc* 江都縣志, 1881 (1743); *Kao-ch'un hc* 高淳縣志, 1881, 5:32a; *P'ing-hu hc* 平湖縣志, 1886, 3:22a; *T'ai-ts'ang cc* 太倉

州志, 1919, 9:7a; *Shao-hsing fc* 紹興府志, 1912, 20:29a; *Yü-hang hc* 餘杭縣志, 1808, 5: 32b; *Yang-chou fc* 揚州府志, 1784 (1778), 16:26b.

25. See appendix; if we include *she-hsueh* built during the first years of Manchu rule mostly by officials, we have the following figures: of the 103 schools, 57 were set up by commoners and 46 by officials (55.3 percent against 44.7 percent).

As for schools incorporated into bigger charitable institutions, we do not have all the data here but a few examples will suffice to show their importance. The famous T'ung-shan T'ang 同善堂 set up in 1745 in Shanghai had a charitable school section; *Shang-hai hc* 上海縣志, 1872, 2:22a–b. The county of Wu-chin also had a similar institution established in 1801; *Wu-chin Yang-hu ho chih* 武進陽湖合志, 1842, 5:33a–34a. The same is true for the county of Hsing-hua, where the general charitable institution established in 1714 had a charitable school; *Hsing-hua hc* 興化縣志, 1852, 1:3a–b). In Chiang-tu too, such an institution was created in 1797; (*Shang Chiang liang hc* 上江兩縣志, 1874, 11:17a–b. We are sure that many more such schools existed in the eighteenth-century Lower Yangtze region.

For the role of local leaders, see A.K.C. Leung, "Ming mo Ch'ing ch'u min-chien tz'u-shan huo-tung ti hsing-ch'i" 明末清初民間慈善活動的興起 (Rise of private charitable institutions during the end of the Ming and the beginning of the Ch'ing periods), *Shih-huo Monthly* 15, no. 6/7 (1986): 52–79. Also A.K.C. Leung, "Organized Medicine in Ming-Qing China: State and Private Medical Institutions in the Lower Yangzi Region," *Late Imperial China* 8, no. 1 (1987): 134–66.

26. Wang Lan-yin, "Ming tai chih she-hsueh," in *Shih-ta yueh-k'an*, pt. 2, 25: 63–75.

27. *(Ch'in-ting) Hsueh-cheng ch'üan-shu*, 73:3a–b. The imperial edict was again based on the 1652 edict of Shun-chih in which *she-hsueh* were to be set up in the cities and were to train gifted youth. According to the *Chen-tse hc* 震澤縣志, 1746, 7:16b, there was practically no response to this edict. The same text also reported that the few *she-hsueh* left over from the Ming were almost not functioning and the edict to end these schools in 1686 by the K'ang-hsi emperor was taken well.

28. *Chiang-yin hc* 江陰縣志, 1878, 5:29b.

29. *Hsueh shih lu* 學仕錄 (Record of bureaucrats) (1867; publisher unknown) 16:34a; *Te-i lu* 得一錄 (Record of charitable deeds) (Soochow: Te-Chien Chai ed., 1869), 10, no. 3:2b.

30. In the 1820s, some three thousand charitable schools on the model of Tai San-hsi were reported to have been newly established nationwide; see *Hsueh shih lu*, 16: 34a. Around mid-century, an idea of a "more flexible" version of charitable schools emerged in which teachers were to travel from village to village to hold temporary classes to teach pupils some one to two hundred characters and a vocabulary permitting them to read simple texts with moral teachings; cf. *Te-i lu*, 10, no. 5: 3b–6b.

31. See A.K.C. Leung, "Ch'ing tai tz'u-shan chi-kou yu kuan-liao ts'eng di kuan-hsi" 清代慈善機構與官僚層的關係 (Charitable institutions and the bureaucracy under the Ch'ing), *Bulletin of the Institute of Ethnology, Academia Sinica* 66 (Aug. 1989): 85–103.

32. Alexander Woodside argues that Chinese education theory, as a kind of ritualized discourse, was shaped and paralyzed by formidable historical precedents, which explains its inability to be readily adapted to vocational training for poor relief, which was more urgently needed by late nineteenth-century Chinese society; Woodside, "Mid-Qing Theorists," 27, 29.

Another possible explanation is that traditional vocational training was so deeply involved with the structure of apprenticeship in various professions that it was technically difficult to extricate it from the old structure and put it into a new one that was not yet well defined. Mathematics, for instance, which is an important subject in modern education for training in abstract reasoning, was taught only to children considered to be less "intelligent" or less qualified for higher education so that they could start early to learn a trade. The teaching of practical mathematics to would-be merchants was described in Terada Takanobu 寺田隆信, *Sansei shōnin no kenkyū* 山西商人の研究 (Study on Shan-hsi merchants) (Kyoto: Society of Oriental Research, 1972), 321–24. Mathematics courses described in the *Huang Ming ching-shih shih-yung pien* were also just commercial mathematics; see "Chen," ch. 26, 7.

33. Rawski, 24–28; Borthwick, 17–18.

34. This is often stated in rules of clan schools, e.g., *Shan-yin An-ch'ang Hsu shih tsung-p'u* 山陰安昌徐氏宗譜 (Genealogy of the Hsu clan of An-ch'ang) (Shao-hsing, Chekiang), (1884); *Yao-shih chia ch'eng* 姚氏家乘 (Genealogy of the Yao clan) (Chia-hsing, Chekiang), 1908. These made it clear that cousins of different surnames could only be accepted exceptionally. When not stated, the exclusivity can likely be taken for granted.

35. Schools of the Yao and Sun clans (the latter established in the earlier eighteenth century) had two classes; see *Yao-shih chia-ch'eng*; *Yang ch'uan Sun-shih tsung-p'u* 陽川孫氏宗譜 (Genealogy of the Sun clan of Yang-ch'uan) (Shao-hsing, Chekiang, 1830), 28:3b. Soochow's Lu clan provided everything except bedding for the pupils, as did the T'u clan school for orphans; see *Lu-shih Feng-men chih-p'u* 陸氏葑門支譜 (Genealogy of the Feng-men branch of the Lu clan) (from Wu-hsien, Kiangsu) (1888), 13:61a; *T'u shih P'i-ling chih-p'u* 屠氏毗陵支譜 (Genealogy of the P'i-ling branch of the T'u clan) (Wu-chin, Kiangsu, 1856), cited in Akigoro Taga 多賀秋五郎, *Chūgoku sōfu no kenkyū* 中國宗譜の研究 (Survey of Chinese genealogies) (Tokyo: Nihon gakujutsu shinkō kai, 1981), 572–73. The Lu and Yao clan schools were boarding schools; the Yao clan school allowed children to go home once a month, while pupils of the Lu clan school simply could not go out "if there is nothing special." The wealthy Yao clan provided pupils with monthly stipends of 160 to 300 cash (800 cash ≅ 1 tael of silver in eighteenth-century Kiangnan), depending on their levels; those who were particularly poor were given extra maintenance grants.

36. *Hung-lou meng*, 紅樓夢 ch. 10.

37. The Lu and Wang clan schools had regular control systems (respectively once a fortnight and during the first five days of the month), whereas the T'u school had irregular controls. The former two schools graded the pupils' performance into three grades. Stationery and money were given as rewards by the Lu and T'u clan schools respectively for good pupils, whereas punishment was not defined among any of the three schools. Only the T'u clan school suggested that poor pupils "feel ashamed and thus make more effort." The diary system was elaborated especially by the Wang clan school; see "Chia-shu," in *Ling-hu Wang-shih chih-p'u* 菱湖王氏支譜 (Genealogy of the Ling-hu branch of the Wang clan) (Wu-hsing, Chekiang), 3a–4b; *Lu-shih Feng-men chih-p'u*, 13:60b–61a; *T'u-shih chih-p'u*, cited in Taga Akigoro, *Chugokū sōfu no kenkyū*, 573.

38. *Yang-ch'uan Sun-shih tsung-p'u*, 28:7a. Similar statements can also be found in genealogies of the Lu, Wang, and Yao clan rules for the schools.

39. This is usually the first article in clan school rules: in *Lu-shih feng-men chih-p'u*, it is stated that every morning before classes began, the pupils, led by the eldest, had to bow before the tablets of Confucius and prominent ancestors of the clan, and the teacher had to lead the pupils to kneel before them on the first and the fifteenth of every month; 13:60b. Similar rituals were required by the Wang clan of Ling-hu; "Jia-shu" (clan school), in *Ling-hu Wang-shih chih-p'u*, 2a.

40. The absence of the bowing and kneeling before the ancestors' tablets in the rules of the orphan school of the T'u clan is revealing: in effect, it is indicated in the rules that most of these fatherless children would probably leave school and learn a craft at twelve or thirteen. They were not expected to become high bureaucrats and glorify the clan. For the Wang clan school of Ling-hu, where this ceremony was performed, although there were also children who would leave school early to learn a craft for a living, it is obvious that the school's emphasis was still on those who would pass the civil examinations as traveling subsidies for candidates were set at the end of the rules and those who succeeded also received various allowances; see "Jia-shu", in *Ling-hu Wang-shih chih-p'u*, 2b, 5b. The school of the Hsu clan of An-ch'ang (established in 1819) was apparently for the poorer members of the clan, but there was no school rule; see "Wen-hai chia-shu chi," in *Shan-yin An-ch'ang Hsu-shih tsung-p'u* (Shao-hsing, Chekiang), 1a–b.

41. The fate of the clan school is naturally linked to that of the charitable estate, a fact convincingly demonstrated by Denis Twitchett, "The Fan Clan's Charitable Estate, 1050–1760," in *Confucianism in Action*, ed. D.S. Nivison and A.F. Wright, (Stanford: Stanford University Press, 1959) 96–133.

42. *Yang-ch'uan Sun-shih tsung-p'u* 28:7a.

43. *Yang-ch'uan Sun-chih tsung-p'u, chüan* 28.

44. The "Ch'ing-shan" charitable school in one village in the county of Wu-chin; *Wu-chin Yang-hu ho-chih*, 1842, 12:50a–b. Also the charitable school in Kao-ch'un, established in 1682; *Kao-ch'un hc*, 1881, 5:32a–b.

45. The charitable school in Tung-t'ai, established in 1808, *Tung-t'ai hc*, 1817, 12:19b.

46. The charitable school in Ju-kao was reconstructed in 1774 under the order of the magistrate and with 660 taels of donation from the local notables; its reorganization was also financed and realized by the local leaders in 1805; two other schools in the same county were similarly created in 1747 and 1816. It is interesting to note that in the latter case, one of the financers of the school regretted that since 1775 the county had produced no *chin-shih* and one of the school's aims was to train would-be bureaucrats. In this sense, it was very similar to the clan schools; *Ju-kao hc*, 1875, 9:64a–68b. In the highly commercialized Soochow county, charitable schools were often financed by rent from donated land as in the case of the two schools in Chen-tze, which were established in 1735 (*Chen-tze hc*, 1893, 7:15b). "Charitable persons" sometimes donated the salaries of a certain teacher, as in the case of the school in Nan-hui, where someone paid the teacher's fees for two years from 1767–1768; *Nan-hui hc*, 1927, 7:33a.

47. As in the case of the above-mentioned Nan-hui school, which ended when the private donation to pay the teacher was ended; *Nan-hui hc*, 1927, 7:33a. Also, as in the case of the Hua-t'ing school, which was established in 1682 by the prefect and was financed and maintained by the magistrates in 1699 and 1737. It collapsed after the lat-

ter date and was briefly restored only in 1795, again with the support of local officials; *Hua-t'ing hc*, 1878, 5:23a.

48. *Ch'en Ch'ueh chi* 陳確集 (Works of Ch'en Ch'ueh) (Peking: Chung-hua shu-chü 1979), 514. One can find many examples of children taught by elder family members in the biographies of famous scholars of the Ming and Ch'ing periods. One other example was Liu Tsung-chou 劉宗周 (1578–1645), the prominent Chekiang thinker, who was educated by his maternal grandfather; see Huang Tsung-hsi 黃宗羲, *Tzu Liu-tzu hsing-chuang* 子劉子行狀 (Life of Master Liu) in *Huang Tsung-hsi ch'üan-chi* 黃宗羲全集 (Complete writings of Huang Tsung-hsi) (Chekiang: Ku-chi ch'u-pan-she, 1985), 1: 208.

49. Mireille Laget, "Petites écoles en Languedoc au XVIIIe siècle," *Annales. Economies. Société. Civilisations.* (Nov.–Dec. 1971), 1398.

50. The main sources used in the following discussion are: Ch'en Fang-sheng 陳芳生, (an experienced early Ch'ing primary teacher of the Ch'ien-t'ang region), "Hsun-meng t'iao-li" 訓蒙條例 (Regulations on primary education); see *T'an-chi ts'ung-shu* 檀几叢書 (Collection of the Sandalwood table) (1695), 2d ser., Hsin-an ed., 13:1a–5b; Liu Tsung-chou 劉宗周 (1578–1645, native of Shan-yin, Chekiang), "Hsiao-hsueh yueh" 小學約 (Primary school rules), in *Liu-tzu ch'uan-shu* 劉子全書 (Complete works of Liu Tsung-chou) (1822), I-Shan T'ang ed., 25:9b–13b; Lü K'un, "Fu-hsing she-hsueh"; Chang Lü-hsiang 張履祥 (1611–74, native of T'ung-hsiang, Chekiang), "Hsueh-kuei" 學規 (School rules), in Ch'en Hung-mou 陳宏謀, (Yang-cheng i-kuei 養正遺規), (Rules on elementary education 1739) in *Wu-chung i-kuei* 五種遺規, Ssu-pu pei-yao ed. (Taipei: Chung-hua shu-chü, 1981) pu-pien:33b–43b; Ts'ui Hsueh-ku 崔學古 (an early Ch'ing educator from Ch'ang-shu, Kiangsu), "Yu hsun" 幼訓 (Regulations for the young), in *T'an-chi ts'ung shu*, 2d ser., 8:1a–13b; Lu Shih-i 陸世儀 (1611–1672, native of T'ai Ts'ang, Kiangsu), "Hsiao-hsueh lei" 小學類 (On primary education), in his *Ssu-pien lu chi-yao* (Excerpts of "Reflections") 思辯錄輯要, (Chiang-su shu-chü, 1877), 1:1a–6b; Wang Yün 王筠 (1784–1854, native of Shantung), "Chiao t'ung-tzu fa" 教童子法; (Method of teaching young children), in *Yün-tzu-tzai k'an ts'ung-shu* 雲自在龕叢書 (Collection of the Yun-tsi-tzai box) (Chiang-yin: Miao ed., Kuang-hsu period [1875–1908]), vol. 2, no. 12:1a–12a; T'ang Piao 唐彪 (eighteenth century, native of Lan-hsi Chekiang), "Fu shih shan yu fa" 父師善誘法 (Good method for the father and for the teacher), in Ch'en Hung-mou, "Yung-cheng Kuei", Li Chao-lo 李兆洛 (1769–1841, native of Wu-chin, Kiangsu), "Hsiang-shu tu-shu fa" 鄉塾讀書法 (Method for the village school), in his *Yang-i chai wen-chi* 養一齋文集 (Collected essays of the Yang-i study) (Li ed., 1878). These major sources will be supplemented with other writings of the time.

51. I am referring to the Yung Shi-ch'iu (Weng Shih-ch'ao 翁仕朝) collection in the Shatin Central Library of Hong Kong. Yung was a village teacher-geomancer-epistolarian doctor of the Hoi-ha (Hai-hsia 海下) village in the late nineteenth century (now situated in the New Territories of Hong Kong), but he did not pass any imperial examination. In the five hundred or so titles of the collection, there are a large number of textbooks for children including various versions (some with illustrations and explanations in the vulgar language) of the *San-tzu ching*, 三字經 *Pai chia hsing* 百家姓, *Ch'ien tzu wen* 千字文, *Ch'ien-chia shih* 千家詩, *Hsiao-ching* 孝經, *Yu-hsueh ku-shih ch'iung-lin* 幼學故事瓊林, *Hsi hsien wen* 昔賢文, commentaries on the Four Books and Five Classics, some of the histories (*Tso chuan* 左傳), vocabulary of the Classics (*Wu ching chi*

tzu 五經集字, *Tza-tzu* 雜字 primers, *Sheng-lü ch'i-meng* 聲律啟蒙, *Jih-chi ku-shih* 日記故事, and some dozen manuals on prose writing, plus a number of popular novels. Except for some more modern (early twentieth century, late Ch'ing period) texts written in Cantonese, these give the impression that they very much reflect the curriculum described by Chang Chih-kung (see n.63) and Evelyn Rawski. A more detailed description of this collection is in Wang Erh-min and Alice N.H. Lun-Ng, "Ju-hsueh shih-su hua chi ch'i tuiyü min-chien feng-chiao chih chin-ju" 儒學世俗化及其對於民間風教之浸濡 (Secularization of Confucianism and its merger with popular culture — the example of Weng Shih-ch'ao at Hong Kong), *Bulletin of the Institute of Modern History, Academia Sinica*, 18 (Taipei, June 1989): 75–94. I would like to thank Dr. David Faure and Dr. Patrick Hase for having introduced me to this fascinating collection.

52. This is specified in Ch'en Fang-sheng, "Hsun-meng t'iao-li," 13:10b.

53. Five different sets of regulations on elementary schools were based on such a daily schedule: Liu Tsung-chou, "Hsiao-hsueh yueh," 25:9b–13b; Lü K'un, "Fu-hsing she-hsueh"; Chang Lü-hsiang, "Hsueh-kui"; Ch'en Fang-sheng, "Hsun-meng t'iao-li"; Huang Liu-hung, *Fu-hui ch'üan-shu* (Complete book concerning happiness and benevolence) (preface dated 1694); Yamane Yukio ed., based on Obato Yukihiro ed. of 1850; Tokyo: Kyūko shoju, 1973) 25:14a–15b.

54. The eight to fifteen age range was the most often mentioned in various primary rules. It was specified in the standard "schedule and curriculum" written by Ch'eng Tuan-li of the Yuan, which was much respected by later educators; see Ch'en Hung-mou, "Yang-cheng i-kuei" 6b–7a. However, some, like T'ang Piao recommended that children start to learn to recognize characters at three or four and attend school at about six once they knew about one to two thousand characters; T'ang Piao, "Fu shih shan-yu fa," 41b. This was also the opinion of Lu Shih-i, "Hsiao-hsueh lei," 1a. There seemed to be less disagreement on the maximum age of fifteen, when one usually had to decide the orientation of one's career: one either continued study in the "big school" (*ta-hsueh*) or learned a trade. In either case, one had to quit the primary school.

55. Liu Tsung-chou, "Hsiao-hsueh yueh," 10b.

56. Rawski, 26–27, 42–43. The experienced teacher Ch'en Fang-sheng reminded parents that elementary teachers had to be reasonably paid so that they "would not have any material worries, and the pupils could benefit [from it and] concentrate on their studies"; "Hsun-meng t'iao-li," 4b–5a.

57. T'ang Piao, "Fu shih shan-yu fa," 40b. Li Chao-lo, in "Hsiao-hsueh," 23a, stated: "People do not pay attention to the employment of an elementary teacher. They only require someone who is a bit literate and do not care about his character." Liu Tsung-chou also warned against the employment of elementary teachers who would stay only for a short year just to get paid; Liu Tsung-chou, "Hsiao-hsueh yueh," 12b–13a.

58. "Inside the classroom, the teacher should discipline [the children], outside the classroom, the father and senior members of the family should discipline them"; Ts'ui Hsueh-ku, "Yu-hsun" 3a.

59. *Cheng Pan-ch'iao chi* 鄭板橋集 (Works of Cheng Pan-ch'iao) (Taipei: Hung-yeh shu-chü, 1982), 209. The original Chinese poem reads:

教館本來是下流,
傍人門戶渡春秋。

半飢半飽清閒客，

無鎖無枷自在囚。

課少父兄嫌懶情，

功多子弟結冤仇。

而今幸得青雲步，

遮卻當年一半羞。

60. *Yang-ch'uan Sun-shih tsung p'u*, 28:10a–11a.

61. See Ch'en Fang-sheng, "Hsün-meng t'ia" 1a.

62. Cf. also Rawski, 15–17, 192.

63. The most detailed descriptions of the origins and the evolutions of the various primers are in Chang Chih-kung 張志公, *Ch'uan-t'ung yü-wen chiao-yü ch'u-t'an* 傳統語文教育初探 (Preliminary survey on the traditional linguistic education) (Shanghai: Shang-hai chiao-yü ch'u-pan-she, 1964), 4–31. See also James T.C. Liu, "Pi 'San-tzu ching' keng tsao di Nan Sung ch'i-meng shu" 比「三字經」更早的南宋啟蒙書 (More ancient Southern Sung primer than the Trimetrical Classic), in *Liang Sung shih yen-chiu hui-pien* 兩宋史研究彙編 (Collected essays on the history of the Northern and Southern Sung) (Taipei: Lien-ching ch'u-pan-she, 1987), 303–6.

64. Ts'ui Hsueh-ku, "Yu hsun," 5b–6a; Wang Yun, "Chiao t'ung-tzu fa," 3b–4a; T'ang Piao, "Fu shih shan yu fa," 41b. These recommended the use of wooden squares (each character on a square) in the teaching of characters to the young child prior to the reading of the three classical primers.

65. Liu Tsung-chou, "Hsiao-hsueh yueh," 11b.

66. On the age at which one should learn to write, Wang Yün recommended that it was not too late to start at eight or nine because at an earlier age the "child's hand is too small and his bones too feeble"; Wang Yun, "Chiao t'ung-tzu fa," 7b–8a. On the correct way to teach calligraphy to beginners, see Ts'ui Hsueh-ku, "Yu-hsun," 10b–11b; Liu Tsung-chou, "Hsiao-hsueh yueh,"11b. See also Chang Chih-kung, *Yü-wen chiao-yü*, 37–39, on the calligraphy models commonly used in elementary schools.

67. The work was said to be written by the late Ming grand academician Li T'ing-chi 李廷機 (*cs* 1583). But there is no direct proof of this. The latest edition of the book is by the Yueh-lu ch'u-pan-she of Changsha, 1988. The late Ming historian and scholar Hsieh Chao-che 謝肇淛 (1567–1624) told us that the historical knowledge he acquired in elementary school was from this kind of primer; cf. Hsieh Chao-che, *Wu tsa tzu* 五雜組 (Five assorted offerings) (Taipei: Wei-wen shu-chü, 1966), 344–45.

68. Chang Chih-kung, *Yü-wen chiao-yü*, 72–73, 87–91, 92–97.

69. Although some educators were against teaching the Classics to children who did not intend to sit for the imperial examination. These texts, according to them, should only be taught at the higher level, the *ching-kuan* (Section of the Classics), of the primary school. See Ch'en Fang-sheng, "Hsun-meng t'iao-li," 5b–7a.

70. T'ang Piao, "Fu shih shan-yu fa," 41b, 43b; Wang Yun "Chiao t'ung-tzu fa," 6a–b; Liu Tsung-chou, "Hsiao-hsueh yueh," 10b–11a.

71. Ts'ui Hsueh-ku, "Yu-hsun," 7b; Lu Shih-i, "Hsiao-hsueh lei," 2a.

72. Ch'en Fang-sheng, "Hsün-meng t'iao-li," 2a–b. Similar methods and principles were employed or recommended by almost all the teachers and educators: Ts'ui Hsueh-ku, "Yu-hsun," 9b–10a; Liu Tsung-chou, "Hsiao-hsueh yueh," 10b; Wang Yun, "Chiao t'ung-tzu fa," 6a–b; T'ang Piao, "Fa shih shan-yu fa," 42a.

73. Ch'en Hung-mou, "I-hsueh hui-chi hsu" 義學彙集序 (Preface for the records concerning the charitable school), in *Hu-hai wen chuan* 湖海文傳 (Collected writings of the lakes and seas), Ching-hsun ed. (1866; reprint of 1837 ed.), 29:3b; T'ang Pin, "Fu-hsing she-hsueh i tuan meng yang kao yü" 復興社學以端蒙養告諭 (Order to restore the *she-hsueh* in order to upright primary education [Kiangsu]) in *T'ang-tzu i-shu* 湯子遺書 (Posthumous writings of T'ang Pin), in *San-hsien cheng-shu* 三賢政書 (Administrative writings of the three wise officials), preface dated 1879, 4:25b.

74. Li Lo, *Chien-wen tza-chi* 見聞雜記 (Miscellaneous records of what I have seen and heard), preface dated 1632 (Shanghai: Ku-chi ch'u-pan-she, 1986) 8:39a.

75. Lu Shih-i, "Hsiao-hsueh lei," 1b. For a detailed description of this text, cf. M.T. Kelleher, "Back to Basics: Chu Hsi's *Elementary Learning*," in W.T. de Bary and J.W. Chaffee, eds., *Neo-Confucian Education: The Formative Stage* (Berkeley: University of California Press, 1989), 219–51. Kelleher also shows that this text was read more by adults and older students than by young children.

76. Li Chao-lo, "Hsiao-hsueh," 19:22b.

77. Ts'ui Hsueh-ku's "Yu-hsun," for instance, mentioned the Classics as texts used, but *Hsiao-hsueh* was not on the list. Ch'en Chueh also mentioned the Classics and the Four Books, as well as the Dynastic Histories, but there was no mention of Chu Hsi's work in his recommendation on primary education; see Ch'en Ch'üeh, *Ch'en Ch'üeh chi*.

78. The poem was written by a certain Kuo Ch'en-yao 郭臣堯, a friend of the Ch'ien-t'ang scholar Liang Shao-jen 梁紹壬 (1792–1837). The third and the fourth verses are the first lines of *Hundred Surnames* and *Thousand Characters*, the poem in Chinese is as follows:

> 一連烏鴉噪晚風，
> 諸徒齊逞好喉嚨。
> 趙錢孫李周吳鄭，
> 天地玄黃宇宙洪，
> 《千字文》完翻《鑑略》，
> 《百家姓》畢理《神童》。
> 就中有個超羣者，
> 一日三行讀《大》《中》。

Liang Shao-jen, *Liang-pan ch'iu-yü an sui-pi* 兩般秋兩盦隨筆 (Miscellaneous writings in the study of autumn rain) (Shanghai: Ku-chi ch'u-pan-she, 1982), 214.

79. The most popular introduction to phonology was of course the *Sheng-lü ch'i-meng* 聲律啟蒙, written by the late seventeenth-century scholar Ch'e Wan-yü 車萬育. Both Liu Tsung-chou and Lü K'un put these exercises in the second morning session; Huang Liu-hung recommended phonology training to be done during the evening session.

80. Ch'en Fang-sheng, "Hsün-meng t'iao-li," 1b–2a.

81. See Sakai Tadao, "Confucianism and Popular Educational Works," in *Self and Society in Ming Thought*, Wm. T. de Bary et al., (New York: Columbia University Press, 1970), 331–64; de Bary, "Mindai no nichiyō ruisho to shomin kyōiku" (Ming family handbooks and popular education) 明代の日用類書と庶民教育, in *Kinsei chūgoku kyōikushi kenkyū*, 27–154.

82. Ch'en Ch'ueh, *Ch'en Ch'ueh chi*, 514.

83. Li Chao-lo, "Hsiao-hsueh," 22a.

84. Lu Lung-ch'i, "Shih tzu-ti t'ieh" 示子弟帖 (Letters to the young), in Ch'en Hung-mou, "Yang-cheng i-kuei," 36b.

85. Liu Tsung-chou, 11b.

86. It is included with Lü K'un's supplement, "Hsü hsiao-erh yü" 續小兒語, in Ch'en Hung-mou, ("Yang-cheng i-kuei," ch.2, 7b–17b). It is also recommended by Li Chao-lo as necessary reading for young children. Other primers of this kind commonly used are described in Chang Chih-kung, *Yü-wen chiao-yü*, 45–53.

87. Li Lo, *Chien-wen tza-chi*.

Li Lo said precisely that Yuan Huang's commentaries on the Four Books were frequently used; on these works, see Sakai Tadao, *Chūgoku zensho no kenkyū* 中國善書の研究 (Studies on Chinese morality books) (Tokyo: Kobundo, 1960), 323–24, 330–32.

88. See Cynthia Brokaw, "Yuan Huang (1533–1606) and the Ledgers of Merit and Demerit," *Harvard Journal of Asiatic Studies*, 47 no. 1(1987): 137–195. Ts'ui Hsueh-ku, "Yu-hsun," 12b–13a.

89. Li Chao-lo, "Hsiao-hsueh", 22b.

90. Sung Chin 宋謹, "Ken-hsin t'ang hsueh-kuei" 根心堂學規 (Rules of the Ken-hsin school), in *T'an-chi ts'ung-shu*, supp. ch., pt.1, 5b–6b, which was divided into two main parts: merits in study and behavior and demerits in study and behavior.

91. Ch'en Wen-shu, "I-hsueh chang-ch'eng," 3a.

92. Wen Hsu 溫序, *Ping yü chang chi* 病餘掌記, cited in Wang Li-ch'i, 王利器, ed., *Yuan-Ming-Ch'ing san-tai chin wei hsiao-shuo hsi-chü shih-liao* 元明清三代禁燬小説戲曲史料 (Materials on the operas and novels forbidden and destroyed during the three dynasties of the Yuan, Ming, and Ch'ing) (Shanghai: Ku-chi ch'u-pan-she, 1981), 246; *Te-i lu*, 11 no.1:11a–b, 2b–3a.

93. The danger that popular literature posed for women who could read a little was described in many family rules and other writings in the Ming and Ch'ing dynasties; see Wang Li-ch'i, *Yuan-Ming-Ch'ing*, 173–80.

94. P'eng Yun-chang 彭蘊章, "Wen-hsin-t'ang shih sheng-t'ung t'iao-yueh 問心堂示生童條約 (Rules for pupils of the Wen-hsin school), cited in Wang Li-ch'i, *Yuan-Ming-Ch'ing*, 292.

95. Jean-Louis Flandrin, *Le sexe et l'Occident* (Paris: Seuil, 1981), 296–99; Philippe Ariès, *L'enfant et la vie familiale sous l'Ancien Régime*. (Paris: Seuil, 1973), 140–76.

96. Lu Shih-i "Hsiao-hsueh lei," 4a.

97. Li Chao-lo, "Hsiao-hsueh," 21b; Ch'en Fang-sheng, "Hsün-meng t'iao-li," 3b–4a.

98. For the details of this discipline, see Ts'ui Hsueh-ku, "Yu-hsun," 4a–5b; Liu Tsung-chou, "Hsiao-hsueh yueh," 10a–b, 12a–b; many of the recommendations were of course simplified or slightly modified versions of Chu Hsi's *Hsiao-hsueh*.

99. On physical punishment, Ts'ui Hsueh-ku gave the most detailed recommendations; cf. "Yu-hsun," 1b–2a, 3b.

100. Ts'ui Hsueh-ku, "Yu-hsun," 1b; Li Chao-lo, "Hsiang-shu tu-shu fa," 29b; T'ang Piao, "Fu shih shan-yu fa."

101. Ts'ui Hsueh-ku, "Yu-hsun," 2b–3b; Liu Tsung-chou, "Hsiao-hsueh yueh," 13a–b; T'ang Piao, "Fu shih shan-yu fa," 44a.

102. Wang Yang-ming, "Hsun-meng ta-i shih chiao tu Liu Po-sung teng" 訓蒙大意示教讀劉伯頌等 (Opinion on elementary education to instructor Liu Po-sung and others), in *Ch'uan hsi lu* 傳習錄, 67–68, in *Wang Yang-ming ch'üan-chi* 王陽明全集 (Taipei: Ta-shen shu-chü, 1983).

103. Lu Shih-i, "Hsiao-hsueh lei," 4b–5a.

104. Yeh Ch'un-chi, *Hui-an cheng-shu*, 361.

105. See Ho Ping-ti, *The Ladder of Success in Imperial China* (New York: Columbia University Press, 1962), 177.

106. Lu Shih-i, "Hsiao-hsueh lei," 4a.

107. Furet and Ozouf, *Reading and Writing*, 123.

108. "Chiao-hua liang ta ti lun" 教化兩大敵論 (On the two big enemies of culture), in *Te-i lu*, 11, no. 2:12a–b.

109. "Shou wei yin-shu chü chang-ch'eng" 收燬淫書局章程 (Regulations of the bureau that collects and destroys licentious books), in *Te-i lu*, 11, no. 1:7a–13b; "I-hua t'ang chang-ch'eng" 翼化堂章程 (Regulations of the I-hua bureau), in *Te-i lu*, 11, no. 2: 1a–21b.

110. A.K.C. Leung, "Ming mo Ch'ing ch'u."

111. In this sense, China's elementary education achieved the opposite goal of that of contemporary Sweden, which reinforced the segregation of social classes and the two cultures: elitist and popular. See Bengt Sandin, "Education, Popular Culture, and the Surveillance of the Population in Stockholm between 1600 and the 1840s," *Continuity and Change* 3, no. 3 (1988): 357–90.

112. Rawski estimates that in the middle and late nineteenth century 30 to 45 percent of the men and 2 to 10 percent of the women in China knew how to read and write; Rawski, *Education and Popular Literacy*, 140.

Regarding changes in England and France, see Furet and Ozouf, *Reading and Writing*, 314, their discussions being based on the famous theory of Jack Goody. For a more recent version of this theory, see Goody, *La logique de l'écriture: Aux origines des sociétés humaines* (Paris: Armand Colin, 1986), esp. 97–102.

113. The idea of a process of "decontextualization" in learning in literate societies is discussed in Jack Goody, *The Interface Between the Written and the Oral* (Cambridge: Cambridge University Press, 1987), 184–85. Interestingly, despite this difference between China and the West, the process of "repetition, copying, verbatim memory" was the same for both civilizations.

114. Borthwick, *Education and Social Change*, 86. According to a 1906 proposal to push forward "modern education," the best way was to "reform the several million *ssu-shu* 私塾 (private schools) that exist"; see "Ssu-shu kai-liang hui chang-ch'eng" 私塾改良會章程 (Regulations of the Society for the reform of private schools) (Shanghai, 1906) in *Chung-kuo chin-tai chiao-yü-shih tzu-liao* 中國近代教育史資料 Materials on the modern history of Chinese education) (Peking: Jen-min chiao-yü ch'u-pan-she, 1961), 103, 105.

GLOSSARY

Chang Ch'ao-jui	張朝瑞	Ch'en Lung-cheng	陳龍正
Chang Hsueh-ch'eng	章學誠	Ch'en Wen-shu	陳文述
Ch'ang-chou	長洲	Ch'en Yü-wang	陳于王
Ch'ang-shu	常熟	*cheng-k'ai*	正楷
Ch'en Ch'üeh	陳確	Cheng Pan-ch'iao	鄭板橋
Ch'en Fang-sheng	陳芳生	Chia Pao-yü	賈寶玉
Ch'en Hung-mou	陳宏謀	*Chia-shan*	嘉善

chiao-hua	教化	Liu Tsung-chou	劉宗周
Chien-lueh	鑒略	Lu Lung-ch'i	陸隴其
Ch'ien-t'ang	錢塘	Lu Shih-i	陸世儀
Ch'ien tzu wen	千字文	Lü K'un	呂坤
chin-shih	進士	Lü Te-sheng	呂得勝
Chin-t'an	金壇	*meng-kuan*	蒙館
ching-kuan	經館	*Ming-wu meng-ch'iu*	名物蒙求
Ch'ing-p'u	青浦	*Pai chia hsing*	百家姓
Chu Hsi	朱熹	*pao-chia*	保甲
chü-jen	舉人	P'ing-hu	平湖
Chü-jung	句容	*San-tzu ching*	三字經
Fu-hui ch'üan-shu	福惠全書	*shan shu*	善書
Hangchow	杭州	Shan-yin	山陰
hao i shih min	好義市民	Shang-yang	上洋
hsiang-yüeh	鄉約	Shao-hsing	紹興
Hsiao-ching	孝經	*she-hsueh*	社學
Hsiao-erh yü	小兒語	*Shen t'ung shih*	神童詩
Hsiao-hsueh	小學	Sheng-hsien	嵊縣
hsien	縣	Sung-chiang	松江
hsien shu	閒書	Ta-kao	大誥
Hsing-hua	興化	Tai San-hsi	戴三錫
Hua-t'ing	華亭	T'ai-hsing	泰興
Huang Liu-hung	黃六鴻	*T'ai-shang kan-ying-p'ien*	太上感應篇
Hui-an	惠安	T'ai-ts'ang	太倉
i-hsueh	義學	Tan-t'u	丹徒
i-hsueh chang-ch'eng	義學章程	Tan-yang	丹陽
Jen p'u	人譜	T'ang Pin	湯斌
Ju-kao	如皋	*Ti-chi lu*	迪吉錄
Kan-ch'üan	甘泉	*Tso chuan*	左傳
Kan-t'ang	甘棠	Ts'ui Hsueh-ku	董學古
Kao-ch'un	高淳	T'ung-hsiang	桐鄉
Kao-yu	高郵	Wang Yang-ming	王陽明
K'un-shan	崑山	Yeh Ch'un-chi	葉春及
lei-shu	類書	Yen Mao-yu	顏茂猷
li	禮	*yin shu*	淫書
Li Chao-lo	李兆洛	Yü-hang	餘杭
Li Lo	李樂	Yuan Huang	袁黃
li-she	里社		

TWELVE

Education and Empire in Southwest China

Ch'en Hung-mou in Yunnan, 1733–38

William T. Rowe

Centuries before the Chinese empire assumed its celebrated role as victim of incorporation into a Western-dominated "world system," it was an established master at imperial domination of peripheral lands and peoples. As was the case in the West, the processes of political subordination and the redirection of local economies were justified by an assumption of cultural superiority, prompting simultaneous attempts to create a "culture of deference" and to foster assimilationist cultural change. As in the West, these attempts were fraught with internal tensions and contradictions; yet, also as in the West, they were usually undertaken by men who were anything but cynical in their faith in their own superior civilization and the nobility of their purpose. An outstanding example of such a process is the subject of this chapter, the founding or rehabilitation of nearly 700 local elementary schools in predominantly non-Han areas of Yunnan province between 1733 and 1738 under the leadership of a young Confucian zealot (and, later, model "statecraft" official), Ch'en Hung-mou.

The intent of this chapter is to look at Ch'en's project for what it says about the empirical and mental universes of the eighteenth-century literati elite. Educational practice is used to shed light on material relations of state and society, center and periphery, and elite and commoner, as well as on the Ch'ing elite's varying conceptions of human nature and of its own role in the world. While one must attempt some assessment of the practical success of the school-founding campaign, I frankly adopt the imperialist perspective in paying little attention to the emotive responses of non-Han peoples to this Ch'ing expansionist drive. That is the task of another study.

The southwest had been nominally a part of China since Han times, and the assimilation of its non-Chinese peoples had for two millennia been considered by Chinese an historical inevitability.[1] However, actual settlement of this area and massive confrontation with local cultures had been forestalled primarily because the ecological and disease environments of the region had proved inhospitable to Chinese under existing technology. The first important population of the southwest by outsiders came only in the fourteenth century, when substantial numbers of Mongol troops were sent there as military colonists. Soon thereafter, Ming T'ai-tsu (r. 1368–98) forcibly removed to Yunnan much of the original Chinese population of the area chosen for his imperial capital, Nanking. But, as James Lee has shown, this "first immigration" disrupted indigenous society only very slightly, since Ming efforts at political and cultural integration were hesitant and noncommittal. A political system of rule by enfeoffed native headmen (*t'u-ssu*), experimented with in earlier eras, was institutionalized, and late in the dynasty sporadic efforts were made to replace this by direct bureaucratic administration (*kai-t'u kuei-liu*). Some Confucian schools were established.[2] In most cases, however, the effects were merely local and severely limited.

The situation changed dramatically following the Manchu conquest of 1644. First, the southwest became an arena of major military action, initially as a haven for Ming loyalist armies and later as the base for the rebellion of erstwhile Ch'ing general Wu San-kuei (1612–78). Then, following the collapse of this rebellion in 1681, the process of incorporation began in earnest. The late seventeenth and early eighteenth centuries saw an unprecedented level of Chinese immigration, part of the broader outward and upward (into highlands) population shift of the mid-Ch'ing that relieved population pressure on the more metropolitan areas and developed new lands for both subsistence and commercialized agriculture. In its size and in its pattern of land settlement and market development, this "second immigration" much more seriously altered the society of the southwest and spawned an increasing incidence of ethnic conflict. Mindful of this, and with an eye toward exploitation of the region's agrarian and mineral resources (notably copper to meet China's expanding currency needs), Ch'ing officials launched an unprecedentedly aggressive program of postrebellion "reconstruction" (*shan-hou*), designed to once and for all eliminate the ecological and cultural frontier that had stood as a barrier to full incorporation. Mines were opened, lands reclaimed, huge numbers of troops permanently stationed in the region, native *t'u-ssu* replaced by Chinese bureaucrats, administrative districts drawn and redrawn, walled cities built, transport and communications infrastructures laid out, and the regional economy effectively monetized.[3] This process both responded to and further precipitated a series of localized but very bloody "uprisings" (the term itself, of course, presumes the legitimacy of imperial purposes in the southwest), including a great rebellion centered on Ku-chou prefecture in Kweichow that was at its height precisely at the time of the school-building campaign in Yunnan.

The program of incorporation gathered momentum throughout the late K'ang-hsi reign but really took off with the accession in late 1722 of the incredibly able, vigorous, and expansion-minded Yung-cheng emperor. Ch'ing southwest policies after this date bore the unmistakable stamp of this remarkable ruler and the corps of energetic "new men," Chinese and Manchu, whom he recruited from outside the normal talent pools of the existing bureaucracy, the imperial clan, and Kiangnan literati networks. Most prominent among these was the highly sinicized Manchu soldier-bureaucrat Oerht'ai, but Yung-cheng's southwest task force also included a host of other men–Yin-chi-shan, Chang Kuang-ssu, Chang Yun-sui, E-mi-ta, Yen Ssu-sheng–who, though diverse in their outlooks and priorities, were all intensely devoted to the cause of imperial incorporation and willing to undertake bold measures to achieve its triumph.[4] For these men their tenure in the southwest was a chance to make their mark, and most, though suffering a setback when the Yung-cheng emperor died young and was succeeded by a different type of ruler, indeed went on to rank among the empire's senior statesmen in the decades to follow. Typical of this group was Ch'en Hung-mou, a supremely confident and ambitious native of frontier Kwangsi province, who had just been promoted from Yangchow Taotai to the critical post of Yunnan Provincial Treasurer. Ch'en set for himself the delicate task of spearheading the province's economic development, while shielding the indigenous peoples from the most vicious forms of Han Chinese exploitation.[5] Whether by assignment or personal initiative, it was also he who took on the task of implementing a Confucian school system in Yunnan. He did so with a degree of singleminded dedication that clearly astounded his contemporaries and effectively made his career.

The extension of empire into southwest China in the eighteenth century involved for Ch'ing officials above all a process of "moral transformation" (*hua*) of the indigenous population, and the goal of school building was one of "transformation via education" (*chiao-hua*). Among the most ancient and pregnant concepts in Confucian discourse, *hua* in the eighteenth century was decidedly a transitive verb; though an introspective moralist such as Ch'en Hung-mou might have been concerned to transform his own temperament through constant study, transformation was far more commonly something done *by* someone *to* someone else.[6] Ch'en wrote repeatedly throughout his career of his duty to "transform the people and perfect local customs" (*hua-min ch'eng-su*) and described the cardinal task of the official as that of "transforming and guiding" (*hua-tao*) the local populace. Though Ch'en tended to weight *hua* equally with *yang* ("nourishing" the people's material needs), in the Yung-cheng reign moral transformation was more often seen as an instrument of control. Ch'en himself at times rhetorically paired "transforming the people" with "extending imperial rule" (*chih-chih*) and wrote of the need to "regulate and transform" (*chih-hua*) by promoting adherence to Confucian social obligation and hierarchy.[7] His Manchu superiors somewhat more bluntly spoke of "governance by education" (*cheng-chiao*), and the emperor himself, who apparently shared few of the moral commitments of his officials, described Confucian education as "mind-washing and thought-cleansing" in the interests of rule.[8]

The goal of Ch'en and his colleagues of "transformation of localistic customs" (*ti-fang feng hua*) presupposed the universal applicability of Chinese social and religious values and the validity for all human society of what Alexander Woodside calls "Confucian uniformity."[9] In this respect, Chinese assumptions of a "civilizing mission" in the southwest differ little from those of Europeans in, for example, nineteenth-century Africa; indeed, in this as in other regards, the Chinese got there first.[10] And, though it lacked such specific elements of Christian imperialist dogma as the imperative to save heathen souls from eternal damnation or the perception of peripheral cultures as the work of Satan, in the right hands the Confucian civilizing mission was every bit as evangelical as its Western counterpart. Ch'en, for example, wrote privately of his duty to bring about "transformative salvation of individuals" (*hua-te i-jen*) and, later in the northwest, to combat Muslim violations of heavenly principle (*t'ien-li*).[11] For Ch'en, moreover, proselytization was clearly seen as one path to his own personal salvation.

A thornier question is that of the degree of ethnic diversity conceived of as allowable within the end-product "Confucian uniformity." Although Oerht'ai and Yin-chi-shan indicated that their goal was to bring southwestern cultural practices "in resonance with those of the center" (*hsieh yü chung*), the widely respected expert on the southwest Yang Shen (1488–1559) had already in the late Ming proposed a model of the Chinese empire as a multiethnic society within which different "peoples" (*min*) could live in moral and social harmony.[12] Racial homogeneity was clearly not a goal of Yung-cheng policy; in the first year of his reign, the emperor had in fact expressly prohibited Han-aborigine intermarriage in the southwest. (Some forty years later we find an elderly Ch'en Hung-mou memorializing the throne to have this prohibition lifted in order to speed the stalled process of incorporation.)[13] Curiously, too, the specific term for "assimilation" (*t'ung-hua*, or "uniformity-producing transformation") never appears in the discourse of educational expansion in Yunnan, though it certainly was available in the contemporary vocabulary.

Nevertheless, the Yung-cheng reign does appear to have been a unique period of universalist emphasis in imperial policy. Faced with an explicit challenge to the idea of Manchu rule in the would-be rebellion of Tseng Ching (1679–1736), the emperor had in 1730 made mandatory reading for all degree-holders his *Ta-i chüeh-mi lu* (Record of righteousness dispelling illusion), a remarkable marshaling of Confucian arguments in defense of the views that the empire and its people were unitary (*t'ien-hsia i-chia, wan-wu i-t'i*) and that ethnic distinctions were artificial and selfishly parochial.[14] This ecumenical drive, a matter both of the imperial sense of mission and of timely political urgency, may well have provided as great a stimulus to cultural initiatives in the southwest as did economic and military considerations.

From the standpoint of the Chinese elite, while Han racial chauvinism clearly provided an undercurrent to the rhetoric of Confucian universalism, it is worth keeping in mind that achievement of moral-cultural uniformity through *chiao-hua* was a persistent theme of Confucian reformers in dealing with folk traditions in Han areas themselves. James Watson and Prasenjit Duara have provided examples of how local deities were "standardized" and tidied up for inclusion in the official pantheon during periods of expanding state control, but the phenomenon went deeper still than this.[15] As the "local customs" chapters of county gazetteers and the reports of activist officials throughout China testify, the popular cultures of common people (*hsiao-min*) were routinely seen by their social betters as sanctioning wasteful, idle, and dissolute behavior. An official with a puritanical streak such as Ch'en Hung-mou would regularly attempt to legislate morality by limiting or banning production of tobacco and alcoholic beverages and performance of local opera. (The Confucian attack on "wasteful" local expenditures on theatrical performances in fact foreshadows the progressive reformist seizure of such funds for the founding of Western-style schools in the twentieth century.)[16] Throughout his career, Ch'en sought to regulate local opera by substituting more orthodox, exemplary librettos for those naturally evolved through the folk tradition.[17] Seen in this light, the process of coerced "civilization" in the southwest was less an assault on non-Han peoples *per se* than part of a larger process of elite assertion of cultural hegemony over commoner populations, Han and non-Han alike.

In the southwest, the Chinese confronted an enormous variety of indigenous peoples, who differed widely from each other in terms of racial stock, culture, religious systems, material civilization, and social and political organization.[18] All engaged in some hunting and gathering, but for most this had long become avocational or secondary to their main economic base, agriculture. Many practiced efficient swidden farming, but others were sedentary cultivators, some employing impressive irrigation systems. Most groups had a relatively sophisticated commercial economy, engaging in both commercial cropping and professional trading. Individually and collectively, the southwest tribes displayed incredible cultural richness in the visual arts, myth, ritual, and oral tradition. Some, like the Lolo and the Na-khi, had developed their own writing systems. Most of these peoples had been gradually pushed up and out from central China over millennia by the expanding Chinese civilization, to which in its formative phase they had in fact contributed many elements.[19]

The perception and depiction of these peoples during the Ch'ing was complex. On the one hand, one finds genuine attempts to comprehend them accurately and even sympathetically; on the other, there is a clearly discernable process of reducing them to a single, mythic "other," a homogeneous negative stereotype against which to contrast the dominant Confucian culture. Responsible Chinese and Manchus of the eighteenth century knew well that they were facing a vast array of diverse peoples; the local customs chapter of the 1736 Yunnan provincial gazetteer, for instance, painstakingly catalogs individual tribes in distinctive detail.[20] And yet, in popular and even official parlance a process had been underway since the Yuan progressively to collapse these peoples into the blanket category "Miao," or "Miao-man," a term the Chinese knew to refer properly to but a small segment of southwestern peoples. As Kweichow Provincial Treasurer E-mi-ta wrote around 1730, the Miao were in fact "not all of a single race" (*chung-lei pu-i*), yet they were all alike in being "primitive" (*sheng-hsing*), "barbarous" (*k'uang-han*), and "savage" (*yeh-wan*).[21] This set of terms recurs with great frequency in Ch'ing official descriptions of the tribes, as do characterizations such as stupid, lazy, weak of physique, listless of spirit, and wasteful of resources — characterizations that were routinely (though less categorically) applied as well to Han populations by development-minded officials and to non-Western peoples by expansionist Europeans.[22]

Although depictions of southwest peoples were universally patronizing, they were not always negative. Claudine Lombard-Salmon has documented a process of progressive "exoticization" of native peoples by Chinese literati travel writers of the Ming and early Ch'ing, a process not unlike the "orientalization" of Asian peoples by Europeans in the early modern era chronicled by Edward Said — by emphasizing their quaint picturesqueness, the peoples are rendered candidates for metropolitan domination.[23] A series of eighty-two paintings done by an eighteenth-century Chinese official in Kweichow thus portrays the natives in a manner that, to my eye, is hardly undignified but rather idyllic and romanticized; they remind one of nothing so much as the verbal portraits of the noble yet doomed savages of North America produced by James Fenimore Cooper.[24] Ch'en Hung-mou himself, a self-conscious man of the frontier who disparaged effete gentry refinements, wrote privately of his admiration for the "rustic virtue" (*ch'un-p'u*) of the southwest peoples, whose stoic self-reliance moved them to reject offers of imperial famine relief.[25] The cant of conquest indeed far more often portrayed the natives as sinned against than sinning, mercilessly exploited by their own headmen, Chinese merchants, and overzealous Ch'ing local bureaucrats, owing to their childlike naïveté. Wrote one expansionist Chinese official, "These people are as guileless as suckling pigs.... Their generous virtue is astonishing." [26]

Similarly complex were prevailing Chinese notions of who or what, in fact, the natives were. The sources of course abound with animal imagery — the debonair Manchu Yin-chi-shan (1696–1771), for instance, described the aborigines as "wriggling and wormlike" (*ch'un*) — but to what extent this represents literal views of such people as biologically subhuman is questionable. That they were held to be racially distinct from Han and Manchu is more likely, but the precise content of the operative Chinese notion of "race" (*chung-lei*) is by no means fully clear.[27] Most telling, and perhaps most widely shared, was the view that the aborigines represented some primeval stage of a unilinear path of human social evolution. Governor Chang Yun-sui, for example, wrote that Yunnan society still appeared "as it had at the dawn of creation."[28] A related notion, given prevalence by the ethnographic studies of the late Ming scholar Chiao Hung (1541–1620), was that aboriginal life offered an accurate picture of how the Chinese themselves had lived in the distant past (indeed, the actual contributions of these groups to the composite Chinese culture must have provided ample evidence for such a view).[29] This of course, in contrast to the view of the southwest peoples as a separate race or species, clearly implied that they were *educable*. As Ch'en Hung-mou wrote, "Han and non-Han are similarly flesh-and-blood. There is no ethnic peculiarity that cannot be overcome."[30]

In sum, the linguistic and imagistic repertoire of eighteenth-century Chinese and Manchus was replete with all the tools familiar from the history of European expansion into Asia, Africa, and the savage-infested New World.[31] All of these portrayals (and they differed according to the perspective and immediate designs of the observer) were alike in taking an instrumental view of the tribal "other." The savage was all that the Chinese (or European) was not —irrational, immoral, and unsophisticated—a contrasting image by which the observer sought to reinforce his own cultural superiority. But the savages also presented a threat, and not simply a military one. By their continuing existence, they constituted a real and present reminder of what civilized man had once been and might become again. As Yin-chi-shan noted, "If savages cherish learning, they may advance to become Han; if Han people neglect learning, they may degenerate into savages."[32] And the historical reality of centuries had been, Ch'ing officials knew well, that far more Chinese had acculturated to aboriginal life than aborigines to Chinese civilization. Even more basically, the existence of these contrasting life-styles raised an implication of cultural relativism, a profound threat to the universalist claims on which rested the very legitimacy of Confucian civilization.

What particular cultural traits of the indigenous peoples most urgently demanded rectification? One was the level of violence in native society. Headhunting and cannibalism were practiced by some groups, but rather few; more troubling were the facts that aborigines routinely carried and used weapons and that aboriginal justice was based on codes of vengeance. During the K'ang-hsi reign, Ch'ing officials had sought to legislate against blood feuds in the southwest and had carried out a massive sword hunt in 1726. In part, the motive was simply a practical prelude to conquest, but the campaign was couched in terms that unquestionably reveal a more deep-seated repulsion against challenges to Confucian standards of rational human conduct. Related to this was the attack on local religious practices, some of which, such as belief in malevolent blood-sucking ghosts and the pervasive *ku*-poison cult, were certainly horrifying. Here too the Chinese assault was partly pragmatic (the undermining of priestly elites, the rechanneling of "wasteful" festival expenditures) but in greater part motivated by defense of basic Confucian sensibilities.

That this attack went beyond the merely utilitarian is shown by the vigorous attempt by Ch'ing authorities to institute Confucian ritual in the southwest. Not surprisingly, in light of the centrality of funerary ritual to Chinese civilization, Ch'en launched a largely successful effort to replace cremation or exposure of the dead by orthodox burial and ancestral sacrifice. More intriguing is his parallel effort to reform marriage practices and sexual morality, a compulsive drive that at times appears to have lain at the very heart of the Ch'ing expansionist effort. Like other expanding metropolitan civilizations, the Chinese found it convenient to denegrate peripheral cultures as sexually lax, and the Han conquest of southern China over two millennia had regularly featured the forced imposition of the patriarchal family and kinship system (*tsung-fa*).[33] But with the ascendance of the Chu Hsi school of Neo-Confucianism in the later dynasties, this imperialist urge had taken on a far deeper religious and psychological urgency. Chu's puritanical concern for sexual propriety, which identified civilization itself with a rigid functional and physical segregation by gender and interpreted the Confucian moral imperative of "shame" (*lien-ch'ih*) in a literal anatomical way, had been internalized by many eighteenth-century Confucian missionaries, none more profoundly than Ch'en Hung-mou himself.

One of the key criteria by which Ch'ing officials pigeonholed southwest peoples was by whether or not they "knew shame" (*chih-ch'ih*). Most, alas, did not.[34] Native dress was immodest, women enjoyed great sexual latitude, spring communal festivals offered sexual license to youth, and domestic units were maintained in an apparently casual fashion incomprehensible to the Chinese. (One pretext claimed for enforced culture change was compassionate concern to ensure adequate care for aboriginal offspring.)[35] Most appalling was the fact that many (by no means all) southwest peoples adhered to a matrilineal and matrilocal social order, within which women enjoyed explicit social and economic dominance. Ch'ing officials went about altering this in many ways. They attempted to impose Chinese-style costume to clothe the native's nakedness. They introduced the use of Chinese family names, inherited, along with property, through the male line. They mandated Confucian wedding ceremonies and paternally arranged child betrothal.[36] Ch'eng Hung-mou personally was at great pains to implant the Chinese virtuous widow cult (*chieh-hsiao*) and, as we shall see, placed instruction in familial virtues at the core of his elementary school curriculum.[37] It is of course possible to see pragmatic ends in this as well; Anthony Jackson, for instance, has suggested that flexible matriarchal systems gave some southwest peoples vehicles for broad communal mobilization to resist Chinese control and so had to be dismantled.[38] But there was more going on than this. The Ch'ing process of expansion into the southwest meant different things to different parties, to be sure, but for Ch'en and many others it was above all a process of reaffirmation of the "natural" social hierarchy that lay at the heart of their own Chineseness. The civilizing mission was at bottom one of "imposing order on chaos.[39]

At the same time, kinship reform was seen as a prerequisite to economic development. The male-headed domestic unit, the practice of sedentary agriculture, and the institution of private (household) property were inextricably linked in a version of agrarian idealism not all that different from that of the Lockean West. In this view, "Man achieved his highest humanity by taking something out of nature and converting it with his labor into part of himself. His private property, conceived in terms of the close, personal relationships of an agrarian society, was his means to social maturity. It gave him stability, self-respect ... and the basis for civilized society itself."[40] Household proprietorship of agricultural land, in China as in the West, was "one of the central notions in the organization of social life" and private landownership "one of the major positive values in the the culture."[41] Proprietorship by the domestic unit brought with it economic stability (*heng-yeh*) and social responsibility, as well as providing the key stimulus to hard work, efficiency, and hence greater productivity. It allowed the introduction of new agrarian technologies that might turn the southwest into an area of agricultural surplus, at least in certain commodities.[42] From the state's point of view, moreover, household proprietorship was basic to Chinese civil law (and thus the shift from tribal to imperial justice) and to fiscal accountability. It also was expected to give rise to an indigenous propertied elite who, given the educational opportunities offered by the new school system, would become the backbone of the new social order.

These cherished myths and fond hopes united policymakers in Yunnan whose goals ranged from the idealistic to the utilitarian. In many cases, they were based on misperceptions, for example of the degree of sedentary agriculture already practiced by Yunnan natives or of the greater efficiency of the alternative production systems local peoples had worked out for themselves over centuries of interaction with their environment. But the transformation of that environment by introduction of the Chinese-style family and of private landholding were hoped to prove irreversible, consolidating the process of Han expansion once and for all.

From the 1380s on, the Ming had announced the establishment of Confucian schools as a cornerstone of its southwest policy, and energetic local officials had periodically launched pilot projects at various points along the aboriginal pale. By one count, Yunnan as a whole saw some seventy-two prefectural and county

TABLE 12.1   Local Schools Established in Yunnan, 1644–1737

Period	No.	Yearly Average
Before 1704	10	0.17
Late K'ang-hsi reign (1704–22)	91	4.79
Early Yung-cheng reign (1723–32)	82	8.20
Ch'en Hung-mou's tenure (1733–37)	465	93.00
Total	648	

SOURCES: *Yun-nan t'ung-chih* (1736), 7:43–60; *Ch'üan-T'ien i-hsueh hui-chi* (1738).

schools, as well as some thirty-three private academies, founded during the Ming period; no more than a fifth of these survived into the Ch'ing.[43] Although the Manchus paid lip service to continuing this Ming initiative from the early years of their rule, it was only in the eighteenth century that serious efforts at school founding in aboriginal areas began, first in Kweichow in 1704–05, then in Ch'en Hung-mou's home province of Kwangsi in 1720.[44] Under Yung-cheng the program was accelerated. Edicts of 1725 ordered the establishment of schools in every county of Yunnan and Kweichow, and later edicts extended this to non-Han areas of Szechwan, Hunan, and Kwangtung. In 1727, an intensive school-founding program was launched by Ortai in Yunnan's Tung-ch'uan prefecture coinciding with abolition of the local headman system there, and a broader project in Kweichow was undertaken by Yin-chi-shan in 1733.[45] The timing of school foundings in Yunnan itself during the Ch'ing's first century (table 12.1) shows clearly that the specific drive undertaken by Ch'en Hung-mou was essentially the culmination of a longer trend, but was wholly unprecedented in its magnitude.

Intimately related to the fits and starts of this school-founding program in the southwest and elsewhere was a protracted debate over nomenclature and, by extension, over the desired character of local educational institutions. The term *i-hsueh* (public, or free, school) was itself new to the Ch'ing, though the type of institution it described was not. Apparently first used in the name of a prefecturally founded secondary school outside Peking in 1701, the term was picked up by the K'ang-hsi emperor in his edict ordering school foundings in Kweichow in 1704 and throughout the empire in 1712.[46] With Yung-cheng's strong endorsement, it became the prevailing term for local schools of the high Ch'ing era.

I-hsueh were something of a compromise between two polar models for local schools available in the late imperial educational repertoire: on the one hand, fully bureaucratic prefectural and county schools (*fu-hsueh*, *hsien-hsueh*) and on the other fully private academies (*shu-yuan*). The former had been the major

instrument in the Ming effort to win the hearts and minds of southwest aborigines and, moreover, had been mandated in every administrative division of
the empire at the founding of the Ch'ing. But their inadequacies were already
obvious by the start of the eighteenth century. Prefectural and county schools
were the most notorious examples of the pervasive trend in late imperial education in which institutions initially created to foster genuine scholarship
gradually fell captive to the narrower dictates of "prepping" for the civil service
examinations, with their initiative as centers of genuine learning eventually
passing to other types of organizations.[47] In the case of *fu-hsueh* and *hsien-hsueh*,
this process had in fact gone one step further so that even their role as examination prep schools had been largely lost, leaving them with a largely ceremonial role in local society but no effective pedagogical function. Thus, when
Ortai began his model school-founding program in Tung-ch'uan in 1727, he
augmented the mandatory prefectural schools with a novel system of *i-hsueh* to
which the tasks of genuine education were entrusted. In Ch'en Hung-mou's
more comprehensive program of the 1730s, the vocabulary of *fu-hsueh* and
hsien-hsueh was dispensed with altogether and even existing prefectural and
county schools were rechristened *i-hsueh*.

Private academies (*shu-yuan*) were of course held in great suspicion by the
early Manchu court as a result of their incendiary role during the last decades
of the Ming. In 1652, the Ch'ing prohibited the founding of new academies and
imposed strict bureaucratic controls on those that survived. In 1723, the
Yung-cheng emperor ordered that all existing *shu-yuan* be renamed *i-hsueh* and
brought under the guidelines for management as such established by his predecessor. Thus, whereas the establishment of private academies had been an
important component of the Ming assimilationist drive in the southwest—having been championed there by no less a figure than Wang Yang-ming (1472–
1529)—they played no comparable role under the Ch'ing. Although the
Yung—cheng emperor opted once again to allow use of the term *shu-yuan* in
1730 and Governor General Ortai had actually established a Yunnan provincial *shu-yuan* at Kunming prior to Ch'en Hung-mou's arrvial, the schools so described bore little relationship to their Ming namesakes. By imperial mandate,
Ch'ing *shu-yuan* followed the earlier experience of prefectural and county
schools: bureaucratization of management, formalization of curricula, and
gradual emasculation as centers of independent scholarly inquiry.[48]

But there was a third, intermediate model of local school in the Ch'ing repertoire, one that bore the special sanctity of association with both the Manchu
court's and Ch'en Hung-mou's Neo-Confucian of choice, Chu Hsi. This was the
so-called "community school" (*she-hsueh*), an institution of primary learning
theoretically established and funded neither by the state nor by private
scholars but by "the people" themselves—by the subcounty local community.
(See Leung for an extensive discussion of this type of school.) Why, given this
exalted pedigree and the hallowed aura that Ch'en throughout his career

attached to local community self-help, was this nomenclature not adopted in Yunnan? It very nearly was. *She-hsueh* had been set up in some aboriginal areas during the Ming and had received strong endorsement from the early Manchu court. As early as 1652, the Shun-chih emperor had called for *she-hsueh* in each county subdistrict (*hsiang*), and it was the reiteration of this edict by the Yung-cheng emperor in 1723–24 that was explicitly cited by Ch'en Hung-mou as his mandate for local school founding.[49] In the Ch'ing official formula, community schools were to be managed by local gentry under the supervision of the centrally appointed county director of studies but were to be free from interference by county subbureaucratic functionaries. They were also to be independent of direct state support, instead financed out of local community contributions and endowments.

But there were problems with the *she-hsueh* model noted by the court itself in an edict of 1685 and by literati reformers throughout the late imperial era. In his pedagogical sourcebook, the *Yang-cheng i-kuei*, Ch'en himself cited the late Ming Kiangnan gentry activist Lü K'un's (1536–1618) critique that so-called community schools too often ignored their rationale of providing "socially useful childhood education" for all local students, devolving instead into examination prep schools for the wealthy or into elitist havens for literati cliques. In settling on *i-hsueh* rather than *she-hsueh* as the term for their new Yunnan schools, then, it seems that Ch'en and his superiors were attempting to draw upon the community-sponsorship elements of the *she-hsueh* tradition but emphasizing more fully than had Chu Hsi or Lü K'un the elements of standardization, orthodoxy, and equalization of opportunity, all under close state supervision.[50]

In other words, the goal in Yunnan was no less than a state-sponsored system of universal male childhood education. Both the Yung-cheng emperor in his call for community schools and provincial authorities in their specific program of *i-hsueh* in Yunnan repeatedly invoked the example of the hallowed *tang-hsiang* system of antiquity, which they conceived in just such a way, nostalgically recalling an age when "no locality was without its school, and no child did not attend."[51]

Embedded in this ideal were two crucial assumptions: that all children were in some measure educable and that it was at least in part the duty of the state to educate them. The assumption of universal educability for late imperial pedagogues involved less a question of innate intelligence than one of innate moral sense. Unlike educators in early modern Europe, with whom they shared a view that children could and should be systematically influenced to do good, Chinese educational theorists had no ground for debate on the basic moral nature of the child.[52] While they differed over the *degree* of educability of different children, the view of the innate goodness and rationality (*liang-chih*) of every human being was, for Confucians, a cardinal item of faith. In both his public utterances and his private correspondence, however, Ch'en Hung-mou repeatedly voiced an unusually impassioned and literal belief that "all men are basically good" (*jen-hsing hsi shan*), that this goodness could never be completely expunged through experience, and that it could be developed or regenerated through careful instruction.[53] Occasionally, he even seems to approach the position, heretical in Christian Europe, of the natural innocence of the child: "Water from mountain streams is perfectly clear, but as it flows down the mountain it becomes muddy and turgid ... However, proceeding through [proper training] children can be brought to reach adulthood while retaining the clarity that the water possessed at its source."[54] Moreover, he made it abundantly plain to his subordinates that this vision of human nature applied to aborigines as well as Han: "I will never entertain such excuses [for foot-dragging] as 'savages will always be savages.'"[55]

Thus, in common with long imperial precedent and with Protestant reformers in early modern Europe, Ch'en held that "mass literacy training" (*kuang-hsing chiao-tu*) was a basic state responsibility.[56] He argued that moral education without a determined effort at universal application was meaningless and concluded that only the state was equipped for this task. Despite his affection for the operation of the market in other areas of activity, for example, he cited the much greater sales of examination cribbooks than of classical texts as evidence of the futility of entrusting popular enlightenment to market forces.[57] In keeping with his deep faith in local societal self-help, he tended to place considerably more emphasis than did his bureaucratic superiors on the supplementary role of household, lineage, and village-community instruction yet argued that offspring of poor or illiterate parents (not to say non-Han peoples) were entitled to state-sponsored education to compensate for what their family and community were incapable of providing.[58] As we shall see, Ch'en placed the burden of this state responsibility squarely on the shoulders of the county magistrate, the lowest rung in the administrative hierarchy. This strategy was not merely pragmatic but was part of a general conception of how to achieve the cultural and political integration of the empire. In the neat formulation of Ch'en's patron, Yin-chi-shan, officially sponsored community schools would simultaneously manifest the principles of "local community self-help", and of "linking the localities with the central state."[59]

Ch'en Hung-mou approached the promotion of the Confucian education in Yunnan in the radically systematic way that was to become a hallmark of his managerial style throughout his long career. The twin anxieties that underlay this approach—well-founded anxieties that were shared by many another Chinese bureaucrat—were that procedures he initiated would be implemented on paper only (*yu-ming wu-shih*) and that they would not survive his own transfer to another post. One key tactic he employed to ensure substance and permanence was the compilation of comprehensive casebooks or registers (*an-ts'e*) that were to include incredibly detailed information about each local institution of a given type, provincewide. The surviving casebook on Yunnan local schools, the *Ch'üan-T'ien i-hsueh hui-chi*, published under Yin-chi-shan's auspices in 1738 and offering data on the location, management, financing, operation, and facilities of each one of Yunnan's local schools, provides a good example of Ch'en's style but in fact comprises only a small fraction of the massive amount of information he accumulated and filed on school matters.[60] His technique was essentially to lay the burden of activism on subordinate local officials and then, through a series of progressively more detailed surveys and questionnaires, to make them increasingly uneasy about discovery and consequences of their noncompliance.

At the time of Ch'en's arrival in Yunnan, nearly two hundred local schools were formally in operation, but his initial investigations revealed that the great majority of these were in practice defunct. Thus, in the spring of 1734 he ordered all local officials to report on actual conditions in the existing schools, as well as to suggest likely locations and means of support for new ones. He met with a chorus of prevarications from local bureaucrats who had no doubt heard similar calls before and were yet to be persuaded of the seriousness of the new provincial treasurer's intent. Lining up the support of his administrative superiors, Ch'en came back to the local officials in ever more threatening terms repeatedly during the next three years. At the time of Ch'en's tenure, Yunnan had about one hundred administrative districts (counties, departments, independent prefectures, military commanderies). His initial plan envisioned one *i-hsueh* in each of the four wards (*hsiang*) of each district, in addition to one in the district seat. The actual final total of nearly seven hundred schools with a combined student body of over twenty thousand, the sponsorship of nearly all of which was credited to local officials, suggests that Ch'en eventually succeeded in conveying his seriousness to the point that enthusiasm for the campaign at the local official level outran its initial aims.[61]

The most distinctive feature of Ch'en's *i-hsueh* foundings in Yunnan, apart from sheer numbers, was their location. Imperial orders for school establishment had of course long specified that schools be outside as well as inside of major urban areas, but this directive had rarely been followed. Ch'en noted that on his arrival *i-hsueh* were disproportionately bunched in the provincial capital and the most developed, Han-dominated counties. Within counties, they were almost exclusively to be found within or just outside the county seat (what Lombard-Salmon not inappropriately terms *villes de colons*). Ch'en set out not only to correct this imbalance but to reverse it. With his own frontier background and deeply ingrained anti-literati bias, he argued that government schools in urban areas primarily served the interests of "accomplished scholars" (*ch'eng-ts'ai*), in other words precisely those who were least in need of state-supported education. His stress was on founding schools in "rural" (*hsiang-ts'un*) and "peripheral" (*pien-fang*) locales, his goal one of in situ education, so that "no one would be too remote to be within reach of a teacher."[62]

TABLE 12.2   Yunnan *I-hsueh* and Population Density
by Prefecture

Prefecture	No. of I-hsueh (1736)	Population Density/km² (1775)
Yun-nan	102	62
Ch'u-ching	56	18
Lin-an	51	9
Ch'u-hsiung	49	10
Ta-li	45	26
Ch'eng-chiang	30	65
Chen-yuan	26	12
Kuang-hsi	25	6
Wu-ting	25	10
Chao-tung	24	16
Ching-tung	16	4
K'ai-hua	12	11
P'u-erh	12	—
Hsun-ning	12	2
Yung-ning	12	7
Yuan-chiang	11	7
Kuang-nan	9	4
Tung-ch'uan	9	16
Meng-hua	7	21
Yung-pei	5	3
Li-chiang	4	—

SOURCES: For *i-hsueh*, *Yun-nan t'ung-chih* (1736), 7:43–60. For population density, James Lee, "Food Supply and Population Growth in Southwest China, 1250–1850," *Journal of Asian Studies* 41, no. 4 (Aug. 1982), 730.

Table 12.2, which correlates by prefecture the number of Yunnan *i-hsueh* as of 1736 with population density as of 1775, indicates the degree to which Ch'en was faithful to his goal of avoiding concentration in metropolitan districts.

Because of the time difference in these two sets of data, what they tell us can be no more than suggestive. Yet the relatively low degree of correlation (coefficient = .612) makes it fairly clear that Ch'en did successfully avoid, and likely reversed, the trend toward metropolitan concentration of local schools.

Similarly, *within* districts Ch'en's newly founded *i-hsueh* lay overwhelmingly outside the county seat, usually being housed in a temple commandeered for the purpose at some crossroads, village, or rural market. For example, in K'un-ming county three schools predated Ch'en's arrival, all located in the county seat; eighteen more were established during his tenure, all in rural temples. In Ch'eng-kung county, the one preexisting school was likewise in the district city, and the additional seven set up under Ch'en were all rural. In remote Yung-pei district, where no schools had existed before, the seven set up under Ch'en all lay in aboriginal areas; the first school in the county seat did not appear until ten years after Ch'en left the province, in 1747.[63]

The most daunting problem facing Ch'en Hung-mou and other school founders in Yunnan was naturally that of financing. The problem was essentially that of funding *operations*, since Yung-cheng era officials (much like their successors in the twentieth century) found it expedient to appropriate for their "transformative" purposes temples built originally by local people for "superstitious" ends. Where such facilities were not available, a grant of property could usually be elicited from a member of the local elite. Thus, the costs with which the founders needed most to be concerned were above all teachers' salaries, though occasionally a small amount was also set aside for stationery or for maintenance and custodial fees. Stipends for *i-hsueh* students were explicitly prohibited by imperial edict.[64]

Budgets for *i-hsueh* operations in Yunnan as elsewhere were considered part of the "public" sphere (*kung*) rather than the private (*ssu*) or official (*kuan*, that is, financed out of formal tax revenues or state appropriations). As with dike maintenance and many other areas of local activism, "public" management of local schools meant that operational responsibility and proprietorship of facilities and endowment trusts (usually but not always agricultural land) were vested in a more-or-less hazily defined local community with more-or-less indirect local official oversight. One of Ch'en Hung-mou's considerable triumphs is that his school-founding program could be completed in Yunnan without drawing directly on land tax revenues, despite the province's great poverty and although such funds later had to be authorized for local schools in tribal areas of Kweichow (1737) and Hunan (1745).[65] The difficulty of maintaining public/community properties free, on the one hand, from private encroachment (*ch'in-yin*), and, on the other, from subbureaucratic engrossment (*chung-pao*) was arguably the single most vexing task facing late imperial field administrators and in the strife-torn southwest was even more difficult than elsewhere. Ch'en immediately discovered that .endowments for previously

founded local schools had in most cases long slipped out of public accountability, and he assumed as a major task the recovery of this property and the
prevention of similar endowment erosion in the future.

He began by ordering local officials to submit detailed budgets for each projected school, specifying in each case from where the revenue was to come. The
wide range of options he suggested for producing endowments creatively
expanded the normal repertoire of means local officials had available for such
purposes. Among them were: (1) use of *kung-ch'ien* or *kung-hsiang*, a local budget
item derived usually from past tax surpluses and retained by magistrates for
repair of city walls and related needs; (2) use of customary fees (*lou-kuei*), the
illegal but often routinized local revenue source on which the actual business of
local government depended; (3) rental income from landed estates attached to
particular bureaucratic posts (*kuan-chuang*); (4) revenue commandeered from
land previously reclaimed by pioneer settlers but hitherto concealed from the
tax collector (*ying-k'en*); (5) income from land newly reclaimed with the use of
official seed money; (6) contributions solicited from the local elite; and (7) surplus proceeds diverted from endowments for other local schools. Ch'en then
evaluated each local official's report and, after singling out several of them for
lack of energy in coming up with funding, he divided Yunnan counties into two
groups based on whether or not they could be expected to finance the requisite
schools out of local resources.[66] To help out those counties with genuinely inadequate resources, he distributed the substantial total of 1252 taels from his
own supplemental salary (*yang-lien*); following this broad hint, many of his
subordinates made similar contributions.[67] Ch'en also recorded his hope that,
in the future, endowments for these schools would be augmented by
contributions from successful alumni.

A better sense of complexities of this system in practice may be gathered
from looking at a few specific cases:

K'un-ming county. In this metropolitan area, seven *i-hsueh* jointly established
by the prefect and magistrate in 1735, along with one founded earlier by local
gentry, were funded out of a collective endowment. This endowment had been
built up in increments, including a large parcel of 919 *mu* donated by the prefect in 1690 (recovered and remeasured under Ch'en's administration at 639
mu), plus smaller amounts contributed in later years by the prefect and by two
local gentrymen. The total revenue after taxes came to 171.8 *tan* of rice, 3.8 *tan*
of which paid for caretakers (for the urban *i-hsueh* only) and the remaining 168
divided into teachers' salaries, paid in grain. Three other *i-hsueh* were set up in
1736 and financed out of a separate endowment contributed by Ch'en
Hung-mou himself. Ch'en's provincial treasurer's office had a landed estate attached, which on his arrival commanded a rent in kind said to be very high.
Ch'en reduced the rent, commuted it to cash, and divided this to cover
teachers' salaries for the three schools.[68]

Ch'eng-kung county. Teachers' salaries for three *i-hsueh* founded by the magistrate in 1734 and for one older school were paid out of a common endowment, including the following: 124 *mu* of land donated long ago to the county by the local military detachment (*tso-wei*), documentation of which had been "recently unearthed" by the magistrate; a parcel of official land (*kuan-ti*) suddenly "turned up" by the magistrate in 1734; taxes from a parcel of land newly reclaimed by the magistrate and rents from another parcel purchased by his contribution; paddy land purchased in 1735 out of a 100-tael contribution by Ch'en Hung-mou and a 40-tael contribution by the magistrate. Four more schools, set up in 1735, were financed by rents from a large piece of seacoast land "discovered" by the magistrate, who recruited tenants, distributed seeds, and remitted taxes on it for perpetuity.[69]

Pao-ning county. Five *i-hsueh* founded by local officials in 1734, plus four earlier ones, were funded out of the following endowment: a 200-tael contribution from Ch'en and a 40-tael allocation from county funds, together used to buy a parcel of rural land; a parcel of land involved in a lawsuit between two county residents and subsequently awarded by the magistrate to the *i-hsueh*; a six-room structure in the county seat contributed by a merchant — three rooms used to house *i-hsueh* students and three rented out for income; and rental income from a large urban copper warehouse.[70]

Yung-pei department. In this peripheral district, seven schools founded variously by the prefect, magistrate, and local native headmen were funded collectively out of an endowment created by a subvention of 302.5 *tan* of rice per year from the prefect's official estate and a parcel of paddy land yielding 28.1 *tan* per year contributed by an aboriginal chief.[71]

From these examples one gets a sense of the flexible arrangements settled on by local officials to satisfy the provincial demand for schools. Sources of endowments included contributions exacted from officials, military, local landholders, sojourning merchants, and native leaders as well as newly reclaimed land, the spoils of lawsuits, and properties variously "rediscovered" by officials as lying in the public domain. Ogawa Yoshiko's conclusion that *i-hsueh* empirewide were overwhelmingly the bequest of lower gentry members who managed their assets in the name of the local community but actually in their own interest thus seems too simplified to explain the case of eighteenth-century Yunnan.[72] Also seen here are the creative use of what Ch'en Hung-mou called the "job-lot system" (*ling-hsing*), with each school supported by a variety of income-producing properties and each property often contributing to several schools.

Under these complex conditions and in order to prevent the sort of endowment attrition that had characterized Yunnan schools in the past, Ch'en instituted new managerial procedures. Collection and disbursement of endowment income were now entrusted directly to the local magistrate rather than left to the teachers themselves or to local school boards, as before. There was to be careful auditing of accounts on official succession, subbureaucratic clerks were to be kept entirely out of the process (Ch'en stipulated that physical collection of endowment rents be conducted by village headmen rather than county functionaries), and the integrity of the *i-hsueh* budget line in county finances was to be tightly maintained (magistrates were cautioned in particular against borrowing from school endowments to make up local land tax shortfalls). Details of each school's property holdings and budget were to be made publicly available in the magistrate's office, kept up to date, and reported to the provincial treasurer's office on a regular basis. They were published for all to see not only in Ch'en's local school casebook but also in the more widely distributed provincial gazetteer. Eventually, Ch'en's new program for regularizing local school finances was adopted as the basis of an empire-wide clean-up campaign launched by the Ch'ien-lung emperor shortly upon his accession to the throne.[73]

How did the complex of Ch'ing goals and fears in the southwest combine to shape curricula in Ch'en's Yunnan *i-hsueh*? Didn't it make sense, for example, to impart to natives via state schools the technical skills they could use to become more economically productive? We have already suggested that in the Yung-cheng emperor's China, as in Victoria's England, the attempt to enforce culture change in peripheral or colonial areas was tied in with a desire to better enable these areas to produce goods for export, to facilitate a trade with metropolitan areas that, in theory at least, would be mutually profitable to both.[74] In the case of Southwest China, a parallel concern was to improve the peripheral region's economy for purposes of fiscal extraction. Ch'en himself was very much concerned during his tenure in Yunnan with introducing new crops and new techniques, in part through a system of officially recognized "model farmers." And yet, remarkably, the notion of using local schools themselves as a vehicle for vocational education seems never to have entered the policy debate.

Instead, the end of primary education in Yunnan was seen very narrowly as, in the words of Ch'en's late Ming model Lü K'un, bringing about "the understanding of moral principles through familiarization with Chinese characters" (*shih-tzu ming-li*).[75] It is worth stressing that literacy was deemed essential *not* out of any modern notion that operating in a literate world made reading skills a practical necessity but rather as a means of acquisition of cultural values.[76] But was there not a fear that too broad a diffusion of classical learning would produce an overabundance of intellectuals and a corresponding shortage of manual labor? I have not seen any articulation in the 1730s of this argument — a common one among European conservatives of that era — but one can infer from Ch'en's various defenses of his program that anxieties on this score had indeed surfaced. He notes, for example, that "it is hardly necessary that the offspring of every peasant should all become examination degree-holders!"[77]

And, as we shall see, a certain tracking mechanism was built into his fully developed educational system. This was both a response to differing human potentials and a matter of practical social need: "Gradually, the literati elite will be able to devote themselves to refined and profound scholarship, while at the same time the doltish masses will be indoctrinated into etiquette and proper behavior."[78] Very characteristically, in Ch'en's scheme it is not that the commoners are given technical training while the elite are granted the opportunity for reflective thought but more nearly the reverse: *all* students are to be trained in ethics and social ritual, but only the more talented progress to study of the technocratic skills associated with the art of governance.[79]

Ch'en's insistence on mass literacy training faced other criticism as well. Although he clearly preferred not to argue in such terms, when pressed Ch'en admitted the utilitarian role of school founding in the broader program of the "pacification of savages" (*fu-i*); literacy training in particular was to enable the aborigines to "transform their barbarous and savage ways."[80] But if the Chinese written language was the marvelously effective enabling instrument that all deeply believed it to be, was it really wise to share it with peoples with whom imperial forces had been constantly at war? This concern was apparently so pervasive that midway through his program Ch'en felt obliged to respond to it in some detail:

> There are those who argue that the savages are crafty and vicious and that compelling them to become literate can only increase their capacity for treachery. Alas! I have always heard that loyalty and fidelity are the best armor and rites and propriety the best weapons, but never that literacy is a provocation to war! If indeed literacy is a tool for devious and self-serving behavior, does it not follow that it should be withheld from Chinese people as well? ... Moreover, the savages who are now in rebellion — are they so because of their exposure to literacy? This argument for keeping the world ignorant and deluding the people is counter to the principles of benevolence and propriety. One is morally bound [as a Confucian] to refute it.[81]

A related question concerned the few aboriginal youths who exhibited great ability in their new educational environment. In late imperial China, education was conventionally seen as serving a dual purpose: moral transformation of the populace and harvesting of the most talented for service of the state. Every official involved in educational development in the southwest professed commitment to the second half of this equation as well as the first, but it is questionable to what extent any of them, including the relatively rustic Ch'en Hung-mou himself, truly believed that this "barbaric and malarial place" (as Ch'en put it) might prove a fertile recruiting ground for great ministers of state. The important thing, at least for Ch'en, was to grant integrity in practice to the Confucian ideal of the universal *search* for talent as well as the principle of ethnic equality of opportunity, that is, of selection of talent "without regard to Han or non-Han origin" (*pu-lun Han-i*).[82] In practical terms, the goal of promoting upward mobility via schooling among the tribesmen was to spawn an elite whose members would return to their native places and serve as role models for other aboriginal youth. The likelihood of creating an educated native elite whose identity and allegiance was still to the ethnic community rather than the empire did not trouble Ch'en Hung-mou, though it may well have occurred to some of his critics. In his mental universe, such conduct for a Confucial scholar, of any ethnic origin, was simply outside the realm of possibility.

Ch'en envisioned Yunnan's school system as a three-tier graded hierarchy. Novice students (*meng-t'ung*) began at the *hsiang*-level rural schools, the more promising advanced to the higher-level *i-hsueh* at the county seat, and the truly gifted were selected for the Provincial Academy (*shu-yuan*) at Kunming, from which they might eventually be promoted further to the Imperial College at Peking. Effectively, students were divided into those deemed suitable merely for general education and those worthy of training for a professional career (*i-yeh*) as scholar-officials. An elaborate monitoring system was set up to determine into which track a student fell and the proper timing of his promotion to a higher-lever school. Here again, the state's role was to overcome the drag of social and economic background on the emergence of true talent; an elaborate system of scholarships was established to allow poor but promising students to attend higher-level schools away from their home areas.[83]

The bulk of Ch'en's attention was concentrated on the lowest-level schools in keeping with his oft-repeated view that nurturing the virtue (*yang-cheng*) of the untaught child was the most sacred task of education. Unlike earlier projects in the southwest, which had concentrated on Confucianizing the sons of tribal chiefs, Ch'en's goal was that *all* local children attend school. While falling short of legislating mandatory school attendance, he ordered that native leaders who obstructed local children from attending be criminally punished and that county officials diligently pursue any means by which the greatest number of local children might be enticed and assisted to attend. At the same time, he adopted an approach that may be described as one of affirmative action in favor of aboriginal students. Employing a parallelism deeply revealing of his thought, Ch'en argued that just as children were more needful of education than adults so too were aborigines more needful than Han Chinese. He accordingly ordered schoolmasters to include in their year-end reports percentages of aborigines versus Han attending each local school and information of the relative progress of students in each group.[84] In the 1720s, special "Miao-Yao" civil service examinations had been instituted throughout Southwest China, and special quotas for passes on regular examinations were established for non-Han peoples in Kweichow in 1734.[85] Ch'en himself seems to have eschewed such transparently patronizing policies, but he did everything possible to guarantee that minority groups would be able to compete for regular civil service degrees on a favorable basis. For example, he prohibited outright the selection of recent Han immigrants for study at the Provincial Academy, and he ordered a crackdown on the practice of Han students changing their legal registration to predominantly aboriginal prefectures in order to compete more favorably for the general quota of examination passes allotted to those areas.[86]

Ch'en's Yunnan schools were primarily intended for children. Although the Yung-cheng emperor in 1723 had identified the target age group for local schooling as boys of twelve to twenty *sui* (eleven to nineteen years of age by Western reckoning), Ch'en himself favored recruiting students of eight *sui* or even younger. This had been the age advocated by Chu Hsi, Lü K'un, and Ch'eng Wei-ch'i, the Yuan dynasty pedagogue whose work had been resurrected by the early Ch'ing champion of Chu Hsi orthodoxy Lu Lung-ch'i (1630–93) and was reprinted by Ch'en himself in 1742.[87] In part because of the tender age of these students and in part out of a deep personal faith in the social utility of ritual, Ch'en devoted a major part of his schools' curriculum to instruction in etiquette and ceremony. He wrote that the students, in addition to literary education, be "trained in the ritual forms of courtesy and deference and the cardinal principles of respectful obedience to the sovereign and to their seniors." Twice a month the teacher led his pupils to worship at the local Confucian temple, where they paid obeisance first to the sage and then to their teacher, and then respectfully greeted each other. Following this, in a rite of bonding with the local community and the imperial state, they were joined by village elders to stand in a circle and hear a local gentry member recite the Sacred Edict.[88]

Ritual practice was a powerful symbolic vehicle on many levels in imperial China. It was on the one hand a visible manifestation of subservience to authority and, as James Watson has recently argued, through standarized practice perhaps the single most important common denominator holding the empire together. It was even more basically an affirmation of one's character as a man (*tso-jen*) and as a properly socialized member of the human community.[89] The most mundane details of human conduct were subject to ritualization. In one of Ch'en Hung-mou's favorite essays of Chu Hsi, "What the Children Ought to Know" (*T'ung-meng hsu-chih*), the latter had written, "The child should first be taught how to put on his clothes, cap, and shoes; then how to speak, walk, and run; and later how to sprinkle, sweep, and clean; and afterwards how to study, write, and other, even the minutist details of what a child should do." On this Ch'en commented, "The novice should start with what can be known and done easily ... beginning with what is necessary for daily life ... in such a way as to avoid corruption of his spirit and to nourish his virtuous nature." Following Chu Hsi's precepts, Ch'en's students were to be repetitively practiced in the forms of personal cleanliness, frugality, decorum, and scholarship: "Everyone should first make his personal appearance correct and proper.... When your clothes are disheveled, your body will be slovenly and ungraceful and you will not command the respect of people." "All clothes which you put on in the daytime should be changed when you go to sleep at night; then the fleas and lice cannot hide in them and they will not be worn out before their time." "Walk slowly, speak quietly." "Whenever you study, you should arrange the things on your table or desk, making them clean, neat, and orderly. Then arrange your book properly, adjust your body, and face the book. Carefully and slowly look at the characters; heedfully and clearly read them out. Read each character loudly and distinctly. Do not read incorrectly; do not miss one; do not add one; do not turn them upside down — no, not even one character."[90]

The language of instruction in Yunnan *i-hsueh* was Chinese, with a standard Mandarin pronunciation (*kuan-yü*). Although Ch'en Hung-mou was not insensitive to the importance of reaching aborigines in their native languages — he decreed, for example, that information on tax assessments be disseminated in native scripts so as to avoid exploitation by Chinese tax collectors — like European colonial administrators he clearly felt "uncivilized" languages unfit media for moral and literary education.[91] Consequently, Ch'en's educational scheme worked in two stages: "first introducing properly spoken Chinese and then only gradually introducing Chinese characters." Over and over again, Ch'en stressed the necessary slowness of this process, with the student building step by step his stock of recognized and reproducible lexical units. He insisted that this process of "opening up" the child's intelligence could be accomplished only by means of a carefully graduated curriculum. In this regard, Ch'en's Yunnan schools accorded with a method that Philippe Ariès identifies as peculiarly "modern" in Europe, achieving educational progress not by the simple expedient of repeating the same text until the student became thoroughly familiar with it but rather by starting with a more basic text and moving on to ever more difficult material and by instituting a system of progressively more difficult year-long "grades" (*fen-nien jih-ch'eng*).[92]

Ch'en's pedagogical theory was already largely formed by the time he was posted to Yunnan and closely reflected his views on the Confucian scholarly tradition. Briefly, his argument was for "substantive learning" (*shih-hsueh*), which he differentiated on the one hand from an aesthetic appreciation of letters for their own sake and on the other from the sort of philological textual study that, under the name Han Learning, formed the dominant intellectual current of his day. Both of these he considered frivolous intellectual indulgences. Nor was *shih-hsueh* for Ch'en identifiable with a simple utilitarian pragmatism (as suggested by the usual English translation, "practical learning"); while Ch'en has justly been identified as an early champion of technological know-how as a necessary component of Confucian scholarship, for him *shih-hsueh* referred as much or more to the study of "substantive" moral values. As applied to primary education, this translated into an emphasis on repeated study of textual passages in order to internalize their message (analogous to the Aristotelian "habit training" revived by Protestant educational theorists in early modern Europe) but *not* a corresponding stress on rote memorization or on oral recitation. Ch'en complained that pedagogues in recent centuries had erred in the directions of "shallow" (*she-lieh*) and "hollow" (*kou-chien*) learning, either denegrating the utility of repetitive study in the interests of broad reading on the one hand or insisting on memorization of countless passages on the other. For him the proper balance entailed slow and careful progress through the text, making sure that the literal meaning and the ethical message of each passage was understood as it was learned, and more generally making sure that "book learning" (*tu-shu*) and the implications for personal conduct (*hsing-chi*) proceeded hand in hand.[93]

Ch'en's own strong ideas in this regard prompted him to personally design the curriculum for his Yunnan local schools. Because of the shortage of books in the province at the time of his arrival, he contributed his own funds for the importing, reprinting, and distribution of texts he deemed appropriate and ordered county officials to do likewise for further reproduction of texts on the local level. Ch'en's personal scholarship during these years was also very active and devoted to the needs he perceived for elementary education; among the works he distributed to Yunnan *i-hsueh* were his own edition of the works of Lü K'un and his abridgements of Ku Hsi-chou's *Kang-chien cheng-shih* and Ch'iu Chün's *Ta-hsueh yen-i pu*.[94] He precisely dictated the pattern of distribution of these works so as to make the most essential (in his view) readily available to all and more difficult works available only at selected locations. In keeping with his desire to make local schools into centers of community life, he ordered that volumes in school libraries be made available for private borrowing so as to direct the content of domestic instruction by househeads and private tutors (at the same time, characteristically, designing a circulation control system to be monitored out of his own office).[95]

The precise contents of the library Ch'en mandated for each of his local schools is given in Table 12.3. We have no direct evidence of just which works were used as instructional materials at each level by teachers in Ch'en's schools, and it is possible that this rather daunting collection was supplemented in practice by more informal materials that have not survived. However, neither is there evidence to suggest that Ch'en, at least, did not fully *intend* that this list of works provide his standard curriculum, and the presence of most of these books in multiple copies at each *i-hsueh* adds support for this assumption.

If indeed this list was designed to serve as his basic teaching curriculum, several striking absences may be noted immediately. First is the lack of any major collection of poetry; Ch'en had an uneasy relationship with China's great poetic tradition, on the one hand acknowledging its cultural importance and on the other disparaging its concern with such frivolities as the beauties of

TABLE 12.3   Textbooks Housed at Each Yunnan *I-hsueh*

Text	Copies
Ku-wen yuan-chien (Reader in classical prose)	24
Kang-chien cheng-shih yueh (Abridged mirror of the dynastic histories)	16
Ta-hsueh yen-i pu chi-yao (Abridgement of the Extended Meaning of the Great Learning and its supplement)	12
Ssu-wen ching-tsui (Essentials of scholarly conduct)	12
Hsing-li ching-i (Essence of writings on nature and principle)	5
Hsiao-hsueh tsuan-chu (Elementary learning, revised and annotated)	4
Chin-ssu lu (Reflections on things at hand)	4
Lü-tzu chieh-lu (Anthology of writings by Lü K'un)	2
Hsiao-ching chu-chieh (Classic on filial piety, annotated)	1
Chu-tzu chih-chia ko-yen (Master Chu's household rules)	1
Sheng-yü kuang-hsun (Sacred Edict, with explanations)	1
Shu-yuan t'iao-kuei (Regulations of the Yunnan Provincial Academy)	1

SOURCES: *Ch'üan-T'ien i-hsüeh hui-chi*, ts'e 2.

nature. Second, despite the goal of preparing minority students for the civil service examinations, the curriculum avoided study of model examination essays that in the view of Ch'en and many others led to the pervasive problem of glib repetitiveness among Chinese literati.[96] Third, the curriculum almost completely neglected the Five Classics, those most ancient of Confucian texts whose centrality had been pointedly reaffirmed by the ascendant Han Learning scholarship. Whereas Ch'en ordered that complete editions of the Classics and Dynastic Histories be maintained only at the district Confucian temples of twelve counties in which "humane letters [were] most developed," the works he chose for his elementary school curriculum were at once more explicitly didactic and more practical in orientation.[97]

Ch'en selected as his basic primer Chu Hsi's compilation *Hsiao-hsueh* (Elementary learning). This was a highly significant choice. Though *Hsiao-hsueh* had of course been extensively used for this purpose ever since the Sung and was periodically endorsed by socially conservative Confucians such as Lu Lung-ch'i, as Angela Leung points out elsewhere in this volume it had in fact been generally displaced during the late Ming and early Ch'ing by less challenging alternatives. Ch'en might have chosen, for instance, the infinitely more accessible *Three-Character Classic* (*San-tzu ching*), which in fact had been recommended by his venerated Lü K'un. But, while similarly Neo-Confucian in spirit, the *San-tzu ching* was not nearly as moralistic as the *Hsiao-hsueh*, which is among the most sternly hierarchical and repressive works in the Confucian Canon. Chu Hsi's fundamentalist attempt to apply ancient social models in the most literal sense to his own more complex twelfth-century world, *Hsiao-hsueh* instructs the novice above all by "clarifying social relationships" (*ming-lun*), which for Chu meant stressing absolutely selfless obedience in the service of elders, husbands, and the ruler as the true way of realizing one's own self-worth (*ching-shen*).[98]

Even more striking was Ch'en's inclusion of "Master Chu's Household Rules" (*Chu-tzu chih-chia ko-yen*), which he attributed — apparently falsely — to Chu Hsi and over ten thousand copies of which he had reprinted for distribution throughout the province. This short work preaches cleanliness in housework, frugality in home economy ("You must be economical in comforts and on no account be extravagant in entertaining guests"), personal modesty ("Train your body to simple habits"), advance thought to provisioning, worship of ancestors, diligent training of children, observance of hierarchy ("A severe decorum should be maintained between elders and juniors and between men and women"), avoidance of litigation with neighbors, and prompt payment of taxes. Ch'en privately conceded that many in his day found these rules old-fashioned and vague but insisted that for him they were timeless. Clearly they were a useful instrument in the Ch'ing campaign for patriarchy and the Chinese family system on the aboriginal pale. Ch'en specifically defended his teaching of them in *primary* school on the grounds that, whereas in the classical age a male was assumed to reach adulthood (*chuang*) at thirty *sui*, in fact most contemporary young men married and assumed househead duties while still in their teens, so that there was no time to waste in imparting this guidance.[99]

If we assume that the relative numbers of copies of works Ch'en supplied to each school library reflects, at least roughly, those works on which classroom instruction was to focus, a truly remarkable emphasis on practical social policy can be detected. By far the most numerous (twenty-four copies) was the 1685 compendium, *Ku-wen yuan-chien*. Compiled by order of the K'ang-hsi emperor to provide students with standard models of classical prose, this work was in substance a selection of political writings — essays, memorials, and imperial edicts — from the late Chou through the Sung; Ch'en explicitly defended his use of it because of its "relevance to political economy (*ching-chi*)."[100] Only slightly down the list (twelve copies) was Ch'en's own *Ta-hsueh yen-i pu chi-yao*, a guide to practical administration in the form of a commentary on the Great

Learning, abridged from the famous Sung compendium by Chen Te-hsiu (1178 –1235) and its Ming supplement by Ch'iu Chün (1421–95).[101] Indeed, even the *Hsing-li ching-i* (five copies), an anthology of Ch'eng-Chu orthodox texts compiled by imperial order in 1715 specifically to serve as the official Ch'ing examination curriculum, subtly reordered the Sung texts so as to emphasize their practical social and political aspects and was appreciated as such by Ch'en Hung-mou himself.[102] Beyond this, Ch'en ordered that lectures and discussions on social policy from the Provincial Academy periodically be printed and distributed for study in lower schools throughout the province.

In sum, Ch'en did far more than continue a received tradition of childhood education. Whereas Ch'eng Wei-ch'i, the Yuan dynasty scholar whose pedagogical theories Ch'en so much admired, had argued for a core curriculum that would proceed seriatim through the Four Books and the Five Classics, Ch'en himself concentrated on far more recent compilations.[103] As he repeatedly stated, the twin emphases of his own syllabus were Neo-Confucian moral cultivation and practical political economy. In other words, like Chu Hsi and many others before him, Ch'en actively reinterpreted the classical tradition to reflect his own and contemporary readings of the Confucian message.

Primarily due to his work in education, Ch'en Hung-mou came to enjoy something of a mythic status in Yunnan, ranking as one of the "seven worthies" of the Provincial Academy and, at least for certain segments of the population, serving as moral and political exemplar. Imperial pronouncements of the Yung-cheng and Ch'ien-lung reigns make it clear moreover that Ch'en's Yunnan school system was promoted as something of a national model, and it continued to be celebrated in the works of nineteenth-century reformist literati.[104] For lack of comparable official initiative, however, no subsequent program remotely matched his in intensity or scope, and the empirewide *i-hsueh* campaign soon fizzled out. Ch'en himself launched a vigorous school-founding drive on reporting to his next duty assignment as Tientsin taotai in 1738, yet this was the last time throughout his long career that *i-hsueh* figured prominently in his administrative approach, despite his continuing deep interest in education generally.[105] By 1751, the Ch'ien-lung court was clearly embarking on a reverse course. In that year it ordered the closing of local community schools in non-Han areas of Kweichow, deriding them as "pottery dogs" (*t'ao-ch'üan*) — decorative but with no bite. In so doing, the court reiterated the litany of racist attitudes and parochial complaints that Ch'en had struggled so hard against: aborigines were congenitally stupid and could not come to understand propriety the way Han people could; if they learned to read they would only waste this skill on lewd or heterodox texts; education of aborigines was in fact a stimulus to seditious movements and thus counter to imperial interests.[106]

In Yunnan itself, the *i-hsueh* system seems to have taken firmer root and did not incur the imperial displeasure of the system in neighboring Kweichow. An

edict of 1761, in fact, reports Yunnan schools operating quite well, singling out
for special mention the effective way in which local school finances continued
to be managed, reported, and audited at the provincial level.[107] (An unstated
reason for imperial approval may well have been that they remained cost-free;
as we have seen, Yunnan schools did not require direct subventions from the
land tax, whereas those of Kweichow and other border provinces did.) As late
as 1835, the *Draft Yunnan Provincial Gazetteer* describes nearly all of Ch'en's
schools still in operation along with a far smaller number that had been added
since his time.[108] All in all, it seems fair to conclude that Ch'en Hung-mou in
Yunnan did achieve a remarkable degree of success in his quest for systemic
safeguards for the substantial and permanent operation of his newly founded
schools.

But did they work? Ch'en himself constantly repeated in both public and
private utterances his expectation that progress would be slow. He wrote:
"This is a task to be accomplished over several generations. My goal is that
among the descendants [of current students] there will be a few who will, by
prolonged exposure to these classical works, succeed in passing the examinations. They will reward our compassion and concern." And again: "If out of
a hundred or a thousand students we succeed in transforming only one or two,
those one or two can in turn serve as models to others by dint of their prestige.
This system will be slow to show results, but its achievements will be real and
long-lasting."[109] The research of James Lee suggests that the first of Ch'en's
goals — producing a few notable examination successes — was stunningly
achieved. In roughly the century following his tenure in the region, more than
seventy non-Han natives of the southwest received the highest civil service degree (*chin-shih*), three times the number for the four preceding centuries
altogether.[110] The number of lower-degree recipients was obviously much
greater still. Yet, to judge by the testimony of officials in Kweichow at the time
of school retrenchment there, the net result was a rather predictable "brain
drain," with few star pupils remaining or returning home to serve as role
models for their fellow aborigines. And one does not have to search far in twentieth-century accounts of the region to be reminded that the educational level
in the southwest remained well below the Chinese average and literacy among
non-Han peoples extremely low.

To what extent did Ch'en's *i-hsueh* contribute to significant cultural change
in Yunnan? Scattered evidence suggests that the process of sinification took
hold differentially within the province, at no place fully penetrating the level of
popular culture. Moreover, where culture change did occur, it was less likely to
bring with it any significant process of "civilization" than one of cultural
demoralization and disintegration, a syndrome unfortunately familiar from
other regions of the world subjected to similar efforts at incorporation.[111] The
best-studied and most celebrated instance is that of the Na-khi tribe in
Yunnan's northwestern Tibetan borderland. According to detailed observation

by Joseph Rock in the 1940s, the long-term result of campaigns to introduce the patriarchal nuclear family and child betrothal during the Yung-cheng reign was a profoundly pathological society with an astronomically high suicide rate among adolescent women and couples. Patriarchal marriage patterns had taken hold among the elite and were enforced among all levels of the society but were still psychologically resisted by large segments of the population. Rock also observed that the related and nearby Hli-khin tribe remained into the 1940s matrilineal (and displayed no abnormal suicide rates), suggesting a still less successful Confucian penetration of their more remote habitat.[112]

It seems on balance that the political and economic incorporation of the eighteenth century was not matched by any significant degree of ethnic assimilation. In the early nineteenth century, a renewed wave of assimilationist measures was launched (including new school foundings), only to be greeted by the greatest incidence of armed resistance since the 1730s.[113] Subsequent drives took place during the early twentieth-century New Policies era and under the Nationalists in the 1930s. Ethnographers, educators, and policymakers associated with these latter-day efforts despaired that Yunnan aborigines still spoke almost no Chinese, held fast to tribal identities, and violently resisted government attempts to alter their life-styles. Such men categorically dismissed all earlier programs of acculturation through education as utter failures.

Looking more closely at this Nationalist effort to transform the peoples of the southwest also allows us a somewhat broadened perspective on the efforts of Ch'en Hung-mou exactly two centuries earlier. The rhetoric of the two drives is similar in many regards but tellingly different in others.[114] Nationalist reformers were, if anything, even less sympathetic than their Confucian predecessors to the cultural distinctiveness of the aborigines — they now had "virtually no culture" or "no culture to speak of." Indigenous peoples lived "like animals," and an emphasis on the need for hygiene education (a prominent theme in this New Life era) provided modernist echoes of Chu Hsi's stress on gentlemanly self-respect in grooming and deportment. The language of race unsurprisingly came up front, though not, as one might expect, to denigrate the aborigines as racial inferiors but rather to emphasize the common heritage of Han and Miao as yellow peoples. Other common ethnic factors, such as the influence of Buddhism, were also highlighted. At the same time it was stressed that a successful modern nation-state — the United States is cited as an example — *may* be ethnically and racially diverse.

The transparent thrust of all this ecumenism was the promotion of the national unit as the end of the educational process, in aboriginal as in Han areas. The two Nationalist educators I have read were equally adamant that education be in standard Chinese (now referred to as "*kuo-yü*") and that the teaching of this "mother tongue" be the first task of aboriginal education; a modern nation must have a unified national language. This and all other elements of the curriculum were to be directed toward "citizenship training" (*kung-min hsun-lien*) and the awakening of "national consciousness" (*min-tsu i-shih*). To this end, one writer despaired of ever achieving proper education for savages in situ and—in sharp contrast to Ch'en Hung-mou's dedication to bringing education to the farthest periphery—proposed that educable Miao be transported to core Mandarin-speaking areas for schooling. Since aborigines "know nothing about production," vocational training had to be made a major part of their education, with all the classism that this implies. Most importantly, instilling patriotism in these "border peoples" was held to be a matter of national security since they provide the only effective buffer against incursions from British Burma.

In a sense, of course, the civilizing mission in the southwest remained very much alive in the 1930s with the content of "civilization" simply redefined from Confucian values to those of nationalism and modernizing progress. But time has brought with it a key change in the mentality of incorporation inasmuch as modernity is not the homegrown ideology that Confucianism was. One reformer accordingly noted that, while "culture" is what distinguishes men from beasts, and while Yunnan was clearly less cultured than other parts of China, China as a whole was similarly less cultured than were Western nations.[115] The reintensified expansionism of the Nationalist era, in other words, was prompted more than anything out of defensiveness and cultural despair.

The doubts and demons that lurked behind the educational drive of Ch'en Hung-mou and his colleagues of the high Ch'ing were more modest and never so openly articulated. Modern-looking in much of its pedagogy and its assumption of state responsibility for mass education, Ch'en's school-founding project was yet essentially traditionalist in its curriculum. Genuinely committed to overcoming exploitation of non-Han peoples and to equality of opportunity for all imperial subjects regardless of ethnic background, it nevertheless presupposed the fundamental error of non-Chinese life-styles and social mores. Through indoctrination in elite cultural values and repeated drilling in ritual practice and the forms of personal relations and conduct, it sought to acculturate natives of the southwest into a rigidly patriarchal, deferential, and puritanical social system—all in the name of order, reason, and human dignity.

In at least two ways, however, Ch'en's educational program in Yunnan rested on idealistic assumptions that were far from universally shared among eighteenth-century Chinese elites. First, as he did throughout his career, Ch'en held stubbornly to a Mencian faith in the innate moral sense of all human beings, a sense which, if properly cultivated, could be relied on to impel them to socially responsible behavior. This found a parallel in Ch'en's views on the education of women—non-Han peoples, like women and the lower classes generally, *should* be educated in order to develop their innate critical judgment rather than simply being mandated to obey externally dictated norms and hierarchical authority.[116] Though Ch'en concurred with more prevalent views in seeing the need for proper ritual practice as an imposed corrective on excessive moral individualism, he was clearly unusual in the degree of his faith in the moral autonomy of all Heaven's creatures.

Related to this was the remarkable extent to which the Yunnan educational drive of the 1730s was designed to bridge rather than reinforce boundaries between privileged and subordinated ethnic groups and between elite and plebeian cultures. Fears over the erosion of such boundaries were common enough in mid-Ch'ing China, as they were in the expanding and industrializing West.[117] Yet the policies of Ch'en and his regional superiors were aimed precisely at the destruction of the most significant cultural boundary of all, that between the literate and the nonliterate, literacy being at once the preeminent badge of Chinese ethnicity and of elite status.

That Ch'en here stood on one side of a major ideological divide within mid-Ch'ing officialdom, and that this divide was related to factional politics, is increasingly clear, although the present state of research does not allow a sure or detailed picture of its contours. A ray of light is thrown on this, however, in a remarkable letter written by Ch'en on his accession to the Shensi governorship in 1744, addressed to Grand Councillor Chang T'ing-yü. Chang, scion of a long line of superliterate prose stylists and high government officials from T'ung-ch'eng, Anhwei, was at once the most powerful Han Chinese political figure of his day and leader of a faction that opposed the patronage network derived from Oerht'ai to which Ch'en belonged. Ch'en's letter is a coy mixture of deference and baiting, contrasting the rustic northwest to the highly refined Lower Yangtze of Chang and his social set. Seeming to deprecate the former, he ends in fact by asserting its superiority. He writes:

> The mentality of the northwest population is obtuse and extremely simple. They are thus easier to govern than the people of the south. At the same time, one must lament their ignorance and accordingly strive to educate them. It seems to me, however, that their very simplicity and rusticity makes them relatively easy to educate. It is perhaps the *un*-rustic [i.e., the Kiangnan elite] who are beyond being educated![118]

The suggestion is clear that it is the cultural elitism of Chang and his party that impedes the progress of such mass education drives as Ch'en's in the southwest.

The populist impulse underlying the *i-hsueh* campaign was particularly strong in Ch'en Hung-mou himself, with his frontier-bred disdain for literati pretense, though it was shared in their own fashion by his Manchu patrons, the Yung-cheng emperor and Governor General Yin-chi-shan. Following Yung-cheng's death and Ch'en's and Yin-chi-shan's reassignment, the skepticism of more conservative bureaucrats reasserted itself and more cautious, protectivist policies increasingly prevailed.[119] By mid-century, the problems of continuing population and economic growth had become so pressing that a general mood of government retrenchment and racial exclusiveness set in, from which educational initiatives were not the least to suffer.[120] Yet for a moment in the 1730s, under a ruler supremely confident in his own abilities and in the superiority of the civilization his rule represented, Ch'en's idealistic brand of Confucianism found a favored place in imperial plans.

NOTES

The author wishes to thank Helen Chauncey, Philip Curtin, Norma Diamond, Louis Galambos, Angela Leung, K.C. Liu, Peter Perdue, and Alexander Woodside for helpful comments on an earlier draft of this chapter.

1. The following paragraphs draw on Herold J. Wiens, *China's March to the Tropics* (Hamden: The Shoe String Press, 1954); Claudine Lombard-Salmon, *Un Example d'Acculturation Chinoise: La Province du Guizhou au XVIIIe Siècle* (Paris: École Française d'Extrême Orient, 1972); James Lee, "The Legacy of Immigration in Southwest China, 1250–1850," *Annales de démographie historique* 1982; 279–304; Lee, "Food Supply and Population Growth in Southwest China, 1250–1850," *Journal of Asian Studies* 41, no. 4 (1982): 711–46. Two older articles of continuing interest on the role of the southwest in Chinese history are J.E. Spenser, "Kueichou: An Internal Chinese Colony," *Pacific Affairs* 13 (1940): 162–72, and Owen Lattimore, "Yunnan, Pivot of Southeast Asia," *Foreign Affairs* 21, no. 3 (1943): 476–93.

2. Huang K'ai-hua 黃開華 , "Ming-tai t'u-ssu chih-tu she-shih yü hsi-nan k'ai-fa" 明代士司制度設施與西南開發 (Establishment of the *t'u-ssu* system in the Ming and opening of the Southwest), *Hsin-ya hsueh-pao* 6, no. 2 (1964): 447–59; John Meskill, "Academies and Politics in the Ming Dynasty," in Charles O. Hucker, ed., *Chinese Government in Ming Times: Seven Studies* (New York: Columbia University Press, 1969), 157.

3. An excellent synopsis of the policy package appears in Yin-chi-shan's memorial of 1734(?), in *Yun-nan t'ung-chih* 雲南通志 (Gazetteer of Yunnan province, 1736; hereafter *YNTC*), 29, no. 6: 29–52.

4. Biographies of many of these individuals appear in Arthur Hummel, ed., *Eminent Chinese of the Ch'ing Period* (hereafter *ECCP*) (Washington, D.C.: Library of Congress, 1943). For a detailed study of Ortai and a general discussion of the Yung-cheng "new men," see Kent C. Smith, "Ch'ing Policy and the Development of Southwest China: Aspects of Ortai's Governor-generalship, 1726–1731" (Ph.D. diss., Yale University, 1970).

5. Ch'en's policies in Yunnan are detailed in Ch'en Hung-mou 陳宏謀, *P'ei-yuan t'ang ou-ts'un kao* 培遠堂偶存稿 (Draft writings from the P'ei-yuan Studio; hereafter *PYTOTK*) (1896), *chüan* 1–4, and in Ch'en Chung-k'o 陳鍾珂, *Hsien Wen-kung-kung*

nien-p'u 先文恭公年譜 (Chronological biography of Ch'en Hung-mou; hereafter *Nien-pu*) (1766), *chüan* 2.

6. Wang Gungwu finds use of the compound *chiao-hua* as early as the third century B.C.; Wang, "The Chinese Urge to Civilize: Reflections on Change," *Journal of Asian History* 18, no. 1 (1984): 3.

7. *PYTOTK*, 3:14, 5:3, 6; Ch'en Hung-mou, preface to *Ch'üan-T'ien i-hsueh hui-chi* 全滇義學彙記 (Casebook of Yunnan local schools; hereafter *IHHC*) (1738); Ch'en Hung-mou, *Hsueh-shih i-kuei* 學士遺規 (Sourcebook on correct scholarship, 1879), 4:86; T'ang Chien 唐鑑, *Kuo-ch'ao hsueh-an hsiao-chih* 國朝學案小識 (Brief account of scholarship in the present dynasty, 1845), 5:11.

8. *YNTC*, 8:1; Hellmut Wilhelm, "Chinese Confucianism on the Eve of the Great Encounter," in Marius B. Jansen, *Changing Japanese Attitudes Toward Modernization* (Princeton: Princeton University Press, 1965), 285.

9. Alexander Woodside, "Some Mid-Qing Theorists of Popular Schools: Their Innovations, Inhibitions, and Attitudes Toward the Poor," *Modern China* 9, no. 1 (1983): 8–10.

10. For the European case, see Philip Curtin, *The Image of Africa: British Ideas and Action, 1780–1850* (Madison: University of Wisconsin Press, 1964); Curtin, *Imperialism* (New York: Walker, 1977).

11. Ch'en Hung-mou, *P'ei-yuan t'ang shou-tu p'ing* 培遠堂手札評 (Private correspondence of Ch'en Hung-mou, with commentary; hereafter *PYTSTP*) (1921), 1:2; Ch'en Hung-mou, *Kuei-t'iao hui-ch'ao* 規條彙鈔 (Compendium of regulations, 1757), 2: 66–68. The evangelical bent in Confucian expansionism is interestingly explored in Hisayuki Miyakawa, "The Confucianization of South China," in Arthur F. Wright, ed., *The Confucian Persuasion* (Stanford: Stanford University Press, 1960), 21–46.

12. James Lee, "Legacy of Immigration," 292.

13. Yen Ju-i 嚴如熤, *Miao-fang pei-lan* 苗防備覽 (Conspectus of the Miao campaigns, 1843), 22:21; Lombard-Salmon, *Example d'Acculturation Chinoise*, 224–225.

14. Yung-cheng emperor, *Ta-i chueh-mi lu* 大義覺迷錄 (1730; reprint, Taipei: Wen-hai, 1969), esp. 1:1–13; *ECCP*, 747–49. The significance of this document is pointed out in several recent studies by Pamela Crossley.

15. James L. Watson, "Standardizing the Gods: The Promotion of T'ien Hou ("Empress of Heaven") Along the South China Coast, 960–1960," in David Johnson, Andrew J. Nathan, and Evelyn S. Rawski, eds., *Popular Culture in Late Imperial China* (Berkeley: University of California Press, 1985), 292–324; Prasenjit Duara, "Superscribing Symbols: The Myth of Guandi, Chinese God of War," *Journal of Asian Studies* 47, no. 4 (1988): 779–95.

16. On one twentieth-century attack, see Roger Thompson, "Statecraft and Self-Government: Competing Visions of Community and State in Late Imperial China," *Modern China* 14, no. 2 (1988): 199–202.

17. *Nien-p'u*, 5:8.

18. For twentieth-century accounts of these peoples, see for example Lin Yueh-hua, *The Lolo of Liang-shan* (New Haven: Human Resources Area Files, 1961); J.F. Rock, *The Life and Culture of the Na-khi Tribe of the China-Tibet Borderland* (Wiesbaden: Franz Steiner, 1963); Inez de Beauclair, *Tribal Cultures of Southwest China* (Taipei, 1974); de Beauclair, *Ethnographic Studies* (Taipei: Southern Materials Center, 1986); Yunnan Provincial Edi-

torial Committee, eds., *Yun-nan Miao-tsu Yao-tsu she-hui li-shih* 雲南苗族瑤族社會歷史 (Social history of Miao and Yao tribes in Yunnan) (Kunming, 1982).

19. See for example E.G. Pulleyblank, "The Chinese and Their Neighbors in Prehistoric and Early Imperial Times," in David N. Keightley, ed., *The Origins of Chinese Civilization* (Berkeley: University of California Press, 1983), 423–29.

20. *YNTC, chüan* 8.

21. Quoted in Lombard-Salmon, *Example d'Acculturation Chinoise*, 355.

22. See for example Curtin, *Image of Africa*, 421.

23. Lombard-Salmon, *Example d'Acculturation Chinoise*, 57–66; Edward W. Said, *Orientalism* (New York: Random House, 1978).

24. *Miao-luan t'u-ts'e* 苗蠻圖冊 (Pictures of Miao life) (Taipei: Institute of History and Philology, 1973). A far less flattering set of caricatures of Miao life, drawn by an unknown Chinese official in the mid-eighteenth century, is reprinted in Chiu Chang-kong, *Die Kultur der Miao-tse* (Hamburg: Museum fur Volkerkunde, 1937).

25. Ch'en Hung-mou, *Ch'en wen-kung-kung shu-tu* 陳文恭公書牘 (Correspondence of Ch'en Hung-mou) (Peking: Ts'an-shu, 1936), 1:3.

26. Cited in Wiens, "China's March," 235. For other examples, see *PYTOTK*, 3:31–34; Chang Yun-sui, cited in J.F. Rock, *The Ancient Na-khi Kingdom of Southwest China* (Cambridge, Mass.: Harvard University Press, 1947) 1, 46–47.

27. For Yin-chi-shan's comment, see *YNTC*, 29, no. 6:30. On the question of racial distinction, see for example Ch'en Hung-mou's comment that the Muslims of northwest China were made up of "various races (*ko-chung-lei*)"; Ch'en Hung-mou, *Kuei-t'iao hui-ch'ao*, 2:65.

28. Chang Yun-sui, preface to *IHHC*.

29. Wang Gungwu, "Chinese Urge to Civilize," 16.

30. *PYTOTK*, 1:33.

31. See esp. the classic work by Roy Harvey Pearce, *The Savages of America: A Study of the Indian and the Idea of Civilization* (Baltimore: Johns Hopkins University Press, 1953). I have also found helpful Gary B. Nash, "The Image of the Indian in the Southern Colonial Mind," *William and Mary Quarterly*, 3d ser., 29 (1972): 197–230; Francis Jennings, *The Invasion of America: Indians, Colonialism, and the Cant of Conquest* (Chapel Hill: University of North Carolina Press, 1975); Alden T. Vaughn, "From White Man to Redskin: Changing Anglo-American Perceptions of the American Indian," *American Historical Review* 87 (1982): 917–53; and Michal J. Rozbicki, "Transplanted Ethos: Indians and the Cultural Identity of English Colonists in Seventeenth-Century Maryland," *Amerika Studien* 28 (1983): 405–28

32. Yin-chi-shan, preface to *IHHC*.

33. For a European counterpart, see Michael Hechter, *Internal Colonialism: The Celtic Fringe in British National Development, 1536–1966* (Berkeley: University of California Press, 1975), 74–75.

34. *YNTC*, 8:8. A recent article by Keith McMahon suggests that, in the eighteenth century, the relatively liberal sexual practices of the southwest tribes were an item of general awareness throughout the empire, serving both as a foil for Confucian moralizing and as a source of titillation for the broader Han population; McMahon, "A Case for Confucian Sexuality: The Eighteenth-Century Novel, *Yesou Puyan*," *Late Imperial China*, 9 no. 2 (1988): 46.

35. *YNTC*, 8:1.

36. Pei Huang, *Autocracy at Work: A Study of the Yung-cheng Period, 1723–1735* (Bloomington: Indiana University Press, 1974), 297–98.

37. *PYTOTK*, 2:13–16, 3:14–15; *PYTSTP* 1:2–3.

38. Anthony Jackson, "Kinship, Suicide, and Pictographs among the Na-khi (S.W. China)," *Ethnos* 36 (1971): 72.

39. Susan Naquin and Evelyn S. Rawski, *Chinese Society in the Eighteenth Century* (New Haven: Yale University Press, 1987), 92.

40. Pearce, *Savages of America*, 68.

41. Rozbicki, "Transplanted Ethos," 423.

42. Wiens, "China's March," 234–35.

43. Huang K'ai-hua, "Hsi-nan k'ai-fa," 463–75.

44. *Ch'in-ting hsueh-cheng ch'üan-shu* 欽定學政全書 (Complete handbook of imperial educational administration) (hereafter *CTHCCS*) (1810), 64:1–2.

45. *CTHCCS*, 64:3–5; *YNTC*, 23:139–44; *Ta-Ch'ing Shih-tsung Hsien-huang-ti shih-lu* 大清世宗憲皇帝實錄 (Veritable records of the Yung-cheng reign), 60:11.

46. *CTHCCS*, 64:1–2.

47. Ichisada Miyazaki, *China's Examination Hell: The Civil Service Examinations of Imperial China* (New Haven: Yale University Press, 1976), 34–35, 117; Thomas H. C. Lee, *Government Education and Examinations in Sung China* (New York: St. Martin's Press, 1985), 53, 263.

48. *PYTOTK*, 2:8–10; *CTHCCS* 64:3; Meskill, "Academies and Politics," 157; Benjamin A. Elman, *From Philosophy to Philology: Intellectual and Social Aspects of Change in Late Imperial China* (Cambridge, Mass.: Harvard University Press, 1984), 119–21. On the Kunming *shu-yuan*, see Ortai's announcement of its founding, reprinted in Ho Ch'ang-ling 賀長齡, *Huang-ch'ao ching-shih wen-pien* 皇朝經世文編 (Writings on statecraft from the present dynasty, 1826), 57:58–61, and Woodside, chap. 13 of this volume.

49. Huang K'ai-hua, "Ming-tai t'u-ssu chih-tu she-shih yü hsi-nan k'ai fa," 451; *CTHCCS*, 64: 1–3; *PYTOTK*, 5:6–7.

50. Ch'en Hung-mou, "Yang-cheng i-kuei" 養正遺規 (Sourcebook on moral education), in *Wu-chung i-kuei* 五種遺規 (Five sourcebooks) (Shanghai: Chung-hua, 1936), 3:29–32. For a somewhat different interpretation of the distinction between *she-hsueh* and *i-hsüeh*, see Leung, chap.11 of this volume.

51. Ch'en Hung-mou, preface, and Yin-chi-shan, preface, *IHHC*; *PYTOTK*, 5:6.

52. See Thomas H.C. Lee, "The Discovery of Childhood: Children's Education in Sung China (960–1279)," in Sigrid Paul, ed., *Kultur-Begriff und Wort in China und Japan* (Berlin: Dietrich Reimer, 1982), 159–89; Gerald Strauss, "The State of Pedagogical Theory, c. 1530: What Protestant Reformers Knew about Education," in Lawrence Stone, ed., *Schooling and Society: Studies in the History of Education* (Baltimore: Johns Hopkins University Press, 1976), 69–94; Joan Simon, *Education and Society in Tudor England* (Cambridge: Cambridge University Press, 1966).

53. *PYTSTP* 1:2–3; *PYTOTK* 1:33.

54. Ch'en Hung-mou, preface to "Yang-cheng i-kuei." For an analysis of the broad-ranging implications of this metaphor, which Ch'en inherited from Chu Hsi, see Donald J. Munro, *Images of Human Nature: A Sung Portrait* (Princeton: Princeton University Press, 1988), 43–57.

55. *PYTOTK*, 1:36.

56. *PYTOTK*, 2:6. Cf. Strauss, "Pedagogical Theory," 87–88; Simon, *Tudor England*, 134. My argument that Ch'en sincerely sought to provide "mass literacy" runs counter to the conclusions of Leung, chap. 11 of this volume. Could Ch'en have realistically held this goal? If we assume Yunnan's population in the 1730s to have been between six and seven million, and the target group of males eight to seventeen years of age to have comprised about 15 percent of this population, Ch'en would have provided a ratio of schools to target population of about one to fifteen hundred. In other words, given social and economic constraints on actual school attendance, his goal of providing educational facilities for all *likely* students seems optimistic but perhaps not unrealistically so.

57. Ch'en Hung-mou, proclamation of Ch'ien-lung 2/11/28, in *IHHC*, *ts'e* 2.

58. Ch'en Hung-mou, preface to *IHHC*; Ch'en Hung-mou, preface to "Yang-cheng i-kuei"; *PYTOTK*, 3:5, 5:6.

59. Yin-chi-shan, preface to *IHHC*.

60. Though the editorship of *IHHC* was attributed to Ch'en, it was actually published shortly after he had been demoted for an unrelated offense and transferred to Tientsin. It seems likely that actual publication was a political act on the part of Ch'en's patron and bureaucratic superior, Yin-chi-shan, intended to salvage Ch'en's reputation in the eyes of the court by giving testimony to his extraordinary administrative energy.

61. *PYTOTK* 2:7; Ch'en Hung-mou, proclamation of Ch'ien-lung 2/12/7, *IHHC*, *ts'e* 2.

62. *PYTOTK* 2:6.

63. *Yun-nan t'ung-chih kao* 雲南通志稿 (Draft Yunnan provincial gazetteer; hereafter *YNTCK*) (1835), 82:27–29, 83:3–4, 87:4–5.

64. *CTHCCS*, 64:1.

65. *CTHCCS*, 64:6–8.

66. It should be noted that, even while driving local officials to greater creativity in uncovering local sources of school funding, Ch'en simultaneously warned them against grabbing legal private land (*min-t'ien*), a concern consistent with his more general policies throughout his career; *Nien-p'u*, 2:8.

67. *PYTOTK*, 4:16. A more modest precedent for this had been set by Kweichow Governor Chang Kuang-ssu (d. 1749) in 1731; Lombard-Salmon, *Example d'Acculturation Chinoise*, 356.

68. *K'un-ming hsien-chih* 昆明縣志 (Gazetteer of K'un-ming county, 1901), 4:18–19; *YNTCK*, 82:27–29.

69. *YNTCK*, 83:3–4.

70. *YNTCK*, 85:1–2.

71. *YNTCK*, 87:4–5.

72. Ogawa Yoshiko 小川嘉子, "Shindai ni okeru gigaku setsuritsu no kiban" 清代に於ける義學設立の基盤 (Social basis of *i-hsueh* founding in the Ch'ing period), in Hayashi Tomoharu 林友春, ed., *Kinsei Chūgoku kyōiku shi kenkyū* 近世中国教育史研究 (Studies in the history of education in modern China) (Tokyo: Kokudosha, 1958), 292.

73. *PYTOTK*, 3:5–11; *CTHCCS*, 64:6; *Yun-nan t'ung-chih*, 20, no. 11:61–68.

74. For a European example, see Curtin, *Image of Africa*, 260.

75. Cited in Ch'en Hung-mou, "Yang-cheng i-kuei," 3:30.

76. On this issue generally, see Philippe Ariès, *Centuries of Childhood: A Social History of Family Life* (New York: Vintage, 1962), 141, 303–5.

77. Ch'en Hung-mou, "Yang-cheng i-kuei," 3:30.

78. *PYTOTK*, 5:7. For a European parallel, see Strauss, "Pedagogical Theory," 79.

79. *PYTSTP*, 1:4.

80. *PYTOTK*, 1:36, 2:6.

81. Ch'en Hung-mou, preface to *IHHC*.

82. *PYTOTK*, 2:9.

83. *PYTOTK*, 2:8–10, 3:5–11.

84. *PYTOTK*, 3:8.

85. *Shih-tsung shih-lu*, 60:11; Yin-chi-shan and Yuan Chan-ch'eng, memorial of Yung-cheng 12/6/1, in *Kung-chung tang Yung-cheng ch'ao tsou-che* 宮中檔雍正朝奏摺 (Palace memorials from the Yung-cheng reign in the Palace Museum) (Taipei: National Palace Museum), 23:141–42.

86. *PYTOTK*, 2:10. In proscribing this practice, Ch'en was merely implementing the imperial policy of making the Yung-cheng emperor's amplified Sacred Edict of 1724 the cornerstone of both primary education and local community ritual. According to Ōmura Kōdō, this emphasis was a function of the major concerns of the Yung-cheng reign: bureaucratic reinvigoration, agricultural development, and extension of Ch'ing direct rule into minority areas. Ōmura Kōdō 大村興道, "Shinchō kyōiku shisō shi ni okeru *Sheng-yü kuang-hsun* no chi'i ni tsuite" 清朝教育思想史に於ける聖諭廣訓の地位につ いて (On the role of the *Sheng-yü kuang-hsun* in Ch'ing educational thought), in Hayashi Tomoharu 林友春, ed., *Kinsei Chūgoku kyōiku shi kenkyū* 近世中國教育史研究 (Studies in, the history of education in modern China) (Tokyo: Kokudosha, 1958), 231–71.

87. Ch'en Hung-mou, "Yang-cheng i-kuei," 3:5–15, 29–32.

88. *PYTOTK*, 3:8–9.

89. See James L. Watson, "The Structure of Chinese Funerary Rites: Elementary Forms, Ritual Sequence, and the Primacy of Performance," in Watson and Evelyn S. Rawski, eds., *Death Ritual in Late Imperial and Modern China* (Berkeley: University of California Press, 1988), 3–19; Thomas H.C. Lee, "Discovery of Childhood," 179.

90. Chu Hsi's text and Ch'en's commentary are in Ch'en Hung-mou, "Yang-cheng i-kuei," 1:5–6. This translation is adapted from that in Evan Morgan, *Wenli Styles and Chinese Ideals* (Shanghai: Christian Literature Society, 1912), 150–63.

91. *PYTOTK*, 3:10–11, 31–34. The classic European example is Macauley's 1835 "Minute," which argued against using "barbaric" tongues such as Arabic or Sanskrit to civilize Britain's colonial charges; see Curtin, *Imperialism*, 178–91.

92. Ch'en Hung-mou, *"Yang-cheng i-kuei,"* 3:40; Ariès, *Centuries of Childhood*, 187.

93. Ch'en Hung-mou *"Yang-cheng i-kuei,"* 3:5–6, 16–17, 31, 35–39.

94. Ch'en Hung-mou, ed., *Lü-tzu chieh-lu* 呂子節錄 (Anthology of works by Lü K'un, 1736); Ch'en Hung-mou, ed., *Kang-chien cheng-shih yueh* 綱鑑正史約 (Mirror of the official histories, 1869); Ch'en Hung-mou, *Ta-hsueh yen-i pu chi-yao* 大學衍義補輯要 (Abridged explication of the Great Learning, 1736). See also *Nien-p'u*, 2:8, 2:19.

95. *PYTOTK*, 4:20–21.

96. *PYTOTK*, 4:3–4.

97. Ch'en Hung-mou, proclamation of Ch'ien-lung 2/11/28, *IHHC*, ts'e 2.

98. M. Theresa Kelleher, "Back to Basics: Chu Hsi's *Elementary Learning* (*Hsiao-hsueh*)," in Wm. Theodore de Bary and John W. Chaffee, eds., *Neo-Confucian Education: The Formative Stage* (Berkeley: University of California Press, 1989), 219–51. See also Thomas H.C. Lee, *Government Education*, 111, and Lee, "Discovery of Childhood," 170–71.

99. *PYTSTP*, 1:1–2. Ch'en reprinted and discussed this work in "Yang-cheng i-kuei," 2:6–7. Translations above follow Morgan, *Wen-li Styles*, 188–93. Authorship of the "Chu-tzu chih-chia ko-yen" is usually ascribed today not to Chu Hsi but rather to the relatively obscure Yuan dynasty scholar Chu Yung-hsien. The fact that Ch'en Hung-mou could misattribute a work so basic to his curriculum, of course, is indicative of the low priority he attached to the issues of textual scholarship central to the intellectual world of his day.

100. Hsu Ch'ien-hsueh 徐乾學, ed., *Ku-wen yuan-chien*, 古文淵鑒, imperial preface dated 1685. See also the biography of Hsu in *ECCP*, 310–12. Ch'en's comment on the work's utility is in *PYTOTK*, 4:17.

101. Chen Te-hsiu's original 1229 work dealt with personal morality and household management on the part of the ruler; Ch'iu Chün's 1487 supplement extended the discussion to questions of practical imperial administration. The former work was a favorite of the Ch'ien-lung emperor but, according to Ch'en Hung-mou's preface to his combined abridgement (1736), it was no longer read by literati of his day, they preferring the more statecraft-oriented supplement by Ch'iu Chün. In his own work, Ch'en characteristically insisted on the complementarity of the two approaches. See Hung-lam Chu, "Ch'iu Chün's *Ta-hsueh yen-i pu* and Its Influence in the Sixteenth and Seventeenth Centuries," *Ming Studies* 22 (Fall 1986): 1–32; Chun-shu Chang, "Emperorship in Eighteenth-Century China," *Journal of the Institute of Chinese Studies* 7, no. 1 (Dec. 1974): 555–56. I have not seen Ch'en's abridgement, but his preface is reprinted in Li Tsu-t'ao 李祖陶, ed., *Kuo-ch'ao wen-lu* 國朝文錄 (Literary records from the current dynasty, 1839), 44:1–2.

102. Li Kuang-ti 李光地, ed., *Hsing-li ching-i* 性理精義, imperial preface dated 1716. See also the biography of Li in *ECCP*, 473–75, and esp. Wing-tsit Chan, "The *Hsing-li ching-i* and the Ch'eng-Chu School of the Seventeenth Century," in William Theodore de Bary, ed., *The Unfolding of Neo-Confucianism* (New York: Columbia University Press, 1975), 543–79.

103. Ch'en Hung-mou "Yang-cheng i-kuei," 3:5–15. This classical curriculum had essentially been followed also in Chang Kuang-ssu's prototype school program in Kweichow, 1729–32; see Lombard-Salmon, *Example d'Acculturation Chinoise*, 356.

104. For the responses of two twentieth-century Yunnan literati, see the preface by Ch'in Kuang-ti 秦光第 and commentary by Liu Shu-t'ang 劉樹堂 in *PYTSTP*. Both Chen's and Yin-chi-shan's prefaces to the *IHHC* were reprinted in Wang Ch'ang's 王昶 1837 compilation of exemplary texts, *Hu-hai wen-ch'uan* 湖海文傳, 29: 1–4.

105. *PYTOTK*, 5:3–7.

106. *CTHCCS*, 64:8–9.

107. *CTHCCS* 64:9–10.

108. *YNTCK, chüan* 82–87. There is of course a well-known tendency for gazetteers simply to reproduce data from their predecessors and so present an anachronistic picture of actual conditions. In the case of the 1835 Yunnan gazetteer, however, the

detailed information it supplies on changes in educational institutions over recent years, as well as the scholarly bent of its chief compiler, Juan Yuan, argues for at least relative reliability.

109. Ch'en Hung-mou, *Ch'en wen-kung-kung shu-tu*, 1:2; *PYTSTP*, 1:4.

110. James Lee, "Legacy of Immigration," 304. Ch'en's success is also lauded in his biography in the *Ch'ing-shih kao* 清史稿 (Draft history of the Ch'ing dynasty) (Peking: Chung-hua shu-chü), 1977, 35: 10558.

111. For a comparable educational program elsewhere facing similar problems and experiencing remarkably similar results, see Colin MacLachlan, "The Indian Directorate: Forced Acculturation in Portuguese America (1757–99)," *The Americas* 28, no. 4 (1972) : 357–87.

112. Rock, *Ancient Na-khi Kingdom*, 2: 391; Rock, *Life and Culture of the Na-khi Tribe*, 32–33; Jackson, "Kinship, Suicide, and Pictographs."

113. Ma Shao-ch'i 馬小伎, *Ch'ing-tai Miao-min ch'i-i* 清代苗民起義 (Miao rebellions of the Ch'ing period) (Wuhan: Hu-pei jen-min ch'u-pan-she, 1956).

114. Pedagogical tracts of the Nationalist era used here are Li Sheng-chuang 李生莊, "Pien-ti chiao-yü chih wo chien" 邊地教育之我見 (My views on education in frontier areas), in *Yun-nan pien-ti wen-t'i yen-chiu* 雲南邊地問題研究 (Studies of frontier problems in Yunnan) (Kunming: Yun-nan sheng-li K'un-hua min-chung chiao-yü-kuan, 1933), 393–411; Fan I-t'ien 范義田, *Yun-nan pien-ti min-tsu chiao-yü* 雲南邊地民族教育 (Survey of education among frontier peoples in Yunnan) (Kunming: Yun-nan sheng-li i-wu chiao-yü wei-yuan-hui, 1936). I am grateful to Joshua Fogel for providing me with a copy of the former article.

115. Li Sheng-chuang, "Pien-ti chiao-yü chih wo chien," 394.

116. Ch'en's most impassioned declaration of his views on women's education is his preface to "Chiao-nü i-kuei" 教女遺規 (Sourcebook on women's education), in *Wu-chung i-kuei*. See also Joanna Handlin, "Lü K'un's New Audience," in Margery Wolf and Roxane Witke, eds., *Women in Chinese Society* (Stanford: Stanford University Press, 1975), esp. 36–38, and Mann, chap. 1 of this volume.

117. See e.g. Dane Kennedy, *Islands of White: Settler Society and Culture in Kenya and Southern Rhodesia, 1890–1939* (Durham: Duke University Press, 1987); Carl F. Kaestle, "Between the Scylla of Brutal Ignorance and the Charybdis of a Literary Education: Elite Attitudes toward Mass Schooling in Early Industrial England and America," in Stone, *Schooling and Society*, 177–91.

118. Ch'en Hung-mou, *Ch'en wen-kung-kung shu-tu*, 2:3.

119. It is indicative of the new direction imperial policy was to take that almost immediately on his succession the Ch'ien-lung emperor recalled and destroyed all known copies of his predecessor's highly universalist tract, *Ta-i chueh-mi lu*; *ECCP*, 749.

120. For but one example of mid-eighteenth-century government retrenchment, see Kao Wang-ling 高王凌, "I-ko wei-wan-chieh ti ch'ang-shih: Ch'ing-tai Ch'ien-lung shih-ch'i ti liang-cheng ho liang-shih wen-t'i" 一個未完結的嘗試－清代乾隆時期的糧政和糧食問題 (Unfinished experiment: the problems of grain administration and food supply in the Ch'ien-lung era), *Chiu-chou hsueh-k'an* 2, no. 3 (1988): 13–40. For the growing mood of racial exclusivity, see the article by Pamela Crossley in this volume.

GLOSSARY

an-ts'e	案冊	i-hsueh	義學
Chang Kuang-ssu	張廣泗	i-yeh	肄業
Chang T'ing-yü	張廷玉	jen-hsing hsi shan	人性昔善
Chang Yun-sui	張允隨	Juan Yuan	阮元
Chen Te-hsiu	真德秀	kai-t'u kuei-liu	改土歸流
Ch'en Hung-mou	陳宏謀	Kang-chien cheng-shih	綱鑑正史
cheng-chiao	政教	Ku Hsi-ch'ou	顧錫疇
Ch'eng-kung	呈貢	Ku-wen yuan-chien	古文淵鑑
ch'eng-ts'ai	成才	kuan-chuang	官莊
Ch'eng Wei-ch'i	程畏齊	kuan-ti	官地
chiao-hua	教化	kuan-yü	官語
Chiao Hung	焦竑	kuang-hsing chiao-tu	廣行教讀
chieh-hsiao	節孝	k'uang-han	狂悍
chih-chih	致治	K'un-ming	昆明
chih-ch'ih	知恥	kung	公
chih-hua	治化	kung-ch'ien	公錢
chin-shih	進士	kung-hsiang	公項
ch'in-yin	侵隱	kung-min hsun-lien	公民訓練
ching-chi	經濟	kuo-yü	國語
ching-shen	敬身	liang-chih	良知
Ch'iu Chün	丘濬	lien-ch'ih	廉恥
Chu-tzu chih-chia ko-yen	朱子治家格言	ling-hsing	零星
Chu Yung-hsien	朱用綫	lou-kuei	陋規
chuang	壯	Lu Lung-ch'i	陸隴其
ch'un-p'u	純樸	Lü K'un	呂坤
ch'un	蠢	meng-t'ung	蒙童
chung-lei	種類	Miao	苗
chung-lei pu-i	種類不一	Miao-Man	苗蠻
chung-pao	中飽	Miao-Yao	苗瑤
E-mi-ta	鄂彌達	min-t'ien	民田
fen-nien jih-ch'eng	分年日程	min-tsu i-shih	民族意識
fu-hsueh	府學	ming-lun	明倫
fu-i	撫夷	Oerht'ai	鄂爾泰
heng-yeh	恆業	Pao-ning	寶寧
hsiang	鄉	pien-fang	邊方
hsiang-ts'un	鄉村	pu-lun Han-i	不論漢夷
hsiao-min	小民	San-tzu ching	三字經
hsieh yü chung	協于中	shan-hou	善後
hsien-hsueh	縣學	she-hsueh	社學
hsing-chi	行己	she-lieh	涉獵
Hsing-li ching-i	性理精義	sheng-hsing	生性
hua	化	shih-hsueh	實學
hua-min ch'eng-su	化民成俗	shih-tzu ming-li	識字明理
hua-tao	化導	shu-yuan	書院
hua-te i-jen	化得一人	Ta-hsueh yen-i pu	大學衍義補

Ta-hsueh yen-i pu chi-yao	大學衍義補輯要	*t'ung-hua*	同化
Ta-i chueh-mi lu	大義覺迷錄	*T'ung-meng hsu-chih*	童蒙須知
tang-hsiang	黨庠	Wang Yang-ming	王陽明
t'ao-ch'üan	陶犬	*yang*	養
ti-fang feng hua	地方風化	*yang-cheng*	養正
t'ien-hsia i-chia, wan-wu i-t'i	天下一家萬物一體	*yang-lien*	養廉
t'ien-li	天理	Yang Shen	楊慎
Tseng Ching	曾靜	*yeh-wan*	野頑
tso-jen	作人	Yen Ssu-sheng	晏斯盛
tso-wei	左衛	Yin-chi-shan	尹繼善
tsung-fa	宗法	*ying-k'en*	應墾
tu-shu	讀書	*yu-ming wu-shih*	有名無實
t'u-ssu	土司	*Yung-pei*	永北

THIRTEEN

The Divorce between the Political Center and Educational Creativity in Late Imperial China

Alexander Woodside

ELITE DISSATISFACTION WITH PUBLIC AND PRIVATE SCHOOL ORGANIZATION

Were the most important differences in the forms of education that premodern Chinese and European societies pursued and publicly rewarded those of content or those of organization? Chinese reformers in the period since 1911 have largely chosen to protest, retrospectively, the differences in content. As one extreme example, Liang Shu-ming (b. 1893) told Shansi schoolteachers in 1922 that from Socrates to Dewey, Western education had exalted the guidance of "knowledge" in human affairs, and the overall supremacy of knowledge-related achievements. Chinese education, in contrast, had devoted itself to the improvement of moral feelings and purposes, and had not made collectively accumulated knowledge of special kinds the important guideline in different fields of action; therefore, an anarchy of individual opinions and experiences still prevailed in such realms as Chinese medicine.[1]

This chapter nevertheless proposes to study one notable form of sub-revolutionary educational discontent in late imperial China that concerned itself as much with the organization of schools as with their content. The first justification for this approach is the search for lost continuities in Chinese political and educational reform impulses before and after the Opium War; the second is that such a focus encourages us to reflect on the organizational differences between Chinese and European school systems, against Liang Shu-ming's Baconian tendency to stress content differences.

The emphasis here on schools as a conceptualized and endlessly reconceptualized institutional system should not be taken to mean that thought about the reform of school curricula, or about reform of the civil service examinations that shaped school curricula, was less important in the Ch'ing period than it had been earlier. As in previous dynasties, the fact that the examinations so often encouraged school study "that was both formalistic and motivated by profit," as Chaffee puts it, was highly offensive to many Ch'ing schoolmen.[2] The major reforms in the content of the examinations that did occur—such as the reform of 1787 that required the rotational testing of all Five Classics as a means of compelling students to master more than just one of them—may well have been the result of academy heads' pressures. It is certain that these reforms were celebrated in the regulations of provincial academies of that time as the potential sources of a dramatic new moral and educational enthusiasm in such schools' students.[3]

In the Ch'ing period, however, if not before, the study of the history of the past organization of schools in China became in itself a striking part of the content of higher learning at the more celebrated academies, in addition to the better known moral education that Liang Shu-ming so stressed. Western scholars tend to see schools as technical agencies of deparochialization or "decontextualization": the process in which students are removed from their families and engaged in increasingly abstract forms of learning that do not have an immediate payoff.[4] But this approach overlooks the fact that schools do more than decontextualize; as institutions, they may embody the more general collective dreams of a society, sometimes of a political kind. In China this was especially true. The educationally conditioned nature of much elite politics constantly threatened to shift political activity to the schools, just as the constitutionally conditioned nature of modern American politics constantly threatens to shift essentially political activity there to the law courts. The court compilers of eighteenth-century China's greatest encyclopedia of classical texts feared, not the ossification of Chinese classical learning but immature intellectuals' pernicious misuse of its wilder features. They warned against unbalanced student antiquarians who might want to revive the well-field system or unstable "Ku Yen-wu followers" who might want to make Chinese speech conform to "ancient sounds."[5] Schools, therefore, played an inevitable part in most efforts, direct or indirect, to retheorize or reimagine some or all aspects of the late imperial political system.

Such attempted retheorizations, or reconstructed pictures of the past with potential retheorizing implications, were—as I have called them—subrevolutionary. They are not as exciting to study as the treatises of the French Revolution. But there were more of them than we usually think, even under a strongman emperor like the Ch'ien-lung emperor. Their importance lies in their evidence of a diffuse dissatisfaction within the intelligentsia that schools were creating, which in turn multiplied or exacerbated the internal complexities of the state ideology, portending the weakening of its self-legitimating capacities in ways more oblique but not less real than peasant heterodoxies in the countryside. Each participant in the government, from the emperor down to the county director of schools, might carry his own unique imaginary map of the ideal government in his head. The very small visible part of this iceberg included the well-known battle between the "feudal" and "bureaucratic" models of politics that engaged Ch'ing thinkers as diverse as Ku Yen-wu (1613–82), the Yung-cheng emperor, and Yuan Mei (1716–98).[6] But there were many other less well-known, more limited efforts by Ch'ing literati to rethink parts of the system. In the Ch'ien-lung era, one academy head proposed that Mongol court institutions be studied and adapted in order finally to end the eunuch evil; another scholar proposed that China proper be fundamentally reorganized as three zones (southern, northern, and central) in order to simulate preimperial political geography and save circulating officials from the more exhausting forms of travel mandated by the "law of avoidance."[7]

The particular reimagining of the empire's institutions considered here had as a principal interest a desire to reshape the organization of education and some of the underlying principles of the process of learning. We might begin at the end of the Ch'ing, with Chang Po-hsi (1847–1907), the architect of imperial China's new school system at the beginning of the twentieth century. Writing in 1902, Chang suggested that the subject matter taught historically in European universities had not differed remarkably from the law, mathematics, and medical education taught in the medieval China of the T'ang and Sung dynasties; that Sung educators such as Ssu-ma Kuang (1019–86) and Chu Hsi (1130–1200) had proposed specialized curricula with fixed terms of study that lent themselves to knowledge accumulation in much the same way as the separate branches of study, and elective subjects, in Western education; and that it was the diverging nature of the structures of education in late imperial China and the West, rather than culturally specific divergences in the conceptualization of educational content, whose negative effects late imperial China now had to struggle the most to overcome. This of course was the opposite of what Liang Shu-ming was to argue in 1922.

The ancient school system of preimperial China, Chang Po-hsi continued, had been a dense, purposeful, four-tiered hierarchy of schools for families, schools for communities of five hundred people, and schools for communities of 12,500 people. These three types of schools had matched Western kindergartens, primary schools, and middle schools respectively. Then at its top, this ancient school system had had schools for whole principalities that matched European universities. From the Han dynasty on, with the rise of civil service examinations, the substance of this system of four tiers of schools had been lost. The whole point of educational reform in 1902 was to devise a modern facsimile of the ancient school system, so that the structures of education in China and the West would again resemble each other.[8]

Our concern here is not with the historical validity of Chang Po-hsi's picture of Chinese and Western schools. No doubt the picture was designed to make the gap between Chinese and Western civilizations seem smaller and more comfortably bridgeable to beleaguered Peking court reformers in 1902, structural change being easier to advocate than radical cultural transformation. Our concern is rather with one of the lesser known modes of elite dissatisfaction with schools in the Ch'ing period—which Chang Po-hsi merely inherited in 1902—and the way in which it could be polemically modernized at the end of the 1800s to stimulate educational change. We normally presume that the Chinese state willingly delegated, to private groups like families and lineages, a power to shape education that European educational traditions would not have permitted them. Obviously, few Chinese Confucian philosophers would have wanted to comment, as Montaigne did in sixteenth-century Europe, that it was a "generally accepted opinion" that children should not be reared by their parents or even by family tutors subject to such parents.[9] But to understand the totality of the critical thought about schools that existed in the Ch'ing, we must recognize that the greater privatization of educational power in China, as compared with Europe, had never gone unchallenged; and early twentieth-century reformers like Chang Po-hsi could build on this fact.

At the theoretical level, there were people like Lu Shih-i (1611–72), one of the most important political theorists of the 1600s and a major rebuilder of imperial Neo-Confucianism after the Ming dynasty foundered. Lu wrote quite categorically that schools ought not to be "privately" created by lesser elements in society. Lu condemned privately established academies (*shu-yuan*), which he said were not in accord with ritual requirements. They were, he thought, symptoms of the improper withdrawal from education by late imperial governments, and were acceptable only in the desperate circumstances caused by the divorce between government power and educational creativity.[10] There is much other evidence that part of the scholar class detested the dispersion of educational powers into private hands, and never fully accepted the alleged congruence between public and private interests in education that seems to us to have marked late imperial China's history. In the 1700s, a notable cultural dictionary even attacked the contemporary use of the term "student" (*hsueh-sheng*), suggesting that its strict early medieval meaning of government school pupil had now been improperly corrupted to describe the disciples of private teachers.[11]

At the practical level, there were conflicts of interest aplenty just beneath the surface. In the famous edict of the year 1733 in which he pretended to explain why he had not authorized the government sponsorship of big provincial academies until then, the Yung-cheng emperor contrasted the type of academy he wanted—one dedicated to "practical government" (*shih-cheng*) and the production of efficient subordinate administrators for his empire—with the provincial gentry's alleged view of academies as instruments for the furtherance of parochial self-aggrandizement and "reputation."[12] On the minority-filled frontiers, there were particularly fierce collisions between the needs of imperial "practical government," in this instance for a multiethnic bureaucracy, and the ambitions of already established provincial Chinese elites. The effort by eighteen Chinese lineages in Hunan in 1767 to usurp Kweichow prefectural degree-holder quotas that the state had set aside for the Miao, and the state's counter-attack against them, were tangible manifestations of this.[13]

More generally, only a minority of Chinese belonged to the powerful lineages that are so often depicted as the state's relatively harmonious partners in education. One anthropologist recently estimated that even in rural Kwangtung, a province notable for its big lineages, no more than 30 percent of the male population at the very most was covered by well-organized lineage groups.[14] This ensured that the poor literati outside the lineages would resent the relatively closed and privileged world of lineage education and would consider ways of revising the educational distribution of power in favor of a stronger state. The notable expansion of this relatively poor provincial intelligentsia throughout the seventeenth, eighteenth, and nineteenth centuries inevitably forced more and more elaborate reconsiderations of the entire late traditional school system, by a crucial segment of the educated classes, and led to a growing interest by educated public opinion in state-led, rather than lineage-led, educational programs.

Reference has already been made to the existence of a myth of a preimperial golden age of education in China. In one version of the myth, derived from the *Chou li* (Rituals of Chou), a text whose interpretation became an obsession with many eighteenth-century literati, ancient China below the county level had had an abundance of public schools, designed to serve communities of twenty-five households, one hundred households, five hundred households, and twenty-five hundred households. In the Ch'ing period, this picture was exalted by influential Neo-Confucian philosophers like Lu Lung-ch'i (1630–93) who clearly feared that lineage education left too many people out and was not itself adequate to preserve the moral standards of Chinese civilization.[15] It was also upheld by high-ranking court officials like Grand Secretary Chang T'ing-yü (1655–1755), who was political to his fingertips and hardly an antiquarian for antiquity's sake.[16]

In another imagined version of the archetypes of ancient education, the preimperial kings of China were thought to have both governed and educated their dependents and feudal associates in one legendary hall. One of the most exacting works of eighteenth-century Chinese scholarship, the *Ming-t'ang ta-tao lu* (Chronicle of the great doctrine of the Hall for the Illumination of the Way) by the Soochow historian Hui Tung (1697–1758), was thought by some to have finally proven the actual existence of this hall, and its perfect fusion or reconciliation of spiritual and temporal power, making it seem almost as real to some of Hui Tung's readers as the far less tidy complex of government buildings then to be found in the Ch'ien-lung emperor's Peking.[17] Such a highly centripetal model of a unity of "government" (*cheng*) and "teaching" (*chiao*), so alien to the tradition in the Christian West of dividing spiritual and temporal power, implied the symbiotic equality of schooling with all other government activities.

When it functioned as a fable of alienation and potential redemption, this dream of a golden age of feudal education could be said to be a rough Chinese equivalent of the legend of Arcadia, or even of the Noble Savage, in European thought in the same period, although it had a less primitivistic flavor. Whereas the credibility of the European legends was reinforced by the discovery of the Americas, and of their supposedly happy but relatively possession-free native inhabitants, the credibility of the Chinese legend was strengthened by the Ch'ing breakthrough in philological skills, and thus in the mastery and apparent understanding of ancient texts, institutions, and geography. Whereas the European legends implicitly criticized inequality and property-owning, the Chinese legend implicitly criticized the dissociation of education from directly exercised political power. In the ancient period, Shao T'ing-ts'ai (1648–1711) wrote, the capacities of all the different strata of upper-class China without exception, from the Son of Heaven to the lowest aristocratic class of feudal "servicemen" (*shih*), had been formed through schools; "the government and teaching of the world had met in oneness."[18]

Imperial China's legend of an all-encompassing ancient school system undoubtedly had, like its European equivalents, fantastic and self-deceiving qualities. But the unfulfilled expectations that it reflected indicate an ineradicable dissatisfaction with the actual educational facts of the 1700s. Moreover, the legend itself could be converted—as the reform official Chang Po-hsi showed in 1902—into an auxiliary paradigm of school reform in China after the Boxer Rebellion. Was such an auxiliary paradigm necessary? We probably exaggerate the fullness and the rapidity of the conversion of all the educated provincial gentry into Westernized state-worshipping nationalists by 1902, or even by 1905. There remained strong provincial vested interests in China at that time that might have favored the continuation of undirected private initiatives in education without extensive national school regulations, let alone a central Ministry of Education. It is not hard to see why Chang Po-hsi thought that the preindustrial myth of a vast public education of antiquity in which nobody went without instruction would, at the very least, make a useful ideological supplement to the newer educational inspirations that were coming to China from the West and from Japan.

The existence of the myth suggests that the weakness of late imperial China's educational organization did not lie in any utterly unclarifiable confusion of state, community, and family interests in which all real power to conceptualize a more forceful and distinct state-led educational mission, or to criticize its absence, had become lost. But the most politically dominant people had little interest in using this power before the end of the 1800s. The desire for an expansion and renewal of public education in Ch'ing China certainly existed before 1840. But in practice it took the form of a centrifugal (though not a pluralistic) diffusion of energies rather than a centripetal or vertical concentration of them. This point will be illustrated, in what follows, by looking at two government-run schools of some importance that were polar opposites of each other in eighteenth-century China. One was a successful frontier academy in Kunming, Yunnan, whose experiments inspired schoolmen in other provinces. The other was the comparatively stagnant Imperial College (*Kuo-tzu chien*) in Peking, right at the center where ideology said reform initiatives should lie but where real reform failed to occur.

The horizontal extension of public education in China before 1840, without much reform at the top or the center, contrasted with the intensification of centralized educational and research leadership in much of Europe, even before the French Revolution. In more political terms, the Ch'ien-lung emperor's perfunctory interest in his Imperial College contrasts with Louis XIV's sustenance of state scientists at the French Academy of Science or Frederick the Great's patronage of the Berlin Royal Academy of Science and Letters. The Manchu emperors' much chronicled association with a handful of European Jesuit astronomers and mapmakers, or their occasional sponsorship of scholarly compilations like the "Four Treasuries" encyclopedia, were not sufficient compensation for this contrast. Thus, it was inevitable that at the end of the Ch'ing the new Chinese interest in the Baconian notion that knowledge is power would inspire attacks on the Chinese emperors for allowing China to fall behind Europe in the accumulation of new knowledge. This was, of course, an anachronistic criticism. But it was one that could feed on and subsume earlier and less modern discontents.

Liang Ch'i-ch'ao's (1873–1929) long disquisition on schools, published in 1896, is perhaps the best example. Beginning with a recapitulation of the myth of an ancient golden age of schools in which nobody within the city-state went without instruction, Liang posited a general decline in Chinese mass knowledgeability and in critical political theory as the result of the formation of a dissent-suppressing empire that did not have to worry about external competitors.[19] And it is true that, compared to European rulers, the Chinese emperors had less need for competitive state-building, either with respect to highly educated international rivals or with respect to the feudal domestic "estates" whose defeat or subordination in Europe evoked a great royal interest there in the training of lawyers, jurists, and scientists. This relative lack of international and domestic state-building pressure, not despotism pure and simple, perhaps stood behind the equally relative underdevelopment of any central Chinese state interest in the crystallization of a more vertically integrated school system, despite the great increase in correspondence and communications among networks of scholars beyond the court. (The great eighteenth-century scholar and teacher Ch'ien Ta-hsin (1728–1804), for example, is supposed to have kept in touch with as many as two thousand friends and disciples in a society in which circulated private letters — it has been aptly suggested — substituted for the learned periodicals that China did not then have.)[20]

At any rate, the emperors of China allowed the extension of public education in the provinces, but they did little from the center to provide it with a permanent validation. The rate of abandonment of provincial academies themselves probably accelerated in the Ch'ing dynasty, as compared to previous dynasties. One study has concluded that of the nineteen hundred or so Ch'ing academies, almost half fell into disuse fairly quickly. Some 306 were lost to "natural" decay and lack of repair; one hundred more were destroyed by warfare or by floods; thirty-four others were converted into temples or government offices; and more than 470 others ceased to function for other reasons.[21] The classic study of academies in Kwangtung province estimates that the average lifespan of a Cantonese academy in the Ch'ing dynasty was a mere fifty-three years. The study agrees, moreover, that the academies' lifespan was declining.[22] The royal academies and universities of eighteenth-century Europe knew nothing like this sort of instability or dissipation of assets. To this one could add that the Chinese court did not create individual professorial chairs in provincial academies such as those created by rulers in European schools that legitimized specialized subjects.

Before the Opium War, Ch'ing literati made little link between educational systems and their international environments. Yet, even before the Opium War, as economic and demographic growth and popular rebellions more and more cruelly exposed the operational inadequacies of the Chinese monarchy, the old belief in a synthesis of "government" and "teaching" stimulated an increased opposition to such a divorce between the political center and educational creativity. Not very far in the background, among the literati, there lurked a diffuse utopian mentality that longed for some sort of education-based reenchantment of the world as a whole. In such a reenchanted world, it was hoped, the monarchy would have to become more subject to the schools. Indeed, in Huang Tsung-hsi's (1610–95) drastic seventeenth-century theoretical attempt to renegotiate the "government-teaching" synthesis, the monarchy would even have had its "rights" and "wrongs" arbitrated by them.

THE IMPORTANCE OF SCHOOLS IN LATE IMPERIAL THOUGHT: THE THEORIES OF HUANG TSUNG-HSI

Politically, in times of trouble, belief in the need to reaffirm the desirability of the homogenization (or more perfect interpenetration) of "government" and "teaching," which the ancient schools ideal made concrete, kept open the whole nature of the relationship between schools and political power rather than ending debate about it. It is possible also that much educational thought in the Ch'ing, if not earlier, reflected the displaced legislative impulses of a large, politically interested, but often relatively powerless intelligentsia whose members were forced to transpose their legislative ambitions from political structures to schools.

The most formidable analysis of the perceived sicknesses of the late traditional empire offers us the best evidence. The reference is, of course, to Huang Tsung-hsi's *Ming-i tai-fang lu*, a difficult title definitively rendered into English as "A Plan for the Prince," written in the 1660s.[23] This work, as is well known, accused emperors of selfishly converting China into an enormous private estate for the use of their own descendants. Thus, thousands of copies of an abridged version of this text were printed and distributed at the Hunan School of Current Affairs in 1897 by Liang Ch'i-ch'ao and other reformers, who saw it as a book that preached limits on despotism. Yet although this book was also read and criticized in the eighteenth century, it was not a major target of the Ch'ing emperors' Literary Inquisition.[24] How could such a potentially subversive thinker as Huang Tsung-hsi blend well enough with his environment to have avoided the full attentions of the imperial book burners? Leaving aside the innumerable controversies about the purposes of the Literary Inquisition or about how much Huang Tsung-hsi was either a Ming loyalist or even a completely secular critic of despotic government, we might agree with his greatest English-language interpreter that while Huang Tsung-hsi's work was "a radical attack on traditional imperial institutions" it was not "at odds" with the general fund of ideas of other literati. Huang "only gave more pointed expression to political views that other thinkers of the day shared with him," Professor de Bary concludes.[25] We might supplement this with the suggestion that Huang's dominant and uncompromising view of schools as the rightful central source of all authority in Chinese politics had at least an abstract legitimacy that the most sensitive emperors could not deny, even if no emperor wanted or would tolerate the immediate situational realization of such a view. The chapters on schools and scholars are possibly the most vital and courageous parts of the *Ming-i tai-fang lu*.

With remarkable audacity, Huang proposed in these chapters the comprehensive reorganization of the imperial political system in such a manner that both highest- and lowest-level government organs would be "school-ized," to use a strange but perfectly appropriate term for it.[26] Schools would become overt legislative and political supervisory organs. "Government" and "teaching" would not merely be united; government would become derivative from schools.

At the very outset of his schools chapter, Huang Tsung-hsi reminded his readers of the most praiseworthy supreme institution of higher learning that the preimperial Chou kings had supposedly created for their capital city and that was known, roughly translated, as the "Moated Sanctuary." (This is a relatively fanciful English translation of the Chinese term "Pi-yung", which more literally means "like a piece of jade surrounded by water;" the term is untranslatable in any way that does justice both to its complexities and to the convenience of Western readers.) The Moated Sanctuary was the wish-fulfilling centerpiece of late imperial China's ancient schools myth, along with memories of other less important ancient centers of higher learning known roughly as the "half-moated sanctuaries" (*pan-kung*, more literally "half palaces" with water on only one side of them), which had allegedly belonged to the hereditary feudal princes below the Chou kings. Avoiding most of the aristocratic details with which less obviously political philologists, especially in the 1700s, liked to embellish the Moated Sanctuary archetype, Huang used it to illustrate his point that the ancient kings had governed the world from schools. Huang stated that the Moated Sanctuary had been the place where Chinese court positions were organized, government orders published, military campaigns planned, and justice discussed and dispensed. But now schools had lost their functions of political governance. They had become marginal dependencies of the emperor and his "vulgar officials."[27]

In order to reform existing schools, Huang Tsung-hsi tried to begin at the top, or at the political center, by making the seventeenth-century Imperial College, the school closest to the emperor, deputize for the ancient Moated Sanctuary in all the mythic plenitude of its reconciliation of government power with the absolute claims of education. In practical terms, Huang demanded that the head of the Imperial College be chosen from among the great scholars of the age and that he be made the equal of the chancellor or the foremost minister of the government. The emperor himself was to visit the Imperial College at least once a month, accompanied by his senior officials. There he was to receive critical lectures about the shortcomings of his policies, with no ritual prohibitions on their content, from the Imperial College head. All the emperor's sons were to be compelled to study at the Imperial College with other students so that they might learn about other people's circumstances, be forced to toil hard, gain empirical experience beyond that found inside their palaces, and thus avoid arrogant self-exaltation.

Huang thus made the Imperial College the matrix and the paramount conscience of an ideally reformulated synthesis of "government" with "teaching." He then argued that the idea that the Imperial College should epitomize — that of the school as the arbiter of politics — should also be extended downward to the counties. Local schools were to become smaller replicas of the revitalized Imperial College. Local officials, like the emperor at the Imperial College, were to be regularly converted into pupils who had to listen to critical lectures about their conduct from more scholarly educational officials. In this proposal, some modern critics of Huang have seen a thinly disguised effort by him to transfer power over schools from officials to an out-of-office provincial intelligentsia.

But this interpretation constrains a major thinker in too narrow a formula. Huang's whole argument about schools suggests that he could barely contain an impatient awareness that the general potentialities of school education had vastly outgrown the ways in which the seventeenth-century school system familiar to him was organized. In this respect, his thought may seem to us to have been prophetic. The *Ming-i tai-fang lu* proposed, for example, that school-based medical education be expanded. Medical education graduates were to be tested and controlled by the provincial commissioner of education. At the end of the year, the mortality rates of their patients were to be recorded in registers, as a result of which the graduates who were least effective doctors were to be dismissed. Huang's faith that government schools could improve even Chinese public health standards was just one more aspect of a gigantic and rather protean optimism about schools as agencies of change.

But there was little that was prophetic about democracy here. While Huang wanted a revival of government schools as centers of moral and political standardization and criticism, he could not see this, in terms similar to Western democratic theory, as a form of independent countervailing power, of "checks and balances." On the contrary, belief in the ideal synthesis of "government" and "teaching" made Huang want to reconcile the schools and the court, to end their estrangement and make their two separate worlds one, admittedly with the monarch as a more morally constrained executive and the Imperial College in Peking as an intermittently intervening sort of educational papacy (without the papacy's separate standing).

Even so, Huang's theories indicated the partial transfer of millenarian expectations, at least of the upper-class variety, away from the monarchy and toward public education. Schools were seen here as the antidote to political decay in a way no court could be. School officials were even delegated by Huang to guarantee the propriety of all the sacrifices, the clothing, and even the popular speech and music in their jurisdictions. Those were the feats of magical purification that kings were still supposed to accomplish in neighboring polities like Java or Burma or Siam.

For Huang's disciples, one sticking point was the anticipated human cost of trying to translate this "school-izing" millenarianism into reality at the end of the 1600s. Shao T'ing-ts'ai, perhaps the most important of these disciples, agreed with Huang that schools were the places where the government of the empire should originate and where the ethical principles on which it was based should be decided. But he abandoned Huang's proposals that famous literati be made omnipotent local school officials and that the Imperial College head be made a schoolmasterly prime minister with the freedom to criticize the emperor to his face. Warning that the literal recreation of such a "school-ized" society would cost too much in taxes and labor, Shao was reduced to offering other, vaguer, more conventional remedies for educational decay. The pedagogical rediscovery of the proper action-directed modes of the internalization of ethics was one; and the abandonment of the metaphysical, word-obsessed, careerist type of education that was allegedly failing in China was another.[28]

CONJECTURAL HISTORIES OF SCHOOLS
AND THE CRISIS OF THE ELITE

Thought about the importance of renewing the power of government schools was multifaceted in late imperial China. There was the relatively egalitarian Neo-Confucian version of the schools legend. As reflected in Huang Tsung-hsi, it was not primarily concerned with differentiating the noble of society from the lowly so much as with extending the Mencian idea that the people were more important than the prince. The influence of the literati and their students was thus to be restored, through a restoration of government schools, as the touchstone of the people's own centrality.

But there was also a contrapuntal and far from egalitarian belief in the need to reaffirm the rightness and clarity of imperial China's heroic transfiguration of the aristocratic privileges of birth and heredity into the essentially post-aristocratic privileges of educational success. It has been justly pointed out that the early establishment of the theoretical supremacy of the wisdom of scholars over the hereditary claims of aristocrats and the wealth of merchants was the Chinese political tradition's outstanding feat. In the premodern West, even Plato's "guardians" had been aristocrats, and learned men had been formally conceded political leadership purely on the basis of their learning only in marginal texts like Thomas More's *Utopia*.[29] But the Chinese political tradition's outstanding feat was never perfectly secure in the eyes of its swelling numbers of aspirant beneficiaries who claimed to be scholars. The contradiction between the emperors' mission as educational expansionists and their unwillingness to share real power or security of social position with the intelligentsia whose formation they had themselves encouraged had become acute by the Ch'ing period, and partly foreshadowed the "crisis of the intelligentsia" in twentieth-century China. The fear of the accelerated erosion of the tangible privileges of educational achievement, with the dangerous consequence that teachers and students might internalize the sense that they were "useless" outsiders, strengthened in the 1700s. As it did so, anxious literati could link their interest in the archetypes of ancient education to a more selfish and far less Mencian interest in some sort of limited refeudalization of the social order, so as to halt the growing insecurity and debasement of the provincial scholar class.

Higher education of the ancient ideal was supposed to have been designed for the "sons of the state" (*kuo-tzu*). This term survived, provocatively, in one of the common names of the formally most important school of higher learning in the Ch'ing empire, the Imperial College. It was also known more literally as the "Directorate for the Sons of the State," or *Kuo-tzu chien*. Who were the "sons of the state"? Eighteenth-century writers showed considerable interest in their social definition. Chin Pang (1735–1801), whose work *Li chien* (Comments on ritual) offers one of the more significant descriptions of ancient schools, made it clear that the "sons of the state" were the sons of the higher Chou dynasty aristocracy. That is, they were the sons of aristocratic officials whose families were entitled to at least three ancestral temples, as contrasted with lesser aristocrats like "servicemen" (*shih*), who were only allowed one ancestral temple, and the ordinary people, who were not then allowed any. Ancient higher learning had comprised only the "sons of the state" and a small admixture of the brightest "district people's children," who had, however, previously been excluded from preparatory royal government schools. Such an arrangement properly maintained the distinctions between the "noble and the mean," Chin Pang wrote.[30]

Eighteenth-century scholars, using their philological skills, produced an unprecedentedly detailed picture of the preimperial "sons of the state." And all the aristocratic splendors of this picture revived the tension between the ancient and the medieval principles in Chinese education. This tension also kept open the nature of the relationship between schools and political power. For an ancient higher education that was dedicated, as Chin Pang suggested, to the preservation of "noble and mean" distinctions in a society in which the numbers of ancestral temples had been strictly rationed by hereditary status, was not full of promises about the potential achievement of individual sagehood for everyone, the staple of many later Neo-Confucian educators.

But many eighteenth-century classicists were less captivated by such promises about sagehood for all than they were by their own detailed descriptions of an omnicompetent preimperial ruling class with great corporate solidarity: the sort of solidarity the eighteenth-century scholar class lacked. As they imagined it, this preimperial ruling class engaged in very broadly conceived educational exercises—ritual, music, archery, riding, writing, and arithmetic—all year long, moving seasonally from one part of the old higher learning complex to another. The ruler himself was a close colleague in these exercises, presiding over the aristocratic dinner parties at which elders were honored and fed and at which the educations of the aristocracy's sons began. In the eyes of the classicists who admired them, ancient schools had not been separate or specialized teaching institutions at all. They had been the complete arena in which the public life and socialization of the aristocracy had occurred: they were not only schools but also assembly halls, council chambers, clubs, and athletic grounds.

This self-sustaining aristocratic communalism, full of feasts and other pageantry, in which schooling itself was a pageant of highly privileged modes of upper-class socialization, was not perfectly compatible with the less class-conscious, more postaristocratic Neo-Confucian passion for the creation of morally responsible individual selves. It was also remote from Western educational concepts like "university," which implied a relatively autonomous corporation confined to teachers and students. Few things more disturbed eighteenth-century student admirers of this remote feudal educational vision than later textual confusions that implied a separation of the functions of governance, education, and feasts and other aristocratic rituals in the ancient world and that thus encouraged the disintegration of the archetype as a whole in people's imaginations. Saving the archetype became a considerable task for students at academies from Soochow to Canton. As lamented one of the students who wrote essays on the Moated Sanctuary at Juan Yuan's famous Ku-ching school at Hangchow at the end of the 1700s, the twisted belief in the later Chinese empire that the Imperial College and the Moated Sanctuary might have been different institutions had led to the latter being misidentified as a place of recreation, not as a school. Thus, it had fallen into neglect.[31]

It would be wrong to assume that eighteenth-century literati all had a common picture in their minds, full of certainty and precision, of how ancient schools had once worked. There were fierce textual disagreements among them, revolving around such matters as the exact locations of ancient institutions within the preimperial royal domain and even whether the term *Pi-yung* had referred to a moated building or just to something like a pond. The esoteric ancient terminology, much of it no longer in use, that had defined the schools and the sorts of people who were involved with them—"sons of the state," "noninheriting sons," "elders of the state," "elders of the people"—baffled even the late imperial theoreticians, like Shao T'ing-ts'ai, who most fancied polemical contrasts between ancient schools and their own.[32]

It would also be wrong to suppose that the leaders of this eighteenth-century scholastic movement that heightened consciousness about the grandeur of the ancient schools had much in common with Huang Tsung-hsi in either political purpose or intellectual method. He was writing speculative political theory in which schools were to help save China and control the emperor. They were writing conjectural history in which schools happened to be more a part of the political center than they were in the real world of the 1700s and in which the ruler discharged his duties within a more intensely pedagogical environment. Much eighteenth-century antiquarian research was pursued for the sheer love of the exercise, without intentional iconoclasm. It would be as unfair to argue that all of it had a crude social and political determination as it might be to propose that something like Einstein's theory of relativity answered obvious social and political needs in our own century.

Yet the imaginative inflation and idealization of the primitive, unspecialized education of China's high aristocratic period, by late imperial intellectuals living thousands of years after it, was mythmaking as well as simple research. Moreover, it was seen as such by its adversaries at the time. Ch'eng Chin-fang (1718–1784), the Yangchow salt merchant's son whose written work was notable for its reverence of the educational program of Sung Neo-Confucianism, derided what he regarded as untrustworthy Han dynasty elaborations of preimperial educational arrangements that exaggerated their scale. Ch'eng stipulated that Mencius was the only guide to follow with respect to what and where ancient schools had been. Ch'eng had fun with contemporary literati who argued that the Moated Sanctuary had stood for a great complex of simultaneously existing schools, but who in the same breath had claimed that its education had been confined to higher aristocrats. Ch'eng deflated ancient education by insisting on its smallness. He pointed out that only one school, not a complex, could possibly have been required for the little group of two hundred or three hundred educable royal and aristocratic children who existed at the time of the first emperors. As the numbers of hereditary officials multiplied later in the ancient period, Ch'eng allowed, some "huts" of higher learning could possibly have been added in order to teach their children too, but nothing greater or more spacious.[33]

Mythmaking invites some political assessment, even if not to the same degree as that which a work like Huang Tsung-hsi's "Plan for the Prince" inspires. The first thing that such a political assessment might do is note the suggestive congruence between the popularity of an extravagant picture of ancient education in which the educated class had great solidarity, had proximity to the political center, and was sharply distinguished from the uneducated and "mean," and the growing anxieties of the actual eighteenth-century Chinese educated class, which enjoyed far less of any of these things. The ideal was so different from the real, by the end of the 1700s, as to disturb the fantasy world of any adolescent provincial academy student.

What was the plight of the Ch'ing degree-holding elite? The ways in which modern analysts—conditioned by industrial society's fondness for social fluidity indexes and the measurement of social mobility—have looked at this problem are not really very dissimilar to the ways in which knowledgeable contemporaries themselves regarded it. We begin with the modern analysts. Ho Ping-ti concludes that it "was much more difficult" for the most senior examination system degree-holders (*chin-shih*) "to attain high official rank during the Ch'ing than during the previous Chinese dynasty."[34] He traces their frustrations particularly to the circumstance that in the self-consciously multiethnic Ch'ing empire highly educated Chinese had to share government positions with Manchus and Mongols, as they had not before 1644. Wang Te-chao also emphasizes the grip of many nonacademic Manchus and Mongols on such positions. On the basis of incomplete statistics, Wang suggests that of some 744 board presidents in the Ch'ing dynasty, only 339 had the top *chin-shih* degrees; of 585 provincial governors general, only 181 had *chin-shih* degrees; and of 989 provincial governors, only 390 had *chin-shih* degrees.[35]

Contemporaries who were knowledgeable about the problem ranged from emperors to maverick intellectuals. They had an almost equally keen statistical awareness of the weakening links between political power and educational achievement. The man at the top was the reluctant ultimate authority on this phenomenon. In 1765, the Ch'ien-lung emperor publicly calculated that China was producing more than five thousand regional degree-holders (*chü-jen*) each decade, if one counted both regular and "special favor" examinations. Yet because fewer than five hundred of these men could be appointed to the coveted position of county magistrate within a single decade, most of them had to wait "for up to thirty or more years" before they could be chosen, by which time they were senescent. Forced by the furious gossip of "ignorant" literati to admit and discuss the problem, the Ch'ien-lung emperor said apologetically that he meditated on their frustration in "the middle of the night."[36] Moving from emperors to well-known and vocal victims of this political depreciation of examination degrees, we encounter Kung Tzu-chen (1792–1841), a high degree-holder who personally failed to gain a position at the Hanlin Academy. Kung calculated that successful scholars had to wait thirty to thirty-five years on average to gain appointments to the Hanlin Academy and another decade after that to become Grand Secretaries. By then, they were elderly and exhausted. Ambitious Manchu and Chinese government appointees in general required thirty to thirty-five years of service to become officials of the first rank, Kung concluded. Thus the "worthy and the knowledgeable" could no longer really rise to the top.[37]

Social change compounded the deficiencies of the government employment machinery, furthering the sense of deprivation of provincial scholars. There was an unprecedented spread of wealth outside the scholar class in the Ch'ing period. This wealth meant that there was growing differentiation in the sources of status legitimization and its rewards. To the degree-holding literati, indeed to the possibly five million or so classically educated male commoners in Ch'ing China who were competing or who had competed for higher status through schooling and examinations, the preeminence of the claim of educational achievement as the criterion for earning higher status that everyone accepted appeared to be gravely jeopardized by such differentiation.[38] Confronted by Peking rice traders whose wealth transcended that of "princes and lords," or by north China plutocrats who could spend more than 100,000 taels on one day's food and lodgings for the visiting Ch'ien-lung emperor and his relatives and servants, the scholar class became more and more visibly anxious about the defense of its own noble titles and noble status attributes (*ming-ch'i*).[39] Significantly, this preimperial term more than twenty centuries old was still in use as a means of characterizing the rank and privileges that the far more recent examination system distributed. The imaginative self-conception of the scholar class was both aristocratic and postaristocratic.

The Ch'ing court's sporadic but barefaced sale of degrees to rich people obviously worsened the scholarly elite's anxieties about the perceived mismanagement of the distribution of noble titles and noble status attributes. The imperial court was supposed to exercise careful control over the status system and its symbolic representation in the interest of preserving respect for the true elite. Most poor lower scholars believed that the titles and peacock feathers of the empire's higher degree-holders were the latterday equivalents of the ranks and chariot dress of the preimperial warrior aristocrats, and should only exist in limited, rationed quantities. Given their psychological aristocratism, few of them could applaud the idea of a diversifying market in government positions. For such scholars, a reconstruction of the practical primacy of the government school system was one possible first step (or first sign of the government's willingness) to begin salvaging the doctrine of "judging the importance of people on the basis of their talent."

Since the stability of any political system rests to a considerable degree on the qualities, real or imagined, of its elite, the Ch'ing court's huge expansion of the sale of examination system degrees as compared to the Ming dynasty's, was both a political and an educational gamble. Degrees were sold to raise money for military campaigns or to obtain the transportation of military supplies. They were sold to raise emergency grain reserves that ordinary government tax collections were too weak to mobilize, especially when central government power receded.[40] Sun Chia-kan (1683–1753), a notable school reformer who despised the sale of student access to the supposedly august Imperial College in Peking, personally investigated the sales system in the 1730s. He discovered that Board of Finance grain procurement was aided by the sale of some forty-three political positions or indulgences, ranging from board department directorships themselves to exemption from capital punishment. What particularly scandalized him was that two-thirds of the one and a half million taels that were annually raised from such sales came from just one item: the purchase of the status of "Imperial College student" (chien-sheng).[41]

In the eyes of thoughtful officials and scholars, the court finally overstepped the boundary of what was tolerable, in the apparent commercial adulteration of the educated elite, in 1833. A rich man named P'an Shih-ch'eng bought a chü-jen degree with a contribution of twelve thousand silver taels to famine relief in Chihli. This was the first time that such an advanced degree status (which carried with it eligibility for high government posts) had been sold rather than earned. The affair triggered a panic among some literati that a political system in which the value of education was nominally supreme was about to mutate irretrievably or fall apart. It is not easy for Western readers to grasp the niceties of all the differences among the degree-holders of the traditional Chinese civil service examinations: "presented scholars," "recommended men," "tribute students," "Imperial College students," and the like. The grandeur of some of the differences perceived among them by Chinese students themselves is suggested by the ancient idiom that one brave Yunnanese censor invoked during this 1833 controversy. Discussing rich people now armed with purchased chü-jen degrees who might try to go a stage farther and even buy chin-shih degrees, he predicted that "having obtained Kansu, they will look covetously toward Szechwan."[42] Here the differing degree levels were imagined, not without justice, to represent whole provinces vulnerable to plunder and conquest.

It is not difficult to see the risks the Ch'ing empire ran with degree sales at a time when thousands of higher degree-holders found themselves barred for decades from the government positions for which they thought they had been educated. Any sociologically minded historian with a knowledge of the consequences of "surplus" intelligentsias in more modern societies could list them. The lowering of the level of ability of the serving bureaucratic elite relative to the increased numbers of highly educated people outside the bureaucracy, or—to put it another way—the greater replaceability of the ruling elite by people outside it, could in the long run be potentially revolutionary portents, given that in an ideologically meritocratic society people prefer to obey people whose abilities are obviously greater than their own.

But that was the long run. In the short run, the devotion of so many eighteenth-century Chinese literati to an archaic, unspecialized aristocratic model of education was hardly revolutionary. Far from wishing to find new identities, such literati were more concerned with repossessing and mastering the rich range of aristocratic and post-aristocratic identities that their educational tradition already permitted them, so that their value could be more fundamentally understood by their rulers, rather than merely accommodated by them. In comparative terms, such literati seem to us to resemble not so much their actual European contemporaries, the Enlightenment thinkers who were then demanding more intellectual freedom, as the ineffectual Plutarch-worshipping antiquarians of the much later Europe of Weimar Germany.

Their Chinese critics at the time, however, saw the problem as one of a discrepancy between a growth in education and the lack of any equivalent growth in the circulation of political information. High officials like Ch'en Hung-mou observed that public opinion in the eighteenth century regarded provincial schoolmen (tu-shu jen) as "useless," because of their addiction to the distant past at the expense of the affairs of the present. But the real cause of their "uselessness," Ch'en Hung-mou wrote, was the provincial scholars' almost total lack of access to the central "court bulletin" (ti-pao) or Peking gazette or to the commercial digests of this gazette, which were also published in Peking. The redemption of the provincial sheng-yuan class, Ch'en further wrote, lay in the installation of court bulletin reading facilities in every town and village school in China, with arrangements made to ensure that even groups of impoverished students had access.[43]

It is noteworthy, however, that while eighteenth-century European universities were being denounced by their critics as useless because their clericalism and medievalism led to scientific sterility, Ch'en Hung-mou and other Chinese critics found the uselessness of Chinese provincial education to lie in its political sterility. Ch'en linked the slow delegitimization of the provincial scholar class to the underdevelopment of the central government's absorption of provincial schools into its own active political world. This was a complaint about the divorce between education and the political center from a slightly different angle, but behind Ch'en's empire-building pragmatism and the less practical schoolmen's antiquarianism one can detect a shared anxiety.

Nor, in more purely educational terms, was the devotion of the literati to an archaic model of education as whimsical as it might seem. China, as was inevitable in a complex civilization, was suffering from an intensifying crisis in the relations between the schools that actually existed, which were based upon artificial book learning, and the "real" world outside the schools. The simpler ancient education had made the school and its outside world coessential, or at least had brought more of the outside world inside the school, thus (it seemed) more effectively encouraging the pupils' sense that their education was meaningful. The reconciliation of the world of the school with that of society outside the school is an eternal educational difficulty. Late imperial apostles of the return of the ancient "sons of the state" who wished to solve it, as well as to make the scholar class more cohesive and the ruler more of a colleague, were hardly just reflecting a hatred of social development rules, as modern critics have sometimes said. Wishful antiquarian research was being used in eighteenth-century China to solve educational problems that today might be consigned to psychologists: the ones who insist that the school must be a form of community life, not just a lesson-dispensing institution.

Altogether, there was a large active or latent desire for a more centrally focused kind of public education. It could be found in everything from the iconoclastic theories of Huang Tsung-hsi to the conjectural history of philologists to the mundane correspondence of officials like Ch'en Hung-mou. It was more a state of mind than a movement. But it was a pervasive state of mind.

THE DIVORCE BETWEEN THE CENTER AND
EDUCATIONAL CREATIVITY IN PRACTICE

Of all existing government schools, the Imperial College had the greatest theoretical promise as a forcing-house of change. Given the vitality of Ch'ing scholarship and the great increase in lateral correspondence and communications among networks of scholars beyond the court, the failure of the Imperial College in Peking to represent and refine these developments in the manner of a European royal academy is one of the most interesting problems in the history of late imperial education.

The Imperial College was the place where a number of ambitious political reformers hoped to begin the renovation of Chinese politics. Huang Tsung-hsi, as we have seen, wanted a politically dominant Imperial College to offer a corrective reality to the artificiality of the imperial family's palaces and to be imitated by smaller government schools in the provinces. Other equally formidable and perhaps more widely read theorists, such as Lu Shih-i, echoed his aspirations in less dramatic ways. Living in the same century as Huang, Lu Shih-i proposed a simplifying reorganization of almost the whole structure of the central government. In this reorganization, such hallowed institutions as the Hanlin Academy, the Imperial Observatory, and the Court of Imperial

Sacrifice were to be abolished and absorbed into the Six Boards; but the Imperial College was to be preserved and elevated to a unique position beyond that of ordinary ministries.[44]

Less politically minded figures such as Sun Hsing-yen (1753–1818), who served as head of southeastern China's famous "evidential research" citadel, the Ku-ching academy at Hangchow, also thought publicly about better versions of the Imperial College. For Sun, the early medieval Imperial College had been an important bulwark against the cultural and other leveling processes that undermined the manifest destiny of the scholar class. Sun pointed to the heroic Imperial College of the T'ang dynasty one thousand years earlier as the place that had given the empire's students a classical knowledge appropriate to their social hegemony. Its students had supposedly had a profound multiple-script working literacy of over ten thousand words, as contrasted with the simpler, more vulgar classical literacy of only two thousand or so words of students in later centuries when the Imperial College was no longer a beacon.[45]

The Ch'ien-lung emperor began his reign by demolishing all such hopes for an ascendant Imperial College. Historians have long assumed that China's Manchu emperors feared the provincial academies and only belatedly accepted their revival by the 1730s. In fact, a powerful Imperial College close to their throne was probably what they really feared. In "A Plan for the Prince," Huang Tsung-hsi had helped to show why by celebrating the alleged thirty thousand students at the Imperial College of the later Han dynasty, "bold in words and profound in discourse," who had menaced high government officials.

The emperor acknowledged in 1736 that the imperial school system was vertically stunted, lacking a properly recognizable "law of academic ascent," or ladder. But he ruled out the possibility that the revitalization of the chief capital city school could supply this, on the thin pretext that the great distances of the empire prevented scholars from all over China assembling in the Imperial College. The Ch'ien-lung emperor was perfectly prepared to enhance the dignity of provincial academies as a substitute for any genuine political restoration of the Imperial College. In 1736, he therefore proposed the official doctrine that provincial academies be considered the modern equivalents of "the schools of the ancient feudal princes' fiefs." He thereby safely located in the provinces the necessary imaginative bridge in education between the contemporary empire and the preimperial aristocratic model of higher education. After six years of study at such latter-day versions of the feudal princes' colleges, the emperor promised, "one or two" of the better academy students could be recommended for government positions.[46]

Even the Ch'ien-lung emperor was not so secure against public opinion that he could neglect the Imperial College completely. It was by now as much a cluster of images that evoked an ideal world as it was an actual school. He refurbished its buildings; and when a censor charged in 1788 that a tutor at the Imperial College was openly selling successful marks in college tests, and that poor students were being driven to borrow money to pay him, the rumors that money had displaced educational achievement at the Imperial College were threatening enough that the emperor brought in one of the great Manchu military commanders, Fu-k'ang-an (d. 1796), fresh from repressing rebellions in Kansu and Taiwan, to control the situation.[47] As part of his famous capital city building program, the Ch'ien-lung emperor even ordered that a literal replica of the ancient Moated Sanctuary as described in the classical accounts of Chou dynasty rituals, be constructed in 1783 at the Imperial College site.[48] This final historical appearance of the *Pi-yung*, as it was imagined to have been, had about as much practical effect as the equally romantic introduction of an Arcadian Academy, with its academicians masquerading as shepherds, in seventeenth-century Rome. Even Board of Rites ministers opposed the physical reappearance of the Moated Sanctuary in eighteenth-century Peking. They told the emperor that "practical government" did not cling to the symbolic past.

To understand the stakes involved in the genuine or merely the make-believe restoration of the Imperial College, it is not enough to look at the theory of Huang Tsung-hsi or Lu Shih-i; the recent past of the actual college must also be appreciated. Searchers after East-West equivalences have compared the Chinese Imperial College to medieval European universities like those in Bologna or Paris or Cambridge.[49] The comparison has some serious difficulties. It never had their relative independence or stood for an equivalent pluralism of learning; and as already noted, its roots lay not in the notion of an exclusive learning corporation, as with Western universities, but in the notion of an aristocratic public life in which political and educational functions were interchangeable.

The Imperial College began to assume its final form in the late fourteenth century, a time both of elation and despair for its partisans then and later. The early Ming emperors maintained two "Directorates for the Sons of the State" —the literal version of the more common of the College's two names—at Peking and Nanking. Ming chroniclers claim that at its peak in 1422 the Nanking Directorate enrolled as many as 9,972 students, but that its enrollment dwindled rapidly to about one thousand students a century later. Whatever its size, the founder of the Ming dynasty in the late 1300s took an obsessive interest in the Imperial College. His involvement evidently extended from personally designing the silk gowns of its students, in order to differentiate them from "bureaucratic underlings," to forbidding its students to enter the school's kitchens and whip the cooks.[50] At this point the Ming Directorate seems to have been an emerging academic powerhouse with the embryonic capacity to function as a medieval school of national administration. Its students were assigned as bureaucratic apprentices to government offices. This made them quite unlike most medieval European university students, but it plausibly reconciled the ancient theoretical concern of uniting government and teaching with the need of the despotic monarchy of the fourteenth century for a new civil service.

Inspired by Sung developments, the Nanking Directorate also established an internal pedagogical structure that survived in various later Imperial Colleges, at least on paper, over the next five centuries. It enshrined a progressive, three-tiered, pyramidal curriculum in which entering students with relatively modest literary abilities and classical understanding were assigned to three preliminary "halls" (t'ang). After a year and a half, they might be promoted to two more advanced halls, and eventually they might gain access to the class or hall at the top of the pyramid, the "accordance with human nature hall" (shuai-hsing t'ang).[51] It is not clear how much genuine educational progress the six halls system guaranteed. Nevertheless, the Ch'ing emperors, while converting the Nanking Directorate into a prefectural school in 1650, kept this internal organization of six halls in their own directorate in Peking.

For defenders of China's central institution of higher learning, its internal organization was not as important as its capacity to demonstrate consistent principles of elitism. When critics of the "Directorate for the Sons of the State" complained about this particular title for the school, it was the word "directorate" (chien) they attacked, not the seemingly anachronistic aristocratic term "sons of the state." In the 1600s, Lu Shih-i condemned the first Ming emperor for first calling the college a "school" but later changing its name back to "directorate," thus reducing its prestige to that of a minor government agency. Lu observed that the fact that the head of the school was officially called a "libationer" (chi-chiu), a form of address for old men, rather than the more reverential "national preceptor" (kuo-shih) as he ought to be, had made matters even worse.[52]

In fact, the very ideal of being one of the "sons of the state," the late imperial equivalent of the heirs of the ancient aristocrats, degenerated into virtual incoherence after the fourteenth century. Students at the early Ming Imperial College had included regional degree-holders selected by the Hanlin Academy, tribute students to the college (kung-chien) nominated by prefectural and county schools, and students through inheritance (yin-chien), the sons of high civil officials. The "inheritance students" most closely approximated the preimperial meaning of "sons of the state." But even this pale and reduced form of the hereditary principle was applied arbitrarily by Ming emperors, who bestowed it as a "favor" without much reference to bureaucratic (let alone aristocratic) status. After 1450, commoner students (min-sheng) bought their way into the Imperial College through donations of grain or money made to the government in times of crisis. With this change, a dignity-sensitive majority of the regional degree-holders began to avoid studying at a school whose student body had become so heterogeneous.

In the Ch'ing period, the whole notion of the "sons of the state" became murkier than ever. Fewer than three hundred students appear to have studied at the Ch'ing Imperial College or attended it for tests at any one time. But thousands of "Imperial College students" (*chien-sheng*) across China, in provinces remote from the college itself, were allowed to hold the title, including the rich men's sons who had purchased it. Connection with the Imperial College had thus become a decentralized, marketable status enablement device rather than a centralized educational (and class socialization) experience.

As the directorate lost educational prestige and the power to clarify social stratification among Chinese students, the respect that foreign rulers paid it by sending more genuinely elite students to it from outside became, proportionately, all the more important to preserving what remained of its disappearing aristocratic mystique. In the seventeenth and eighteenth centuries, the foreign students at the Imperial College who notably helped to keep alive the older, stricter, less marketplace-oriented concept of the "sons of the state" were the impeccably upper-class sons of the kings and ministers of the Ryukyu kingdom. In return, the Okinawan students were treated with great liberality. By a lucky accident, we know that they enjoyed a sufficiently exalted position to be able to hold conversations on their own initiative with the Vietnamese ambassador during his visit to Peking in 1760–61.[53]

In the highest government school, whose student body was supposed to forecast the nature of the elite future, the increasingly meaningless heterogeneity of the Imperial College's Chinese students robbed it of what one might call its educational teleology, the sense that it was part of a continually unfolding educational and political purpose. Barring the sudden conversion of the emperors to the ideas of Huang Tsung-hsi or Lu Shih-i, the only way this teleological sense could be revived was by making the college a more concentrated sort of school of national administration.

The intent of the most important reforms attempted at the college between 1644 and 1905, those of Board of Justice president Sun Chia-kan in 1737, fell short of this but could have been a beginning. The Yung-cheng emperor's publicly stated suspicion, already mentioned, that academies in the provinces would promote local interests rather than "practical government" gave Sun and other reformers their cue. Drawing on the ideas of the Sung dynasty school reformer Hu Yuan (993–1059), Sun asked that the numbers of students that provincial schools sent to the Imperial College be strictly limited to three hundred or fewer. This more carefully chosen student body was then to be directed into two specialized "studios" or divisions of learning: the "classical meanings" (*ching-i*) division and the "administration of affairs" (*chih-shih*) division. Within the former division, students could specialize on one Confucian Classic or cover many. Within the latter division, students would study such subjects as laws, border defense, the control of water resources, historical modes of taxation, and mathematics, again specializing on one of these "affairs" or covering many.[54]

The reforms for the Imperial College that Sun Chia-kan proposed in 1737 were applied only superficially; they apparently soon became a dead letter. It is worth asking why. On the one hand, the emperors themselves in the eighteenth century had no obvious need for anything like Chinese equivalents of the university-trained jurists whom Max Weber identified, in his famous treatise *Politics as a Vocation*, as being indispensable to state consolidation in the more pluralistic and competitive national politics of Europe: the royal and parliamentary jurists of seventeenth-century England, for instance, or the French crown jurists who helped the French monarchy to weaken the rule of aristocratic seigneurs. So the political need for something like a more specialized school of national administration was relatively weak. Inevitably, Sun Chia-kan stressed the nonpolitical social need. He portrayed his educational reforms as a remedy for the existing marginalization of the Imperial College's graduates rather than as any attempt at a formal reordering of the organization of knowledge. With the creation of a specialized "two studios" system, for example, Sun wanted to give the head of the Imperial College more power within the bureaucratic labyrinth to secure speedy employment for his best graduates as county magistrates, instead of having them languish for decades as county directors of schools.

On the other hand, this refinement of educational elitism at the political center necessarily threatened to aggravate the displacement and marginality of the thousands of young schoolmen outside the college who would not get this specialized administrative education. Their more traditional classical educations would then seem even less relevant in the eyes of themselves and others, eighteenth-century academicians warned.[55] Given the need to palliate the worries of the surplus provincial intelligentsia who would remain outside the latter-day "sons of the state," there was not sufficient support for Sun's ideas among the higher bureaucrats.

Like other provocative educational ideals, the spirit of innovation that Hu Yuan and Sun Chia-kan represented withered in the capital but was kept alive in the provinces. Discussions of it became themselves educational subject matter. For instance, at Juan Yuan's Sea of Learning Hall (Hsueh-hai T'ang), founded at Canton in 1820, minor Cantonese students wrote laudations of Hu Yuan. Significantly, such student essays attacked the prejudice that books about politics were "impure" and suggested that a specialized education in administrative affairs could rehabilitate the lives of middling quality scholars or would-be scholars who were not bright enough to become "evidential research" super-classicists.[56] This was a brave attempt to show how the revival of the power of the schools through the introduction of Hu Yuan's more specialized teaching arrangements might benefit thousands of nameless provincial students, rather than the reverse. But the Hu Yuan cult apparently remained confined to the provinces and to academy students' wishful essays after Sun Chia-kan left the scene; most of the higher officials who managed upward mobility in a period of generally declining prospects resisted it.

One should add that Hu Yuan's ideas, and Ch'ing extensions of them, did not amount to a recognition that the sphere of politics could be a distinct branch of moral philosophy, and thus echo an old Western assumption that the influence of thinkers like Machiavelli, and the ineradicable pluralism of the West's various political and religious authorities, kept reinforcing. Yet despite the Confucian empire's refusal formally to separate politics from ethics or to assume, like European Machiavellianism, that politics might possess a set of laws of its own separate from moral or religious theory, some sort of indigenous concept of a more formidable, more specialized school of national administration still lay not very far beneath the surface of the ideal of the unity of "government" with "teaching." Machiavellianism was perhaps not as necessary a midwife to the birth of such education as some Westerners might assume. And the restoration of the commanding position of the Imperial College at the top of the government school system—the most important event that failed to happen in the history of Ch'ing higher education before 1840—clearly could have been a key to such a school's successful discovery and elaboration.

With the unarrested decline of the Imperial College, China became a more educationally polycentric society. The most interesting school experiments occurred in the provinces and on the frontiers. Only on very rare occasions did the court itself encourage these school experiments, as in its intermittent attempts at the linguistic deparochialization of the official ruling class in the interest of greater empirewide fluency of indoctrination. There were, for example, the ill-fated Mandarin speech schools the court sponsored after 1728 in Kwangtung and Fukien for students (future exponents of Sacred Edicts) who could not understand the spoken Chinese of the rest of China. (According to the famous academician Yü Yueh (1821–1906), every county in Fukien had an "orthodox speech academy" in the Yung-cheng reign; but local officials' neglect of them ensured that only one survived, and in name only, by the late 1800s.)[57] There was also the use of government educational officials and schools in Honan in the late 1770s to teach phonological orthodoxy—the prosodic rules of Chinese poetry based on tonal distinctions—to Honanese students whose inadequate aural literacy annoyed the court.[58]

On the frontiers, officials could play a more totalistic role as teachers trying to create an educational communalism that might revive some of the communal spirit of the aristocratic socialization that heartland scholars associated with the golden age. But they did this without promoting the aristocratic principles themselves. The frontier academy reaffirmed that the acquisition of certain intellectual as well as moral qualities was within the reach of everyone rather than confined to members of socially or culturally superior milieus. That the maturation of late imperial society did not lead to a consolidation of pseudo-aristocratic expectations about higher education, as it very well might have given its declining upward mobility rates, is due in part to its expanding frontiers and the schools they brought into existence. If the frontier school experiments contrast sharply with the absence of any great investment in a pyramidal school system that consolidated knowledge accumulation at the empire's center, they still deserve attention for more positive reasons.

Oerht'ai's (1680–1745) Kunming academy of the Yung-cheng reign (1723–35) is a good example; how many other government academies there were like it we do not yet know. Certainly, the governor of Kwangtung in 1732 admired it enough to regard it as an educational pilot project for such enterprises as the transmission of spoken mandarin in his own province, asking that Kwangtung be allowed to rebuild the Yüeh-hsiu academy and use Oerht'ai's Yunnanese teaching methods at it.[59]

The problem that Oerht'ai was addressing in Yunnan was that both Yunnanese and outside officials posted there regarded the far southwest as backward and devoid of educable people. So frontier academies of Oerht'ai's Kunming kind were concerned with enormous tasks of socialization and adaptation, such as the actual creation of reading habits and the initiation of poor Yunnanese men with good memories and quick comprehension into an initially exotic realm of academic association. They were less concerned with intellect development as an end in itself or with the emulation of ancient hegemonic "sons of the state" about which most Yunnanese knew little. Oerht'ai said that he wanted his academy to nurture not sages or worthies but "adults." This term captures perfectly the socializing or adaptational quality of his school, as contrasted with the more aristocratically emulative types of academies elsewhere. When he mentioned it, Oerht'ai's version of the ancient schools myth was socially denatured enough to suit the southwest frontier. Thus Oerht'ai drew his students' attention to the inspiringly large enrollments that the ancient schools were alleged to have had—several thousand students as contrasted with the disgracefully small number of examination candidates then in Yunnan. But he said nothing about the social positions of the students of antiquity, who had thus become, in his presentation of them, almost classless.[60]

A more educationally polycentric society, with weak central schools, did not necessarily imply greater pluralism in learning. The need for imperial coherence expressed in the China wide examination system required the continuous reproduction of the same classical values on a wider and wider geographical front, as well as continuous anxiety about their possible entropy. In this milieu, socialization and power were identical, not—as in the Baconian worldview— knowledge and power. Together with the absence of international pressures that might have compelled the stronger vertical consolidation of higher education, this need to reproduce classical values on expanding frontiers offers a major way of explaining the history of late imperial schools.

Given this need, Oerht'ai's curriculum made it clear that "adulthood" at his academy was based on the reading of the Thirteen Classics in their entirety.

Yet, in this adaptational type of frontier academy, although the curriculum resembled those elsewhere in the empire, history and politics took on a much greater importance. Understanding the reasons for the rise and fall of dynasties, or external political events, was stressed far more than more introverted Neo-Confucian "finding it in oneself" explorations of pure ethical principles. One interesting feature of Oerht'ai's educational agenda in Kunming appears to have been its attempted development of learning categories directly related to the endless, fluctuating political struggle for mastery over geographical and cultural frontiers. When his Yunnanese students read the accounts of border peoples in the *Shih-chi* or the Han histories, Oerht'ai directed them to study the separate "uses" of kindness and terror; he said little about the intrinsic morality of such things. When Oerht'ai students read the monographs in these works on laws and punishments and warfare, they were told to examine the relative worth of their "great methods," not their eternal principles. In addition, the struggle to create educational motivation among the Yunnanese, as well as a serviceable intelligentsia on the frontier, evidently required types of academies with more generous criteria for admission and less intricate internal testing than their counterparts in southeast China, as well as less metaphysics or philology. Oerht'ai personally paid for the recruitment to his academy of degreeless Yunnanese (at big established academies, entering students held degrees, even if they were only "junior students" or *t'ung-sheng*); he also scrapped the medieval, but pervasive, system of internal tests within Ch'ing academies in which individual students progressed through tests from an "outer studio" (*wai-she*) to an "inner studio" (*nei-she*) to an "upper studio" (*shang-she*).

To say that the ultimate values of Chinese higher education in the 1700s were similar in Peking and Kunming, therefore, would be true but would obscure some significant distinctions in educational practice. Oerht'ai's Kunming academy was devoted, as Oerht'ai put it, to "the glory of the country" (*kuo jung*) and to carrying out a "people of talent plan" for the "state" (*kuo-chia*). This was language that was rarely used anymore about the central Imperial College. In this sense, within a general Confucian framework, the frontier school still came closer than did the weakened Imperial College to the modern utilitarian definition of higher education as an asset of state power that expands its recipients' capacity to master the external world.

In the fall of 1901, the post-Boxer Rebellion school reformer Chang Po-hsi was to muse that the high-ranking schoolmen of Peking were formally the cream of an empirewide educated class of more than ten thousand students in each province, yet that uneducated "coastal Chinese" in contact with foreigners knew more than such Peking schoolmen did about current events.[61] A look at the earlier educational system suggests that its structural peculiarities partly accounted for this, as well as a more general situation of degrees of cultural exposure to the West after 1839 that favored coastal Chinese. A divorce between the political center and educational innovation had been accepted before 1839 by a despotic monarchy with no scholastically advanced international enemies and an immense need to project Confucian values to the geographical edges of a growing empire rather than to consolidate knowledge accumulation at the center. This does not alter the fact that such a divorce violated a widespread hunger among the literati for a much greater closeness between politics and education. After the Opium War, the lack of this closeness could be recast not just as a painful deviation from the corporate solidarity of the legendary kings and aristocrats of ancient China but as a major source of China's contemporary vulnerability to imperialism. The new era confirmed, rather than undermined, the old importance of fusing "government" with "teaching."

EPILOGUE

During the 1898 reforms, K'ang Yu-wei (1858–1927) directly attacked the underdevelopment at the center of state control over Chinese education. He asked that the court order provincial officials to make the first national inventory in Chinese history of the numbers of academies, charitable schools, and community schools in China, their numbers of students, and their funds. For him the traditional academies were inadequate not because they contrasted with aristocratic school archetypes of antiquity but because they were part of a poorly coordinated political order whose investment in education was too small when compared with American educational expenditures.[62] An era of competitive state-building in education based on international standards had finally arrived for the Chinese throne.

In 1905, at the time the examination system was liquidated, Chang Po-hsi and his associates created a Ministry of Education in Peking into which the ineffectual Imperial College was finally absorbed. On paper, the divorce between the political center and provincial educators was at an end. The 1905 Ministry of Education was China's earliest modern central organ of educational administration. No one could doubt that behind the new ambition to create a capital city ministry with the power to impose Chinawide school regulations, inspect provincial schools, and supervise their budgets there lurked not the ideas of Huang Tsung-hsi but a host of imported foreign ideas. Education was the foundation of a strong state, Yen Fu (1853–1921) wrote, thinking of Bacon and Newton. Yuan Shih-k'ai (1859–1916) and others told the throne in 1905 that "people who knew" attributed Prussia's military victory over France in 1871 and Japan's more recent victory over Russia to good national primary school teachers: schools, not examinations, were the source of national prosperity.[63]

Yet if we are to gain an intellectually multidimensional sense of the educational changes in China at the end of the empire, we must look, not just at the most adventurous Westernizing theorists, but also at officials in the second and third tiers of the government who needed stronger imaginative bridges between the past and the future than Yen Fu or K'ang Yu-wei could provide. Their conversion to the notion of intensified government control of education was critical, although it is often overlooked. There is every reason to believe that for more obscure officials like Shansi governor Hu P'in-chih, who helped to end the traditional academies after 1896, the vivid picture such men had in their minds of a legendary alternative school system of the preimperial period was still important to their conversion.

To put it another way, the provincial academy system in China was far from an educationally spent force at the end of the 1800s (see Keenan); even a young communist revolutionary like Mao Tse-tung (1893–1976) was nostalgic for them after they vanished, insisting in 1921 that his Hunan Self-Study University adopt the strong points of both the "ancient *shu-yuan* and contemporary schools."[64] So the sudden overthrow of such academies before 1911 requires more explanation than it often gets. The rapidity of the expansion of new schools between 1901 and 1911 is usually attributed to shock at the Boxer Rebellion and at continued foreign aggression. But the fact also counted that for centuries a significant number of literati had had theoretical expectations about the possibilities of government schools that were almost millenarian in their intensity. Chang Po-hsi, the architect of the new education ministry, was the ultimate educational insider. He had been regional examiner in Shantung, Szechwan, and Kiangsi; provincial director of education in Shantung and Kwangtung; head of the Imperial College; and tutor to imperial princes, all before he became the court's master school reformer in 1901. He is also one of the best examples of the not entirely Westernized conversion process we are discussing with respect to educational change. We have already noted his argument in 1902 that the first priority must be a modernizing revival of China's ancient tradition of schools, and his belief in the similarity of the dense networks of schools in Chinese antiquity with modern Western school types ranging from primary schools to universities. Chang's belief in this similarity presumably generated at least some of his passion to create universities in China. It also made the creation of China's first modern universities anything but an unequivocal act of "Westernization," given the continued influence of the belief in the synthesis of "government" and "teaching."

The assimilation of Western educational stimuli by the more traditional imagined alternatives to late imperial education, such as the ancient schools archetypes, helps to explain why Chang and other late Ch'ing reformers did not understand certain features of modern Western universities and failed to adopt them. Such features included the relative autonomy of Western universities in deciding what to teach, the importance to them of pure research, and the separation of Western universities from the direct processes of civil service recruitment.

Moreover, the foundation of the ancient schools legend, with its picture of multitiered educational communities of different sizes in ascending order, was a vision of communal intimacy and understanding, as in the feasting rituals that the lost aristocratic order had embraced as part of schooling. The legend made little allowance for the possibility that the reproduction of such a multitiered educational system might breed not intimacy but alienation. Moved by this ancient ideal of achieving political and educational closeness through schools, Chang Po-hsi and his associates may not have appreciated the political risks the Ch'ing court ran with its sudden commitment to the more alienating forms of modern educational expansion. Many of these risks were to be confirmed and illustrated by the Revolution of 1911.

NOTES

1. Liang Shu-ming 梁漱溟, "Tung-Hsi jen ti chiao-yü chih pu-t'ung" 東西人的教育之不同 (Dissimilarities in the education of Eastern and Western people), *Chiao-yü tsa-chih* (Shanghai, 20 Mar. 1922), 1–5.

2. John W. Chaffee, "Chu Hsi in Nan-k'ang: *Tao-hsüeh* and the Politics of Education," in W.T. de Bary and J.W. Chaffee, eds., *Neo-Confucian Education: The Formative Stage* (Berkeley: University of California Press, 1989), 423–24.

3. See, for example, the discussion of the 1787 examination system reforms in the 1789 rules of the Yu-chiao Academy in Kiangsi; Wang Ch'ang 王昶, *Ch'un-jung t'ang chi* 春融堂集 (Literary collection of the Ch'un-jung Hall), (1807), 68:9–9b.

4. As two relatively random examples of modern Western scholars who stress the decontextualizing effects of schools, see Jerome Bruner, *The Relevance of Education* (New York: W.W. Norton and Co., 1973), 12; Jack Goody, *The Interface between the Written and the Oral* (Cambridge: Cambridge University Press, 1987), 184–85.

5. *Fan-li* 凡例 (General rules), *Ch'in-ting ssu-k'u ch'üan-shu tsung-mu* 欽定四庫全書總目 (General index of the imperially authorized library of the Four Treasuries) (Kuang-tung shu-chü 1868 ed.). 9–9b (rule 14).

6. The outstanding study is by Min Tu-ki, *National Polity and Local Power: the Transformation of Late Imperial China* (Cambridge, Mass.: Harvard Council on East Asian Studies, 1989), ed. P.A. Kuhn and T. Brook, 89–136.

7. Ch'u Ta-wen 儲大文, "Shih-chung chih chih" 侍中之職 (Post of palace attendants), in Ho Ch'ang-ling 賀長齡, comp., *Huang-ch'ao ching-shih wen-pien* 皇朝經世文編 (Compilation of the statecraft essays of the present court; hereafter *CSWP*) (Taipei: Wen-hai, 1972), 13:13b–14; Wang Hsin-ching 王心敬, "Ta wen hsuan-chü 答問選舉 (Answers and questions about selection and promotion), in *CSWP*, 17:9b–10.

8. For the text of Chang Po-hsi's memorial, dated 15 Aug. 1902, see the *Shih-erh ch'ao Tung-hua lu: Kuang-hsu ch'ao* 十二朝東華錄：光緒朝 (Tung-hua Gate records of the Kuang-hsu reign), comp. Chu Shou-p'eng 朱壽朋 (Taipei: Wen-hai, 1963), 9:4884–85.

9. Michel de Montaigne, *Essays*, trans. J.M. Cohen (London and Baltimore: Penguin Books, 1958), 58–59.

10. Lu Shih-i 陸世儀, *Ssu-pien lu chi-yao* 思辨錄輯要 (Summary version of the chronicles of careful thought and clear distinctions), 20:4b, in *Lu Fu-ting hsien-sheng i-shu*

陸桴亭先生遺書 (Bequeathed works of Lu Shih-i), comp. T'ang Shou-ch'i 唐受祺 (Peking, 1900).

11. Chai Hao 翟灝, *T'ung-su pien* 通俗編 (Compilation for the comprehension of customs), (1751), 7:11.

12. For the text, see *Ta Ch'ing shih-tsung hsien-huang-ti shih-lu* 大清世宗憲皇帝實錄 (Veritable records of the Yung-cheng reign) (Tokyo: Okura shuppan kabushiki kaisha, 1937), 127:7b–8b.

13. Ou To-heng 歐多恆, "Ch'ien-hsi Ch'ing-tai Kuei-chou chiao-yü fa-chan ti yuan-yin" 淺析清代貴州教育發展的原因 (Limited explanation of the reasons for educational expansion in Ch'ing dynasty Kweichow), *Kuei-chou she-hui k'o-hsueh* 2 (Kweiyang, 1985): 103.

14. James L. Watson, "Chinese Kinship Reconsidered: Anthropological Perspectives on Historical Research," *The China Quarterly* 92 (London, Dec. 1982): 606.

15. Lu Lung-ch'i 陸隴其, *San-yü t'ang wen-chi* 三魚堂文集 (Prose collection of the Hall of the Three Fishes) (1701; reprint, 1867), *wai-pien* (Outer compilation), 3:19b–22.

16. Chang T'ing-yü 張廷玉, *Ch'eng-huai yuan wen-ts'un* 澄懷園文存 (Preserved prose works of the Ch'eng-huai garden) (reprint, Taipei: Wen-hai, 1970), 10:37–39.

17. See the comments of Wang Ch'ang, "Hui Ting-yü hsien-sheng mu-chih ming" 惠定宇先生墓志銘 (Epitaph inscription for Hui Tung), in Wang, *Ch'un-jung t'ang chi*, 55:2–2b.

18. Shao T'ing-ts'ai 鄧廷采, "Hsueh-hsiao lun" 學校論 (On schools), in Shao, *Ssu-fu t'ang wen-chi* 思復堂文集 (Literary collection of the Ssu-fu Hall) (1712), 8:7–11.

19. Liang Ch'i-ch'ao 梁啟超, "Hsueh-hsiao tsung-lun" 學校總論 (General discussion of schools), in Shu Hsin-ch'eng 舒新城, comp., *Chin-tai Chung-kuo chiao-yü tzu-liao* 近代中國教育資料 (Materials in modern Chinese educational history), (Peking: Jen-min chiao-yü ch'u-pan-she, 1962), 3:936–44.

20. Sugimura Yūzō, *Ken-ryū kōtei* (Ch'ien-lung emperor) (Tokyo: Nigensha, 1961), 141–42; Benjamin A. Elman, *From Philosophy to Philology: Intellectual and Social Aspects of Change in Late Imperial China* (Cambridge, Mass.: Harvard University Press, 1984), 203.

21. Ch'en Yuan-hui 陳元暉 et al., *Chung-kuo ku-tai ti shu-yuan chih-tu* 中國古代的書院制度 (China's ancient system of academies) (Shanghai: Shang-hai chiao-yü ch'u-pan-she, 1981), 97.

22. Liu Po-chi 劉伯驥, *Kuang-tung shu-yuan chih-tu yen-ko* 廣東書院制度沿革 (Evolution of the academies system of Kwangtung) (Changsha: Commercial Press, 1939), 116–17.

23. I borrow this translation from the essential, trailblazing early Western study of this work, which of course is W.T. de Bary, "Chinese Despotism and the Confucian Ideal: A Seventeenth-century View," in J.K. Fairbank, ed., *Chinese Thought and Institutions* (Chicago and London: University of Chicago Press, 1957), 163–203.

24. See, for example, the critique of Huang by Ch'eng Chin-fang 程晉芳 (1718–84) in Ch'eng Chin-fang, "Tu Jih-chih-lu" 讀日知錄 (Reading the "Chronicles of Daily Knowledge"), in *CSWP*, 2:11–11b; Hsieh Kang 謝剛, "Ming-i tai-fang lu yü Ch'ing-ch'u wen-tzu yü 明夷待訪錄與清初文字獄 ("A Plan for the Prince" and the early Ch'ing Literary Inquisition), *Chung-kuo shih yen-chiu* 3 (Peking, 1983), 71–84.

25. Wm. Theodore de Bary, *The Liberal Tradition in China* (New York: Columbia University Press, 1983), 3. On the relationship between Huang and his own age, see also

Lynn A. Struve, "Huang Zongxi in Context: a Reappraisal of His Major Writings," *Journal of Asian Studies* 47, no. 3 (Aug. 1988), 474–502.

26. I borrow this term for Huang's ideas from Ch'iu Ch'un 邱椿, *Ku-tai chiao-yü ssu-hsiang lun-ts'ung* 古代教育思想論叢 (Collected essays on ancient educational thought), (Peking: Pei-ching shih-fan ta-hsueh ch'u-pan-she, 1985), 2:97.

27. Huang Tsung-hsi 黃宗羲, "Ming-i tai-fang lu: hsüeh-hsiao" 明夷待訪錄：學校 (Plan for the Prince: schools), in *Huang Tsung-hsi ch'üan-chi* 黃宗羲全集 (Complete works of Huang Tsung-hsi) (Hangchow: Che-chiang ku-chi ch'u-pan-she, 1985), 1:10–14.

28. Shao T'ing-ts'ai, "Hsueh-hsiao lun"; Hu Ch'u-sheng 胡楚生, "Shao Nien-lu 'Hsueh-hsiao lun' hsi-i" 邵念魯學校論析義 (Explanation of the meaning of 'On schools' by Shao T'ing-ts'ai), in Hu, *Ch'ing-tai hsueh-shu shih yen-chiu* 清代學術史研究 (Studies in the history of Ch'ing dynasty learning) (Taipei: Tai-wan hsueh-sheng shu-chü, 1987), 148–50.

29. Yü Ying-shih, 余英時 *Chung-kuo ssu-hsiang ch'uan-t'ung te hsien-tai ch'uan-shih* 中國思想傳統的現代詮釋 (Contemporary exegesis of Chinese intellectual tradition) (Taipei: Lien-ching ch'u-pan shih-yeh kung-ssu, 1987), 35.

30. Chin Pang 金榜, "Ta hsueh" 大學 (Higher learning), in *Huang Ch'ing ching-chieh* 皇清經解 (Exegesis of the Classics of the imperial Ch'ing; hereafter *HCCC*) (Canton, 1829; reprint, 1861), 556:15–16, 23.

31. Sun T'ung-yuan 孫同元, "Pi-yung t'ai-hsueh shuo" 辟雍太學説 (Discussion of the Moated Sanctuary and the Imperial College), in Juan Yüan 阮元 et al., eds., *Ku-ching ching-she wen-chi* 詁經精舍文集 (Prose collection of the Ku-ching school), (1801), 2:32–33b.

32. Note, for example, Shao's confusion about the term *shu-tzu* 庶子 (noninheriting sons of aristocratic families, who were more lowly than the "sons of the state" to which ancient higher education was oriented) and his teacher Mao Ch'i-ling's reply, in Mao Ch'i-ling 毛奇齡, "Ching wen" 經問 (Questions about the Classics), in *HCCC* 165:1–2b.

33. Ch'eng Chin-fang 程晉芳, "Ku hsueh-hsiao k'ao" 古學校考 (Examination of ancient schools), in *CSWP*, 57:1b–2b.

34. Ping-ti Ho, *The Ladder of Success in Imperial China: Aspects of Social Mobility, 1368–1911* (New York: Sciences Editions, John Wiley and Sons, 1964), 119–20.

35. Wang Te-chao 王德昭, *Ch'ing-tai k'o-chü chih-tu yen-chiu* 清代科舉制度研究 (Study of the Ch'ing examination system) (Hong Kong: Chung-wen ta-hsueh ch'u-pan-she, 1982), 58–61.

36. *Ta Ch'ing Kao-tsung ch'un-huang-ti shih-lu* 大清高宗純皇帝實錄 (Veritable records of the Ch'ien-lung reign; hereafter *CKTSL*) (Tokyo: Okura shuppan kabushiki kaisha, 1937), 745:17b–19b.

37. Kung Tzu-chen 龔自珍, "Ming liang lun" 明良論 (On the elucidation of excellence) in *Kung Tzu-chen ch'üan-chi* 龔自珍全集 (Collected works of Kung Tzu-chen) (Shanghai: Jen-min ch'u-pan-she, 1975), 33.

38. I borrow this estimate from the essay by David Johnson, "Communication, Class, and Consciousness in Late Imperial China," in D. Johnson, A. Nathan, and E. Rawski, eds., *Popular Culture in Late Imperial China* (Berkeley: University of California Press, 1985), 59–60.

39. Examples from the memoirs of the Ch'ien-lung reign by Chao-lien 昭槤, *Hsiao-t'ing hsu-lu* 嘯亭續錄 (Continued chronicles of the Hsiao pavilion), ed. Ho Ying-fang 何英芳 (1880; reprint, Peking: Chung-hua shu-chü, 1980), 2:434.

40. The classic study is Hsu Ta-ling 許大齡, *Ch'ing-tai chüan-na chih-tu* 清代捐納制度 (Purchase of offices and degrees system of the Ch'ing dynasty) (Peking: Harvard-Yenching Institute, 1950; reprint, Hong Kong: Lung-men shu-tien, 1968), 85–86.

41. Sun Chu 孫鑄, comp., *Sun Wen-ting kung tsou-shu* 孫文定公奏疏 (Memorials of Sun Chia-kan 孫家淦), in *Chin-tai Chung-kuo shih-liao ts'ung-k'an* 近代中國史料叢刊 (Collected publications of modern Chinese historical materials), comp. Shen Yun-lung 沈雲龍 (Taipei: Wen-hai, 1970), no. 55, *chüan* 4:19–19b.

42. Chu Tsun 朱嶟, "Ch'ing shen chung ming-ch'i shu" 請慎重名器疏 (Memorial requesting the taking of great care with noble titles and status attributes), in Sheng K'ang 盛康, comp., *Huang-ch'ao ching-shih wen hsu-pien* 皇朝經世文續編 (Continuation of the compilation of statecraft essays of the present court) (Taipei: Wen-hai, 1972), 66:78–79b.

43. Ch'en Hung-mou 陳宏謀, "Chi Chang Mo-chuang shu" 寄張墨莊書 (Letter to Chang Mo-chuang), in *CSWP*, 2:9b–10.

44. Lu Shih-i, *Ssu-pien lu chi-yao*, 13:7b–8.

45. Sun Hsing-yen 孫星衍, *Wen-tzu t'ang chi* 問字堂集 (Literary collection of the Hall for Questioning Written Words) (1795; 1886), 4:19–21.

46. *CKTSL*, 20:2b–3b.

47. *CKTSL*, 1312:28–29b, 44–46b, 1313:4b–6b, 7b–10.

48. *CKTSL*, 828:1b–3b, 1174:16–16b.

49. For example, Liu I-cheng 柳詒徵, "Wu-pai-nien ch'ien Nan-ching chih kuo-li ta-hsueh" 五百年前南京之國立大學 (Nanking's state university of five hundred years ago), *Hsueh-heng* (Shanghai, Jan. 1923), 1–12, (Feb. 1923), 1–24.

50. I rely here on Liu I-cheng, ed., *Nan-yung chih* 南雍志 (Gazetteer of the southern Imperial College) (Nanking: Chiang-su sheng-li kuo-hsueh t'u-shu-kuan ed., 1931), 1:44b, 9:5–5b. The first version of this work was compiled in the fifteenth century; the best-known version was compiled by Huang Tso 黃佐, himself the head of the college in the mid-sixteenth century.

51. Liu I-cheng, *Nan-yung chih*, 9:7b–8. For the Sung dynasty antecedents of the internal structure of the college, as defined by Wang An-shih 王安石, see the excellent essay by Thomas H.C. Lee, "Sung Schools and Education before Chu Hsi," in de Bary and Chaffee, *Neo-Confucian Education*, 105–36.

52. Lu Shih-i, *Ssu-pien lu chi-yao*, 13:10b-11.

53. Hsiung Ming-an 熊明安, *Chung-kuo kao-teng chiao-yü shih* 中國高等教育史 (History of Chinese high-level education) (Chungking: Ch'ung-ch'ing ch'u-pan-she, 1983), 292–94. For an early Ch'ing view of the Okinawan students at the directorate by the school's head in the 1680s, see Wang Shih-chen 王士禎, "Chi Liu-ch'iu ju t'ai-hsueh shih-mo" 紀琉球入太學始末 (Account from first to last of the Okinawans at the Imperial College), in *Tai-ching t'ang chi* 帶經堂集 (Literary collection of the Tai-ching Hall) (1712), 51:23–25. For the Vietnamese envoy's account of his conversation with the Ryukyu students, see *Le Quy Don toan tap; tap II: Kien van tieu luc* (Complete works of Le Quy Don, volume two: the small chronicle of things seen and heard) (Hanoi: Nha xuat ban khoa hoc xa hoi, 1977), 223.

54. *CKTSL* 48:10–11b. For a slightly different version of Sun's memorial, see the *Ch'in-ting Kuo-tzu chien tse-li* 欽定國子監則例 (Imperially authorized rules of the Directorate for the Sons of the State), (1824), 34:6–7. On Chu Hsi's view of Hu Yüan, see W. T. de Bary, "Chu Hsi's Aims as an Educator," in de Bary and Chaffee, *Neo-Confucian Education*, 200–201.

55. Wang Ch'ang 王昶, "Ching-i chih-shih i-t'ung lun" 經義制事異同論 (On the similarities and differences between general classical study and the study of administrative affairs), in *Ch'un-jung t'ang chi* 春融堂集 33:1–2. See also *CSWP*, 1:14–14b.

56. For example, Wu Chien 吳鑑, "Hu An-ting hsien-sheng lun tsan" 胡安定先生論贊 (Discussion and praise of Hu Yüan), in Chin Hsi-ling 金錫齡, ed., *Hsueh-hai t'ang ssu-chi* 學海堂四集 (Essays from the Sea of Learning Hall, Fourth Series), (1886), 16:47–49.

57. Yü Yüeh 俞樾, "Cheng-yin shu-yüan" 正音書院 (Orthodox speech academies), in Yü, *Ch'a-hsiang shih hsu-ch'ao* 茶香室續鈔 (Continuation of notes of the Ch'a-hsiang chamber) (1883), 15:15–16.

58. *CKTSL*, 907:50b–51b.

59. *Chu-p'i yü-chih* 硃批諭旨 (Vermilion endorsements and edicts of the Yung-cheng reign), 1738; Yang Yung-pin 楊永斌 Memorials, vol. 16, chüan 4:17–18.

60. See Oerht'ai 鄂爾泰, "Cheng Tien shih ju shu-yüan ch'ih" 徵滇士入書院敕 (Orders summoning Yunnan scholars to enter the academy), *CSWP*, 57:18–19b.

61. Cited in Hsiung Ming-an, *Chung-kuo kao-teng chiao-yü shih*, 346.

62. For the text of K'ang's memorial, see, inter alia, Chien Po-tsan 翦伯贊 et al., comps., *Wu-hsu pien-fa* 戊戌變法 (Reforms of 1898) (Shanghai: Shang-hai jen-min ch'u-pan-she, 1957), 2:219–22.

63. Chu Shou-p'eng, *Shih-erh ch'ao Tung-hua lu: Kuang-hsu ch'ao* 9:5372–75.

64. On Mao's admiration for traditional academies, see Wang Shu-pai 汪澍白, ed., *Wen-hua Ch'ung-t'u chung te chüeh-tse* 文化衝突中的抉擇 (Choices within cultural conflict) (Changsha: Hu-nan jen-min ch'u-pan-she, 1989), 426–27.

GLOSSARY

Chang Po-hsi	張百熙	*Fu-k'ang-an*	福康安
Chang T'ing-yü	張廷玉	Hsueh-hai T'ang	學海堂
cheng	政	*hsueh-sheng*	學生
Ch'eng Chin-fang	程晉芳	Hu P'in-chih	胡聘之
chi-chiu	祭酒	Hu Yuan	胡瑗
chiao	教	Huang Tsung-hsi	黃宗羲
Chiao-yü wan-neng shuo	教育萬能説	Hui Tung	惠棟
chien	監	K'ang Yu-wei	康有為
chien-sheng	監生	*Ku-ching ching-she*	詁經精舍
Ch'ien Ta-hsin	錢大昕	*kung-chien*	貢監
chih-shih	治事	Kung Tzu-chen	龔自珍
Chin Pang	金榜	*kuo-chia*	國家
chin-shih	進士	*Kuo-jung*	國榮
ching-i	經義	*kuo-shih*	國師
Chou li	周禮	*kuo-tzu*	國子
chü-jen	舉人	*Kuo-tzu chien*	國子監

Li chien	禮箋	*Shih-chi*	史記
Liang Ch'i-ch'ao	梁啟超	*shu-yuan*	書院
Lu Lung-ch'i	陸隴其	*Shuai-hsing t'ang*	率性堂
Lu Shih-i	陸世儀	Sun Chia-kan	孫嘉淦
Mao Tse-tung	毛澤東	Sun Hsing-yen	孫星衍
min-sheng	民生	*t'ai-hsueh*	太學
ming-ch'i	名器	*t'ang*	堂
Ming-i tai-fang lu	明夷待訪錄	*ti-pao*	邸報
Ming-t'ang ta-tao lu	明堂大道錄	*tu-shu jen*	讀書人
ming-t'i ta-yung	明體達用	*t'ung-sheng*	童生
nei-she	內舍	*wai-she*	外舍
Oerht'ai	鄂爾泰	Wang Ch'ang	王昶
pan-kung	泮宮	Wang Te-chao	王德昭
P'an Shih-ch'eng	潘仕成	Yen Fu	嚴復
Pi-yung	辟雍	*yin-chien*	蔭監
po-hsueh	博學	Yu-chiao	友教
shang-she	上舍	Yuan Mei	袁枚
Shao T'ing-ts'ai	邵廷采	Yuan Shih-k'ai	袁世凱
shih	士	Yü Yueh	俞越
shih-cheng	實政	Yueh-hsiu	粵秀

Lung-men Academy in Shanghai and the Expansion of Kiangsu's Educated Elite, 1865–1911

Barry Keenan

POST-TAIPING ACADEMY EXPANSION IN KIANGSU

Renewal of Confucian scholarship together with the renovation of educational institutions was integral to the basic policy of imperial restoration in the T'ung-chih (1862–74) reign.[1] In the populous and culturally advanced Lower Yangtze region, this policy fostered a revival of classical academies that lasted from 1862 to 1900. Analysis of this expansion in academy education reveals that the rationale for the Restoration revival of Confucian education was not the Ch'ing court's blind reassertion of the old order after the Taiping defeat. Rather, the expansion countered new social and political tensions brought into being by both the social dislocation of the war and other postwar policies. One such postwar policy was the sale of offices and the increase in civil service degree quotas brought about by the financial exhaustion of the empire. Another was the national imperative to fend off increasing foreign encroachment by adopting the military technology of the West.

After the Taiping suppression and up to 1911, some two thirds of all officials with titles of appointment in China had received their posts without following the regular route of the examinations.[2] Magistrates in turn passed along the expense of many of these purchased offices by selling lucrative yamen clerkships that were under their control.[3] In Kiangsu province in the 1860s, social dislocation also increased when the court raised the quota of *sheng-yuan* (government students) who qualified as local elite —which the state did because of Kiangsu's contributions to the war effort. The lower gentry increased by an added 360 *sheng-yuan* every time the prefectural examinations were held, resulting in a 30 percent increase of Kiangsu *sheng-yuan* by the end of the Ch'ing.[4] This increasing cohort of lower degree-holders needed offices to hold and needed more academies just to make it possible for them to prepare for the *chü-jen* (elevated person) degree.

In addition, a post-Taiping policy authenticated some new alternatives to the orthodox means of gaining social advancement through mastery of the Confucian Classics. This policy was the introduction of foreign military and industrial technology in a national program of self-strengthening usually termed Western affairs (*yang-wu*). There is no question Ch'ing officials recognized the efficacy of Western weapons during and after the war.[5] Arsenals, interpreters' schools, and the introduction of Western transportation and communication technology became a part of dynastic restrengthening in the T'ung-chih period. Even such controlled westernization, however, increased the appeal of unorthodox alternatives for success. Founding academies provided attractive student stipends and addressed the increasing need to validate Confucian learning and its official institutions as the restoration of bureaucratic authority took place.

A decade of disruption in the Lower Yangtze had also created a significant backlog of aspirants who had been searching for opportunities to gain the status of a government student (*sheng-yuan*). The career pattern of the father of Hu Shih (1891–1962) illustrates the problems of the wartime generation. Hu Ch'uan (*Tzu*, or courtesy name, hereafter T., Tun-fu, 1841–95) was coming of age in Hui-chou prefecture in Anhwei province when the preliminary examinations there were disrupted by the arrival of the Taiping army in 1853. His lineage was active in commerce; and Hu Ch'uan had already begun carrying family tea down to the mouth of the Yangtze to sell it in Ch'uan-sha, Kiangsu, by that time. In 1859, Hu Ch'uan took and passed the county preliminary qualifying examination in Shanghai near his family tea business.[6]

His scores on the Sung-chiang prefectural examination that followed the qualifying examination in Shanghai, however, were not competitive enough to win him *sheng-yuan* status. The buildup of talent in the relatively pacified area around Shanghai made passage extremely difficult. Only after the war in 1865, at age twenty-four and six years later, was Hu Ch'uan able to qualify for the *sheng-yuan* in the reestablished examinations back at his native prefecture in Anhwei.[7]

After that he tried the provincial examinations unsuccessfully and finally elected to examine into the newly established *Lung-men shu-yuan* (Dragon Gate Academy) in Shanghai where he qualified to renew his annual stipend support for the next three years. When he left Lung-men Academy in 1871, he was still unable to get through the provincial examinations, but he had acquired three years of superb higher education, which undoubtedly helped him qualify and succeed in the private secretary post (*mu-fu*) to a significant national official where he served for the next six years.[8]

Academy Expansion

The expansion of academies in several provinces including Kiangsu suggests that the Tung-chih Restoration succeeded in encouraging the growth of academy education throughout the country. Professor Grimm's statistics for

Kwangtung report a rate of construction from 1850 to 1874 averaging twenty-four or twenty-five academies per decade, which was unprecedented in Kwangtung province in Ming or Ch'ing history.[9] Statistics for Anhwei confirm another trend implicit in the Kwangtung figures. Commercial capital and urbanization correlate with the areas in both provinces where academies expanded most rapidly.[10]

Financial exhaustion in post-Taiping China seems also to have allowed increasing local control over the founding of academies. Privately financed academies mushroomed in prosperous regions of certain provinces that had long-term increases in commercial capital during the 1700s. In the Ch'ien-lung period, Chekiang province gentry—many of whom were connected to producing and trading silk cloth—contributed to academies in unprecedented numbers.[11] Furthermore, as Angela Leung demonstrates in this volume, community control over elementary education in the Lower Yangtze provinces increased steadily in the 1700s. This increased the role of the gentry and provided the needed initial conditions for the expanded role of local elites after 1865.

Kiangsu's neighboring province Chekiang showed a marked increase in the pattern of academy construction from 1850 to 1900. Mary Backus Rankin's careful study of the province in this period notes the peculiarity of this increase if one contrasts the contemporaneous downturn in *chin-shih* (presented scholar) degrees received by Chekiangese. Burgeoning commercial towns had more than their share of the new academies, and Rankin drives home the intriguing thesis that post-Taiping academy expansion signified "a weakening rather than a strengthening of ties with the state."[12] As bureaucratic ties of the central government to localities loosened in the post-Taiping era, the organization of a variety of institutions by the local elite in Chekiang expanded and continued to develop up to 1911.[13]

In Chekiang, T'ung-chih recovery policies often served to pull together new public institutions into matrices of local elite activism. The new managerial elite working in welfare institutions after 1864, for example, could easily overlap with persons running new educational institutions.[14] If Chekiang is representative, the response of local elites to the national crisis of the Taiping suppression and its aftermath gradually generated a new activism in public management within both rural and urban areas. One new development was the increasing prominence of gentry managers (*shen-tung*)—individuals of varied social backgrounds—running local institutions. Local social status was gradually expanded in Chekiang well beyond scholarly validation by the central government.[15]

The new managerial elite was active in founding new academies.[16] In Chekiang from 1850 to 1900, newly established or revived academies averaged 16.8 per decade, which was the province's highest rate compared to any other period in the Ch'ing. In Kiangsu province during the same era, new foundings

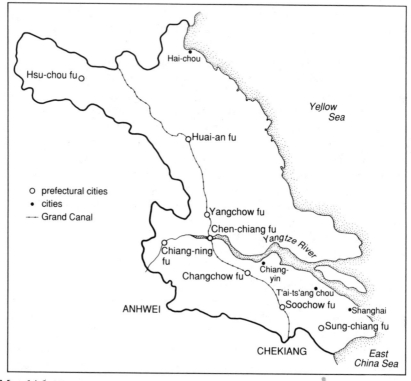

Map 14.1 Kiangsu

SOURCE: Adapted from David Faure, "The Rural Economy of Kiangsu Province, 1870–1911"
(Hong Kong: Institute of Chinese Studies, Chinese University of Hong Kong, 1978), 366.

including renovations averaged an almost equally high number of 16 per decade. In the same period in Kwangtung, the rate of new foundings and renovations was 22 per decade. Comparison with figures in the Ch'ien-lung era (1736–95) demonstrates the significant rise of new academy foundings in all three provinces:[17]

	Ch'ien-lung	1850–1900
Kwangtung	17.2 per decade	22 per decade
Kiangsu	10.3 per decade	16 per decade
Chekiang	8.8 per decade	16.8 per decade

The peculiarity of Kiangsu in terms of academy growth was that the most prosperous core counties south of the Yangtze in Kiangsu were precisely those most affected by the Taiping violence. This Taiping destruction in Kiangsu south of the Yangtze had been most acute in Chiang-ning prefecture near the Anhwei provincial border (map 14.1) The effects of destruction were gradually

TABLE 14.1.   Number of Academies in
Southern Kiangsu Province, by Prefecture

Date	Prefectures (East to West)					Total
	Sung-chiang[a]	Soochow[b]	Changchow[c]	Chen-chiang[d]	Chiang-ning[e]	
1900 (all built or renovated since 1862)	20 (20%)	32 (31%)	29 (29%)	10 (10%)	10 (10%)	101 (100%)
1820[f]	8 (18%)	11 (25%)	10 (23%)	7 (16%)	8 (18%)	44 (100%)

a *Sung-chiang fu hsu-chih* 松江府續志 (1884; reprint, 1974), 1646–47, 1673–81, 1703–35. *Hua-t'ing hc* 華亭縣志 (1878; reprint, 1970), 406–9; *Lou hsien hsu-chih* 婁縣志 (1879; reprint, 1974), 285–89; *Feng hsien hc* 奉賢 (1878; reprint, 1970), 337–40; *Chin-shan hc* 金山 (1878; reprint, 1974), 631–32; *Nan-hui hc* 南滙 (1927; reprint, 1970), 647–48, 660, 665; *Ch'ing-p'u hc* 青浦 (1879; reprint, 1970), 701–9; *Ch'ing-p'u hsien hsu-chih* 青浦縣續志 (1934; reprint, 1975), 403–23; *Ch'uan-sha t'ing-chih* 川沙廳志 (1879; reprint, 1975), 104–9; *Ch'uan-sha t'ing-chih* 川沙廳志 (1937; reprint, 1974), 283; *Shang-hai hc* 上海 (1882; reprint, 1975), 686–700; *Shang-hai hsien hsu-chih* 上海縣續志 (1918; reprint, 1970), 637–52.

b See Wang Shu-huai, *Chung-kuo* 57, and revised totals from *Su-chou fc* 蘇州 (1883; reprint, 1970); *Wu hc* 吳 (1933; reprint, 1970), 410–16; *K'un Hsin liang hsien hsu-hsiu ho-chih* 崑新兩縣續修合志 (1880; reprint, 1970), 80–82; *Ch'ang Chao ho-chih kao* 常昭合志稿 (1904; reprint, 1974), 779–90. *Wu-chiang hsien hsu-chih* 吳江縣續志 (1879), 3, 4a–5a.

c *Ch'ang-chou fc* 常州 (1886), 14a–16a; *Wu-chin, Yang-hu hc* 武進, 陽湖 (1906; reprint, 1968), 5, 5b–7b; *Wu-hsi, Chin-kuei hc* 無錫金匱 (1881; reprint, 1970), 114–17; *I-hsing, Ching-hsi hsien hsin-chih* 宜興荊溪縣新志 (1882; reprint, 1974), 425–30; *I-hsing hsu-chih* 宜興續志 (1920; reprint, 1970), 109–10, 172–83; *Chiang-yin hc* 江陰 (1878; reprint, 1968), 5, 19–28; *Chiang-yin hc* 江陰 (1921; reprint, 1970), 361–88.

d *(Hsu tsuan) Chiang-ning fc* (續纂)江寧 (1880; reprint, 1970), 51–52; *Ch'iang-p'u pei-ch'eng* 江浦塊乘 (1891), 12, 10a–12a; *Li-shui hc* 溧水 (1905; reprint, 1970), 539–540; *Kao-ch'un hc* 高淳 (1881), 5, 33a–36a; *(Hsu tsuan) Chü-jung hc* (續纂)句容 (1904; reprint, 1974), 154–56, 296–97, 307–8; *Liu-ho hc* 六合 (1883) 3, 12a, 4, 9a.

e *Tan-t'u hc* 丹徒 (1879; reprint, 1970), 3, 39ab, 351–53; *Chin-t'an hc* 金壇 (1885), 5, 7, 14ab, 41b, 106, 300–302; *Tan-yang hsien hsu-chih* 丹陽縣續志 (1885; reprint, 1974), 10, 10a–11b; *Tan-yang hc* 丹陽 (1927; reprint, 1961), 102–6; *Li-yang hsien hsu-chih* 溧陽縣續志 (1899; reprint, 1971), 5, 6a–8a.

f Wang Shu-huai, *Chung-kuo*, citing *I t'ung chih* 一統志 (Unified gazetteer, Chia-ch'ing revision) (1820; rev. ed., 1844; reprint, Taipei: Commercial Press, 1966), 6, 106.

reduced eastward through Chen-chiang prefecture to Changchow prefecture, Soochow prefecture, and finally to Sung-chiang prefecture, which included Shanghai county on the Pacific coast.[18] Rehabilitation of academies occurred after 1865 at a rate proportional to the prosperity of the prefectures and went from rapid development of many post-Taiping academies in eastern Kiangsu to slower development and fewer academies in the war-torn and less affluent western part of the province.[19]

Table 14.1 shows by prefecture the academy reconstruction that took place south of the Yangtze in Kiangsu, from 1862 to the end of such reconstruction in 1900. The totals of post-Taiping academies are compared to those that existed in that prefecture according to the national gazetteer of 1820. These figures make clear changes in geographical distribution. In 1820, for example, Sung-chiang prefecture on the east coast had about the same number of academies as the two westernmost prefectures, but by 1900 Sung-chiang had twice the number of academies present in either Chen-chiang or Chiang-ning in the west. All five prefectures had by 1900 increased in absolute value the number of academies they had in 1820. The three easternmost prosperous and populous core prefectures expanded dramatically—doubling the academy number in the case of Sung-chiang and tripling it in the cases of Soochow and Changchow.

In Changchow prefecture, academy foundings increased as reconstruction continued into the Kuang-hsu era (1875–1908). Rebuilding destroyed facilities and building from scratch took more time further west from Shanghai. While only about half of the twenty-nine post-Taiping Changchow founding dates (some are restorations) are given in the gazetteer entries, note how many of those given are academies founded after the T'ung-chih period ended in 1874:

> Tao-nan Academy (1869)
> Kao-shan Academy (1875)
> Li-yen Academy (1877)
> Ch'ang-yin Academy (1878)
> Hsi-nan Academy (1878)
> San-chin Academy (1879)
> Chin-tai Academy (1880)
> Chu-hsi Academy (1880)
> Hsien-yang Academy (1881)
> Lin-chih Academy (1881)
> Nan-ching Academy (1884)
> Tao-hsiang Academy (1885)

The two western prefectures of Chen-chiang and Chiang-ning had to finance more elaborate reconstruction than was necessary in the eastern part of Kiangsu. Demobilization of Ch'ing troops also drained local resources so that many counties simply had no financial means to reconstruct former academies or finance new ones. In the prefectural capital of Chiang-ning, for example, Kuei-kuang Academy was never rebuilt, nor was Ying-hua Academy in nearby Chiang-p'u county. Kao-p'ing Academy in Li-shui county had been demolished and the financially strapped magistrate could not rebuild. He decided instead to commit the remaining endowment to finance the travel of local candidates to take *chü-jen* or *chin-shih* examinations.[20]

The largest expense was that of rebuilding student dormitories and libraries; then came endowments for monthly stipends. In eastern Kiangsu, magistrates coordinated and supplemented resources gathered for the expenses from lineages, villages, guilds, and wealthy individuals. Sometimes local notables even got all the gazetteer credit for founding an academy. In western Kiangsu local managers from villages sometimes approached a magistrate, as happened in Kao-ch'un county in 1863; then the magistrate had to find the resources to slowly endow an academy. In Chiang-ning prefecture, it often took the tenure of two or three magistrates (at three years each) in a locality to accumulate enough endowment to fully reopen an academy. That both Chen-chiang and Chiang-ning prefectures reconstructed ten academies was a credit to the persistence of local administrators who had few resources outside of their own budgets to call on.[21]

Despite the financial strain of academy reconstruction, by 1900 all five southern Kiangsu prefectures had exceeded pre-Taiping totals. If one isolates the total number of academies in Kiangsu's southern five prefectures, the density of post-Taiping academy expansion becomes clear. By 1900 there were 101 as compared with a total of only 44 academies in 1820.[22] The academy growth in southern Kiangsu after 1862 averaged a record-breaking 25.3 academies founded per decade, which would have averaged a total of 3 academies in each of the thirty-five counties by 1900 had they not been concentrated toward the populous easternmost counties.[23] Adding the northern prefectures back in with the rest of the province produces a total of about 168 academies in 1900 as compared with 70 in 1820.[24]

Official sponsorship is claimed in almost all of the 101 foundings in the southern Kiangsu prefectures. The fact that private foundings are insignificant in number follows a trend in Kiangsu throughout the Ch'ing: official sponsorship had been dominant in Kiangsu, although it is also clear the local educated gentry had provided the funding.[25] The redistribution of post-Taiping academies makes it equally clear that the involvement of a concentrated local elite in the highly urbanized core area of eastern Kiangsu determined where academies flourished. The pent-up aspirations of a generation with commercial capital and managerial skills accounts for the mushrooming of academies in southeastern Kiangsu from 1862 to 1900. What was harder to see at the time was that the expansion of institutions of higher education to meet the needs of postwar social dislocation, including a backlog of students in 1865, was going to produce an oversupply of local educated elite members by 1895.

Students leaving after an average period of three years joined that important stratum of nonofficial local society called the local educated elite. All degree-holders below *chü-jen* were included in this stratum, whose largest component was the multitude of *sheng-yuan* or first degree-holders. Legitimate access to office for the some 53,754 *sheng-yuan* in post-Taiping Kiangsu was limited to a national quota of 87 admitted to *chü-jen* status every three years.[26] The remainder were left as a rural intelligentsia naturally interested in educational innovations or management opportunities that could utilize its talents.

LUNG-MEN ACADEMY IN THE T'UNG-CHIH RESTORATION

In 1733, the Yung-cheng emperor had ended a period of dynastic consolidation that repressed private academies by funding a provincial academy in each provincial capital. In Kiangsu, the 1733 edict established two elite academies because the administration of the province was split into one center in Chiang-ning prefecture supervising Kiangsu's northern counties and another supervising the Kiangnan core prefectures centered at Soochow. These institutions were sophisticated models for some sixty-two more at the prefectural, department, and county levels that were founded or restored during the sixty-year Ch'ien-lung reign that followed. Gentry contributions were important in allowing founding officials to establish lasting endowments in land or in interest-bearing bank accounts at pawnbroker houses to maintain these new institutions.[27]

The necessity of official-gentry collaboration in financing academies provided the distance from state control needed to prevent oppressive political domination of these institutions. Academy directors were not classified as officials and, once appointed, they worked of necessity within the realities of the local society in which they were located. Much local variation resulted, even in enrollments, which varied from a minimum of 10 students to around 130. The quality of the academy director and the quality of financial succor from official and private sources at any point in time generally determined the quality of learning in an institution.[28]

T'ung-chih Restoration policy explicitly called for the founding of academies.[29] In Kiangsu, one high-quality regional academy rose above the many county-level restorations and foundings that followed. Lung-men (Dragon Gate) Academy drew students from the culturally and economically rich Yangtze Delta, as it was established by the Taotais in Shanghai. The Taotais—who founded and initially supported Lung-men Academy, along with its eminent director for its first fourteen years—made its quality competitive with the two official provincial academies in Soochow and Chiang-ning that had been founded in 1733.

The officials who founded Lung-men Academy in 1865 were important figures in the Kiangsu Restoration. Ting Jih-ch'ang (T. Yu-sheng, 1823–82) and Ying Pao-shih (T. Min-chai, b. 1821, *chü-jen*, 1844) succeeded each other as the Military Taotais of eastern Kiangsu (*Su-Sung-T'ai pei-ping*) from 1864 to 1868. They are often placed by historians with Li Hung-chang (1823–1901) and his adviser Feng Kuei-fen (T. Lin-i, 1809–74) as modernizers who, after 1860, pushed to their institutional limits proposals on Western affairs.[30] In their roles as founders of the academy, they are revealed, however, as primarily concerned with the disastrous effect Western values and commercialism were leaving in coastal Kiangsu.

As Kiangsu's governor from 1868 to 1870, Ting Jih-ch'ang worked tirelessly to reestablish an effective central government—from the village lecture system up to model standards of provincial judicial and fiscal probity. Along the way, he made sure heterodox Western ideas did not compromise the strengths of the Confucian state.[31] As Taotai in 1864, he allocated one thousand taels of silver to establish a sophisticated academy in Shanghai city. His successor as Taotai the following year, Ying Pao-shih, carried out this design and saw to it that neither vocationalism nor pedantry became the standard at the new institution but rather rigorous training to produce moral, competent, and effective students. Lung-men Academy, noted Ying in his reminiscence of its founding, was to generate talented scholars who would make a significant contribution to their country.[32]

The top student in Lung-men's entering class was contacted by Taotai Ying for an interview after his admission. Shen Hsiang-lung (T. Yueh-chai) later wrote what Taotai Ying told him about his purpose in founding the academy: "[Mr. Ying] thought that from the time Shanghai had begun being active as a commercial port its atmosphere had changed too rapidly. In order to stem the tide before it became disastrous, he founded the [Lung-men] academy."[33] In his own reminiscence of Lung-men Academy as well, Taotai Ying carefully described the Sung tradition of academies dedicated to the best in Confucian values. He then explained the need for a distinctively Confucian academy in Shanghai: "The conditions of this coastal port are such that Chinese and foreign affairs are so mixed together that ... there is a special need for orthodox learning.... In this way I hope to contribute in a small way to the fulfillment of Mr. Ting's original intentions.[34]

When the bylaws of Lung-men Academy were framed, the first academy director wrote a draft and Taotai Ying consulted one of the most respected Han Learning scholars of the day, Yü Yueh (T. Ch'ü-yuan, 1821–1907) to assess their quality. Yü was then teaching at Soochow's 1733 Tzu-yang Academy. Yü praised the bylaws he was asked to review as superior to those at Tzu-yang Academy and noted: "Not only will it [Lung-men Academy] be a blessing for the scholars of the southeast, but the benefits of literary and military strengthening will accrue to the Restoration (chung-hsing).[35]

The relationship of scholars of Yü's status to the state was, however, an issue Restoration architects must have viewed with some apprehension. Yü had been permanently disbarred from holding official positions in the 1850s for posing a provincial examination question judged by a censor to be insulting to the empress.[36] But the uneasy Ch'ing accommodation of scholars to state interest in controlling academic life entered a new phase after 1864. While needing to discipline unruly scholars, the state also needed desperately to produce more loyal literati. Men selected to become directors of Lung-men Academy in the future included a variety of eminent scholars, some of whom had consistently rejected official appointment, excused themselves from further public service, or in the case of Sun Ch'iang-ming (Hao or literary name, hereafter H., Chu-t'ien, 1817–1900, see table 14.2) had gravitated to the academic community after censure in the mid-1860s for inappropriate criticism of a county magistrate.[37]

Largely because the course of the fourteen-year war of suppression was centered in the middle and Lower Yangtze provinces, Shanghai had become a national center of Western knowledge and its propagation. Western arsenals and troops had been centered there and were used carefully by the Ch'ing government in rooting the Taipings out of Kiangsu. Li Hung-chang began the Shanghai Interpreters' College in 1863 and established the Kiangnan Arsenal in Shanghai in 1865. Translation bureaus and publishing houses then developed in Shanghai.[38] In the midst of such Westernization in treaty port Shanghai, Lung-men Academy's founding in 1865 reasserted the primacy of an elite form of traditional Confucian training.

Good stipends supported the *sheng-yuan* who took examinations to be admitted. In place of direct training to prepare for the civil service exams, Lung-men's pedagogical philosophy was reminiscent of that practiced in the earlier Hsueh-hai-t'ang (Sea of Learning Hall) academy in Canton. Lung-men required that two diaries be kept by students each day, one a daily schedule of books and passages chosen to be studied that day and the other a record of intellectual reactions to one's reading. The reading centered on analyses of the Classics, philosophical texts from the Sung *Hsing-li hsueh* (school of principle), and analyses of historical texts. Poetic compositions were omitted from the curriculum. An independent-study learning environment resulted in which it was assumed that self-cultivation through studying the Classics and related works would prepare dedicated teachers, scholars, and public leaders of intellectual and moral excellence rather than job-seeking bureaucrats.[39]

Lung-men's ideals and founding principles, again following the famous Hsueh-hai-t'ang, also make clear that scholars explicitly protected their own interests in this restoration institution. When its bylaws were revised in or about 1870, defiant language appeared regarding the possibility of Lung-men Academy's ever teaching the eight-legged essay. The revised bylaws were deposited in the governor general's office in Chiang-ning as proof that this was forbidden.[40] Scholars had been given an opening five years earlier to establish a serious academy, and in 1870 they protected their scholarly prerogative against corrosion from either the political needs of the state or the vocationalism of students:

> In the future, the regulations of the academy will be clear to the governor general and to the governor. If in the future an official wants to implement the contemporary-style essay (*shih-wen*), the trustees and enrolled students can refer to the principles [written here]. Or if the trustees and students want to study the contemporary-style essay (*shih-wen*) or poetry, an official can refer to these precepts and make them public. What is essential is that an academy is made to produce talent. Principles and their implementation combine to define real learning. Study here is not only aimed at becoming an official. As for the

fascination with the popular essay, there are other local and regional academies for that purpose.[41]

Lung-men Academy Trustees

Lung-men Academy was under the supervision of the Taotai of the Su-Sung-T'ai region in eastern Kiangsu until the Ch'ing dynasty fell in 1911. By 1867, Taotai Ying had moved the institution from borrowed facilities at Jui-chu Academy and built a campus with fifty dormitory rooms, which housed the original twenty-six residential students on stipend. In 1871, Taotai T'u Tsung-ying (H. Lang-hsuan, 1810–94) was able to add twelve thousand treasury taels to Ying's ten thousand and deposit them with a reputable pawnbroker bank in Shanghai. This investment yielded steady interest for operating expenses.[42] By 1876, thirteen more dormitory rooms were added, and in 1880 the number of residential scholarship students rose to thirty-six.[43]

There was a local board of trustees for Lung-men Academy composed of prominent citizens. While the term for trustee appears in no gazetteer records of this Taotai-sponsored official institution, the academy regulations reveal some of the functions trustees (*tung-shih*) actually carried out. Chief among their functions was the administration of the endowment.

The business of investing the Taotai's endowment was handled not by underlings in his office but by responsible persons in the office of the Shanghai county government. The county officials selected responsible pawnbrokers and received a formal bank book for recording all transactions, including interest accrued.[44] When these financial arrangements were made, the county officials were required to notify the local board of trustees. The trustees, along with one administrator of the academy itself, could then request that a certain amount of money be withdrawn for use in running the academy.

Each time there was a withdrawal, the Taotai's office was notified. The four responsible units—the academy administrators, the academy board of trustees, the county official, and the office of the Taotai—formed a kind of checks-and-balances relationship with one another. Should any trustees resign, for example, the remaining local gentry (*ti-fang shen-shih*) on the board themselves selected replacement trustees who were upstanding and able (*cheng lien ming*) and notified both the Taotai and county officials concerned. The new trustees had to be formally approved by the Taotai's office before they could assume their responsibilities. Similarly, when a change in personnel occurred in either the county or Taotai office, the departing official had to balance the books, write an exit report to the trustees, and provide an official transcript of the exit report on academy affairs to the new incoming official.[45]

With an average of three county-level academies appearing in each county of southern Kiangsu by 1900, many of the local educated elite of the region were engaged by academies as trustees. The trustees' role was local, but because the functional role of the average county academy in Kiangsu related directly to passing stages of the national civil service examinations, academies in principle enlisted local elite in the promotion of national rather than more local interests. But it is equally clear that the local educated elite and particularly the sophisticated scholarly elite of the Lower Yangtze had interests of their own. They rejected the vocationalism of students and the role of the academy as preparatory school for the civil service examinations. The various academy directors could agree with founding and supporting officials regarding the need for upholding Confucian standards in westernizing Shanghai. Many of those same scholars, however, had also been alienated from official power and were not adverse to criticizing the government itself for not adequately upholding Confucian standards.

LEARNING AT LUNG-MEN ACADEMY

Lung-men's Founding Commitment to Ch'eng-Chu Learning, 1865–70

The opening of Lung-men Academy in 1865–66 was far from smooth. The first director hired by Taotai Ying Pao-shih was a Chekiangese, Ku Kuang-yü (H. Fang-hsi 1779–1866), who died within two months of assuming his duties. The second director, Wan Hu-ch'uan (T. Ch'ing-hsuan 1807–1904), taught for only a half year because the death of his father required that he return to Hupei for the customary three years of mourning. Then in 1866 Taotai Ying appointed a Kiangsu native of exceptional renown, Liu Hsi-tsai (T. Jung-chai, 1813–81), who established the high reputation of Lung-men Academy during his fourteen years of leadership.[46]

Analysis of the backgrounds of these initial headmasters reveals some of the objectives of the early Restoration in Kiangsu. Perhaps the most salient fact about the first two men selected as directors was their fervent commitment to Ch'eng-Chu Neo-Confucianism. What also emerges is the compatibility of this emphasis with the regional leadership of the Restoration by Tseng Kuo-fan, who assumed the post of governor general in Chiang-ning city after the Taiping defeat in 1864.

The first headmaster, Ku Kuang-yü, stood out in his era for not promoting *Han-hsueh* (Han Learning), but rather emphasizing the Ch'eng-Chu school still orthodox in the examination system.[47] His reputation was built not on success in the civil service examinations—because, in part, the Taiping Rebellion had interrupted his progression through the examination system, but he was famous primarily for his writings, as well as years of tutorial teaching.[48] He had studied with Yao Ch'un (T. Ch'un-mu) from Sung-chiang prefecture in Kiangsu, who himself was a student of Yao Nai (T. Hsi-pao, 1730–1815), the composition master of the famous T'ung-ch'eng school.[49] T'ung-ch'eng writers generally adopted *Sung-hsueh* (Sung Learning) as their fundamental credo, and his training with Yao Ch'un set Ku's primary scholarly direction along Ch'eng-Chu lines.[50]

The second appointee of Taotai Ying Pao-shih was a well-reputed scholar of the Ch'eng-Chu school. Standard biographies of Wan Hu-ch'uan in Ch'ing compilations repeat a story that seems to have given his scholarly identity an almost sagelike quality. When the Taiping rebels were crossing from Kiangsi into his home province of Hupei, Wan opted to stay at home in Hsing-kuo county and to continue his teaching of the Classics in a modest school. As the rampage of destruction reached his hut, the Taiping soldiers found him sitting erect reciting a passage, which apparently caught the invaders by surprise. The rebels left him untouched and soon left his village as well. Such rectitude was seen by his villagers as exceptionally principled living and impressed many officials, who thereafter awarded him rank and attempted to appoint him to office. Tseng Kuo-fan and Li Hung-chang both tried to give him jobs during the war. He represented to them a model of heroic Confucian resistance. But Wan refused all official appointment and remained an academy teacher and scholar the rest of his life.[51]

Meanwhile, Taotai Ying in Shanghai moved up to the post of Kiangsu Judicial Commissioner (*Chiang-su an-ch'a shih*) in 1869. The man who replaced him as Taotai was mentioned above as handsomely renewing the endowment of Lung-men Academy. He was T'u Tsung-ying, a young official admired by Tseng Kuo-fan. T'u had been the student of a fellow Anhweiese, Wu T'ing-tung (H. Chu-ju, 1793–1873).[52] Once in the lucrative Taotai post at Shanghai, T'u commissioned the resigned second Lung-men headmaster, Wan Hu-ch'uan who had traveled to Hupei to prepare a comprehensive collated edition of Chu Hsi's works, *Chu-tzu ta-ch'üan* (Complete works of Master Chu).[53]

T'u's promotion of Sung Learning continued from a select group of high officials including Tseng Kuo-fan who had been trying to reconcile the important philological discoveries of the Ch'ing period with a commitment to Ch'eng-Chu expositions of moral philosophy. (For a demonstration of some Chinese scholars' intellectual animosity to the allegedly "empty" Ch'eng-Chu school that such officials had overcome, see especially Brokaw on Tai Chen, chap. 8 of this volume; for a fuller analysis of the complex thought of Tseng Kuo-fan, see Liu, chap. 3 of this volume). The leader of the original Hanlin coterie uniting them in Peking, T'ang Chien (1778–1861), and his follower the impressively self-disciplined Wo-jen (T. Ken-feng, 1804–71), had been given conspicuous posts as the Restoration began.[54] Lung-men Academy's history helps trace the continuing importance of their ideals in early T'ung-chih Restoration ideology. They acknowledged the same intellectual lineage as the first two headmasters of Lung-men Academy; namely, the early, Ch'ing advocates of Ch'eng-Chu moral philosophy, Chang Lü-hsiang (T. K'ao-fu, 1611–74), Lu Lung-ch'i (T. Chia-shu, 1630–93), and Chang Po-hsing (T. Hsiao-hsien, 1652–1725).[55] T'ang Chien praised Lu Lung-ch'i as the legitimate successor to Chu

Hsi's work in the Ch'ing, and the man who had transmitted the orthodox study of the *tao* to the Ch'ing dynasty.[56] The other two, along with Lu Shih-i (T. Tao-wei, 1611–72), comprised the four major proponents of Ch'eng-Chu thought in the early Ch'ing.[57] In the year of Wo-jen's death, 1871, "on the petition of a high official" that may well reflect the influence of this group of high officials, Chang Lü-hsiang was officially canonized in the Confucian Temple of China, and Chang Po-hsing joined him in 1878.[58]

T'u Tsung-ying's teacher, Wu T'ing-tung, and Tseng Kuo-fan had both been students of T'ang Chien. One of Tseng's first acts once he took up residence in the former Taiping capital in 1867 had been to invite Wu T'ing-tung—whom he referred to as one of China's three living sages—to come there as a distinguished visiting lecturer.[59] Tseng presented Wu T'ing-tung as a model scholar-official who could be emulated by Restoration administrators.

Tseng had hoped Wu's personal example and his lectures on the principles of Confucianism would prove inspirational and be a model of exemplary Confucian leadership as Taiping heterodoxy was expelled. Tseng had experienced such inspiration in the Peking group of friends years before. Tseng's diary records the kind of standards T'ang Chien had discussed with the coterie: "[With regard to self-examination,] my teacher said, 'In recent years, Wo-jen has been the most dedicated one. Every day he records each word he said, each move he made, and even each meal he ate. He also records his bad behavior and the lusts that he fails to overcome. After hearing all this, I felt like a blind man who has just been given the ability to see the world again.'"[60]

One of Wo-jen's final acts before he died was to praise Taotai T'u Tsung-ying's 1871 addition to Lung-men Academy's endowment.[61] It was the hope of the academy's official Restoration founders and its scholarly directors that this lived environment of moral philosophy would be a microcosm of a society whose leaders had learned how to transcend self-interest.

Student Selection and Pedagogy at Lung-men Academy

Admission to Lung-men was competitive and brought with it substantial stipends of support. By 1870, twenty-six residential scholarships were awarded, and admission was also granted to another twenty-four students who lived off campus. The residential scholarship consisted of four taels of silver a month. While off-campus students received no stipend, they could, however, compete for the substantial monetary awards given for each of the eight monthly essay prizes.[62] To be among the fifty academy students, with or without scholarships, required passing the rigorous entrance examination given each November. To renew one's student status for a second year depended on the grades one had accumulated on the eight monthly essays completed before the eleventh month, when the next year's class was decided.

For an outside candidate to become one of the twenty-four off-campus students, two former examination papers from another academy (or a civil service examination) were submitted. These were followed by the sit-down examination on campus. If the off-campus applicant later wanted to become one of the elite twenty-six residential students with stipends, he had to notify the trustees of the institution. All his monthly essays were then submitted and reviewed, as well as his marks on his original entrance examination. It was also essential to have a personal recommendation from one of the current residential students in order to be transferred from off campus to residential stipend status. Such letters commented on the candidate's scholarship and moral character. Competition among several off-campus students for a residential scholarship was decided by the academy director in consultation with the Taotai.[63]

Eight monthly essays and daily independent study before the essay topics were announced were the primary pedagogy at the academy. Once a topic was announced—always on the thirteenth of each month—residential students had two days to finish the essay, with progressively longer times allowed for off-campus students returning essays from as far away from Shanghai as Soochow. In addition, the academy director and master teacher lectured on selected topics every five days.[64]

Before the thirteenth of each month, the student at Lung-men Academy submitted his diaries twice to his teacher (*shih*) —once on the fifth day of the month and again on the tenth. The teacher was the director of the academy, and he tutored each student. The teacher reacted to what the student had logged as reading and to the student's journal of ideas. The teacher's critical assessment and dialogue with the student were on a tutorial basis.[65]

The printed bylaws of the academy described the diaries as a method of daily discipline:

Precept Three: Daily Discipline

This includes all students recording their activities in a diary and keeping a scholarly journal. The activities diary must include early morning, prenoon, afternoon, and after the lights are lit—four divisions of the day, with appropriate subjects in each division. Basically, the combined morning hours should be spent on the Four Books (one must go to a second book only when the first is mastered) and *Hsing-li* (nature and principle) (every day one should study a few chapters).[66] In the afternoon, the student should study the histories and Chu Hsi's *Outline* and [Ssu-ma Kuang's (1019–86)] *Mirror* (selecting one book and reading from the beginning, with no skipping) and should study the noncanonical Chou philosophers (the selection of essential points to be studied must be made judiciously).[67] Also, one may read current affairs (but only about real events). With extra effort one can write compositions (but they must concern principle and not be careless compositions or poetry). One can also practice calligraphy (but only *k'ai* style). After the lights are on, one might work on civil service career preparation (one must know how former scholars explained the principles of morality (*i-li*).

Although there are differences in divisions of the day, one must always be busy. Every subject and activity must be recorded so that what is learned from study and what one questions must be recorded daily in the notation book. What one records must not be fabricated and must not be written in tedious detail. One must avoid pretexts for not making entries. Every fifth and tenth day one must submit the diaries to the teacher and get advice. The teacher will direct activity and give reactions. Every month there will be a topical essay, and at the end of the year they will be ranked according to the depth or superficiality of the essay, and students evaluated for promotion or demotion.[68]

One explicit pedagogical ideal at Lung-men Academy was living or putting into practice what one learned. The central conception of how moral principles (*t'i*) and their implementation (*yung*) were part of the institution is illustrated by the following sections of the 1865 founding precepts on the curriculum, which were required to be posted at the upper right of each student's desk. The Confucian conception of *t'i* and *yung* as expressed in these academy precepts makes clear what violence Chang Chih-tung (1837–1909) did to them at the end of the century by proposing foreign technology could become the *yung* without disturbing essential Chinese values (*t'i*):

Precept One: Personal Behavior

Emphasize implementation. Those studying classical texts should begin with rigorous analysis of the content and then should complete the learning by practicing it.

To know and be able to practice that knowledge is real knowledge. According to the *Doctrine of the Mean*, to study broadly, inquire, analyze, and clearly argue an issue should result in earnest practice of what one has learned. Those who want to attain knowledge through learning must reflect to reach the real objective. In establishing an academy, we ask the students who study the orthodox tradition to better themselves and thereby not pass along what is bad in one's self. In this way, gradually and through reflection, one can attain sincerity.

If you do not fix your will, you cannot firmly implement what is sought and practice it. In this case, what is analyzed will be of no use. All students should often analyze their own behavior and see if it is in conformity with what they study in their books. One must keep them in conformity or there will be self-recrimination.

Precept Two: Serious Study

Studying should be systematic. First study the *tao* in the Four Books, then expand your knowledge by studying all the histories, *Tzu-chih t'ung-chien* (The comprehensive mirror), and Master Chu's *Kang-mu* (Outline). Then one can use the following compilations as ladders for assistance: *Hsiao-hsueh* (Elementary primer); *Chin-ssu lu* (Reflections on things at hand); collections of materials on nature and principle.[69] In this way one can use understanding the subtle essence of the principles of morality (*i-li*) to direct oneself in a pattern of behavior.

Selections from the one hundred philosophers and the Classics, histories, and all related practical volumes can be studied according to the ability of the

TABLE 14.2   Headmasters of Lung-men Academy, 1865–1904

Period in Office	Name (Tzu or Hao)	Native Place
1865	Ku Kuang-yü (H. Fang-hsi)	Chekiang, P'ing-hu
1865–66	Wan Hu-ch'uan (T. Ch'ing-hsuan)	Hupeh, Hsing-kuo
1866–80	Liu Hsi-tsai (H. Jung-tsai)	Kiangsu, Hsing-hua
1881–84	Pao Yuan-shen (T. Hua-t'an)	Anhwei, Hu-chou
1884–94	Sun Ch'iang-ming (H. Ch'ü-tien)	Chekiang, Jui-an
1894–98	Chu Hsiao-t'ang (T. Hsien-t'ing)	Kiangsi, Kuei-hsi
1898–1900	Wu Ta-ch'eng (T. Ch'ing-ch'ing)	Kiangsu, Soochow
1900–1904	Weng T'ao-fu (T. Pin-sun)	Kiangsu, Ch'ang-shou
1904	T'ang Shou-ch'ieng (T. Chen)	Chekiang, Shan-yin

student. After that, remaining energy can be used on composition and on prep-aration for the civil service exams. One cannot be lazy or interrupt, and one can-not read carelessly in a variety of books. One progresses according to one's own ability, clarifying the *t'i* (principles, or substance) and attaining the *yung* (im-plementation, or function). This will lead to real benefit, and is the right way to approach study.[70]

Synthesis of Confucian Schools under Later Directors

Table 14.2 above lists the directors of Lung-men Academy, 1865–1904. The longest and most renowned contributions were made by Liu Hsi-tsai, director for the fourteen years from 1866 to 1880, and Sun Ch'iang-ming, director from 1884 to 1894. Of Liu's uniquely exemplary career, two items may be extracted to characterize his contribution to the academy.

First, his diligence in assessing student diaries is remarked on by the great Kiangnan scholar Yü Yueh, whom Ying Pao-shih consulted when the academy was founded. In his affectionate epitaph for Liu Hsi-tsai, Yü Yueh says that for fourteen years Liu reviewed student submissions, critically analyzing them one by one. Director Liu's advice eliminated the weaknesses and encouraged the strengths of each student. Yü Yueh noted with admiration that this man, who had tutored the Hsien-feng emperor, would sometimes at 2 or 3 A.M. personally check to be sure his students were in their dormitories.[71]

Secondly, Yü Yueh described Liu Hsi-tsai's teaching as not stressing one factional school of Chinese scholarship to the exclusion of another. Liu did not teach according to the Sung or Han school exclusively but stressed the contributions each could make to a student's ethical development. Yü himself evidently agreed with this viewpoint. In an intellectual synthesis that seemed more accommodating than the self-discipline fostered by T'ang Chien's coterie in 1865, Yü's position represented a syncretism of Confucian factions that was shared by the manifestos of most serious Kiangsu academies by the 1880s: "I believe in selecting the good parts from past scholarship rather than condemning inadequacies," Yü said in agreement with Director Liu of Lung-men. "The Han and Sung schools cannot be in total opposition in my view."[72]

The synthetic Confucian philosophy taught at Lung-men Academy in the 1870s had been continued by Tseng Kuo-fan when he returned to Chiang-ning a second time in 1867. When Tseng addressed the question of which philosophical positions should be taught at academies, he insisted upon a synthesis of Han- and Sung-Learning schools of scholarship. Tseng wanted to avoid any debilitating factionalism at this critical moment in the reconstruction of the Ch'ing dynasty. Later academies, building on Tseng's reputation, called for the integration of *Sung-hsueh*, *Han-hsueh*, and T'ung-ch'eng composition, which Tseng had praised in the work of Yao Nai. These elements Tseng saw as woven into a synthetic ideology that promoted both substantial and practical scholarship (*shih-hsueh*).[73] Self-cultivation in Ch'eng-Chu moral philosophy was the core of the post-Taiping synthesis promoted by Tseng, and this element influenced the nineteenth-century Confucian consensus.[74] A theme common in Tseng's thought, the Kiangsu academy revival, as well as some *ch'ing-i* (pure opinion) sentiment was the axiom that the restored Confucian state implied renovation of a highly centralized government based on the holding power of an unfractured common political ideology.[75]

In Sun Ch'iang-ming's decade of dedication to the academy, it is important to notice a biographical fact that accounts for a man of his extraordinary ability choosing to head the academy. Following his *chin-shih* degree he accepted official posts; then from 1853 to 1862 he worked in his home locality of Jui-an, Chekiang, primarily leading the militia defending against the Taiping invaders and related rebels.[76] In 1863, he began to supervise examinations as he had in Kwangsi before the war, but he could not contain his criticism of the poor local administration of Jui-an. The incompetence Sun attacked was probably one case of the lamentable *hsien* (county) administration, compounded by the increasing sale of such offices, that Ting Jih-ch'ang was soon to try to correct further north in Kiangsu.[77] Speaking out of place, however, caused supervisors to censure Sun and prevented him from holding official posts until he was finally rehabilitated in 1896 at age seventy-nine.

The process and aftermath of the Taiping suppression affected the Lower Yangtze for years. Liu Hsi-tsai, when given the opportunity in 1866, excused himself from public service of the highest grade on the pretext of poor health to devote his life to academic teaching and scholarship. In Sun Ch'iang-ming's case, censure had the effect of moving a man of exceptional talent from official posts to a new classical academy in the region that was itself dedicated to producing more men of exceptional talent for the future.[78] In 1900, Sun Ch'iang-ming was presented an honorary title on the sixtieth anniversary of his 1841 *chin-shih* degree. Rehabilitation was probably welcome to this man, and when the court retreated to Hsi-an in 1900, this seasoned militia leader from the Taiping era wept openly. He subsequently fell ill and died the same year.[79] The legacy these directors left to two generations of Lung-men students facing the twentieth century was the practice of Confucian principle and the appeal to a moral leadership that transcended all factionalism.

THE TRANSITION TO MODERN PUBLIC SCHOOLS IN THE LOWER YANGTZE REGION, 1895 – 1911

The trauma of national defeat by Japan in 1894–95 had an important effect on the local educated elite in the Lower Yangtze. For nearly two generations, the revival of academies in Kiangsu had expanded the opportunities and initiative of the educated in localities throughout the province. The Japanese military blow in 1895 stunned the centralized government, and the Ch'ing Court released its control over many national institutions. While decentralizing reform initiatives accompanying this change were viciously repressed after the Hundred Days of 1898, the local elite was nevertheless impelled to expand its range of activities as crisis management discontinued many central government functions. The New Policies then attempted to reimpose centralized controls in 1901.

In 1895, the expanded local educated elite in the Lower Yangtze was already working outside those orthodox routes to social mobility envisaged by the T'ung-chih Restoration. Of the many able students at Lung-men Academy, Chang Huan-lun (T. Ching-fu) is one good example of how a member of the Shanghai local elite gradually redirected his energies and expanded the range of his professional contributions after 1865. He was a student of Liu Hsi-tsai and in 1876, when the Shanghai Taotai founded a new classical academy in Shanghai much like Lung-men, was appointed director. Much like leaders at Lung-men Academy itself, he was also sought after by high officials to take appointments to public office. Tseng Chi-tse (1839–90) and Chang Chih-tung both tried unsuccessfully to appoint Chang to office.[80]

What Chang Huan-lun preferred to do was not lead the classical academy but found a reformist academy of his own in Shanghai. In 1878, he began a school whose objectives stretched to the breaking point the premises on which classical academies such as Lung-men were founded. His new school, Cheng-meng (Correcting youthful ignorance) Academy, taught moral principles, but students tied them to current affairs.[81] Except for Ch'eng-Chu learning, no subject matter relating to the examination system was taught. Foreigners were hired to head academic departments, and military training was part of the curriculum. Further, English and French were both taught.[82]

Two other former Lung-men students went with Chang Huan-lun from Lung-men Academy to set up the dissenting academy and at least another was soon hired to teach there. Local gazetteers reveal that soon one of these young men even went to teach at an explicitly national strengthening institution, Shanghai's Kiangnan Arsenal, where other former Lung-men students also eventually taught.[83]

The decade after the defeat by Japan, 1896 to 1906, was decisive in increasing the autonomy and power of the Lower Yangtze educated elite, many of whom were like Chang Huan-lun experimenting with new organizations. In the first half of this period, national crisis generated a de facto increase in local autonomy. The birth of the first municipal government in Shanghai resulted, for example, from the inability of Ch'ing officials to carry out long-standing projects already underway such as widening narrow streets to increase public safety. The 1894–95 war with Japan diverted the time and resources of officials in charge, and in 1896 the Shanghai municipal government became managed by default for the first time by local officials.[84]

In 1896, there existed in the city a branch of the strident self-strengthening organization the *Ch'iang-hsueh hui* (Learning for strength society). In the next few years, several early revolutionary organizations also formed, fueled by students returning from Japan and also by Shanghai students at the new *Nan-yang kung-hsueh* (Nan-yang public school). This school had been set up by Sheng Hsuan-huai (1844–1916) in 1896 but was soon managed by Chang Huan-lun, the same former Lung-men student who founded the reformist Cheng-meng Academy in 1878.[85]

Many educational institutions, societies, and clubs had been founded in Shanghai and throughout the country after 1895, and after the repression of the reformers of 1898 most continued inconspicuously and with no national support. After 1900, local educators formed new organizations in Shanghai at a surprising rate, and while most were without an explicit political platform, their formation at all indicated the increased role of the local elite in education.[86]

In 1902, for example, a Shanghai Education Society (*Hu-hsueh hui*) formed with monthly contributions required of members. They established a charitable elementary school, a physical education society, and a night school that taught a wide spectrum of subjects. In 1905, the society was joined by another, staffed primarily by former Lung-men Academy students, that would eventually combine with the *Hu-hsueh hui* in 1908 to form the Shanghai County Educational Society (*Shang-hai hsien chiao-yü hui*). The 1905 society was called the Education Research Society (*Chiao-yü yen-chiu hui*) and was cofounded by Yuan Hsi-t'ao (b. 1865), a Lung-men student important in Lung-men's own transformation into a teacher training school—a process that began the preceding year.[87]

Provincewide organization of professionally committed educators was also centered at Shanghai by 1905. The predecessor of the Kiangsu Educational

Association (*Chiang-su sheng chiao-yü hui*) was formed there by October 1905 with the doyen of Kiangsu education, Chang Chien (T. Chi-chih, 1853–1926), elected chairman.[88] This gave some provincewide organizational voice to Kiangsu's educated elite. In the next few years, conflicts over prerogatives exercised by organized Kiangsu educators, and prerogatives claimed by government officials continued. The many compromises between them jolted reforms forward.[89]

Policies in the year 1906 contained revealing compromises. It became clear that the need of New Policies officials to control proliferating public schools had adjusted to the reality that only the existing local elite was going to make new schools work. In 1906, edicts established China's first detailed provincial educational administration. It included county-level educational units that were run basically by the local educated elites. While supervised by the county magistrate, the Offices to Encourage Education (*Ch'üan-hsueh so*) that were required to be established in each *hsien* beginning in 1906 were openly agreed to be managed by the local elite (*shih-shen*) in each school district.[90]

The other revealing school regulation of 1906 was the Ch'ing court's promotion of the provincial educational associations that were cropping up. With the examination system abolished the previous September, it was clear the new schools would now become a focus of activism within the local elite. The New Policies reformers tried to harness some of this local activism and in fact tried to separate it from the increasing threat of provincial self-direction. As Marianne Bastid has demonstrated, the links of educational association members with provincial assembly members by 1909 made this aim fail. Perhaps most importantly, the extraordinary proliferation of these associations from 1906 to 1911 and their connection to 1890s *hsueh-hui* (study societies) make clear that an all but irrepressible organization of Kiangsu's local educated elite was taking place.[91]

The expanded local educated elite of the Lower Yangtze gained the initiative in education from the government in the first decade of this century. By early 1902, provincial officials in Kiangsu began implementing the national edict of 1901 converting all academies to public schools and founding brand-new schools. From an initial 67 public schools existing in Kiangsu at the end of 1902, the number doubled annually to reach 564 in 1905. Then in 1906, with the examinations abolished and official policy acknowledging the leadership of the local elite and their associations in organizing new schools, the total doubled again in one year to 1,182. The trend continued after 1911, and by 1915 official reports listed 5,982 public elementary schools, secondary schools, and colleges in Kiangsu.[92] As the government gradually acknowledged the need to have the local elite manage local public schools after 1900, the expanded educated elite of the post-Taiping era was ready to take charge.

EPILOGUE: LUNG-MEN NORMAL SCHOOL

The conversion of Lung-men Academy to a Taotai-sponsored normal school was completed in the fall of 1904. At the time, four Shanghai-area scholars were sent to Japan by local authorities to survey normal schools there. Two former Lung-men Academy students from this mission Shen En-fu (T. Hsin-ch'ing) and Yuan Hsi-t'ao, became the first and second presidents respectively of the new Lung-men Normal School.[93] An affiliated elementary school was also quickly established. But the transition was far from smooth.

In early 1904, the established and progressive Chekiangese scholar T'ang Shou-ch'ien (T. Chen 1857–1917) accepted the academy's appointment as its new director.[94] From the 1870 regulations on, Lung-men Academy had insisted on its relative independence from government dictation. When rumors of conversion of the academy to a normal school spread on the campus in 1904, the director T'ang requested that the supervisor (*kuan-ch'a*) concerned report T'ang's dissenting views to the authorities. Declaring the academy a teacher training school would have placed it under close government control, which T'ang resisted.[95] But instead of setting up a timetable for negotiations, official response was to begin renovations to expand the dormitory and classroom capacity of the academy for its new functions as a normal school. Lung-men Academy's last director resigned in open dissent.

Shen Hsiang-lung, the student cited earlier at the top of Lung-men's first entering class of 1865, sympathized with the resignation of 1904. He reflected on the forty years he had watched Lung-men's progress under various eminent directors and felt that much was lost in the normal school transformation that took place in the early Republic. He commented around 1915: "All the headmasters were pure Confucians, basing their work on the Ch'eng-Chu school. All the disciples stressed high character and studied moral principles. The traditions studied asked the students to live their learning while in residence. Later, when modern schools (*hsueh-t'ang*) were begun and Western studies introduced, the study of *hsing-li* (Sung school of principle) was considered outmoded and impractical. So such academies were changed to teacher training schools. But can the new schools equal the quality of the teaching of the previous era? Can they produce followers of open heart and sincere feelings like those who followed the teachings of [directors] Liu or Pao?"[96]

Hu Shih was a proponent of some of the most advanced pedagogical methods in the American progressive education movement, but he later joined this Ch'ing student (for somewhat different reasons) in lamenting the sacrifice that the transformation of Lung-men Academy represented. In the 1920s, Hu Shih singled out the regional Lung-men Academy along with the two other provincewide Kiangsu academies as late models of the best in the Ch'ing classical tradition of academies. He lamented that a hundred-year-old German tradition of public schools came at the turn of the twentieth century to replace a thousand-year-old Chinese tradition, the classical pedagogy of which, at least, was of vastly superior quality.[97]

Whatever strengths later interpreters saw in Lung-men Academy's classical pedagogy, T'ang Shou-ch'ien resigned in 1904 for a principle that had become widespread among the local elite of the Lower Yangtze. From 1865 on, when academy expansion in Kiangsu began, academics in the Lower Yangtze had laid claim to the aims of education for its own sake in reconstructing post-Taiping institutions. For two generations, directors, trustees, and students enjoyed the relative autonomy of founding new institutions that themselves then further expanded the educated elite in each locality. The national crisis after 1895 continued to liberate and finally organize the local educated elite of the Lower Yangtze. By 1906 in Kiangsu, the local educated elite that had evolved in the preceding forty years had made local self-determination an end in itself. It was not surprising that T'ang Shou-ch'ien soon supported constitutionalism and then Sun Yat-sen's republican government.[98]

NOTES

Abbreviations

fc — *fu-chih* 府志 (prefecture gazetteer)

hc — *hsien-chih* 縣志 (county gazetteer)

CTCC — *Ch'ing-tai chuan-chi ts'ung-k'an* 清代傳記叢刊 (Collectanea of Ch'ing biographies) 206 vols. (Taipei: Ming-wen shu-chü, 1985).

SHSTCK — *Shang-hai shi t'ung-chih kuan ch'i-k'an* 上海市通志館期刊 (Journal of the provincial gazetteer office of Shanghai city) (1933–34; reprint, Hong Kong: Lung-men shu-tien, 1967).

A revised version of this chapter will appear in Barry Keenan, *Imperial China's Last Classical Academies: Social Change in the Lower Yangzi, 1864–1911,* China Research Monograph 42 (Berkeley: Institute of East Asian Studies, University of California, 1994).

1. Mary Wright, *The Last Stand of Chinese Conservatism: The T'ung Chih Restoration, 1862–1974* (New York: Atheneum, 1969), 130.

2. This figure was only about 50 percent before the Taiping revolutionary movement. See Marianne Bastid-Bruguiere, "Currents of Social Change," in *The Cambridge History of China,* ed. John K. Fairbank and Kwang-Ching Liu (Cambridge: Cambridge University Press, 1980), 11, no. 2:538; Chung-li Chang, *The Chinese Gentry* (Seattle: University of Washington Press, 1970), 116–37.

3. Kwang-Ching Liu, "The Ch'ing Restoration," in *The Cambridge History of China,* ed. John K. Fairbank (Cambridge: Cambridge University Press, 1978) 10, pt. 1: 479.

4. Chang, *Chinese Gentry,* 88, 100.

5. Liu, "Ch'ing Restoration," 425–35; Ting-yee Kuo and Kwang-Ching Liu, "Self-strengthening: The Pursuit of Western Technology," in *The Cambridge History of*

China, ed. John K. Fairbank (Cambridge: Cambridge University Press, 1978), 10, no.1: 496–500, 519–25.

6. Hu Ch'uan 胡傳, "Tun-fu nien-p'u" 鈍夫年譜, (Chronological biography of Hu Chuan), in Hu Shih, *Ssu-shih tzu-shu* (Autobiography at forty) (Taipei: Yuan-liu, 1991), 189–91.

7. Hu Ch'uan, "Tun-fu nien-p'u," 191, 228. See also Hu Shih 胡適, *Hu Shih k'ou-shu tzu-chuan* 胡適口述自傳 (Hu Shih's oral history autobiography) trans. with notes by T'ang Te-kang (Taipei: Chuan-chi wen-hsueh ch'u-pan she, 1986), 11–14.

8. Hu Ch'uan, "Tun-fu nien-p'u," 221–28; Hu Shih, *Hu Shih k'ou-shu*, 12–15.

9. Tilemann Grimm, "Academies and Urban Systems in Kwangtung," in *The City in Late Imperial China*, ed. G. William Skinner (Stanford University Press, 1977), 481.

10. Ibid., 484.

11. Ōkubo Eiko 大久保英子, "Shindai kōsetsu chihō no shoin to shakai" 清代江浙 地方の書院と社會 (Academies and society in the Chiang-che region in the Ch'ing period), in Akigorō Taga, ed., *Kinsei to Ajia kyōiku shi kenkyū* 近世とアジア教育史研究 (Research on the history of education in East Asia in modern times) (Tokyo: Gakujutsu sho shuppansha, 1970), 246, 384–88.

12. Mary Rankin, *Elite Activism and Political Transformation in China: Zhejiang Province, 1865–1911*, (Stanford: Stanford University Press, 1986), 53.

13. Ibid., 54.

14. Ibid., 98.

15. Ibid., 18–21.

16. Ibid., 97.

17. For Kiangsu, see Ōkubo, "Shindai kōsetsu," 239; for Kwangtung, see Grimm, "Academies," 481; for Chekiang, see Rankin, *Elite Activism*, app. B. These figures provide a gauge of the amount of activity over time in establishing or reestablishing local academies. The gross numbers of academies at any point in time is particularly hard to discern, as one county's gazetteer reporting them will appear at a time years apart from the gazetteer of the next county. Ōkubo's statistics give little sense of the total number of academies in Kiangsu. Wang Shu-huai breaks down academies by prefecture and time period. The nearly sixty academies present in northern counties would not have been destroyed in the Taiping violence and are probably under-reported in Ōkubo's record of new foundings and renovations. See Wang Shu-huai 王樹槐, *Chung-kuo hsien-tai hua ti-ch'u yen-chiu: Chiang-su sheng 1860–1916* 中國現代化地區研究：江蘇省 1860–1916 (Regional studies on Chinese modernization: Kiangsu province 1860–1916) (Taipei: Chin-tai shih yen-chiu so, 1984), 57.

18. Liu Shih-chi 劉石吉, *Ming-Ch'ing shih-tai Chiang-nan shih-chen yen-chiu* 明清時代 江南市鎮研究 (Studies in urban Kiangnan in the Ming-Ch'ing period) (Shanghai: Chung-kuo she-hui k'o-hsueh ch'u-pan she, 1987), 73–80, 94; Yeh-chien Wang, "The Impact of the Taiping Rebellion on Population in Southern Kiangsu," *Papers on China* (Cambridge, Mass.: Harvard University Press, 1965), 19:120–29.

19. See Liu Shih-chi, *Ming-Ch'ing shih-tai*, 89–97, and table 14.1. Sung-chiang prefecture on the coast became increasingly urbanized right through the Taiping depredations, as did Soochow prefecture and T'ai-ts'ang Department. Migrations of families from other parts of the Lower Yangtze to avoid the Taiping violence accounted for some of this steadily increasing and largely urban population.

20. *Chiang-ning fc*, 51; *Chiang-p'u pei-ch'eng*, 12, 1a–2b; *Li-shui hc*, 539–41.

21. *Chiang-ning fc*, 52; *Kao-ch'un hc*, 5, 33a–36b; Jonathan Ocko, *Bureaucratic Reform in Provincial China: Ting Jih-ch'ang in Restoration Kiangsu, 1867–1870* (Cambridge, Mass.: Harvard Council on East Asian Studies, 1983), 137; *Chü-jung hc*, 154–55, 297–98; *Liu-ho hc*, 3, 12.

22. See table 14.1 and Wang, *Chung-kuo*, 57.

23. This rate appears somewhat artificially high in southern Kiangsu because a baseline of zero academies must be assumed for 1862 when the Taipings had basically closed all normal operation of academies and destroyed most of them in their rampage across these five prefectures. There was a general Ch'ing regulation that each county have at least one academy, and that indeed was the average for this time period in Chihli province; (see Richard Orb, "Chihli Academies and Other Schools in the Late Ch'ing: An Institutional Survey," in *Reform in Nineteenth-Century China*, ed. John Schrecker and Paul Cohen [Cambridge, Mass.: Harvard University Press, 1976], 236; see also Rankin, *Elite Activism*, 49). Only Chiang-ning prefecture in southern Kiangsu had an actual distribution as low as one academy per county. It is instructive to note that an equal period of such rapid growth as southern Kiangsu experienced occurred once in Kwangtung province. From 1851 to 1861, perhaps for reasons related to escapism from Taiping violence elsewhere, academy foundings reached twenty-five per decade and private foundings also skyrocketed; Grimm, "Academies," 481.

24. Wang Shu-huai cites the national gazetteer *I t'ung chih* for this figure. I have tested the statistics given in the *I t'ung chih* for prefectures in Kiangsu by checking more detailed county gazetteers that were contemporaneous and found it reliable. See my Table 14.1 and add to Wang's figures for prefectures north of the Yangtze to get the provincial total. See Wang Shu-huai, *Chung-kuo*, 57.

25. Ōkubo, "Shindai kōsetsu," 245–47; Ogawa Yoshiko 小川嘉子, "Shindai ni okeru gigaku setsuritsu no kiban" 清代における義學設立の基盤 (Basis for charitable school founding in the Ch'ing), in Hayashi Tomoharu 林友春, ed., *Kinsei Chūgoku kyōiku shi kenkyū* 近世中國教育史研究 (Research on Chinese education in the modern era) (Tokyo: Kokudosha, 1958), 292, 305.

26. Min Tu-ki, *National Polity and Local Power* (Cambridge, Mass.: Council on East Asian Studies, 1989), 21–49; Chang Chung-li, *The Chinese Gentry*, 100; Etienne Zi (Siu) *Pratique des Examens Littéraires en Chine*, (Shanghai: Imprimerie de la mission Catholique, 1894), no. 5, 118.

27. Ōkubo, "Shindai kōsetsu," 239–46; Benjamin A. Elman, "Imperial Politics and Confucian Societies in Late Imperial China: The Hanlin and Donglin Academies," *Modern China*, 15, no. 4 (1989): 392–402; Elman, *From Philosophy to Philology: Intellectual and Social Aspects of Change in Late Imperial China* (Cambridge, Mass.: Harvard University Press, 1984), 119–30; Ch'en Yuan-hui 陳元暉 et al., *Chung-kuo ku-tai ti shu-yuan chih-tu* 中國古代的書院制度 (China's premodern academy system) (Shanghai: Shanghai chiao-yü ch'u-pan she, 1981), 91. See also n. 50 below.

28. Alexander Woodside, "State, Scholars, and Orthodoxy: The Ch'ing Academies, 1736–1839," in *Orthodoxy in Late Imperial China*, ed. Kwang-Ching Liu (Berkeley: University of California Press, 1990), 166–71. Liu, "Ch'ing Restoration," 485.

29. Liu Chin-tsao, comp., *Huang-ch'ao hsu wen-hsien t'ung-k'ao* 皇朝續文獻通考 (Continuation of collection of imperial documents), 400 vols. (Shanghai, 1936), 100: 8591.

30. Knight Biggerstaff, *The Earliest Government Schools in China* (Ithaca, N.Y.: Cornell University Press, 1961), 8; Chao-ying Fang, "Ting Jih-ch'ang," in Arthur Hummel, ed., *Eminent Chinese of the Ch'ing Period* (hereafter *ECCP*) (Washington, D.C.: Government Printing Office, 1943), 722.

31. Lu Pao-ch'ien 陸寶千 *Ch'ing-tai ssu-hsiang shih* 清代思想史 (History of Ch'ing period thought) (Taipei: Kuang-wen shu-chü, 1983), 349–61; Ocko, *Bureaucratic Reform*, 61. Ting had played a role in the government's recapture of Soochow and Changchow as well as in the disbanding of the allied Ever Victorious Army of Charles "Chinese" Gordon. He was promoted to the rank of prefect and in 1864 achieved the post of Military Taotai of Eastern Kiangsu; Ocko, *Bureaucratic Reform*, 18; *Shanghai hc*, 9, 34a. In 1867, he was promoted from the office of salt controller for the Lianghuai region to financial commissioner (*pu-cheng shih*) of the province of Kiangsu. A native of Kwangtung, Ting had won the patronage of Li Hung-chang as a county magistrate in Kiangsi, and his fortunes rose steadily after the war. In 1868, Ting was made governor of Kiangsu where he served until resigning to mourn his mother's death in 1870. Throughout the years 1864–70, Ting was a leader of the T'ung-chih Restoration in the prosperous Yangtze Delta.

32. Ying Pao-shih 應寶時, "Hsun-tao Ying Pao-shih Lung-men shu-yuan chi" 巡道 應寶時龍門書院記 (Taotai Ying Pao-shih's account of Lung-men Academy), in *Shang-hai hsien-chih* 上海縣志 9, 693–94.

33. Shen Hsiang-lung 沈祥龍, "T'an-tung tsa-shih" 潭東雜識 (Miscellaneous points from the eastern T'an), *Wen-i tsa-chih* 文藝雜誌, no. 7 (1914–15): 69; no. 9 (1914–15):83.

34. Ying Pao-shih, "Hsun-tao Ying Pao-shih," 34b.

35. Yü Yueh 俞樾, "Yü Ying Min-chai t'ung-nien" 與應敏齋同年 (To Ying Min-chai who passed the examinations in the same year as myself) in Yü Yueh, ed., *Ch'un-tsai t'ang ch'üan-shu* 春在堂全書 (Complete works from the Arrival of Spring Hall), vol. 414 (Taipei: Wen-hai, 1968), 502-4; *Hsu-ting Shang-hai Lung-men shu-yuan k'o-ch'eng liu-tse* 續定上海龍門書院課程六則 (Six provisions of the revised curriculum of Lung-men Academy in Shanghai) (Shanghai: Lung-men Academy, 1870), 4b.

36. Rankin, *Elite Activism*, 134.

37. Miao Ch'üan-sun, 繆荃孫, "Ch'ing ku shih-lang hsien Han-lin yuan shih-tu hsueh-shih Sun hsien-sheng mu-chih ming-pei" 清故侍郎銜翰林院侍讀學士孫先生墓志銘碑 (Funerary inscription of the Han-lin academician Sun Ch'iang-ming), *CTCC*, 120 (1985): 545–48.

38. Kuo and Liu, "Self-strengthening," 499; Biggerstaff, *Earliest Government Schools*, 35–36, 157; *SHSTCK*, 506–25.

39. Ying Pao-shih, "Hsun-tao Ying Pao-shih," 34b; *SHSTCK*, 503; Hu Ch'uan, "Tun-fu nien-p'u," 221–22. Cf. Elman, *From Philosophy*, pp. 174–76.

40. *Hsu-ting Shang-hai Lung-men shu-yuan chang-ch'eng liu-tse* 續定上海龍門書院章程六則 (Six provisions of the revised by-laws of Lung-men Academy in Shanghai) (Shanghai: Lung-men Academy, 1870), 1a.

41. Ibid., 1b–2a.

42. *Shang-hai hc*, 9, 695; P'an Min-te 潘敏德 *Chung-kuo chin-tai tien-dang-yeh chih yen-chiu,* 1644–1937 中國近代典當業之研究 1644–1937 (Study of the Modern Chinese Pawnshop, 1644–1937), monograph ser. 13. (Institute of History, National Taiwan Normal University, 1985), ch. 2.

43. *SHSTCK*, 1:503; *Sung-chiang*, 17:1704.

44. The system of using pawnbroker houses to provide interest on public funds was called *fa-shang sheng-hsi*. For a full account, see P'an Min-te, *Tien-dang-yeh*, ch. 2. The two pawnbrokers in Shanghai used for Lung-men's initial ten thousand tael endowment produced 1,140 taels as annual interest; *Hsu-ting k'o-ch'eng liu-tse*, 3b–4a; T.S. Whelan, *The Pawnshop in China* (Ann Arbor: Center for Chinese Studies, University of Michigan, 1979), 10.

45. *Hsu-ting Chang-ch'eng liu-tse*, 3b–4a.

46. Lu Pao-ch'ien, *Ssu-hsiang shih*, 36; Shen Hsiang-lung, "T'an-tung tsa-shih," 83, 85.

47. *CTCC*, 104, 332.

48. Ibid., 17: 593, 104:332.

49. Shen Hsiang-lung, "T'an-tung tsa-shih," 85; *CTCC*, 17:593, 94:757.

50. Ch'ien Mu 錢穆, *T'ung-ch'eng p'ai wen-hsueh shih* 桐城派文學史 (History of the literature of the T'ung-ch'eng faction) (Hong Kong: Lung-men shu-tien, 1975), 5.

51. *CTCC*, 19:885–89, 7:633–39.

52. Hao Chang, "The Anti-foreignist Role of Wo-jen (1804–1871)," *Papers on China* (Cambridge, Mass.: Harvard University Press, 1960), 14:6; *CTCC*, 202:507.

53. Wan may have petitioned T'u for the project because the eminent diplomat Wu Ta-ch'eng (T. Ch'ing-ch'ing, 1835–1902) had already convinced Wan to do it. Wu had previously been a student of Wan's and in 1898 was himself to become the director at Lung-men Academy; see *CTCC*, 4:887, 895.

54. Liu Kwang-Ching, "Ch'ing Restoration," 423; Tseng Kuo-fan 曾國藩, "T'ang Ch'ueh-shen kung mu-chih ming" 唐確慎公墓志銘 (Funerary inscription of T'ang Ch'ueh-shen), in *Tseng Wen-cheng kung ch'üan-chi* 曾文正公全集 (Complete works of Tseng Wen-cheng) (Taipei: Wen-hai, 1974), 12918.

55. *CTCC*, 4:887, 104:332; Chang, "Wo-jen," 5–6; *CTCC*, 7:241; Andrew Cheng-kuang Hsieh, "Tseng Kuo-fan, A Nineteenth-Century Confucian General" (Ph.D. diss., Yale University, 1975), 19; Thomas Watters, *A Guide to the Tablets in a Temple of Confucius* (Shanghai: American Presbyterian Mission Press, 1879), 235, 243.

56. See *CTCC*, 2:76–77. See also Carsun Chang, *The Development of Neo-Confucianism in China* (New York: Bookman, 1962), II:318, citing T'ang Chien 唐鑑, *Kuo-ch'ao hsueh-an hsiao-shih* 國朝學案小史 (Records of dynastic scholarship) (Shanghai, 1935), preface, 4. Lu Lung-ch'i was canonized in the Confucian Temple in 1724; see Watters, *Temple of Confucius*, 242.

57. See *Kuo-ch'ao hsueh-an hsiao-shih* in *CTCC*, 2:85–151. See also Wing-tsit Chan, "The *Hsing-li ching-i* and the Ch'eng-Chu School of the Seventeenth Century," in *The Unfolding of Neo-Confucianism*, ed. W.T. de Bary (New York: Columbia University Press, 1975), 549.

58. Watters, *Temple of Confucius*, 234. It is interesting to note that one of the coterie, Tseng Kuo-fan, who died in 1872, was discussed for canonization in 1903. Chang Chih-tung successfully opposed that recommendation ostensibly because of Tseng's punishment by death of eighteen Chinese for their role in the Tientsin Massacre of 1870. See Chang Ta-hsiang and Li Shih-sun 張達驤, 李石孫, "Chang Chih-tung shih-chi shu-wen" 張之洞事蹟述聞 (Oral traces of Chang Chih-tung), in *Wen shih tzu-liao hsuan-chi* 文史資料選輯 (Selections of source materials on literature and

history), no. 99 collection, (Peking: Wen shih tse-liao ch'u-pan she, 1984) 87. See also *ECCP*, 52.

59. Feng Hsu 馮煦, *Hao-an sui-pi* 蒿庵隨筆 (Varied writings from Hao-an) (Taipei: Wen-hai, 1966), 67–68.

60. Hsieh, "Tseng Kuo-fan," 27, citing *Tseng Wen-cheng shou-shu jih-chi* 曾文正手述日記 (Manuscript diary of Tseng Kuo-fan) (reprint, Taipei, 1965), 149–51.

61. Lu Pao-ch'ien *Ssu-hsiang shih*, 331–34.

62. Each month a total of 32.5 taels of silver was awarded as prize money. The top student got a maximum of 2 taels and the lowest award was 0.5 tael. Forty out of the fifty students were given some monetary award each month; see *Hsu-ting chang-ch'eng liu-tse*, 6a.

63. Ibid., 6b.

64. Hu, "Tun-fu nien-p'u," 222.

65. See the praise given Liu Hsi-tsai by the student Shen Hsiang-lung in Shen, "T'an-tung tsa-shih," 83–84. See also Yü Yueh on Lin's reading of student work; Yü, "Tso-ch'un-fang," 2.

66. See Chan, "*Hsing-li ching-i*," 543. Parentheses contain material written in small print in the original text, much like commentaries on the Classics.

67. This is Chu Hsi's historical textbook, *T'ung-chien kang-mu* (Outline and details of the comprehensive mirror). For further definition, see Chang, "Wo-jen," 17.

68. *Hsu-ting k'o-ch'eng liu-tse*, 2a

69. *Hsing-li chu-shu* in the text refers to works in general in *hsing-li* instead of a single book title.

70. *Hsu-ting k'o-ch'eng liu-tse*, 1b.

71. Yü, "Tso-ch'un-fang tso-chung-yun Liu chün mu-pei" 左春坊左中允劉君墓碑 (Funerary inscription of Liu Hsi-tsai), in Yü Yueh, *Ch'un-tsai t'ang ch'üan-shu* 春在堂全書, vol. 414, *tsa-wen*, 4, no. 3 (Taipei: Wen-hai 1968), 2.

72. Ibid., 3.

73. Chiang Mu 姜穆, *Tseng Kuo-fan ti mu-liao ch'ün* 曾國藩的幕僚群 (Private bureaucracy of Tseng Kuo-fan) (Taipei: Li-ming wen-hua shih-yeh kung-ssu, 1987), 101–3; Huang T'i-fang 黃體芳, "*Nan-ching shu-yuan pei chi*" 南菁書院碑記 (Nan-ching Academy stele inscription) (Chiang-yin: stele, 1885, ninth lunar month); Kwang-Ching Liu, "The Ch'ing Restoration," 487; Hao Chang, *Liang Ch'i-ch'ao and Intellectual Transition in China, 1890–1907* (Cambridge, Mass.: Harvard University Press, 1971), 42.

74. Hao Chang, *Chinese Intellectuals in Crisis: Search for Order and Meaning* (1890–1911) (Berkeley: University of California Press, 1987), 15.

75. Chang, "Wo-jen," 5; Bastid, "*Ch'ing-i* and the Self-strengthening Movement," in *Ch'ing-chi tzu-ch'iang yun-tung yen-t'ao hui lun-wen chi* 清季自強運動研討會論文集 (Papers from the conference on the Ch'ing self-strengthening movement) (Taipei, Institute of Modern History, Academia Sinica, 1988): 877–79; Lu Pao-ch'ien, *Ssu-hsiang shih*, 331–33; John E. Schrecker, "The Reform Movement of 1898 and the *Ch'ing-i* Reform as Opposition," in John E. Schrecker and Paul Cohen, eds., *Reform in Nineteenth-Century China* (Cambridge: Harvard University Press, 1976), 290; Liu, "Ch'ing Restoration," 487.

76. Sun had led local gentry himself in suppressing the Gold Coin Society rebellion during the Taiping era. See Rankin, *Elite Activism*, 116, citing Liu Chu-feng 劉祝封,

"Ch'ien-fei chi-lueh" 錢匪紀略 (Brief account of the Gold Coin rebels), *Ou-feng tsa-chih* 甌風雜誌 (The Wen-chou Miscellany) (1924), 8–11.

77. Frank A. Lowjewski, "T'ing Jih-ch'ang in Kiangsu: Traditional Methods of Surmounting Dysfunction in Local Administration during the Late-Ch'ing Period," *Chin-tai shih yen-chiu so ch'i-k'an* (Bulletin on the Institute of Modern History, Academia Sinica), 8 (1979): 235–53; Ocko, *Bureaucratic Reform*, ch. 6.

78. Miao, "Sun hsien-sheng mu-chih ming pei," 3a–3b.

79. Ibid., 3a.

80. *SHSTCK*, 1, *chüan* 2:504.

81. The name is taken from Chang Tsai's (1020–77) most important work. See Chu Hsi, *Reflections on Things at Hand* (New York: Columbia University Press, 1967), xxvii.

82. *SHSTCK*, 1, *chüan* 2:504.

83. *Shang-hai hc*, 18:42–44; *Shang-hai hsien hsu-chih*, 50.

84. *SHSTCK*, 2, *chüan* 4:1213–15.

85. The revolutionary activity centered in the Chinese Education Society (*Chung-kuo chiao-yü hui*) and in the Patriotism Society (*Ai-kuo hsueh-she*) until both were quieted in the suppression of the *Su-pao* newspaper in 1903; *SHSTCK*, 2, *chüan* 3:832–40. Chang Huan-lun ran another school in Shanghai in 1904 called *Mei-hsi hsueh-t'ang* whose curriculum was simple but progressive. Hu Shih attended that school because of the Lung-men Academy friendship between his father and Chang Huan-lun. See Hu Shih, *Ssu-shih tzu-shu* (Taipei: Yuan-liu, 1991), 47–50; *SHSTCK*, 1, *chüan* 2: 628–29, 2, *chüan* 3:832–40; *Shang-hai hsien hsu-chih*, 18: 42a-43b.

86. Rankin, *Elite Activisim*, 197–201; *SHSTCK*, 2, *chüan* 2, 531; Frederick Wakeman, "The Price of Autonomy: Intellectuals in Ming and Ch'ing Politics," *Daedalus*, 102, no. 2 (1972): 61.

87. *SHSTCK*, 2, *chüan* 3:842–46.

88. Bastid, *Educational Reform*, 246 n.1.

89. Ibid., 57.

90. Chiang Wei-ch'ao 蔣維喬, "Chiang-su chiao-yü hsing-cheng kai-k'uang" 江蘇教育行政概況 (Kiangsu educational administration) (Shanghai: Commercial Press, 1924), 2; Bastid, *Educational Reform*, 43. The English version of the section of Bastid's French work on the 1906 regulations translates the role of the magistrate too strongly. The original Chinese is *chien-tu*, to oversee or supervise. It is true the salary of the local elite managers was ultimately paid by the magistrate's budget, but in the Chinese regulations of 1906 the local District Inspector of Education (*hsien shih-hsueh*) selected one local person who was then responsible for each school district in the county. That person was chosen from those among the local gentry who were "concerned about education, competent, and of high moral character." See Taga Akigorō 多賀秋五郎, comp., *Kindai Chūgoku kyōiku shi shiryō* 近代中國教育史資料 (Materials on the history of education in modern China) (1972; reprint, Taipei: Wen-hai ch'u-pan she, 1976), 1:423; H.S. Brunnert and V.V. Hagelstrom, *Present Day Political Organization of China* (Shanghai: Kelly and Walsh, 1912), 409.

91. Bastid, *Educational Reform*, 62–64; Wakeman, "Price of Autonomy," 55–60.

92. See Bastid, *Educational Reform*, 44, citing *Chiao-yü t'ung-chi t'u-piao* (Charts on educational statistics) (1907), 27. See also Chiao-yü pu 教育部, *Chung-hua min-kuo ti-san tz'u*

chiao-yu t'u-piao 中華民國第三次教育圖表 (The third educational statistics in the Republic of China) (1915; reprint, Taipei: Wen-hai, 1986) 98, no. 10, 203.

93. Shen served as the first president from 1905 to 1907, when he resigned to become the manager of Shanghai's *Chung-kuo t'u-shu kung-ssu* (China Book company), which later published school textbooks. Shen remained a trustee until 1911. Yuan ran the school from 1907 to 1909, when a third member of the mission, Hsia Jih-ao (T. Lung-yun), took over. See "Chiang-su sheng-li ti-erh shih-fan hsueh-hsiao" in *Chiang-su sheng-li ti-erh shih-fan hsueh-hsiao erh-shih chou-nien ts'e* 江蘇省立第二師範學校二十週年冊 (Twentieth anniversary book of the number two normal school in Kiangsu province) (Shanghai: Number Two Normal School in Kiangsu Province, 1925), 1.

94. T'ang, a *chin-shih* of 1895, was a reformer with strong ties to his native Chekiang and had published extensively on philology; Rankin, *Elite Activism*, 261–62; *CTCC*, 16: 509. See Shen, "T'an-tung tsa-shih," 84, for the account of T'ang's connection with Lung-men that follows.

95. Bastid, *Educational Reform*, 121.

96. Shen, "T'an-tung tsa-shih," 84.

97. Hu Shih 胡適, "Shu-yuan chih ti shih-lueh" 書院制的史略 (Historical sketch of the academy system) in *Chiao-yü hui-k'an* 教育彙刊 (Educational collection) (1924), 2:1. Hu Shih himself edited and published another recording of this lecture; Hu Shih, "Shu-yuan chih-tu shih-lueh" 書院制度史略 (Outline history of the academy system), *Tung-fang tsa-chih*, 21, no. 3 (Feb. 1924): 142–46. *ECCP*, 722.

98. Rankin, *Elite Activism*, ch. 7; Elman, "Hanlin and Donglin Academies," 392–402.

GLOSSARY

Ai-kuo hsueh-she	愛國學社	*Chin-t'ai shu-yuan*	金臺書院
Chang Chien (T. Chi-chih)	張謇(季直)	*Ching-yeh shu-yuan*	敬業書院
Chang Huan-lun	張煥綸	*ch'ing-i*	清議
(T. Ching-fu)	(經甫)	*Chu-hsi shu-yuan*	竹西書院
Chang Lü-hsiang	張履祥	*Chu Hsiao-t'ang*	朱小唐
(T. K'ao-fu)	(考夫)	(T. Hsien-t'ing)	(獻廷)
Chang Po-hsing	張伯行	*chü-jen*	舉人
(T. Hsiao-hsien)	(孝先)	*chu-sheng*	諸生
Ch'ang-yin shu-yuan	常陰書院	*chu-tzu ta-ch'üan*	朱子大全
Changchow	常州	*Ch'üan-hsueh so*	勸學所
Chen-chiang fu	鎮江府	*ch'üan-hsueh yuan*	勸學員
Cheng lien ming	正廉明	*chung-hsing*	中興
Cheng-meng shu-yuan	正蒙書院	*Chung-kuo chiao-yü hui*	中國教育會
Chiang-ning fu	江寧府	*Chung-kuo t'u-shu*	中國圖書
Chiang-su an-ch'a-shih	江蘇按察使	*kung-ssu*	公司
Chiang-su sheng chiao-yü hui	江蘇省	*fu*	賦
chiao-yü hui	教育會	*Han-hsueh*	漢學
chiao-yü yen-chiu hui	教育研究會	*Hsi-nan shu-yuan*	溪南書院
chien-shen chih yao	檢身之要	Hsia Jih-ao	夏日璈
chien-tu	監督	(T. Lang-yun)	(琅雲)
chin-shih	進士	*Hsiao-hsueh*	小學
Chin-ssu lu	近思錄	*hsien*	縣

hsien shih-hsueh	縣視學	Shen Hsiang-lung	沈祥龍
Hsien-yang shu-yuan	峴陽書院	*shen-tung*	紳董
hsing-li	性理	Sheng Hsuan-huai	盛宣懷
hsing-li hsueh	性理學	*sheng-yuan*	生員
hsiu-ts'ai	秀才	*shih*	師
hsueh-cheng	學政	*shih-fan hsueh-t'ang*	師範學堂
Hsueh-hai-t'ang	學海堂	*shih-hsueh*	實學
hsueh-hui	學會	*shih-shen*	士紳
Hsueh-pu	學部	*shih-wen*	時文
hsueh-t'ang	學堂	*Su-pao*	蘇報
Hu Ch'uan	胡傳	*Su-Sung-T'ai pei-ping*	蘇松太備兵
(T. Tun-fu)	（鈍夫）	Soochow fu	蘇州府
Hu-hsueh hui	滬學會	Sun Ch'iang-ming	孫鏘鳴
Hu Shih	胡適	(H. Chu-t'ien)	（渠田）
Huang T'i-fang	黃體芳	Sun Yat-sen	孫逸仙
(T. Shu-lan)	（漱蘭）	Sung-chiang fu	松江府
i-hsueh	義學	*Sung-hsueh*	宋學
i-li	義理	*ta-hsueh-t'ang*	大學堂
Jui-chu shu-yuan	樂珠書院	T'ai-tsang chou	太倉州
k'ai	楷	*Tao-hsiang shu-yuan*	道鄉書院
Kang-mu	綱目	*Tao-nan shu-yuan*	道南書院
Kao-p'ing shu-yuan	高平書院	T'ang Chien	唐鑑
Kao-shan shu-yuan	高山書院	T'ang Shou-ch'ien	唐壽潛
Ku-ching ching-she	詁經精舍	(T. Chih-hsien)	（蟄仙）
Ku Kuang-yü	顧廣譽	(Chen)	（甄）
(H. Fang-hsi)	（訪溪）	*ti-fang shen-shih*	地方紳士
kuan-ch'a	觀察	*t'i*	體
Kuei-kuang shu-yuan	奎光書院	*t'i-hsueh shih*	提學使
Li-yen shu-yuan	禮延書院	Ting Jih-ch'ang	丁日昌
Lin-chin shu-yuan	臨津書院	(T. Yü-sheng)	（雨生）
Liu Hsi-tsai)	劉熙載	Tseng Chi-tse	曾紀澤
(T. Jung-chai)	（融齋）	Tseng Kuo-fan	曾國藩
Lu Lung-ch'i	陸隴其	*tu-shu chih yao*	讀書之要
(T. Chia-shu)	（稼書）	T'u Tsung-ying	涂宗瀛
Lu Shih-i (T. Tao-wei)	陸世儀（道威）	(T. Lang-hsuan)	（朗軒）
Lung-men shu-yuan	龍門書院	*tung-shih*	董事
Nan-ching shu-yuan	南菁書院	T'ung-ch'eng	桐城
Nan-yang kung-hsueh	南洋公學	T'ung-wen kuan	同文館
Pao Yuan-shen	鮑源深	*Tzu-chih t'ung-chien*	資治通鑑
(Hua-t'an)	（華潭）	*Tzu-yang shu-yuan*	紫陽書院
San-chin shu-yuan	三近書院	Wan Hu-ch'uan	萬斛泉
Shang-hai hsien	上海縣	(T. Ch'ing-hsuan)	（清軒）
chiao-yü hui	教育會	Weng T'ao fu	翁勠夫
She-hsueh	社學	(T. Pin-sun)	（斌孫）
Shen En-fu	沈恩孚	Wo-jen (T. Ken-feng)	倭仁
(T. Hsin-ch'ing)	（信卿）	(T. Ken-feng)	（艮峯）

Wu Ta-ch'eng	吳大澂	*Ying-hua shu-yuan*	英華書院
(T. Ch'ing-ch'ing)	（清卿）	Ying Pao-shih	應寶時
Wu T'ing-tung	吳廷棟	(T. Min-chai)	（敏齋）
(H. Chu-ju)	（竹如）	Yü Yueh	俞樾
yang-wu	洋務	(T. Ch'ü-yuan)	（曲園）
Yao Ch'un	姚椿	Yuan Hsi-t'ao	袁希濤
(T. Ch'un-mu)	（春木）	(T. Kuan-lan)	（觀瀾）
Yao Nai	姚鼐	*yung*	用
(T. Hsi-pao)	（惜抱）		

AFTERWORD

The Expansion of Education in Ch'ing China

Alexander Woodside and Benjamin A. Elman

Writing less than five years after the Ch'ing dynasty collapsed, the Chinese educational reformer Huang Yen-p'ei (1878–1965) surveyed the educational landscape the Ch'ing emperors had bequeathed the Chinese people and pronounced it bankrupt. He charged that Western education esteemed the natural and imparted a proper sex education to both male and female pupils; late imperial Chinese education based itself on coercion, segregated the sexes, and was reticent about human reproduction. Western education permitted an individualistic diversity among its students and schools and promoted creativity; late imperial Chinese education required uniformity in everything from student uniforms to calligraphy and prized imitation. Western education exalted the public good and service to society and taught its pupils to do good; Chinese education exalted the perfection only of the self and taught its pupils merely not to behave badly.[1]

Ever since Huang delivered this verdict, less politically engaged scholars in both China and the West have been questioning the historically prejudiced antitheses, so typical of the early Chinese revolution, on which his comparison and others like it relied. There is room for some sympathy with the rhetorical despair of patriotic intellectuals, but it is not the best conceptual tool with which to analyze the history of education in seventeenth-, eighteenth-, and nineteenth-century China. At its conclusion in June 1989, members of our conference were under no illusion that we completely understood all the changes that had occurred in the educational world of the Ch'ing dynasty, even those occurring before dynastic decline became evident. But these changes did have one keynote whose significance we all recognized: the quantitative and qualitative educational expansion, particularly of Confucian education, in the Ch'ing period. It is by no means clear that this expansion kept up with the growth of Chinese population at the same time; and it is true that no Ch'ing ruler ever surpassed, in the grandeur of their rhetorical ambition to impose elementary schools on young Chinese children, earlier rulers like the founder of the Ming dynasty. For examination system candidates, upward mobility prospects actually declined in this period. Nevertheless, education—both as organized socialization from above and as the acquisition of knowledge through highly literate forms of learning—gained in variety and in geographical and epistemological reach between 1644 and 1911.

School building was the most obvious form of this expansion. Compared to the Ming dynasty, there was a marked increase in the types of schools in China and in the numbers of schools that were publicly sponsored.[2] We have to begin with the extraordinary reverence for schools as an instrument of policy that China's Manchu emperors exhibited. The Manchus' whole state-within-a-state was to be reproduced through a variety of schools: academies for each of the Eight Banners at Peking in the middle 1600s; Imperial Clan Academies; the Gioro academy for the descendants of the paternal uncles of Nurgaci (1559–1626); the Imperial Household Department officer schools; the Eight Banners officer schools for Banner commoners in Peking; and finally, provincial Manchu garrison schools. The varied educational strivings of the Ch'ing emperors suggest that they saw the ceaseless conditioning of the elite of their own badly outnumbered people, by schools, as the one sure check against the atrophy of the Manchu hegemony in China.

The field broadens when we come to the provincial academies that supported and educated a minority of the Chinese elite in training. The conservative scholar Kuan T'ung (1780–1831), who worried that the Ch'ing provincial scholar class was too large, gloomily estimated that academies supplied student stipends to no more than about 8 percent of the students in any given county.[3] But compared to the Ming dynasty, there was a marked increase in academies. The best estimates suggest that there were about twelve hundred academies in Ming China but over nineteen hundred academies in Ch'ing China.[4] The real significance of this expansion lies not just in its numbers but in the fact that the geographical scope and ecumenicity of Chinese academy education had widened. In established southeastern commercial centers, Ch'ing academies did not necessarily surpass their Ming predecessors. On the frontiers, with academies appearing in Yunnan, Kansu, and even Sinkiang in the 1700s and 1800s, it was a different story.[5] In Kweichow province, one can trace the origins of academies back to the twelfth century; nevertheless, the outstanding contemporary specialist on late imperial education in Kweichow asserts that the tempo of academy development there was much more impressive in the Ch'ing than in the Ming. Between 1736 and 1851, Kweichow supported at least 130 academies, the majority of which were new, a greater number than that of a southeastern province like Anhwei (98) in the Ming dynasty.[6]

Loyal gentry families and salt merchants contributed to the sustenance of academies, at least in the southeast, as part of an intimate cooperation between local interests and the imperial government. This cooperation makes it difficult for modern analysts strictly to isolate the role of the "state" from the "public sphere" in the expansion of such higher education. Nevertheless, the practice in European educational history seems to be to call universities "state universities" even when they were sponsored by noble estates rather than by kings, as with Göttingen University in eighteenth-century Hannover.[7] By these standards, it is permissible to say that the Ch'ing period completed a growing extension of state influence over the academies. Their very locations were now far more likely to be provincial capitals than isolated mountains and forest groves, as in the earlier period. One group of Chinese scholars has recently calculated that of the nineteen hundred or so examinable Ch'ing academies, only 182 (or fewer than 10 percent) were operated by private interests wholly outside the government sector.[8] We still have to explain why, given this trend of the extension of state influence over the academies between the fourteenth and the nineteenth centuries, the trend was not even stronger, and why there was not more political consolidation of higher education at the very top. Compared to the German universities of their era, which also trained government bureaucrats, the state control that late imperial Chinese academies experienced was underdeveloped and indirect, even if it was true that a completely "private" higher education had only the most marginal existence in Ch'ing China.

With elementary schools, which occupy the most important position in the history of Ch'ing educational expansion, the matter of state involvement seems less opaque. Back in 1958, the Japanese scholar Ogawa Yoshiko drew our attention to the emergence of many "charitable schools," as public elementary schools were then predominantly known, in China in the eighteenth and nineteenth centuries. She also reminded us that such schools were aimed specifically at poor children and at the children of ethnic minorities, that they became considerably more numerous than academies or earlier elementary "community schools," and that, as the conversion of at least twenty-five Shanghai charitable schools into more modern schools in the early twentieth century indicates, their existence eventually helped China to make its transition to a post-Confucian educational order.[9]

Contemporaries themselves welcomed the formation of charitable schools across the empire. The Fukien poet Kuo Ch'i-yuan (n.d.), writing of a charitable school that he himself financed in Anhwei in 1741, thought such schools were evidence of both the superiority of Ch'ing education to that of previous dynasties and imperial China's capacity to approximate the networks of rural schools of an earlier golden age.[10] Here, state involvement appears to have been conditioned by region and by the regional availability of large elites with strong attachments to Confucian ideals. In the prosperous Lower Yangtze region of China, the charitable schools exemplified the growth of a philanthropic movement for which local community leaders were responsible. But in the capital city and in its surrounding area, and on the frontiers where non-Chinese minorities lived, the Ch'ing emperors intervened directly to order the creation of charitable schools. The K'ang-hsi emperor wrote the tablet inscription for a major Peking charitable school established in 1702, and by 1705 he had required the development of charitable schools in every prefecture and county of Kweichow, for the purpose of educating both the heirs of the minority peoples' headmen and the "children of Miao people who want to go to school." The Yung-cheng emperor renewed the effort to build charitable schools in Kweichow in 1725 and moved to compel minority children to attend charitable schools and learn mandarin speech in parts of Szechwan in 1730. In 1742, the emperor Ch'ien-lung ordained the creation of charitable schools for the Tai-speaking Li people of south Kwangtung. Publicly run charitable schools appeared in the 1700s for the Tibeto-Burman Yi or Lolo people of Yunnan, the Yao people from Hunan west, the Muslim people of Shensi and Kansu and Shantung, and even the Turkic peoples of newly conquered Sinkiang, which did not become a province until 1884.[11]

At least some of the impetus for this elementary school expansion, particularly among the minorities of the southwest, may be traced back to pre-Ch'ing figures like the late Ming philosopher Wang Yang-ming, who had served in the southwest in the early 1500s. Wang Yang-ming had ardently preached (although he had not originated) the doctrine that everything in heaven and earth was of one body; the peoples of the empire were all educable and there were not real differences among them. From this point on, the southwest became a pedagogical laboratory for the "one body" doctrine, giving the Miao, Yao, and Yi peoples a greater importance than they could claim through sheer numbers. Ch'en Hung-mou was to reapply and refine this notion that Chinese and non-Chinese were "of one body" when he began his huge expansion of charitable schools in Yunnan in 1733. But it is equally clear that the three major Manchu emperors — K'ang-hsi, Yung-cheng, and Ch'ien-lung — regarded such school expansion as part of a program of imperial unification that they pursued with unprecedented vigor. Their vulnerability was that many of the anonymous local Chinese officials on whom they relied to carry out their program did not share such grandiose educational ambitions, but "made excuses, dodged out of sight, or answered questions that had not been asked of them," as Ch'en Hung-mou was to complain, memorably, in 1733.[12]

THE QUESTION OF THE LIMITS
OF CH'ING EDUCATION EXPANSION

It is one thing to insist on the dynamic quality of late imperial Chinese education. It would be another matter to pretend that Ch'ing school expansion offered China the beginnings of a completely unobstructed pathway to the late twentieth-century apotheosis of educational "modernity" in which one out of every five people on the planet is a student, three quarters of the world's primary-school-age children are enrolled in something called a school, and there is an intimate link between the establishment of independent nation states and their enactment of compulsory education laws. The expansion of education in Ch'ing China had political, social, and cultural limits.

Education was not compulsory in Ch'ing China. Nor was there much serious premonition of the modern idea that it ought to be. Even among the ruling Manchus, as Crossley points out, efforts to "enforce systematic education were made only at the capital and affected only a tiny portion of the adult males of the banner population." As to the Chinese, the famous scholar and palace tutor Hu Hsu (1655–1736) estimated that all the empire's schools reached no more than about 2 or 3 percent of the Chinese people in the first half of the 1700s. He lamented that this left vast masses of peasants, gardeners, artisans, merchants, woodcutters, fishermen, and peddlers in a limbo of ignorance. We cannot in fact know what percentage of the population schools reached, although this projection may not be unreasonable. That people so close to the emperor as Hu Hsu should have drawn such anguished pseudostatistical pictures of the inadequacies of schooling does show the scope of the ambitions for mass popular improvement that circulated among the elite. But Hu Hsu was not necessarily a mass educator like Ch'en Hung-mou. His proposed solution to the inadequate coverage of the schools was not that illiterate peasants be schooled, but that those among them who were moral paragons be identified and honored for their superior morality by being given the privileges of lesser gentry. He and others like him did not mechanically associate virtue with the school experience or with literacy.[13]

Partly because virtue was not mechanically associated with literacy, the imperial state and its local agents rarely tried to guarantee the long-term stability of the schools that actually were built. This failure was important because the funds even for state-sponsored schools came largely from local economic assets—land rents, pond rents, salt taxes, gentry subscriptions—which were coveted for other purposes by people other than the apostles of education. Angela Leung speaks of the "precarious" and "discontinuous" existence both of the charitable schools and of private clan schools in the Lower Yangtze region. More generally, Igarashi Shōichi has disagreed with Ogawa's optimistic conclusion that the numbers of charitable schools progressively increased to the end of the Ch'ing dynasty; the evidence suggests the opposite, namely, that even northern Chinese charitable schools had difficulty sustaining themselves over several centuries.[14] Woodside has contrasted Ch'ing China, a society whose values permitted unbridled private competition for the landed resources that might have supported schools, with eighteenth-century Burma and Siam, countries with high premodern literacy rates whose economically privileged Buddhist monasteries probably protected rural schooling more effectively.[15]

The treatment of girls exposes the limits of Ch'ing school expansion in quite a different way. Chinese charitable schools wholly excluded girls, in contrast to their eighteenth-century English namesakes, the religiously inspired charity schools that taught religion, literacy, and manual labor to children of both sexes. It is proof of the importance of private family education that, as Susan Mann shows, the Ch'ing period still witnessed a steady rise in the numbers of daughters, wives, and mothers from literati families who were literate, had serious literary interests, and now wrote for the first time in vernacular Chinese.

Personal identity when defined in gender terms significantly altered the meaning and perception of the role of education for the sexes and predetermined how the organization of cultural tasks to be learned was transmitted differently for men and women from generation to generation. The automatic subordination of women meant that certain social and cultural categories were imposed on the different sexes by virtue of their sexually based social reality. Education in the late imperial Chinese state and society, whether public or private in nature, contributed significantly to the personal and group structuring of gender identity. Through rituals, language, and educational differences for men and women, gender identities were constructed and transmitted. The social and historical experiences of men and women were mediated through acceptable notions of what forms of behavior were appropriate for each sex. The sexual objectification of women and men through differently defined educations points to the latent forms of "gender ideology" that pervaded elite and popular cultural life.[16]

Education for men and women thus meant different things, granting boys competitive access to political, social, and economic hegemony in society while at the same time defining women in subordinate roles as wives, mothers, and matriarchs. Control over and access to material and cultural resources were gender specific, which the kinship system, labor market, schools, and state offices took for granted in theory and practice. Consequently, several of the chapters in this volume demonstrate the degree to which gender was a primary mode for legitimating the authority of patriarchal power autochthonous to the differential forms of education for men and women in China from 1600 to 1900.[17]

The expansion of literacy itself in the Ch'ing period has ambiguities that must be carefully sifted. That some expansion occurred is now difficult to doubt. Pioneering social surveys of the Republican period carried out within a few decades of the overthrow of the Ch'ing dynasty began to erode the old assumption, always more rhetorical than a proven fact, that 80 percent or more of the Chinese population was completely illiterate. By the early 1930s, for example, a study of a group as lowly as the Chengtu city rickshaw coolies had revealed that 57 percent of such coolies could read at least some written characters.[18] In a definitive work based on gazetteer research, Evelyn Rawski has recently systematized, enriched, and greatly expanded this emerging post-Ch'ing consensus that traditional Chinese literacy rates were indeed higher than earlier writers, Chinese and Western alike, had claimed. Rawski concludes that in the 1800s 30 to 40 percent of all Chinese men and 2 to 10 percent of all Chinese women may have known how to read and write, even if for most of them such skills were primitive.[19] Another scholar has made a comparative analysis of what Chinese fiction in the sixteenth and seventeenth centuries hinted at with respect to the literacies of its stock commoner characters such as clerks, secretaries, merchants, soldiers, jailers, restaurant owners, silversmiths, and servants. This research has upheld Rawski's conclusion that many people outside the scholar class were literate in varying degrees and that literacy was slowly increasing.[20]

None of this meant that the imperial political system was as hospitable to ever-rising levels of literacy as most modern states devoted to science and industry would be. Dynastic governments had little quarrel with increases in account-keeping literacy of the sort used in shops, on junks, or in big households. However, such governments showed every interest in controlling the growth of politically empowering literacy of the kind needed for reading classical books on astronomy or warfare, or of the kind that encouraged aspirations that might destabilize a society without heredity-based social classes, and whose employer bureaucracy was not infinitely expandable. Emperors, for example, did not want professional soldiers to become scholars, although there were examinations for officers. The fear was that, with no feudal command structure compelling them to be soldiers, they might then desert their occupation.[21] One may look in vain in late imperial China for highly literate "little corporals" of artillery of the young Napoleon Bonaparte type.

Outside the government, many members of the provincial scholar class agreed that politically marketable literacy should be controlled. They were becoming more and more anxious about the preservation of the exclusive "noble titles and noble status attributes" that their own classical literacy as degree-holders was supposed to earn them. They did not wish to share such things with an indefinite number of others. In modern societies, government leaders characteristically want to reduce the ranks of intellectuals seeking government jobs, while lowly students themselves press to increase them. In contrast with this, many "poor literati" in late imperial China, given their psychological aristocratism and their sense of the limited quantity of accessible social assets and career opportunities, actually wanted to see the student intelligentsia of which they were a part diminished in numbers. Resisting pressures from Peking police officials, the Manchu emperor in 1803 invoked the sanctity of scholars' "noble titles and noble status attributes" as his reason for excluding the sons of government policemen from the examination system. Since such discrimination contradicted the Neo-Confucian emphasis that all people were good, the emperor lamely explained that his decision belittled the policemen's occupations, not themselves as human beings.[22] Politically active literacy in China of the type needed to understand constitutions and parliamentary elections was presumed to be so small in 1908 that the Japanese-style education ministry that had been newly set up in Peking calculated that it would take until 1917 to make even 5 percent of the Chinese people adequately literate in such terms.[23]

When Huang Yen-p'ei criticized the legacy of late imperial education in 1916, however, he concerned himself not with its limits on literacy, its treatment of females, or the precarious existence of its schools. He complained instead about the whole quality of its educational experience. Judgments about educational quality embody so many cultural, social class, and time period biases that no short appreciations or denigrations of such a thing may safely be attempted. But it may be worth mentioning that our conference itself probed the part that massive memorization played in Ch'ing classical education. One of our discussants, Tetsuo Najita, stirred our meetings with his suggestion that all the memorization may have reflected enormous cultural anxiety. Was the memorization, perhaps, a venture into the "defensive articulation" on a very large scale of "who we are" and "who we are not," a mission that compelled millions of examination-taking people to adopt a certain identity?

The memorization to which Najita referred was part of a Chinese reading program to which elite youths were supposed to devote themselves between the ages of eight and twenty-five. During the early Mongol empire, one of this reading program's chief architects, Ch'eng Tuan-li (1271–1345), had written a curriculum for his own family school with the title "Daily schedule of reading according to the ages of pupils." This became the standard educational plan in many Chinese elite schools from the fourteenth through the nineteenth centuries.[24] It required even small children to perform cycles of the reading and recitation of sections of the Four Books and Five Classics in a certain sequence, a hundred times each. Ch'eng himself conceded that his plan might seem unreal but said that education demanded the same sort of effort as that involved in growing and harvesting crops. The early Ch'ing primary school teacher Ch'en Fang-sheng, whom Angela Leung quotes, makes it clear how much the endless demonstration of successful memorization was thought to be the touchstone of children's intelligence, in keeping with Ch'eng Tuan-li's plan. The remarkable educational correspondence of Tseng Kuo-fan to which Kwang-Ching Liu introduces us is a rich repository of the more sophisticated moral and epistemological justifications for the sheer patience on which so much memorization had to rely.

Memorization to internalize exactly the required Confucian curriculum tested in examinations was a cultural act of great meaning for Han Chinese elites. As in early modern Europe, where stress on order and conformity ensured that rote learning (e.g., the catechism) played a fundamental role in the educational process, late imperial Chinese state educators prized orthodoxy and the rote reception of that orthodoxy. Repetition as a habit of learning was the key to developing the memory as a pedagogic tool to produce uniformity by education. The Oboi regents, for example, backed down from their efforts to delegitimate the Four Books and Five Classics in state examinations of 1663 when Han Chinese challenged such curricular reforms. To instill a fixed set of ideas and facts, rulers, officials, and examiners all believed or became convinced that the pious recital of the Four Books and Five Classics by Han Chinese students represented an act of faith in Confucian moral values and submission to imperial political sovereignty. Inculcation of the classical language by mastering verbatim canonical ancient texts in theory created acceptable dispositions that were structured by classical attitudes, concepts, and beliefs.

Modern critics, aghast at all the seemingly wasted centuries of memorizing and reciting, have sometimes imagined themselves to be giants standing on the shoulders of dwarfs. In the famous essay on schools that he published in 1896, Liang Ch'i-ch'ao charged that Chinese emperors, more free from external challenges than European rulers, had dedicated themselves to the elimination of all independent domestic political theorists by using the examination system to exhaust intellectuals' talent and ensure their political quietism. Liang implied that the processes of the examination system, including memorization, were deliberately designed to enervate the minds and bodies of Chinese students, for political reasons.[25]

When modern writers have defended memorization, they have often done so for technical reasons of a kind quite remote from the intellectual world of a Tseng Kuo-fan. Three primers—the *Trimetrical Classic,* the *Hundred Names Classic,* and the *Thousand Character Classic*—dominated, as a mostly inseparable trio, Chinese elementary education from the thirteenth to the twentieth centuries. Looking at them, one scholar has concluded that the very nature of the Chinese written language made it virtually inevitable that Chinese children be compelled to memorize the roughly two thousand individual characters in these three primers before they could begin to read meaningful connected discourse. There was no alphabet, as in European languages, to permit the early acceleration of word or phrase recognition. And the forms of Chinese written words changed little in response to their changing grammatical functions, making the memorized recognition of individual characters all the more important.[26]

Against such opinions, what must not be overlooked is that memorization was essential to classical education in Europe as well as in China for many centuries, even if it survived longer in China. For European humanists, the memorization of texts was part of the desirable imitation of ancient philosophers, orators, and poets like Aristotle, Cicero, and Virgil. Reaction against so much memorization occurred earlier in Europe in part because partisans of the living colloquial languages of the various European kingdoms mounted patriotic challenges to the classical Greek and Latin written languages in which the memorized texts were written; there were no equivalent links between patriotism and colloquial languages in the politically unsubdivided, more universally minded Chinese empire.

Furthermore, at least some of the European educators who attacked the imitation and memorization in medieval European humanist education attacked particularly its assumption that most human beings, as natural equals, would benefit from philosophical instruction. Montaigne, for example, compared fourteen or fifteen hours a day of syllogisms and memorization to the work of a porter, and wished to put in its place a new version of the syllogism-free education that Aristotle had given Alexander.[27] Successful memorization, though it may trouble modern liberal educators, was at least a proof of educational achievement that was within the reach, theoretically, of almost any industrious and literate person, porters as well as princes. As such, its educational prominence was necessarily a guarantee of the postaristocratic chances for upward mobility that the Chinese examination system offered. Eighteenth-century Chinese academy leaders, like Wang Ch'ang at his academy at Nanchang, Kiangsi in 1789, went out of their way to remind their incoming students of the total number of words in each Classic: 40,848 in the *Poetry Classic;* 27,134 in the *Documents Classic;* 24,437 in the *Changes Classic;* 98,994 in the *Record of Rituals;* 15,984 in the *Spring and Autumn Annals.* This was a message of encouragement, not of intimidation. Wang Ch'ang explained enthusiastically that it would take students only 690 days, or less than two years, to master the recitation of all these texts. He added that he would expel from his academy only those students whose inability to recite showed that they were dull and lazy.[28]

THE PROBLEM OF THE CAUSES
OF CH'ING EDUCATIONAL EXPANSION

The causes of the expansion of education may be as difficult to explain as its effectiveness or its degeneration. Is, for instance, the rise of modern mass education all over the world in the past century principally the result of the struggle to legitimate new sorts of social orders, or the result of the compulsion to provide the cognitive skills for technological change and industrialization, or the logical accompaniment of the spread of new values of "universalistic individualism?"[29] The subject is so broad as to suffer from an almost incurable lack of definition. Looking at the way the most famous British journal of social history has treated the subject of education since it first appeared, Joan Simon recently suggested that the authors of papers in *Past and Present* characteristically used the history of education to resolve analytical stalemates that had arisen elsewhere. Simon contends that scholars preoccupied with such issues as "growth" and "modernization" once concerned themselves largely

with economic categories such as capital, labor, and resources, but their "failure to arrive at any general theory of growth in these terms brought a turn of
attention to the variables on the sidelines" such as education. Sometimes this
meant that they looked at education only as a means of throwing light on industrialization or social mobility without "seeking a closer understanding of
education itself."[30]

For preindustrial education, historians of European education have found
the problem of causation more easy to manage. In Lawrence Stone's almost
too quotable generalization, the bitter rivalry of the various Christian churches
and sects for control of people's minds "did more to stimulate education in the
West between 1550 and 1850 than any other single factor."[31] This is a more
complex argument than the earlier one that attributed European preindustrial
educational growth to Protestantism. But its theme, that open ideological or
religious struggle among different groups for the right to socialize new
generations was the key to the formation of educational systems, is, at least at
first glance, difficult to transfer meaningfully to late imperial China. Supposedly late imperial China had no equivalent competitive religious pluralism.

We must begin with the obvious. In part, Ch'ing educational expansion was
the symptom of a more general social, political, and economic expansion. The
empire of China doubled its size under Manchu rule to include substantial
Mongol, Muslim, Tibetan, and Manchu minorities; its Chinese population
growth was also startling, the population probably doubling in the 1700s.
Urumchi's acquisition of a charitable school in 1780 thus accompanied the
consolidation of unprecedented ties between China and Sinkiang, including the
spread of Ch'ing military colonies there and a boom in textile exports from
southern China to the Kazakhs. South of Sinkiang, the development of the
Kweichow economy under Ch'ing rule also provided a better material foundation for schools than ever before. Between 1658 and 1812, the clearing of
nearly nine million Chinese acres of Kweichow land and the rise of Chinese
landlordism in the southwest as a consequence of the disestablishment of the
hereditary chiefs of the various minorities meant the emergence of many new
local subscribers of capital for school creation. By the end of the dynasty, this
new Kweichow Chinese elite was strong enough to found 628 modern schools
of all types just between 1897 and 1911.[32]

The incremental or accumulative effects of a purely intellectual growth
should also not be overlooked. Compared to the Ming dynasty, there was a dramatic increase in the quantity and quality of knowledge in the lives of literate
Chinese. A far richer awareness of the technical authenticity of written texts
emerged, leading in some quarters to tremendous excitement about the possibility of finally recovering the "real" messages of the Classics after thousands
of years of presumed error. Kwang-Ching Liu shows in detail how even Tseng
Kuo-fan, a practicing Neo-Confucian, eagerly experimented with evidential research. Tseng, in fact, told one of his sons in 1859 that he thought the Ch'ing

dynasty was a cultural epoch of distinction, having inaugurated a third imperial ethos of learning, as compared with the first ethos of learning from the Han to the T'ang dynasties and the succeeding ethos of learning from the Sung to the Ming dynasties.[33]

At least some crucial aspects of Ch'ing educational expansion may be attributed to the ideals of educational universalism of Neo-Confucianism that William Theodore de Bary's many books have done so much to unveil for Western audiences. In the Ch'ing period, such educational universalism was stimulated by its contention with a wider popular print culture whose most noteworthy product was the vernacular novel. The great official Ch'en Hung-mou seems to have been a living exemplar of Chu Hsi's educational creed. He was driven throughout his career by what Rowe calls his impassioned assertions that all men, including the southwest aborigines, were good and that education could help them restore the pristine clarity of their natures. De Bary has shown us how Chu Hsi's *Elementary Learning,* a "manual of ritual conduct for the young" compiled under Chu Hsi's direction in the 1180s, was supposed to be the staple of a broadly based education among the young "extending down to the lowest levels of society."[34] Ch'en Hung-mou quite literally did the extending. As Rowe points out, he adopted this work as the "basic primer" for multiethnic education in eighteenth-century Yunnan, despite the availability of less challenging alternatives and controversies over its difficulties even among Chinese teachers.

It is less simple to judge the actual effects of the spread of Neo-Confucian educational ideals. We have to begin with female education. The repressive Neo-Confucian cult of female virtue and the decline of the Buddhist monasteries that had educated Chinese women outside their home restricted the public learning of women, as Susan Mann emphasizes. One of the keys to this restriction, however, may lie not in the texts of Chu Hsi themselves so much as in what Mann calls the "rich repertoire" of "nonliterate education" that achieved its fullest expression in the late empire after Chu Hsi's death. Here, the futility of maintaining any old-fashioned division between formal and informal modes of education is most acute. The ideal of the "virtuous woman," which contradicted the earlier classical ideal of "female scholar," had to be reinforced outside the schoolroom by Double Seven Festivals and elaborate dowry processions that endlessly shaped women's and men's consciousness — to say nothing of their very expectations of female achievement.

The results may be inferred by looking at the remarkable fact that not one of the Chinese woman writers of the late imperial period to whom Mann refers ever won in their lifetimes the cultural prominence and fame that great poetesses like Ho Xuan Huong and Ba Huyen Thanh Quan won in the late 1700s and early 1800s in the smaller neighboring Confucian kingdom of Vietnam. Yet Vietnam was also governed by emperors and examinations and by the texts of Chu Hsi. It had also adopted the formal hierarchical

Neo-Confucian ideology that subordinated women. The difference is to be explained precisely with reference to degrees of development of the nonliterate conditioning that Mann discusses. In the poorer, less urbanized Vietnam, where even the Confucian intelligentsia lived closer to the villages than their Chinese gentry counterparts, the symbolic indoctrination of nonliterate education for women never acquired the social depth or the psychological weight that it attained in big, rich Chinese cities like Ningpo.

What one discussant bluntly called the "uselessness" of the Chinese education that Ch'ing officials offered minorities like the Miao also became an issue at our conference. This education was accompanied by the drastic loss of the minorities' political and psychological self-confidence. Indeed, the extension of Ch'ing state power into the southwest in the form of the accelerated replacement of hereditary Miao "indigenous minority officers" by Chinese and Miao "circulating bureaucrats" itself prompted educational expansion, albeit of a morally less ambitious kind than Ch'en Hung-mou favored. The introduction of nonhereditary bureaucratic power into huge regions from which it had previously been almost absent clearly required a local flow of examination system degree-holders to legitimize and sustain it.

In dealing with the "uselessness" issue, we still have to distinguish between two possibilities. One is that the demoralization of the Miao peoples throughout this period was the direct result of state pressures that Confucian education reinforced. The other is that it was the result of noneducational forces that overwhelmed the Neo-Confucian educators, who tried at least to palliate the demoralization if not halt it. The great land hunger of poor Chinese in the 1700s and 1800s, combined with the Ch'ing government's relative tolerance of peasant mobility, led to an invasion of the southwest by masses of Szechwan, Hunan, and Kwangtung peasants. One recent study of the southwest Tai-speaking minority known in China today as the Chuang (Zhuang) nationality has estimated that between the mid-1500s and the early twentieth century the ratio of Chuang to Chinese people in Ch'en Hung-mou's home province of Kwangsi went from eight to two in favor of the Chuang to six to four in favor of the Chinese.[35] Under such dramatic circumstances of minority dispossession, the more generous, ethnicity-blind side of Neo-Confucian ideals may never have had much chance in the southwest. The Chinese migrants used their superior legal and moneylending skills to deprive the minority upper classes of their lands, and thus sabotaged what willingness they might have had to convert themselves into a minority Confucian gentry of the hill country.

Eventually, the dispossession of the minorities certainly brought with it its own educational nemesis. It facilitated the European projection into China of the competitive religious pluralism in education that had earlier promoted the spread of literacy in Europe itself. By the end of the Ch'ing dynasty, the Christian missionaries that the London Mission Society sent to southwest China after 1887 had made their headquarters at Chengtu into the real educational capital for many of the region's minorities. They created an effective separate school system, including middle schools, in terrain that earlier Confucian educational evangelists had never fully won over. The missionaries themselves were amazed by how quickly they acquired Miao congregations in Yunnan and Kweichow. They hopefully attributed it to a genuine hunger for Christianity. More secular historians may detect in it a genuine Miao hunger for a serviceable written language of their own. By about 1905, the English missionary Samuel Pollard had completed the development of a Miao written language, into which missionaries quickly translated Christian texts. But the number of literate Miao Christians now multiplied so rapidly that the use of the new Pollard Alphabet expanded beyond its religious focus to cover all of Miao life and thought.[36] However generous the instincts of Confucian school builders might have been, they were not prepared to devise new written languages for subject minorities. In this respect the Confucian educational evangelism of the late empire, unable to separate the dissemination of Confucian ethics from the internalization of orthodox Chinese linguistic models, was not "useless," but was less competitively adaptable than the alternative European religio-educational systems, more accustomed to competition, that now challenged it.

It would be wrong to conclude from this that Confucian educational expansion had suffered absolutely no competition at all of the pluralistic European kind before the Opium War. Members of our conference agreed that far more work needs to be done with respect to the modes and processes of "alternative education" in late imperial China. But certain observations are possible even now.

So far as we can tell, the regular Buddhist clergy and its temples were not regarded as much of either a threat or a stimulus by late imperial Confucian schoolmasters. The Ch'ing court itself issued hundreds of thousands of ordination certificates to Buddhist and Taoist monks (six hundred thousand monks and novices being legitimated between 1736 and 1739 alone). It justified the acceptance of such a monkhood by complacently and unflatteringly characterizing it as a necessary vocational outlet for the larger and larger numbers of lower-class people who were incapable of farming. Ch'ing academy heads publicly argued that the Buddhist religion was inoffensive and even helped the state to deter banditry.[37] Their condescension concealed the historical fact that Confucian academy education had borrowed something of its form from the great Buddhist temples of earlier centuries. The Buddhist education of the Sui and T'ang dynasties had probably been the first fully to systematize the fusion of teaching and scholarly research in such a comprehensive way that a large temple might become a self-contained outpost of lecturing, book collecting, the translation and authentication of scriptures, the holding of prayers and sacrifices, and the eating and other living activities of its devotees. Confucian literati, determined to compete with Buddhist temples on their own terms, had seen to it their own academies made use of this multifaceted temple tradition of research and teaching while giving it a Confucian content.[38]

But by the 1700s, the exchange of educational inspirations had reversed direction. Buddhism was having to learn its educational initiatives from Confucianism. The great lay Buddhist educator P'eng Shao-sheng (1740–96), himself the son of a well-known Confucian academy head, tried to redeem the decay of Buddhist studies in China by establishing the Chien-yang Academy for this purpose. In so doing, he borrowed back the academy formula, even though teaching in P'eng's academy was evidently by verse riddles and by doubt-resolving chants. P'eng's academy was the first independent Buddhist school, not attached to a temple, to be founded in late imperial China by an educator outside the clergy. As such, it paved the way for an even more considerable lay Buddhist educator, Yang Wen-hui (1837–1911), who created the Buddhist Press in Nanking in 1866. It also foreshadowed the rise of Buddhist educational associations at the end of the Ch'ing. Yet Yang Wen-hui's dream of supplying Chinese Buddhist education with the millions of copies of printed scriptures it needed in order to coexist on less unequal terms with state Confucianism reveals only too sharply the disabilities under which Buddhist teachers labored.[39]

The real competition for Confucian schoolmasters lay with the more heterogeneous but at least partly Buddhist popular religious sects, especially those which were affiliated, however loosely, with the White Lotus religious tradition. The expansion of this religious tradition, partly through tumultuous seventeenth-century migrations that gave the sects more of a Chinawide constituency than they had ever previously had, was one of the major events of Ch'ing dynasty history. As one example of this widening transmission of alternative sectarian education through migration, the "incense-smelling sect," which began the 1600s more or less as a northern sect centered in one Hopei village, had spread by the end of the 1600s to Kiangsu, Chekiang, Anhwei, Hupeh, Kiangsi, and even Szechwan. Its votaries had had to flee to the south and the west to escape the consequences of a failed rebellion at the end of the Ming dynasty.[40]

The White Lotus sects had their own creation mythology. They had their own system of historical time. As a matter of particular sensitivity to Confucian schoolmasters, they had more egalitarian views about age and sex than those offered in ordinary charitable schools. The texts with which they taught their followers included scriptures, most of them evidently written near the end of the 1500s, as well as handbills, placards, burial certificates, and even the written registers that organized their memberships.[41] Sect literature was often handcopied and circulated furtively, a little like *samizdat* works in the former Soviet Union. But any broad definition of the Chinese educational world in the 1700s and 1800s must recognize that it comprised hundreds or even thousands of private teaching networks that thrived far outside the reach of official public education. One rural sect teacher who led a rebellion against the Ch'ing court in 1774 may have had as many as three hundred pupils, mostly lower-class: monks, traveling actresses, hired laborers, cart pushers, sellers of fish or dried beancurd or horses, moneyshop owners, and yamen clerks.[42]

The sects did not give older Chinese women a radically new educational power so much as formalize hidden educational power that they already possessed. What one might call the informal curriculum in Chinese education, such as the stories mothers and grandmothers imparted to their daughters, and their sons when they returned home from school, had long been, to an important degree, a female creation. Occasionally, we catch eminent people in the public celebration of this fact. Li Lien-ying (1856–1911), the last major court eunuch in Chinese history, erected a stone tablet to his paternal grandmother years after her death on which he inscribed his gratitude for her vivid tales about local medieval officials who had battled with ghosts and demons in their youth; her imagination, not the village schoolmaster's texts, had supplied him with his role models. The religious sects reflected the considerable femaleness of the informal educational curriculum in the village milieus from which politically influential if culturally lowbrow figures like Li Lien-ying came. In the sects, women educated women—and men. But the sects also represented something of an uncontrolled underground mutation of the earlier Buddhist monastery education for elite women to which Susan Mann refers. This unnerved Confucian educators. Many of the sects were led by women. The fact that the sects freed women from their normal subordinate roles and welcomed female religious powerfulness could not but be a blow to the more orthodox educators who wrote the didactic treatises that sought, in Mann's words, to control younger women.

It is certain that Ch'en Hung-mou, who was also one of the two primary figures in formal women's education in mid-Ch'ing times, deeply feared open and exhibitionistic participation in religious rituals by younger women at Buddhist and Taoist temples. He tried to block it in Kiangsu in 1760 by arresting the temple monks who permitted it and exposing them in cangues before their own temples.[43] The obvious context of this fear was the fragility of poor women's respect for authority in hard times: Kiangsu was also the home of all-female mobs that blockaded government offices with demands for food relief, as the emperor himself had angrily discovered in 1748.[44] There was a significant feminization of the content of lower-class religion after the 1500s. The supreme deity of the White Lotus sects in late imperial China, the Eternal Venerable Mother, was an idealized model of the suffering but resourceful Chinese peasant mother. One scholar suggests that the Ch'ing dynasty may well have been unique for its proliferation of female deities who took motherhood as their theme, and that the primitive memories of an earlier matriarchy that may have been behind the Eternal Venerable Mother cult could have been pressed into service in this period as the "references" for at least a minor degree of female liberation.[45]

Whatever truth there may be in such speculations, sectarian expansion clearly disturbed elite educators enough to make a major school-based counterattack by state Confucianism seem likely. Yet there was none comparable to the school-based strategies of religious warfare in Europe, such as those waged by the Jesuits against Lutheranism or Calvinism.

Individual Ch'ing state officials certainly considered such strategies. Huang Yü-p'ien, the Hopei county magistrate of the 1830s who became a famous intelligence-gathering adversary of the sects, deplored their mingling of the sexes.[46] He quite specifically built charitable schools as an antidote to the White Lotus religion. But there is little evidence that his activities ever broadened into an empirewide campaign. That the reflexes of educational expansion as an antidote to heterodoxy existed in China, but were weaker there than they were in Europe, is probably to be explained by the isolation of China and by the nature of the sects as much as by Confucianism's famous tolerance. Obviously, the White Lotus religion was not the state creed of international enemies of China. As Susan Naquin has pointed out, it was also not a monolithic organization but small scattered groups of believers who depended on "long and loose chains of teachers and disciples."[47] Some of the White Lotus religion's most popular scriptures actually echoed the contents of the "Sacred Edicts" of the Ch'ing emperors. These echoes vindicated the judgment of the emperors that regular oral expositions of such edicts to the common people were the only educational means of containing the sects that they really needed.[48]

The construction of Confucian educational defenses against Chinese Islam, another important form of alternative education, reveals a similar pattern. Individual officials could be found who, seemingly like European religious crusaders, wished to use schools to counteract this "outsider" religion in China. Lu Yueh (1723–85), a bureaucrat in Shantung in the 1770s, proposed the establishment of charitable schools in all Chinese Muslim (*Hui*) settlements of a few dozen households or more in the province. He saw this as part of a thirty-year program to efface the separate Hui culture in Shantung. Again, his proposal was not broadened into an empirewide campaign. Moreover, Lu's suggestion that Shantung Hui children be paid stipends to study the three charitable school staples of what he called the "teaching of China"— the *Elementary Learning* of Chu Hsi, the *Filial Piety Classic*, and the emperors' Sacred Edicts—did not reflect any deeply troubled sense about the intractable separateness of the Hui people. He saw the Hui problem as being one of their inadequate socialization as Chinese rather than their membership in an exclusive, demanding religious community whose center was outside China. So the parallel between Lu's proposed Islam-effacing schools and the European use of schools in religious struggles is not a perfect one.[49]

But the assumption that the alternative education of a religion like Islam was no real threat to a monochromatically Confucian empire was permitted in part by China's isolation. This was to change. A mature system of Islamic education—as embodied in separate schools, a professional clergy of real quality, and an adequate supply of multilingual texts—was just beginning to be transferred to China in the 1700s. The acceleration of this transfer and the breakdown of China's isolation ultimately altered the whole relationship of Islam to late imperial Chinese education in the century after Lu Yueh's death.

The education of the southwest Muslims, who became a critically important and rebellious part of Chinese Islam in the nineteenth century, epitomizes the trend, and the emergence of previously almost unimagined contradictions among ethnic Chinese educators. Islam had probably created transprovincial educational networks of its own within China, linking Yunnan with Kansu and Shensi, by no later than the Yuan dynasty. The southwest, nonetheless, did not produce its own commanding Islamic teachers able to write Arabic, Persian, and classical Chinese until the late 1600s when Ma Chu compiled a guide to Islam of over 100,000 words and began to set up mosque schools. This was probably the dawn of formal Islamic mosque education in the Chinese language in the southwest, although it is only from the beginning of the 1800s that documents become numerous enough to allow us to study Yunnan's Islamic schools. The Yunnan Muslim scholar Ma Te-hsin (1794–1874) was the first to link the Chinese southwest directly to the theological scholars of Egypt and Turkey. He did so personally by studying in those countries in the 1840s. When he returned to Yunnan, Ma wrote the textbooks and the Chinese-language digests of more complex Middle Eastern works in science and philosophy that were necessary to end the textual poverty of Chinese mosque education. By the end of the Ch'ing dynasty, Yunnan mosques had embarked on the development of their own self-contained school system, which included colleges, middle schools, and primary schools. The green-robed and white-turbaned graduates of Yunnan's mosque colleges were a new phenomenon in the Chinese educational landscape. For multilingual Chinese Muslim educators like Ma Te-hsin, who eventually became the martyred leader of a separate Islamic kingdom in Yunnan, Singapore (the Asian clearinghouse of Islam), not Peking, was now the real center of the world.[50]

The rise of multiple educational capitals within Chinese civilization, whether Chengtu with its Christian schools for minorities or Singapore with its modernist mosques, tested the sinocentric premises of the imperial Confucian education whose expansion we are studying as they had never been tested before. But this occurred very late. The educational alternatives to imperial education—whether Buddhist, Christian, or Islamic—began to acquire the mass textual accessibility and the concentrated international stimuli they needed to compete with it only in the second half of the 1800s. Religio-educational warfare of the European type, therefore, cannot be regarded as the paramount factor in the growth of Confucian education in late imperial China.

In advancing a broader, more multicausal explanation of this growth, which we favor and which we have outlined above, it remains for us to consider the enormous if enigmatic influence of the civil service examinations. Nineteenth-century Western observers in China marveled at the examinations. They took it for granted that the examinations were not only an educational process but the embodiment of the socially necessary myth that reconciled the Chinese people to the political system that lay beyond their schools. As one Victorian doctor and treaty port sinologist wrote excitedly in 1886: "How has it come to pass that such a dense proletariat should through so many ages contentedly accept their situation? ... The labourer can descry no brand on his son's brow indicative of inferiority and exclusion from positions to which the sons of the great aspire. The air of the examination hall is as free as the air of heaven, and there, in competition, labourers and rich men's sons are on an equality. Herein lies the secret of the success of Chinese administration, the explanation of the contentment of half-starved artisans and labourers...."[51]

Unfortunately, the price that twentieth-century scholars have paid for their proper skepticism about such Chinese proletarian "contentment" has been considerable. The whole field of meaning that the civil service examinations did create has not received our sufficient attention. Some of our own conference members remained politely unpersuaded that the examinations even deserved much of a place in a conference about education. The written answers to examination questions were hardly regarded by contemporaries as major documents in intellectual history, one of our discussants argued, and no well-educated literatus ever called his examination essays his life's masterpiece. Recent scholarship has also made it clear that there was a growing number (some would call this a "public sphere") of literate people in late imperial China, ranging from poetesses to pettifoggers, that had little directly to do with the examinations. The discovery of this sphere has sometimes worked to reduce the significance of the examinations in our eyes.

But high Ch'ing politicians themselves, while they rarely flattered themselves about the "contentment" of the lower classes, emphatically asserted the existence of a necessary link between the examinations and the desire for educational self-improvement, even if they deplored the examinations' effect on broader learning. In the "Exhortation to Learning" essay that he wrote in 1898 as a rebuke to popular rights theorists, Chang Chih-tung reached the extreme of speculating that without an autocratic bureaucratic government that supplied such a "ladder of advancement" the Chinese people might be utterly unwilling to go to school. In an age that favors popular social history, we might also remember that the Chinese civil service examinations were, at least vicariously, far more of a mass enterprise than the more austere civil service entry examinations of modern Western countries. In nineteenth-century southern China, for example, gentry, peasants, artisans, merchants, women, and even foot soldiers and yamen messengers all celebrated the triennial regional examinations and more local ones by engaging in a pervasive gambling lottery called "examination hall surnames" (*wei-hsing*), in which they placed bets on the names of forthcoming winners. In this respect, the examinations became a mass-based theater of social fantasies and economic exchanges, and could enjoy an imaginative prominence even in the poorest rural areas.[52]

EDUCATION AND EXAMINATIONS IN COMPARATIVE CONTEXT

Educational thought in late imperial China, whether Confucian (Han Learning oriented) or Neo-Confucian (Sung Learning oriented) in form, presupposed in practice that young Chinese males (particularly from elite families with sufficient cultural resources) were "mainstreamed" into a classical education whose ultimate goal was preparation for the imperial civil service examinations. Cultural prestige and political power were the prerogative of Chinese males, even when girls in elite families matched their male siblings in literary talent and classical erudition.[53]

Many important forms of literate and nonliterate education existed independent of the glamorous civil service examinations, however. Hence, it would be a mistake to take the Confucian/Neo-Confucian curriculum of state examinations as the most pervasive aspect of education in late imperial society. This point made, it would nonetheless be equally mistaken to regard the civil examinations merely as a superficial "lottery" competition with little educational substance or cultural meaning. The linkages between Neo-Confucianism as educational philosophy and classical literacy as a means for educationally empowering Chinese elites in social and political life are historically significant.

Unlike contemporary Europe and Japan where social barriers between nobility and commoners prevented the significant translation of commercial wealth into elite status, landed affluence and commercial wealth in Ming-Ch'ing China were intertwined with examination status. Empowerment of elites in premodern Korea and Japan and the role of Neo-Confucianism in that empowerment were substantially different from China precisely because the semiaristocratic nature of Yi dynasty Korean society and the full aristocratic pedigrees in Muromachi-Tokugawa Japan prevented the establishment of a thorough Confucian meritocracy as in China. Without a civil service examination, Japanese Confucianism was institutionally practiced among elites, nobles, warriors, and priests in ways fundamentally different from those of late imperial China. As the prerogative of semiaristocratic military and the civil *yangban* elites, Neo-Confucianism in Korea generally did not permit (other than by warfare, social chaos, etc.) the social inclusion and political enfranchisement through meritocratic means of nonaristocratic groups such as merchants as happened in China.[54]

These different social and institutional patterns meant that the same theories of Neo-Confucianism during the Ming and Ch'ing dynasties were applied not only differently in China, Korea, and Japan but also far less broadly in educational terms in Korea and Japan. A Zen Buddhist student of Ch'eng-Chu philosophy in Muromachi Japan or a Confucian *yangban* in Yi Korea may have shared the textual world of Ming dynasty literati, but the same constellation of moral tenets for self-cultivation when mastered by priests, elites, and aristocrats in Korea and Japan versus mandarins and commoners in imperial China belied the fundamentally different social and political groups to which those educational tenets applied. In refusing to borrow China's examination system, Japanese Confucians remained committed to their native, aristocratic traditions.

Although Yi Korea established civil service examinations in 1392 dominated by the semiaristocratic *yangban*, Vietnam, not Korea, was the most faithful borrower of China's invention of meritocracy based on examinations. The Vietnamese examination system lasted from 1075 to 1919 and gradually caused the replacement of hereditary strongmen in Vietnamese villages by a Confucian scholar-gentry remarkably similar to China's. The poor scholar who subsisted on rice and sweet potatoes while learning how to write Chinese prose poems in assigned metrical and rhyme patterns became as much a part of the traditional political and social life of eastern Indochina as he was of that of Peking and Hangchow. Vietnam observed and responded to changes in the Chinese examination curriculum—it being easier for outsiders to study Chinese intellectual life this way than through inventories of the activities of hundreds of far-flung academies—and shared the changing tastes in texts that Chinese examiners espoused. (For example, China's enlarged interest in the *Rituals of Chou* in the 1700s spread to Vietnam.) The mystique of the Chinese meritocracy was so potent that the Vietnamese envoy to Peking in 1760, as part of an ongoing technology transfer effort, even investigated and measured the heights of the stone monuments at the Peking Imperial College that honored past Chinese palace examination winners.

Differences in the dynamics of educational supply and demand, however, meant that literati in Vietnam enjoyed a more aristocratic kind of prestige than their Chinese counterparts, even if, as in China, they lacked a hereditary aristocratic class basis. The Vietnamese civil service was proportionately larger to the size of its population than the Ch'ing bureaucracy was to the swelling population of China. Yet the absence in Vietnam of rich cities or of a big landlord class equivalent to China's that could invest in the expansion of Confucian culture meant that there was a smaller supply of Vietnamese candidates for degree status, and certainly no surplus. Hence, Vietnamese men who passed higher examinations received honors from their government that their late imperial Chinese counterparts could only envy. Peasants were conscripted to build luxurious residences for them; the government also gave them "glorious return" parades of welcome to their native villages, complete with flags and huge palm leaf fans and other regalia and bands of drum players and other musicians.[55]

EXAMINATION MYSTIQUE AND IMPERIAL REALITY

Many chapters in this volume describe how civil service examinations in late imperial China represented the focal point through which state interests, family strategies, and individual hopes and aspirations were directed. Once set in place and granted legitimacy, the recruitment system based on Confucian classical studies achieved for education in China a degree of national standardization and local importance unprecedented in the premodern world. Imperial control over elite education was premised on the state's prerogative to select and promote officials. In fact, the state was more concerned with organizing and codifying examination competitions than it was with monitoring schools or training teachers. Allan Barr's survey of the depiction of the village schoolmaster in a late imperial novel points to the huge gap between the Confucian ideal of respect for teachers and the social reality of a teacher's diminished status in an educational world where teachers were viewed as "failed" examination candidates. After creating functional units in officialdom to be filled through competitive selection, the emperor was willing to allow the actual process of education in classical Chinese and training for the examinations to drift out of state schools into the private domain of village schoolmasters, tutors, academies, or lineage schools.

Because education for the civil service was premised on social distinctions between literati, peasants, artisans, and merchants in descending order of rank and prestige, licensing examinations stood as a purposive barrier sealing in at best semiliterate masses from fully classically literate elites. Until the Ming, for instance, sons of merchants were not legally permitted to take the civil service examinations. Futhermore, occupational prohibitions, which extended from so-called "mean peoples" to all Taoist and Buddhist clergy, kept many others out of the civil service competition. The state's vision of elite education changed only enough in the late fourteenth century to enfranchise sons of merchants in the examination competition. Despite the rhetoric of impartiality and egalitarian Confucian ideals, success in the examinations evolved as a prerogative of the wealthy and powerful in local communities. In the contest for local quotas and examination success, artisans, peasants, and clerks were poorly equipped to take advantage of the theoretical openness of the civil service. During the late empire only 1.6 to 1.9 percent of the total population of China belonged to the gentry class.[56]

Imperial support of education and examinations was contingent on the success of the examination process in supplying talented and loyal men for the empire to employ. The state's minimum requirement that the educational system reinforce and inculcate political, social, and moral values that would maintain the dynasty in its present form was inseparable from Confucian rhetoric exalting the sanctity of learning and the priority of civilian values as the measure of social and moral worth. The mandarin official took precedence over the teacher. Loyalty to the ruling house was cemented by the requirement that a final "palace examination" be administered by the emperor himself to test those who had successfully passed the highest-level metropolitan examination. The emperor in effect became the empire's premier examiner, symbolically demanding oaths of unswerving allegiance from successful candidates for public office. In a tightly woven canvas of loyalties encompassing state and society, even emperors became educated in the Confucian rationale for their imperial legitimacy — by tutors selected from the civil service examinations![57]

Those who participated in the selection process perceived the examination system, not education per se, as the most prestigious means to achieve personal success. The examination hierarchy in effect reproduced acceptable social hierarchies by redirecting wealth and power derived from commerce or military success into the civil service. Educational success, however, required substantial investments of time, effort, and training. The state's mechanisms for political selection from the pool of examination candidates translated into targets of local strategies for the long-term social success of families, clans, and lineages. Nonelite schools also emerged under their umbrella of support.

The national school system established since the Sung dynasty was limited to candidates already literate. Community schools for the poor depended on the charity of exceptional officials such as Ch'en Hung-mou, gentry, merchants, and the leading clans in local society. The goal of mass literacy was never entertained. To achieve status and prestige, the passport to officialdom and high culture was the Mandarin spoken dialect and classical Chinese. Similar to the Latin/vernacular divide that demarcated secondary from primary education in early modern Europe, the spoken (Mandarin) and written (classical) languages of higher education in late imperial China were alien to everyday speech and taught to a minority as elite disciplines.

Those who could afford the financial and labor sacrifices needed to prepare young men for the examinations did so without question. Careerism usually won out over individual idealism among talented young men who occasionally were forced to choose between their social and career obligations to their parents and relatives and their personal aspirations. Wealth and power provided the resources for adequate linguistic and cultural training that would in turn legitimate and add to the wealth and power of a successful candidate in the examination cycle. Merchant families as much as official families saw in the civil service the route to greater wealth and orthodox success and power.

Because the civil service examinations tested classical learning based on ancient texts drawn from an antiquity nearly fifteen hundred years earlier, they were essentially tests administered in a written language that diverged from the vernacular Chinese of late imperial China. In addition, the Mandarin vernacular required of candidates as the official spoken dialect diverged from other spoken dialects, which were treated as subordinate languages. To acquire the legitimate cultural training necessary to qualify for local gentry status or the civil service, most students preparing for the examinations essentially were mastering a new spoken dialect (Mandarin) as a second language and a written language (classical Chinese) whose linguistic terseness, thousands of unusual written graphs, and archaic grammatical forms required memorization and constant attention from childhood.

Frequently, the rites of passage from child to young adult in wealthy families were measured by the number of ancient texts that were mastered at a particular age. "Capping" of a young boy between the ages of sixteen and twenty-one, for example, implied that he had mastered all of the Four Books and one of the Five Classics, the minimum requirement for any aspirant to compete in the civil service examinations. If he could cope with such rote training, a student could try his hand at passing the licensing examinations as early as age fifteen, although most young men rarely achieved licentiate status before age twenty-one. Unequal social distribution of linguistic and cultural resources meant that those from families with limited traditions of literacy were unlikely to compete successfully in the degree market with those whose family traditions included classical literacy.

Rare successes by a few humble candidates were the stuff of legends, stories, and propaganda for the mystification of the examination process. In the popular imagination, "fate" was typically used to explain the educational mortality of the lower classes. Those excluded from the selection process were asked to acknowledge that their academic fates were due to their lack of mental gifts. The classically trained elites in turn could blame the classically illiterate for their ignorance.

The Confucian dream of social mobility was a masterpiece of social, political, and cultural idealism. As an institution that demanded anonymity for examinee test papers and renounced hereditary transfer of social and political status, the examination system diverted attention from the de facto elimination that took place without examinations. Measurement of social mobility through examinations thus contains an unforeseen trap. By isolating those who were graduates from the larger pool of examination candidates, and then proceeding to reconstruct the social backgrounds only of the former, we are left with a skewed population of "survivors" in the examination process. Focus on the opposition between those who passed and failed examinations is the source of a limited perspective on the overall function of a classical education in the civil service selection process. Such analysis misses the relation between examination licentiates and those who were excluded because of their inferior educations or legal status. The gatekeeping function of the civil service examinations was an unspoken social goal of the process of selection.[58]

Illusions concerning the social neutrality of the state and the cultural autonomy of the educational system papered over the reality of the social structure of classical literacy during the Ming and Ch'ing dynasties. Examination selection effected an elimination process that was more thorough the less advantaged the social class. Exclusion of the masses of peasants, artisans, clerks, Buddhists, and Taoists—not to mention all women—from even the licensing stage of the selection process eliminated all but the culturally advantaged. This ensured that those who competed in the competition were a self-selected minority from Confucianized families, lineages, or clans with sufficient cultural resources to invest in their male children.[59]

The civil service competition successfully created a national curriculum for elites. The curriculum in turn consolidated gentry families all over the empire into a culturally and legally defined social stratum. By requiring mastery of archaic forms of classical Chinese, state authorities initiated young males into a select world of political and moral discourse drawn primarily from the Confucian Classics, the Four Books, and the Dynastic Histories. Intellectually conservative literati such as Fang Pao sought to maintain the curriculum on its orthodox Neo-Confucian course. Others endeavored to introduce Han Learning changes into the examination requirements. Whether Han or Sung Learning, classical discourse remained the monopoly of the classically trained elites.

Moral values such as filial piety and ancestor worship certainly transcended class and cultural barriers in late imperial China. Moreover, popular literacy in vernacular Chinese was widely prevalent among nonelites. Nonetheless, the dominant values, ideas, questions, and debates that prevailed in court and among officials were translated into a restricted classical language whose pronunciation was shrewdly based on the standard Mandarin dialect of the capital region in northern China and not on the dialects of the more populous and prosperous south. These "state languages" were written and spoken forms that only the privileged could fully grasp after years of training. Preparation for the civil service thus entailed long-term internalization of orthodox schemes of classical language, thought, perception, appreciation, and action. In class and individual terms, social and political reproduction yielded both "literati culture" and the literatus as a "man of culture." Southern Chinese whose native dialects differed from the dominant, official language of Mandarin were able to overcome their initial linguistic disadvantages vis-à-vis northern Chinese through the translation of wealth into superior educational resources and facilities.[60]

Fang Pao's efforts to enlist imperial support to publish examination essays on the Four Books championing Neo-Confucian orthodoxy reflected his goal of using a pedagogical manual to thwart cultural threats to Neo-Confucian orthodoxy and undercut the political positions of literati whom Fang vilified as heterodox. Similarly, the "invention" of the T'ung-ch'eng school represents the frightened response of elite lineages there to the growing influence of what they deemed heterodox Han Learning in the prosperous Yangtze Delta and the concomitant need to reassert local prestige through appeals to orthodox Neo-Confucianism. Convergence of state ideological interests and T'ung-ch'eng literati goals was the result.

Local lineages, for example, were able to translate social and economic strength into civil service examination success, which in turn correlated with their dominant control of local cultural resources. Coming from a family with a strong tradition of classical scholarship and Mandarin-speaking credentials had inherent local advantages for future social and political advancement as compared with the prospects of sons of lesser families and lineages. Hence, proficiency in spoken Mandarin and classical literacy was a vital element for kinship strategies. Private lineage initiatives in schooling coincided with the public needs of the state. Like European elites in the fifteenth and sixteenth centuries who crossed over from their vernaculars to classical Latin as the language of instruction in secondary education, most Ming and Ch'ing Chinese subordinated their native tongues if they entered higher education.

Merchants also became known as cultured patrons of classical scholarship. In fact, they became almost indistinguishable from the gentry elite, although hereditary designations as "merchant families" remained in force until the twentieth century. In the Yangtze Delta, for instance, they supplied resources for establishing local schools and private academies. The result was a merging of literati and merchant social strategies and interests. Classical scholarship flourished due to merchant patronage, and books were printed and collected in larger numbers than ever before.[61]

Subordination of the content of the civil service examinations to elite literary culture was further cemented through strict enforcement of requirements that all candidates' essays be composed in the rigid parallel-prose styles known as "eight-legged essays." Such cultural expectations were heightened by the gentlemanly requirements that candidates be adept in the art of calligraphy, one of the most esoteric and yet most characteristic cultural forms of training to master written Chinese. State examinations required expert calligraphy on special paper free of smudges or cut-and-paste graphs. Although students had to prepare calligraphically acceptable answers using only the officially recognized "regular" script, the man of culture was also expected to master "cursive," "running," and by the Ch'ing even ancient "seal" forms of writing. Seal and cursive script were unintelligible to all but the most erudite.[62]

Primacy was given to the social function of classical, literary, and calligraphic forms of cultural expression rather than to technical expertise as the measure of the educated man. An "amateur ideal" that equated cultural values with social status took precedence among elites and precluded nonelite participation in the ways of leisure. Although legal, medical, and fiscal specialties were tested during the T'ang and Sung dynasties, the end of specialty examinations in the civil service selection process during the

Southern Sung and thereafter marked the state's withdrawal of social and political prestige from technical subjects. Thereafter, training in law, medicine, astronomy, and fiscal affairs became the preserve of commoner clerks, secretaries, aides, and even Muslims and Europeans, who staffed the technically oriented yamens of the bureaucracy.[63]

Reproduction of classical attitudes among candidates for public office meant that gentry from all over the empire had more in common with each other culturally than with other social groups in their native areas. After years of classical training, for instance, Cantonese literati from southeastern China shared decisive linguistic (Mandarin) and discursive (classical) commonalities with other literati all over the empire, whether from Shantung in the north, Szechwan in the southwest, or any other area whose native dialect was distinctively different from that of Kwangtung. Institutionalization of the Mandarin dialect as the official spoken language (more an ideal than a reality) and ancient Confucian texts in the civil service examination process had generated class cleavages between thoroughly Confucianized elites and nonelite natives.

The Confucian curriculum chosen for the civil service, consequently, represented a cultural repertoire of spoken forms, linguistic signs, and conceptual categories that ensured that elite political power and social status throughout the late imperial period would be defined in prescribed terms acceptable to the state. Sung Neo-Confucianism provided the cultural content for political legitimation of the dynasty and the social prestige of its dominant status group. The precise linkages between civil examinations, political legitimacy, and cultural orthodoxy point to the bittersweet wedding of Confucian/Neo-Confucian moral discourse to an imperially prescribed view of state power drawn from classical Legalism, which subordinated the people under the ruler.[64]

A hierarchy of conservative social and political values, whether Sung or Han Learning, transmitted from one generation to the next through the elevation of spoken Mandarin and the subordination of regional dialects gave content to the classical methods of instruction in legitimate culture. Rote memorization of the Four Books and the Classics in Mandarin pronunciation by examination candidates, sometimes deplored but never rejected, represented the programmed transmission of the habit-forming rituals and culture of the dominant class in late imperial China. Yet, as Elman shows, there was room for change in the content and forms of cultural transmission.[65]

Accordingly, study of the educational impact of civil service examinations in late imperial China provides us with the crucial historical example germane to contemporary society and its high valuation of personal merit as measured by written examinations. No other comparable materials on education and examinations exist outside of China that give ready access to the study of the long-term role of examinations in the history of education. We learn how state examinations first prioritized a certain domain of Confucian knowledge, which then enabled gentry and merchant elites to translate their financial advantages into cultural resources for the literate mastery and reproduction of the special knowledge tested. Such mastery over generations yielded the long-term social and political success of Chinese gentry families and lineages.

So all-absorbing a system also caused many individual miseries of a kind similar to but on a far vaster scale than the famous list of the miseries of scholars in Samuel Johnson's *The Vanity of Human Wishes:* toil, envy, want, the patron, and jail. The examination system's most notorious victims commanded large rebellions against the dynasty whose examiners had rejected them. The leader of the Taiping movement in the 1850s is the most memorable example. More obscure victims joined an underground of opposition to the system whose requirements or workings were thought to abuse them. Some literati of the 1600s and 1700s publicly declined ever to take a single civil service examination, on the grounds that they felt demeaned, or treated like bandits rather than like a potential ruling class by the body searches to which soldiers guarding provincial examination sites subjected them.

What is remarkable about the court debate in Peking between 1903 and 1905 that ended the examination system is how heavily the ultimate destroyers of the examinations, the high officials Yuan Shih-k'ai and Chang Chih-tung, drew on the arguments of critics of the examinations in previous centuries, particularly the eighteenth century. The most notable of these arguments, which the Ch'ien-lung emperor himself had expressed in 1744, was that the examination system constantly threatened to become as much a welfare-dispensing instrument as a process of education and that too many of the students it produced had neither adequate practical knowledge nor morality. The new schools of the early 1900s, such high officials hoped, could imprint proper moral behavior more effectively than the examinations had ever done. For them, the abolition of the examinations in 1905 was not a blow struck against the centrality of moral indoctrination in education but an effort to reconfirm it.[66]

CULTURAL TENSIONS IN INTELLECTUAL CHANGE

Faced with the loss of the Han Chinese "homeland" first to Mongols in the thirteenth century and then to Manchus in the seventeenth, native Chinese expressed through orthodox and heterodox forms of Confucian cultural practice significant racial and intellectual unease. Debates over what should be taught and how Confucianism/Neo-Confucianism should be defined and practiced under native and conquest dynasties indicate that the Ch'ing empire was for Han Chinese a period of emotional turmoil in terms of their own internal intellectual debates and vis-à-vis the threat of barbarian culture to the millennial integrity of Han Chinese civilization. Behind the Confucian facade of cultural omniscience (voiced through elite education and the cutthroat competition for success in the civil service examinations) lurked a fear that the very continuity of Han Chinese culture was threatened in the post-Mongol empire. Behind the veil of political arrogance (expressed by the dragon throne and its mandarins) lurked a disquieting sense that Han Chinese now served a hostile barbarian kingdom that had co-opted Confucian/Neo-Confucian discourse as its own.

Among Ch'ing dynasty Confucians seeking what Kai-wing Chow describes as nativist and fundamentalist relief from the successful Manchu co-option of a barbarian-inspired (that is, Buddhistic) Neo-Confucian orthodoxy, the Han Learning versus Sung Learning controversy threatened to engulf the Neo-Confucian cultural consensus enshrined in civil service examinations. During the Ch'ing dynasty, evidential research scholars advocated a program that would resume the interrupted conversation with antiquity. Moving back in time, they first sought out T'ang and then Later Han dynasty sources to overcome limitations they found in Sung and Ming dynasty forms of Neo-Confucianism. Because Later Han dynasty classical sources were relatively unaffected by Neo-Taoist and Buddhist notions that had influenced T'ang, Sung, and Ming Confucians, Han Confucians increasingly received respect and attention from purists during the seventeenth and eighteenth centuries.

The debate between those who favored Han dynasty classical scholarship, that is, "Han Learning," and those who favored the Neo-Confucian school, that is, "Sung Learning," was philologically very technical but its political repercussions were considerable. Han Learning represented more than just an antiquarian quest. Its advocates indirectly cast doubt on the Confucian ideology that Manchu rulers had enshrined in their official legitimation of imperial power. Rediscovery of the political message contained in the *Mencius* by Tai Chen, among others, allowed Confucians to gainsay Neo-Confucian orthodoxy as untrue to the ideals of ancient Confucianism. When tied to classical studies, philology thus had a political component and translated into new educational agendas.

Manchu rulers were adept at co-opting these Chinese literati debates and rendering them politically harmless. Early in his reign, the Ch'ien-lung emperor added his imperial authorization to Fang Pao's efforts to publish model examination essays loyal to Chu Hsi's vision of the Four Books. In the 1770s, the emperor honored critical scholars such as Tai Chen for their precise scholarship and even granted imperial patronage to the Han Learning agenda for classical studies. In the process, the examination system itself evolved under the dual influence of Sung and Han Learning. Orthodox Neo-Confucianism remained the measure for essays on the Four Books in session one of the provincial and metropolitan examinations. After 1750, however, questions on the Five Classics and the policy questions on sessions two and three began increasingly to reflect the inroads of evidential research and Han Learning views on the Confucian Canon. Such compromises in the examination curriculum were emblematic of the broader intellectual efforts of nineteenth-century Ch'ing Confucians to mitigate the Han versus Sung Learning controversy and seek common ground by building on the moral strengths of Sung Learning and the scholarly advantages enjoyed by Han Learning.

A trivial analysis of the end of imperial education would see a static and hopelessly discredited system as having been buried by a new doctrine of "saving the country through education;" as propounded by such thinkers as K'ang Yu-wei, Liang Ch'i-ch'ao, and Yen Fu, this doctrine suggested that Western-style schools were the basis of national wealth and power. Our conference did not have the time to consider the educational upheaval at the end of the Ch'ing in any detail, but its findings suggest that education had always tried to save the country, or empire, and that traditional imperial education never stood still. It continued to expand according to its own logic, even in the late 1800s when it was being ravaged both by foreign imperialism and by the decay of the political and military institutions to which it was bound.

As late as the 1870s, for example, Governor General Tso Tsung-t'ang, charged with governing the Chinese, Mongols, Tibetans, and Hui people of Kansu, still heroically struggled to stretch the facilities of the examination system as far as Lanchow so that the mixed Sino-Muslim scholar gentry whom he saw as the key to the northwest's political future would not be discouraged by having to travel hundreds of miles by cart or camel to compete for degrees in north-central China. As Tso saw it, Confucianism was still the only way to create political loyalty on the frontier. And the desire to pursue "fame" through examination success was the only real way to create a mass interest in the northwest in Confucianism or in the Sino-Muslim charitable schools that taught it.

A quarter of a century later, during the 1898 reforms, K'ang Yu-wei asked the emperor to begin to introduce mass education for all commoners, male and female, from childhood. The purpose of this mass education was to encourage Chinese duplications of such alleged American phenomena as the yearly production of twenty thousand new books and three thousand new gadgets and enjoyment of the national power that came with these accomplishments, despite the apparent restriction of American military budgets to a mere 10 percent of American educational expenditures. (This was 1898.) The money for K'ang's new education was to come in part from the reclamation of "surplus funds" in the post-rebellion reconstruction bureaus, commercial promotion agencies, and telegraph services of China's outer provinces. We may observe that the difference between these 1873 and 1898 educational visions did not expose a China that was undergoing a simple changeover from static tradition to dynamic modernity. It revealed a far more complex transition, yet to be fully understood, in which one form of educational expansion, oriented toward the reproduction of Confucian values on continuously widening multiethnic frontiers, was displaced by another form of educational expansion, based—haltingly—on the production of new kinds of knowledge, and the state's formal mobilization of all of its citizens.

NOTES

1. Huang Yen-p'ei 黃炎培, "Tung-hsi liang ta-lu chiao-yü pu t'ung chih ken-pen t'an" 東西兩大陸教育不同之根本談 (Discussion of the roots of the differences in Eastern and Western education), *Chiao-yü tsa-chih* (Shanghai, 15 Jan. 1916), 4–8.

2. This point is discussed category by category in T'ao Yü-ch'uan 陶愚川, *Chung-kuo chiao-yü shih pi-chiao yen-chiu* 中國教育史比較研究 (Comparative study of Chinese educational history) (Tsinan: Shan-tung chiao-yü ch'u-pan-she, 1985), 389–90. See also E. A. Kracke, Jr., "The Expansion of Educational Opportunity in the Reign of Hui-tsung of the Sung and its Implications," *Sung Studies Newsletter* 13 (1977): 6–30, for an earlier period of educational expansion.

3. Kuan T'ung 管同, "Shuo shih" 說士 (Discussion of the scholars), in Ko Shih-chun 葛士濬, comp., *Huang-ch'ao ching-shih wen hsü-pien* 皇朝經世文續編 (Continued compilation of the statecraft essays of the present court) (1888; reprint, Taipei: Wen-hai ch'u-pan-she, 1972), *chüan* 53: 1–2.

4. Ch'en Yuan-hui 陳元暉 et al., *Chung-kuo ku-tai ti shu-yuan chih-tu* 中國古代的書院制度 (China's ancient system of academies) (Shanghai: Shang-hai chiao-yü ch'u-pan-she, 1981), 86–87, 97.

5. Ch'en Yuan-hui, *Chung-kuo ku-tai ti shu-yuan chih-tu*, 97–98.

6. Ou To-heng 歐多恆, "Ch'ien-hsi Ch'ing-tai Kuei-chou chiao-yü fa-chan ti yuan-yin" 淺析清代貴州教育發展的原因 (Limited explanation of the reasons for educational development in Ch'ing dynasty Kweichow), *Kuei-chou she-hui k'e-hsueh* 2 (Kweiyang, 1985): 102; Ch'en Yuan-hui, *Chung-kuo ku-tai ti shu-yuan chih-tu*, 64.

7. Charles E. McClelland, *State Society and University in Germany 1700–1914* (London and New York: Cambridge University Press, 1980), 36–37.

8. Ch'en Yuan-hui, *Chung-kuo ku-tai ti shu-yuan chih-tu*, 97.

9. Ogawa Yoshiko, 小川嘉子 "Shindai ni okeru gigaku setsuritsu no kiban" 清代に於ける義學設立の基盤 (Basis of the establishment of charitable schools in the Ch'ing dynasty), in Hayashi Tomoharu 林友春, ed., *Kinsei Chūgoku kyōiku shi kenkyū* 近世中國教育史研究 (Studies in the educational history of modern China) (Tokyo: Kokudosha, 1958), 273–308.

10. Kuo Ch'i-yuan 郭起元, *Chieh-shih t'ang wen-chi* 介石堂文集 (Prose collection of the Chieh-shih Hall) (1754), 6:1–2.

11. Wang Te-chao 王德昭, *Ch'ing-tai k'e-chü chih-tu yen-chiu* 清代科舉制度研究 (Study of the Ch'ing examination system) (Hong Kong: Chung-wen ta-hsueh ch'u-pan-she, 1982), 101.

12. Ch'en Hung-mou 陳宏謀, *P'ei-yuan t'ang ou-ts'un kao* 培遠堂偶存稿 (Draft archives of the P'ei-yuan Hall) (1872), 1:33–35b.

13. Hu Hsu 胡煦, "Ch'ing po chu hsiao-ti shu" 請博舉孝弟疏 (Memorial requesting the broad recommendation of filial sons and devoted brothers), in Ho Ch'ang-ling 賀長齡, comp., *Huang-ch'ao ching-shih wen-pien* 皇朝經世文編 (Compilation of the statecraft essays of the present court) (1826; reprint, Taipei: Wen-hai, 1972), 57: 15–15b.

14. Igarashi Shōichi 五十嵐正一, *Chūgoku kinsei kyōikushi no kenkyū* 中國近世教育史 の研究 (Researches in the modern educational history of China) (Tokyo: Kokusho kankōkai, 1979), 400.

15. Alexander Woodside, "Some Mid-Qing Theorists of Popular Schools," *Modern China* 9, no. 1 (Jan. 1983): 5–6.

16. Cf. Joan W. Scott, "Gender: A Useful Category of Historical Analysis," *American Historical Review* 91, no. 5 (Dec. 1986): 1053–75.

17. Cf. Charlotte Furth, "Androgenous Males and Deficient Females: Biology and Gender Boundaries in Sixteenth and Seventeenth-Century China," *Late Imperial China* 9, no. 2 (Dec. 1988): 1–25.

18. Yung Ming 詠霓, "Ch'eng-tu shih ti jen-li ch'e-fu" 成都市的人力車夫 (Rickshaw pullers of Chengtu municipality), *Lao-kung yueh-k'an*, (Nanking, 1 Mar. 1935): 1–22.

19. Evelyn S. Rawski, *Education and Popular Literacy in Ch'ing China* (Ann Arbor: University of Michigan Press, 1979), 140.

20. Lu Hung-chi 陸鴻基 (Bernard Luk), *Chung-kuo chin-shih ti chiao-yü fa-chan* 中國近世的教育發展 (Modern educational development of China) (Hong Kong: Hua-feng shu-chü ch'u-pan-she, 1983), 74–78.

21. For a more detailed presentation of this argument, see Alexander Woodside, "Real and Imagined Continuities in the Chinese Struggle for Literacy," in Ruth Hayhoe, ed., *Education and Modernization: The Chinese Experience* (Oxford and New York: Pergamon Press, 1992), 23–46.

22. *Ta Ch'ing Jen-tsung Jui-huang-ti shih-lu* 大清仁宗睿皇帝實錄 (Veritable records of the Chia-ch'ing reign) (Tokyo: Okura Press, 1937–38), 123: 29b–31.

23. Woodside, "Real and Imagined Continuities," 39.

24. See John Meskill, *Academies in Ming China: A Historical Essay* (Tucson: University of Arizona Press, 1982), 160–66.

25. Liang Ch'i-ch'ao 梁啟超, "Hsueh-hsiao tsung-lun" 學校總論 (General discussion of schools), in Shu Hsin-ch'eng 舒新城, comp., *Chin-tai Chung-kuo chiao-yü shih tzu-liao* 近代中國教育史資料 (Materials in modern Chinese educational history) (Peking: Jen-min chiao-yü ch'u-pan-she, 1962), 3:936–44. See also R.A. Houston, *Literacy in Early Modern Europe: Culture and Education 1500–1800* (New York: Longman, 1988), 56–58, 156–58.

26. For a consideration and partial historical rebuttal of theories of this kind, see Woodside, "Real and Imagined Continuities."

27. Eugenio Garin, *L'éducation de l'homme moderne 1400–1600* (Paris: Fayard, 1968), 100–102; Michel de Montaigne, *Essays*, trans. J.M. Cohen (London and Baltimore: Penguin Books, 1958), 70–71.

28. Wang Ch'ang 王昶, *Ch'un-jung t'ang chi* 春融堂集 (Literary collection of the Ch'un-jung Hall) (1807), 68:9–9b. Other Confucians had different totals of graphs for each Classic.

29. For something of this debate, see John Boli, Francisco Ramirez, and John W. Meyer, "Explaining the Origins and Expansion of Mass Education," *Comparative Education Review*, Chicago, 29, no. 2 (May 1985): 145–70.

30. Joan Simon, "The History of Education in *Past and Present*," *Oxford Review of Education* 3, no. 1 (1977): 71–86.

31. Lawrence Stone, "Literacy and Education in England, 1640–1900," *Past and Present*, 42 (1969): 81.

32. Ou To-heng, "Ch'ien-hsi Ch'ing-tai Kuei-chou chiao-yü," 104–5.

33. *Tseng Wen-cheng-kung chia-hsun* 曾文正公家訓 (Family instructions of Tseng Kuo-fan), in *Tseng Wen-cheng-kung ch'üan-chi* 曾文正公全集 (Complete works of Tseng Kuo-fan) (1952; reprint, Taipei: Shih-chieh shu-chü, 1965), 4:9–10.

34. Wm. Theodore de Bary, *The Liberal Tradition in China* (New York: Columbia University Press, 1983), 27–32. See also de Bary and John Chaffee, eds., *Neo-Confucian Education: The Formative Stage* (Berkeley: University of California Press, 1989).

35. Fan Hung-kuei 范宏貴 et al., *Chuang-tsu lun-kao* 壯族論稿 (Essays on the Chuang nationality) (Nan-ning: Kuang-hsi jen-min ch'u-pan-she, 1989), 51.

36. On the Pollard Alphabet and its historical effects, see Wang Fu-shih 王輔世, "Miao-tsu wen-tzu kai-ke wen-t'i" 苗族文字改革問題 (Problem of the reform of the Miao written language) in Hu Ch'i-wang 胡起望 et al., *Miao-tsu yen-chiu lun-ts'ung* 苗族研究論叢 (Collection of essays in the study of the Miao nationality) (Kweiyang: Kui-chou min-tsu ch'u-pan-she, 1988), 467–72.

37. Alexander Woodside, "State, Scholars, and Orthodoxy: The Ch'ing Academies, 1736–1839," in K.C. Liu, ed., *Orthodoxy in Late Imperial China* (Berkeley: University of California Press, 1990), 163, 165.

38. Ting Kang 丁鋼, *Chung-kuo Fo-chiao chiao-yü: Ju-Fo-Tao chiao-yü pi-chiao yen-chiu* 中國佛教教育：儒佛道教育比較研究 (Chinese Buddhist education: a comparative study of Confucian, Buddhist, and Taoist education) (Chengtu: Ssu-ch'uan chiao-yü ch'u-pan-she, 1988), 146, 152, 172–73. Erik Zürcher describes how ordination examinations were required by the T'ang state; see his "Buddhism and Education in T'ang Times," in de Bary and Chaffee, eds., *Neo-Confucian Education*, 32–35. Such examinations presumably continued into the late empire.

39. Ting Kang, *Chung-kuo Fo-chiao chiao-yü*, 198–200.

40. See the analysis in Daniel L. Overmyer, *Folk Buddhist Religion: Dissenting Sects in Late Traditional China* (Cambridge: Harvard University Press, 1976), 103–4.

41. Susan Naquin, *Millenarian Rebellion in China: The Eight Trigrams Uprising of 1813* (New Haven: Yale University Press, 1976), 20–24.

42. Susan Naquin, *Shantung Rebellion: The Wang Lun Uprising of 1774* (New Haven: Yale University Press, 1981), 41–45.

43. On Li Lien-ying's early education, see Ts'ai Shih-ying 蔡世英, *Ch'ing-mo ch'üan-chien Li Lien-ying* 清末權監李蓮英 (Powerful eunuch Li Lien-ying of the end of the Ch'ing) (Shihchiachuang: Ho-pei jen-min ch'u-pan-she, 1986), 1–20, esp. 9; on Ch'en and female religious behavior, see Ch'en Hung-mou, *P'ei-yuan t'ang ou-ts'un kao*, 47:14–14b.

44. *Ta Ch'ing Kao-tsung Ch'un-huang-ti shih-lu* 大清高宗純皇帝實錄 (Veritable records of the Ch'ien-lung reign) (Tokyo: Okura Press, 1937–38), 313: 24b–25.

45. Yü Sung-ch'ing 喻松青, *Ming-Ch'ing pai-lien-chiao yen-chiu* 明清白蓮教研究 (Researches on the White Lotus religion of the Ming and Ch'ing) (Chengtu: Ssu-ch'uan jen-min ch'u-pan-she, 1987), 299-301.

46. For Huang's importance, see Overmyer, *Folk Buddhist Religion*, 29.

47. Naquin, *Millenarian Rebellion in China*, 2.

48. For the sects' scriptural absorption of the message and language of the Sacred Edicts, see Yü Sung-ch'ing, *Ming-Ch'ing pai-lien-chiao yen-chiu*, 214. The outstanding study

of the Sacred Edicts themselves is that of Victor H. Mair, "Language and Ideology in the Written Popularizations of the Sacred Edict," in David Johnson, A.J. Nathan, and Evelyn S. Rawski, eds., *Popular Culture in Late Imperial China* (Berkeley: University of California Press, 1985), 325–59.

49. Woodside, "Some Mid-Qing Theorists of Popular Schools," 20–21.

50. These paragraphs are heavily indebted to Na Chung 納忠, "Ch'ing-tai Yun-nan Hui-tsu jen yü I-ssu-lan wen-hua" 清代雲南回族人與伊斯蘭文化 (Hui nationality people of Ch'ing dynasty Yunnan and Islamic culture), in Chinese Academy of Social Sciences Nationalities Research Institute et al., *Hui-tsu shih lun-chi* 回族史論集 (Collection of essays on the history of the Hui nationality) (Yinchwan: Ning-hsia jen-min ch'u-pan-she, 1984), 92–97.

51. D.J. MacGowan, "Chinese Guilds or Chambers of Commerce and Trade Unions," *Journal of the China Branch of the Royal Asiatic Society*, 21, no. 3–4 (Shanghai: 1886, issued March 1887), 192.

52. See the memorial by censor Teng Ch'eng-hsiu 鄧承修 that describes the gambling in Ch'en T'ao 陳弢, comp., *T'ung-chih chung-hsing ching-wai tsou-i yueh-pien* 同治中興京外奏議約編, (Summary compilation of capital and provincial memorials of the T'ung-chih Restoration) (1875; reprint, Shanghai: Shang-hai shu-tien, 1984), 4: 37–38b.

53. Mark Elvin, "Female Virtue and the State in China," *Past and Present* 104 (1984): 111–52; Joanna Handlin, "Lu K'un's New Audience: The Influence of Women's Literacy on Sixteenth-Century Thought," in Margery Wolf and Roxanne Witke, *Women in Chinese Society* (Stanford: Stanford University Press, 1975), 13–38.

54. On Korea, see Yong-ho Ch'oe, "Commoners in Early Yi Dynasty Civil Examinations: An Aspect of Korean Social Structure, 1392–1600," *Journal of Asian Studies* 33, no. 4 (Aug. 1974): 611–31, which tries unsuccessfully to present Yi Korea as a Confucian meritocracy, while along the way conceding that merchants, artisans, and "mean peoples" were not permitted to take civil examinations there. On the semiaristocratic nature of *yangban* elites, Ch'oe's conclusion that the avenue to officialdom was accessible to obscure clans is undercut by the finding that 26.2 percent of examination graduates came from only fifteen clans, while clans as a whole produced 69.6 percent of all graduates. Cf. June-ho Song, "The Government Examination Rosters of the Yi Dynasty," in *Studies in Asian Genealogy* (Provo, Utah: Brigham Young University Press, 1969), 154, where Song notes that the thirty-eight leading clans produced 52 percent of the graduates in 745 examinations held over 503 years from 1392 to 1894.

55. Alexander Woodside, *Vietnam and the Chinese Model* (Cambridge, Mass.: Harvard University Press, 1988), 169–233.

56. David Johnson in "Communication, Class, and Consciousness in Late Imperial China," in Johnson, Nathan, and Rawski, eds., *Popular Culture in Late Imperial China*, 59, estimates there were at least five million classically educated male commoners in Ch'ing times, or roughly 5 percent of the adult male population in 1800 and 10 percent in 1700. See also Hsiao-tung Fei, *China's Gentry: Essays on Rural-Urban Relations* (Chicago: University of Chicago Press, 1953), 71–72.

57. Cf. Pierre Bourdieu and Jean-Claude Passeron, *Reproduction in Education, Society, and Culture*, trans. Richard Nice (Beverly Hills: Sage Publications, 1977), 194–210. On China, see Wolfram Eberhard, *Social Mobility in Traditional China* (Leiden: E.J. Brill, 1962), 22–23.

58. Bourdieu and Passeron, *Reproduction*, 141–67.

59. For examples of systematic examination success, see Benjamin A. Elman, *Classicism, Politics, and Kinship: The Ch'ang-chou School of New Text Confucianism in Late Imperial China* (Berkeley: University of California Press, 1990), 6–15, 42–73, 97–100.

60. Rawski, *Education and Popular Literacy*, 1–23. See Willard Peterson, *Bitter Gourd: Fang I-chih and the Impetus for Intellectual Change* (New Haven: Yale University Press, 1979), 25–35, Peter Bol, "Chu Hsi's Redefinition of Literati Learning," in de Bary and John Chaffee, eds., *Neo-Confucian Education*, 151–85. Cf. Houston, *Literacy in Early Modern Europe*, 138–39.

61. Ping-ti Ho, "The Salt Merchants of Yang-chou," *Harvard Journal of Asiatic Studies* 17 (1954): 130–68, and Ōkubo Eiko, *Min-Shin jidai shoin no kenkyū* (Research on academies in the Ming-Ch'ing period) (Tokyo: Kokusho kankōkai, 1976), 221–361.

62. Ching-i Tu, "The Chinese Examination Essay: Some Literary Considerations," *Monumenta Serica* 31 (1974–75): 393–406; Alexander Woodside, "Some Mid-Qing Theorists of Popular Schools," 11–18; Lothar Ledderose, *Mi Fu and the Classical Tradition of Chinese Calligraphy* (Princeton: Princeton University Press, 1979); Benjamin A. Elman, *From Philosophy To Philology: Social and Intellectual Aspects of Change in Late Imperial China* (Cambridge, Mass.: Harvard University Press, 1990), 191–97.

63. Robert Hymes, "Not Quite Gentlemen? Doctors in Sung and Yuan," *Chinese Science* 7 (1986): 11–85; Jonathan Spence, *To Change China: Western Advisers in China, 1620–1960* (Middlesex: Penguin Books, 1980), passim; Joseph Levenson, "The Amateur Ideal in Ming and Early Ch'ing Society: Evidence from Painting," in John Fairbank, ed., *Chinese Thought and Institutions* (Chicago: University of Chicago Press, 1957), 320–41.

64. Cf. Wm. Theodore de Bary, *Neo-Confucian Orthodoxy and the Learning of the Mind-and-Heart* (New York: Columbia University Press, 1981), 1–66; James T.C. Liu, "How did a Neo-Confucian School Become the State Orthodoxy?" *Philosophy East and West* 23, no. 4 (1973): 483–505.

65. Cf. Pierre Bourdieu, "Systems of Education and Systems of Thought," in Michael Young, ed., *Knowledge and Control: New Directions for the Sociology of Education* (London: Collier Macmillan, 1971), 190–201.

66. See *Shih-erh ch'ao Tung-hua lu: Kuang-hsu ch'ao* 十二朝東華錄：光緒朝 (Tung-hua Gate records of the Kuang-hsu reign), comp. Chu Shou-p'eng 朱壽朋 (Taipei: Wen-hai Press, 1963), 9:4979–82. For a brief discussion of the 1744 debate as seen in 1903, see Wolfgang Franke, *The Reform and Abolition of the Traditional Chinese Examination System* (Cambridge, Mass.: Harvard University East Asian Monographs No. 10, 1968), 56–57.

GLOSSARY

Ch'eng Tuan-li	程端禮	Li Lien-ying	李蓮英
Hu Hsu	胡煦	Liang Ch'i-ch'ao	梁啟超
Huang Yen-p'ei	黃炎培	Lu Yueh	陸燿
Huang Yü-p'ien	黃育梗	Ma Chu	馬注
Hui	回	Ma Te-hsin	馬德心
Igarashi Shōichi	五十嵐正一	Ogawa Yoshiko	小川嘉子
K'ang Yu-wei	康有為	P'eng Shao-sheng	彭紹升
Kuan T'ung	管同	Pi Yuan	畢沅
Kuo Ch'i-yuan	郭起元	Sun Hsing-yen	孫星衍

Tso Tsung-t'ang	左宗棠	Yang Wen-hui	楊文會
Wang Ch'ang	王昶	Yen Fu	嚴復
wei-hsing	闈姓	Yuan Shih-k'ai	袁世凱

INDEX

A-kuei [Janggiya], 374 n38
abacus, 230, 251 n53
aborigines: assimilation of, 417–18, 420, 445; culture of, 423–24, 450 n34; culture of, 9, 10, 419–21, 424–25, 436–37, 444–46, 528, 537–38; stereotypes about, 421–23, 450 n24. *See also specific tribes by name*
academies, 4, 7, 10, 13, 144, 249 n23, 426–27, 459, 461, 465, 471, 485, 486, 538–39; directors of, 500, 521 n90; and education of Manchus, 349, 357, 358; expansion during late Ch'ing, 494–500, 516 n17, 517 n23, 526–27; financing of, 495, 498–99, 500, 503, 526–27; of Imperial Household Department, 355, 526; internal tests in, 484, 506–7, 520 n62; and modern public schools, 513–15, 552; purposes of, 510; student stipends, 494, 498, 502, 526. *See also specific academies by name*
Academy of Mathematics, 231, 238–39, 240
agriculture, 30, 228, 418, 421, 425, 453 n86
Ai Nan-ying, 187
Aisin Gioro clan, 353
Altaic, 344
Analects, 55, 124, 125, 126, 141, 164, 342
Anderson, Mary, 38
Anhwei, 214 n127, 244, 539; academies of, 495, 526
archeology, 247
Ariès, Philippe, 439
astrology, 105 n98
Astronomical College, 236
astronomy, 98, 105 n98, 203, 224, 234, 353, 364; and cosmology, 227–28; in Han dynasty, 226, 249 n17; and the idea of progress, 246–47; and Jesuits, 229; and politics, 225–26; reform of, 229–30; and ritual, 226. *See also* mathematics and mathematical sciences

Ba Huyen Thanh Quan, 536
baksi (erudites), 343, 350, 351
banner education, 243, 340, 348–59, 526; and Chinese classical studies, 348; of commoners, 356–59; costs and fees, 358–59, 363; curriculum, 353, 359, 360–65; elementary education, 352, 358; of the elite, 354–55, 362; in the garrisons, 358, 362–63, 366; and military arts, 351, 354, 361; and private academies, 358, 363; reform of, 359–65; and state schools, 116, 354–57, 362–64; and stipends, 359
banner examinations, 116, 344, 349; ethnic quotas in, 349, 350–51, 352, 363; format of, 350–51; and garrison examinations, 357–58, 363; purposes of, 349; subjects examined, 350, 351
bannermen, 348, 349, 369 n1
Bastid, Marianne, 513
Begging to Teach, 67–68
betrothal, 32, 35
bikuni, 37
bithesi (scribes; banner clerks), 350, 351, 355
Board of Appointments, 113, 344, 350, 355, 362
Board of Finance, 474
Board of Justice, 302, 309, 480
Board of Punishments. *See* Board of Justice
Board of Rites, 83, 113, 136, 157, 192, 478
bondservants, 355, 369 n1
Boxer Rebellion, 486
Buddha, 126
Buddhism and Buddhists, 1, 8, 130, 134, 285

Buddhism and Buddhists (*continued*)
    n19, 445, 538, 546, 553, 557 n38
Buddhist education, 1, 529, 536, 538–39
bureaucracy, 113, 326 n27, 344, 418, 472–75.
    See also officials
Burma, 446, 468, 529

Cabuhai, 344, 345, 353
calendrical reform, 228, 229, 230, 236
calligraphy: in civil service examinations,
    114, 138, 550; in elementary education, 393–
    94, 412 n67
Canton, 24, 29–30, 481
cartography, 224
casebooks (*an-ts'e*), 429–30
Central Asia, 112, 347, 376 n79
Cha Shen-hsing, 41 n15
Cha Ssu-t'ing, 41 n15, 323 n9
Chan, Wing-tsit, 5
Ch'an Buddhism, 8
Chang Chao, 232
Chang Ch'ao-jui, 383
Chang Ch'i, 41 n15
Chang Chien, 513
Chang Chih-tung, 123, 511, 543, 552
Chang, Chung-li, 66
Chang Hsia, 115–16
Chang Hsueh-ch'eng, 12, 195, 202, 390; and
    historical scholarship, 201; on women's
    education, 24–26, 27–28, 38, 39
Chang Huan-lun, 511, 512, 521 n85
Chang Hui-yen, 41 n15
Chang Juan-lin, 213 n106
Chang Kuang-ssu, 452 n67, 454 n103
Chang Liang-chi, 87
Chang Lü-hsiang, 185, 505, 506
Chang Po-hsi, 460–61, 463, 484, 485, 486, 505
Chang Po-hsing, 187
Chang T'ing-hsiang, 309
Chang T'ing-yü, 197, 447, 462
Chang Tsu, 325 n26
Chang Ying, 196, 197, 213 n113
Chang Yun-sui, 423
Changchow (prefecture), 130, 135, 199, 215
    n140 n141; academies of, 497, 498
Change Classic (*I ching*; also cited as *Book of
    Changes*, and *Changes Classic*), 115, 119, 139,
    174, 190, 235, 342, 534
Chao Ping, 170–72, 177
charitable schools. See *i-hsueh*
Ch'e Wan-yü, 413 n9
Chekiang, 129, 198, 199, 200, 201, 539;
    academies of, 495, 496
Chen-chiang (prefecture), 497, 498, 499
Chen Te-hsiu, 443
Ch'en Chin, 140
Ch'en Chin-hsin, 254 n125

Ch'en Ch'ueh, 210 n64, 391, 396
Ch'en Fang-sheng, 393, 394, 411 n56, 532
Ch'en Hao, 116, 119
Ch'en Hua-ch'ü, 27
Ch'en Hung-mou, 9–10, 85, 447, 452 n60,
    475, 476, 536, 537; background of, 419; and
    Chiao-nü i-kuei, 21; on curriculum, 424, 438,
    440, 446; and education of women, 21–22,
    446–47; endows schools, 433, 440; on
    ethnic differences, 423, 528; and *hua*, 419–
    20; on human nature, 428–29; and legal
    education, 329 n52; on literacy training,
    435–36, 452 n56; management style of,
    429–30, 434–35; pedagogical theory of,
    439–40; on ritual, 438–39; and school
    financing, 432–33, 452 n66; writings of,
    442–43
Ch'en Li-ch'ü, 27
Ch'en Lung-cheng, 383
Ch'en P'ei-chih, 27, 43 n27
Ch'en Ti, 290 n96
Ch'en T'ien-hsi, 303–9
Ch'en Wen-shu, 26, 27, 388
Ch'en Yü-wang, 383
Ch'en Yung-kuang, 205, 217 n170
Cheng Hsieh, 51, 58
Cheng Hsuan, 136, 139
Cheng-meng Academy, 511, 512
Cheng Pan-ch'iao, 392
Cheng-te emperor, 130
Ch'eng Chin-fang, 201, 471, 472
Ch'eng-Chu school, 2, 13, 113, 116, 118, 126,
    130, 138, 152, 185–86, 187–88, 190, 209
    n36; in Lung-men Academy, 504, 505; Tai
    Chen on, 258–59, 282; and Tseng Kuo-fan,
    78, 87–88. *See also* Neo-Confucianism
Ch'eng I, 2, 113, 115, 119, 127, 169, 173;
    views on the *Spring and Autumn Annals*, 71
    n12
Ch'eng-kung county, 434
Ch'eng Ta-wei, 230, 243, 245
Ch'eng Tuan-li, 4, 411 n54, 532
Ch'eng Wei-ch'i, 438, 443
Chengtu, 537
Chi Fu-hsiang, 141
Chi Yun, 64, 141, 142, 198, 259
ch'i (energy; vitality; material force), 125,
    127, 165; Ming thinkers on, 290 n96; Tai
    Chen on, 261, 266, 276
ch'i-she, 348, 351, 353, 354, 358, 359, 363, 364;
    defined, 373 n28; Hung-li emperor on, 360,
    361
Chia-ch'ing emperor, 4, 130, 363
Chia-hsun ch'un-yen (Family instructions and
    earnest words), 51, 57, 61–62
chiang-chang (study aids; primers), 185, 192,
    553. See also *Ch'in-ting Ssu-shu-wen*

Chiang Ch'en-ying, 187
Chiang Fan, 200–201, 215 n136
Chiang-ning (prefecture), 498, 499
Chiang Yung, 200, 201, 244, 258, 269
chiao ("teaching"), 3–4, 5, 20
Chiao Hsun, 4
chiao-hua (culture; "transformation via education"), 401, 419–20, 421, 449 n6
Chiao Hung, 290 n96, 423
chieh-hsiao (virtuous widow cult), 424
Chien-chou, 343
chien-sheng, 351, 474, 480
Chien-wen emperor, 116
Chien-yang Academy, 539
Ch'ien Ch'en-ch'ün, 41 n15
Ch'ien I-pen, 130–31
Ch'ien-lung emperor, 5, 60, 116, 132, 151, 157, 175, 232, 367, 464, 472–73, 528, 552, 553; and banner education, 359–61; and Imperial College, 464, 477–78; and Manchu education, 9, 340; and Manchu language, 9, 341, 361, 362–63, 366; on Manchu military arts, 361; and provincial academies, 477
Ch'ien Ta-hsin, 57, 141, 202, 245, 259, 464
Chih (robber baron), 169, 170, 171
Chihli, 474, 517 n23
Chin (dynasty), 342, 374 n43
Chin Pang, 201, 469
Chin p'ing mei (Golden lotus), 62, 373 n26
chin-shih, 23, 113–14, 350, 351, 472, 474; of Chekiang, 495
Ch'in Hui-t'ien, 86, 93
Ch'in-ting Ssu-shu-wen, 150–51, 160, 170–75, 193–95, 196; organization of, 162–68
ching-chi, 4, 102 n46, 442
Ch'ing (dynasty), 2, 3, 4, 552–55; innovations in bureaucracy, 344. *See also* officials
Ch'ing Code, 295, 297, 299, 300, 309, 327 n34; commentaries on, 308; criminal code, 296, 317; statutes and substatutes of, 307
ch'ing-i (pure opinion), 510
Ch'iu Chün, 440, 443
Chou (dynasty), 234, 466, 467, 469–70, 478
Chou Li (Ch'ing literatus), 141
Chou-li (Rites of Chou), 21, 79, 462, 545
Chou Tun-i, 85, 173, 174
ch'ou-jen, 225, 246–47, 248 n12
Ch'ou-jen chuan (Notices on mathematicians and astronomers), 225, 228, 231, 244, 254 n125
Christianity and Christian schools, 99, 535, 542. *See also* missionaries
chronology, 224, 226, 227
Chu Hsi, 2, 3–4, 113, 115, 124–25, 126, 129, 132–33, 134, 169, 235, 267, 438, 460, 536; on desire, 125, 126, 285 n19; on education

and study, 275–78; on enlightenment, 290 n95; on human nature and principle, 128–29, 141; and *li-hsueh*, 127, 267–68; on mental discipline, 280; on the mind, 130–31; on moral instruction, 52; on sagehood, 280–81; on sexual propriety, 424
Chu I-tsun, 187
Chu Shih, 193
Chu Shih-hsiu, 217 n170
Chu Tsai-yü, 226
Chu-tzu chi-chu, 115
Chu-tzu chih-chia ko-yen, 442
Chu-tzu ch'üan-shu, 78, 190
Chu Yuan-chang, 112
Chu Yun, 141, 198, 259, 279
Chu Yun-ssu, 95
Chu Yung-hsien, 454 n99
chü-jen, 113, 122, 351, 472, 474; in Kiangsu, 493, 499
Chuang (minority), 537
Chuang Ts'un-yü, 135
Chuang-tzu (philosopher), 126
Chuang-tzu (text), 89, 94, 95, 186
Ch'un-ch'iu. See *Spring and Autumn Annals*
chün-tzu, 169
Chung-shan Academy, 203
chung-shih, 354
Ch'ung-chen li-shu, 229, 232
civil service examinations, 1, 2, 3, 50, 72 n27, 531–32; abolition of, 552; child examinees, 61, 548; in Ch'ing dynasty, 116–23, 552; in comparative context, 544–46; and corruption, 72 n27, 120–21, 214 n114; court examinations, 121, 122; and cribbooks, 79–80, 160, 185, 429 (see also *chiang-chang*); cultural resources and examination success, 197–201, 206, 549–50, 552; educational content of, 111; educational importance of, 11–12, 543–44, 551–52; ethnic quotas in, 437, 461–62; and examiners, 118, 121, 123, 129, 131, 132, 142, 185, 194, 214 n114, 323 n9, 324 n18; format of, 114–16, 117–23, 135–37, 294, 323 n7; functions of, 111–12, 123, 143–44, 151, 163, 168, 175–77; in Jurchen language, 342; local examinations, 117; metropolitan examinations, 118–22 *passim*, 140–43; in Ming dynasty, 112–16, 123, 125; and numbers of licentiates, 117, 122; and orthodoxy, 111, 112, 113, 116, 118, 119, 123–33, 135–42 *passim*, 258, 553–54; palace examinations, 121, 132, 136, 143, 153, 324 n19, 547; *p'an* questions in, 294, 295–96, 325 n26, 326 n27; policy questions in, 7, 114, 115, 118, 119, 121, 135, 142, 143, 162–63, 295, 324 n17, 325 n20; provincial examinations, 55, 117–22 *passim*, 137–40,

civil service examinations (*continued*)
198; quotas for official families, 198;
reform of, 119–20, 122, 123, 458–59;
regional quotas, 117, 123, 493, 499, 546;
regional rates of success, 122, 123, 136,
197, 200, 205, 214 n127; and sale of
degrees, 113, 473–74, 479, 494, 510; in
Shantung, 124, 136, 137; in Shensi, 136,
139–40; specialty examinations, 550–51;
and state ideology, 111, 123, 124, 131, 132,
134, 203, 546–47, 550, 552; subjects
examined in, 55–57, 114, 115–16, 117, 118,
119, 120, 121, 122, 125, 135–43, 162–64,
183, 185, 198, 294–96, 323 n8, 550–51; in
Sung dynasty, 550–51; in Szechwan, 136,
138; in T'ang dynasty, 323 n7, 325 n26,
550; translators' examinations, 116, 351–
52, 356, 362, 364, 374 n38; and writing
style, 5, 168–69, 186–88, 211 n87, 325 n26,
547–48; in Yuan dynasty, 123. *See also*
banner examinations; *Documents Classic*;
eight-legged essay; Han Learning; Sung
Learning
clan schools, 389–91, 401, 408 n35 n37, 409
n39 n40, 529
Classic of Filial Piety (*also cited as* Filial Classic),
52, 55, 69, 114, 119, 120, 351, 395–96, 402
Classics: in civil service examinations, 55–56,
114–44 *passim*, 294–95, 549, 553; in legal
education, 297, 310, 320; in women's
education, 21, 22–24. *See also specific titles*
clerks, 299, 305, 329 n51 n52, 336 n146, 435;
income of, 311, 494
community schools (*she-hsueh*), 9, 382–84,
386–87, 405 n5, 427–28, 527; financing of,
382–83, 384, 427, 428, 547; purposes of,
382, 384
concubines, 27, 42 n26, 43 n27
Confucianism, 125, 129, 130, 176–77, 204,
227, 328 n40; and moral philosophy, 111,
112, 137; and ritualism, 190–92; in
Vietnam, 536–37. *See also* Neo-
Confucianism
Confucius, 1, 26, 85, 124, 428
cosmology, 131, 226, 227; and
Neo-Confucianism, 228
"Counsels of Yü the Great" ("Ta Yü mo"),
128, 135, 136, 138, 139
Court of Imperial Sacrifice, 476–77
courtesans, 24, 36, 42 n26
curriculum, 13, 56, 57, 69, 511, 532; and civil
service examinations, 7, 56, 57, 111, 113,
114, 123, 134, 136, 184, 443, 549–52; in
elementary schools, 393–96, 424, 435, 439;
informal curriculum, 540; in Japan, 37; in
legal education, 307–13, 320–21; in
mathematics and astronomy, 231–46; in

state schools, 114. *See also* women's
education

Dagai [Giolca], 343
de Bary, Wm. T., 4, 466, 536
discipline: in elementary education, 398–400,
402, 438–39; in Lung-men Academy, 507–
8
Doctrine of the Mean, 141
Documents Classic (*Shu-ching*), 56, 126, 128,
136, 342, 534. *See also under* Old Text
Double Seven Festival, 28–30, 39, 536
dowry, 20, 21, 31, 32–34, 536
Dream of the Red Chamber, 22, 38, 41 n13, 389,
391
Duara, Prasenjit, 421
Dynastic Histories, 113, 117, 133, 549

education: of commoners, 5, 9, 356–59, 529,
540–41; defined in Ch'ing, 3–5, 420; role
of diversions in, 58; and economic
transformation, 2, 435, 534–35; role of
fathers in, 53, 96; and human nature, 428–
29; and manual labor, 58; role of mothers
in, 22, 23; and peers, 54, 81; and physical
exercise, 36, 249 n23; purposes of, 419–20,
423–25, 428–29, 432, 435–37, 445–47,
459, 461–68, 470–76, 481–82, 527–29,
537–38; and religious sects, 539–41; and
ritual, 470–71; social environment in, 53–
54, 546–47; and specialization in studies,
57, 81; state funding of, 1, 352, 382–83,
529; state role in, 1, 9, 11, 113–44, 340–69
passim, 381–84, 385, 400, 402, 425, 527–28,
546–47; in teenage years, 54, 411 n54; and
vocation, 52, 80, 364, 436; Western
influence in, 485–87, 511–12, 537–38;
Western views on, 2–3, 68, 537–38, 543.
See also banner education; educational
organization; elementary education;
women's education
educational organization: and ancient schools
myth, 460, 462–63, 464, 466–67, 469, 470–
71, 483, 487; in China and the West
compared, 429, 458, 459, 460, 462, 463,
464, 465, 469, 470, 475, 486, 525–26, 527,
533–34, 544–46 *passim*; and crisis of the
Ch'ing elite, 122, 469–76, 526; debate over
public vs. private, 458–68; and elite
politics, 185, 459–60; late Ch'ing reform
of, 485–87, 511–15, 554–55; and lineages,
461–62, 552; and polycentrism, 476–85,
541; and role of the state, 460–63, 458–65
passim, 469, 485–97, 527–29; and state
ideology, 459, 527–28; and synthesis of
government (*cheng*) and teaching (*chiao*),
462, 466, 470–71, 475, 486. *See also*

Imperial College; *kuo-tzu*

Eight Banners, 344–45, 355, 369 n1; education of, 356–57; officers' schools of, 356, 365, 373 n37, 526

eight-legged essay, 5, 51, 61, 114, 118, 119, 121, 169–70, 187, 189, 194, 202, 203, 326 n27, 502, 550

Eight Masters (T'ang-Sung), 186, 187

elementary education, 9, 358, 485, 495, 527, 528; age of students, 392, 438; and decontextualization, 402–3, 459; discipline in, 398–400, 402, 438–39; elementary schools in early Ch'ing, 385–87; form and methods of, 391–93, 411 n53, 425–48 *passim*, 533; and imperial examination system, 382, 384, 389, 400; and moral training, 396–400, 429, 439; purposes of, 399–400, 424–25, 428–29, 435–36, 527; and ritual, 438–39; teaching methods in, 393–96; and tests, 361, 389, 408 n37; textbooks, 393, 394, 395, 397, 413 n77, 440–43, 533, 536. *See also* banner education; community schools; *i-hsueh*

Elements of Geometry (Euclid), 98, 99, 250 n42

elites, 3, 5, 51, 114, 199, 418, 421; crisis of Ch'ing elite, 469–76; in Hunan, 205, 461–62; in Japan, 544; in Kiangsu, 499, 503–4, 513, 515; in Korea, 372 n24, 544–45, 558 n54; in Kweichow, 535; and the law, 318; in Lower Yangtze region, 495–515 *passim*; as promoters and managers of academies, 495, 499, 521 n90, 526–27; as promoters and managers of charitable schools, 385–86, 432; in T'ung-ch'eng county, 152, 197–98, 205–6, 447, 549–50; in Vietnam, 545–46; and women, 31, 540. *See also* literati

embroidery, 31–32

epigraphy, 203, 247

Erdeni, 343

eremitism, 112

Eternal Venerable Mother, 540

etymology, 143

eunuchs, 460, 540

Ever Victorious Army, 518 n31

evidential (*k'ao-cheng*) scholarship, 7, 13, 125, 133, 134, 135, 136, 139–40, 184, 190–91, 195, 198–99, 200, 202, 203; and science, 226–28

"examination hall surnames" (*wei-hsing*) lottery, 544

Fa-shih-shan, 41 n15

factionalism, 132–33, 147 n59, 153, 159, 165, 459

Fakjingge, 346

family: role in education, 53–54, 215 n142, 388, 400–401, 410 n48; role in legal education, 303, 329 n52; schools, 11 (*see also* clan schools); in women's education, 25, 530; women's role in, 21, 22, 104 n89, 540

Family Letters, 76, 77, 96

Fang Chou, 51, 152, 166, 193

Fang Chung-t'ung, 243–44

Fang Hsi-yuan, 258

Fang Hsiao-pao, 154

Fang Pao, 6, 7, 118, 198, 549, 553; and Ch'eng-Chu orthodoxy, 188–90, 191; and Ch'ien-lung emperor, 157–62; defends Neo-Confucianism, 152, 172, 191; edits ritual texts, 158–60, 193; family background of, 152; and Hanlin Academy, 155; intellectual interests of, 153, 159, 165, 188–89, 194; and K'ang-hsi emperor, 151–54; as student in Peking, 153, 188; and Tai Ming-shih, 154, 188–89, 209 n47; and T'ung-ch'eng school, 184, 195; and Wei Ting-chen, 153–54; and writing style, 167, 188–89, 208 n19, 209 n47; writings of, 153, 162, 170 n24; and Yung-cheng emperor, 155–57

Fang Tse, 201

Fang Tung-shu, 201, 205

Feng Kuei-fen, 500

filial piety, 30, 79, 318, 549

Five Classics, 532; in civil service examinations, 56, 57, 61, 69, 113, 114, 117, 119, 127, 133, 141, 158, 162–63, 278, 459; in elementary schools, 394, 443

Five Phases (*wu-hsing*), 131, 223

Five Relations (*wu-lun*), 80, 88, 395

Foochow, 29

footbinding, 21, 28, 47 n72

Foreign Language Colleges (*t'ung-wen kuan*), 364

foreign language instruction, 511. *See also* translation

Foucault, Michel, 206 n3

Foucquet, Jean-François, 238–39, 240

Four Books, 7, 35, 56, 57, 113, 114, 115, 117, 125, 127, 133, 141, 162, 163, 532; in elementary schools, 394, 443; Tai Chen on, 278; in translators' examinations, 351

"Four Treasuries." See *Ssu-k'u ch'üan-shu*

fu-dao. See under women's education

fu-hsueh (prefectural schools), 426–27

Fu hsueh ("Women's Learning"), 24–26

Fu-hui ch'üan-shu, 315, 384–85, 387

Fu-k'ang-an, 478

Fukien, 482

funeral rituals, 424

Fung Yu-lan, 50

Gagai, 343

Garin (Kang-lin) [Suwan Gūwalgiya], 344, 345
gentry, 87, 147 n59, 434, 495, 500, 537, 551, 552; size of, 546; of Vietnam, 545. *See also* elites
Gioro Academy, 354–55, 526
Giyanghedei, 344, 353
Gold Coin Society rebellion, 520 n76
granaries, 383–84
Grand Secretariat, 83
Great Learning, 141
Great Ritual Debate, 130
Gubadai, 242

Han Learning, 5, 7–8, 10, 13, 111, 121, 122, 125, 194–95, 196, 549; and debate over Sung Learning, 123, 133–43, 202–5, 553–54
Han-shu, 79–80, 89, 93, 114, 186, 342
Han T'an, 152, 193
Han Yü, 80, 84, 85, 92, 167
Hangchow, 23, 26, 199
Hanlin Academy, 116, 136, 192, 473, 476; and instruction in Manchu, 345
Heilungkiang, 343
higher education, 547; and the ancient schools myth, 466–72 *passim*, 478; in China compared to the West, 460, 464, 470, 475, 478, 481, 486, 527; in law, 294–96, 299, 321; of Manchus, 352–55, 362–63; of Mongols, 352, 355, 356, 373 n37, 374 n43; of Muslims, 542; in science and mathematics, 231–46; role of the state in, 479, 500, 526–27. *See also* academies; banner education; civil service examinations; *specific schools by name*
Hli-khin, 445
Ho Ch'i-jui, 132
Ho Kuo-tsung, 241, 242, 243
Ho, Ping-ti, 117, 472
Ho Xuan Huong, 536
Honan, 70, 482
Hong Kong, 2
Hopei, 539
Hou-Han shu, 80
Hsi-hsiang chi (Romance of the western chamber), 35, 62
hsi-hsueh (Western learning/studies), 10, 224, 228, 229, 502
hsi-hsueh chung-yung (Chinese origins of Western knowledge), 231, 235
Hsi-yang hsin-fa li-shu, 229
Hsia Jih-ao, 522 n93
hsiang-shih, 350, 363
hsiang-yueh. See village lecture system
Hsiao-ching. See Classic of Filial Piety
Hsiao-hsueh (Elementary education;

Elementary learning; "Lesser Learning"), 51, 69, 86, 352, 395, 397, 402, 441–42, 536
Hsieh Chao-che, 412 n67
Hsien-an Palace Officers' School, 355–56, 373 n37
hsien-hsueh (county schools), 426–27
hsin-fa (mental discipline), 132
Hsing-an hui-lan, 309, 328 n43, 335 n143
Hsing-li (Principles of Nature), 351, 352
Hsing-li ching-i, 443
Hsing-shih yin-yuan chao, 59
Hsiung Po-ling, 166
Hsiung Tsu-li, 158, 178 n11
Hsu Ho-ch'ing, 143
Hsu Kuang-ch'i, 30, 228, 230, 233, 243, 245
Hsu P'eng-shou, 142–43
Hsu Sheng, 25
Hsu Shou, 98
hsueh ("learning"; study), 3–4, 266; and women, 20
Hsueh Feng-tso, 243
Hsueh-hai T'ang, 24, 481, 502
Hsueh Hsuan, 290 n96
hsueh-t'ang. See modern schools
Hsueh Yun-sheng, 328 n48
Hsun-tzu (philosopher), 1, 264, 280
Hsun-tzu (text), 186
Hu An-kuo, 115, 119
Hu Chi-t'ang, 329 n48
Hu Ch'uan, 494
Hu Hsu, 529
Hu Shih, 205, 494, 514–15, 521 n85
Hu Wei, 190
Hu Yuan, 480, 481, 482
hua ("moral transformation"). See *chiao-hua*
Hua Heng-fang, 98
Huang Liu-hung, 315, 384–85, 413 n79
Huang Tso, 490 n50
Huang Tsung-hsi, 290 n96, 465–68, 469, 471, 476
Huang Yen-p'ei, 525, 532
Huang Yü-p'ien, 541
Hui. *See* Muslims
Hui-chou (prefecture), 13, 199, 200, 201, 258
hui-shih, 350, 351, 354
Hui Tung, 134, 194, 259, 462
Hunan, 123, 426, 432, 537
Hunan School of Current Affairs, 466
Hunan Self-Study University, 486
Hundred Days reforms (1898 reforms), 511, 554
Hundred Surnames (*Pai chia hsing*; also identified as *Hundred Names Classic*), 393, 533
Hung-li. *See* Ch'ien-lung emperor
Hung Pang, 201
Hung T'ai-chi, 343–44, 345, 349

Hung-wu emperor, 112, 115, 346; on community schools, 382
Hupeh, 539
Huters, Theodore, 205

I-ching. See Change Classic
i-fa ("moralizing methods"), 189, 194
I-hsing [Aisin Gioro], 346
i-hsueh (charitable schools; public, or free, schools), 9, 11, 358, 375 n53, 384–88, 389, 390, 397, 430–32, 527–29, 530, 539; financing of, 387–88, 390–91, 409 n46 n47, 432–33, 527–28, 529; and itinerant schools, 407 n30; management of, 385–88, 428, 434–35; origin of the term, 426; and private academies, 406 n21, 426–27; purposes of, 385, 387, 441, 527, 541; role of the state in, 384, 385, 386–87, 406 n21, 428
I-huan (Prince Ch'un), 364
i-li (philosophy, moral philosophy), 187, 190, 203, 257. *See also* moral philosophy *under* Tai Chen
identity, 12, 530, 532
ideology, 111–12, 192, 206 n5, 446, 530, 550; and Ch'ing multilingualism, 347–48. *See also* civil service examinations
Igarashi Shōichi, 529
immigration and immigrants, 200, 418, 438, 535, 537
Imperial Board of Astronomy, 8, 226, 228, 230, 232, 236, 237–38
Imperial Clan Academy, 353–54, 361, 362, 526
Imperial Clan Court, 362
Imperial College (*Kuo-tzu chien*), 8, 231, 236, 238, 352, 437, 469, 471, 474, 485; compared to Western schools, 464, 478, 481; contending views on, 476–82; curriculum of, 479; foreign students in, 480; in Ming dynasty, 113, 478–79; and political reform, 467, 468, 476–85; in Sung dynasty, 479; in T'ang dynasty, 477. *See also* Moated Sanctuary
Imperial Household Department, 355, 375 n47
Imperial Observatory, 476
Islam. *See* Muslims

Jackson, Anthony, 425
Japan, 11–12, 36–47, 463, 511–12, 514; and Confucianism, 544–45; language of, 341
Java, 468
jen (humaneness), 261
Jen Ta-ch'un, 195
Jesuits, 224, 229, 232, 248 n8, 464; as imperial tutors, 238, 239, 240, 252 n79; scientific writings of, 229, 231, 232; service

at court, 230; as teachers, 237, 239–40, 243–44
Ju-lin wai-shih (The scholars), 50, 66, 70
Juan Yuan, 24, 89, 199, 228, 231, 246, 471, 481
Jui-chu Academy, 503
Jung-lu [Suwan Gūwalgiya], 365
Jurchens, 343, 344, 366, 367, 368, 369 n1, 374 n43; language of, 342, 343. *See also* Chin (dynasty)

Kang I, 308
K'ang-hsi emperor, 8, 116, 117, 120, 151, 152, 153–54, 158–59, 190, 192; and education, 348; and charitable schools, 528; and community schools, 385; on Manchu military arts, 348; and science, 225, 231, 236, 237, 238, 239, 240, 245
K'ang Yu-wei, 485, 486, 554
Kansu, 478, 526, 542, 554
Kao P'an-lung, 101 n16, 290 n96
Kao-p'ing Academy, 498
Kazakhs, 535
Kiangnan, 70, 122, 244, 364, 388, 419, 500
Kiangnan Arsenal, 502, 512
Kiangsu, 29, 198, 199, 214 n129, 493, 512–13, 539; academies of, 494–98, 510, 511, 514, 515, 517 n23
kindergartens, 460
Kitans, 368, 376 n79; language of, 342, 370 n7. *See also* Liao (dynasty)
knowledge, 12–13, 458, 535; scientific knowledge, 223–24, 229–31; technical knowledge, 8; transmission of, 245
Ko, Dorothy, 42 n21
ko-wu (investigation of things), 191
Kögler, Ignatius, 232
Korea, 343, 371 n12; and Confucianism, 544–45; language of, 341, 370 n7; translators in, 346, 372 n24
Ku-ching academy, 471, 477
Ku-chou (prefecture), 418
Ku Hsi-chou, 440
Ku Hsien-ch'eng, 101 n16, 130
Ku Kuang-ch'i, 41 n15
Ku Kuang-yü, 504
Ku-liang, 115
Ku Tsung, 242
ku-wen. See Old Text
Ku-wen yuan-chien, 442
Ku Yen-wu, 4, 56, 94, 185, 270, 460
Kuan T'ung, 205, 526
Kuan Yun, 27
Kuei-kuang Academy, 498
Kuei Yu-kuang, 187, 196, 204
K'un-ming county, 433–34
Kung Kung-hsiang, 345

kung-sheng, 351
Kung Tzu-chen, 345, 473
Kung-yang, 115
K'ung An-kuo, 135
K'ung Shang-jen, 52, 60, 61
K'ung Ying-ta, 136
Kunming, 427, 464; academy of, 483–84
Kuo Ch'i-yuan, 527
Kuo Sung-tao, 78
kuo-tzu ("sons of the state"), 469–70, 476, 479–80, 483, 489 n32, 490 n50
Kuo-yü (text), 186
Kwangsi, 419, 426, 537
Kwangtung, 24, 38, 123, 426, 465, 482, 537; academies of, 495, 496, 517 n23
Kweichow, 418, 426, 432, 437, 443, 452 n67, 454 n103, 461–62, 526, 528, 535

Lamp at the Crossroads, 52, 53, 61, 70
Lan Ting-yuan, 21, 22, 38, 316
landlordism, 535, 545
Lao-tzu, 126, 337 n159; text, 342
law, 13, 321 n1, 425, 481; and appeals, 315, 319; and bribery, 319; and case records, 304–5; and civil law and civil matters, 316, 318, 335 n145, 425; in civil service examinations, 114, 294–96, 299, 323 n7, 326 n27; and clan rules, 298, 336 n145; customary law and rules, 299, 308, 322 n1; the judicial process, 304–6, 315; legal texts, 293–94, 303, 307, 309–10; natural law, 322 n1; numbers of practitioners of, 315–16, 317; popular attitude toward, 315, 317, 318–19; in popular culture, 297, 298; positive law, 292, 317, 318, 321 n1, 328 n40; role of precedent in, 308–9; and provincial and local regulations, 308; source materials for the study of, 293; and suicide, 315, 318, 334 n143 n144; and torture, 312, 336 n145; and trials, 306, 312; types of people involved in, 292–93, 322 n3; and women, 312. *See also* norms
Lee, James, 418
legal education, 13, 319–21, 460; and case reports, 297, 298, 309; of the common people, 293–98, 320; and ethics, 321; informal education, 297–98; of law apprentices, 304–13, 320; in modern China, 320, 321; public education, 296–97; school education, 293–96, 297; and texts, 294, 301, 303, 320; of those in the legal system, 298–313. *See also* legal secretaries
legal secretaries, 8–9, 292, 299, 336 n146; as apprentices, 304–13; duties of, 302, 304–7, 309; education of, 302–13, 319–20; ethical education of, 310–13; practical training of, 304–7; readings of, 307–10; relations with

clerks, 305, 311; role in legal system, 302; salaries of, 311, 331 n66; social origins of, 303; and the state, 302
Legalism, 551
lei-shu (family handbooks), 396
Lei Tsu (goddess of sericulture), 31
li (moral principles; principle), 125, 127; Chu Hsi on, 286 n33; Ming thinkers on, 290 n96; Tai Chen on, 261, 262, 267, 273, 275, 276, 277, 280, 282
li (rules of propriety), 292, 297
Li Chao-lo, 396–97
Li-chi (Book of rites; Record of Rites; Record of Rituals), 79, 115–16, 119, 225, 342, 534
Li chien (Comments on ritual), 469–70
Li Chih, 185
Li Chih-tsao, 243
Li Ch'ü, 52
Li Chung-chien, 140
Li Hai-kuan, 6; background of, 50–51; on civil service examinations, 51, 61, 69–70; on the Classics, 52; educational philosophy of, 51–52, 55, 57, 58, 69–70; on fiction, 52, 62; on moral instruction, 52; and Neo-Confucianism, 64; reformist goals of, 70; on teaching, 52, 55, 58, 70
li-hsueh, 63, 92, 127, 129, 183
Li Hung-chang, 500, 502, 505
Li K'ai-hsien, 347, 372 n26
Li Kuang-ti, 152, 159, 166, 185, 189, 193, 244, 245
Li Kung, 191, 210 n64, 290 n96
Li Lien-ying, 540
Li Lo, 397
Li Meng-yang, 130
Li Shan-lan, 98
Li Yen-chi, 346
Li Yü-huang, 52
Li Yuan-tu, 90
Liang Chi, 345
Liang Ch'i-ch'ao, 464, 466, 533, 554
Liang Shu-ming, 345, 458, 459, 460
Liang Te-sheng, 26–27
Liao (dynasty), 342, 368
libraries, 7, 214 n121, 215 n130, 440–43, 498
licentiates. See *sheng-yuan*
Lin Chao-t'ang, 142
lineages, 461–62, 549, 550, 552; and scholarly traditions, 215 n140 n142; schools of, 11, 20; of scientists, 244–45. *See also* T'ung-ch'eng county
Ling Shu-hua, 32
Ling T'ing-k'an, 201, 203
literacy, 530–32, 549; as a goal of education, 429, 435–36, 447, 529, 547; rate of, 381, 402, 415 n112, 529, 530–32, 558 n56; among southwest tribes, 421, 444; of

women, 22, 38
Literary Inquisition (Ch'ing dynasty), 192, 466
literati, 161–62, 175–76, 192, 193, 468, 531, 549. *See also* educational organization; elites
literature: Ch'ing anecdotal literature, 64; and culture, 5; and moral education, 52; recreational literature in Manchu, 345; as source material, 51; travel literature, 422; and women's education, 20–26, 414 n93
litigation, 325 n26; cost of, 336 n145; extent of, 314–15, 316–17; in Manchu language, 341; subjects of, 315; traditional attitude toward, 317, 335 n143, 336 n145
litigation masters (*sung-shi*) and tricksters (*sung-kun*), 300–301, 316, 317, 318, 337 n160
Liu Ch'ing-chih, 51
Liu Ch'uan-ying, 88
Liu Feng-lu, 41 n15
Liu Heng, 315
Liu Hsi-tsai, 504, 509, 510, 511
Liu Hsiang, 21
Liu Hsien-t'ing, 186
Liu I, 76
Liu Jung, 78, 84, 87, 94, 105 n96
Liu K'ai, 205
Liu Sheng-mu, 204
Liu Ta-k'uei, 195, 196
Liu Tsung-chou, 290 n96, 394, 397, 410 n48, 413 n79
Liu T'ung-hsuan, 198
Liu Tzu-chuang, 166
Lo Ch'in-shun, 290
Lo Jen-chung, 296, 325 n26
Lo Tse-nan, 105 n96
Lolo. *See* Yi
Lombard-Salmon, Claudine, 422, 430
London Mission Society, 537–38
Lower Yangtze region, 246, 381, 385–86, 402, 447, 510, 516 n19, 527, 529; academies in, 493–511; as center of female erudition, 23–24; transition to public schools in, 511–14. *See also specific places by name*
Lu Hsun, 65
Lu K'en-t'ang, 125, 131, 324 n19
Lu Lung-ch'i, 185, 188, 397, 438, 442, 462, 505
Lu Shih-i, 54, 401, 461, 506; proposals for political reform, 476–77, 479
Lu-Wang school, 289 n91
Lu Wen-ch'ao, 184
Lu Yueh, 541
Lü Ch'ien-hung, 172–75, 177
Lü K'un, 40 n7, 384, 397, 406 n18, 413 n79, 428, 435, 438

Lü-li yuan-yuan, 231–32, 236, 239, 242, 245
Lü Liu-liang, 185, 186, 187, 188, 189, 192
Lü Te-sheng, 397
Lü-ying (Green Standard), 304
Lun-yü. See Analects
Lung-men Academy, 10, 13; and Ch'eng-Chu Learning, 504–6; curriculum of, 502, 508, 509–11; educational philosophy of, 500–501, 502, 509–10; financing of, 503, 505; founding of, 500; headmasters of, 501, 504–6, 509–11, 514–15; becomes normal school, 514–15; pedagogical methods of, 506–9; stipends, 502, 506; trustees of, 503–4

Ma Ch'i-ch'ang, 196
Ma Chu, 542
Ma Tsung-lien, 214 n126
Ma Yü, 200
Macartney, Halliday, 98
Machiavellianism, 482
magistrates, 292, 304, 305, 317, 318, 356, 481, 521 n90; staff of, 336 n146. *See also* bureaucracy; officials
Manchu language, 9, 341–42, 344, 347, 376 n73; Ch'ien-lung emperor on, 9, 341, 361, 362–63, 366; dialects of, 341; as an invention of the state, 9, 12, 340, 367; as medium of diplomatic communication, 345, 372 n18; orthography of, 342, 343–44, 361; pedagogical aids for the study of, 346; Sibo dialect, 341, 342; symbolic role in state culture, 340, 344–45, 347, 359–60, 365–67. *See also under* translation
Manchus, 535; in Board of Astronomy, 237; and civil service examinations, 116, 296 (*see also* banner examinations); culture of, 340, 365–66; defined, 369 n1; education of, 9, 10, 345; in Hanlin Academy, 116; and Sibo, 370 n7 (*see also under* Manchu language); and technical knowledge, 237, 362–65, 367–68; women, 366. *See also* banner education
Mandarin vernacular (*kuan-yü; kuo-yü*), 439, 445, 528, 547–48, 549, 550, 551; and Mandarin speech schools, 482
Mao Ch'i-ling, 191
Mao K'un, 187
Mao Tse-tung, 486
marriage practices, 10, 31, 32; companionate marriage, 23, 43 n27; among southwest aborigines, 424, 445; in upper class, 23. *See also* dowry
mathematics and mathematical sciences, 13, 99, 203, 353, 364; and astronomy, 226; Chinese tradition of, 230, 231, 233, 234; in civil service examinations, 114, 225, 242; curriculum in Imperial College, 231–32; in

mathematics and mathematical sciences
(*continued*)
elementary education, 408 n32;
independent scholars of, 226, 227, 243–46;
and Neo-Confucianism, 226; and official
careers, 241–43; regional centers of study
of, 225, 244; and the state, 227, 228, 236–
43, 245–46; in Sui and T'ang, 225; in Sung
and Yuan, 226; and Tai Chen, 279; texts,
230–35, 245, 251 n62. *See also* astronomy;
cosmology
matriarchy, 424–25, 445
McMahon, Keith, 450 n34
medical education, 468
Mei Chueh-ch'eng, 233, 240, 241–42, 243,
244
Mei Tseng-liang, 205, 217 n170
Mei Wen-ting, 226, 227, 228, 231, 233, 234,
241, 244, 245
memorization: Ch'en Hung-mou on, 440; and
civil service examinations, 120, 342, 533,
551; and cultural anxiety, 11–12, 532; in
elementary education, 394–95; and
identity, 532–34; and legal secretaries, 307
Mencius (philosopher), 1, 81, 85, 263
Mencius (text), 4, 141, 164, 168–69, 186, 553
Meng-tzu tzu-i shu-cheng, 258, 260, 275. *See also*
Tai Chen
merchants, 199, 200, 473, 526–27; and civil
service examinations, 544, 546, 547, 550,
552
metaphysics, 468, 484
metropolitan examinations. *See* civil service
examinations
Miao (minority), 360, 422, 445, 446, 528, 537;
language, 538; and "Miao-Yao" civil service
examinations, 437, 461–62
Miao Ch'üan-chi, 307, 329 n52
middle schools, 460, 538, 542
military examinations, 352, 531
military training, 356, 360, 364, 511, 531. See
also *ch'i-she*
Ming (dynasty), 2, 3, 112, 113, 185, 186, 342
Ming An-t'u, 233, 242, 243, 244, 246–47, 254
n125
Ming Hsin, 244
Ming-i tai-fang lu ("A Plan for the Prince"),
466, 468, 472, 477. *See also* Huang
Tsung-hsi
Ming-shih, 242
Ming T'ai-tsu, 418
Ming-t'ang ta-tao lu (Chronicle of the great
doctrine of the Hall for the Illumination of
the Way), 462
Ministry of Education, 485
Ministry of Personnel. *See* Board of
Appointments

Ministry of Rites. *See* Board of Rites
minorities. *See* aborigines
missionaries, 537–38. *See also* Jesuits
Mo-tzu, 1
Moated Sanctuary ("Pi-yung"), 466–67, 471–
72, 478
mobility. *See* immigration and immigrants;
social mobility
modern schools, 10, 99–100, 511–15, 535,
552
Mongol language, 341, 343, 347; in imperial
documents, 346–47
Mongolian Bureau, 347
Mongolian Hanlin Academy, 352
Mongolian National University (*kuo-tze chien*;
also identified as Mongolian Imperial
University), 352, 374 n43
Mongols, 535, 554; in civil service
examinations, 116, 350, 351, 352; culture
of, 368; education of, 352, 355, 356, 373
n37, 374 n43; nobility, 347, 352; in the
southwest, 418. *See also* Yuan (dynasty)
Montaigne, 534
mourning rituals, 30
Mukden, 351
Muslims, 112, 230, 365, 369 n1, 420, 528, 535,
551, 554; and banner companies, 355;
education of, 11, 541–42

Na-khi, 421, 444–45
Nan-yang kung-hsueh (Nan-yang public school),
512
Nanking, 24, 115, 122, 200, 418, 478, 479, 539
Naquin, Susan, 541
National Academy, 352–53, 362
National University. *See* Imperial College
Nationalists, 445–46, 528
Needham, Joseph, 248 n8; and "the
Needham problem," 223
Neo-Confucianism, 469, 471, 536, 537; in
Japan, 544; in Korea, 544–45, 558 n54; as
orthodoxy, 2, 3, 7, 183, 187, 191, 193–94,
258; in Vietnam, 545–46. *See also*
Ch'eng-Chu school; *li-hsueh*; *Tao-hsueh*
New Culture Movement, 205
New Life, 445
New Policies, 445, 511, 513, 521 n90
New Text. *See* evidential (*k'ao-cheng*)
scholarship
Nieh Chi-kuei, 100
Nien Rebellion, 97
Ningpo, 29, 32, 537
Nivison, David, 25
norms, 292, 294, 297, 299, 317, 318, 319
novels, 396, 397–98; and educational issues,
50–70; in legal education, 298, 328 n46;
and women's education, 22. *See also*

literature

nü-shih (female scholars), 19, 20; contrasted to *chen-nü*, 23, 24–25. *See also under* women

Nung-cheng ch'üan-shu, 30–31, 228

Nurgaci, 343, 344, 367, 526

Oboi regents, 119, 120, 236, 533

Oerht'ai, 159, 420, 426, 427, 447, 483–84

"Offices of Chou" ("Chou kuan"), 126, 127, 128

officials, 460; and mathematical sciences, 241–43; as promoters of local schools and academies, 382–84, 385–87, 390, 420, 425–48, 467, 482–83, 499; recruitment of, 112–44 *passim*, 152, 176, 296, 472–75, 478, 546; tenure of, 299, 329 n51; use of Manchu language by, 345. *See also* magistrates

Ogawa Yoshiko, 434, 527

ohariya, 37

Old Text (*ku-wen*): 82, 167, 168, 186; and civil service examinations, 187–88; controversy over *Documents Classic*, 134–35, 141, 142; debate with Han Learning, 133–36, 184, 190–91, 194–96. *See also* Han Learning; Sung Learning; T'ang-Sung ancient prose

Opium War, 14, 364

orphans, 390, 409 n40

"orthodox speech academies," 482

Ou-yang Hsiu, 92, 152, 186, 208 n19

pa-ku wen. See eight-legged essay

p'ai-lou, 20

palace examinations. *See* civil service examinations

Palace School for Princes (*Shang-shu-fang*), 241

Pan Chao, 21, 23, 25, 30

p'an (hypothetical judicial decisions), 294, 295–96, 325 n26, 326 n27

P'an Cheng-chang, 246

P'an Lei, 226–27, 246

P'an P'ing-ko, 191, 210 n64

P'an Shih-ch'eng, 474

pao-chia (police security system), 383

Pao-hsi, 365

Pao-ning county, 434

Pao T'ing-po, 200

Parrenin, Dominique, 242–43

pawnbrokers, 500, 503, 519 n44

The Pedant's Lament, 67

Peking, 5, 115, 116, 121, 225, 341, 478, 542

P'eng Shao-sheng, 539

philanthropy, 401–2, 407 n25, 527. See also *i-hsueh*

philology, 95, 105 n104, 116, 133–39 *passim*, 191, 198, 202, 463, 470, 484; and Ming thinkers, 290 n96

phonology, 142, 247, 396, 413 n79, 482

Pi Yuan, 4–5, 198–99

Pi-yung. See Moated Sanctuary

poetry, 203; and Ch'en Hung-mou, 440–41; in civil service examinations, 121, 203; women as authors of, 23, 27, 45 n38; in women's education, 22

Poetry Classic. See Shih-ching

policemen, 531–32

Pollard, Samuel, 538

popular culture, 9, 11, 13, 30, 401, 402, 421, 444, 536; and civil service examinations, 543–44

popular religion, 4, 424, 538. *See also* religious sects

Porter, Jonathan, 247

Privy Council, 355

Prospect Hill Officers' School, 355

provincial examinations. *See* civil service examinations

P'u Sung-ling, 50, 66–67

Qoninci, 368

Rankin, Mary Backus, 495

Rawski, Evelyn, 66, 243, 381, 530–31

religious sects, 539–41. *See also* White Lotus sect

Restoration Society, 165

Revolution of 1911, 487

revolutionary activity, 512, 521 n85

Ricci, Matteo, 233, 234, 244

Ricoeur, Paul, 206 n5

Rock, Joseph, 445

runners (of local government), 292, 300, 336 n146

rural schools, 430–48 *passim*, 529. *See also* elementary education

Ryukyu kingdom, 480

Sacred Edicts, 438, 453 n86, 461, 500, 541

Said, Edward, 422

Satō Ichirō, 209 n47

schoolteachers, 6, 55, 58, 485; in Ch'ing anecdotal literature, 64; income of, 65–66, 70, 392–93, 411 n56, 432, 434; reputation of, 64, 411 n57; social origins of, 65; status of, 65–68, 392, 546; and venality, 59, 411 n57; as village schoolmasters, 65–68

science: adoption of Western science, 230–31, 248 n8; defined, 223–24; in Europe, 224, 228, 250 n39; expansion in Ch'ing, 224–25, 228; and the idea of progress, 246–47; and natural philosophy, 224

scriveners, 299–300, 315

Sea of Learning Hall. *See* Hsueh-hai T'ang

self-cultivation, 63, 132; in elementary

self-cultivation (*continued*)
education, 395, 398
self-strengthening, 493, 512
Seven Classics, 277, 278
sex education, 35, 525
sexual morality, 23, 35, 39, 424
shan-shu (books of good deeds; morality
books), 334 n136, 397, 401
Shang (dynasty), 234
Shang-shu, 158, 174
Shanghai, 502, 511, 512
Shanghai Interpreters College, 502
Shantung, 541
Shao T'ing-ts'ai, 463, 468
Shao Yung, 235
she-hsueh. See community schools
Shen Ch'ang-yü, 131–32
Shen Chia-pen, 328 n48
Shen En-fu, 514, 522 n93
Shen Fu, 43 n27
Shen Hsiang-lung, 501, 514
Sheng Hsuan-huai, 512
sheng-yuan, 65, 117, 314, 337 n156, 351, 353,
364, 475; in Kiangsu, 494, 499
Shensi, 542
Shenyang, 341
Shih-chi, 88, 114, 186, 246, 342
Shih Ching (Ch'ing literatus), 270
Shih-ching (Poetry Classic; Book of poetry),
79, 119, 137, 534
shih-hsueh ("concrete studies"; practical
scholarship; "substantive learning"), 226,
227, 228, 249 n23, 439–40, 510
shih-wen ("present style of writing";
contemporary-style essay), 187, 502
shu-hsi t'i (familiar questions), 295, 324 n17,
325 n20, 326 n27
Shu-li ching-yun, 233–35, 240
shu-yuan. See academies
Shun (sage-king), 126, 127, 128, 129, 135,
169, 170, 171
Shun-chih emperor, 117, 385, 407 n27, 428
Shun-t'ien (prefecture), 349
Shuo-wen (Explication of writing), 138
Siam, 468, 529
Simon, Joan, 534
Singapore, 2, 542
Sinkiang, 370 n4, 526, 528, 535
Sivin, Nathan, 223–24, 231
Six Arts, 225, 226, 399
Six Boards, 477
Six Classics, 272
Smith, Arthur F., 66
Smogulenski (Polish Jesuit), 244
social mobility, 400, 437–38, 482–83, 511,
526, 537, 544–46, 547, 548
socialization, 10, 483, 526, 541, 548

Soochow (prefecture), 23, 125, 194, 199, 245,
497, 500, 516 n19
southwest China, 417–18, 528, 537; economy
of, 418, 421; state administration in, 418.
See also specific provinces by name
Spring and Autumn Annals, 52, 114, 119, 186,
342, 534
Ssu-k'u ch'üan-shu, 195, 213 n107, 215 n130
n131, 228, 254 n125, 464; and Manchu and
Mongolian skills, 345
Ssu-ma Ch'ien, 91, 186, 189
Ssu-ma Kuang, 91, 460
Ssu-wen ching-hua (Essential anthology of
refined literature), 80
state-building, 123, 129, 151, 190, 464; and
banner education, 348–59; and Ch'ien
Lung and Chia-ch'ing reforms, 359–61;
and Ch'ing cultural policies, 367–68; and
Ch'ing expansionism, 417–21, 453 n86;
and imperial universalism, 340–41, 345–
47, 367, 420–21, 423; in Ming dynasty, 382;
and Nationalist expansionism, 445–46, 528
state schools, 113, 116, 529, 546; and
mathematical sciences, 236–43. *See also
specific schools by name*
statecraft, 36, 102 n46, 136, 140, 224; and
science, 240
Stone, Lawrence, 535
Story of the Stone. See Dream of the Red Chamber
Su Shih, 80, 84, 92
Suan-ching shih-shu (Ten Mathematical
Classics), 225, 251 n62
Suan-fa t'ung-tsung, 230, 245
suicide, 47 n76, 315, 318, 334 n143 n144, 445
Sun Chia-kan, 474, 480–81, 482
Sun Ch'iang-ming, 501–2, 509, 510, 511
Sun Hsing-yen, 5, 24, 137, 203, 477
Sun-tzu, 89
Sung (dynasty), 1, 112, 113, 460, 547;
translators in, 346
Sung-chiang (prefecture), 497, 516 n19
Sung Jo-chao, 23
Sung Learning, 8, 10, 13, 111, 123, 133–34,
138, 196, 203, 213 n107, 549. *See also*
Neo-Confucianism
Sungyun, 376 n73
Supreme Ultimate, 63, 131
Swatow, 38
Szechwan, 426, 528, 536

Tai Chen, 8, 13, 125–26, 195, 200, 201, 215
n136, 228, 244; on Chu Hsi, 267–68, 275–
76; on the Classics, 259, 269–73, 275, 276–
78, 279, 282; on desire and feeling, 262–64,
274, 280, 282; on education, 261–62, 263,
264, 266, 272, 275; and evidential research,
257, 259, 268, 278–79; on goal of learning,

279–83; and Han Learning, 259, 268, 269, 286 n38; on human nature, 262–63, 264, 265, 266, 284–85 n14, 288 n61; influence of, 283 n6; intellectual interests of, 259, 271; on knowledge, 265–66, 270–71, 276, 277, 279; moral philosophy of, 257, 258, 259, 262; affinity for Neo-Confucianism, 258, 264, 282; critique of Neo-Confucianism, 64, 126, 258–59, 260, 262–63, 267, 275–78, 280, 553; on perception, 264, 282; and philology, 269–71, 279; philosophical writings of, 258, 259, 272–73, 275; on principle, 266–68, 269, 274, 277, 280–81; program of learning of, 257, 260–75, 275, 280. See also *Meng-tzu tzu-i shu-cheng*

Tai Ming-shih, 56, 154, 184, 186, 188–89, 196, 205, 209 n47, 375 n48

Tai San-hsi, 387

T'ai-chou school, 125

T'ai-shang kan-ying p'ien, 334 n136

Taiping Rebellion, 87, 97, 517 n23; and civil service examinations, 122–23, 494, 552; in Kiangsu, 496–97

Taiwan, 2, 478

Tan-hsin tang-an (Archive of Tan-shui subprefecture and Hsin-chu district), 300, 301, 316, 335 n144

T'ang (dynasty), 239, 323 n7, 460; translators in, 346

T'ang Chien, 78, 505–6, 510

T'ang Piao, 411 n54

T'ang Pin, 158

T'ang Shou-ch'ien, 514, 515, 522 n94

T'ang Shun-chih, 187

T'ang-Sung ancient prose, 186–89, 193, 202–3, 204, 216 n149, 217 n162. See also Old Text

tao (the Way; moral teachings), 22, 201, 292

Tao-hsueh (Studies of the Way), 2, 147 n59. See also Neo-Confucianism

Tao-kuang emperor, 364

Tao-t'ung, 129

Taoism and Taoists, 134, 285 n19, 538, 546

taxation, 432–33, 468, 474

teachers: foreign teachers, 511; of legal secretaries, 303–4; in National Academy, 354–55. See also Jesuits; schoolteachers

Temple of Eminent Statesmen, 158

terakoya, 37

Thirteen Classics, 483

Thousand Character Classic (*Ch'ien tzu wen*), 393, 533

Three-Character Classic. See *Trimetrical Classic*

t'i (substance; moral principles), 76, 508

Tibetans, 112, 535, 554; language of, 347

tien-shih, 351

T'ien Wen-ching, 157–58

Ting Ch'ü-chung, 244

Ting Jih-ch'ang, 500–501, 510, 518 n31

Toghto, 368

Tokugawa period, 37, 46 n72. See also Japan

translation, 502, 538; of Chinese works into Jurchen, 342; into Manchu, 344, 345–46; and role in state ideology, 346–47; of Russian, 372 n18; translators' bureaus, 343, 346, 347, 371 n10, 372 n25

translators, 346–47, 364, 367, 373 n25

Treaty of Aigun, 345

Trimetrical Classic (*San-tzu ching*), 61, 393, 442, 533

Ts'ai Shen, 127–28

Ts'ai Shih-yuan, 193

ts'e. See policy questions *under* civil service examinations

Tseng Chi-fen, 100

Tseng Chi-hung, 77, 88, 95, 99

Tseng Chi-tse, 77, 78, 88–96, 97, 98, 103 n53, 105 n103, 511

Tseng Ching, 192–93, 420

Tseng Kuang-chün, 99

Tseng Kung, 166–67

Tseng Kuo-ch'üan, 77, 78, 79–80, 87, 97–98, 105 n96

Tseng Kuo-fan, 6–7, 8, 10, 13, 216 n161, 504, 505, 519 n58; on academies, 150; career of, 77, 83, 86, 87; concern for status, 79; daughters of, 96, 100; defends examination system, 81–82; diaries of, 77, 78, 79, 83, 87, 506; early life, 77–78; on eight-legged essays, 81, 82; and evidential scholarship, 88, 93, 505, 535–36; and family affairs, 85; favored literature of, 78, 79–80, 84, 85, 86–87, 89–90, 92–94, 98; habits of, 78–79; and Hanlin Academy, 77, 78, 83; on *ku-wen*, 82, 205; letters of, 4, 81, 88–95, 98; and Neo-Confucianism, 78, 81, 88; and poetry and calligraphy, 77, 81, 90; on predestination, 80, 84, 88, 96, 102 n36; on purposes of study, 80, 82; on ritual, 86–87, 92; and self-cultivation, 78, 79, 80, 82, 84, 102 n39; sense of purpose, 81–82; and statecraft, 86, 102 n46; on Sung and Han Learning, 84, 88; tutors brothers, 79–81; tutors sons, 87–92; writings of, 76, 84, 91, 92, 93, 96, 101 n16

Tseng Kuo-hua, 77, 81, 85, 87, 103 n49

Tseng Kuo-huang, 77, 85, 87, 103 n49

Tseng Kuo-pao, 77, 85, 86, 87, 103 n49

Tseng Lin-shu, 81, 85

Tseng Pao-sun, 99–100

Tseng Yueh-nung, 100

Tso Ch'iu-ming, 142

Tso-chuan, 94, 115, 142, 186, 397

Tso Mou-ti, 347
Tso Tsung-t'ang, 554
Ts'ui Hsueh-ku, 397
Ts'ui Shu, 24, 41 n15, 43 n27
Tu, Ching-i, 169
Tu Fu, 80, 84
Tu Wei-ming, 4
Tu Yu, 92
t'u-ssu (native headmen), 418, 426
T'u Tsung-ying, 503, 505, 506
Tuan Yü-ts'ai, 89, 94, 202, 272
Tung Chung-shu, 142
Tung Hai University, 100
Tung-lin Academy, 130
Tung Yu-ch'eng, 247
T'ung-ch'eng county, 152, 192, 193, 196; and
    civil service examinations, 197; prominent
    lineages of, 152, 197–98, 201, 206, 447
T'ung-ch'eng school, 5, 7, 93, 183–206, 504–
    5; influence of, 204–5; origins of, 184, 195–
    96, 201, 212 n100, 549
T'ung-chih Restoration, 123, 493, 505; and
    expansion of academies, 494–95, 500, 511;
    and Kiangsu, 504
T'ung-shu, 173, 174
tutors, 55, 89, 96, 193, 391, 401, 477–78
tzu-ti (male dependents of Manchu
    servicemen), 353, 354, 358, 360, 361;
    defined, 374 n44
tzu-wen tzu-ta (to ask a question and answer it
    oneself), 295, 324 n17
Tzu-yang Academy, 245, 501
tz'u-chang (literary writing), 203

Uigur language, 347, 370 n7
Urumchi, 535

Verbiest, Ferdinand, 232, 237, 238, 239, 252
    n79
Vietnam and Vietnamese, 480, 536–37; civil
    service system of, 545–46
village lecture system, 296–97, 383, 401, 500
vocational training, 80, 364, 407–8 n32
Voltaire, 224

Wan Hu-ch'uan, 504, 505, 519 n53
Wan-nan school, 244
Wan Ssu-t'ung, 210 n50 n64
Wang An-shih, 84
Wang Ch'ang, 141, 534
Wang Ch'i-shu, 200
Wang Chung, 203
Wang Fu, 200
Wang Hsi-shan, 227, 244
Wang Hui-tsu, 8, 9, 338 n163; advice of, 312;
    background of, 313–14; character of, 313–
    14; on employers, 311; teachings of, 310–

13; writings of, 303, 309, 334–35 n136
Wang Hung-hsu, 125
Wang Kuo-wei, 345
Wang Lun, 124, 146 n32
Wang Ming-sheng, 141, 259
Wang Mou-hung, 189, 191
Wang Nien-sun, 88, 92, 93
Wang Te-chao, 472
Wang Tuan, 26–27
Wang Tzu-lan, 27
Wang Wan, 187, 188
Wang Wei-han, 309
Wang Yang-ming, 125, 130, 134, 185, 194,
    275, 528; on children's education, 399, 400
Wang Yin-chih, 93, 142
Wang Yu-huai, 309
Wang Yuan, 186
Wang Yun, 412 n67
Watson, James, 421, 438
Weaving Maid (Chih-nü), 28, 29, 30, 45 n53
Webster, Noah, 3
Wei Chi-jui, 187
Wei Hsi, 187
Wei Li, 187
wei-so system, 342
Wei T'ing-chen, 155–57, 161
well-field system, 459
wen ("culture"; "literature"), 3–4, 5, 76, 201;
    contrasted to *wu*, 348, 359; and women, 20
Wen Ching-yü, 27
Wen-hsiang [Suwan Gūwalgiya], 365
Western learning. See *hsi-hsueh*
White Lotus sect, 112, 539, 540, 541
widows, 20, 24, 39, 40 n7, 47 n76
Wo-jen, 79, 505
women: as authors, 23, 27, 38, 42 n21 n22, 45
    n38, 536–37; class differences among, 20;
    gender roles of, 19, 23, 104 n89, 530; and
    handicrafts, 28, 30–31; in Japan, 36–37, 46
    n72; as leaders of religious sects, 540;
    literacy rate of, 38–39, 415 n112, 531; and
    manual labor, 28, 34, 37, 39; marital status
    of educated women, 24, 26, 43 n27; and
    painters, 24, 42 n26, 43 n27; physical
    exercise, 36; as procreator, 34–35, 37;
    regional patterns of female erudition, 23–
    24, 42 n22 n23; in the Renaissance, 35–36;
    and rites of passage, 28; as scholars, 19,
    26–27, 39, 536–37, 544; socialization of,
    12; among southwest peoples, 424; as
    tutors of sons, 22, 41 n15; women's work,
    28–35. *See also* family
women's education, 1, 2, 5, 6, 414 n93, 536–
    37, 554; in childhood, 27–28; and classical
    learning, 22–24; decline of, 25–26; and
    didactic texts, 20, 21–22, 23, 30, 40 n6, 40
    n9, 41 n13; literate education, 20, 22–25;

moral instruction in, 20; nonliterate education, 12, 20, 21, 28, 540; patrons of, 27, 45 n38; purposes of, 20–21; rationale for, 22–23; and religious sects, 540; in the Renaissance, 35–36; and ritual, 25, 27, 29, 30, 31, 37, 530; and sexual segregation, 20, 424, 525, 541; source materials on, 20; and wifely training (*fu-dao*), 21, 27–39

Women's Learning (*nü hsueh*), 21, 22, 38, 40 n6

"Women's Learning." See *Fu hsueh*

Woodside, Alexander, 381, 407 n32

Wu Ch'in, 129–30

Wu Ching-tzu, 50, 51, 70

Wu Kuang-yao, 316

Wu San-kuei rebellion, 154, 418

Wu Ta-ch'eng, 519 n53

Wu T'ing-tung, 79, 505, 506

Wylie, Alexander, 98

Yang Kuang-hsien, 236

Yang Shen, 420

Yang Wen-hui, 539

yangban (Korean elite), 372 n24, 544, 545, 558 n54

Yangchow (prefecture), 24, 125, 199

Yangtze Delta, 7, 8, 9, 13, 111, 120, 121, 123, 136, 140; as center of evidential research, 133, 136, 140, 163, 550. *See also individual places by name*

Yao (minority), 528

Yao (sage-king), 128, 129, 254 n113

Yao Ch'un, 504–5

Yao Nai, 7, 13, 84, 93, 184, 198, 201, 203–5, 504; and the T'ung-ch'eng school, 195–97

Yao Wen-jan, 197

Yeh Ch'un-chi, 383, 384, 400

Yelu Dashi, 376 n79

Yen Fu, 485, 486, 554

Yen Jo-chü, 134, 190–91

Yen Mao-yu, 397

Yen Yuan, 124, 125, 191, 290 n96

Yi (also identified as Lolo) (minority), 421, 528

Yi (Korean dynasty), 343, 372 n24, 544–45, 558 n54

Yin-chi-shan, 420, 422, 426, 430, 447–48

yin-chien ("inheritance students"), 479

Yin-chih, Prince, 240, 253 n95

Yin-lu, Prince, 232, 240–41, 253 n95

Ying-hua Academy, 498

Ying Pao-shih, 500, 504, 505, 509

Yü (sage), 126, 128, 274–75

Yü, Ying-shih, 201

Yü Yueh, 68, 482, 501, 509

Yuan (dynasty), 2, 112, 113, 230, 342, 542; translators in, 346

Yuan Hsi-t'ao, 512, 514, 522 n93

Yuan Huang, 397

Yuan Mei, 24–25, 26, 27, 39, 44 n31, 73 n35, 460

Yuan shan (On the Good), 258, 259

Yuan Shih-k'ai, 365, 485, 552

Yuan Ts'ai (Sung literatus), 21

Yuan ts'ai ("On the Origins of Talent"), 76

Yueh Chung-ch'i, 192

Yueh-hsiu academy, 483

yung (function; implementation), 76, 508

Yung-cheng emperor, 4, 121, 132, 151, 155, 156, 157, 175, 192, 193, 240, 447–48, 453 n86, 460; and charitable schools, 528; and civil service examinations, 323 n9; and community schools, 387; on goals of education, 419–20; on *shu-yuan*, 461, 480, 500

Yung-lo emperor, 115

Yung-pei department, 434

Yunnan, 419, 425, 428, 447, 483–84, 526, 542; administrative districts in, 430; local schools in, 425–26, 430, 437, 443–44, 536, 542; population density in, 431–32, 452 n56; Provincial Academy of, 437, 438, 443. *See also* Ch'en Hung-mou; *i-hsueh*; Oerht'ai; *specific places by name*

Compositor:	Central Typographers
Text:	10/12 Baskerville
Display:	Baskerville
Printer:	Thomson-Shore, Inc.
Binder:	Thomson-Shore, Inc.